D1087515

Wandering, Begging Monks

THE TRANSFORMATION OF THE CLASSICAL HERITAGE

Peter Brown, General Editor

Wandering, Begging Monks

Spiritual Authority and the Promotion of Monasticism in Late Antiquity

Daniel Caner

UNIVERSITY OF CALIFORNIA PRESS

Berkeley   Los Angeles   London

University of California Press
Berkeley and Los Angeles, California

University of California Press, Ltd.
London, England

© 2002 by the Regents of the University of California

Library of Congress Cataloging-in-Publication Data

Caner, Daniel.
    Wandering, begging monks : spiritual authority and the
promotion of monasticism in late antiquity / Daniel Caner.
        p. cm.—(The transformation of the classical heritage ; 33)
    Includes bibliographical references and index.
    ISBN 0–520-23324-7 (alk. paper)
    1. Monastic and religious life—History—Early church, ca. 30–
600. 2. Messalians. I. Title. II. Series.

BR195.M65 C36 2002
271'.009'015—dc21

                                                    2002016559

Manufactured in the United States of America
10 09 08 07 06 05 04 03 02
10 9 8 7 6 5 4 3 2 1

The paper used in this publication is both acid-free and totally
chlorine-free (TCF). It meets the minimum requirements of ANSI/
NISO Z39.48–1992 (R 1997) *(Permanence of Paper).* ∞

For Ann

CONTENTS

ACKNOWLEDGMENTS

I began this book six years ago as a doctoral dissertation in the Graduate Group in Ancient History and Mediterranean Archaeology at the University of California, Berkeley. It was conceived with the encouragement and direction of Susanna Elm and helped along the way by conversations with my friend Bill North. I am indebted to Peter Brown, Susan Ashbrook Harvey, and Philip Rousseau for their generous suggestions and corrections. Several colleagues sent me copies of their unpublished work: Robert Doran, Robert Kitchen, and Kevin van Bladel provided Syriac translations, Michael Gaddis and Wendy Mayer their dissertations, and Susan Ashbrook Harvey an article on Rabbula. Helen Sillet, Allen Ward, and my copyeditor, Jennifer Eastman, deserve special thanks for their careful attention to revision drafts. I alone am responsible for the errors and excesses that remain. Finally, I want to thank Kate Toll and David Gill at the University of California Press for their support, and my family, who may still wonder why this project has kept me happy for so long.

These acknowledgments would not be complete without expressing my gratitude to three holy men who first inspired me years ago in Greece: thanks to Brother John of Athos, Abba Christophoros of Zografou, and Demetri, a wandering exorcist whom I met late one night in an Athenian soup kitchen.

ABBREVIATIONS

The following abbreviations are used for items frequently cited in footnotes and the bibliography. I cite critical editions and translations in my footnotes by giving the name of editor(s) or translator and page number of the texts, sometimes with series name and line number (indicated by commas) added. Full citations are given in the bibliography. All translations are my own except where indicated.

AASS	*Acta Sanctorum*
AB	*Analecta Bollandiana*
ACO	*Acta Conciliorum Oecumenicorum*. Ed. E. Schwartz
ACW	Ancient Christian Writers (translation series)
ANF	Ante-Nicene Fathers (translation series)
BZ	*Byzantinische Zeitschrift*
CCSL	Corpus Christianorum, Series Latina
CIL	Corpus Inscriptionum Latinarum
CJ	*Codex Justinianus*. Ed. P. Krüger
CS	Cistercian Studies (translation series)
CSCO	Corpus Scriptorum Christianorum Orientalium
CSEL	Corpus Scriptorum Ecclesiasticorum Latinorum
CTh	*Codex Theodosianus*. Ed. Th. Mommsen and P. M. Meyer
DACL	*Dictionnaire d'archéologie chrétienne et de liturgie*
DHGE	*Dictionnaire d'histoire et de géographie ecclésiastique*
DSp	*Dictionnaire de spiritualité*
Ep.	*Epistula, Epistulae*
GCS	Die griechischen christlichen Schriftsteller der ersten Jahrhunderte

Hefele-Leclerq	C. J. Hefele and H. Leclerq, *Histoire des conciles d'après les documents originaux*. Vols. 1.1–2.2.
HE	*Historia ecclesiastica*
HL	Palladius, *Historia Lausiaca*
HM	*Historia monachorum in Aegypto*
HR	Theodoret of Cyrrhus, *Historia religiosa*
JbAC	*Jahrbuch für Antike und Christentum*
JECS	*Journal of Early Christian Studies*
JEH	*Journal of Ecclesiastical History*
JRS	*Journal of Roman Studies*
JThS	*Journal of Theological Studies*
Lampe	G. W. H. Lampe, *A Patristic Greek Dictionary*
LCL	Loeb Classical Library
LH	Nestorius, *Liber Heraclidis*
NPNF	Nicene and Post-Nicene Fathers (translation series)
OCA	Orientalia Christiana Analecta
OCP	*Orientalia Christiana Periodica*
PapETSE	Papers of the Estonian Theological Society in Exile
PG	Patrologia Graeca
PL	Patrologia Latina
PLRE 1	*The Prosopography of the Later Roman Empire*. Vol. 1 (A.D. 260–395). Ed. A. H. M. Jones, J. R. Martindale, and J. Morris.
PLRE 2	*The Prosopography of the Later Roman Empire*. Vol. 2 (A.D. 395–527). Ed. J. R. Martindale.
PLS	Patrologiae Latinae Supplementum
PO	Patrologia Orientalis
PS	Patrologia Syriaca
PTS	Patristische Texte und Studien
REB	*Revue des études byzantines*
RHE	*Revue d'histoire ecclésiastique*
RHR	*Revue de l'histoire des religions*
RevSR	*Revue de science religieuse*
ROC	*Revue de l'Orient chrétien*
SC	Sources chrétiennes
SH	Subsidia Hagiographica
SM	*Studia Monastica*
SP	*Studia Patristica*
TS	Text and Studies
TU	Texte und Untersuchungen
VC	*Vigiliae Christianae*
ZKG	*Zeitschrift für Kirchengeschichte*
ZPE	*Zeitschrift für Papyrologie und Epigraphik*

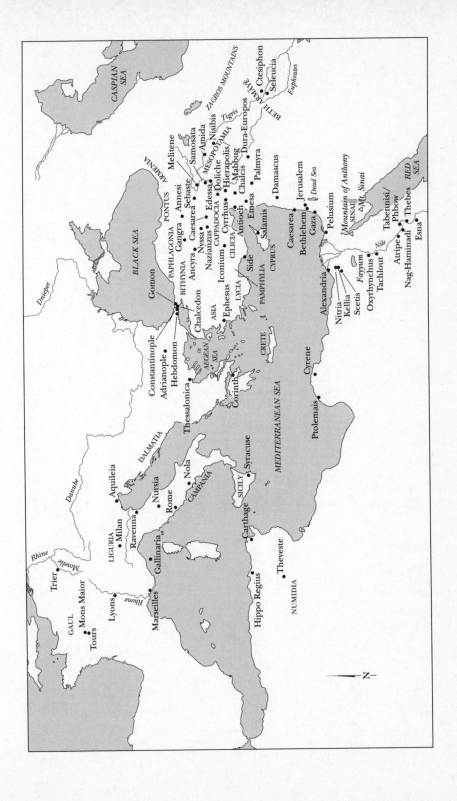

Introduction

This book explores social and economic concerns that contributed to the promotion of certain forms of Christian monasticism over others between roughly 360 and 451 C.E. Its focus is ascetic poverty and competing claims to material support made by ascetic laymen and church leaders. The monastic movement was just taking shape: How should monks interpret scriptural pronouncements on poverty? What relation was there between early monastic practice and apostolic tradition? What were the implications for members of the clergy? To what extent, and on what conditions, was material dependency acceptable in late Roman society?

Although we will pursue these questions mainly in Asia Minor, Syria, and Egypt, the issues involved are best introduced by the warning that Augustine, bishop of Hippo, sent to monks of Carthage in 401:

> Slaves of God, Soldiers of Christ, may you thus ignore the deceits of that most fervent enemy, who, desiring with his customary foulness to obscure in every way your good reputation, . . . has scattered everywhere so many hypocrites in the garb of monks, who wander around the provinces never sent, never stationary, never settled, never stable. . . . all seek, all demand either the expenses of their profitable poverty or a reward for their pretended holiness. . . . Under the general name of monks your good and holy profession, which in the name of Christ we desire to spread throughout Africa as it has through other lands, is being reviled.[1]

---

1. Augustine, *De opere monachorum* 28.36; ed. Joseph Zycha, pp. 585–86: O servi dei, milites Christi, itane dissimulatis callidissimi hostis insidias, qui bonam famam vestram . . . omni modo cupientes obscurare putoribus suis, tam multos hypocritas sub habitu monachorum usque-quaque dispersit, circumeuntes provincias, nusquam missos, nusquam fixos, nusquam stantes, nusquam sedentes. . . . et omnes petunt, omnes exigunt aut sumptus lucrosae egestatis aut

Augustine bears witness here to the pervasion of wandering monks throughout the Roman Empire at the turn of the fifth century. Such hypocrites, he claims, feigned holiness to reap material gains. Their begging threatened to discredit monasticism as a whole. Against their example he implored his readers to "show people you are not seeking an easy meal in idleness, but that you are seeking the kingdom of God through the straight and narrow life of [this monastic] profession."[2] That meant manual labor, practiced within the confines of a monastery.

In these passages Augustine reveals a preoccupation with the impact of wandering, begging monks on public opinion and the problems they raised for the social acceptance of the "good and holy" monastic profession he wished to promote in North Africa. Similar concerns for public opinion were shared by church and monastic authorities throughout the Roman Empire, as we shall see. But the issues raised by such monks in the late fourth and early fifth centuries were far more complex. Augustine wrote *On the Work of Monks* not simply to exhort his readers toward a more respectable form of monastic life, but also to discourage them from emulating certain long-haired, itinerant ascetics who had reportedly gained a considerable following as spiritual teachers among local monks and ordinary Christian laymen. Such "long-hairs" did not work, that is, they did not practice manual labor. Instead they offered admirers spiritual edification in exchange for material support, while seeking to live like the "birds of the sky" that "neither sow nor reap," or the "lilies of the field" that "neither toil nor spin," in literal accordance with the "freedom from care" that Jesus encouraged his disciples to embrace in his Sermon on the Mount (Mt 6: 25–34; cf. Lk 12:22–31). It was against their notions of ascetic propriety that Augustine composed his treatise. In his view, they had not only misinterpreted and abused evangelic precepts by refusing to work, but by claiming a right to material support on the grounds that they were teachers, they were also claiming for themselves the apostolic privileges that rightfully belonged only to vested members of the clergy.

Inasmuch as it served to discredit such ascetic teachers, Augustine's depiction of "hypocrites in the garb of monks" must not be taken at face value. The same goes for denouncements of wandering "pseudomonks" made by his Eastern counterparts at this time. As we shall see, such accusations and condemnations of ascetic vagrancy and begging were often expressions of

---

simulatae pretium sanctitatis . . . sub generali nomine monachorum vestrum propositum blasphematur, tam bonum, tam sanctum, quod in Christi nomine cupimus, sicut per alias terras, sic per totam Africam pullulare. Trans. adapted from Mary Sarah Muldowney, p. 384, who reads *cupiens* for the *cupientes* of CSEL.

2. Augustine, *De opere*, ed. Zycha, p. 586: ostendite hominibus non vos in otio facilem victum, sed per angustam et artam vitam huius propositi regnum dei quaerere.

a rivalry for social and spiritual authority. Indeed, often what caused concern was that the monks in question had gained prestige not only among their ascetic peers but also among the Christian laity, who rewarded them with alms. So observes the emperor Julian, whose treatise *To the Cynic Heracleius* preserves our earliest (ca. 361) explicit testimony for wandering monks:

> Long ago I gave you a nickname, and now I think I will write it down. It is *apotaktistai* [renouncers], a name applied to certain persons by the impious Galilaeans. They are for the most part men who by making small sacrifices gain much, or rather everything, from all sources, and in addition secure honor, crowds of attendants, and services. Something like that is your method, except perhaps for uttering divine revelations. . . . And perhaps too there is this difference, that you have no excuse for levying tribute on specious pretexts as they do; which they call *eleēmosynē* [alms], whatever that may mean. But in other respects your habits and theirs are very much alike. Like them you have abandoned your homeland and wander all over. . . . [3]

Julian's sketch is, of course, as much a caricature as Augustine's, meant to chasten ascetics of his own calling. It nevertheless makes plain what Augustine and other Christian writers only imply: certain wandering monks received both popular acclaim and alms by virtue of their material renunciations (i.e., their ascetic poverty) and their charismatic behavior or utterances (here specified as prophesying). From an ecclesiastical perspective, such acclaim could prove challenging indeed. At Constantinople it became pivotal in a series of confrontations between church officials, whose claims to spiritual authority derived mainly from their church office, and monks, who derived both apostolic authority and aristocratic patronage by virtue of their ascetic practices and spiritual services.

As vagrant beggars, spiritual teachers, or charismatic "enthusiasts," wandering monks raised the basic question of what it meant to be a monk wherever they appeared. When the Council of Chalcedon in 451 issued the first church canons that addressed the movements of monks and placed their activities under episcopal control, monasticism was still an evolving phenomenon. One purpose of this study is to demonstrate that the sequestered form of monastic life that the Council favored, as well as the self-

---

3. Julian, *Oratio* 7.224BC; ed. and trans. adapted from Wilmer C. Wright, p. 122: πάλαι μὲν οὖν ἐθέμην ἐγὼ τοῦτο τὸ ὄνομα, νυνὶ δὲ αὐτὸ ἔοικα καὶ γράψειν. ἀποτακτιστάς τινας ὀνομάζουσιν οἱ δυσσεβεῖς Γαλιλαῖοι· τούτων οἱ πλείους μικρὰ προέμενοι πολλὰ πάνυ, μᾶλλον δὲ τὰ πάντα πανταχόθεν ξυγκομίζουσι, καὶ προσκτῶνται τὸ τιμᾶσθαι καὶ δορυφορεῖσθαι καὶ θεραπεύεσθαι. τοιοῦτόν τι καὶ τὸ ὑμέτερον ἔργον ἐστί, πλὴν ἴσως τοῦ χρηματίζεσθαι. . . . ἴσως δὲ καὶ διὰ τὸ μηδὲν ὑμῖν εἶναι πρόσχημα τοῦ φορολογεῖν εὐπροσώπως, ὁποῖον ἐκείνοις, ἣν λέγουσιν οὐκ οἶδ' ὅπως ἐλεημοσύνην, τὰ δ' ἄλλα γε ἐστιν ὑμῖν τε κἀκείνοις παραπλήσια. καταλελοίπατε τὴν πατρίδα ὥσπερ ἐκεῖνοι, περιφοιτᾶτε πάντη. . . .

sufficient, work-based ideal that authorities like Augustine promoted, were in fact novel developments in monastic history, supplanting an earlier, widely practiced ideal in which an ascetic elite, observing apostolic principles, provided spiritual edification to Christian communities in return for their material support. But this book is also a study in cultural history that explores why certain Christian holy men became recognized as legitimate, while others, who embraced Jesus' most demanding precepts for Christian perfection, became marginalized and repudiated in this most crucial period for the establishment, spread, and acceptance of monastic institutions.

THE MODEL HOLY MAN

With the victories of Constantine in the first quarter of the fourth century, a cultural revolution gained supremacy in the Roman Empire that would eventually transform or supplant traditions held for centuries. The process of Christianization that followed is most notorious for its violence against pagan temples, sacred groves, and statuary, and for imperial legislation against the practice of ancient rites. Yet this process required more penetrating suasion than could be effected by the swift and irregular destruction of outward symbols of the cultural past or imposed by the threat of capital punishment.[4] Ancestral customs tended to reassert themselves where neglected by church and imperial forces.[5] Christianization required that imaginations be reoriented toward new cultural icons, based not only on scriptural examples but also on living exemplars who vividly embodied the ideals that the Scriptures described.[6] At the same time, church leaders had to acknowledge and accommodate the sensibilities of their large congregations, now being filled with the mainstream of Roman society.[7] The pressures on these leaders to persuade and accommodate were exerted in turn upon a figure that rose to prominence in the rhetoric, literature, and society of the late fourth century: the Christian monk.

4. These are the aspects of Christianization discussed by Ramsey MacMullen, *Christianizing the Roman Empire, A.D. 100–400* (New Haven: Yale University Press, 1984), 68–119 and Frank Trombley, *Hellenic Religion and Christianization, c. 370–529*, vols. 1–2 (Leiden: Brill, 1993–1994). For threats of capital punishment see *CTh* 16.10.6 (issued in 356) and 16.10.13.2 (395).

5. For an instructive example, see John of Ephesus, *Lives of the Eastern Saints* 16 (PO 17.233–37). For methodological problems in assessing Christianization see esp. Robert Markus, *The End of Ancient Christianity* (Cambridge: Cambridge University Press, 1990), 1–17.

6. See Peter Brown, *Authority and the Sacred: Aspects of the Christianisation of the Roman World* (Cambridge: Cambridge University Press, 1995), 3–26, 57–78 and Averil Cameron, *Christianity and the Rhetoric of Empire: The Development of Christian Discourse* (Berkeley and Los Angeles: University of California Press, 1991).

7. See Markus (1990): 63–83.

In previous centuries Christians had already celebrated men and women within their communities who made sexual and material renunciations in order to distance themselves from the ordinary "world" and prepare themselves for the world to come.[8] But as Christianity gained a more central position in Roman society after Constantine, church rhetoric increasingly favored those solitaries whose *askēsis* (spiritual exercises, practices, renunciation, or mode of life) placed them outside the normal (urban or village) course of human interactions and concerns. Around such *monachoi* crystallized the most otherworldly ideals. "To go to the monastery of a holy man," John Chrysostom told congregations in Antioch (modern Antakya) in the 380s or 390s, "is to pass as if from earth unto heaven," for in that solitude visitors would find neither the self-indulgence of luxuries nor the burdens of ordinary living.[9] And none seemed to offer a better example than the monks of the Egyptian desert:

> If you go now to the desert of Egypt, you will see that this desert has become better than any paradise, with countless choruses of angels in human form. . . . They display the same strictness *[akribeia]* in the great diligence of their lifestyle as they do in their doctrine of faith. For though they have stripped themselves of all possessions and crucified themselves to the whole world, they push themselves still further, nourishing those in need through their own physical labors. For though they fast and keep vigils, they don't think it right to be idle during the day; instead they devote their nights to holy hymns and watches, applying themselves during the day to prayers and the work of their hands together at once, imitating the apostles' zeal.[10]

Anyone would know this who went to Egypt, Chrysostom says; but if they could not, he suggests they consult the biography of "him whom Egypt brought forth after the apostles, namely the great and blessed Antony." By reading his *Life* they would learn precisely "what sort of lifestyle Christ's laws demand."[11]

8. See J. C. O'Neill, "The Origins of Monasticism," in *The Making of Orthodoxy: Essays in Honor of Henry Chadwick*, ed. R. Williams (Cambridge: Cambridge University Press, 1989), 270–87.

9. John Chrysostom, *In epistulam I ad Timotheum homilia* 14.3 (PG 62.575).

10. Chrysostom, *In Matthaeum homilia* 8.4–5 (PG 57.87–88): καὶ νῦν ἐλθὼν εἰς τὴν ἔρημον τῆς Αἰγύπτου, παραδείσου παντὸς βελτίω τὴν ἔρημον ταύτην ὄψει γεγενημένην, καὶ χοροὺς ἀγγέλων μυρίους ἐν ἀνθρωπίνοις σχήμασι. . . . Διὰ δὴ τοῦτο μετὰ τῆς τοσαύτης ἀκριβείας τῶν δογμάτων, καὶ τὴν ἀπὸ τοῦ βίου πολλὴν ἐνδείκνυνται σπουδήν. Τὰ γὰρ ὄντα ἀποδυσάμενοι πάντα, καὶ τῷ κόσμῳ σταυρωθέντες παντί, καὶ περαιτέρω πάλιν ἐλαύνουσι, τῇ τοῦ σώματος ἐργασίᾳ πρὸς τὴν τῶν δεομένων ἀποχρώμενοι τροφήν. Οὐδὲ γὰρ ἐπειδὴ νηστεύσουσι καὶ ἀγρυπνοῦσιν, ἀργεῖν μεθ᾽ ἡμέραν ἀξιοῦσιν· ἀλλὰ τὰς μὲν νύκτας τοῖς ἱεροῖς ὕμνοις καὶ ταῖς παννυχίσι, τὰς δὲ ἡμέρας εἰς εὐχάς τε ὁμοῦ καὶ τὴν ἀπὸ τῶν χειρῶν ἐργασίαν καταναλίσκουσι, τὸν ἀποστολικὸν μιμούμενοι ζῆλον.

11. Chrysostom, *In Matthaeum hom.* 8.5 (PG 57.88–89): εἰ δέ τις οὐδέποτε ἐπέβη τῶν σκηνῶν ἐκείνων, ἐννοείτω τὸν μέχρι νῦν ἐν τοῖς ἁπάντων στόμασιν ὄντα, ὃν μετὰ τοὺς Ἀποστόλους ἡ Αἴγυπτος

The homilies Chrysostom and other preachers delivered before urban Christians in this period often praised "those of the hills" who proved that worldly transcendence and apostolic ideals were possible for ordinary human beings. Through their rhetoric such "holy ones" found place beside the martyrs as heroes of the new culture.[12] The homily cited above also attests the extraordinary impact ("now on everyone's lips") that Athanasius' biography (written ca. 357) of the Egyptian hermit Antony had on the conception of monasticism held by easterners and westerners alike in the late fourth century.[13] Inspiring not only for ordinary Christians, it also exerted profound influence as a normative text describing how monks should practice their vocation. As Gregory of Nazianzus remarked in 380, Athanasius' biography provided "legislation for the monastic way of life in narrative form."[14] What that meant is sketched by Sozomen, a church historian writing at Constantinople in the middle of the fifth century:

> Whether or not the Egyptians or others were the first to exhibit this philosophy [i.e., monasticism], it is agreed by all that the great monk Antony brought this course of life to the highest pitch of discipline and perfection, with the appropriate ethics and bodily exertions. . . . He bestowed his patrimony on his villagers and distributed the rest of his property to the poor, since he realized that it is the mark of a serious philosopher not just to strip oneself of wealth, but to disperse it properly. . . . He tempered the intensity of those who conversed with him and moderated their habits. . . . He never allowed himself to be idle, but required each who intended to live in goodly fashion to work. . . . He endeavored to be unknown and to remain unseen in desert places, but if ever forced to enter a city for supplies, he immediately went back out to the desert when he had fulfilled his purpose, for he used to say that . . . just as fish lose their lives when cast on dry land, so do monks lose their dignity when they go into towns.[15]

ἤνεγκε, τὸν μακάριον καὶ μέγαν Ἀντώνιον. . . . τοιοῦτον ἐπεδείξατο βίον, οἷον οἱ τοῦ Χριστοῦ νόμοι ζητοῦσι. Καὶ τοῦτο εἴσεταί τις μετὰ ἀκριβείας, ἐντυχὼν τῷ βιβλίῳ τῷ τὴν ἱστορίαν ἔχοντι τῆς ἐκείνου ζωῆς.

12. The classic study is Peter Brown, "The Rise and Function of the Holy Man in Late Antiquity," *JRS* 61 (1971): 80–101; revised in *id., Society and the Holy in Late Antiquity* (Berkeley and Los Angeles: University of California Press, 1982), 103–52. See also *id.,* "The Rise and Function of the Holy Man in Late Antiquity, 1971–1997," *JECS* 6 (1998): 353–76.

13. Chrysostom, *In Matthaeum hom.* 8.5 (PG 57.89): . . . μέχρι νῦν ἐν τοῖς ἁπάντων στόμασιν ὄντα . . . The traditional attribution of the *Vita Antonii* to Athanasius remains probable though problematic. See Bernadette McNary-Zak, *Letters and Asceticism in Fourth-Century Egypt* (Lanham, Md.: University Press of America, 2000), 88–97. For its impact on fourth- and fifth-century monasticism see Samuel Rubenson, *The Letters of St. Antony: Monasticism and the Making of a Saint* (Minneapolis: Fortress Press, 1995), 163–84 and Timothy Fry, *RB 1980: The Rule of Saint Benedict in Latin and English with Notes* (Collegeville, Minn.: Liturgical Press, 1981), 311–13.

14. Gregory of Nazianzus, *Oratio* 21.5 (PG 35.1088A): συνέγραψε τοῦ μοναδικοῦ βίου νομοθεσίαν ἐν πλάσματι διηγήσεως.

15. Sozomen, *Historia ecclesiastica* 1.13.1–10; ed. Joseph Bidez and revised Günther C. Han-

The characteristics that Sozomen identifies with Antony are worth repeating. By placing as much emphasis on distributing wealth as on renouncing it, by promoting moderation in ascetic behavior, by practicing manual labor instead of "idleness" *(argia)*, and by striving to live in isolation so as to preserve the "dignity" *(semnotēta)* befitting a monk, Athanasius' Antony epitomized strict monastic discipline *(akribeia)* for this fifth-century reader. Thus Athanasius' narrative established Antony as the model Christian holy man.

Athanasius' depiction of Antony may have borne little resemblance to the historical Antony,[16] but the practices associated with him and other Egyptian monks soon set the standard for monks living elsewhere in the Roman Empire. We may see how such "Egyptian" practices were idealized, schematized and promoted by western authors reporting to readers back home. As Jerome (ca. 347–420) informed his Roman protégé Eustochium in 384, in Egypt there were three kinds *(genera)* of monks.[17] *Coenobites* lived together and regulated their prayer, fasting, and manual labor in obedience to superiors in their communities. *Anchorites* were those who had withdrawn far from society and lived alone in deserted regions after training in *coenobia*. Antony had made such anchorites famous, but their way of life could be traced back to John the Baptist. There was still another kind of monk, which Jerome labels the *remnuoth:*

> These men live together in twos or threes, seldom in larger numbers, and live according to their own will and ruling. A portion of what they make they contribute to a common fund which provides food for all. In most cases they live in cities and fortress villages, and anything they sell is very expensive, as if it were their craftsmanship that was holy rather than their way of life. Quarrels are frequent among them, for while they supply their own food, they refuse to subordinate themselves to anyone. It is true that they compete with one another in fasting, making a fuss about achievements which should be kept secret. Everything among them is done for effect: loose sleeves, big boots, rough cloaks, constant groaning, visiting virgins, slandering clergy. Whenever a feast day comes they stuff themselves till they vomit.

sen, pp. 27–29: εἰς ἄκρον ἀκριβείας καὶ τελειότητος ἤθεσι καὶ γυμνασίοις τοῖς πρέπουσιν ἐξήσκησε ταυτηνὶ τοῦ βίου τὴν διαγωγὴν Ἀντώνιος ὁ μέγας μοναχός ... σπουδαίου γὰρ εἶναι φιλοσόφου κατεῖδεν μὴ μόνον ἑαυτὸν γυμνῶσαι χρημάτων, ἀλλὰ καὶ εἰς δέον ταῦτα ἀναλῶσαι. ... τῶν ὁμιλούντων αὐτῷ τὸν τόνος ἐκίρνα καὶ τοὺς τρόπους ἐρρύθμιζε. ... ἀργεῖν δὲ οὔτε αὐτὸς ἠνείχετο καὶ τὸν μέλλοντα καλῶς βιοῦν ἐργάζεσθαι παρεκελεύετο ... ἐσπούδαζεν ἀγνοεῖσθαι καὶ ἐν ταῖς ἐρημίαις λανθάνειν. ... τοὺς μὲν γὰρ ἰχθύας ἔλεγε. ... ξηρᾶς ἁπτομένους τὸ ζῆν ἀπολιμπάνειν, τοὺς δὲ τὴν μοναστικὴν σεμνότητα ἀπολλύειν τοῖς ἄστεσι προσιόντας.

16. See Rubenson (1995): 185–91; Michael A. Williams, "The *Life of Antony* and the Domestication of Charismatic Wisdom," in *Charisma and Sacred Biography* (Chico, Calif.: Scholars Press, 1982), 23–45; and Hermann Dörries, "Die Vita Antonii als Geschichtsquelle," in *Worte und Stunde*, vol. 1 (Göttingen: Vandenhoeck und Ruprecht, 1966a), 145–224.

17. For the *genera monachorum* tradition, see Fry (1981): 313–20.

According to Jerome, such remnuoth were regarded in Egypt as "most inferior and despised," but "in our own province," he remarks, "they are the chief if not the only kind" of monk—an observation to which we shall return.[18]

The Egyptian *genera monachorum* that Jerome defined became more developed when John Cassian (ca. 360–435) described Egyptian practices for fledgling monastic communities outside Marseilles. As he wrote around 428, "in Egypt there are three kinds of monks, of which two are excellent, while the third . . . must be completely avoided."[19] Like Jerome, he identifies the first two kinds as coenobites and anchorites, but the third he calls *sarabaites;* he also provides a history for each. According to Cassian, coenobitic monasticism originated with the apostles, whose common use of property is described in Acts 2:45 and 4:32–35. However, as Christian leaders began to relax the original discipline of their communities, those who sought apostolic perfection were forced to move away from cities. These recluses, he asserts, were the earliest monks, and vestiges of their way of life could still be seen in strict *coenobia*.[20] Like Jerome, Cassian says that anchorites originated with Antony but found their prototypes in John the Baptist and Old Testament figures. Cassian, however, also insists that the anchoretic lifestyle evolved from the coenobitic.[21]

Against these two *genera* Cassian contrasts the *sarabaites*. These, he says, hasten to be called monks, but fail to observe coenobitic discipline or submit to the will of a superior; they make renunciations only for show, and live at home, without a superior, either alone or in groups of two or three; they wander about at will, and work only to provide themselves with luxu-

---

18. Jerome, *Ep.* 22.34; text and trans. (adapted) F. A. Wright, pp. 136–37: tertium genus est, quod dicunt remnuoth, deterrimum atque neglectum et quod in nostra provincia aut solum aut primum est. Hi bini vel terni nec multo plures simul habitant suo arbitratu ac dicione viventes et de eo, quod laboraverint, in medium partes conferunt, ut habeant alimenta communia. Habitant autem quam plurimum in urbibus et castellis, et, quasi ars sit sancta, non vita, quidquid vendiderint, maioris est pretii. Inter hos saepe sunt iurgia, quia suo viventes cibo non patiuntur se alicui esse subiectos. Re vera solent certare ieiuniis et rem secreti victoriae faciunt. Apud hos affectata sunt omnia: laxae manicae, caligae follicantes, vestis grossior, crebra suspiria, visitatio viginum, detractatio clericorum, et si quando festior dies venerit, saturantur ad vomitum.

19. John Cassian, *Collatio* 18.4; ed. E. Pichery (SC 64), p. 14: duo sunt optima tertium . . . omnimodis evitandum.

20. Cassian, *Collatio* 18.5; ed. Pichery (SC 64), pp. 14–16: Istud ergo solummodo fuit antiquissimum monachorum genus . . . cuius etiam nunc adhuc in districtis coenobiis cernimus residere vestigia.

21. Cassian, *Collatio* 18.6; ed. Pichery (SC 64), pp. 16–18: ita ergo processit ex illa qua diximus disciplina [i.e., the coenobitic] aliud perfectionis genus, cuius sectatores anchoretae id est secessores merito nuncupantur.

ries.[22] Cassian links them historically to Ananias and Sapphira, who had declined to give all their property to the original apostolic community (Acts 5:1–4), but he also suggests that most sarabaites were driven to the monastic profession "by necessity."[23] Like Jerome, he notes that their kind of monasticism was about the only one found outside of Egypt.[24] Cassian, however, adds that a fourth kind of monk had recently emerged. Though he gives them no name, he says they pretend to be anchorites, but refuse to submit to the governance of superiors after a brief period of training in coenobitic monasteries.[25]

Whether or not Cassian was familiar with Jerome's letter to Eustochium, it was his version of the Egyptian *genera monachorum* that provided the general profiles by which monks would be classified and evaluated in the Western monastic tradition. Early in the sixth century (ca. 500–530) an anonymous writer used Cassian's distinctions of good and bad monks in his *Rule of the Master*.[26] While this writer felt no need to amplify his brief entries on coenobites, anchorites, and sarabaites, he went much farther than Cassian in describing a fourth kind of monk, applying a Greek and Latin hybrid term to describe them: *gyrovagi* (those who wander in circles).[27]

> They spend their entire life in different provinces visiting different cells or monasteries for three or four days . . . demanding that their hosts perform the precept of the Apostle which says "Give hospitality to strangers" [Rom 12:

22. Cassian, *Collatio* 18.7; ed. Pichery (SC 64), pp. 19–20: ad publicam tantummodo id est ad hominum faciem renuntiantes. . . . districtionem ut diximus coenobii declinantes bini vel terni in cellulis commorantur . . . hoc praecipue procurantes, ut absoluti a seniorum iugo exercendi voluntates suas ac procedenti vel quo placuerit evagandi agendiue quod libitum fuerit habeant libertatem.

23. Cassian, *Collatio* 18.7; ed. Pichery (SC 64), pp. 18–19: hi igitur dum inbecillo animo rem summae virtutis adfectant, vel necessitate ad hanc professionem venire conpulsi.

24. Cassian, *Collatio* 18.7; ed. Pichery (SC 64), p. 21: per alias provincias . . . istud tertium Sarabaitorum genus abundare ac prope esse cogouimus.

25. Cassian, *Collatio* 18.8; ed. Pichery (SC 64), pp. 21–22.

26. More precisely, he used Cassian's distinctions transmitted by the *Rule* of Eugippius (511–ca. 535), abbot of a monastery near Naples. For the relation of the *Regula Eugippii* to the *Regula magistri [RM]*, see Conrad Leyser, *Authority and Asceticism from Augustine to Gregory the Great* (Oxford: Clarendon Press, 2000), 108–18. I focus on the *RM* because of its influence on Benedict and his *Rule*.

27. The term *gyrovagi* derives from the Greek γῦρος (circle) and Latin *vagus* (wanderer, vagrant). It is first attested in *Regula Eugippii* 27.13–18 (a passage used and amplified by the *RM*), but its origin is not known. In the late fourth century, Evagrius Ponticus used the term κυκλευτής to describe monks who "circulate" from one superior to another in the Egyptian desert: see below ch. 1. For the social problems associated with *gyrovagi* in the *RM*, see Maribel Dietz, *Travel, Wandering, and Pilgrimage in Late Antiquity and the Early Middle Ages* (Ph.D. diss., Princeton University, 1997), 121–31.

13]. Taking advantage of this precept, they ask to rest their restless feet after journeying; using travel as a pretense, what they really desire is to relieve not their feet but their bellies. . . . Never staying put, they are forced by traveling every day to beg, sweat and groan, instead of living and working in one place. . . . they prefer to travel than stay still. Ever wandering through different lands, they have no idea where they might support their weariness, or even where they might find their burial.[28]

It was this anonymous *Rule of the Master* that provided Benedict of Nursia (writing ca. 530–560) with a typology for rounding off the *genera monachorum* at the beginning of his own more famous sixth-century *Rule*.[29] For Benedict it sufficed to note that in addition to coenobites, anchorites, and sarabaites,

> there exists a fourth kind of monk called gyrovagi, who spend their entire life in different provinces visiting different cells for three or four days, ever wandering, never settled, enslaved to their own wills and debauched bellies, worse than sarabaites in all ways. Better to keep silent than to speak about these and their wretched way of life.[30]

As sarabaites served as a negative foil for coenobitic monks, so too did gyrovagi serve as a negative foil for the anchoretic life. The *Benedictine Rule* enshrined this extension of John Cassian's original schema for posterity, providing a stereotype by which ascetic wandering and begging would be understood and disparaged into the medieval period.[31] But Augustine's treatise shows that this form of monastic life could already be considered a widespread problem by the end of the fourth century.

The near uniformity of this *genera monachorum* tradition might suggest there was agreement in late antiquity over what constituted good and bad ascetic practices and monastic types. It is therefore important to note another anonymous, but less well-known, version of the *genera monachorum,*

28. *RM* 1,32–49,163–173; ed. Adalbert de Vogüé (SC 105), pp. 332–46: numquam persistantes acti sunt cotidie ambulando mendicare, sudare et gemere, quam uno loco stando laborare et vivere. . . . eligunt magis ambulare quam sistere. Qui per diversa semper vagando ignorant apud quem tedia sua suscipiant, et quod est ultimum, nesciunt ubi suam constituant sepulturam.

29. On the relationship between the two *regulae,* see Fry (1981): 79–83 and Leyser (2000): 118–20.

30. Benedict of Nursia, *Regula* 1.10–12; ed. Timothy Fry et al., p. 170: Quartum vero genus est monachorum quod nominatur gyrovagum; qui tota vita sua per diversas provincias ternis aut quaternis diebus per diversorum cellas hospitantur, semper vagi et numquam stabiles, et propriis voluntatibus et gulae illecebris servientes, et per omnia deteriores sarabaitis.

31. See Ernest McDonnell, "Monastic Stability: Some Socioeconomic Considerations," in *Charanis Studies: Essays in Honor of Peter Charanis,* ed. A. E. Laiou-Thomadakis (New Brunswick: Rutgers University Press, 1980), 136–38.

written probably in southern Gaul around 410.[32] It was written partly in response to a view apparently held by many at that time, namely that monks were "worthy of hatred" even by Christians.[33] The author of the *Discussions of Zacchaeus and Apollonius* attributes this view to the practices of certain deviant monks who feigned fasting and chastity while creeping among women, whom they seduced "with vain notions" in order to obtain gifts and reap "the shameful profits of greed."[34] He then goes on to describe those *genera* of monks he considered true. Like Jerome and John Cassian, he identifies these as monks who either lived alone or together in a communal arrangement, shunning inactivity in the belief that their "food had to be derived through work alone."[35] In contrast to Jerome and Cassian, however, this author assumes that the communal monks he praises might also be found in urban areas and says nothing about obedience to superiors. (He also includes mere celibates among those who "truly pursue their monastic profession," though he deems these to be inferior to others: "their faith is hot, but not burning; while religious in disposition, they are not wholly consumed with religion.")[36] Here lies the importance of his version of the *genera monachorum*. Not only does the *Discussions of Zacchaeus and Apollonius* attest the variety of monastic life to be found in cities of the early fifth century. It also indicates that Jerome and Cassian were using the Egyptian monastic tradition to reform monastic practices considered acceptable by at least some Western authorities: for the loosely organized monastic communities its author describes seem to be exactly what Jerome and Cassian

32. For date (ca. 408–10) and milieu (Suplicius Severus' circle) of the *Consultationes Zacchaei et Apollonii*, see Jean Louis Feiertag, *Les Consultationes Zacchaei et Apollonii. Étude d'histoire et de sotériologie* (Fribourg: University Press, 1990), 38–125; summarized in *id., Questiones d'un Païen à un Chretien (Consultationes Zacchaei christiani et Apollonii philosophi)*, vol. 1 (Paris: Éditions du Cerf, 1994), 16–31.

33. *Consultationes Zacchaei et Apollonii* 3.3.1; ed. Jean Louis Feiertag and Werner Steinmann (SC 401), p. 178: quam ob causam etiam nostrorum odiis digni habeantur. For pagan antipathies toward monks in this period, see D. H. Raynor, "Non-Christian Attitudes to Monasticism," *SP* 18 (1989): 267–73.

34. *Consultationes Zacchaei et Apollonii* 3.3.6; ed. Feiertag-Steinmann (SC 401), p. 180: primum studiis lubricae familiaritis irrepunt, captasque mulierculas vanis opinionibus inludentes, in usum miserae cupiditatis illiciunt; dum aut muneribus inhiant, et foeda avaritiae lucra conquirunt.

35. *Consultationes Zacchaei et Apollonii* 3.3.13–15; ed. Feiertag-Steinmann (SC 401), p. 184: Locis primum remotioribus habitant, etiamsi in urbibus degant. . . . cunctis exsecrabilis torpor, et victus nisi labore non congruens.

36. *Consultationes Zacchaei et Apollonii* 3.3.9–12; ed. Feiertag-Steinmann (SC 401), pp. 180–84: Hi autem vere modum professionis istius exsequuntur. . . . Quidam etiam velut in postremo sectae istius gradu parva observatione contenti tantum caelibes vivunt. . . . fides calida est, non tamen fervens; et mens religiosa non religioni penitus addicta.

were complaining about when they noted the prevalence of remnuoth or sarabaite monasticism outside Egypt.[37]

NORMATIVE TRADITION AND HISTORICAL REALITIES

*If monks [are single ones], why so many? If so many, how then can they be
    solitaries?*
Oh multitude of monks that gives the lie to monachism!
    PALLADAS, late fourth to early fifth century[38]

Tracing the early history of Christian monasticism in the Roman Empire remains a vexed problem, not least because Athanasius' portrait of Antony and the writings of authors like Jerome and Cassian continue to influence monastic studies.[39] Many scholars continue to assume that "a distinction must be made between an ascetic and a monk, as every monk is an ascetic, but not every ascetic is a monk."[40] Yet the *genera monachorum* tradition demonstrates that making such distinctions was not so easy in the late fourth and early fifth centuries, and that early monastic history was itself a process of sorting out which practices were to be identified with legitimate monks, and which were not.

In the *genera monachorum* two practices are held to be defining features of monastic legitimacy: social isolation and economic self-sufficiency. Both depended on the practice of manual labor, which enabled a monk to live independently from mainstream society. Indeed, Paul had admonished Christians to "work with your own hands" for this very reason, "that you

37. For this objective of Cassian's *De institutis* and *Collationes,* see Columba Stewart, *Cassian the Monk* (Oxford: Oxford University Press, 1998), 17. Stewart suggests *De institutis* 10.23 was aimed at practices associated with Martin of Tours (see below, ch. 3) and Sulpicius Severus. That Jerome and Cassian were discussing the same phenomenon under the labels *remnuoth* and *sarabaites* is clear. Both labels probably derive from the Coptic word *auāet* (company): see Fry (1981): 318 n. 39.

38. Palladas, *Anthologia Graeca* 11.384; trans. adapted from William R. Paton, *The Greek Anthology,* vol. 4 (LCL 84; Cambridge: Harvard University Press, 1926), 255: εἰ μοναχοί, τί τοσοίδε; τοσοίδε δὲ, πῶς πάλι μοῦνοι; / ὦ πλῆθυς μοναχῶν ψευσαμένη μονάδα. A distich "mocking the discrepancy between theory and practice": Alan Cameron, "Wandering Poets: A Literary Movement in Byzantine Egypt," *Historia* 14 (1965): 474.

39. For their influence on modern studies see esp. James E. Goehring, "The Origins of Monasticism," in *Eusebius, Christianity, and Judaism,* ed. H. W. Attridge and G. Hata (Leiden: Brill, 1992), 235–55.

40. S. Abou Zayd, *Ihidayutha* (Oxford: ARAM, 1993), 93. The attempt to distinguish between monk and ascetic is modern. When distinctions were drawn in late antiquity, they were drawn between true and false monks. I cannot agree with Karl Heussi in *Der Ursprung des Mönchtums* (Tübingen: Mohr, 1936), 53–54, who argues that a *Sonderwelt* created by isolation (in a hermitage, cloister, etc.) from the world distinguished a monk from an ascetic. Physical withdrawal was a contested criterion for monastic legitimacy in this period; see below, chs. 3–5.

may behave properly towards outsiders and be dependent upon no one" (1 Thess 4:11–12). Yet we must not take this ascetic emphasis on manual labor for granted. Although numerous studies have focused on the way "orthodox" monastic authorities of this period like Jerome, Augustine, and Cassian promoted its practice as an ascetic ideal,[41] few have sufficiently addressed the alternatives to that normative tradition that existed and were also espoused at the time.[42] Indeed, modern studies have tended to identify objections to manual labor with marginal or heretical ascetic groups such as "Manichaeans," "Messalians" or "circumcellions." Moreover, they have treated such groups as separate historical phenomena, or rather, as distinct and isolated historical "movements." In this way scholarship has perpetuated the labels, distinctions, and typologies that late antique authorities used to discredit and marginalize beliefs and practices contrary to their own. As a result, we have lost a balanced perspective (if not complete sight) of a conflict between different notions of ascetic propriety that arose in the late fourth and early fifth centuries. This conflict had bearing not only on the development of the normative monastic tradition, but also on the place and privileges that monks could assume in the late Roman ecclesiastical and social structure.

This book approaches early monastic history as a series of conflicts and reforms that arose over such practices as wandering, begging, and enthusiastic behavior (e.g., prophesying or ostentatious prayer and fasting) as well as the justifications made in their defense. I attempt to circumvent late antique typologies by taking a comprehensive approach that draws on a

41. See Heinrich Holze, *Erfahrung und Theologie im frühen Mönchtum. Untersuchungen zur einer Theologie des monastichen Lebens bei den ägyptischen Mönchsvätern, Johannes Cassian, und Benedikt von Nursia* (Göttingen: Vandenhoeck und Ruprecht, 1992), 107–32; the articles in S. Felici, ed., *Spiritualità del lavoro nella catechesi dei Padri del III–VI secolo* (Rome: Libreria Ateneo Salesiano, 1986); A. Quacquarelli, *Lavoro e ascesi nel monachesimo prebenedettino del IV e V secolo* (Bari: Istituto di letteratura cristiana antica, Universtità degli studi, 1982); and Arthur Geoghegan, *The Attitude towards Labor in Early Christianity and Ancient Culture* (Washington, D.C.: Catholic University Press, 1945). Studies on ascetic poverty have focused on the same late antique authorities: e.g., Georg Jenal, *Italia Ascetica atque Monastica. Das Asketen-und Mönchtum in Italien von den Anfängen bis zur Zeit der Langobarden, ca. 150/250–604* (Stuttgart: Hiersemann, 1995), 474–94 and Adalbert de Vogüé, "Le pauvreté dans le monachisme occidental du IVe au VIIIe siècle," *Collectanea Cisterciensia* 46 (1984): 177–85.

42. True even for more nuanced studies of ascetic attitudes to manual labor in this period, e.g., Antoine Guillaumont, "Le travail manuel dans la monachisme ancien: contestation et valorisation," in *Aux origines du monachisme chrétien* (Bégrolles-en-Mauges: Abbaye de Bellefontaine, 1979a), 117–26 and Birgit van den Hoven, *Work in Ancient and Medieval Thought: Ancient Philosophers, Medieval Monks, and Theologians and the Concept of Work, Occupations, and Technology* (Amsterdam: J. C. Gieben, 1996), 117–52. Philippe Escolan, *Monachisme et Église. Le monachisme syrien du IVe au VIIe siècle: un ministère charismatique* (Paris: Beauchesne, 1999), 183–201, notes that manual labor was the exception to the norm in the Syrian milieu, and identifies this rejection of labor with an "apostolic" ideology rather than with specific heretical groups.

wide range of sources, while focusing primarily on ascetic wandering and material dependency. Thus problems specifically identified with certain monks in the East (e.g., Messalians) will be clarified by comparison to problems associated with monks in the West who in the same years were being criticized for similar practices, but under different labels. I also attempt to expose the rhetorical strategies used by critics of such "pseudomonks" by noting similarities to satirical tropes used by Greco-Roman authors to discredit philosophic rivals in earlier periods. Furthermore, my point of departure is social history, especially (although I begin with desert communities in Egypt) the urban social history of the late Roman Empire. That is because monks who wandered or refrained from manual labor were not considered a problem if they remained in the wilderness. It is also because most of our sources were written by members of urban societies who were keenly aware of the attitudes of their fellow urban citizens. Indeed, too often monasticism in this period has been treated as if it developed wholly detached from the late Roman social mainstream, as if monks themselves neither blended into nor were affected by the late Roman urban environment and social structure.[43] But these were the historical realities that most concerned the authorities who wrote our sources.

It will become clear that an apostolic ascetic lifestyle characterized by wandering and material dependency was widely advocated and practiced in the fourth and fifth centuries all around the Roman Empire.[44] This form of monastic life went back at least to the third century and was justified by a literal understanding of certain New Testament passages (e.g., Mt 6:26–34, Lk 10:38–42, Jn 6:27, Acts 6:1–4, and 1 Thess 5:17).[45] It was based on the notion that strict imitation of Jesus and his apostles (meaning absolute poverty, prayer, and spiritual teaching) was the highest form of Christian life. Though its most radical proponents in this period became identified

43. A notable exception is McDonnell (1980). Two important discussions of wandering as an early ascetic practice are Antoine Guillaumont, "Le dépaysement comme forme d'ascèse dans le monachisme ancien," *École Pratique des Hautes Études, Ve section: Sciences religieuses, Annuaire 1968–1969* 76 (1968): 31–58 and Hans von Campenhausen, "The Ascetic Ideal of Exile in Ancient and Early Medieval Monasticism," in *Tradition and Life in the Church*, trans. A. V. Littledale (Philadelphia: Fortress Press, 1968), 231–51. They do not, however, discuss the social and economic implications of the practice.

44. In this respect my study differs from Escolan (1999), which treats "apostolic" monasticism only as a Syrian phenomenon, restricted to the Roman East.

45. To clarify, I will not link this apostolic form of monastic life directly to first-century Christian *Wanderradicalismus*, on which see Gerd Theissen, "The Wandering Radicals," in *Social Reality and the Early Christians: Theology, Ethics, and the World of the New Testament*, trans. M. Kohl (Minneapolis: Fortress Press, 1992), 33–60. Instead, I argue that this apostolic lifestyle arose from the way Christians (in different places, at different times) read or heard their Scriptures and aspired to imitate them.

as heretics (e.g., "Manichaeans," "Eustathians," "Messalians"), it was also represented by those ascetics whom Augustine and others identified as "pseudomonks," who offered urban patrons spiritual services in exchange for material support. We shall see how this form of monastic life was marginalized by church and monastic authorities either through accusations of heresy or through their insistence (justified by giving different interpretations to the scriptural passages cited above, or by placing greater emphasis on such passages as Acts 4:32–35, 5:1–4, Eph 4:28, and 2 Thess 3:6–10) that withdrawal from urban areas, manual labor, and moderate poverty truly constituted strict monastic discipline and apostolic *mimēsis*. This study therefore establishes that authorities like John Chrysostom who have been most associated with promoting Christian asceticism in this period were not promoting asceticism per se, but rather certain kinds of asceticism. In addition, we shall see that their reasons for doing so derived not merely from spiritual principles but from social preoccupations as well.

The late fourth and early fifth centuries were troubled times for the Roman Empire. Though still prosperous, it was not a world in which many could easily attain *amerimnia* (freedom from care), a word that wealthy citizens of Antioch inscribed in the floors of their suburban villas.[46] Barbarian invasions and pressures of heavy taxation troubled all levels of society. Nothing reflects these developments more starkly than the imperial legislation preserved for our horror in the Theodosian and Justinian Codes. With authoritarian certitude successive emperors sought to guarantee stability by prescribing a social order in which professions were made hereditary obligations, where "anyone who tried to seek improvement of his status or make for pastures new was promptly dragged back to the place and calling of his *origo*."[47] Thus at the lowest levels of society Emperor Theodosius I in 393 decreed that peasant tenants of large estates in Thrace,

> even though they appear freeborn by natural condition, shall nevertheless be regarded as slaves to the very land on which they were born, and shall have no right to take off wherever they like or to change their place of inhabitation.[48]

His successors forbade even urban guild members to change their occupations and residences in concern that many such skilled laborers had

---

46. Jean Lassus, *Sanctuaires chrétiennes de Syrie* (Paris: Geuthner, 1947), 265.

47. Cameron (1965): 484, caricaturing a standard take on late Roman society.

48. *CJ* 11.52.1; ed. Paul Krüger, p. 443. Cf. *CJ* 11.51.1, issued seven years earlier. For such laws, see A. H. M. Jones, "The Caste System in the Later Roman Empire," *Eirene* 7 (1970): 79–96 and *id.*, *The Later Roman Empire, 284–602: A Social, Economic, and Administrative Survey* (Oxford: Basil Blackwell, 1964), 795–803, 809–12.

already "deserted the service of the cities to pursue a life in the country, taking off for hidden and out-of-the-way regions."[49] Official policy was no less rigid toward citizens whose birth and resources qualified them to serve on local city councils. Edicts were issued nearly every year from 313 to 418 to stem the "flight of the councilors," that is, to restore the many *decurions* who sought to evade this financial burden (formerly assumed by local elites as a matter of voluntary competition, and the main basis for urban prosperity in earlier centuries) by slipping into the imperial administration and other professions, or by simply wandering off on *peregrinatio* (travel abroad).[50]

Historians are rightfully skeptical whether such legislation was enforced or had any real effect on late Roman society.[51] The imperial laws nonetheless illustrate a deep concern for establishing a fixed socioeconomic hierarchy (and thus a dependable tax base) for the late Roman world, and that *stabilitas loci* was a guiding ideal for promoting economic and social stability in the imperial domain before it became advocated in monastic circles. We may be sure that such civic policies and concerns influenced the contemporary church leaders, many of whom now came (especially in the East) from decurion social ranks or higher.[52] It has often been observed that church leaders of this period identified ascetic practices such as rejection of manual labor, male and female cohabitation, liberation of slaves, and the wearing of long hair (by men) or short hair (by women) with heresy partly because such practices effaced commonly recognized categories on which the Roman social order and hierarchy was based.[53] But the monastic movement also challenged notions of proper social order in less dramatic ways.

Although historians have recognized that monasticism provided a new way by which late Roman citizens might improve their social standing,[54] few have studied how contemporary monastic leaders responded to this sudden confluence of men and women from different social origins, or how such

49. *CTh* 12.19.1 (issued in 400) and 14.7.2 (issued in 409 or 412); ed. Theodor Mommsen and Paul Meyer, pp. 733 and 785.

50. See *CTh* 12.1, the largest collection of edicts in the *CTh* under a single heading. For *peregrinatio* see *CTh* 12.1.143–144 (both issued in 395). For the "flight of the councilors," see Jones (1964): 737–63 and J. H. W. G. Liebeschuetz, *Antioch: City and Imperial Administration in the Later Roman Empire* (Oxford: Clarendon Press, 1972), 167–86.

51. See Jones (1970): 96; Cameron (1965): 484; and Ramsey MacMullen, "Social Mobility and the Theodosian Code," *JRS* 54 (1964): 49–53.

52. See Frank D. Gilliard, "Senatorial Bishops in the Fourth Century," *Harvard Theological Review* 77 (1984): 153–75 and *id., The Social Origins of Bishops in the Fourth Century* (Ph.D. diss., University of California at Berkeley, 1966).

53. Evelyne Patlagean, *Pauvreté économique et pauvreté sociale à Byzance, 4–7ème siècles* (Paris: Mouton, 1977), 136–45.

54. MacMullen (1964): 49.

mobility influenced contemporary monastic discourse. Yet it is apparent from Augustine's letters as well as his treatise *On the Work of Monks* that "social inequalities were maintained" in monasteries that he and his peers established around Hippo and Carthage.[55] Describing the proper distribution of labor in the monastery, Augustine explained that monks who came from humble origins *(ex paupertate)* should continue to perform the manual labors that characterized their former existence, but those who came from affluent backgrounds *(ex divite)* must not be required to perform such physical toils: they should be given administrative duties instead.[56] Augustine sought to promote compassion between rich and poor members of his monasteries rather than to break down existing social categories. For it would "in no way be decent" *(nullo enim modo decet),* he reasons, that men of senatorial ranks who adopted monasticism should become laborers while workmen became idle, or that peasants *(rustici)* should live luxuriously in monasteries where landed gentry *(praediorum domini)* had retired after renouncing such a life. Thus Augustine accepted and reinforced the distinctions of social rank, status, and privilege of the secular world within his monastic "commonwealth of Christians."[57]

Few monastic writers of this period make such overt reference to social rank and decorum as Augustine does here. However, the criticism that Nilus of Ancyra laid against wandering, begging "pseudomonks" in Eastern cities of the early fifth century responded to similar concerns. These monks, as we shall see, pursued patronage by offering themselves as ascetic teachers to wealthy urban Christians, which Nilus attributes to their having no source of support from home. Yet urban households were not the only venue through which the *gyrovagi* of this period could achieve upward social mobility. While commenting on the wayward practices of certain bishops under his jurisdiction, Pope Siricius of Rome (384–399) complained that

> it is hard to imagine anything more illicit than the fact that [certain bishops] refuse to provide sustenance to those who pass through (whether they really are or simply pretend to be monks, as they call themselves), but rather make these men—whose way of life and baptism we can know nothing about, and

55. W. H. C. Frend, *The Donatist Church: A Movement of Protest in Roman North Africa,* 3d ed. (Oxford: Clarendon Press, 1985), 328 n. 5, referring to Augustine, *Ep.* 211.6.

56. Augustine, *De opere* 25.33; ed. Zycha, pp. 579–80: si nolent [to perform manual labor] quis audeat cogere? quibus tamen invenienda sunt opera in monasterio etiamsi a corporali functione liberiora, sed vigilanti administratione curanda.

57. Augustine, *De opere* 25.33; ed. Zycha, p. 580: omnium enim christianorum una respublica est. . . . illi autem, qui etiam praeter istam sanctam societatem vitam labore corporis transigebant . . . si nolunt operari, nec manducent. . . . nullo modo enim decet, ut in ea vita, ubi senatores fiunt laboriosi, ibi fiant opifices otiosi, et quo veniunt relictis deliciis suis qui fuerant praediorum domini, ibi sint rustici delicati. On Augustine's concerns in this passage see Leyser (2000): 8–19.

whose faith we consider uncertain and unproven—their deacons, or hasten to ordain them as priests, or, what is more serious, do not hesitate to make them bishops. . . . Since [such ordained monks] are not used to restraint, they first exult in pride, then soon fall into falsehood; for those who are complete strangers to the world cannot be assumed to have learned true faith in churches.[58]

Such readiness to hustle wandering monks into church service is otherwise unattested. Siricius' letter points out, however, what was happening in church dioceses outside our view, as well as the ease with which some monks assumed positions of authority in the ecclesiastical domain. It was not until the mid-fifth century that monks (and other laymen) were expressly forbidden to preach.[59] Siricius bears witness to two problems we shall find repeatedly associated with wandering monks of the East: questionable orthodoxy and a vexing ability to gain recognition as leaders in Christian communities. His letter alerts us that in the late fourth and early fifth centuries, the boundaries between the ecclesiastical and the monastic worlds, as between orthodox and non-orthodox belief, were still often remarkably fluid.

58. Siricius, *Ep.* 6.2 (4) (PL 13.1165B–1166A): quantum illicitum sit illud. . . . ut transeuntes (sive simulent, sive sint monachi, quod se appellant), quorum nec vitam possumus scire nec baptismum, quorum fidem incognitam habemus nec probatam, nolint sumptibus adjuvare, sed statim aut diaconos facere, aut presbyteros ordinare festinent, aut, quod est gravius, episcopos constituere non formident. . . . Non retenti, inde in superbiam exaltantur, inde insuper ad perfidiam cito corruunt; quia fidem veram in ecclesiasticis toto orbe peregrini discere non asseruntur. For the context of Siricius' letter see Jenal (1995): 694–97.

59. As stated by Pope Leo, *Ep.* 210.6. See Roger Gryson, "The Authority of the Teacher in the Ancient and Medieval Church," *Journal of Ecumenical Studies* 19 (1982): 176–87, esp. 179–80.

1

Wandering in the Desert and the Virtues of Manual Labor

It was said of Abba Agathon that he once spent much time building a cell with his disciples. When they had finished it they went to settle there. But in the first week he saw something that seemed harmful and he said to his disciples, "Get up, let's get away from here." They became very distressed and said, "If you were intending to move on all along, why did we take so much trouble to build the cell? People will be scandalized at us and say, 'Look, they've moved again: what unsettled, restless men!'" Seeing them distressed he said, "Even if some are scandalized, others will be edified and say, 'Such men are blessed because they move from place to place for the sake of God, scorning all else.' But whoever wants to come let him come. I'm already going."[1]

This vignette from the *apophthegmata patrum* (sayings and stories attributed to pioneers of Egyptian desert monasticism) presents two very different attitudes toward wandering monks in the late fourth or early fifth century, and introduces questions that are central to our entire study. It assumes that monks would likely cause a scandal if seen repeatedly *(palin)* moving or changing residence: Why? Who would be scandalized by such behavior? Does the label *akathistoi*—the "unsettled," "restless," or perhaps "unstable" ones—imply other behavior that caused alarm? If so, what sort of behavior? At the same time, why might other people consider such monks *makarioi* (blessed) and be edified by them, as Agathon so confidently asserts?

Agathon was an Egyptian anchorite, and this chapter explores these

---

1. G Agathon 6 (PG 65.109D–111A): μέλλουσι πάλιν οἱ ἄνθρωποι, σκανδαλισθέντες εἰς ἡμᾶς, λέγειν· Ἰδοὺ μετέβησαν πάλιν οἱ ἀκάθιστοι.... Εἰ καὶ σκανδαλίζονταί τινες, ἀλλὰ πάλιν οἰκοδομηθήσονται ἕτεροι, λέγοντες· Μακάριοι οἱ τοιοῦτοι, ὅτι διὰ τὸν Θεὸν μετέβησαν, καὶ πάντων κατεφρόνησαν. For the method of apophthegmata citation, see below, n. 7.

questions strictly within his desert milieu.[2] As Agathon's story makes clear, that means surveying the full range, cause and context of ambivalence. Egyptian desert tradition offers enough examples of respected wandering monks to demonstrate that wandering was not simply an outlandish, typically "Syrian," or otherwise deviant form of ascetic behavior, but rather a practice with its own principles, aims, and priorities, which might be pursued wherever conditions allowed.[3] Yet the Egyptian tradition needs closer examination, precisely because Egypt became almost uniformly identified by outsiders with *stabilitas loci* and industrious self-sufficiency.[4] Although the actual practice of these virtues among Egyptian monks was probably exaggerated,[5] the normative tradition associated with Egypt clearly favored an ascetic lifestyle based on cell-sitting and manual labor over one characterized by wandering and material dependency. To appreciate why that was so, we must set the ideals and problems identified with ascetic wandering against their presumed backdrop, the Egyptian desert.

This tradition and its setting nevertheless pose difficulties for historical analysis. By the fifth century, Egypt had become something of a monastic dreamworld shaped by the ideals of those who described it. While the *apophthegmata patrum* have long been regarded as the most faithful representation of the attitudes of the earliest Egyptian desert fathers, this literature has been passed down through several stages of oral and written transmission. Many of the apophthegmata may have been deliberately altered or placed in this Egyptian tradition to meet the concerns of a later monastic audience.[6] Even if we can identify the earliest apophthegmata in

2. The ideals and problems associated with wandering in Egypt are mainly found in the apophthegmata (i.e. anchoretic) tradition. Therefore, I will discuss Pachomius and coenobitic practices only in passing; evidence for their impact on anchoretic tradition is slight. See Philip Rousseau, *Pachomius: The Making of a Community in Fourth-Century Egypt* (Berkeley and Los Angeles: University of California Press, 1985) and Bernward Büchler, *Die Armut der Armen. Über den ursprünglichen Sinn der mönchischen Armut* (Munich: Kösel, 1980).

3. See, e.g., Guillaumont (1968): 49–50; Campenhausen (1968): 234–36; Peter Nagel, *Die Motivierung der Askese in der alten Kirche und der Ursprung des Mönchtums* (Berlin: Akademie Verlag, 1966), 70–71, 94–96; Arthur Vööbus, *History of Asceticism in the Syrian Orient*, vol. 2 (Louvain: Secrétariat du CorpusSCO, 1960b), 269–71; and Richard Reitzenstein, *Historia Monachorum und Historia Lausiaca. Eine Studie zur Geschichte des Mönchtums und der frühchristlichen Begriffe Gnostiker und Pneumatiker* (Göttingen: Vandenhoeck und Ruprecht, 1916), 50–69.

4. E.g., Athanasius, *Vita Antonii* 3; *Historia monachorum in Aegypto* prol. 7–8; Chrysostom, *In Matthaeum hom.* 8.4–5; and Jerome, *Ep.* 22.36 and 125.11.

5. Ewa Wipszycka, "La monachisme égyptien et les villes," *Travaux et mémoires* 12 (1994), reprinted in *id.*, *Études sur le christianisme dans l'Égypte de l'antiquité tardive* (Rome: Institutum Patristicum Augustinianum, 1996), 325–27 offers a critique of the stereotypes of Egyptian monasticism in ancient tradition and modern scholarship.

6. See esp. Rubenson (1995): 152. Apophthegmata collections already circulated in Egypt by the late fourth century. Our collections seem to derive from one set down in Palestine in

the extant collections,[7] their precise attributions and chronology are difficult, if not impossible, to pin down.[8] For these reasons some historians now doubt whether the apophthegmata can be used to reconstruct Egyptian anchoretic history at all.[9] Dispute has arisen in particular over when, or to what extent, we can say that the desert elders ever condoned a wandering lifestyle. Philip Rousseau has argued that this practice had been a normal part of early desert existence until population growth in the late fourth and early fifth centuries caused a "hardening of attitudes" against movement, in order "to safeguard, amidst growing pressure, the atmosphere of tranquility" the desert had formerly provided.[10] Graham Gould counters, however, that it is impossible to reconstruct the attitudes of the desert fathers toward wandering in terms of historical development; he

the early fifth century and (probably) transmitted by monks, connected with Abba Poimen, who fled Scetis (described below) after its devastation by barbarians in 407: see Graham Gould, *The Desert Fathers on Monastic Community* (Oxford: Clarendon Press, 1993), 13–17; Jean Gribomont, "Les apophthègmes du désert," *Rivista di storia e letteratura religiosa* 13 (1977a): 534–35; and Wilhelm Bousset, *Apophthegmata: Studien zur Geschichte des ältesten Mönchtums* (Tübingen: Mohr, 1923a), 68–71. It is possible that the tension found in many apophthegmata between wandering, cell-sitting, and manual labor was introduced by later authors and does not reflect the concerns of the earliest desert fathers: see Peter Nagel, "Action-Parables in Earliest Monasticism: An Examination of the Apophthegmata Patrum," *Hallel* 5 (1977/1978): 251–61. At least two apophthegmata pertaining to wandering and manual labor show how the tradition might be altered by later redactors: see Philip Rousseau, *Ascetics, Authority, and the Church in the Age of Jerome and Cassian* (Oxford: Oxford University Press, 1978), 44–45 (on G Antony 10); another instance is PJ 4.17 (PL 73.866D), a story about an itinerant monk's resistance to stealing cucumbers, which a later version (PG 73.742CD) amplifies with a soliloquy on the virtues of manual labor.

7. For this approach, see Bousset (1923a) and Jean-Claude Guy, *Recherches sur la tradition grecque des Apophthegmata Patrum* (Brussels: Société des Bollandistes, 1984). Opinions differ over criteria and methodology for assessing priority for the different MSS and different versions of individual apophthegmata: see Rubenson (1995): 145–52; Gould (1993): 5–25; and, more generally, James Goehring, "Monastic Diversity and Ideological Boundaries in Fourth-Century Egypt," *JECS* 5 (1997): 61–65.

I cite the collections whose priority is generally accepted: the systematic Latin [PJ]; the alphabetical Greek [G]; the anonymous Greek [N, #133–369]; the Ethiopian [Eth.Coll.]. Each apophthegm is cited by its collection's abbreviation, followed by its name and / or number in that collection. Another valuable source for apophthegmata and early Egyptian anchoretic practices is Isaiah's *Asceticon*. Though compiled in the late fifth century, it probably reflects earlier Scetic tradition: see Derwas Chitty, "Abba Isaiah," *JThS* n.s. 22 (1971): 68.

8. Bousset (1923a): 60–66 and Chitty (1971) discuss chronology for the fathers identified in the sayings and for the different generations they represent.

9. A position stated categorically by Rubenson (1995): 188; see also Ewa Wipszycka, "Les aspects économiques de la vie de la communauté des Kellia," in *Le site monastique des Kellia: Sources historiques et explorations archéologiques* (Geneva, 1986); reprinted in Wipszycka (1996): 339.

10. Rousseau (1978): 44–53, quoted 45, 51.

also does not think any apophthegm shows an elder readily condoning the practice.[11]

Our sources offer a view of Egyptian desert monasticism that is impressionistic at best: it is easier to scan the range of attitudes and personalities attributed to the desert fathers than to place them confidently in a historical framework. Yet the monks who became known as desert fathers were part of a historical process, and stories about them can, to some degree, be anchored upon contemporary testimony. There is, for example, the Coptic *Life of Phif.* Probably written in the middle of the fourth century, this narrative records the movements of the anchorites Phif and Apollo. Together they wandered "all over the mountains like animals" and from village to village in Middle Egypt, building cells and staying for a year or so before moving on. Sometimes they received hospitality from monks along the way; otherwise, their disciple Papohe (the author of the narrative) took care of their material needs. Wherever they went, local monks sought from them their spiritual wisdom. After Phif's death, God directed Apollo to settle in a monastery near Tachlout (modern Dashlut). He was to have no fear: "Everyone will hear of you and come and give you gifts in your sanctuary . . . all will say, 'Come, let us go to the mountain of the Master.' "[12]

The *Life of Phif* provides a rare glimpse of the kind of monks who inspired some of the stories in Egyptian anchoretic tradition. Unlike the *Life of Phif,* however, that tradition is set mainly in the desert, using the desert to contextualize its explanations of various ascetic attitudes and practices, including wandering. Even if its original setting cannot be reconstructed in detail, we must probe the logic of this highly influential desert mentality.[13] Clearly it developed its own historical understanding of its origins:

> A brother went to Abba Sisoes from Petra [the disciple] of Abba Antony and said to him, "Father, what should I do? The brothers ridicule me saying, 'You wander about and have made a practice of racing from place to place: you refuse either to stay put or to do the work of your own hands.' " Abba Sisoes replied, "If the brothers of these days had seen us elders in our day racing from place to place with our sheepskins, they would have mocked us too and said 'Those men are possessed by a demon.' "[14]

11. Graham Gould, "Moving on and Staying Put in the *Apophthegmata Patrum,*" *SP* 20 (1989): 231–37, esp. 237 n. 35; also Gould (1993): 154–57, 163 n. 101.

12. Papohe, *Life of Phif* 5–14, ed. Tito Orlandi and trans. Antonella Campagnano, pp. 22–33; for date, p. 16. Tachlout and all the other villages they visited were in the Schmun/ Hermopolis Magna nome; the "mountains" were escarpments along the Nile valley edge.

13. James Goehring traces the early history of this mentality in "The Encroaching Desert: Literary Production and Ascetic Space in Early Christian Egypt," *JECS* 1 (1993): 281–96.

14. Eth.Coll. 14.37; trans. Victor Arras, 87: Deambulas et circumcursas et edoctus es circumcursare de loco in locum, nec cupis manere et operari opus manuum tuarum. . . . Fratres

As a second-generation desert monk, then some ninety years old,[15] Abba Sisoes would have been exceptionally qualified to observe what changes had occurred in the desert since his arrival there in the early fourth century. To think this apophthegm actually preserves his own reflections is perhaps naïve. Yet even if it merely reflects the nostalgia of later monks for a lost or imaginary way of life,[16] we should not discount the historical perspective or reasoning it represents. Not only does it assume that wandering had been a defining feature of early Egyptian desert existence, but it also suggests that this practice had become repudiated and even misunderstood by a later generation of monks whose lifestyle and outlook were confined by their cells.

The Sisoes apophthegm justifies an exploration of why monks themselves imagined that such a change had occurred over the first three generations of Egyptian desert monasticism (ca. 330–430). One starting point is clear: the desert father tradition reflects a need to reconcile an ideology of solitary withdrawal with the pressures of an increasingly populated desert world.[17] The conflicting goals of solitude and communal stability made wandering a controversial practice. Yet the very telling of stories about early wanderers in the Egyptian tradition indicates a readiness to accommodate as well as to censure this alternative lifestyle. Such stories seem to have been preserved because they not only expressed fundamental spiritual ideals, but also communicated what principles and behavior might render this lifestyle compatible with communal monastic needs and, therefore, acceptable. The Sisoes apophthegm, however, directs us toward a problem that was particularly associated with wandering monks and raised concern. A wandering monk was suspected to be a monk who did not engage in the practice most commonly recommended to ensure both individual and communal tranquility: manual labor.

This fairly obvious complaint against wandering monks in Egyptian tradition has attracted little notice,[18] but it is crucial for understanding why

---

harum dierum, si invenissent nos seniores nostris diebus . . . huc illuc circumcursantes, nos ludibrio habuissent dicentes: isti viri daemonium habent.

15. From the 340s to the 430s, according to Chitty (1971): 59.

16. Gould (1993): 16 n. 65 believes this apophthegm to be one of several that present a later, nostalgic perspective, formulated after barbarian raids (in 407, 410, and 434) had devastated the desert settlements and forced inhabitants to move to more secure areas. Gould believes the apophthegmata generally represent the idealized projections of later diaspora communities on early monastic history.

17. See Gould (1989): 233–36 and (1993): 153. Although Gould explains the impulse to wander in the desert by reference (as Rousseau does) to the historical circumstance of overcrowding, he does not concede that such overcrowding may have also resulted in a change of attitude to that practice.

18. Hermann Dörries, "Mönchtum und Arbeit," in *Worte und Stunde*, vol. 1 (Göttingen: Vandenhoeck und Ruprecht, 1966b), 279–80, notes a conflict between the ideals of wandering

wandering became generally repudiated as an ascetic vice. No doubt the dominant emphasis on manual labor and self-sufficiency was to some degree determined by certain scriptural exhortations,[19] but it was also taught by difficulties that arose from communal ideals and economic needs. Though some Egyptian wanderers embodied the Gospel's ideal of living "free from care" (Mt 6:25–34; Lk 12:22–34), many represented a life of dependence on others. Criticism of monks who did not work remind us that securing adequate provisions remained a constant worry for monks in the desert. Anxieties common enough in more affluent regions of the Roman Empire were greatly amplified by desert conditions, in which the prayer "give us this day our daily bread" had special urgency. This was particularly true in the Egyptian desert, where "to survive at all . . . the [monk] had to transplant into it the tenacious and all-absorbing routines of the village" and "remain in one place, earning his living from manual labor."[20] This background of desert scarcity clarifies the Egyptian tradition's ambivalence toward the wandering lifestyle by casting the ascetic virtues and vices that desert wanderers represented in starkest possible relief.

XENITEIA IN THE DESERT

By the late third century an ascetic movement marked by varying degrees of *anachōrēsis* (withdrawal) had begun to flourish among Christians in Egypt.[21] The *Life of Antony* informs us that before Pachomius established (ca. 320) his famous coenobitic community in a deserted town of Upper Egypt, Antony the Great had already heeded the Gospel's call to "care not

and manual labor in the Egyptian tradition, but does not attempt to explain it. Nagel (1966): 95–101 treats the subjects separately.

19. E.g., Ps 128:2; 1 Thess 2:9, 4:11–12; and 2 Thess 3:6–12. The tension between the Pauline passages and Mt 6:25–34 will be discussed below, ch. 3; here I wish to describe other points of tension. Few apophthegmata quote Paul directly, but allusions to his stance on manual labor are clear enough (e.g., as 2 Thess 3:8 justifies manual labor πρὸς τὸ μὴ ἐπιβαρῆσαι τινα, so G Poemen 10 justifies it διὰ τὴν ὄχλησιν). Nagel (1977/1978): 256–58 believes many apophthegmata that justify manual labor (e.g., G John Colobus 2; Silvanus 5; Isaias 5) were products of later times.

20. Brown (1982): 110.

21. Derwas Chitty, *The Desert a City: An Introduction to the Study of Egyptian and Palestinian Monasticism under the Christian Empire* (Oxford: Basil Blackwell, 1966), remains standard; recent studies emphasize the close and regular contact Egyptian monks maintained with villages. I have found especially helpful Wipszycka (1994); Rubenson (1995): 89–125; James E. Goehring, "The World Engaged: The Social and Economic World of Early Egyptian Monasticism," in *Gnosticism and the Early Christian World. In Honor of James M. Robinson*, ed. J. E. Goehring et al., vol. 2 (Sonoma: Polebridge Press, 1990), 134–44; and E. A. Judge, "The Earliest Use of Monachos for 'Monk' (P. Coll. Youtie 77) and the Origins of Monasticism," *JbAC* 20 (1977): 72–89.

for tomorrow" and set the ascetic movement on its most heroic, solitary course.[22] After imitating more experienced "renouncers" *(apotaktikoi)* living at the edge of his village, Antony began to seek more ambitious measures of social withdrawal, culminating with his departure (ca. 313) to the "Inner Mountain," some eighty-five miles from the Nile toward the Red Sea.

Before Antony, "no monk at all knew the distant desert" in Egypt.[23] The *Life of Antony* produced the most influential account of how that desert was won for Christian monasticism. It captures the spirit that motivated many fourth- and fifth-century Egyptians to seek out the desert frontiers in order to become strangers to "the world." *Xeniteia* was the term that became used for the voluntary alienation by which ascetics sought release from material and social circumstances that might hinder their ability to trust in God and make spiritual progress thereby.[24] Christians had traditionally achieved *xeniteia* in Egypt by withdrawing to the confines of their homes or to the outskirts of their villages.[25] Over time, however, increasing numbers sought a more dramatic fulfillment by relocating, like Antony, to the stark otherworld of the desert. Here, beyond the sights and sounds of the world, it was believed a monk might find spiritual stillness or tranquility *(hēsychia)*.[26] But life in the desert was far from serene. As Antony himself may have warned, its demons never ceased to make war on a monk's heart,[27] and its pitiless environment relentlessly challenged its new inhabitants' ability to stay still, remain tranquil, and "care not for tomorrow."

Not until foreigners began to write travel accounts of Egypt in the late fourth and early fifth centuries do the monastic settlements of the desert come into focus.[28] The settlements of Nitria (Kom al-Barnugi), Kellia (Kou-

22. Athanasius, *V.Antonii* 3.1; ed. G. J. M. Bartelink, p. 134: ἤκουσεν ἐν τῷ εὐαγγελίῳ τοῦ Κυρίου λέγοντος· Μὴ μεριμνήσητε περὶ τῆς αὔριον (Mt 6:34); sect. 11 and 49–50.

23. Athanasius, *V.Antonii* 3.2.

24. The term originated from scriptual references to Christians as "strangers and travelers on earth" (e.g., Heb 11:13, 1 Pet 2:11): see Guillaumont (1968): 33–35 and Campenhausen (1968): 231–51. Antony himself wrote that Abraham's departure (Gen 12:1) from home and family "is the model for the beginning of this way of life. . . . wherever and whenever souls endure and bow to it, they easily attain the virtues, since their hearts are ready to be guided by the Spirit of God." Antony, *Ep.* 1; ed. and trans. Rubenson, p. 197.

25. Athanasius, *V.Antonii* 3–11. See Wipszycka (1996): 283–87; Graham Gould, "The *Life of Antony* and the Origins of Christian Monasticism in Fourth-Century Egypt," *Medieval History* 1 (1991): 3–11; Goehring (1990); and Judge (1977): 80–86.

26. G Antony 11 (PG 65.77C).

27. G Antony 11 (PG 65.77C), with Antoine Guillaumont, "La conception du désert chez les moines d'Egypte," *RHR* 188 (1975): 19 n. 2.

28. Not to say sharp focus: see Georgia Frank, *The Memory of the Eyes: Pilgrims to Living Saints in Christian Late Antiquity* (Berkeley and Los Angeles: University of California Press, 2000), 49–69, for narrative strategies and motifs in the *Historia monachorum in Aegypto* and Palladius, *Historia Lausiaca*. For John Cassian's description of monks of Nitria, Kellia, Scetis, and other regions, see Stewart (1998): 8–12, 133–40.

sour al-Robbeyat), and Scetis (Wadi Natrun), all founded southwest of Alexandria from 330 to 340, were the most accessible and became the most famous, providing the setting for the writings of Evagrius Ponticus, Palladius, and John Cassian as well as for many of the apophthegmata.[29] Monks who clustered here around the cells of their chosen spiritual masters enjoyed far more independence for ascetic experimentation in pursuit of hēsychia than did those who entered the more regulated Pachomian coenobitic institutions along the Nile. As Palladius describes life at Nitria (ca. 388–398/400), "men on the mountain have different ways of living, each as he is able and as he wishes."[30] But freedom in these frontier settlements was never absolute. Certain precepts evidently circulated more than others, and monks were expected to conform, to some degree, to the balanced way of life that their masters promoted for both individual and communal tranquility.

Within such communities evolved the Egyptian desert tradition and the normative "spirit of . . . classical Egyptian anachoretism," which shunned "the fantastic and superhuman" ascetic feats usually associated with Syria.[31] Yet the moderation so often identified with Egyptian tradition evolved through a process of weighing options to determine what ascetic practices might best suit monks and their needs within the desert settlements. We glimpse how monks imagined that process through an apophthegm that tells how an elder at Kellia made his confession to Ammonas, a disciple of Antony: "Three thoughts weigh me down: should I wander in the desert, move away to some foreign land where no one recognizes me, or lock myself in a cell and not greet anyone, and eat only every other day?" "Sit in your cell," Ammonas advised, ". . . and you will be saved."[32] While promoting moderation, this apophthegm surveys more extreme options that some of the earliest desert monks "prone to a hard life" were imagined to have tried in order to maintain their xeniteia and "be saved." It has been

29. For Nitria and Scetis, see Hugh G. Evelyn-White, The Monasteries of the Wadî'n Natrûn. Part 2: The History of the Monasteries of Nitria and Scetis (New York: Metropolitan Museum of Art, 1932). For Kellia, see below, n. 43. Gould (1993): 13 believes that the apophthegmata collections G and N were compiled to preserve a "clear view of Scetiote monasticism" before its diaspora. Evagrius, Palladius, and John Cassian visited or lived in these communities before 400.

30. Palladius, Historia Lausiaca [HL] 7.2; ed. G. J. M. Bartelink, p. 38. For differing views on the relative contrasts between anchoretic "freedom" and coenobitic "constraints," see Bousset, "Das Mönchtum der sketischen Wüste," ZKG 42 (1923b): 9; Rousseau (1978): 51; and Gould (1989): 231.

31. Campenhausen (1968): 234.

32. G Ammonas 4 (PG 65.120BC): τις γέρων πονικὸς εἰς τὰ Κελλία . . . τρεῖς λογισμοὶ ὀχλοῦσί μοι· ἢ τὸ πλάζεσθαι ἐν ταῖς ἐρήμοις, ἢ ἵνα ἀπέλθω ἐπὶ ξένης ὅπου οὐδείς με ἐπιγινώσκει, ἢ ἵνα ἐγκλείσω ἑαυτὸν εἰς κελλίον καὶ μηδενὶ ἀπαντήσω, διὰ δύο ἐσθίων.

suggested that this vignette illustrates the victory of "classical" Egyptian asceticism over non-Christian Egyptian religious traditions,[33] or over radical Christian tendencies promoted by such ascetic literature as the *Acts of Thomas* or Manichaean "Psalms of the Wanderer."[34] The story more clearly responds, however, to the basic premise, that withdrawal to settlements like Nitria and Kellia did not guarantee the solitude or the salvation expected of the desert. There was often an impulse to seek a more extreme *xeniteia*. What were conditions in these communities actually like, and how did they affect Egyptian desert tradition?

Looming just beyond the green Nile valley, the Egyptian desert was always something of an imaginary terrain for the monks who lived there and visitors who described it.[35] Its magnitude is best evoked by Palladius, for whom the *panerēmos* (open desert) extended from Nitria "as far as Ethiopia, Mazicae, and Mauretania": that is, to the limits of the sub-Mediterranean world.[36] But this stark expanse served more as an inspirational backdrop than as an actual residence for the monks who produced the desert tradition. Necessity restricted their cells to regions close enough to the Nile to allow access to water seeping up through the sand. Those who tried to push farther risked breakdown, if not death.[37] Need for supplies also kept them close to the villages and towns of the world they had renounced.[38] This

33. So Bousset (1923b): 19–23 and 31. Nagel (1966): 90–94 surveys non-Christian parallels. Late antique Egypt's various religious traditions would have informed the ascetic thinking of monks who moved to the desert, but their impact on local monastic practices can be glimpsed only through the fifth-century writings of Shenoute in Upper Egypt. See David Frankfurter, *Religion in Roman Egypt: Assimilation and Resistance* (Princeton: Princeton University Press 1998), 264–84.

34. Both discussed below, ch. 2. For the possibility of Manichaean influences, see Rubenson (1995): 122–23 and Rousseau (1985): 28–36, both expressing caution. Fragments of a Coptic *Acts of Thomas* have been edited by Paul-Hubert Poirier, *La version copte de la Prédication et du Martyre de Thomas* (Brussels: Société des Bollandistes, 1984).

35. Peter Brown, *The Body and Society: Men, Women, and Sexual Renunciation in Early Christianity* (New York: Columbia University Press, 1988), 214–23, evokes the real and imaginary impact of the desert on Egyptian anchoretic thought. Guillaumont (1975): 7–13 discusses the ambivalence toward this setting in the apophthegmata. Idyllic descriptions of the desert all come from foreigners appealing to Greek and Roman sentiments: see Frank (2000): 29–101 and Stefan Rebenich, *Hieronymus und sein Kreis. Prosopographische und sozialgeschichtliche Untersuchungen* (Stuttgart: Franz Steiner, 1992), 86–98. Wipszycka (1996): 330–36 and Goehring (1990): 135–36 note the influence of such romantic literature upon modern scholarship.

36. Palladius, *HL* 7.2. Roger Bagnall, *Egypt in Late Antiquity* (Princeton: Princeton University Press, 1993), 144, notes the sharp contrast between the fertile green and black of the Nile valley and the desert's dry reddish hues.

37. Exemplified by the fate of Ptolemy, a monk who lived eighteen miles beyond Scetis in "a place where no one can live": see Palladius, *HL* 27. Near the desert edge, water could be tapped beneath the surface: Papohe, *Life of Phif* 9.

38. Wipszycka (1996): 324–25; Goehring (1990): 138–39; and Bagnall (1993): 144, 295

range of viable desert solitude was reduced even further by increased settlement and development.

By the late fourth century, monastic settlements had in fact transformed previously empty wastelands. Around the year 400, one visitor wrote in his *History of the Monks in Egypt*, "You can see them scattered in the desert like true sons awaiting Christ their father . . . a boundless multitude of monks of all ages, inhabiting the desert and countryside in numbers impossible to count."[39] Other visitors corroborate his impression that monks were populating the desert in remarkable numbers. About 3,000 inhabited Nitria alone when Rufinus visited in 373.[40] Fifteen years later Palladius reckoned that number at 5,000. He also says there were two communities at Nitria with as many as 150 and 210 monks each, and records that by then 600 more had moved into the open desert at Kellia.[41]

While impressive to visitors, this influx was remembered as a problem in the apophthegmata tradition. Kellia was first settled, we are told, when a sense of crowding forced Nitria's original founder, Amoun, to find a new region "far off" where he and others might continue to live in tranquility.[42] This solution was only temporary. The fourth- to eighth-century remains of the new settlement, named Kellia after the brick cells that dotted the desert slopes, have recently been exposed by excavators. The site resembles nothing less than a densely packed suburb, with over fifteen hundred walled *laurae* (two or more cells linked by a central hall or court) burrowed down and sprawled across a seven-mile strip of sand, all constructed around wells tapping seepage from the Nile.[43]

---

discuss distances of monasteries from cultivated land. The most distant (Scetis) was a twenty-four-hour journey west of the Nile, in Wadi'n Natrun, where water was available.

39. *Historia monachorum in Aegypto [HM]* prol. 7–10; ed. André-Jean Festugière, pp. 7–8 (cf. Num 24:5–6). This Greek *HM* purports to record what Palestinian travelers saw in Egypt in 394. It may be based in part on a lost description by Timothy of Alexandria, used by Sozomen in *HE* 6.29.2. Rufinus' Latin version is edited by Eva Schulz-Flügel, *Tyrannius Rufinus. Historia monachorum sive De vita sanctorum patrum* (Berlin: Walter De Gruyter, 1990), who thinks Rufinus also used a Greek text based on an actual journey. The two versions differ markedly on Nitria and Kellia, perhaps because a Greek redactor excised portions later associated with Origenism. See Caroline Bammel, "Problems of the *Historia Monachorum*," *JThS* n.s. 47 (1996): 99–101.

40. Rufinus, *HE* 2.3; cf. *id.*, *HM* 21.1.2.

41. Palladius, *HL* 7.2 and *id.*, *Dialogus de vita Iohannis Chrysostomi [Dial.]* 17. See also Evelyn-White (1932): 18, 84.

42. G Antony 34 (PG 65.85D): ἐπληθύνθησαν οἱ ἀδελφοὶ καὶ θέλουσί τινες αὐτῶν οἰκοδομῆσαι κελλία μακρὰν ἵνα ἡσυχάσωσι. Chitty (1966): 29 dates this foundation to 338.

43. See Antoine Guillaumont, "Les fouilles françaises des Kellia, 1964–1969" and Rodolphe Kasser, "Fouilles suisses aux Kellia: passé, présent, et futur," both in *The Future of Coptic Studies*, ed. R. McL. Wilson, 203–8 and 209–19, respectively (Leiden: Brill, 1978); also Rodolphe Kasser, "Sortir du monde: réflexions sur la situation et le développement des établissements monastiques aux Kellia," *Revue de théologie et de philosophie* 26 (1976): 111–24; C. C.

Rufinus says that Kellia's dwellings in the 370s were constructed "out of eyesight and earshot" from each other,[44] and it remains unclear how far the site's excavated structures reflect fourth-century conditions.[45] They reveal, nonetheless, that an influx of monks could nearly make the desert a city,[46] and cast doubt on the degree of solitude and simplicity often associated with Kellia and other desert settlements.[47] In fact, the people who moved to this new frontier represented a variety of backgrounds and ties to "the world." An imperial law of the early 370s reveals that some maintained substantial property in the Nile valley while living in the desert.[48] Some may have also brought slaves with them.[49] Nitria was developed to handle a growing tourist traffic: Palladius notes that in his day there was a guesthouse near the main church where visitors could stay up to two or three years (they had to work in the kitchen or garden after the first week). Within the church itself one could see three whips dangling from palm trees: these were kept to deal with fallen monks and thieves who came by. Nitria also had seven bakeries, as well as doctors and pastry cooks. Wine, too, was sold.[50]

Palladius attests how intensively monks were domesticating the regions closest to the Nile by the late fourth century. The amenities he saw at Nitria were not found at the desert's farthest outpost, the twenty-mile-long depression called Scetis, but increasing numbers evidently made changes felt there too. In the fourth century a priest named Isidore announced to his

---

Walters, *Monastic Archaeology in Egypt* (Warminster: Aris and Phillips, 1974), 7–18; and Denis Weidmann, "Kellia: Swiss Archaeological Activities," in *The Coptic Encyclopedia*, ed. A. S. Atiya, vol. 5 (New York: Macmillan, 1991), 1400–1406.

44. Rufinus, *HM* 22.2; ed. Schulz-Flügel, pp. 358–59: eremus enim est vasta et cellulae. . . . neque in conspectu sibi invicem neque in vocis auditu sint positae.

45. Excavations suggest the greatest density occurred after the fifth century. Only one fourth- or fifth-century complex has been conclusively identified (Qusur 'Isa 1), with small rooms under later structures. The quantity and distribution of such primitive structures is unknown; see Weidmann (1991): 1402–5.

46. Athanasius, *V.Antonii* 14.7; ed. Bartelink, p. 174: ἡ ἔρημος ἐπολίσθη ὑπὸ μοναχῶν. More accurately, "the desert was civilized by monks," which conveys the point that the transformation of the desert was not so much a matter of building new structures as of imagining its domestication.

47. See Wipszycka (1996): 337–38 and François Daumas, "Les travaux de l'institut français d'archéologie orientale pendent l'année 1966–67," *Comptes rendus de l'Académie des inscriptions et belles-lettres 1967* (Paris, 1968): 448.

48. *CTh* 12.1.63 (issued at Beirut, 370 or 373); see below, ch. 5 n. 48. For this law and the social origins and status of Egyptian monks generally, see Wipszycka (1996): 329–36 and (1996): 353–60.

49. Wipszycka (1996): 358–59; e.g., PJ 14.16 (PL 73.951A): Senex quidam solitarius habuit quemdam ministrum manentem in possessione.

50. Palladius, *HL* 7.2–4; ed. Bartelink, p. 38. Fallen monks: εἰς λόγον μοναζάντων πταιόντων. See also Wipszycka (1996): 255–57.

congregation one day that he intended to leave Scetis because it no longer provided the hardship for which he had come.[51] Once when another monk at Scetis complained, "I want to find *hēsychia,* but the brothers won't let me," he was advised to move to the remote "inner desert" of Scetis called Petra.[52] But already by the mid-fourth century Sisoes reportedly had fled Petra because of its crowding.[53] By the late fourth century one region of Scetis alone had five hundred monks.[54] There were also frequent visits from family members and strangers seeking cures, blessings, and general edification from desert elders. Macarius the Great was rumored to have dug a half-mile tunnel under Scetis just to escape his crowds of admiring visitors.[55]

No doubt such attention was often secretly welcomed, but an increase in desert traffic and domestication could easily erode the precious sense of distance that monks needed to imagine themselves separated from the world. Palladius was shown a cell of an early monk at Nitria that had been abandoned because it was now considered "too close to civilization—he had built it when the anchorites were few and far between."[56] Such perceptions of the desert's shrinkage help explain the desert tradition's ambivalence toward the practice of wandering. Not only does the need to pursue further measures of *xeniteia* become more understandable through this sense of the desert's domestication, but the stories that monks told about Egypt's wandering pioneers become more poignant too.

STORIES OF THE WANDERING PIONEERS

While touring monasteries along the Nile, the author of the *History of the Monks of Egypt* says he learned about John, an elder known for "surpassing all the monks of our own time in virtue." John was still alive, but could never be easily found because he was "always moving from place to place in the desert."[57] According to local tradition, John had stood motionless for three years under a rock in prayer. Eventually his feet cracked and an

51. G Poemen 44 (PG 65.332D): νῦν οὐκ ἔτι ἔχει κόπον. See also Eth.Coll. 13.27.

52. G Macarius Aeg. 22 (PG 65.272B). Evagrius Ponticus notes that the demon of vainglory attacked monks in the form of "crowds of people who touch their clothes" or "men knocking at the door, seeking audience with them": *Practicus* 13; trans. James Bamberger, p. 19.

53. G Sisoes 28 (PG 65.402AB): ἐν τῷ ἄρξασθαι πληθύνεσθαι τὴν Σκῆτιν. John Cassian, *Collatio* 19.5 also describes the crowding as well as the pressures it inflicted on a monk who eventually left it.

54. Palladius, *HL* 20.1 (for a region called Pherme).

55. Palladius, *HL* 17.10.

56. Palladius, *HL* 16.1; ed. Bartelink, p. 64: τὴν κέλλαν, εἰς ἣν ᾤκει οὐκέτι μὲν οὐδεὶς διὰ τὸ ἐγγυτέρω αὐτὴν εἶναι τῆς οἰκουμένης· ἐκεῖνος γὰρ τότε αὐτὴν ἔκτισιν ὅτε σπάνιοι ἦσαν οἱ ἀναχωρηταί. Trans. Robert Meyer, p. 52.

57. *HM* 13.3; ed. Festugière, p. 99: οὐδεὶς ταχέως εὑρεῖν δύναται διὰ τὸ ἀεὶ μεταβαίνειν αὐτὸν τόπον ἐκ τόπου ἐν ταῖς ἐρήμοις.

angel appeared. The angel healed him, then ordered him to move on. "Thereafter he lived wandering in the desert, eating wild plants."[58]

To younger contemporaries, John's lifestyle and virtue classed him among the wandering pioneers; he belonged to "another age."[59] The Sisoes apophthegm notes with irony how later monks naturally would believe their wandering predecessors to have been "possessed by a demon." By the late fourth century, many did in fact explain such behavior in terms of possession. But the Sisoes apophthegm seems to use the motif of possession for the specific purpose of criticizing that view. It suggests that monks "of these days," despite their more developed theories and practices, failed to understand or appreciate their predecessors' spirituality. The apophthegmata often use fantastic imagery to register the difference in spiritual capacities between one generation and the next. As Abba Elias measured Agathon (a monk of the third generation), "compared to his own generation he is fine, but compared to the ancient ones—I have seen a man in Scetis who could make the sun stand still in the heavens."[60] This power over the elements that God had given his champions in biblical times was also attributed to two of the wandering pioneers. The fantastic stories about these pioneers show how monks liked to think about those who had first ventured into the desert, before so many had made it a city. Such stories recaptured the grandeur of early desert *anachōrēsis*. By describing how early monks had penetrated the wild wastes where only angels, beasts, and demons had dared tread, they reminded their listeners of the desert's open expanses and preserved imaginative dimensions constantly imperiled by human encroachment. But they were not told only for entertainment; they also provided inspiration for monks afflicted by the physical limitations and spiritual doubts that were part of their desert existence.

"Nothing is wondrous about my own achievements when compared to our fathers' way of life." In this way the accomplished wonder-worker Abba Copres introduced his stories about Patermuthius, the first monk to appear in the Thebaid. This pioneer astonished his village priests by living on plants in the desert for three years.[61] He had the gift of mobility at will: as he roved between desert and cultivated land, "frequently if there was somewhere he wished to be, he suddenly found himself there." Once he made

---

58. *HM* 13.8; ed. Festugière, p. 100: διῆγεν δὲ κατὰ τὴν ἔρημον λοιπὸν περιάγων καὶ ἐσθίων βοτάνας. Rufinus says John was also ordered to go around the desert visiting and edifying other monks: eremum circumeuntem visitare etiam alios fratres et aedificare eos in verbo et doctrina domini: Rufinus, *HM* 15.2; ed. Schulz-Flügel, p. 337.

59. *HM* 13.3; ed. Festugière, p. 98: ἄλλης μὲν λοιπὸν ἡλικίας. Frank (2000): 54–55 analyzes such descriptions in the *HM* and *HL* as literary tropes.

60. G Elias 2 (PG 65.184B). Chitty (1971): 58 dates Agathon's death to 444. See Josh 10: 12–14 for Joshua making the sun stand still.

61. *HM* 10.2, 10.7.

the sun stand still, since the Gospel advised him to walk only during sun-
light; another journey transported him directly to paradise.[62]

This heroic generation was imagined to have passed beyond the limits
of human endurance. Its most colorful representative was Macarius the
Citizen,[63] a former Alexandrian street vendor and priest of Kellia who was
said to be a "lover of the desert more than anyone else." Palladius (who
"actually saw" him three years before he died) reports that Macarius kept
four cells around the desert as around the points of a compass; he was said
to have "explored its farthest, inaccessible regions."[64] His most famous quest
brought him to the legendary desert garden of Jannes and Jambres: in this
way Macarius, like Patermuthius, was believed to have visited paradise,
which he found after nine days of following stars, "traversing the desert as
if on the open sea." One version of the story emphasized the need to rely
on God for navigation: to teach Macarius to trust only in miraculous signs,
as Moses had done in the wilderness, God allowed a demon to remove the
reeds Macarius had carefully planted to mark his path back.[65] Another version tells how an angel led him to the garden after he had been lost for
three weeks. Two naked men lived there, who fed him the "fruits of Paradise." When Macarius asked if he could guide others to their garden from
the world, they forbade him, "because the desert extends far without mark-
ings and has many demons throughout who make monks wander and destroy them, as has happened to many others who wished to come here and
have been destroyed." Nonetheless, Macarius later showed the garden's
marvelous fruits to other monks of "the inhabited world" in hope that they
might follow him back. But their elders feared for their souls, refused to
let the monks go, and persuaded Macarius not to return.[66]

Such stories warned of the perils ordinary monks faced if they lost themselves in spiritual quests too ambitious or solitary. Yet they also showed how
extraordinary monks had overcome such perils by utterly trusting that God
would care for them and provide for their needs.[67] They not only provided

62. *HM* 10.12–21; ed. Festugière, pp. 80–84; citing Jn 11:9, 12:35. After living in the desert
for three years eating wild plants, Patermuthius astonished his church priests "for having
achieved the highest degree of ascesis": *HM* 10.7; ed. Festugière, p. 78.

63. Palladius, *HL* 18.1. Evelyn-White (1932): 55–58 dates his birth ca. 296, entry to Nitria
ca. 330, priesthood at Kellia ca. 355–74, and death ca. 396.

64. Rufinus, *HM* 29.1; ed. Schulz-Flügel, p. 369: amatorem fuisse eremi super omnes ceteros, ita ut etiam ultima et inaccessibilia deserti perscrutatus sit loca. Palladius *HL* 18.10 locates
his cells at Nitria, Kellia, and Scetis, and one "toward Libya."

65. Palladius, *HL* 18.6–10; ed. Bartelink, pp. 80–84. Jannes and Jambres were magicians
who had contested Moses' powers in Ex 7:11–22.

66. *HM* 21.6–9; ed. Festugière, pp. 125–26. The Greek *HM* confuses Macarius the Great
with Macarius the Citizen, but Rufinus' *HM* assigns the story to the latter.

67. E.g., *HM* 1.47, 10.23, 11.5, 12.4, 12.15; Palladius, *HL* 18.8–9.

the boldest examples of *xeniteia* in the desert but demonstrated that elusive ideal that first propelled Antony on his course, *amerimnia* (freedom from care).[68]

For outsiders, all monks who braved the Egyptian desert exemplified this ideal. As readers are told at the beginning of the *History of the Monks in Egypt,*

> Where they live there is no care for food or concern for clothing. . . . If one of them lacks his basic necessities, he does not turn to a city or village, or to a brother, a friend, a relation, or to his parents, children, or family to get what he needs, for his will by itself suffices. When he raises his hands and utters words of thanksgiving to God with his lips, all these things are instantly provided for him.[69]

The desert wanderers exemplified this ideal on the most elemental level. That was especially thought true of Abba Bessarion, another member of Scetis' pioneering generation, whose "way of life was like that of birds of the sky or fish in the sea or animals on land, since he passed all the years of his life free of care and anxiety."

> No concern for a dwelling troubled him, nor did any desire for a particular place ever control him, nor did the enjoyment of delights, possession of houses, or reading of books. Instead he seemed completely detached from all passions of the body, being nourished on the hope of things to come and supported by the strength of his faith; he lived like a prisoner led here and there, suffering cold or scorched by the sun's heat, being ever exposed to the open air in his nakedness. He afflicted himself along the desert's edge like a vagabond.[70]

Like Macarius, Bessarion was believed to have traversed the desert like a ship on the open sea. Like Patermuthius, he was said to have made the sun stand still so he could complete a journey, and like John, he was remembered for having stood still for an astonishing length of time in great pain.[71]

These monks share a superhuman profile that is unusual in Egyptian tradition (Macarius' *askēsis* was "so excessive," we are told, that he went almost totally bald).[72] Yet however eccentric they may seem, they simply

68. Athanasius, *V.Antonii* 3.1; so also Gould (1989): 237 and Guillaumont (1968): 34.

69. *HM* prol. 7–8; ed. Festugière, p. 7: οὐ φροντὶς ὑπάρχει παρ' αὐτοῖς, οὐκ ἐσθῆτος, οὐ βρωμάτων μέριμνα . . . ὅταν τις αὐτῶν ἐν ταῖς ἀναγκαίαις χρείαις ἐλλείπηται, οὐ πόλιν ἐπιζητεῖ. . . .

70. G Bessarion 12 (PG 65.141D–144AC): ἀμερίμνως πάντα τὸν τῆς ζωῆς αὐτοῦ χρόνον διατελέσαντα. Οὐ γὰρ φροντὶς οἴκου παρ' αὐτοῦ ἐμελετᾶτο, οὐ τόπων ἐπιθυμία κεκρατηκέναι ἔδοξε τῆς τούτου ψυχῆς, οὐ κόρος τρυφῆς, οὐ κτίσις οἰκημάτων, οὐ βίβλων περιφοραί· ἀλλ' ὅλος δι' ὅλου τῶν τοῦ σώματος παθῶν ἐφάνη ἐλεύθερος, ἐλπίδι τῶν μελλόντων τρεφόμενος. For Bessarion, see Bousset (1923a): 61.

71. G Bessarion 3, 8, and 6; PJ 7.4.

72. See Palladius, *HL* 18.3–4, 18.24, 18.28.

represented to their admirers a dramatic fulfillment of the "freedom from possessions, *askēsis,* and flight from men" that all Egyptian monks considered essential for spiritual advancement.[73] What made them superhuman was their ability to live as Jesus had exhorted his disciples to live, "free from care":

> Care not for your life, what you will eat or drink, nor for your body, what you will wear. Is not life more than food and the body more than clothes? Look at the birds of the sky; they neither sow nor reap nor gather into storehouses, yet your heavenly Father feeds them. Are you not worth more than they? . . . So do not worry and say, What shall I eat? What shall I drink? . . . But strive first for God's kingdom and his righteousness, and all these things will be given to you. Care not for tomorrow, for tomorrow will care for itself.[74]

This passage from the Sermon on the Mount, with its premise that God cares and that dedication to God and God's kingdom will relieve Christians from bodily and material worries, is fundamental to the stories of Bessarion, Patermuthius, John, and Macarius. Roaming where the Spirit moved them and trusting in its care, such early desert supermonks embodied the spirit of *amerimnia* in the most dynamic fashion.

Hence the confidence that some people would be edified by Agathon and his disciples and would regard them as "blessed because they move about for the sake of God, scorning all else." Each of the desert wanderers discussed above is said to have edified other monks, and edification seems to have been the main point of circulating tales about them.[75] Indeed, desert monks had special need for exemplars of freedom from care. The anxieties that persistently troubled them were documented in a spiritual self-help book written by Evagrius of Pontus (ca. 345–99), the great ascetic theorist of late-fourth-century Kellia. His *Counter-Sayings* provided scriptural citations to be recalled and recited whenever a monk was troubled by his thoughts. Many concerned the most basic fears:

> Against the thought of a soul worn out and distressed in hunger from scant bread and water: Isa 30:20.[76]

73. G Theodore of Pherme 5 (PG 65.183D): τὴν ἀκτημοσύνην, τὴν ἄσκησιν, καὶ τὸ φεύγειν τοὺς ἀνθρώπους.

74. Mt 6:25–33; ed. Kurt Aland et al., pp. 20–21: μὴ μεριμνᾶτε τῇ ψυχῇ ὑμῶν τί φάγητε [ἢ τί πίητε], μηδὲ τῷ σώματι ὑμῶν τί ἐνδύσησθε. οὐχὶ ἡ ψυχὴ πλεῖόν ἐστιν τῆς τροφῆς καὶ τὸ σῶμα τοῦ ἐνδύματος; ἐμβλέψατε εἰς τὰ πετεινὰ τοῦ οὐρανοῦ ὅτι οὐ σπείρουσιν οὐδὲ θερίζουσιν οὐδὲ συνάγουσιν εἰς ἀποθήκας, καὶ ὁ πατὴρ ὑμῶν ὁ οὐράνιος τρέφει αὐτά· οὐχ ὑμεῖς μᾶλλον διαφέρετε αὐτῶν; . . . μὴ οὖν μεριμνήσητε λέγοντες, Τί φάγωμεν; ἢ Τί πίωμεν; . . . ζητεῖτε δὲ πρῶτον τὴν βασιλείαν [τοῦ θεοῦ] καὶ τὴν δικαιοσύνην αὐτοῦ, καὶ ταῦτα πάντα προστεθήσεται ὑμῖν. μὴ οὖν μεριμνήσητε εἰς τὴν αὔριον, ἡ γὰρ αὔριον μεριμνήσει ἑαυτῆς. Cf. Lk 12:22–32. The influence of this passage on early monastic practice will be discussed more fully in the next three chapters.

75. See *HM* 10.9; 13.10; *HL* 18.12–16; G Bessarion 12 (PG 65.144AC).

76. Evagrius Ponticus, *Antirrheticus [Ant.]* 1.42; ed. with Greek retroversion Wilhelm Fran-

Against the thought being anxious over food and water, being concerned about where to get these: Ps 55:22.[77]

Against the thought telling me that hunger or great affliction will soon arise: Prov 10:3.[78]

Against thoughts that arise in us because of great need, that gradually break down the resolve of the soul: 2 Cor 4:8–11.[79]

Evagrius' scriptural citations provided relief for monks who could read. For others, the wandering monk of desert mythology provided a more personalized and perhaps more accessible relief,[80] reminding listeners of God's boundless care for them. As Bessarion reminded a disciple who was afraid of thirst on one of their travels, "God is here; God is everywhere."[81]

Thus, stories told of the wandering pioneers met the spiritual needs of monks anxious in their cells. They also provided sanction for monks of later generations who felt the need to move around. For example, when Abba Daniel, a monk of the third generation, was asked when he might build a cell and settle down, he justified his continued travel with Bessarion's rationalization: "God is in the cell; God is outside as well."[82] At the same time, this apophthegm indicates that justification was needed for movement in a place where monks were so often judged by their ability to stay put in their cells.

SETTLING THE DESERT

To turn from stories of the wandering pioneers to the actual practice of desert wandering is to pass from ideals of rugged solitude to the pragmatic constraints under which most monks lived. We do not know how many Egyptian monks actually lived like Patermuthius or Bessarion,[83] but desert wisdom mostly weighed against trying. Evagrius himself offered a scriptural remedy:

---

kenberg, pp. 480–81. For Evagrius' activities at Kellia (ca. 385–99), see Guillaumont (1972b): 29–56 and Michael O'Laughlin, "The Bible, the Demons, and the Desert: Evaluating the *Antirrheticus* of Evagrius Ponticus," *SM* 34 (1992): 201–15.

77. Evagrius, *Ant.* 1.16; ed. Frankenberg, pp. 476–77. See also *Ant.* 1.8.

78. Evagrius, *Ant.* 1.21; ed. Frankenberg, pp. 476–77.

79. Evagrius, *Ant.* 1.55; ed. Frankenberg, pp. 482–83.

80. See Peter Brown, "The Saint as Exemplar in Late Antiquity," *Representations* 1 (1983): 15–20.

81. G Bessarion 1 (PG 65.140A).

82. G Daniel 5 (PG 65.156B).

83. The Coptic *Life of Phif* indicates that there were more wandering monks in Egypt than our Greco-Roman sources reveal: see Wipszycka (1996): 325–27.

> Against the rash thought that prompts us to stretch out our way of life beyond what is necessary, so that we go out to a waterless place with sackcloth tied around our loins, and live continually under the sky, and eat desert roots; that repeatedly urges us to flee the sight of people who are calling us or are being called by us: Eccl 7:16.[84]

Similar caution is expressed in a story of Macarius the Great, the reputed founder of Scetis (not to be confused with Macarius the Citizen). For five years he was said to have held out in his cell against the impulse to "go to the desert to see what I could see," fearing lest his impulse had come from demons. Eventually he went out and discovered two naked monks living with animals far off by a pool of water. Totally isolated and ignorant of "the world," these monks represented the ultimate in desert *xeniteia*. "God has made this way of life for us," they told him. "We neither freeze in winter, nor does summer cause us harm." So Macarius asked,

> "How can I become a monk?" They said to me, "Unless you renounce everything in the world you cannot become a monk." I said, "But I'm weak and cannot live like you." And so they said to me, "If you can't live like us, sit in your cell and weep for your sins." Macarius knew that their renunciations were beyond him.

Accepting the more sheltered alternative, he conceded, "I have not yet become a monk, but I have seen monks."[85]

This story conveys the Egyptian tradition's profound ambivalence toward the open-air existence associated with such deep-desert marvels. It recognizes that their extreme form of *xeniteia*, though ideal, was beyond even the heroic founder of Scetis. In desert tradition Macarius the Great represents a cautious alternative to his wandering counterpart, Macarius the Citizen. In fact, the Egyptian desert demanded an ascetic lifestyle more tempered for human frailties. Exposure to its harsh environment posed severe risk: "An elder was asked, 'Why am I afraid when I walk into the desert?' He replied, 'Because you're still alive.' "[86] The dangers of pursuing *xeniteia* far into that desert were summed up by the scriptural remedy that Evagrius offered against such extremism: "Do not be too righteous, do not act too wise: why should you destroy yourself?" (Eccl 7:16).

Consequently most monks adopted a more settled, silent mode of *xeniteia* that helped ensure spiritual progress within communal circumstances. When Macarius the Great once dismissed monks at Scetis with the instruc-

---

84. Evagrius, *Ant.* 1.37; ed. Frankenberg, pp. 478–79.

85. G Macarius Aeg. 2 (PG 65.260B–261A). Trans. adapted from Benedicta Ward, pp. 125–26.

86. N 90.

tion to flee, an elder asked him, " 'Where can we flee beyond this desert?' Macarius put a finger to his mouth and said, 'Flee this.' Then he went to his cell, shut the door, and sat down."[87] Numerous apophthegmata similarly equate *xeniteia* with keeping silent and sitting in one's cell.[88] Besides being safer than desert wandering, this form of *xeniteia* promoted social harmony in desert settlements, which were all too often afflicted by the tensions and rivalries common to any small village. In the heated social world of the desert, tempers grew short: judgmentalism, backbiting, and anger were constant problems.[89] One elder admitted that the only thing harder than saying nothing mean to a brother was to leave a meal still hungry.[90] Moving from place to place was a natural response to such tensions.[91] But the desert fathers saw spiritual discipline and social restraint to be one and the same. They urged their followers to accept social reconciliation as a necessary part of their spiritual challenge:

> The fathers used to say that if temptation came upon you where you dwell, do not leave that place . . . for wherever you go, you will find what you flee. Be patient until the temptation passes, so that your withdrawal in time of peace will also not raise a scandal and so that your moving away does not cause affliction for those who dwell in that place.[92]

In this testy environment, movement could easily be interpreted as an insulting judgment against others and, therefore, might cause a scandal, as Agathon's disciples were aware. Keeping silent was a better way to minimize tensions. Bessarion advised a monk who was troubled living with other brothers to keep silent and to refrain from measuring himself against them.[93]

Silence and cell-sitting, however, could prove too much for even the hardest ascetics. In a vision attributed to Pachomius (Egypt's leading authority on the problems of communal life) the only monks seen in hell were monks "quite pure as regards to the body," but who were also "idlers who go about in places where brothers live as anchorites. They speak evil

87. G Macarius Aeg. 16 (PG 65.269B).

88. E.g., G Ammonas 4 (cf. Biare 1); G Arsenius 2; G Macarius Aeg. 16, 27, 41; and G Theodore 14 equate flight from men with sitting in one's cell or silence. G Andrew 1; G Longinus 1; G Tithoes 2; PJ 4.44, 15.43; and Isaiah, *Asceticon* 6.6b equate *xeniteia* with silence. For this form of *xeniteia*, see Guillaumont (1968): 52–55 and Gould (1993): 150–64.

89. Gould (1993): 112; Rousseau (1978): 51–53.

90. Eth.Coll. 14.17; trans. Arras, p. 83.

91. N 194, on which see Rousseau (1978): 44 and Gould (1989): 235 n. 27.

92. N 200: ὑπόμεινον ἕως οὗ παρέλθῃ ὁ πειρασμός, ἵνα ἀσκανδάλιστος γένηται ἡ ἀναχώρησίς σου καὶ ἐν καιρῷ εἰρήνης, ὅπως μηδὲ τοῖς κατοικοῦσι τὸν τόπον θλίψιν τινὰ ποιήσει ὁ χωρισμός σου. See also N 194 and Gould (1993): 99–101.

93. G Bessarion 10 (PG 65.141C); see also G Poemen 79.

of the other brothers living near [those they are visiting], knowing that the latter are not on good terms with the former, and thus they think they will find favor on account of their slanders, with a view to getting food and drink."[94] Such monks, Pachomius saw, would be "cast into hard torments that never cease." Evagrius warns that "the monk who wanders around will practice false sayings—he will contradict his own father."[95] Evagrius and the Pachomian vision make plain what the apophthegmata otherwise imply: wandering and social disturbances were believed to go together. By the end of the fourth century a decidedly negative image of wandering had emerged in the desert.

WANDERING IN DEJECTION AND THE SOLACE OF MANUAL LABOR

> The monk who wanders around is like a dry bush in the desert: he achieves stillness *[hēsychia]* for a time, but is then blown about, whether willing or not. A plant yields no fruit if transplanted, and a monk who wanders will bear no fruit of virtue. . . . Just as a single woman will not suffice for a man who loves pleasure, a single cell will not suffice for a monk afflicted by *akēdia.*[96]

Desert monasticism prompted the first serious discussion of depression and its disabling effects. In Evagrius' writings, monks who habitually wander around had succumbed to a desperate kind of bored depression or despondency known as *akēdia.* For monks who had to face the same barren cell alone each day, deprived of adequate sleep and food, with little hope of stimulation beyond their tedious contemplative routine, *akēdia* was a familiar, predictable, and merciless condition.[97] So regular were its assaults that monks equated it with the "sickness that wastes at noonday" mentioned in their ninetieth psalm, and called it the "noontime demon."[98] At this hour

94. Bohairic *Life of Pachomius* 88; ed. and trans. Armand Veilleux, pp. 114–15. On this Bohairic version of Pachomius' *vita,* see Rousseau (1985): 38–44.

95. Evagrius, *Ad monachos* 81; ed. Hugo Grossman, in Jeremy Driscoll, *The "Ad Monachos" of Evagrius Ponticus: Its Structure and a Select Commentary* (Rome: Abbazia S. Paolo, 1991), 59: Κυκλευτὴς μοναχὸς μελετήσει ῥήσεις ψευδεῖς / τὸν δὲ ἑαυτοῦ παραλογίσεται πατέρα. Though probably written for Rufinus and Melania's community at Jerusalem (see Driscoll, 37–43), the *Ad monachos* probably reflects Evagrius' experience at Kellia.

96. Evagrius, *De octo spiritibus malitia* 13 (PG 79.1160A): κυκλευτὴς μοναχὸς, φρύγανον ἐρημίας, ὀλίγον ἡσύχασε καὶ πάλιν φέρεται μὴ βουλόμενος. Φυτὸν μεταφερόμενον οὐ καρποφορεῖ, καὶ μοναχὸς κυκλευτὴς οὐ ποιήσει καρπὸν ἀρετῆς . . . Φιληδόνῳ οὐκ ἀρκέσει μία γυνὴ, καὶ ἀκηδιαστῇ μοναχῷ οὐκ ἀρκέσει μία κέλλα. Though preserved under the name of Nilus of Ancyra, this work is now attributed to Evagrius.

97. G Poemen 149 (PG 65.360A). John Cassian, *De institutis coenobiorum [Inst.]* 10.1 notes that it especially afflicted solitaries and desert dwellers.

98. Cassian, *Inst.* 10.1. Cassian is referring to Ps 91:6 of the RSV.

a heavy malaise spread over a monk,[99] causing those who could not resist either to fall asleep or to impose upon themselves extreme remedies of self-denial, such as excessive fasts or extreme *anachōrēsis* to remote, uninhabited places—"urging them," says Evagrius, "to imitate John the Baptist or that first anchorite, Antony."[100] Experience with this form of possession helped shape negative attitudes toward wandering monks in Egyptian tradition and the early monastic world.

Evagrius gives a detailed description of how this "most oppressive of all demons" could lead a monk astray.[101] Under its influence time seemed to stand still, and the desire to leave the cell became increasingly hard to resist.

> First of all [the demon] makes it seem that the sun barely moves, if at all, and that the day is fifty hours long. Then he constrains the monk to look constantly out the window, to walk outside the cell, to gaze carefully at the sun. . . . then he instills in the heart of the monk a hatred for the place, a hatred for his very life itself, a hatred for manual labor.[102]

Once in its grip, Evagrius explains, a monk begins to think that nobody cares for him; and if a fellow monk had ever caused him a slight, the demon of *akēdia* would remind him to nurture his grudge. Finally the demon would seduce him to abandon his cell with a rationalization often found in the apophthegmata: "This demon drives him along to desire other sites where he can more easily procure life's necessities. . . . He goes on to suggest that, after all, it is not the place that is the basis of pleasing the Lord: God is to be adored everywhere."[103] In the apophthegmata ascribed to Bessarion and Daniel, the conviction that God was everywhere provided a pious justification for wandering. For Evagrius, however, this sounded more like a demonic Siren's call to spiritual negligence. Evagrius considered it another way that the demon of *akēdia* might entice a monk either to abandon his cell and wander aimlessly in the desert, or to head home and give up monasticism for good.[104]

To hold out in the cell against a force so powerful a monk needed to

99. G Theodora 3 (PG 65.201C).

100. Evagrius, *De malignis cognitationibus* 25 (PG 79.1229D): ἀκροτάτην ἀναχώρησιν τῷ καρτερικῷ ὑποβάλλων, εἰς τὸν ζῆλον προσκαλούμενος Ἰωάννου τοῦ Βαπτιστοῦ, καὶ τῆς ἀπαρχῆς τῶν ἀναχωρητῶν Ἀντωνίου. See also Siegfried Wenzel, "Ἀκηδία: Additions to Lampe's Patristic Greek Lexicon," *VC* 17 (1963): 173–74.

101. Evagrius, *Practicus* 12; ed. Antoine and Claire Guillaumont (SC 170), pp. 520–22: Ὁ τῆς ἀκηδίας δαίμων. . . . πάντων τῶν δαιμόνων ἐστὶ βαρύτατος.

102. *Ibid.;* ed. A. and C. Guillaumont (SC 170), pp. 522–23; trans. Bamberger, pp. 18–19.

103. *Ibid.* Ed. A. and C. Guillaumont (SC 170), p. 524: οὐκ ἔστιν ἐν τόπῳ τὸ εὐαρεστεῖν τῷ Κυρίῳ προστίθησιν· "πανταχοῦ γὰρ," φησί, "τὸ θεῖον προσκυνητόν." Trans. Bamberger, p. 19.

104. See Evagrius, *Ant.* 6.4, 15, 24, 26, 33, 39, 41, 43–44, 52–53, 57.

train himself in using the "tools of God."[105] Chief among them was manual labor.[106] Egyptian monks liked to believe that this most mundane part of their life had divine origins: according to legend, it had first been introduced to Antony by an angel to help him withstand the assaults of the demon of *akēdia*.[107] Work generated spiritual staying-power: indeed, Egyptian tradition justifies the practice of manual labor primarily as a contemplative aid by which a monk might subdue his body and focus his mind on prayer.[108] Manual labor became such a mainstay of desert spirituality that some monks virtually equated it with sitting in the cell and salvation itself. "An elder was asked, 'What is necessary to do to be saved?' He was making rope, and without looking up from the work, he replied, 'You're looking at it.' "[109] The ability to spend long hours sitting weaving reeds into ropes attributed to Scetis' founder, Macarius the Great, was admired as a sign of spiritual energy and prowess.[110] Novice monks had to be warned not to make it a matter of rivalry.[111] Some elders worried that their fixation on manual labor threatened to supplant the contemplative activity it was meant to support. As one complained, "When I was at Scetis our main work was the work of the soul, and we regarded manual labor as a secondary work. Now the works of the soul have become secondary, and what was secondary is the main work."[112]

By at least the fifth century, manual labor was being specifically prescribed as an antidote for the impulse to wander around in a spiritual malaise.[113] It is perhaps no surprise that monks who embraced the spiritual rationale for this work ethic might regard wanderers as possessed by a demon. But they also had material grounds for complaint. The idlers in Pachomius' vision were said to spread gossip for the sake of getting food and drink. Such behavior was also attributed to the influence of *akēdia*:

> Whenever it begins to conquer anyone . . . it drives him out of his cell beaten, unstable, wandering about, negligent toward all work, and makes him contin-

105. S John Colobus 4; ed. Guy, p. 24. Cf. Gould (1993): 151.

106. For the emphasis of manual labor in Egyptian anchoretism, see esp. Dörries (1966b) and Wipszycka (1996).

107. G Antony 1.

108. E.g., Achilles 5; Isidore 5; and John Colobus 11. See also Nagel (1966): 100.

109. N 91; trans. Columba Stewart, p. 35. Manual labor and cell-sitting: G Poemen 168 (PG 65.361C): τὸ ἐν τῷ κελλίῳ καθίσαι, τὸ φανερόν, τοῦτό ἐστι τὸ ἐργόχειρον. Cf. Isaiah, *Asceticon* 5.20.

110. G Macarius Aeg. 4.

111. Isaiah, *Asceticon* 7.212; 8.12.

112. G Theodore of Pherme 10.

113. Isaiah, *Asceticon* 11.51; ed. René Draguet, p. 170: ἐὰν εἶ ἀποτακτικός . . . καὶ ἴδῃς σεαυτὸν θέλοντα κυκλῶσαι ἔτι ὄντος σου ἀσθενοῦς ταῖς αἰσθήσαι . . . κοπίασον ἔργῳ χειρῶν σου. The advice is included in a section explaining how not to become a burden on other monks.

ually go around the brothers' cells and monasteries for no other purpose but
to discover where, or with what excuse, he can procure refreshment in the
future. For an idler's mind cannot think of anything but food and the belly.[114]

In reading such descriptions, however, it is difficult to tell whether the main
concern was the problems *akēdia* caused an individual, or that idleness
caused a community. While depression challenged every monk in the desert, failure to overcome it presented a burden for the community as a
whole. The demonization of wandering in ascetic theory may have caused
some monks who wandered on principle to be misunderstood and mocked
by their peers. So the Agathon and Sisoes apophthegmata suggest. Nevertheless, whether or not they were considered demon-possessed, monks who
wandered the Egyptian desert in search of others to feed them would have
posed an unwelcome burden on monks already anxious about feeding
themselves.

WANDERING AND SUSTENANCE IN THE DESERT

In describing how a settlement was prepared for a thousand monks in
Upper Egypt's Thebaid, the *History of the Monks in Egypt* explicitly links
desert wandering with material need:

> Abba Or had spent much time in practicing the ascetic life as a solitary in the
> farther desert. Afterwards he organized hermitages in the nearer desert and
> planted a marsh-ground with his own hands . . . so that there would be a plen-
> tiful supply of timber in the desert . . . so that the brothers who gathered
> round him would not be forced to move around on account of any need.
> Instead he made every provision for them . . . so that they should not lack any
> necessity and would have no excuse for negligence.[115]

Although some wanderers, like John and Patermuthius, may have foraged
enough wild vegetation to survive in the deep desert for some time,[116] most
probably lived, like Phif, Bessarion, and other loners, along the escarp-

114. Cassian, *Inst.* 10.6; ed. Jean-Claude Guy, p. 390: excussum exinde instabilem de cet-
ero reddet ac vagum, et ad omne opus desidem cellas fratrum iugiter faciet ac monasteria
circumire nihilque aliud procurare. . . . mens enim otiosi nihil aliud cogitare novit quam de
escis ac ventre. See also Evagrius, *Ant.* 6.33 and 57.

115. *HM* 2.2–3; ed. Festugière, pp. 35–36: ἐφύτευσεν δὲ τοῦτο ἵνα μὴ διά τινα χρείαν οἱ
συνερχόμενοι πρὸς αὐτὸν ἀδελφοὶ ἀναγκασθῶσιν περιάγειν. ἀλλὰ πᾶσαν πρόνοιαν αὐτῶν ἐποιεῖτο.
. . . ἵνα ἐν μηδενὶ λείπωνται τῶν ἀναγκαίων καὶ μὴ πρόφασις αὐτοῖς ῥαθυμίας τις γένηται. Trans.
adapted from Norman Russell, p. 63.

116. *HM* 10.6; ed. Festugière, p. 78: τριετῆ διάγων χρόνον κατὰ τὴν ἔρημον . . . πρὸς τροφὴν
ταῖς ἀργίαις βοτάναις ἠρκεῖτο. It is not clear what is meant by desert here: perhaps the margins
of the cultivated zone. Nonetheless, deep desert survival must not be discounted as legendary:
HM 1.46 lists plausible ways to survive for short periods in the remote desert.

ments of the Nile valley. Their ridges offered plenty of tombs and niches for shelter, as well as a quick descent to fields, houses, and village trash-heaps for easy pickings.[117] But a more self-sustaining lifestyle and predict-able economy was needed to sustain large groups of monks and keep them from wandering in search of food or supplies. That was especially true in farther desert regions, like Scetis, where the "dearth of necessities" was so extreme that "even among lazy monks, neither gluttony nor indifference can be found."[118] In such desert settings, as much as in Pachomian mon-asteries along the Nile, a communal work ethic developed that eventually became normative in Egyptian tradition.[119] The apophthegmata portray inhabitants of Scetis routinely working in groups to produce ropes and baskets to sell for raw materials and food. Here manual labor was not just a spiritual discipline but a virtue of necessity.

At Scetis only if a monk were sick and displayed compunction with tears would he not be compelled by his peers to get out of his cell and work.[120] Fear kept them busy: it has been estimated that all the industry that made Egyptian monks so famous kept them just ahead of starvation.[121] Beyond the difficulty of feeding themselves, ascetic etiquette obliged monks to pro-vide hospitality for the "multitude of brothers rushing in" on visits.[122] Eva-grius' *Counter-Sayings* records how such concerns at Kellia gave rise to un-charitable thoughts:

> Against the thought telling me that the things collected for myself do not suffice for both me and the brothers who come to visit me: 2 Kings 4:43–44.[123]

> Against the thought telling me to guard my treasures for myself, being un-willing to use them to relieve any brother who asks: Deut 28:18.[124]

117. G Bessarion 12 (PG 65.144C); Bagnall (1993): 142–47 describes this marginal area and its inhabitants (shepherds, monks, tax evaders, outlaws).

118. Palladius, *HL* 17.5; ed. Bartelink, p. 72: οὐδὲ παρὰ τοῖς ῥᾳθύμοις ἔστιν εὑρεθῆναι ἀδηφαγίαν ἢ ἀδιαφορίαν ἐν τοῖς τόποις ἐκείνοις . . . διὰ τὴν σπάνιν τῶν χρειῶν. Marshes made Scetis inhabitable, providing reeds for weaving: see Evelyn-White (1932): 31–33.

119. Guillaumont (1979b): 119–25.

120. G John Colobus 19 (PG 65.212C): πολλάκις ἔρχεται ἀδελφὸς λαβεῖν με εἰς ἔργον . . . ἐὰν εὑρῶσί σε πενθοῦντα, οὐκ ἀναγκάζουσί σε ἐξελθεῖν. See Evelyn-White (1932): 173–76, 182–88 for monastic economies at Scetis and Kellia. Wipszycka (1996): 337–62 and (1996): 324–27 provide general surveys of Egyptian monastic economies.

121. So Wipszycka (1996): 350–52; for a more optimistic assessment, Aline Rousselle, *Porneia: On Desire and the Body in Antiquity*, trans. F. Pheasant (Oxford: Basil Blackwell, 1988), 169.

122. Cassian, *Collatio* 19.5–6.

123. Evagrius, *Ant.* 1.10; ed. Frankenberg, pp. 476–77.

124. Evagrius, *Ant.* 3.10; ed. Frankenberg, pp. 494–95. See also 1.28, 47, 49; 3.5, 57.

This "burden which generally weighs on all: the ordinary anxiety of providing food" helps explain the Egyptian tradition's distinctive emphasis on supporting oneself through manual labor.[125] Awareness of this burden produced the work ethic that fostered economic stability and social harmony in communities afflicted by scarcity. Thus Abba Poemen refused to stop pleating ropes at Scetis because of the burden he might otherwise cause.[126] Certain elders were presented as exemplars of self-sufficiency, like Agathon, "self-sufficient in all things: manual labor, food, and clothing," or Abba Pambo, who claimed he had never eaten bread that he had not earned with his "own hands," or Abba Zeno, who "had always refused to receive anything from anyone at all."[127]

Yet this ethic of self-sufficiency must not be taken for granted, nor can its widespread practice be certain.[128] Egyptian monks never confused practicing manual labor with a paradisial existence, the life of angels, or freedom from care. After all, one of the first lessons monks learned from their Scriptures was that the need to work had arisen from disobedience in Eden. Some yearned to transcend this daily reminder of original sin. One day, for example, John the Dwarf took off his clothes and, walking off toward the desert, told his elder, "I want to be free of care like the angels . . . who do not work but ceaselessly offer worship to God." This was a dangerous aspiration anywhere, but especially in the desert. John returned to his cell within a week, but his elder refused to recognize him: "John has become an angel and is no longer among men. . . ." John was left outside the cell in distress until the elder opened the door and reminded him, "You are human and must work to eat."[129] John humbly prostrated himself on the floor and asked forgiveness.

John's lesson was fundamentally about pride. Such cautionary tales rec-

---

125. See John Cassian, *Collatio* 19.6; ed. Pichery (SC 63), p. 43: hoc generale cunctorum pondus, id est communem parandi victus sollicitudinem. Isaiah, *Asceticon* 11 preserves rules especially sensitive to the problem of material support.

126. G Poemen 10 (PG 65.324C): οὐκ ἤθελε λαμβάνειν παρά τινός τί ποτε διὰ τὴν ὄχλησιν.

127. G Agathon 10 (PG 65.112C): αὐτάρκης ἐν πᾶσιν, ἔν τε τῷ ἐργοχείρῳ καὶ τῇ τροφῇ καὶ τῇ ἐσθῆτι. G Pambo 8 (369D): ἐκτὸς τῶν χειρῶν μοῦ οὐ μέμνημαι ἄρτον φαγών. G Zeno 2 (176C): ἀπ᾽ ἀρχῆς οὐκ ἤθελε λαβεῖν παρά τινός τί ποτε. See also PJ 6.15, 17, 20 and the interesting account of Agathon's virtues in Isaiah, *Asceticon* 6.5.

128. Dörries (1966b): 279–81 and van den Hoven (1996): 118. Rousseau (1985): 184 warns against assuming that Pachomius emphasized manual labor to the degree it was emphasized in later tradition. See also Wipszycka (1996): 350–57.

129. G John Colobus 2 (PG 65.204D–205A): Ἤθελον ἀμέριμνος εἶναι ὡς οἱ ἄγγελοι ἀμέριμνοί εἰσι, μηδὲν ἐργαζόμενοι, ἀλλ᾽ ἀδιαλείπτως λατρεύοντες τῷ θεῷ. . . . Ἄνθρωπος εἶ, χρείαν ἔχεις πάλιν ἐργάζεσθαι ἵνα τραφῇς. Trans. adapted from Ward, p. 86. Cf. Eth.Coll. 14.52. Nagel (1977/ 1978): 257 argues that this apophthegm was told in later times to promote manual labor against the wandering lifestyle.

ognized the yearning of dedicated monks to live free of care, but also warned against forgetting one's place and making the same mistake as Adam had made in Paradise. That was a problem especially associated with monks who pursued *hēsychia* alone in the farther desert. One such elder reportedly had almost attained "a trace of a life without a body,"

> for he did not till the earth, nor did he worry about food, or seek plants or even grass to satisfy his bodily needs. . . . Instead, from the day he abandoned the world for the desert he was filled with confidence in God and took no thought how to nourish his body.

God supplied him with bread until he fell from grace. After spending years this way in prayers, hymns, and meditations, the monk "began to think himself superior to most men . . . and began to trust in himself." Increasingly self-satisfied, he began to neglect his prayer. Soon the bread that God provided began to change too, first appearing gray, then half-baked or gnawed by mice. Finally he went back toward the Nile, scanning the horizon, until he found a group of monks who received him and invited him to share what they had. "From that time on he spent the rest of his life in sorrow . . . and gained his bread from his own labor." An angel warned him not to be deceived in the future, but since he had repented, his monastic brothers would continue to console him with food.[130]

These fantastic stories addressed a real problem. As Evagrius observed, "we have received no command to work constantly . . . but we do have the obligation to pray without ceasing."[131] In fact, some desert solitaries benefited from arrangements that relieved them from manual labor. Evagrius himself earned his bread mostly by writing his guides and treatises,[132] but aristocratic connections and fame also brought daily visitors who left him alms in gratitude for their spiritual edification.[133] Others were maintained by their families or servants, or (like Phif and Apollo) were supported by

---

130. *HM* 1.44–58; trans. adapted from Russell, pp. 59–61.

131. Evagrius, *Practicus* 49; ed. A. and C. Guillaumont (SC 171), p. 610: ἐργάζεσθαι μὲν διὰ παντὸς . . . οὐ προστετάγμεθα, προσεύχεσθαι δὲ ἡμῖν ἀδιαλείπτως νενομοθέτηται. Trans. Bamberger, p. 29.

132. Palladius, *HL* 38.10.

133. Evagrius, *Ep.* 31 and 32; the Coptic *HL* records that Evagrius received five or six "pilgrims from afar . . . attracted by his wisdom and asceticism" each day, and "everything that was sent to him was kept by the steward [of Kellia] who always served in his house": see Cuthbert Butler, *The Lausiac History of Palladius. Part 1: A Critical Discussion together with notes on Early Egyptian Monasticism* (Cambridge: Cambridge University Press, 1898), 144. Wipszycka (1996): 356 suggests that enough alms were distributed at Kellia to attract beggars. Kellia was perhaps special, since it was the most accessible abode of famous desert masters. *HL* 7.2 notes they were supplied with bread from Nitria.

attendant monks *(diakonētēs)* in a kind of work-study discipleship.[134] Such arrangements, however, fostered a sense of ascetic privilege that could generate serious tensions. We are told that Pachomius disapproved of those who let others support them while devoting themselves to prayer and fasting: "We often see them served by others worse off than themselves and see that they are proud, or faint-hearted, or vain, in search of human glory."[135] Monks supplied Antony the Great at his Inner Mountain "as children who were mindful of their father," until Antony realized that "some were annoyed and suffered hardship." Therefore he began to cultivate a garden.[136]

We do not know how extensively such arrangements of privileged dependency were practiced in Egypt, or if they ever fell out of fashion. By the early fifth century, however, such behavior evidently stood out sufficiently to attract the notice of Bishop Cyril of Alexandria. In a letter to a bishop of Fayyum (south of Scetis) Cyril complained about monks there who

> go about claiming to devote their time to prayer and doing no work; wrong in their ideas, they make religion a means of livelihood, an excuse for avoiding work. . . . If they think it is a good thing to have nothing to do with work, who is going to provide for them if everybody imitates their behavior? The people in question are making it their alleged duty to devote their time solely to prayer and to do no work at all an excuse for idleness and gluttony.[137]

This was a problem found elsewhere in the early monastic world, as we shall see. That Egyptian tradition generally emphasized manual labor and self-sufficiency instead of such "idleness" and dependency may be partly explained by the communal imperatives of desert existence. Beyond providing food, manual labor had a sociological function. In settlements that brought together people of diverse economic backgrounds, the notion that all members should perform manual labor provided a means of leveling

134. Support by family, Evagrius, *Ant.* 1.61 and Ps-Athanasian canons 102–4; by slaves, Wipszycka (1996): 358–59; by disciples, Evelyn-White (1932): 182 and *V.Antonii* 50.3–5, PJ 14.16, G Arsenius 17, G Sisoes 7, Eth.Coll. 13.9. Kellia cell configurations may reflect this arrangement. See Daumas (1968): 440–42.

135. *Bohairic Life of Pachomius* 35; ed. and trans. Veilleux, p. 60.

136. Athanasius, *V.Antonii* 50.4–5; ed. Bartelink, p. 270: ἐφρόντιζον ἀποστέλλειν αὐτῷ. . . . προφάσει τοῦ ἄρτου σκύλλονταί τινες καὶ κάματον ὑπομένουσιν. Antony's manual labor is otherwise noted only when he was still near Nile villages in *V.Antonii* 3.

137. Cyril of Alexandria, *Letter to Calosirius* [*Ep.* 83]; ed. and trans. adapted from Lionel Wickham, p. 218–19: Περιέρχονται δὲ καὶ ἕτεροί τινες . . . προσποιούμενοι μόνῃ σχολάζειν τῇ προσευχῇ, καὶ οὐδὲν ἐργαζόμενοι, καὶ ὄκνου πρόφασιν καὶ πορισμοῦ ποιοῦνται τὴν εὐσέβειαν. The letter is not dated. Cyril was bishop of Alexandria 412–44 and Calosirius is otherwise known only from the transcript of the Second Council of Ephesus (449).

out social differences and fostering communal solidarity. Surely it was no coincidence that in Pachomian communities the biennial Remissions ceremony, a special period of reconciliation and forgiveness, was also the time when monks rendered accounts for the manual labors they had performed that year.[138] To participate in a community's manual labors was to accept one's human condition and display a proper sense of humility.[139] It thus promoted economic stability and social harmony in a testy environment. Privileged dependency, on the other hand, not only placed an extra burden on monks already hard-pressed to support themselves, but could also be resented as entitlement and pride.

Such resentment also would have been directed toward unknown wandering monks, no matter how "pure as regards to the body" they happened to be. Those who Cyril complains had made themselves known at Calamus, on the edge of the Fayyum region, may have lived as Abba Bessarion was said to have lived, free from care, without practicing manual labor:

> He afflicted himself along the desert's edge like a vagabond. . . . If he happened to come upon pleasanter places where there were brothers who lived a common life, he would sit weeping outside their gate like someone who was shipwrecked. . . . If a brother came out and found him sitting there like a beggar and one of the world's poor, [the brother would be] filled with compassion . . . and ask, "Why are you weeping? If you need something, we will see you receive it as far as we can. Only come in, share our table, and rest yourself."

After fabricating a tale to edify his hosts and win their charity, Bessarion would depart on his way.[140] Evidently this behavior was what people expected from a monk who adopted a life of radical *xeniteia:*

> I know a brother who was practicing *xeniteia*. He was at a church, and when the time came, sitting down to eat with the brothers, he presented himself for the communal meal. But some said, "Who invited that one here?" and said to him, "Get up and get out." So he stood up and left. But others were grieved and called him back. Afterwards they asked him, "What's in your heart, now that you've been cast out and called back?" He replied, "I put it in my heart that I'm like a dog that goes out when kicked but comes back when called."[141]

138. For the Remissions ceremony, see McKnary-Zak (2000): 53–69. Büchler (1980): 92–97 explains the famous Pachomian work ethic by reference to Pachomius' sense of solidarity with the poor.

139. See Isaiah, *Asceticon* 5.12; 6.5; 8.4; 11.51. N 375 notes that calligraphy (scribal writing) is inferior to weaving baskets, because it generates vainglory.

140. G Bessarion 12 (PG 65.144AC); trans. adapted from Ward, pp. 42–43. Gould (1989): 237 notes that the narrative is allegory.

141. N 306. See also PJ 15.64.

In these stories wandering, begging monks became exemplars of abject humility and represented an ideal quite distinct from the pride associated with wanderers who did not work, such as John the Dwarf or the deep-desert elder of the cautionary tales. Such humility was edifying and necessary. Egyptian desert tradition aspired to be charitable: many monks viewed their manual labor as a way of providing the means to help anyone in need.[142] Bessarion was said to have sought out monks who lived in more fertile regions, and perhaps the monks whom Cyril criticized in the Fayyum were doing so too. But the kind of charity Bessarion and others sought was, no doubt, in shorter supply in more remote areas already strained by scarcity. In fact, Evagrius warns against becoming violent toward a brother at a meal as if he were "one of those who wander around" only to leave "once satisfied with bread."[143] But these stories probably tell how such monks were usually received: when one appeared unknown at the brothers' table, their first impulse was to drive him out.

WANDERING AND COMMUNAL STABILITY IN THE DESERT

Christians who moved to the Egyptian desert quickly learned that to sit and concentrate on prayer was itself hard work, requiring discipline of the highest degree. There was a constant temptation to leave the cell in hope of discovering how life might be sustained more easily than by endlessly weaving baskets and ropes. Wandering always represented an alternative, and some notable desert fathers advised and practiced it in pursuit of freedom from care: Abba Zeno, who roamed between Egypt, Sinai, and Palestine, even warned, "Never stay in a place, or lay a foundation where you might build yourself a cell."[144] Yet that way of life seems to have been generally discouraged. Communal necessity and material needs recommended a spiritual life of physical stillness supported by manual labor instead.

There was a desire among late antique writers to romanticize the Egyptian desert and the solitude of its early settlers. However, the apophthegmata indicate that the more monks moved there, the more it was necessary to enforce cooperation and communal solidarity. Though often depicted as a symptom of ascetic failure, wandering caused concern in part simply

---

142. See Gould (1993): 98–100; Nagel (1966): 99; and Dörries (1966b): 284.

143. Evagrius, *Tractatus ad Eulogium* 26 (PG 79.1128B): Ὅταν λογισμὸς ἐγκόψῃ σε, μὴ ἄγαν βιάσασθαι τῇ τραπέζῃ τὸν ἀδελφόν. . . . σοὶ μὲν γὰρ ἴσως ὑποβάλλει τῶν κυκλευτῶν ἕνα τὸν ἀδελφὸν ὑπάρχειν, καὶ ὅτι ἄρτοις ἀρκεσθεὶς ἀφικέσθω. See also Isaiah, *Asceticon* 10.50.

144. PJ 8.5 (PL 73.906C): Nunquam maneas in loco . . . neque mittas fundamentum ut aedifices tibi cellam aliquando. Zeno is identified as "one who wanders around, turns in a circle, gyrates" (*metkarrkānā*) in the Syriac translation of John Rufus, *Plerophoriae* 8 (PO 8.20), possibly rendering κυκλευτής.

because it suggested a refusal to submit to an elder's authority: "A beginner who goes from one monastery to another is like a mule which bolts this way and that for fear of the halter," says Abba Isaiah.[145] Yet this problem was not identified only with novices. Palladius describes how one monk named Ptolemy lived alone in a distant part of Scetis called the "Ladder." He managed to survive there for fourteen years by carrying water in pots or collecting dew with sponges, but this "unreasonable" manner of solitary survival eventually left him

> completely estranged *(apoxenōtheis)* from the teaching, company, and aid of the holy men, and from the continuous communion of the mysteries, so that he reached such a degree of nonsense as to say these things were nothing. It is said that he is borne about Egypt suspended aloft in his pride and has given himself over to gluttony and wine-drinking, holding no society with anyone.[146]

Ptolemy's case warned how Egyptian loners who practiced extreme forms of *xeniteia* could become social outcasts. If monks insisted on living such an open-air life, they had to follow better examples—hence the stories of good wanderers whose lifestyle was reconciled with the ideals of established communities. Bessarion and Macarius both proved themselves capable of remaining still for long periods; John began to wander only after an angel ordered him to cease standing still. These stories demonstrated that wandering and stillness were not incompatible, but also that wandering was not a lifestyle for novices. Furthermore, its exemplars demonstrated both humility and a willingness to conform. John, for example, returned to the same place every Sunday to receive communion and weave harnesses "according to the custom of those parts." Macarius the Citizen illustrated his willingness to submit to his elders and perform penance if he had overstepped his bounds, while Bessarion was known for sharing the humiliation of fellow monks.[147] Finally, some wanderers, like Agathon and Zeno, were idealized for their self-sufficiency.[148] If, however, monks sought support from others, they had to do so with humility, not pride, as Bessarion did, and they had to do it in places where monks lived more comfortably and might benefit from exposure to those in need. As another apophthegm

145. G Isaiah 3 (PG 65.181A); see also Isaiah, *Asceticon* 10.50, where readers are warned not to allow a κυκλευτὴς μοναχός to eat with other brothers.

146. Palladius, *HL* 27.1–2; ed. Bartelink, p. 140: ὃς ἀποξενωθεὶς διδασκαλίας καὶ συντυχίας ἀνδρῶν ὁσίων καὶ ὠφελείας ... ἀλλ' ἢ φέρεσθαι μετέωρος ἄχρι ... μηδενὶ μηδὲν ὁμιλοῦντα. Trans. adapted from Meyer, p. 88.

147. G Bessarion 7; stories about Macarius' submission to both Pachomius and Macarius the Great imply contrast and subordination between different ascetic lifestyles: see *HL* 18.12–16 and G Macarius Aeg. 21.

148. Isaiah, *Asceticon* 6.5 says Agathon was neither preoccupied with manual labor nor distressed when in need of alms.

suggests, discretion was the necessary precondition for those who moved about and wished to be received as "workmen for God."[149] In these ways Egyptian desert tradition made some accommodation for individuals who followed their impulse to roam free of care.

By the early fifth century, however, Egyptian monks were more often identified with their cells and could be caricatured as having an almost banausic devotion to manual labor.[150] Their diligence won admirers like John Cassian, who promoted a philosophic Egyptian (or more specifically, Evagrian) regimen of isolated withdrawal, manual labor, and silent stillness among monastic readers in southern Gaul.[151] But enthusiasm for Egyptian monastic practices was not shared by all. After hearing that John Cassian had come down to Egypt from a monastery in Syria, one Egyptian elder expressed concern:

> We have known some people have come from your region in order to go around to the monasteries of the brothers . . . not in order to receive the rules and institutes for which they came here, or, while sitting apart in their cells, to attempt to put into practice what they had seen or been told. Holding onto the behavior and concerns to which they have been accustomed, they are thought to have changed provinces not for the sake of progress, but from a need to escape poverty, and some have reproached them for this. . . . Since they changed neither their way of fasting nor their manner of psalmody nor even the clothes that they wore, why should they be thought to have come here for anything than just to supply their food?[152]

Who were these vagrants, and why were they specifically identified with Syria? What were their practices of fasting and psalm-singing, and was there any justification for suspecting that they had set out on their travels only for the sake of food? With these questions we pass to the next chapter and a radically different Christian ascetic tradition.

---

149. Eth.Coll. 13.4; trans. Arras, p. 62: si ibi transmigaveris cum discretione cito vinces et operarius eris propter Dominum.

150. See Synesius of Cyrene, *Dio* 7; ed. Antonio Garzya, p. 680.

151. See Stewart (1998): 11–12, 17.

152. Cassian, *Collatio* 18.2.2; ed. Pichery (SC 64), pp. 12–13: qui mores suos ac studia quibus inbuti fuerant retentantes, ut eis exprobrari a nonnullis solet, non profectus sui gratia, sed vitandae egestatis necessitate existimati sunt provincias conmutasse. . . . cum enim nec ieiuniorum morem neque psalmorum ordinem nec ipsorum denique indumentorum habitum permutasset, quid aliud in hac regione sectari quam sola victus sui conpendia crederentur? Trans. adapted from Ramsey, p. 636. With this passage Cassian introduces his *genera monachorum*.

2

Apostolic Wanderers of
Third-Century Syria

Writing in Constantinople in the middle of the fifth century, the church historian Sozomen believed the first monks of Syria were those who had "emulated the monks of Egypt in the practice of philosophy" by scraping a raw existence off the mountains, near the Persian frontier.

> When they first began such philosophy they were called *boskoi* [grazers] because they had no homes, ate neither bread nor meat and drank no wine, but dwelt constantly in the mountains, continually praising God with prayers and hymns according to the law of the Church. At the usual meal hours they would each take a sickle and wander in the mountains, feeding off wild plants as if they were grazing. This was their kind of philosophy.[1]

Such primitive, open-air "philosophy" understandably fascinated urbane writers of the fifth and sixth centuries. Not only did it resonate deeply with old Greco-Roman commonplaces about how human beings must have lived, uncorrupted, before cities were built, but it also recalled the ways of Hebrew prophets "of whom the world was not worthy," who "wandered in deserts and mountains, and in caves and holes in the ground" (Heb 11: 38). Wrapped in goatskins or straw mats, *boskoi* monks pursued a decidedly

---

1. Sozomen, *Historia ecclesiastica [HE]* 6.33.2; ed. Joseph Bidez and revised Günther Christian Hansen, p. 289: τοῖς ἐν Αἰγύπτῳ φιλοσοφοῦσιν ἀμιλλώμενοι... τούτους δὲ καὶ βοσκοὺς ἀπεκάλουν, ἔναγχος τῆς τοιαύτης φιλοσοφίας ἄρξαντας· ὀνομάζουσι δὲ αὐτοὺς ὧδε, καθότι οὔτε οἰκήματα ἔχουσιν οὔτε ἄρτον ἢ ὄψον ἐσθίουσιν οὔτε οἶνον πίνουσιν, ἐν δὲ τοῖς ὄρεσι διατρίβοντες, ἀεὶ τὸν θεὸν εὐλογοῦσιν ἐν εὐχαῖς καὶ ὕμνοις κατὰ θεσμὸν τῆς ἐκκλησίας. τροφῆς δὲ ἡνίκα γένηται καιρός, καθάπερ νεμόμενοι, ἅρπην ἔχων ἕκαστος, ἀνὰ τὸ ὄρος περιιόντες τὰς βοτάνας σιτίζονται. Trans. adapted from Charles Hartnaft, p. 370. Sozomen refers to mountains above Carrhae (modern Harran).

counter-cultural *anachōrēsis*.[2] Hunters were believed to have sometimes mistaken them for strange animals, and no wonder: their matted mass of hair made their heads appear like eagles with wings outspread for flight, and their fingernails curled down like the talons of birds of prey.[3] As celebrated in Syriac chant,

> Those who graze on grass and roots instead of delicacies,
> and in place of lofty dwellings, live in caves. Like birds they go up to live on rocky ledges, . . .
> Wherever one of them goes . . . he enjoys the herbs he picked in faith; he leaves the rest behind and moves on from there,
> because he has heard the saying, "Do not be anxious about tomorrow."[4]

Such zealots for "freedom from care" not only avoided artificial shelter and clothing, but rejected all the ordinary labors by which human beings obtained their food.[5]

According to Sozomen, this "strict philosophy, off the beaten track of mankind" had been introduced to Syria by a monk named Aones, "just as Antony had introduced it to Egypt."[6] Aones is otherwise unknown, but the ascetic lifestyle associated with him is familiar from what we have already seen of Bessarion and other wanderers in Egypt.[7] In fact, testimony from

---

2. For *boskoi* anchoretism, see Arthur Vööbus, *History of Asceticism in the Syrian Orient,* vol. 1 (Louvain: Secrétariat du CorpusSCO, 1958b), 150–57 and *id.,* (1960b): 22–35, 262–64, though much of the evidence Vööbus cites is now dated later than he believed it to have been (see below, n. 4). Such monks may have been classed among the *abile* (mourners), an ascetic elite associated with the beatitude, "Blessed be those who mourn, for they shall be comforted" (Mt 5:4): see Andrew Palmer, *Monk and Mason on the Tigris Frontier: The Early History of the Tur Abdin* (Cambridge: Cambridge University Press, 1990), 85.

3. A hagiographic topos: e.g., John Rufus, *Plerophoriae* 31 (PO 8.73) on Heliodorus of Tarsus; apophthegm G Milesius 2.

4. Ps.-Ephrem, *On Solitaries,* trans. in Vööbus (1960b): 27; and Ps.-Ephrem, *On Hermits and Desert Dwellers,* trans. Joseph Ammar, pp. 70,65–69 and 73,233–41. Both *mêmrē* were probably written by Isaac of Antioch in the mid- to late fifth century: see Edward G. Matthews, "'On Solitaries': Ephrem or Isaac?" *Le Muséon* 103 (1990): 91–110.

5. E.g., Theodoret of Cyrrhus on Jacob of Nisibis, *Historia religiosa [HR]* 1.2; ed. Pierre Canivet and Alice Leroy-Molinghen (SC 234), p. 162: τροφὴν δὲ εἶχεν, οὐ τὴν μετὰ πόνου σπειρομένην καὶ φυομένην, ἀλλὰ τὴν αὐτομάτως βλαστάνουσαν. See also Matthews (1990): 103–4 and Callinicus, *Vita Hypatii* 3.6.

6. Sozomen, *HE* 6.33.4; ed. Bidez-Hansen, p. 289: Ἀώνην τῆς ἐκτὸς πάτου ἀνθρώπων καὶ ἀκριβοῦς φιλοσοφίας ἄρξαι παρὰ Σύροις. Despite the skepticism of Jean-Maurice Fiey, "Aonès, Awun, et Awgin (Eugène) aux origenes du monachisme mésopotamien," *AB* 80 (1962): 52–81, Sozomen's "Aones" may be the earliest reference to Mar Awgen, legendary introducer of Egyptian monasticism to Syria.

7. By the seventh century, Abba Bessarion had become an exemplar for Mesopotamian *boskoi* called *mshannyanē* (people who move from place to place): see the Syriac apophth-

the western Mediterranean to northern Mesopotamia shows that the lifestyle attributed to only a few Egyptian monks was one that many adopted wherever there was enough vegetation to survive. It especially came into vogue in Syria, Mesopotamia, and Palestine.[8] Here, monks could easily follow the footsteps of their Old Testament forebears (the patriarchs and the prophets) and imitate their nomadic patterns.[9] Near Eastern hinterlands offered more possibilities for healthy sustenance than the Egypt desert did: nuts, asphodel roots, and a juicy thistle *(mannouthia)* that grew on the desert fringe may even account for the reported longevity of many who took up the diet.[10] In cultivated regions they could live by scavenging garden fruits and vegetables.[11] They may have also picked tares off the ground or used their sickles to reap uncut corners of fields set aside for the poor to glean in accordance with ancient charitable custom.[12] Although one admirer in the fifth century expressed concern that some *boskoi* were settling down and taking up agriculture,[13] their ascetic lifestyle (as distinct from other forms of *anachōrēsis*) would long persist among Christian monks, both male and female. Late into the sixth century they could still be glimpsed roaming along the Dead Sea coast or foraging in the Palestinian desert naked, "like animals, . . . no longer human in the way they thought."[14]

---

egmata collection, *Paradisus patrum,* ed. Paul Bedjan, p. 907; trans. Ernest Wallis-Budge, p. 383, with Guillaumont (1968): 55 n. 3.

8. For Syro-Mesopotamia, see (besides Ps.-Ephrem) Theodoret, *HR* 1.2 (James of Nisibis), 21.3 (James), 22.2 (Limnaeus), 23.1 (John); at 16.1 he says this "open-air way of life" was introduced to Cyrrhus (northeast of Antioch) at the end of the fourth century. For Palestine, see below, nn. 11–12 and 14.

9. Brown (1982): 112 and Vööbus (1960b): 16; see e.g., *Vita Alexandri* 26.

10. See Yizhar Hirschfeld, "Edible Wild Plants: The Secret Diet of Monks in the Judean Desert," *Israel Land and Nature* 16 (1990): 25–28, which came to my attention through Peter Brown; also John Binns, *Ascetics and Ambassadors of Christ: The Monasteries of Palestine, 314–631* (Oxford: Clarendon Press, 1994), 107–8. Grazing on the wrong plants could also kill a monk, as nearly happened to Martin of Tours foraging hellebore on the island of Gallinaria: *Vita Martini* 6.5. Repeated famines would have made many inhabitants of the Near East familiar with this *boskoi* diet: see Gildas Hamel, *Poverty and Charity in Roman Palestine* (Berkeley and Los Angeles: University of California Press, 1990), 17–18. For differences between Syrian and Egyptian deserts, see Brown (1982): 110–12.

11. A problem noted in North Africa by Augustine, *De opere monachorum* 23.28, and in Palestine by apophthegm G Zeno 6.

12. As suggested by Vööbus (1960b): 263. For the Hebrew custom of "gleanings" (based on Lev 19:9–10, 23:22, and Deut 14:28–29), see Hamel (1990): 128–29, 153, and 217, and Roger Brooks, *Support for the Poor in the Mishnaic Law of Agriculture: Tractate Peah* (Chico, Calif.: Scholars Press, 1983), and the ordinances governing *pe'ah, leket,* and *shikhah* in the Babylonian Talmud, *Seder Zera'im.* The Syriac *Life of Symeon Stylites* 11 attests its practice among Christian landowners in fifth-century Syria.

13. Matthews (1990): 109.

14. Evagrius Scholasticus (ca. 592–594) *Historia ecclesiastica [HE]* 1.21; ed. Joseph Bidez

There is no reason to doubt that *anachōrēsis* took the wild form that Sozomen says it did among early Syrian recluses. To accept his word that such *boskoi* were the first Syrian monks is, however, to be overly influenced, as he was, by Antony's model of desert withdrawal as the touchstone of strict monastic life. Long before such recluses took to the mountains, Christian communities scattered from the eastern Mediterranean to western Persia had already grown accustomed to the homeless wanderings of ascetic exemplars similarly guided by the Holy Spirit. Although excluded from most ancient and modern accounts of early monastic history, these third-century ascetics must be recognized as precursors of fourth-century Syrian monks, or rather—since their sexual and material renunciations were virtually the same as those of later monks—as early monks themselves.[15] The main difference between these third-century wanderers and those Sozomen identifies as the first "monks" was that the earlier ones lived in or between cities and villages rather than in mountains and deserts. Nonetheless, it was these early, indigenous monks, as much as the emulators of Antony, who set the standards for which Syrian and Mesopotamian monks would later become famous, or, for some, infamous.

This chapter therefore steps back from the fourth and fifth centuries to examine the earlier tradition of Christian ascetic wandering in towns and villages of the third-century Near East. Regrettably, little information exists about the Syriac-speaking Christian communities that extended, by the third century, from the eastern Mediterranean coast to Mesopotamia and western Persia (an area today spread over southeastern Turkey, Syria, northern Iraq, and western Iran).[16] Although a late-second-century epitaph

---

and Léon Parmentier, p. 30. John Moschus' *Pratum Spirituale* makes several references to *boskoi* ranging from Cilicia to Egypt in the late sixth and early seventh centuries.

15. Important discussions of early Syrian ascetic tradition include Sidney Griffith, "Asceticism in the Church of Syria: The Hermeneutics of Early Syrian Monasticism," in *Asceticism*, ed. V. L. Wimbush and R. Valantasis (Oxford: Oxford University Press, 1995), 220–45; Robert Murray, "The Features of the Earliest Christian Asceticism," in *Christian Spirituality: Essays in Honor of Gordon Rupp*, ed. P. Brooks (London: S.C.M., 1975a), 65–77; Sebastian Brock, "Early Syrian Asceticism," *Numen* 20 (1973): 1–19; Aelred Baker, "Syriac and the Origins of Monasticism," *Downside Review* 86 (1968): 342–53; and Jean Gribomont, "Le monachisme au sein de l'Église en Syrie et en Cappadoce," *SM* 7 (1965): 7–24. For the preference to reserve the term "monk" for ascetics who practice physical withdrawal, see Griffith (1995): 237 and *id.*, "Monks, 'Singles,' and the 'Sons of the Covenant,'" in *Eulogema: Studies in Honor of Robert Taft, S.J.*, ed. E. Carr et al. (Rome: Pontificio Ateneo S. Anselmo, 1993), 157–58. The distinction is maintained by Escolan (1999): 11–12.

16. By the late fourth and early fifth centuries the Syriac-speaking Christian milieu included the late Roman provinces of Syria (I and II), Euphratensis, Mesopotamia and Osrhoene (today mostly in southeastern Turkey) as well as the Persian territories of Adiabene and eastern Mesopotamia (Iraq, western Iran). For general introduction, see Fergus Millar, *The Roman Near East, 31 B.C.–A.D. 337* (Cambridge: Harvard University Press, 1993), 225–63, 437–523; Susan Ashbrook Harvey, *Asceticism and Society in Crisis: John of Ephesus and the Lives of the Eastern*

informs us that Christians could be found "everywhere" from the Syrian plain to Nisibis (modern Nusaybin) across the Euphrates river, they seem to have remained a minority at least into the fourth century, especially outside the major cities.[17] Certainly there were more Jews living in these regions than Christians. Excavations at Dura-Europos, a Euphrates fortress town destroyed by Persian forces in 256, have revealed that third-century Christians lived nestled among pagans and "at the door of the Jews like poor relations not on speaking terms."[18] While their house church (ca. 232–256) could only accommodate sixty to seventy people standing, an ornate synagogue down the street could seat nearly twice as many.[19] Moreover, there is scant record (unlike in the West at this time) for a centralized ecclesiastical administration or assertive clergy among third-century Syrian Christian communities, even at Edessa (modern Urfa), which was a major Christian center.[20] Instead, the figures who dominate the record into and

---

Saints (Berkeley and Los Angeles: University of California Press, 1990), 1–21; Jean-Maurice Fiey, *Jalons pour une histoire de l'Église en Iraq* (Louvain: Secrétariat du CorpusCSO, 1970); and Judah B. Segal, *Edessa "The Blessed City"* (Oxford: Clarendon Press, 1970), 62–109. Problems besetting historical reconstruction of earlier periods are summarized by Robert Murray, "The Characteristics of the Earliest Syriac Christianity," in *East of Byzantium: Syria and Armenia in the Formative Period,* ed. N. G. Garsoïan et al. (Washington D.C.: Dumbarton Oaks, 1982), 4–5: "The rise of Syriac-speaking Christianity is bafflingly obscure, and the earliest literary works help us little. They are too difficult to date, to place, or to interpret historically." Robert Murray, *Symbols of Church and Kingdom: A Study in Early Syriac Tradition* (Cambridge: Cambridge University Press, 1975b), offers guidance to its spiritual and imaginative context.

17. Epitaph of Abercius Marcellus (ca. 190), ll. 10–11: καὶ Συρίης πέ[δον εἶδα] καὶ ἄστεα πάντα, Νισῖβιν / Εὐφράτην διαβ[ὰς πάν] τῃ δ' ἔσχον συνο[μαίμους]. Text and commentary in Wolfgang Wischmeyer, "Die Aberkiosinschrift als Grabepigramm," *JbAC* 23 (1980): 22–47. Extensive Christianization outside the cities Abercius visited may not have begun until the late fourth and fifth centuries: see J. H. W. G. Liebeschuetz, "Problems Arising from the Conversion of Syria," in *The Church in Town and Countryside,* ed. D. Baker (Oxford: Basil Blackwell, 1979), 18.

18. Murray (1975b): 19; see also H. J. W. Drijvers, "Jews and Christians at Edessa," *Journal of Jewish Studies* 36 (1985): 88–102. Dura-Europos excavators also found shrines for Adonis, Aphlad, Atargatis, Artemis Azzanathkona, Artemis-Nanaia, Jupiter Dolichenus, Zeus Kyrios, Zeus Megistos, Zeus Theos, Mithras, and the Gaddē.

19. See Carl H. Kraeling, *Excavations at Dura-Europos Final Report 8,* part 1: *The Synagogue,* 2d ed. (New York: KTAV Publishing House, 1979), 33 and *id., Excavations at Dura-Europos Final Report 8,* part 2: *The Christian Building* (New Haven: Yale University Press, 1967), 109.

20. See Walter Bauer, *Orthodoxy and Heresy in Earliest Christianity,* ed. and trans. R. A. Kraft and G. Krodel, 2d ed. (Philadelphia: Fortress Press, 1971), 20–43; also Escolan (1999): 20–28, 61–63; H. J. W. Drijvers, *Bardaisan of Edessa* (Assen: Gorcum, 1966), 216; and Vööbus (1958b): 161. Dionysius of Alexandria (247–64) *apud* Eusebius, *Historia ecclesiastica* 7.4–5, attests churches in Syria, Arabia Nabataea, and Mesopotamia in the mid-third century, but does not mention any bishop outside Antioch. The sixth-century *Chronicle of Edessa,* though based on earlier sources, does not list any bishop at Edessa before 312; although the first listed (Qwona) may represent only the first whom the chronicler believed orthodox, or the first to erect a major church building after Constantine's conversion: see Millar (1993): 465. Nothing

during the third century are individual, competing teachers, the most eminent being Marcion, Tatian (who had a strong following in western Syria by the late second and third century), Bardaiṣan (at Edessa ca. 154–222), and Mani (whose missionaries had reached Syria by the 260s).[21]

What is clear is that from earliest times asceticism played an integral and affirming role in the communities and the faith of Syrian Christians. This "radical consensus" meant, above all, that discipleship of Christ, lived out by laymen and women through varying degrees of sexual and material renunciation, constituted the highest expression of Christian life.[22] The writings of Aphrahat "the Persian Sage" (fl. 336–346) and Ephrem (at Nisibis to 363, then at Edessa until 373) reveal that mainstream Syriac communities of the fourth century granted a privileged position to ascetics who sought to pattern their life after Jesus, the great Iḥidāyā (Single or Only-Begotten One).[23] Within such communities, male and female iḥidāyē (single, solitary ones) formed an "informal class of believers" called the Bnay and Bnāt Qyāmā (Sons and Daughters of the Covenant). By "taking a stand" (aqim) in the "singleness" (iḥidāyutā) of celibacy and mind they assumed at baptism, such "covenanters" were thought to have entered a special relationship with Christ, and apparently served as exemplars for other members of their community, whom they edified "as a living icon of Paradise restored."[24]

Scholars have focused on fourth-century treatises concerning the Bnay and Bnāt Qyāmā for their reflection of a "pre-monastic" Syrian ascetic norm. Some believe this norm should be distinguished from "the other main strand in Syriac asceticism, that which stressed above all the following of

in our sources suggests any clerical establishment east of Antioch comparable to that recorded for Rome by Eusebius, HE 6.43.

21. For Marcion's and Tatian's influence on Syriac spirituality, see Vööbus (1958b): 31–54 and Brown (1988): 83–101; for Bardaiṣan, see Drijvers (1966). For Manichaean activities, see below.

22. Quotation from Brown (1988): 88; see also Murray (1975a): 68–69 and Harvey (1990): 4–6. Many took vows of celibacy at their baptism: see Robert Murray, "The Exhortation to Candidates for Ascetical Vows at Baptism in the Ancient Syriac Church" New Testament Studies 21 (1974/1975): 59–80 and Escolan (1999): 36–44.

23. Iḥidāyā was the Syriac word used to translate μονογενής (only begotten one) in Jn 1: 18. For its use and connotations, see Griffith (1995): 223–29; id., (1993): 142–45; and Antoine Guillaumont, "Monachisme et éthique judéo-chrétienne," RevSR 60 (1972a): 199–218, reprinted in id., (1979a). For Syrian traditions privileging ascetics (esp. the ascetic poor), see Escolan (1999): 1–69 and Alessio Persic, "La Chiesa di Siria e i 'gradi' della vita cristiana," in Per foramen acus. Il cristianesimo antico di fronte alla pericope evangelica del "giovane ricco" (Milan: Vita e Pensiero, 1986), 208–63.

24. Griffith (1995): 229, 234; see also id. (1993): 145–53 for the terms Bnay and Bnāt Qyāmā and their relation to the term iḥidāyā. For the possible derivation of the "covenant" (qyāmā) institution from Judaic tradition, see George Nedungatt, "The Covenanters of the Early Syriac-Speaking Church" OCP 39 (1973): 191–215, 419–44.

Jesus in his homelessness and poverty."[25] There are no sure grounds, however, for maintaining a hard distinction between ascetic wanderers and covenanters. Although the evidence for the wanderers of the Syrian ascetic tradition is restricted mostly to the apocryphal *Acts of Thomas* and the Pseudo-Clementine *Letters to Virgins*, these two texts by themselves provide substantial evidence for ascetic imagination and practice in third-century Syria. Their links to the later, more settled, "covenant" tradition are apparent, for while the *Letters to Virgins* guided readers in the proper practice of a lifestyle of ascetic wandering, they also urged them to present themselves on their travels as "a beautiful pattern to believers, and to those who shall believe."[26] The *Bnay* and *Bnāt Qyāmā*, as depicted in the fourth century, belonged to the same ascetic tradition, albeit under increased organization, supervision, and control by local church leaders.

More importantly, the wanderers of third-century Syria introduce a motive for practicing Christian asceticism that is different from anything we have found preserved in Egyptian desert tradition. Like Egyptian desert wanderers, these Syrian wanderers embraced celibacy, poverty, and homeless wanderings in pursuit of freedom from care, but their ascetic lifestyle was based on apostolic precedent rather than on the example of Antony the Great. For them, following Christ meant active engagement, as Christ's representatives, with the "world" they had renounced, rather than permanent social withdrawal. Few scholars have taken their apostolic presumptions seriously, believing that their concerns were directed more toward achieving their own salvation than toward teaching others.[27] But this criticism is misplaced. For such wanderers, to emphasize and display strict ascetic behavior—to exhibit "demonstrative piety" (as one scholar has described the feats of the later Syrian pillar monk, Symeon Stylites)[28]—was an apostolic imperative. It not only authenticated their apostolic endeavors and attendant claims to Christian leadership, but also the economic as-

25. Murray (1975a): 70. Giuseppe Visonà, "Povertà, sequela, carità. Orientamenti nel cristianesimo dei primi secoli," in *Per foramen acus. Il cristianesimo antico di fronte alla pericope evangelica del "giovane ricco"* (Milan: Vita e Pensiero, 1986), 12–21, 75–77, draws similar distinctions. Readers should be aware that Murray, Griffith, and others who base their discussions of early Syrian asceticism primarily on Aphrahat and Ephrem offer a more conservative reconstruction than my own.

26. *Epistulae ad virgines / de virginitate* I.3.1 (PG 1.383B); trans. Pratten, p. 55. For the phrase, see below, n. 80. Geoffrey G. Harpham, *The Ascetic Imperative in Culture and Criticism* (Chicago: University of Chicago Press, 1987), xiv, considers it an "entire ideology . . . condensed."

27. A view introduced by Adolf von Harnack, "Die pseudoclementinischen Briefe De virginitate und die Entstehung des Mönchthums," *Sitzungsberichte der königlich-preussischen Akademie der Wissenschaften zu Berlin* 21 (1891): 381–82, reiterated by Campenhausen (1968): 233 and Nagel (1966): 71.

28. Millar (1993): 520.

sumptions that went with them. This connection between the apostolic vocation and demonstrative asceticism is pronounced in both the *Acts of Thomas* and the *Letters to Virgins,* and needs special emphasis here. For the evangelic inspiration that put such ascetic exemplars on the road did not expire with the third century. Their assumptions, practices, and the expectations they set must be examined to appreciate not only the wanderings of the later *boskoi,* but also of other ascetic enthusiasts whose apostolic aspirations raised alarm in cities, towns, and villages of the late fourth and early fifth centuries.

AN APOSTOLIC PARADIGM FOR ASCETIC WANDERERS: *THE ACTS OF THOMAS*

Though little known in Christian traditions of the Greco-Roman world, Judas Thomas, the brother of Jesus,[29] was regarded as the premier apostle of the Syrian milieu, having converted lands as far east as Persia and India. By the late fourth century his shrine was one of the great Christian monuments of Edessa. When the Spanish pilgrim Egeria visited it in spring of 384, she venerated the saint not just with prayers, but also by reading what she believed to be his own words.[30] She may have been reading portions of the apocryphal *Acts of Thomas,* a work that probably originated in the environs of Edessa in the first half of the third century.[31] While its appeal lies partly in its highly imaginary settings and events, the *Acts of Thomas* also sets forth an apostolic program of celibacy, poverty, and homelessness that may have reflected, and certainly inspired, the practices of many Syrian ascetics from the third century onward.

According to the *Acts of Thomas,* when the world was divided up among the apostles, India fell to Thomas. Sold by Jesus as a carpenter-slave to a merchant traveling for an Indian king, Thomas soon makes himself known by the hymns he sings, the miracles he performs, and the celibacy he preaches en route. Once in India he receives gold and silver from King

---

29. On the identification of Judas Thomas (Judas "the twin") as Jesus' brother, see John Gunther, "The Meaning and Origin of the Name Judas Thomas," *Le Muséon* 93 (1980): 113–48.

30. Egeria, *Itinerarium* 19.2, ed. Pierre Maraval, p. 203: et aliquanta ipsius sancti Thomae ibi legimus. This probably refers to the *Acts of Thomas,* not the *Gospel of Thomas:* see Maraval's commentary. On Thomas' cult at Edessa, see Segal (1970): 174–76.

31. For date and testimony for the *Acts of Thomas [ATh],* see A. F. J. Klijn, *The Acts of Thomas, Introduction, Text, Commentary* (Leiden: Brill, 1962), 18–26 and H. J. W. Drijvers, "The Acts of Thomas," in *New Testament Apocrypha,* ed. E. Hennecke, W. Schneemelcher, and R. McL. Wilson, 2d ed., vol. 2 (Westminster: John Knox Press, 1992), 322–38. Originally written in Syriac, it survives in both a Greek and a Syriac version. In this chapter I follow the Greek version (which seems to reflect the original text more closely than the Syriac version), but I note where the Syriac may illumine the ascetic implications of a passage.

Gundaphor (a historical ruler of northern India) to build a sumptuous palace, but eventually people noticed that he was using these resources to serve a different sort of king. As Gundaphor learns, "He has neither built a palace nor has he done anything else . . . but he goes about the towns and villages, and if he has anything he gives it all to the poor, and he teaches a new God."[32] The apostle is imprisoned as a sorcerer until Gundaphor learns the true value of his craft and requests baptism. Then Thomas moves on, preaching throughout India, attracting a large following through his miracles, exorcisms, and songs. Finally in another kingdom he establishes himself as a teacher in the house of a military officer whose wife and daughter he had saved from demons. Here too the apostle attracts many followers, but his success in preaching celibacy to Mygdonia, the wife of the brash Prince Karish, lands him in prison for sorcery again. Once released, Thomas continues to preach his "doctrine which both gods and men abhor," despite stern warnings from the local king, Masdai.[33] Thomas even baptizes Masdai's wife and son. For these last acts the apostle is executed, but he dies happily, his mission accomplished: "Lord, I have fulfilled thy work and thy command. I have become a slave; therefore today do I receive my freedom. . . ."[34]

This narrative conveys, with exotic flair, the ascetic ideals and expectations of the Syrian Christians who produced it.[35] For them, salvation required not merely firm belief in Christ but strict imitation of Christ. That did not simply mean celibacy. Although the plot revolves around the adoption of celibate "holiness" by its characters (and for that reason has often been treated as a manifesto of radical encratism, the notion that adopting Christianity required practicing celibacy), what distinguishes the *Acts of Thomas* from other apocryphal acts is its emphasis on homeless poverty adopted in imitation of Jesus. Thus Thomas is repeatedly called a "stranger," and he identifies himself primarily by the material renunciations he has made in service to Christ:

> Look upon us because for Your sake we have left our homes and those of our fathers' goods, and for Your sake have gladly and willingly become strangers. Look upon us, Lord, because we have left our own possessions for Your sake, so that we might possess You, the possession that cannot be taken away. . . .

32. *ATh* 20; trans. Drijvers, p. 347.
33. *ATh* 126; trans. Drijvers, p. 389.
34. *ATh* 167; trans. Drijvers, p. 404.
35. For possible context, see H. J. W. Drijvers, "East of Antioch: Forces and Structures in the Development of Early Syriac Theology," in *East of Antioch: Studies in Early Syriac Christianity* (London: Variorum, 1984a), 1–27; A. Hamman, "*Sitz im Leben* des actes apocryphes du Noveau Testament," *SP* 8 (1966): 62–69; and *id.*, "Le *Sitz im Leben* des Actes de Thomas," *Studia Evangelica* 3 (1964): 383–89.

Look upon us, Lord, who have left our fathers, mothers, and the ones who gave us nurture, so that we might behold Your father and be satisfied with His divine nourishment.[36]

I boast of poverty, love of wisdom, humility, fasting, prayer, and the community of the Holy Spirit. . . . [37]

I believed in Your revelation and remained in the poverty of the world. . . . I have become poor and needy and a stranger and a slave, despised, imprisoned, hungry and thirsty, naked and weary.[38]

The *Acts of Thomas* casts its Christian exemplar as a wandering, begging ascetic.[39] As he asks one curious visitor, "What have you come to see? A strange, poor man, one easily despised, a beggar, with neither wealth nor possessions? But I have one possession which neither king nor rulers can take away. . . . Jesus, the savior of all humanity."[40]

What Jesus was this whom Thomas possessed, obeyed, and imitated? Certainly not the immaculate Jesus of most modern conceptions. The *Acts of Thomas* reflects an ancient Christology that emphasized Jesus' identity as a homeless vagrant "who has nowhere to lay his head" (Mt 8:20). This was a God whose majesty assumed human dimensions by adopting the most despicable form of human existence, "who, though being in the form of God . . . emptied Himself by taking the form of a slave, coming to be in human likeness; and once found human in appearance, humbled himself, becoming obedient until death" (Phil 2:6–8). By stooping so low, God had rendered his power and promise of salvation accessible to all humanity. As Paul explains, "for your sake he became poor *[ptōcheusen]*, though he was rich, so that with his poverty *[ptōcheia]* you might become rich" (2 Cor 8: 9). By "poverty," Paul may have simply ment "humanity." However, the terms he used were significant for later readers. A *ptōchos* was a person who

36. *ATh* 61; ed. Maximilian Bonnet and R. A. Lipsius, pp. 177–78: διὰ σὲ κατελείψαμεν τοὺς οἴκους ἡμῶν καὶ τὰ γονικὰ ἡμῶν, καὶ διὰ σὲ ξένοι γεγόναμεν ἡδέως καὶ ἑκόντες. Trans. adapted from Drijvers, p. 364.

37. *ATh* 139; ed. Bonnet-Lipsius, p. 246: καυχῶμαι ἐπὶ πενίᾳ καὶ φιλοσοφίᾳ καὶ ταπεινότητι καὶ νηστείᾳ καὶ εὐχῇ καὶ τῇ κοινωνίᾳ τοῦ ἁγίου πνεύματος. Trans. adapted from Drijvers, p. 394.

38. *ATh* 145; ed. Bonnet-Lipsius, p. 252: ἐν τῇ τοῦ κόσμου πενίᾳ παρέμεινον. . . . γέγονα πένης καὶ ἐνδεὴς καὶ ξένος καὶ δοῦλος καὶ καταπεφρονημένος καὶ δεσμώτης καὶ λιμώττων καὶ διψῶν καὶ γυμνὸς καὶ κεκοπιακώς. Trans. adapted from Drijvers, p. 397. The Syriac version of sect. 107 adds the prayer, "For Thy sake I have been a recluse and an ascetic *(sriqā)* and a pauper *(meskēnā)* and a wandering mendicant *(ḥādurā)*. Let me then receive the blessing of the poor, and the rest of the weary." Trans. Klijn, p. 120; for the Syriac terms, see pp. 38, 272–73.

39. The Greek version uses the term ξένος (stranger) 16 times. The Syriac version's *aksnāyā* may specifically mean "wandering Christian": see Klijn, pp. 165–66.

40. *ATh* 136; ed. Bonnet-Lipsius, p. 242: ξένον ἄνθρωπον καὶ πένητα καὶ εὐκαταφρόνητον καὶ πτωχόν, μήτε πλοῦτον ἔχοντα μήτε κτῆσιν. Trans. adapted from Drijvers, p. 393.

lived in absolute poverty, whose destitution made him crouch in need or fear like a beggar, in contrast to the more relative poverty of a *penēs*, who, though dependent on others, could nonetheless scrape by in a menial occupation.[41] In Paul's emphasis on Christ's voluntary humility and poverty, many ascetics believed they found their key to imitating Christ and entering his Kingdom.[42] After all, nothing had been lost in this act of divine condescension. Believers knew that Jesus' humble, unremarkable appearance (cf. Mt 11:29; Lk 24:13–35; Jn 20:15) concealed awesome power. The *Acts of Thomas* calls on Jesus as one who "lives in need like [a poor man] but saves like one without need . . . rests from a journey in exhaustion as man, but walks on the waves of the sea as God."[43] If anything, Jesus' humble appearance even magnified his powers by giving him an element of surprise. As a demon confessed after suffering his vengeance,

> We believed we could bring him under our yoke like the rest, but he turned and held us in his grip. For we did not know him: he deceived us by his despicable form, by his poverty and indigence. When we looked upon him as such, we believed him to be a man bearing flesh, not knowing him to be the one who gives life to mankind.[44]

This ancient Christology found its force by inverting the expected order of things: "God chose what is low and despised in the world . . . to bring to nothing things that are" (1 Cor 1:28). It thus also had the potential to surround imitators of Christ—ascetics like Thomas who might otherwise be ignored—with an aura of supernatural power.

As a freeborn man who also became a slave and labored for the Kingdom, the Apostle Thomas represented ascetic imitation of Jesus par excel-

41. 2 Cor 8:9; ed. Aland, p. 636: γινώσκετε γὰρ τὴν χάριν τοῦ κυρίου . . . ὅτι δι᾽ ὑμᾶς ἐπτώχευσεν πλούσιος ὤν, ἵνα ὑμεῖς τῇ ἐκείνου πτωχείᾳ πλουτήσητε. For the classical distinction, see Patlagean (1977): 25–36. See Hamel (1990): 167–76 for biblical usage and bibliography. For the special emphasis in Syrian Christianity on Christ's physical, material poverty, see Visonà (1986): 12–17 and Michael Mees, "Pilgerschaft und Heimatlosigkeit. Das frühe Christentum Ostsyriens," *Augustinianum* 19 (1979): 65–73.

42. For the significance of 2 Cor 8:9 for late antique Christology and ascetic ideology, see Pius Angstenberger, *Die reiche und der arme Christus. Die Rezeptionsgeschichte von 2 Kor 8,9 zwischen dem zweiten und dem sechsten Jahrhundert* (Bonn: Borengässer, 1997), esp. 51–56 and 363–68. In Greco-Roman tradition it was also believed that imperial rulers might leave their palaces to roam the streets at night in disguise: e.g., Ammianus Marcellinus, *Res Gestae* 14.1.9.

43. *ATh* 47; ed. Bonnet-Lipsius, p. 164: ὁ ἐπιδεόμενος ὥσπερ <. . . . > καὶ σῴζων ὡς ἀνενδεής . . . ὁ ἐπαναπαυόμενος ἀπὸ τῆς ὁδοιπορίας τοῦ καμάτου ὡς ἄνθρωπος καὶ ἐπὶ τοῖς κύμασι περιπατῶν ὡς θεός. The Syriac supplies "poor man": see Klijn, p. 89.

44. *ATh* 45; ed. Bonnet-Lipsius, p. 162: ἔσχεν ἡμᾶς τῇ μορφῇ αὐτοῦ τῇ δυσειδεστάτῃ καὶ τῇ πενίᾳ αὐτοῦ καὶ τῇ ἐνδείᾳ.

lence.[45] In the *Acts of Thomas* the two often meld into one, leaving ambiguous any distinction between Jesus and his follower.[46] "You are a man of two forms," remarks a young man whom Thomas has saved from a demon. "Wherever you wish [to be], there you are, and no one holds you back."[47] It has been suggested that this feature was intended to inspire readers to effect their own assimilation to Christ, guided by Thomas' example.[48] His apostolic way of life was to be adopted by ordinary Christians, "to whom he [Thomas] teaches a new doctrine, saying that no one can live, unless that person be released from all belongings and become a renouncer like himself. And he is determined to make many his partners. . . ."[49] Thus, as Jesus provided the example for Thomas' voluntary poverty and homeless wanderings, so Thomas' apostolic way of life provided a model for his readers' imitation. In this way, the *Acts of Thomas* encouraged readers to fulfill an ideal summed up in the *Gospel of Thomas*'s simple command, "Be passersby!" In other words, become transient.[50]

Such material renunciations brought intimations of salvation in this world as in the one beyond. Among these was *amerimnia* (freedom from care), which Thomas regularly preached along with renunciations. This condition might be achieved once readers fully renounced their "service to the belly,"

> which casts the soul into worries and cares and sorrows, so that it becomes anxious lest it should come to want, and ponders things that are far from it. But when you free yourself of these, you become without worries, sorrows, or fears: and there remains for you that which was said by our savior, "Take no care for the morrow, because the morrow will take care for itself," and, "Look upon the ravens," and, "Consider the birds of the sky which neither reap nor

45. For this aspect of their identity, see Klijn (1962): 161, noting that in the Syriac *ATh* 143 Jesus is called "a slave and a poor [man]."

46. Thomas is either assimilated to or mistaken for Jesus in sect. 45, 65, and 88 (at 160 he explains that he actually is not Jesus); Thomas turns into Jesus and vice-versa in sect. 11, 54–55, 57, 118, and 151. See Klijn (1962): 37.

47. *ATh* 34; ed. Bonnet-Lipsius, p. 150: ἄνθρωπος γὰρ εἶ δύο μορφὰς ἔχων.

48. Thus Drijvers (1984a): 16 and *id.*, "Facts and Problems in Early Syriac-Speaking Christianity," *The Second Century* 2 (1982a): 172.

49. *ATh* 100; ed. Bonnet-Lipsius, p. 213: οὐδεὶς δύναται ζῆσαι ἐὰν μή τις ἀπαλλαγῇ πάντων τῶν ὑπαρχόντων καὶ γένηται ἀποτεταγμένος ὥσπερ καὶ αὐτός· καὶ σπουδάζει πολλοὺς κοινωνοὺς ἑαυτῷ ποιῆσαι. See also sect. 143. The Syriac version has "ascetic and wandering mendicant" (*mgazzyā w-ḥādurā*) for the Greek ἀποτεταγμένος (renouncer): see Klijn (1962): 116.

50. *Gospel of Thomas* 42; trans. Thomas Lambdin, p. 131. For this gospel's relation to the Syrian milieu and *ATh* ascetic model, see Mees (1979): 57–58 and Gilles Quispel, "The Syrian Thomas and the Syrian Macarius," *VC* 18 (1964): 235. The fact that the Coptic borrows the Greek verb περιάγω, frequently used to describe Jesus' transience (e.g., Mt 4:23, 9:35), suggests that the phrase was not supposed to simply mean "be detached."

store away in holds, and God cares for them; how much more then for you of little faith?"

Jesus, he told his followers, would provide for their needs: he would become the refuge and healer for all who "endured the heat and burden of the day" for his sake, their "fellow-traveler in this land of error."[51] Both freedom from care and celibacy typified Jesus and were to be imitated.[52] These conditions prepared an ascetic to obtain a higher goal, the sublime state of *praotēs* (meekness, gentleness, understood by Syriac translators as *makkikutā* [lowliness, humility]), which not only typified Jesus, but was also considered his special "boast."[53] This was how Jesus chose to flex his power in the world, "not with swords or with legions of angels," but with the mighty gentleness of a supreme God: "Gentleness has overcome death, bringing it under authority. Gentleness has enslaved the enemy. . . . Gentleness fears no man and does not offer . . . resistance."[54] *Praotēs* was in fact the quality that Jesus associated with those who would "inherit the earth." While bringing spiritual rest, it could also prove effective through its disarming appearance of weakness. By imitating Jesus' gentle humility through the voluntary adoption of poverty, ascetics might share in his unexpected force. So Thomas, like Jesus, also vanquished demons on earth: "Why do you want to rule over us, especially when you teach others not to rule so? . . . Why are you like the Son of God who wronged us? You resemble him very much, as if you were born of him."[55]

In other words, an ascetic's combination of poverty, humility, and gentleness could generate charismatic power.[56] These qualities became regarded as cardinal virtues for wandering ascetics in the later fourth and fifth centuries. They enhanced an ascetic's power of empathy, enabling him to become, like Paul, "all things to all people" (1 Cor 9:22). Material renunciations that fostered these virtues also fortified an ascetic with *par-*

51. *ATh* 28 and 60; trans. Drijvers, pp. 350, 364. *Amerimnia* is a recurring theme: see sect. 34, 42, 85–86, 142, 144–45.

52. *ATh* 86; ed. Bonnet-Lipsius, p. 202: μείνατε οὖν ἐν τῇ ἁγιωσύνῃ καὶ δέξασθε τὴν ἀμεριμνίαν καὶ ἐγγὺς γίνεσθε τῆς πρᾳότητος· ἐν γὰρ τούτοις τοῖς τρισὶν κεφαλαίοις εἰκονογραφεῖται ὁ Χριστός. In the *ATh*, ἁγιωσύνη (holiness, chaste purity) means celibacy.

53. *ATh* 86; ed. Bonnet-Lipsius, p. 202: ἡ δὲ πρᾳότης καύχημα αὐτοῦ ἐστιν, alluding to Mt 26:52. For the Syriac translations of the πρᾳότης as "humility," see Klijn (1962): 265–67. The Syriac Peshitta uses *makkikē* (the lowly, the humble) to render the words οἱ πραεῖς of Mt 5:5: see G. Winkler, "Ein bedeutsamer Zusammenhang zwischen der Erkenntnis und Ruhe in Mt 11, 17–19 und dem Ruhen des Geistes auf Jesus am Jordan. Eine Analyse zur Geist-Christologie in syrischen und armenischen Quellen," *Le Muséon* 96 (1983): 267–326.

54. *ATh* 86; trans. adapted from Drijvers, p. 373.

55. *ATh* 45; ed. Bonnet-Lipsius, p. 162.

56. *ATh* 66; the Syriac *ATh* makes clear the link between poverty, humility, and exercising power: see Klijn (1962): 88–89, 109–10, 207–8, 265–67.

rhēsia, the bold self-confidence needed to confront people of higher social station or office with candid freedom of speech. This power of the Hebrew prophets was available to all Christians if they imitated Jesus: "Perfect these things in us to the end," asks Thomas of Jesus, "so that we may have the *parrhēsia* that is in you."[57] In return for his ascetic renunciations, Thomas was asking Jesus to grant him a degree of *parrhēsia* that went beyond the *parrhēsia* of courtiers or philosophers who addressed an emperor at court. This was a supernatural *parrhēsia* "that neither passes away nor changes," the charismatic boldness of accomplished ascetics whose renunciations gave them access to God and nothing else to lose.[58] Filled with the Spirit, such Christians could speak with God "as the Son of God speaks with His Father," or face down demons.[59] On the human level, *parrhēsia* armed them to speak without fear to all members of society. What demons found out when they mistook Jesus and his apostle in the *Acts of Thomas* for contemptible figures, opponents of their later ascetic imitators learned as well. What they saw before them was definitely *not* what they got.[60]

Readers of the *Acts of Thomas* also learned that genuine Christian exemplars were most surely identified by their demonstrative piety, that is, through their ascetic conduct. As a complete stranger who comes performing miracles, exorcising demons, and wrecking marriages in the service of a "new God," Thomas is accused of being a *magus* (sorcerer or charlatan) wherever he goes.[61] Only his visible commitment to asceticism, especially to ascetic poverty, allays suspicion and secures his recognition as an authentic representative of Christ. So Gundaphor's advisors explain:

> We think he is a *magus.* But his works of compassion and the healings which he has done for free, and moreover his simplicity and kindness and his piety show that he is righteous or an apostle of the new god whom he preaches. For continually he fasts and prays, and eats only bread and salt, and his drink is water, and he wears a single garment whether in fine weather or foul, and takes nothing from anyone, and what he has he gives to others.[62]

As Peter Brown has noted, in this passage we glimpse how late antique

57. *ATh* 61; ed. Bonnet-Lipsius, p. 177: τέλεσον οὖν εἰς ἡμᾶς ταῦτα ἕως τέλους, ἵνα ἔχωμεν παρρησίαν τὴν ἐν σοί. Trans. adapted from Drijvers, p. 364.

58. *ATh* 103; trans. Drijvers, p. 379. For the history of the term, see Erik Peterson, "Zur Bedeutungsgeschichte von Παρρησία," in *Festschrift Reinhold Seeberg,* vol. 1, ed. W. Koepp (Leipzig: Werner Scholl, 1929), 283–97 and Peter Brown, *Power and Persuasion in Late Antiquity* (Madison: University of Wisconsin Press, 1992), 61–68. For its attribution to Christian holy men, see Brown (1982): 136–37.

59. Syriac homily cited in Peterson (1929): 295.

60. See the description of Alexander Akoimētos at trial, *V.Alex* 48.

61. *ATh* 16, 20, 89, 96, 98–101, 104, 106, 114, 116–17, 123, 134, 138–39, 151, 162–63.

62. *ATh* 20; ed. Bonnet-Lipsius, p. 131: σημαίνει ὅτι δίκαιός ἐστιν ἢ ἀπόστολος τοῦ θεοῦ τοῦ νέου ὃν αὐτὸς καταγγέλλει. Trans. adapted from Drijvers, p. 347.

communities identified their holy men.[63] Thomas' fasting and commitment to poverty distinguish him as a righteous stranger, even as an apostle, against a less reputable class of itinerant charmers. These ascetic practices were so important for establishing Thomas' credentials that his adversaries had to discredit them first in order to prove Thomas a deceiver. "That he neither eats nor drinks, do not think that it is for righteousness' sake. . . . This he does because he has no possessions. For what should he do who does not ever have his daily bread? And he has only one garment because he is poor."[64] But others who benefited from his services accepted such behavior as clear proof that Thomas was indeed the real thing: "He did not seek rewards, but demands in return only belief and chaste purity. . . . What he eats is bread and salt, and his drink is water from evening to evening, while he devotes himself to prayer."[65]

The question of legitimacy is raised in other apocryphal *Acts,* but it is never tied so closely to ascetic practice, as it is in the *Acts of Thomas.*[66] This emphasis implies a special concern or warning for readers who might wish to pursue a similar apostleship: as itinerant strangers, they would also have to demonstrate celibacy, fasting, and poverty to prove themselves legitimate representatives of Christ in the communities they entered. As if to underscore this point, the *Acts of Thomas* also notes how to identify illegitimate apostles:

> There shall come false apostles and prophets of lawlessness . . . who preach and ordain that men should flee from impieties but are at all times found in sins themselves. . . . not satisfied with one wife, they corrupt many women. . . . not ⟨content⟩ with their own possessions, [they] wish that all trifles be ministered to them alone, proclaiming themselves to be his (Christ's) disciples . . . who exhort others to abstain from fornication, theft and avarice, but ⟨secretly practice these things themselves⟩.[67]

63. Peter Brown, *The Making of Late Antiquity* (Cambridge: Harvard University Press, 1978), 22.

64. *ATh* 96; trans. Drijvers, p. 376.

65. *ATh* 104; trans. Drijvers, p. 379.

66. For the theme, see P. Poupon, "L'accusation de magie dans Les Actes apocryphes," in *Les Actes apocryphes des apôtres,* ed. F. Bovon (Geneva: Labor et Fides, 1981), 71–93. The other second- and third-century *Acts* (which are not wholly preserved) often depict apostles preaching sexual and material renunciations, but none stress fasting and poverty as proof of apostolic authenticity.

67. *ATh* 79; ed. Bonnet-Lipsius, pp. 194–95: οἱ μὴ ἐπαρκούμενοι τῇ ἑαυτῶν κτήσει ἀλλὰ θέλοντες πάντα τὰ ἀχρειώδη αὐτοῖς ἐξυπηρετεῖσθαι μόνοις, ἐπαγγελλόμενοι ὡς μαθηταὶ αὐτοῖς. Trans. adapted from Drijvers, pp. 370–71, whose emendations to lacunae are enclosed in angle brackets.

More than a paraphrase of Jesus' warning against false apostles and prophets (Mt 7:15–20), this description suggests real experience with wandering teachers who did not practice what they preached. Its message is reinforced when Thomas, after discussing the connection between voluntary poverty, compassion, and humility, affirms that "even we, if we do not ⟨bear⟩ the burden of the commandments, are not worthy to be preachers of his name."[68]

A similar concern is found in another text that comes from this Syrian milieu, the Pseudo-Clementine *Letters to Virgins*. Because of numerous correspondences between Thomas and the wanderers described in the *Letters to Virgins*, some scholars have suggested that the *Acts of Thomas* describes standards that contemporaries hoped to find in itinerant Christian ascetics.[69] The *Letters* not only demand that such ascetics prove themselves worthy "preachers of Jesus' name," but also assume that strict asceticism would prove them worthy of receiving support from communities they visited. This assumption needed no further explanation in a Christian milieu in which it was customary to honor ascetics and to recognize, as Thomas asserts, that pleasing God required "reaching to the poor, supplying those in want, and sharing with those in need, especially with those who conduct themselves in holiness."[70]

A MANUAL FOR APOSTOLIC WANDERERS: PSEUDO-CLEMENT'S *LETTERS TO VIRGINS*

Traditionally ascribed to Clement, first bishop of Rome, the *Letters to Virgins* offer detailed evidence for the actual practice of ascetic wandering before the fourth century.[71] Although their exact date and provenance remain

---

68. *ATh* 66; trans. Drijvers, p. 367.

69. See esp. Georg Kretschmar, "Ein Beitrag zur Frage nach dem Ursprung frühchristlicher Askese" *Zeitschrift für Theologie und Kirche* 61 (1964): 34–35, listing correspondences. Vööbus (1958b): 84–90 draws on both for a composite picture of ascetic ideals and practices in third-century Syria.

70. *ATh* 85; ed. Bonnet-Lipsius, 200–201: εὐάρεστοι γίνεσθε τῷ θεῷ . . . τῷ διὰ χειρὸς ὀρέγοντι τοῖς πένησιν καὶ πληροῦντι τὸ ἐνδεὲς . . . μεταδιδοῦσα τοῖς δεομένοις· μάλιστα τοῖς ἐν ἁγιωσύνῃ πολιτευομένοις.

71. Originally written in Greek, the *Epistolae ad virgines / de virginitate* [*EV*] are mostly preserved in a single Syriac MS edited by Th. Beelen in 1856 (PG 1.379–451). Greek fragments subsequently discovered were published along with Beelen's Latin trans. of the Syriac text (superior to the Latin trans. in PG 1; I refer to its subsections in my citations of the text) by F. Diekamp in *Patres Apostolici* 2.2. Coptic fragments were published by Louis-Théophile Lefort, "Le 'de virginitate' de S. Clément ou de S. Athanase?," *Le Muséon* 40 (1927): 260–64; id., "S. Athanase, Sur la virginité," *Le Muséon* 42 (1929): 265–69; and Enzo Lucchesi, "Compléments aux pères apostoliques en Copte," *AB* 99 (1981): 405–8. Almost all belong to the "first" letter. For observations towards a new critical edition, see Antoine Guillaumont, "Christianisme et

unknown, scholarly consensus has assigned them to third-century Syria.[72] By the late fourth century they had attained quasi-canonical status as testimony of the chaste *mores* of the apostolic age. Cited in defense of celibacy against fourth-century detractors, the two letters (originally a single treatise) in fact preserve one of the earliest Christian discourses on that practice.[73] Yet they discuss celibacy only in order to address broader issues. Their author is chiefly concerned with the ministries provided by itinerant ascetics to scattered Christian communities.[74] His *Letters* suggest remarkable independence from official supervision, referring only once to the church as a source of authority,[75] and making no reference to clergy, only to other "brothers" (other male ascetics).[76] They draw inspiration from Jesus' appointment of the seventy apostles, sent in pairs from town to town without purse, pouch, or sandals to heal the sick and proclaim that the Kingdom was at hand (Lk 10:1–16). Since "the harvest is great but the workmen are few," the author of the *Letters* similarly seeks to enlist respectable virgins as "workmen who shall be such as the apostles," in order to "dispense the word of truth."[77]

To qualify, readers had to "imitate Christ in everything."[78] They had to "express his likeness in their thoughts, in their whole life and in all their behavior." Their faith had to be known from their deeds—words could not

---

gnoses dans l'orient préislamique," *Annuaire du Collège de France 1981–1982* (Paris, 1982), 432–33.

72. Harnack (1891): 363–73 assigns their date and origins to third-century Syria or Palestine on the basis of the earliest testimony to them (from the fourth-century East) and their linguistic peculiarities. Support for Syrian origin is presented by Arthur Vööbus, "Ein merkwürdiger Pentateuchtext in der pseudo-klementinischen Schrift De virginitate," *Oriens Christianus* 44 (1960a): 54–58. Alfred Adam, "Erwägungen zur Herkunft der Didache," *ZKG* 68 (1957): 24, prefers a late second-century date. Harnack believes their attribution to Clement was made in the middle of the fourth century.

73. Guillaumont (1982): 432. The *EV* is cited by Epiphanius of Salamis, *Panarion* 30.15; Jerome, *Ad Jovinianum* 1.12; and *Constitutiones Apostolorum* 8.47.85, compiled in Antioch ca. 380 (see below, ch. 5, no. 66).

74. Harnack (1891): 374 and Adam (1957): 25 note that the author's "eigentlicher Zweck" comes in *EV* I.10–II.6, which discusses ascetic conduct during travel.

75. *EV* I.11.10 (PG 1.407A): "declare the gift which you received in the church for the edification *[mawhabtā d-qabbelt b-ʿēdtā l-benyānā]* of the brothers in Christ." Trans. adapted from B. P. Pratten, p. 59. Reitzenstein (1916): 54 notes the lack of emphasis on church supervision in these letters, and believes the ascetics of the *EV* acted on their own after baptism; so too Kretschmar (1964): 38 and William Telfer, "The Didache and the Apostolic Synod of Antioch," *JThS* 40 (1939): 268–69.

76. Although female as well as male virgins are addressed in *EV* I.2.1, the *EV* discuss ministrations provided only by other "brothers."

77. *EV* I.13.3–4; trans. Pratten, p. 60, quoting Lk 10:2, Mt 9:37–38, and 2 Tim 2:15.

78. *EV* I.6.1.

suffice.[79] Indeed, the *Letters* place striking emphasis on the outward display of ascetic virtue. Readers were not to keep their celibacy concealed. This was asceticism expressly practiced in the service of apostleship. The reader needed to "crucify" himself, so that "while preaching to others, he may be a beautiful example and pattern to believers, and . . . so that he may 'not be cast away' [1 Cor 9:27] but may be approved before God and before men."[80] Ideally, such apostolic exemplars would inspire believers as both messengers and the message, bringing light to "those who sit in darkness."[81] Their ascetic practices would serve as their credentials, identifying them as true representatives of Christ: "for all who see you will 'acknowledge that you are the seed which God has blessed' [Is 61:9]; . . . a seed honorable and holy; . . . a 'priestly kingdom' " [1 Pet 2:9].[82]

Such emphasis on sexual abstinence as proof of integrity was perhaps not surprising for a milieu in which the revised standard version of the Gospels was Tatian's *Diatessaron*—a harmonized epitome of the four Gospels that emphasized the chastity of Jesus and his apostles.[83] What the *Letters to Virgins* actually represent is a manual written to instruct wandering Christian ascetics how to conduct themselves with corresponding behavior in the villages and towns along their itinerary. The author clearly felt the need for such a manual:

> We have spoken thus in consequence of evil rumors and reports concerning shameless men, who, under the pretext of fear of God, have their dwelling with maidens . . . and walk with them along the road and in solitary places—a course which is full of dangers . . . such as ought not to be among believers, especially among those who have chosen a life of holiness. . . . Others wander around the houses of virgin brothers and sisters under the pretext of visiting them, reading the Scriptures to them, or exorcising and teaching them. . . . They pry into things which ought not to be inquired into and with persuasive words make their living on the name of Christ.[84]

Such faults would be routinely found in later polemics against wandering monks. In this case, however, the critic was a wanderer himself, to whom

79. *EV* I.7.1; trans. Pratten, p. 57. Emphasis on deeds over words: I.2.2, 3.1.
80. *EV* I.9.1, trans. Pratten, p. 58. "Pattern" translates the Syriac *dmutā* (PG 1.397D); the original Greek was τύπος. The phrase is also found at I.3.1 and II.64. Harpham (1987): xiv suggests it communicated that "only through certain physical acts acknowledged to constitute 'mastery' over the body . . . could virtue be acquired, attested to, or proven." For general discussion of Christian holy men as exemplars bearing a new ideology, see Brown (1983): 1–25.
81. *EV* I.2.4.
82. *EV* 1.9.4; trans. Pratten, p. 58.
83. See Vööbus (1958b): 39–45 and Brown (1988): 87–88.
84. *EV* I.10.1–5; trans. adapted from Pratten, p. 58.

it was perfectly acceptable that his readers should travel from town to town, "edifying and confirming" both male and female Christians "in the faith of one God."[85] In fact, the spiritual services that he expects them to offer on the road are practically the same as those of the "shameless" men he criticizes: singing hymns and psalms, reciting Scriptures, uttering prophesies, performing exorcisms, raising prayers.[86] Like the apostle Thomas, they would exhort whoever received them to be "'free from anxious care in everything' [Phil 4:6] as is fit and right for the people of God."[87] And they were to pay special attention to the poor.[88]

The author's complaint was not about the services being offered but the way they were being performed. His *Letters* are clearly intended to promote discretion among his readers, "as is becoming and suitable to our calling and profession."[89] For this reason the author offers a description of the conduct in Christ that he and his own ascetic company had adopted for their visits to both Christian and non-Christian communities of every size or type, "if it chance that the time for rest overtake us in a place, whether in the country, or in a village, a town, a hamlet, or wherever we happened to be."[90] His guiding rule is to avoid ever being alone in the company of women: "With [female] virgins we do not dwell or have anything in common; with these we neither eat nor drink, nor do we sleep wherever a virgin sleeps."[91] Communities in which the resident virgins were male offered the safest lodgings: "There we call together all the brothers, and speak to them words of encouragement and comfort," sharing a room until dawn with one who was celibate.[92] Care was needed in mixed communities. Females in the room had to be separated from males "in all modesty and becoming behavior"; when leaving they placed the kiss of peace on cloth-covered hands. "Then we go where God permits."[93] If all the Christians were female and "they press us to pass the night," then he secured lodgings somewhere through "a woman who is aged and the most modest among them." But if the sole Christian in a community were female, "Then we do not stop there, nor pray there, nor read the Scriptures there, but flee as if before the face of a serpent."[94]

---

85. *EV* I.13.1; trans. Pratten, p. 60.
86. Recitations: *EV* II.2.1, 4.2, 6.2; psalm-singing: II.6.3; prophesy: I.11.10; exorcisms: I.12.2; prayers: I.12.3.
87. *EV* II.1.3; trans. Pratten, p. 61.
88. *EV* I.13.8.
89. *EV* I.13.6; trans. Pratten, p. 60.
90. *EV* II.1.3; trans. adapted from Pratten, p. 61.
91. *EV* II.1.2.
92. *EV* II.1.4; trans. Pratten, p. 61.
93. *EV* II.2.2–5; trans. Pratten, p. 61.
94. *EV* II.4.–5.1; trans. Pratten, p. 62.

Such circumspection was necessary, the author felt, "so that we may be without reproach in everything, lest anyone be offended or scandalized by us."[95] He held a pessimistic view of the capacity for trust that his readers would encounter in communities they visited. "The hearts of men are firmly fixed on evil," he warns, and therefore itinerant brothers had to be careful to avoid any situation that might give rise to slander.[96] Cohabitation and travel by male and female ascetics was his most immediate concern, as was only natural, considering the notice this would have received in conservative villages of the Near East.[97] There also was need to rein in their charismatic powers. Exorcisms performed "with terrible words" that terrified their patients, prophesies that went off on strange tangents, and utterances that went beyond familiar teachings had to be discouraged.[98] The author insists that when his own company traveled, only "those gifted in speaking" spoke with Jesus' gentleness and humility, and that they only used "words as are earnest, serious, and chaste."[99] There were far too many, he notes, who simply "hunt after words and consider this virtue and correct behavior," or worse, "take the name of Christ falsely," and "do not practice what they preach" (Mt 23:3).[100] Of equal concern, however, was the economic motive that the author believed drove many to adopt his profession in the first place: "They wish to be teachers and to display themselves as skillful in speaking, because they traffic in iniquity in the name of Christ—which is not right for slaves of God to do."[101] His indignation on this point is pronounced; he prays that God not send forth any more "workmen" who merely work "'for the food which perishes' [Jn 6:27], not workmen who 'sell their services' [Jn 10:12], not workmen to whom the fear of God and righteousness appear to be gain, not workmen who 'serve their bellies' [Rom 16:18] . . . not workmen who traffic in Christ."[102] Thus the *Letters to Virgins* expresses the same concern for establishing apostolic legitimacy found in the *Acts of Thomas*. In fact, the author's main reason for discussing

95. *EV* II.3.2; trans. adapted from Pratten, p. 62.

96. *EV* II.5.2–3; trans. Pratten, p. 62.

97. For context, see Brown (1988): 140–59. Scholarship on the *EV* has focused on its polemics against *virgines subintroductae* (virgins snuck in), i.e., male and female ascetic cohabitation: e.g., Kretschmar (1964): 33; Hugo Duensing, "Die dem Klemens von Rom zugeschriebenen Briefe über die Jungfräulichkeit," *ZKG* 63 (1950): 50; and Harnack (1891): 374–75, 382. For this custom and its later history, see Susanna Elm, *"Virgins of God": The Making of Asceticism in Late Antiquity* (Oxford: Clarendon Press, 1994), 48–51.

98. *EV* I.11–12; trans. Pratten, pp. 58 and 59: prophesy should be reserved for "spiritual brothers who know the words are those of the Lord" (11.10; 8.59).

99. *EV* II.1.3, 2.4; trans. Pratten, p. 61; also I.12.4.

100. *EV* I.11.1 and 8; trans. adapted from Pratten, pp. 59–60.

101. *EV* I.11.2; (PG 1.404D): *meddem d-lā zādeq l-'abdaw d-alāhā*. Trans. adapted from Pratten, pp. 58–59.

102. *EV* I.13.4–5; trans. Pratten, p. 60.

virginity in his manual was to emphasize how readers must distinguish themselves from the many false workmen "who imitate the children of light, while being not light but darkness."[103]

The problem he addressed already had a long history. His very phrase, "traffic in Christ," derives from an earlier Christian manual known as the *Teachings of the Twelve Apostles,* or *Didache.*[104] Probably written in western Syria in the late first century, the *Didache* informed Christians how to distinguish true charismatic figures who wandered into their communities from false ones.[105] Such help was necessary, since it was acknowledged that "every true prophet who wishes to dwell among you is worthy of his food," as was every "true" apostle, teacher, or workman.[106] They were entitled to a community's produce when they came (as had been provided for Levite priests under Mosaic law [Num 18:21–28]) and to a day's supply of bread when they left. The guidelines offered by the *Didache* were simple. If any teacher, prophet, or apostle tried to stay longer than two days or asked for money, he was false.[107] It gave similar advice for giving hospitality to any other tramp who came "in the name of the Lord." Those who wished to stay more than two or three days had to work for their food. Any prophet, apostle, or beggar who stayed longer and remained "idle," refusing to work, the *Didache* calls a "Christmonger," warning readers, "beware of such."[108]

To appreciate such warnings and advice, we must consider some norms of charity and entitlement that by this time had become diffused throughout the Roman Near East. In the first place, it was generally recognized that privileged treatment was owed to those who dedicated themselves to edifying society, from Jewish sages who studied Torah (seen as a service to Yahweh) to Cynic street philosophers.[109] There were also scruples that charged even common beggars with a certain numinous aura, to be treated

103. *Ibid.* On this point, see also Mees (1979): 60–61.

104. See Adam (1957): 16 and Telfer (1939): 269, with *Didache* 12.5 (below).

105. For date and provenance, see Willy Rordorf and André Tuilier, *La Doctrine des Douze Apôtres (Didachè)* (SC 248; Paris: Éditions de Cerf, 1978), 91–99. Aaron Milavec, "Distinguishing True and False Prophets: The Protective Wisdom of the *Didache,*" *JECS* 2 (1994): 121–25, argues that its itinerant teachers were not official community leaders, but ascetics of eschatological fervor who occasionally served alongside such leaders.

106. *Didache* 13.1–2; ed. Rordorf and Tuilier, p. 190.

107. *Didache* 11.5–6, 12.

108. *Didache* 12.2 and 5; ed. Rordorf and Tuilier, p. 188: Εἰ μὲν παρόδιός ἐστιν ὁ ἐρχόμενος, βοηθεῖτε αὐτῷ ὅσον δύνασθε· οὐ μενεῖ δὲ ὑμᾶς εἰ μὴ δύο ἢ τρεῖς ἡμέρας,. . . . Εἰ δ᾽ οὐ θέλει οὕτω ποιεῖν, χριστέμπορός ἐστι· προσέχετε ἀπὸ τῶν τοιούτων.

109. Study of Torah was indirectly supported by tithes (and said to ensure the fertility of the land): see Hamel (1990): 111, 168 and W. S. Green, "Palestinian Holy Men: Charismatic Leadership and Rabbinic Tradition," in *Aufstieg und Niedergang der römischen Welt* II/19.2 (Berlin: Walter de Gruyter, 1979), 641–42. For Cynic philosophers, see Dio Chrysostom, *Or.* 32.9. I thank Susan Ashbrook Harvey for this reference.

with charitable caution. Gathered at the edge of synagogues and temple sanctuaries, their appearance could rouse ancient fears of pollution, representing what might happen with a sudden reversal of fortune.[110] Indeed, beggars themselves were believed to be able to bring about such reversals upon those who did not heed them. "Despise not the voice of the poor and give him not cause to curse you," later Christians were warned, "for if he curse whose palate is bitter, the Lord will hear his petition."[111] That they might cast an evil eye on more fortunate passers-by remained a clear and present danger in Jewish, pagan, and Christian traditions.[112] Charity extended toward them was not necessarily given in sympathy.

Not far removed from common mendicants were holy beggars devoted to the service of a particular deity. Best known among them are the ascetic Galli, who attached themselves to the "Great Mother" Cybele or to Atargatis, the "Syrian goddess." The latter especially prepared the ground in the Near East for many a Christian holy man. In the second century, devotees of the Syrian goddess could be seen performing their inspired songs and rites of self-mutilation in the precinct just outside Atargatis' home temple in Hierapolis/Mabbug (modern Membidj).[113] They otherwise apparently spent their lives as collectors, traveling around the Mediterranean and Near East in bands, gathering food and coins from astonished villagers "by which they supported themselves and looked after the goddess." They were also known for making prophesies and divinations.[114] Moving under the shadow of more staid civic priesthoods (it is not certain whether they were officially recognized as priests themselves), their ecstatic behavior and begging received little credit for religious sincerity from Greco-Roman ob-

110. Cf. Artemidorus, *Oneicritica* 3.53 and Philostratus, *Vita Apollonii* 4.10. For treatment of beggars and the possibility of their ritual impurity in Jewish tradition, see Hamel (1990): 55–56, 68–70, 216–19 and Milavec (1994): 127 n. 14, citing Mishnaic advice on charity similar to the *Didache*'s. For beggars outside pagan temples: Ps.-Clement, *Recognitiones* 7.13.

111. Ephrem, *Homily on Admonition and Repentence* 16; trans. A. E. Johnston, p. 334.

112. For discussion and bibliography, see Frank (2000): 129–31; Brigitte Kern-Ulmer, "The Power of the Evil Eye and the Good Eye in Midrashic Literature," *Judaism* 40 (1991): 344–53; and Arthur Hands, *Charities and Social Aid in Greece and Rome* (Ithaca: Cornell University Press, 1968), 46–47, 76–85. Peter Brown has kindly referred me to John Chrysostom, *In epistulam I ad Thessalonicenses V hom.* 9.3 (PG 62:465), describing beggars who solicited young women by appealing to their husbands, children, or beauty: i.e., things by which they might be especially provoke the envy of "the Eye."

113. Lucian, *De dea Syria* 50–51. For Hierapolis, see Millar (1993): 242–48 and Godefroy Goossens, *Hiérapolis de Syrie: essai de monographie historique* (Louvain: Bibliothèque de l'Université, 1943). For the question of continuity between behavior in this shrine and practices of later Christian holy men, see David Frankfurter, "Stylites as *Phallobates:* Pillar Religions in Late Antique Syria," *VC* 44 (1990): 168–98.

114. Ps.-Lucian, *Asinus* 37; ed. and trans. Matthew D. MacLeod, p. 111. Cf. Apuleius, *Metamorphoses* 8.27–29 and 9.8–9.

servers.[115] Yet an inscription found near Damascus proudly proclaims in simple Greek how one such "slave" of the Syrian goddess, Lucius the Pious, had made over forty successive trips "sent by Lady Atargatis," and had brought back more than a hundred "purses," all of which he recorded for her on the inscribed altar.[116] It would be wrong to dismiss such enthusiastic journeying and solicitations as self-serving. Evidently the people who contributed did not. Indeed, those who "gladly" housed them and the image they carried may have seen in their begging the goddess herself crying out, not for alms, but for sacrifices due.[117]

Such behavior and sense of charitable obligation would have set expectations for the Christian reception of strangers who appeared offering spiritual services "in the name of the Lord" from the first century onward. Jesus' prohibition against taking a "purse on the road" (Mt 10:10, cf. Lk 10:4) may have been intended to distinguish his own apostles from other holy slaves and beggars of the East; yet at the same time Jesus proclaimed his own homeless, needy "workmen" to be worthy of their pay (Lk 10:7). Therefore, there was a need for guidelines to help Christians distinguish the true wandering apostles, prophets, and teachers from false. The second-century East was known to abound with apocalyptic figures who wandered begging around cities and army camps, each declaring "I am God (or a Son of God, or a divine Spirit). And I have come."[118] The reception and reverence extended to one such charismatic figure named Peregrinus ("the Stranger") by a Christian community in second-century Palestine became the butt of satire after he later went off to immolate himself at the Olympic

115. Nor from modern scholars: cf. A. Pauly and G. Wissowa, *Real-Encyclopädie der classischen Altertumswissenschaft* 1 (Stuttgart: J. B. Metzlerscher, 1894), 915–17, s.v. "Agyrtes." To my knowledge, religious begging in the Hellenistic and Roman Near East has received little study. See the notes to Arthur Darby Nock, "Eunuchs in Ancient Religion," in *Essays on Religion in the Ancient World*, ed. Z. Stewart, vol. 1 (Oxford: Clarendon Press, 1972), 13–15.

116. Ed. H. Fossey, "Inscriptions de Syrie," *Bulletin de Correspondence Hellénique* 21 (1897): 60: Θεᾷ Συρίᾳ Ἱερα[π]ολιτῶν Λούκιος δοῦλος αὐτ[ῆ]ς . . . εὐσεβ[ὴ]ς καὶ πεμφθεὶς ὑπὸ τῆς κυρία[ς] . . . ἀ[π]οφόρησε ἑκάστη ἀγωγὴ πήρας . . . ἔνονται. I thank Peter Brown for this reference. For another inscription by a Syrian traveling at the behest of a god (exactly which is not clear), see C. P. Jones, "A Syrian in Lyon," *American Journal of Philology* 99 (1978): 336–53.

117. For the housing of the image of the goddess and the Galli who carried it, see Ps.-Lucian, *Asinus* 39; cf. Apuleius, *Met.* 8.30, 9.8. The Galli are described as "compelling the goddess to beg": τὴν θεὸν ἐπαιτεῖν ἀναγκαζόντων, Ps.-Lucian, *Asinus* 35; ed. Macleod, p. 108. Problems of interpreting such behavior are illuminated by J. D. Y. Peel, "Poverty and Sacrifice in Nineteenth-Century Yorubaland: A Critique of Iliffe's Thesis," *Journal of African History* 31 (1990): 469–72. Peel shows that what Christian missionaries believed to be religious begging in West Africa was actually understood by locals to be a god demanding sacrifices through its priests. I thank Peter Brown for directing me to this article.

118. Celsus *apud* Origen, *Contra Celsum* 7.9, referring to prophets in second-century Palestine and Phoenicia. Trans. Henry Chadwick, p. 402.

games as a Cynic philosopher.[119] By the third century, internerant enthusiasts who took money for spiritual services were commonly charged by
critics as being sorcerers or charlatans.[120] Christian apologists recognized
the need to defend their own enthusiasts who continued to travel and
preach in cities, villages, and army camps. As Origin wrote in 248:

> One could not say they did this for the sake of wealth, since sometimes they
> do not even accept money for the necessities of life, and if ever they are
> compelled to do so by want in this respect, they are content with what is
> necessary and no more, even if several people are willing to share with them
> and to give them more than they need.[121]

This, then, was the background of the *Letters to Virgins*. Their author had
good reason to be worried by rumors circulating about "workmen who traffic in Christ." One striking feature of his manual is its assumption that his ascetic readers would be dependent upon other Christians for their material
support. Indeed, the account he gives of his own wanderings makes clear
that he himself expected the communities he visited to provide for him and
his band in return for spiritual services they offered. For example, he claims
that, upon entering a community that already had its own holy man,

> that same brother will provide and prepare whatever is necessary for us; and
> he himself waits upon us, and he himself washes our feet for us, and anoints
> us with ointment, and he himself gets ready a bed for us, that we may sleep
> in reliance on God. All these things will that consecrated brother, who is in
> the place in which we tarry, do in his own person.[122]

But if no such brother is to be found, "all those who are there will receive
the brother who comes to them, and care for his wants in everything, as-
siduously, with good will."[123] If there were only women, then the eldest

---

119. Lucian, *De morte Peregrini* 11–14, 16; on his depiction of Proteus Peregrinus, see James
A. Francis, *Subversive Virtue: Asceticism and Authority in the Second-Century Pagan World* (University
Park, Penn.: Pennsylvania State University Press, 1995), 55–58 and M. J. Edwards, "Satire and
Versimilitude: Christianity in Lucian's *Peregrinus*," *Historia* 38 (1989): 89–98.

120. For charges against itinerant Cynic, Jewish, and Christian teachers, see W. L. Liefeld,
The Wandering Preacher as a Social Figure in the Roman Empire (Ph.D. diss., Columbia University,
1967), 245–71.

121. Origen, *Contra Celsum* 3.9; ed. Marcel Borret (SC 136), p. 30: τινες γοῦν ἔργον
πεποίηνται ἐκπεριέρχεσθαι οὐ μόνον πόλεις ἀλλὰ καὶ κώμας καὶ ἐπαύλεις, ἵνα καὶ ἄλλους εὐσεβεῖς τῷ
θεῷ κατασκευάσωσι. καὶ οὐκ ἂν πλούτου τις ἕνεκα φήσαι αὐτοὺς τοῦτο πράττειν, ἔσθ᾽ ὅτε μὲν οὐδὲ
τὰ πρὸς τροφὴν λαμβάνοντας, εἴ ποτε δὲ ἀναγκάζοιντο ὑπὸ τῆς ἀπορίας ταύτης, τῇ χρείᾳ μόνῃ,
ἀρκουμένους, κἂν πλείους αὐτοῖς κοινωνεῖν ἐθέλωσι καὶ μεταδιδόναι τὰ ὑπὲρ τὰς χρείας. Trans.
Chadwick, pp. 133–34. It is telling that Origen's remarks here (written in 248) were not
prompted by anything the pagan critic Celsus had specifically written on this point.

122. *EV* II.2.1–2; trans. Pratten, p. 61.

123. *EV* II.3.1; trans. Pratten, p. 61.

among them would, from her "love of the brothers," "bring whatever is requisite for the service of brothers who are strangers."[124] According to his examples, he never took money or stayed long in the communities he visited: only if pressed "by their affection for strangers" did he spend the night, and then he expected from his hosts only "bread, water, and that which God provides."[125] A passing reference to home and neighbors indicates that he was not himself homeless, and suggests that they supported him when he was not on the road.[126] But nowhere else does he otherwise explain how he and his company supported themselves. Their dependence on Christian goodwill is simply assumed to be part of their apostolic profession. Hence the tension that runs through the *Letters to Virgins*. Their author was himself potentially implicated in the same delicate issue of material support for wandering prophets and teachers that the *Didache* addresses.

This was also the reason for his concern that his readers "imitate Christ in everything" and prove themselves to be "a priestly kingdom" through proper ascetic conduct. That alone would distinguish them from "traffickers in Christ." Already the *Didache* had advised Christian communities to examine the behavior of the charismatic figures who came to them: "Not everyone who speaks in the Spirit is a prophet, but only if he has the ways of the Lord. . . . If he does not practice what he preaches, he is a false prophet."[127] The author knew his readers would be similarly scrutinized for "ways of the Lord" by communities expected to support them. Asceticism would prove each to be "a true teacher. . . . like the workman, worthy of his food."[128]

In Pseudo-Clement's *Letters to Virgins* we encounter the example and concerns of a wandering Christian ascetic who was openly dependent on those whom he visited for his material support and was, therefore, sensitive to the suspicions that surrounded wanderers. His *Letters* must not be read simply as a discourse on virginity, but rather as a manual intended to establish norms of ascetic conduct for others who chose to venture on such an apostolic profession. In condemning the behavior reported about some of his contemporaries, the author not only recalls the *Didache*'s warnings about false apostles, but anticipates some of the charges that church offi-

---

124. *EV*II.4.4 (PG 1:425D): *l-teshmeshthon d-aḥē aksnāyē.* Trans. adapted from Pratten, p. 62.
125. *EV*II.2.1; trans. Pratten, p. 61.
126. *EV*II.2.1; trans. Pratten, p. 61: "if we be distant from our homes and our neighbors." Reitzenstein (1916): 53 suggests that the *EV* reflects tensions between propertied and homeless ascetics.
127. *Didache* 11.8; ed. Rordorf and Tuilier, pp. 184–86: οὐ πᾶς δὲ ὁ λαλῶν ἐν πνεύματι προφήτης ἐστιν, ἀλλ' ἐὰν ἔχῃ τοὺς τρόπους κυρίου. Ἀπὸ οὖν τῶν τρόπων γνωσθήσεται ὁ ψευδοπροφήτης καὶ προφήτης. 11.10: εἰ ἃ διδάσκει οὐ ποιεῖ, ψευδοπροφήτης ἐστί.
128. *Didache* 13.2; ed. Rordorf and Tuilier, p. 190: διδάσκος ἀληθινός ἐστιν ἄξιος καὶ ὥσπερ ὁ ἐργάτης τῆς τροφῆς αὐτοῦ.

cials in the next century would raise against "hypocrites in the garb of monks." Indeed, their enthusiastic behavior contained the seeds for a typology of heresy ("Messalianism") that we shall discuss in the next chapters.[129] Yet Pseudo-Clement's concerns must not be taken as evidence for any sort of decline. On the contrary, the author reveals that his apostolic vocation was flourishing in the third-century Roman East—if anything, too many Christians were answering the call. Moreover, his *Letters* demonstrate the practice and assumed propriety of an apostolic arrangement for leadership and support, whereby ascetic exemplars served scattered Christian communities informally alongside or in the place of (but not necessarily against) ordained clergy. Such figures provided edification and charismatic services, though perhaps not church sacraments like the Eucharist or baptism—at least they are not mentioned in the *Letters*. Far from attesting any decline in apostolic ideals or ascetic enthusiasm, the Pseudo-Clementine *Letters to Virgins* make clear that wandering ascetics kept the apostolic pulse alive along the roads of third-century Syria.

As for those accused of "trafficking in Christ" and working in the "service of their bellies," we perhaps get a glimpse of what the author meant when he explains what *not* to do if stuck for a few days in a non-Christian town, especially at festival time:

> We do not sing psalms to the heathens, nor do we read to them the Scriptures, that we may not be like common singers . . . or like soothsayers, as many are who follow these practices and do these things, that they might sate themselves with a scrap of bread and, for the sake of a sorry cup of wine, go about "singing the songs of the Lord in a strange land" [Ps 137:4] of the Gentiles. . . . [130]

Clearly one danger of wandering in this third-century countryside was the possibility of going native. The pagan festivals of rural villages would have posed opportunities and temptations for talented but needy Christian ascetics to show off their skills, make some conversions, and leave after receiving some sustenance. As far as the author was concerned, the problem with Christian ascetics performing at pagan festivals lay not with the compensation they received, but with the fact that their performances easily blurred distinctions between Christian and non-Christian holy men, and obscured the distinct Christian "pattern" he hoped to promote in pagan as well as Christian communities.

Those who did "sing the songs of the Lord in a strange land" might have taken comfort by thinking of the apostle Thomas and the songs he was said to have sung at pagan feasts while heading east. In fact, the themes that they themselves may have sung eventually came back in the form of Man-

---

129. As noted by Mees (1979): 63–64; Adam (1957): 26; and others.
130. *EV* II.6.3–4; trans. adapted from Pratten, p. 63.

ichaean songs that were written down on papyri in Egypt.[131] The Coptic *Manichaean Psalm-Book* preserves a collection or cycle of ancient spirituals called "Psalms of the Wanderers." The title apparently alludes to both the physical transience and the spiritual yearnings of the ascetics who sang them. These celebrated freedom from care in antiphonal refrains.[132] Jesus was their model, guide, and refuge; and songs of the Spirit were their sustenance:

> It is Jesus that we seek, on whom we have modeled ourselves.[133]

> In the midst of the sea, Jesus, guide me.
> Do not abandon us that the waves may not seize us.
> When I utter Thy name over the sea it stills the waves.

> I trusted in Thy hope, I trusted not in gold and silver.
> I looked forth in the world, I found no harbor save Thy harbor. . . .
> I have found no rest save Thy rest.
> The provision of the Holy Spirit are these prayers, these songs, and these
>   psalms.[134]

They encouraged themselves in the pursuit and power of their "holy poverty":

> He that humbleth himself shall be received,
> He that [exalteth] himself shall be humbled.

> Poverty . . . has received a great name; it has been made wealth:
> It is holy poverty.
> Therefore, my brethren, let us love poverty and be poor in the body but
>   rich in the spirit.
> And let us be like the poor, making many rich,
> as having nothing, possessing power over everything.
> What shall we do with gold and silver? Let us love God.[135]

Those who sang such psalms simply identified themselves as "strangers" who had left their homes and families to follow Jesus.[136] Yet this was no

---

131. Thus Murray (1975b): 28–29 and 161. These psalms probably date ca. 400: see I. M. F. Gardner and Samuel N. C. Lieu, "From Narmouthis (Medinet Madi) to Kellis (Ismant El-Kharab): Manichaean Documents from Roman Egypt," *JRS* 86 (1996): 149. See also Audré Villey, *Psaumes des errants: Écrits manichéens du Fayyûm* (Paris: Cerf, 1994) and Peter Nagel, "Die Psalmoi Sarakoton des manichäischen Psalmbuches," *Orientalistische Literaturzeitung* 62 (1967): 123–30.

132. *Psalmoi Sarakoton,* ed. and trans. Charles R. C. Allberry, p. 161, 3–5; cf. the *Psalms of Heracleides,* ed. Allberry, p. 192, 12–13. Murray (1975b): 28 n. 3 characterizes these psalms as "responsorial shanties."

133. *Psalmoi Sarakoton,* trans. Allberry, p. 170, 16–18.

134. *Psalmoi Sarakoton,* trans. Allberry, pp. 151, 4–10 and 184, 22–27.

135. *Psalmoi Sarakoton,* trans. Allberry, pp. 157, 3–9 and 159, 15–16.

136. Cf. *Psalmoi Sarakoton,* trans. Allberry, pp. 175, 26–27 and 182, 13.

mountain-top or desert *anachōrēsis*. As expressed in one refrain, they conceived their estrangement from the world as ideally pursued in the service of humanity: "Thou art a stranger to the world. Be . . . a sojourner on the earth for men."[137] It was partly through the efforts of such vagrant psalm-singers, one must suppose, that the Holy Spirit reached the far-flung villages and towns of third-century Syria and Mesopotamia.[138]

THE CONTINUING INFLUENCE OF THE APOSTOLIC PARADIGM

By the time these verses had been set down on papyri (ca. 400), their Manichaean singers had become a disturbing presence in the Roman Empire, denounced by Christian and imperial authorities alike as alien subversives spreading poison from the Persian East.[139] Though portrayed as utterly un-Christian, Mani was actually born and raised in a Judeo-Christian baptist sect of southern Mesopotamia. He and his followers considered themselves genuine successors to the apostles: they did not identify themselves as "Manichees" (a name coined by their adversaries), but rather as consummate Christians representing the true Church of Jesus Christ.[140] Setting forth with missionary zeal from Mesopotamia as early as 244,[141] Mani's followers made themselves known through their songs, public debates with other Christian leaders, and pronounced ascetic ethic of fasting, poverty, and homelessness founded on the apostolic model:

137. *Psalmoi Sarakoton*, trans. Allberry, 181, 22–23.

138. Thus Brown (1988): 196–97. David A. Aune, *Prophesy in Early Christianity and the Mediterranean World* (Grand Rapids: Eerdsmans 1983), 84, suggests that the songs of early wandering Christian prophets entered church liturgies.

139. See Diocletian's rescript to Julianus, proconsul of Africa, probably dating to 302 (text in S. Riccobono, *Fontes Iuris Romani Anteiustiniani* 2.580–81; for date, see J. D. Thomas, "The Date of the Revolt of L. Domitius Domitianus," *ZPE* 22 [1976]: 261–62) and Eusebius, *HE* 7.31. L. J. van der Lof, "Mani as the Danger from Persia in the Roman Empire," *Augustiniana* 24 (1974): 75–84, surveys the imagery that Roman authorities from Diocletian to Augustine used to portray Manichaean alterity.

140. For Mani's identification of himself and his disciples as Jesus' apostles, see Gardner and Lieu (1996): 167–68; Samuel N. C. Lieu, *Manichaeism in the Later Roman Empire and Medieval China,* 2d ed. (Tübingen: Mohr, 1992), 28–59; Brown (1988): 197–202; and *id.,* "The Diffusion of Manichaeism in the Roman Empire," *JRS* 59 (1969), reprinted in *id., Religion and Society in the Age of St. Augustine* (London: Faber and Faber, 1977), 96–99. For the role of Jesus in Manichaean theology, see Manfred Heuser, "The Manichaean Myth According to the Coptic Sources," in *Studies in Manichaean Literature and Art,* ed. Manfred Heuser and Hans-Joachim Klimkeit, trans. Majella Franzmann (Leiden: Brill, 1998), 66–74, 92–93.

141. See Samuel N. C. Lieu, "From Mesopotamia to the Roman East: The Diffusion of Manichaeism in the Eastern Roman Empire," in *Manichaeism in Mesopotamia and the Roman East* (Leiden: Brill, 1994), 23–53: missions reached the Syrian frontier as early as the 260s. For their third-century context in the Roman Empire, see Robin Lane Fox, *Pagans and Christians* (New York: Knopf, 1987), 562–71.

They withered through fasting, . . . [they] took up the cross upon them, went from village to village.

They went into the roads hungry, with no bread in their hands. . . . No gold, no silver, no money did they take with them on their way.

They went into villages, not knowing anybody.

They were welcomed for His sake; they were loved for His name's sake.[142]

Like other fourth-century apostolic Christians, Mani's followers drew inspiration from the *Acts of Thomas* as well as the Gospels.[143] By combining strict asceticism with missionary endeavors and by imitating Christ's homeless poverty and assuming that others would provide them with material support in return for the spiritual edification they offered, Manichaeans became the most notorious heirs to the apostolic paradigm for Christian life that had guided the author of the *Letters to Virgins* and continued to inspire Christian ascetics of the Roman East in the fourth and fifth centuries.[144]

More will be said in the next chapter about Manichaean and other monastic arrangements derived from this apostolic paradigm. What must be emphasized here is the continuing influence of this paradigm on Syro-Mesopotamian ascetic practice. Its remarkable vitality in this milieu may be explained by a lack of strong ecclesiastical structure or assertive church hierarchy in the third-century East, a condition perhaps exacerbated (or created) by renewed warfare between Rome and Persia.[145] Here wandering ascetics may have filled a vacuum, assuming an active, if informal, role as representatives of the Christian faith. That is the impression given by the *Letters to Virgins*. Like later itinerant priests called *periodeutae,* who in the next century would be sent to make liturgical rounds and represent distant

142. *Psalms of Heracleides,* trans. Allberry, p. 195, 6–13. Cf. 1 Cor 4:28. Manichaean ascetic practices are described in detail by Vööbus (1958b): 115–24.

143. See Epiphanius of Salamis, *Panarion* 47.1.5 (the "Encratites") and 61.1.5 (the "Apostolic Ones," celibates who renounced all possessions in Pamphylia, Cilicia, and Phrygia). Manichaean use of the *ATh* is discussed by Peter Nagel, "Die apokryphen Apostelakten des 2. und 3. Jahrhunderts in der manichäischen Literatur. Ein Beitrag zur Frage nach den christlichen Elementen im Manichäismus," in *Gnosis und Neues Testament,* ed. K.-W. Trögen (Berlin: Gutenslohor, 1973), 173–77.

144. See Brown (1988): 202 and H. J. W. Drijvers, "Odes of Solomon and Psalms of Mani: Christians and Manichaeans in Third-Century Syria," in *Studies in Gnosticism and Hellenic Religions Presented to Gilles Quispel,* ed. R. van den Broek and M. J. Vermaseren (Leiden: Brill, 1981), 117–30.

145. This condition may be apparent rather than actual, but see above, n. 20. For third-century warfare in these regions, see Millar (1993): 141–73. Murray (1975b): 157–58, 274–75, 340–47 notes an individualistic streak in Christian spirituality in Syriac literature of the period, in contrast to the institutional emphasis of much Christian literature being written around the Mediterranean at this time.

bishops in the rural Syrian hinterland, these wandering ascetics met pastoral needs in the countryside.[146] Their enthusiasm to do so may have even been welcomed by official church leaders, considering the limited reach of their pre-Constantinian budgets and numbers.

The continuing circulation of such apostolic figures may also explain the distinctive ascetic bent in Syro-Mesopotamian Christianity. In the past, scholars have turned to possible influences from Judaic sects encouraging celibacy;[147] to the "dualist" cosmologies disseminated by followers of Marcion, Tatian, and Mani;[148] to eschatological fervor;[149] or more generally, to a Syriac "tendency to literalize symbols."[150] What needs to be added is the recognition that ascetic behavior might serve sociologically "as a marker, as a sign of belonging, to one sect rather than another, to one community rather than another."[151] We must remember the proximity of Eastern congregations to more established Jewish communities and ideas. The zealous kind of *imitatio Christi* celebrated in Syria bears striking resemblance to the Judaic expectation that disciples would imitate their rabbinic masters— each of whom was viewed as "living Torah"—in everything they did or said.[152] At the same time the need that Paul felt in the first century to distinguish Christians from Jews through distinctive ascetic practice would presumably still have been felt by third-century Christians who continued to live under the shadow of a larger Jewish population and culture.[153] Both the *Acts of Thomas* and the *Letters to Virgins* communicated a need for Christian leaders to mark themselves off from non-Christians through intense

146. Trombley (1993–1994): vol. 2, 250 argues from epigraphical evidence that congregations east of Antioch lacked resident priests and deacons, and therefore depended on such *periodeutae* during most of the fourth century. Eusebius' reference to "priests and teachers of the brethren in villages" may be evidence of ascetic teachers in third-century Egypt: *HE* 7.24.6; ed. Gustave Bardy, p. 203: πρεσβυτέρους καὶ διδασκάλους τῶν ἐν ταῖς κώμαις ἀδελφῶν, but Bardy believes διδασκάλους is just a gloss on πρεσβυτέρους.

147. E.g., the Qumran sect, which espoused celibacy for its members and referred to itself as the "covenant." See Murray (1975b): 17–18 and Vööbus (1958b): 23–30.

148. A thesis asserted in Vööbus (1958b): 158–69.

149. E.g., Mees (1979): 65–73.

150. Thus Harvey (1990): 5 suggests that in the Syriac Church "Literal and figurative aspects of [scriptural] interpretation were seen to be the same, and so too were one's actions and their symbolic meanings."

151. Dianne M. Bazell, "The Politics of Piety," in *Asceticism,* ed. V. L. Wimbush and R. Valantasis (Oxford: Oxford University Press, 1995), 499.

152. See Robert Kirschner, "The Vocation of Holiness in Late Antiquity," *VC* 38 (1984): 114–19. Milavec (1994): 131 believes *Didache* 11.8 derives from Jewish notions of the rabbi as "living Torah," who trains disciples "as much by what he does as by what he says." For Judaic notions of religious poverty comparable to those associated with Jesus, see Hamel (1990): 161, 194–96.

153. Kretschmar (1964): 65–66 believes contact between Christians and Jews made ascetic perfectionism central to Syrian Christianity.

imitatio Christi. But the need to prove oneself through ascetic discipline would have extended to interaction between Christians as well. This was of utmost importance in a region characterized by competition between Christians of different stripes, all seeking to establish themselves as representatives of "true" Christianity.[154] Manichaean missionaries in particular were known to impress as much through the pale charm of their ascetic rigors as through the cogency of their cosmic speculations.[155] In this respect their success merely confirmed the lessons laid out by the *Acts of Thomas* and *Letters to Virgins:* for many Christians, apostolic legitimacy depended upon demonstrative ascetic conduct. Thus apostolic ambitions and rivalries helped shape notions of what it meant to be an exemplary Christian in these regions, and helped promote the high ascetic tone of Syrian spirituality.

Finally, just as it is historically unwarranted to view the Manichaeans as an outside catalyst for the Christian ascetic ferment in third- and fourth-century Syria and Mesopotamia (rather than the other way around),[156] it is also unwarranted to regard the ascetic tradition depicted in the *Acts of Thomas* or the *Letters to Virgins* as historically unrelated to the Syrian institution of the *Bnay* and *Bnāt Qyāmā,* even as it is described in the fourth century. Though it was clearly an ancient institution, we do not know how such "Sons and Daughters of the Covenant" lived or what specific role they played before the fourth century. It would be a reasonable conjecture, however, to suppose that the itinerant ascetics addressed and described in the *Letters to Virgins* were themselves "covenanters," branching out from some unknown Syrian community.[157] Indeed, Aphrahat's sixth *Demonstration* (336/337), our earliest source specifically addressed to members of a *Bnay* or *Bnāt Qyāmā,* suggests that he assumed covenanters would similarly serve an informal role as spiritual instructors of their community:

154. For examples of competition between ascetic Christian groups in Syria, see Vööbus (1958b): 160–62.

155. See Lieu (1992): 143–44, citing Augustine, *De moribus ecclesiae catholicae et moribus manichorum* 1.2 and Ephrem, *Contra haeresis* 1.12 (Mani's pale complexion deceives the unwary) and 23.7.5–10 ("He seduces simple women through diverse pretenses: he catches one by fasting, the other by sackcloth and leguminous plants"). Cf. Chrysostom, *In Genesim hom.* 7.4 (PG 54.613) and Mark the Deacon, *Vita Porphyri* 87.

156. Vööbus (1958b): 158–69, unaware that Mani was born and raised in a Christian community, surmised that Manichaean asceticism derived from Hindu (i.e., not Christian) traditions, and that Manichaean missionaries passed Hindu ascetic traditions to Christians in Syria, thereby revitalizing "archaic" Christian ascetic practices. This "Vööbus thesis" was first refuted by Gribomont (1965); see also Griffith (1995).

157. Lane Fox (1987): 359–60 and Telfer (1939): 269 identify the ascetics of the *EV* with "covenanters." As Segal (1970): 136 notes, the covenant institution probably varied from place to place.

Let us be poor in the world, that we may enrich many with the teaching of the Lord.[158]

In an acceptable time, let him speak his word; otherwise, let him be silent . . . [and] to such a one as fears God let him reveal his secret; but let him keep himself from the evil man.[159]

Aphrahat was writing for a Christian community in Persian territory that expected its spiritual elite to practice strict asceticism and edify others. As spiritual exemplars, their lives were expected to reflect the voluntary poverty and humility of Christ:

Let us take our pattern, my beloved, from our Savior, Who though He was rich, made Himself poor, and though He was lofty, humbled His majesty, and though His dwelling place was in heaven, He had no place to lay His head.[160]

Although Aphrahat focuses mainly on sexual renunciations, fasting, and prayer,[161] his exhortations that covenanters imitate Christ's homeless poverty indicate that pronounced material renunciations continued to define what it meant to follow Christ and serve as his representatives in the early fourth century. Aphrahat's proximity to the apostolic ascetic tradition described in the *Letters to Virgins* is also indicated by his urging of covenanters to identify with the poor in their community,[162] and by his warning that a covenanter should not "for his belly's sake make himself despised by his begging" while teaching others.[163] Aphrahat does not discuss how his covenanters should support themselves, but fifth-century regulations make clear that local church leaders and communities were expected to supply their needs,[164] as earlier had been done for the itinerant ascetics of the *Letters to Virgins*.

By the fifth century (and perhaps earlier) the *qyāmā* had become a

158. Aphrahat, *Demonstratio* 6.1 (PS 1.246); trans. John Gwynn, p. 363.

159. Aphrahat, *Demonstratio* 6.8 (PS 1.275.1–4); trans. Gwynn, p. 369. Cf. 6.8 (274.25–27).

160. Aphrahat, *Demonstratio* 6.9 (PS 1.275–78); trans. Gwynn, p. 369. Cf. 6.1 (PS 1.242). For Aphrahat's use of this phrase, see Angstenberger (1997): 199–207.

161. For Aphrahat's ascetic ideals, see Diana Juhl, *Die Askese im Liber Graduum und bei Afrahat* (Weisbaden: Harrassowitz, 1996), 129–59. Like the author of the *EV*, Aphrahat addresses the problem of male and female ascetic cohabitation at length: see *Demonstratio* 6.4–7 and Griffith (1993): 154–56.

162. Aphrahat, *Demonstratio* 20.9 and 17; see Angstenberger (1997): 203–4 and Persic (1986): 211–14. See *EV* I.12.8 for a similar admonition to wanderers.

163. Aphrahat, *Demonstratio* 6.8 (PS 1.275,2): *lā nebsē napsheh b-shelteh.* Trans. Gwynn, p. 368 (amplifying Rom 16:18).

164. See Arthur Vööbus, "The Institution of the *Benai Qeiama* and *Benat Qeiama* in the Ancient Syrian Church," *Church History* 30 (1961): 21–22, based on fifth-century canons attributed to Rabbula, *Rules for the Clergy and the Bnay Qyamâ* 12, 19, 25, and 27.

formal institution from which might be drawn candidates for lower orders of the church hierarchy in Syrian and Mesopotamian regions.[165] As church institutions strengthened in the post-Constantinian era and asceticism came more into vogue, a new category of "Single Ones" came to be recognized, called *monachoi* in Greek. [166] Those most celebrated by this name were ascetics like Antony, Aones, and the *boskoi* who withdrew to mountains and deserts, severing themselves from all contact with human society. Why did such *anachōrēsis* become the touchstone of this new form of monastic vocation? What happened to those who continued to pursue the old apostolic model of ascetic life through cities, towns, and villages of the newly Christianized empire? These questions will be the focus of the next two chapters.

165. See Escolan (1999): 46–58; Susan Ashbrook Harvey has kindly let me read her unpublished discussion of later church regulations pertaining to the *qyāmā*, "Bishop Rabbula: Ascetic Tradition and Change in Fifth-Century Edessa."

166. The Greek μοναχός (solitary, single one) may have originally been used to translate the Syriac *iḥidāyā* (single one): see Françoise Morard, "Encore quelques réflexions sur Monachos," *VC* 34 (1980): 395–401 and Griffith (1995): 228–29.

3

In Support of "People Who Pray"

Apostolic Monasticism and the Messalian Controversy

In 431 church officials at the Council of Ephesus condemned what they called "the most noxious heresy in memory," namely that of the "Messalianites or . . . the Euchites or . . . the Enthusiasts, or however else . . . it is known."[1] Sixteen years earlier, in 415, despite previous efforts to expel "this disease" from eastern regions,[2] Jerome could designate "Messalians" as the "heretics of nearly all Syria."[3] From seemingly obscure beginnings first noticed in the last quarter of the fourth century, Messalianism had become regarded as one of the most tenacious and exasperating heresies in the eastern Roman Empire. In response, the Council of Ephesus called for a systematic round-up "throughout each and every province" of anyone "even suspected of such disease, whether clerics or laymen,"[4] and for their anathematization of the heresy. But Messalianism proved to be a recurring challenge. Church leaders continued to issue new canons against Messalian heretics and to record their activities for the next two centuries and beyond.[5]

The late fourth and early fifth centuries were a crucial time for subor-

---

1. *Acta Conciliorum Oecumenicorum [ACO]* 1.1.7 [80]; ed. Eduard Schwartz, p. 117,4–7: περὶ τῶν λεγομένων Μεσσαλιανιτῶν εἴτε οὖν Εὐχιτῶν ἢ γοῦν Ἐνθουσιαστῶν εἴτε ὁπωσοῦν ἡ μιαρωτάτη μνημονευθέντων αἵρεσις σαφηνισθείη. At which session this was raised is not known: see Carl J. Hefele and Henri Leclerq, *Histoire des conciles d'après les documents originaux*, vol. 2 (Hildesheim: Georg Olms, 1973), 340–42.

2. Theodoret of Cyrrhus, *Haereticarum fabularum compendium [HFC]* 4.11 and *Historia ecclesiastica [HE]* 4.10.8.

3. See below, n. 36.

4. *ACO* 1.1.7 [80]; ed. Schwartz, p. 117,10–16. For text, see below, n. 45.

5. See Klaus Fitschen, *Messalianismus und Antimessalianismus: Ein Beispiel ostkirchlicher Ketzergeschichte* (Göttingen: Vandenhoeck und Ruprecht, 1998), 272–341.

dinating ascetic laymen to the institutional authority of church leaders. This involved the promotion of orthodox monastic arrangements and the marginalization of those deemed heretical.[6] In this and the next chapter we will examine the evolution of the Messalian profile that church authorities in the eastern Roman Empire generated and applied to many ascetics who continued to pursue the apostolic model for monastic life discussed in the last chapter. Underlying the earliest characterizations of "People Who Pray" (*mṣallyānē* in Syriac, usually rendered "Messalians" or "Euchites" in Greek) are the same ascetic assumptions, behavior, and problems that the *Letter to Virgins* had criticized a century earlier in the East. The fact that People Who Pray became identified as heretics with specific doctrines by church authorities in the late fourth century does not mean that we are dealing with a new ascetic phenomenon. Rather, we are dealing with a post-Constantinian ecclesiastical process of defining, consolidating, homogenizing, or rejecting forms of Christian life and expression that now came under the direction of a largely Mediterranean-based, Greco-Roman hierarchy with its own institutional perspective and concerns.

The heretical profile constructed by Eastern church authorities has had its intended effect of marginalizing such People Who Pray from the mainstream of early church and monastic history. Nearly all historians continue to assume that there arose in the late fourth century a more or less distinct "movement" with specific "leaders" who propagated a coherent set of ideas and an antiecclesiastical outlook ("Messalianism"), which allegedly originated in Mesopotamia and spread into western Syria, and then on to Asia Minor, Armenia, Egypt, perhaps even North Africa.[7] This line of interpretation follows the westward progress of church actions and official definitions drawn against Messalians in the late fourth and early fifth century. Starting at Antioch, where certain "leaders" of the heresy and their notions

6. This ecclesiastical process is sketched in broad strokes by Rita Lizzi, *Il potere episcopale nell' Oriente romano: Rappresentazione ideologica e realità politica (IV–V sec. d.C)* (Rome: Edizioni dell' Ateneo, 1987). For its impact on Syrian ascetic groups generally, see Escolan (1999): 71–123. It has been well discussed in relation to gender issues: see Elm (1994): 184–223 and Virginia Burrus, *The Making of a Heretic: Gender, Authority, and the Priscillianist Controversy* (Berkeley and Los Angeles: University of California Press, 1995).

7. Fitschen (1998) and Escolan (1999): 91–123 assume that a specific Messalian group or movement existed outside polemics. This assumption guides Fitschen's approach to Messalian history, which employs meticulous source-criticism to identify "true" Messalians and Messalian doctrine. See Fitschen (1998): 12–15, 238 and Columba Stewart, Review of *Messalianismus und Anti-Messalianismus,* by Klaus Fitschen, *JEH* 50 (1990): 552. The representations of Messalians in polemical sources cannot, however, be trusted for accuracy: that is clear from the different descriptions given by Theodoret and Severus of Antioch of Adelphius' testimony (see below). Nor can we assume that contemporary authorities drew sharp distinctions between ascetic behavior that looked Messalian but which (according to modern historians) was not really Messalianism.

were condemned, it further narrows its historical scope by regarding as Messalian only those ascetics specifically labeled as such by late antique authors, and by discounting from serious consideration all those not explicitly described as adhering to the specific doctrinal teachings that were added to the Messalian profile. Consequently many studies continue to treat Messalianism not only as an isolated movement, but also as a historical novelty of the late fourth and early fifth centuries, and as a problem strictly limited to doctrinal concerns.

Works written to identify and condemn Christian heretics, however, cannot be taken as objective or accurate any more than hagiographies can. Not merely tendentious, they tend to construct histories that are false or misleading by their specificity and systematic organization: groups totally unrelated in time or place become assimilated under specific heretical labels (e.g., Apotactites, Encratites) simply because their ascetic practices appear similar, or they become linked to specific heretical leaders (e.g., the "heresiarchs" Tatian, Mani), despite the lack of any demonstrable connection.[8] By constructing such heretical genealogies, church authorities defined and marginalized a disturbing or competing "other." To follow this ancient methodology—seeking to understand Messalian phenomena only by reference to specific leaders and doctrines described in heresiological literature—risks missing the broader historical dynamic and the social issues reflected in the Messalian controversy.

This dynamic and the social issues involved come into view only through an alternative methodology that focuses on behavioral aspects of the Messalian profile: in particular, on their alleged refusal to perform manual labor and their claim to material support from others. By focusing on behavioral rather than doctrinal features (thus shifting the usual focus of Messalian scholarship), it will become apparent that what church leaders were confronting under the "Messalian" label was not in fact a novel movement, but rather a complex of ideals, practices, and assumptions deeply rooted in the apostolic model for Christian ascetic life and leadership outlined by the Gospels themselves.

Given the ascetic tradition that we have seen already flourishing in Syria and Mesopotamia in the third century, it is not surprising that most of the testimony for Messalian phenomena directs us back towards these and

8. This rhetorical strategy was applied by both Jerome and Epiphanius of Salamis to ascetic groups in this period. See Susanna Elm, "The Polemical Use of Genealogies: Jerome's Classification of Pelagius and Evagrius Ponticus," *SP* 33 (1997): 311–18 and Aline Pourkier, *L'hérésiologie chez Épiphane de Salamine* (Paris: Beauchesne, 1992), esp. 341–61, 486–92. Such strategies developed out of second- and third-century heresiological practices: see Alain Le Boulluec, *La notion d'hérésie dans la littérature grecque (IIe–IIIe siècles)* (Paris: Études Augustiniennes, 1985), vol. 1: 162–73, 178–86; vol. 2: 549–54.

neighboring regions. Yet precisely because the practices associated with People Who Pray were derived from the Gospels rather than specific "Messalian" leaders, the behavior and assumptions identified with "Messalianism" in the Roman East could be found (although without the Messalian label) wherever aspiring Christian ascetics turned to the Gospels for direction during the post-Constantinian monastic boom.

Indeed, late-fourth-century church leaders in Carthage encountered among their monks a "pestiferous contagion" of practices and assumptions (e.g., refusal to work, claim to material support from others) that were similar to those being labeled "Messalian" at this time in the East. Although it has been surmised that Augustine wrote his treatise *On the Work of Monks* to suppress Messalian monks who had moved to Africa to escape persecution in the East, this view is historically unwarranted and methodologically unsound. His treatise instead demonstrates that the Messalian controversy must not be understood in isolation, or as a phenomenon sui generis, but rather as the Eastern crystallization of a conflict that arose between church officials and ascetic laymen all around the Mediterranean in the late fourth and early fifth centuries. The ecclesiastical alarm raised by such People Who Pray went beyond doctrinal concerns: by their uncompromising assertion of apostolic poverty, and by the claims they made based on their spiritual activities, such ascetics forced the question of who might legitimately claim apostolic privileges (and, therefore, apostolic authority) in this crucial period for defining the prerogatives of the church hierarchy in Roman society.

THE EVOLUTION OF THE MESSALIAN PROFILE

The Messalian profile received its first detailed exposition around 377, when Bishop Epiphanius of Salamis on Cyprus completed his *Panarion* (Medicine Chest), a massive catalogue of the eighty heresiarchs and heretical groups he reckoned had sprung up since the Flood.[9] Numerically inspired by the eighty concubines distinguished from the "only one" in Song of Songs 6:8, Epiphanius used written documents, personal encounters, and hearsay in order to relate "Judaic," "Samaritan," "Hellenic," and "Barbarian" doctrines and practices that constituted deviations from godliness. Last and most recent of all came a "totally ridiculous" sect that he called the "Massalians":

9. For Epiphanius' background, see Jon F. Dechow, *Dogma and Mysticism in Early Christianity: Epiphanius of Cyprus and the Legacy of Origen* (Macon, Ga.: Mercer University Press, 1988), 25–124. For the date, sources, and methodology of his *Panarion*, see Pourkier (1992): 341–61.

These people think it good [to mingle] in the same place, men and women, saying (if you believe it!) they have utter faith in Christ, since they have renounced the world and have completely abandoned their own things. Whenever summer comes they sleep mixed together, men with women and women with men, right in the same spot—in public thoroughfares, in fact—because, they claim, they have no possession on earth. They show no restraint and stretch out their hands to beg, on the grounds that they have no livelihood and no possessions.[10]

As in their begging, "Massalians" showed no self-restraint in their fasting, ceasing their "supposed devotion to prayer" whenever they wished for food and drink.[11] Epiphanius also notes their readiness to identify themselves as prophets, patriarchs, and angels—"whatever you might want"—even Christ.[12]

Epiphanius' description seems to have been based on hearsay, and the origin of their heresy truly puzzles him. Unlike other sects which he defines by the practice that he mostly associated with them, he has difficulty identifying these People Who Pray and their "supposed devotion to prayer" with any known Christian heresiarch, sect, or text. To make sense of their practices he suggests instead that they were imitating certain "pagan Massalians" who had appeared during the reign of Emperor Constantius II (324–361). From these and other pagan groups the "Christian Massalians," he argues, probably derived their own peculiar practices, "devoting themselves to praying and hymn-singing" in the open air.[13] Yet Epiphanius remains perplexed: "Christian Massalians have no beginning or end, no top or bottom, but are unsettled in every way, without leaders, and utterly deluded. They entirely lack the support of a name, a law, a location, or a legislation."[14]

Epiphanius therefore pursues their origin in another direction. After noting that Messalians could be found "also in Antioch, having come in

---

10. Epiphanius, *Panarion* 80.3.4; ed. Karl Holl and revised Jürgen Dummer, p. 487: εἰς Χριστὸν πεπιστευκέναι λέγοντες, ὡς ἀποταξάμενοι τῷ κόσμῳ καὶ τῶν ἰδίων ἀνακεχωρηκότες.... καθεύδοντες, ἐν ῥύμαις μὲν πλατείαις, ὁπηνίκα θέρους ὥρα εἴη, διὰ τὸ μὴ ἔχειν, φησί, κτῆμα ἐπὶ τῆς γῆς. ἀκώλυτοι δέ εἰσι καὶ ἐκτείνουσι χεῖρας μεταιτεῖν ὡς ἀβίωτοι καὶ ἀκτήμονες. Epiphanius spells the name "Massalians;" after him "Messalians" becomes conventional.

11. Epiphanius, *Panarion* 80.3.6; ed. Holl-Dummer, p. 488: δῆθεν εἰς τὴν εὐχὴν ἐσχολακότες.

12. Epiphanius, *Panarion* 80.3.5; ed. Holl-Dummer, pp. 487–88: ἐκεῖνον ἑαυτὸν φάσκει οἷον δ᾽ ἂν ἐθέλοις. Cf. Sulpicius Severus, *Vita Martini* 23.3–24.3 on Western ascetics who variously identified themselves as Elijah, Christ, and John the Baptist at this time.

13. Epiphanius, *Panarion* 80.1.3; 3.2; ed. Holl-Dummer, p. 487: τὰ ἴσα ἐν ὑπαίθρῳ ἐξαγόμενοι... ἐπὶ τὸ εὔχεσθαι καὶ ὑμνεῖν ἐσχολάκασιν.

14. Epiphanius, *Panarion* 80.3.3; ed. Holl-Dummer, p. 487: οὔτε ἀρχὴ οὔτε τέλος οὔτε κεφαλὴ οὔτε ῥίζα... ἀστήρικτοι καὶ ἄναρχοι καὶ ἠπατημένοι, μὴ ἔχοντες ὅλως στηριγμὸν ὀνόματος ἢ θεσμοῦ ἢ θέσεως ἢ νομοθεσίας.

from Mesopotamia,"[15] Epiphanius shifts focus to the "extreme simpleness" of certain "respectable brothers" in Mesopotamian monasteries.[16] Epiphanius holds them responsible for encouraging these ascetics in the practice that would become the most commonly recognized feature of the Messalian profile: their refusal to practice manual labor.

> They got this baleful presumption from the extreme simpleness of certain brothers . . . [who] though orthodox, do not know moderation in Christian conduct, which bids us to renounce the world, give away our money and property, sell what we have and give to beggars, but . . . not to be idle, or without work, or to eat at the wrong times: not to be like a drone among honey-bees, but to "work with one's own hands" [1 Thess 4:11] just like the holy apostle Paul, who, though he renounced the world, was a herald of truth, "whose hands sufficed not only for himself, but for those who were with him" [Acts 20:34] . . . teaching us in the plainest words: "He that does not work, let him not eat" [2 Thess 3:10].[17]

Epiphanius also criticizes these Mesopotamian monks for growing hair long "deliberately . . . like a woman's," and for conspicuously wearing sackcloth. Such practices, he says, demonstrate their *philonikia* (spirit of contentious rivalry), a characteristic he attributes to Messalians as well.[18]

Thus Epiphanius ascribes to Messalian heretics a broad range of enthusiastic and (in his view) undisciplined behavior, reflecting both Christian and non-Christian precedents. But of all the traits that he identifies with Messalians, it is their *argia* (idleness) that causes the most dismay. Only priests and bishops, he argued, were entitled to receive their daily bread from others, because, like the apostles, they preached, performed the liturgy, and administered the church.[19] But ascetic "slaves of God" who had "truly been founded on the rock of truth"—like those of Egypt, where Epiphanius received monastic training—obtain their sustenance, he maintains, performing "light tasks with their own hands, each according to his

15. Epiphanius, *Panarion* 80.3.7; ed. Holl-Dummer, p. 488: καὶ ἐν Ἀντιοχείᾳ εἰσὶν ἀπὸ τῆς Μέσης τῶν ποταμῶν ὁρμώμενοι. Fitschen (1998): 24 cites this as evidence that Epiphanius' Messalians practiced *stabilitas loci* and were "not wild gyrovagi."

16. Epiphanius, *Panarion* 80.6.5.

17. Epiphanius, *Panarion* 80.4.1–2; ed. Holl-Dummer, p. 488: τὸ βλαβερὸν τοῦτο φρόνημα ἀπὸ τῆς ἀμετρίας τῆς τινων ἀδελφῶν ἀφελείας. . . . μὴ γινώσκοντες τὸ μέτρον τῆς ἐν Χριστῷ πολιτείας, τὸ κελεῦον ἀποτάσσεσθαι τῷ κόσμῳ, κτημάτων τε ἰδίων καὶ χρημάτων ἀποξενοῦσθαι, πωλεῖν τε τὰ ἴδια, καὶ μεταδιδόναι πτωχοῖς . . . μὴ <εἶναι> ἀργὸν μήτε ἄεργον.

18. Epiphanius, *Panarion* 80.6.5–7.5, arguing (80.7.3) that the propriety of long hair had ceased with Paul (e.g., 1 Cor 11:16). Long hair was one of the conceits Augustine associates with begging monks: *De opere* 31.39–32.40.

19. Epiphanius, *Panarion* 80.5.6.

skill."[20] Laying full emphasis on Paul's admonitions to perform manual labor, Epiphanius dismisses any possible appeal to Jesus' command, "work not for the meat that perishes, but for the meat that endures to eternal life."[21] In fact, Epiphanius does not recognize any connection between their attitude toward work and their devotion to prayer and hymn-singing. Instead, he treats these traits separately, associating their prayer with pagan exemplars, their idleness with simple-minded Mesopotamian monks. Although he admits the latter to be orthodox Christians, he suggests that they "had learned this [argia] from Mani." Thus Epiphanius sought to discredit the Messalian trait he found most reprehensible by linking it with the great Mesopotamian heresiarch.[22] His message was clear: "the divine word tells us to mark such people who do not work."[23]

"A heresy has been established," Epiphanius concludes, "through the horridness of idleness and other evils."[24] Wandering, cohabitation of males and females, total renunciation of material possessions (aktēmosynē), irregular prayer and fasting, literal identification with spiritual exemplars, and above all, argia—refusal to work and its consequent begging—these were the traits that characterized Messalian heretics for him. It is notable that Epiphanius' criticisms are purely concerned with matters of ascetic practice rather than doctrine. Epiphanius, of course, may well have been ignorant or inaccurate about the ascetics he describes as "Messalian." What matters is that his Panarion established a profile that would guide readers in identifying Messalians from the late 370s onward. Although his successors added doctrinal features to it, the behavior he identified would remain more or less constant. And although Epiphanius did not specifically link Messalian argia with Messalian devotion to prayer, the equation he makes between rejection of manual labor, poverty, and claims to support by others (through outright begging, in his example) is most important for understanding later criticisms of ascetic argia.

20. Epiphanius, Panarion 80.4.4–6; ed. Holl-Dummer, p. 491. For Epiphanius' monastic background and outlook, see Dechow (1988): 32–36.

21. Epiphanius, Panarion 80.4.4, quoting Jn 6:27.

22. Cf. Pourkier (1992): 361. Others think Epiphanius dissociated their prayer and argia simply because he was dealing with something foreign to his way of thinking: e.g., Jean Gribomont, "Le dossier des origines du Messalianisme," in Epektasis: Mélanges patristiques offerts au Cardinal Jean Daniélou, ed. J. Fontaine and C. Kannengiesser (Paris: Beauchesne, 1972), 613–14 and Hermann Dörries, "Die Messalianer im Zeugnis ihrer Bestreiter. Zum Problem des Enthusiasmus in der spätantiken Reichkirche," Saeculum 21 (1970): 215–16.

23. Epiphanius, Panarion 80.4.3; ed. Holl-Dummer, pp. 490–91. For comparable Manichaean practices see below, p. 120–21.

24. Epiphanius, Panarion 80.7.5; ed. Holl-Dummer, p. 493: κατέστη αἵρεσις ἐν δεινότη<τι>ἀργίας.

Epiphanius, however, was not the first church authority to note these strange People Who Pray or associate them with Mesopotamia. Already by 373, a hymn written by Ephrem to educate Mesopotamian congregations about heretics around Edessa or Nisibis had finished with a reference to "the *mṣallyānē*, who are debauched."[25] Ephrem's single line of verse provides little information about these People Who Pray, except, perhaps, that their manner of prayer might be considered overly boisterous or agitated.[26] Still, even though Ephrem probably wrote this hymn at Edessa, where certain "Messalian leaders" were later apprehended, he, like Epiphanius, does not identify Messalians with any specific doctrines.

Indeed, the history and definition of Messalianism becomes more elaborate only through actions taken against certain Mesopotamian monks in the 380s and 390s at synods held in Antioch and Side (modern Selimiye).[27] When Bishop Flavian of Antioch (381–404) heard of Messalian activities in the region of Edessa, he initiated a search for possible leaders. Suspects were hauled in: Adelphius, "neither a priest nor a monk but one of the laity," "Sabas the Castrated, who wears a monk's garb," and several others. The elderly Adelphius acted as their spokesman in the hearings that followed.[28] Adelphius allegedly confided to Flavian their opinion that

> there is no benefit from holy baptism for those who receive it, but only zealous prayer can drive out the indwelling demon. For each person descended from the forefather [Adam] derives from him an enslavement to demons along with [human] nature. But when these are driven away by assiduous prayer, then the All-Holy Spirit comes, giving sensible and visible signs of His own presence. . . . not only is he, to whom this happens, liberated from the agitations of the body, but he can also clearly foresee things to come, and behold the holy Trinity with his own eye.[29]

25. Ephrem, *Contra haereses* 22.4; trans. Columba Stewart, *"Working the Earth of the Heart": The Messalian Controversy in History, Texts, and Language to A.D. 431* (Oxford: Clarendon Press, 1991), 15. Stewart dates it before 373, Fitschen (1998): 19 before 363.

26. Stewart (1991): 15–16 notes that *ezdallal* (here translated "debauched") can mean "to jump" or "to be agitated," and that the root-verb of *ṣl'*, from which *mṣallyānē* is formed, means "to incline" or "to bend." He suggests that Ephrem may have been "mocking the pose of these people who claim devotion to prayer, saying, in effect, 'And the bow-ers [= pray-ers], who can't stay still.'" In other words, Ephrem seems to have been criticizing an enthusiastic style of prayer rather than a distinct heretical group.

27. For the chronology and contributions of these two synods I follow Stewart (1991): 24–42.

28. Photius, *Bibliotheca* 52; ed. René Henry, p. 37. Theodoret names fewer "leaders" in *HE* 4.11.2 and *HFC* 4.11. For Photius' and Theodoret's sources and representation of these synod meetings, see both Stewart (1991): 25–32 and Fitschen (1998): 25–39, 51–53 (with background material on Adelphius, 25–29).

29. Theodoret, *HE* 4.11.7; ed. Léon Parmentier and revised Günther Christian Hansen,

This sounded like blasphemy. Not only had Adelphius suggested the inefficacy of a basic church sacrament (baptism), but he had also conjured the almost Manichaean specter of a congenitally indwelling demon, an innate source of evil that could only be exorcised through constant prayer. Adelphius and his companions were excommunicated and expelled from Syria; the synod dismissed as insincere their offer to renounce such beliefs since they continued to communicate with other Messalians. Then Flavian sent notice of his findings to church leaders in Osrhoene (the province where the monks had originated) and lower Armenia.[30] Here bishop Letoïus of Melitene (modern Eski Malatya) responded by zealously burning monasteries he suddenly discovered to be "convulsed by this disease;" he followed up his actions by contributing his own letters to the anti-Messalian campaign.[31] Meanwhile Adelphius and company relocated up the Mediterranean coast to Pamphylia and "filled it with outrage."[32] Therefore Amphilochius, the redoubtable bishop of Iconium (373–394), summoned another synod to deal with them in the Pamphylian capital of Side. The same monks were apprehended and their Messalian errors recorded again in synodal *acta,* or memoranda.

These two synods raised awareness of Messalian monks by circulating official synodal *acta* and letters that identified what specific behavioral traits and doctrinal errors marked ascetics out as such. Indeed, records taken either from Antioch or Side preserve some actual utterances *(phōnai)* of Adelphius himself, speaking for his fellow Messalians (as they now were identified).[33] Apparently Adelphius did not maintain that baptism was entirely unbeneficial (that was just the polemical spin put on his testimony). However, while he believed that baptism cut out one's "growth of sinful deeds" committed during one's lifetime, he did not believe it could remove a person's deeper "root of sin," which he described as an "indwelling demon" (an anticipation, it seems, of the notion of "original sin"). Only the "energy" generated by continuous prayer could extinguish this innate

p. 231: μόνην δὲ τὴν σπουδαίαν εὐχὴν τὸν δαίμονα τὸν ἔνοικον ἐξελαύνειν.... τούτων δὲ ὑπὸ τῆς σπουδαίας ἐλαυνομένων εὐχῆς, ἐπιφοιτᾷν λοιπὸν τὸ πανάγιον πνεῦμα, αἰσθητῶς καὶ ὁρατῶς τὴν οἰκείαν παρουσίαν σημαῖνον.... ἀλλὰ καὶ σαφῶς τὰ μέλλοντα προορᾷ καὶ τὴν τριάδα τὴν θείαν τοῖς ὀφθαλμοῖς θεωρεῖ.

30. Photius, *Bibliotheca* 52.

31. Theodoret, *HE* 4.11.3 and Photius, *Bibliotheca* 52. Metilene was the metropolitan city of ancient Lesser Armenia.

32. Theodoret, *HE* 4.11.8; ed. Parmentier-Hansen, p. 231.

33. Theodoret, *HFC* 4.11 (PG 83.431C): ὑπομνήμασιν ἐντεθεικὼς αὐτῶν τὰς φωνὰς ἐναργῶς δηλούσας τοῦ δόγματος τὴν διαφοράν. For the origin of these *acta* and their accuracy, see Stewart (1991): 31–32. I follow his translation and discussion of Severus of Antioch's *Contra additiones Juliani* at pp. 35 and 243–50.

source of evil thoughts and passions; once expelled, it would be replaced by the Spirit, whose visitations an ascetic could feel or even see.[34] More importantly, the synodal *acta* attest that Adelphius and company did not identify themselves as "Messalians," but as *pneumatikoi* (Spiritual Ones). Because they identified themselves as such, we are told, they did not work, but "pretended" to devote themselves to prayer instead.[35]

Whether these particular Spiritual Ones were actually related to the People Who Pray who had troubled Ephrem and Epiphanius will be discussed below. What matters here is that these synods, by focusing on the same group of ascetics (who vanish from history after these proceedings), generated an official Messalian profile that added specific heretical doctrines to ascetic behavior that had already caused alarm. Awareness of this profile is thereafter attested by Jerome, writing from his Bethlehem monastery in 415. Now identifying Messalians as the "heretics of nearly all Syria," he linked them to his own set of pagan and Christian heresiarchs who believed in the possibility of attaining detachment from all emotional flux, or *apatheia:*

> Some assert that *pathē*, which we call perturbations—sorrow, joy, hope, fear— can be uprooted and eradicated from the human mind, while others assert that these can be broken in, ruled, moderated, and coerced like horses bridled with the right bits. These opinions Cicero explains in his *Tusculan Disputations,* and Origen tries to blend with Christian truth in his *Stromata,* so I can pass over the Manichaeans, Priscillians, Evagrius from Ibora, Jovianus, and the heretics of nearly all Syria, whom they perversely called "Messalians" in their own language, "Euchites" in Greek. The opinion held by all these is this, that it is possible for human virtue and knowledge to attain perfection, by which I mean not merely likeness, but equality with God; wherefore they thoughtlessly and ignorantly assert that they can sin, once they have reached this pitch of consummation.[36]

In Jerome's view Messalians represented a recent addition to the ranks of pagan philosophers and heretical Christian thinkers who vainly believed that human spiritual perfection and assimilation to God could be achieved

---

34. Theodoret, *HFC* 4.11 (PG 83.429BC): ἡ δὲ ἐνδελεχὴς προσευχὴ...τὸν ἐξ ἀρχῆς συγκληρωθέντα πονηρὸν δαίμονα τῆς ψυχῆς ἐξελαύνει.... οὔτε ἄλλο τι δύναται τῆς ψυχῆς ἐξελάσαι, ἀλλὰ μόνη τῆς προσευχῆς ἐνέργεια.

35. Theodoret, *HFC* 4.11 (PG 83.429C): οὕτως ἐξαπατηθέντες οἱ τρισάθλιοι ἔργον μὲν οὐδὲν μετιᾶσι (πνευματικοὺς γὰρ ἑαυτοὺς ὀνομάζουσι) τῇ δὲ εὐχῇ δῆθεν ἐσχολακότες. For the term πνευματικοί, see Stewart (1991): 28 n. 33. Discovery of how Adelphius and company identified themselves did not change their official identification as Messalians.

36. Jerome, *Dialogus adversus Pelagianos,* prol. 1; ed. C. Moreschini, pp. 3–4: totius paene Syriae haereticos, quos sermone gentili διεστραμμένως, id est perverse, Massalianos, graece Εὐχίτας vocant. For the context, see Elizabeth Clark, *The Origenist Controversy: The Cultural Construction of an Early Christian Debate* (Princeton: Princeton University Press, 1992), 223–26.

through *apatheia*. Optimism for achieving this condition through ascetic exertions was hardly uncommon at this time, as the eulogy for the Egyptian desert wanderer Abba Bessarion attests.[37] Although neither Ephrem nor Epiphanius allude to this notion, the testimony associated with Adelphius suggests he had articulated a similar belief at Antioch or Side. Jerome's notice not only suggests familiarity with a Messalian profile defined in doctrinal terms,[38] but also indicates that, by the second decade of the fifth century, Messalianism could be regarded as endemic to the Syrian East.

Now, in fact, the heresy began to receive attention at the highest levels. Sometime during his tenure at Constantinople (406–425) Bishop Atticus urged episcopal colleagues in Pamphylia "to expel Messalians from everywhere as an accursed abomination."[39] Then, on the ordination of his episcopal successor, Sisinnius, in 426, another synod was held at Constantinople to address the problem. It may have been at this time that the label "Enthusiast" was officially added to the Messalian profile and became synonymous with "Messalian."[40] The bishops were clearly exasperated with failures to eradicate the problem. Suspicions now fell upon clergy for possibly harboring Messalian heretics. Communicating with Pamphylian bishops, the synod ordered the deposition of any cleric caught "saying or doing anything that rendered him suspect of this disease," and refused such clerics any restoration to office, "even if he offer to pay out ten thousand times the penance imposed on those who repent."[41] Two years later (May 30, 428) Emperor Theodosius II included "Messalians, Euchites, or Enthusiasts" among the most objectionable heretical and schismatic groups who were now being forbidden by law to assemble or pray anywhere on Roman soil.[42] Finally, in 431 the Council of Ephesus raised the problem of "Messalianites, Euchites, or Enthusiasts" before the assembled authorities of the imperial church. Here Pamphylian and Lycaonian representatives submit-

37. G Bessarion 12 (PG 65.144A): ὅλος δι' ὅλου τῶν σώματος παθῶν ἐφάνη ἐλεύθερος. For Bessarion, see ch. 1, p. 33.

38. For differing views on Jerome' testimony, see Stewart (1991): 41–42 and Fitschen (1998): 40.

39. Photius, *Bibliotheca* 52; ed. Henry, p. 38: πανταχόθεν . . . ὡς ἄγη καὶ μύση. The circumstances of this letter are unknown: see Fitschen (1998): 40–41.

40. Fitschen (1998): 41, 52 suggests that the label "Enthusiasts," first attested in the law of 428, may have originated from the 426 synod.

41. Photius, *Bibliotheca* 52; ed. Henry, p. 38. Photius does not preserve the whole synodal letter. As Stewart (1991): 44 n. 72 observes, it is not clear whether this hard-line position represents the position of all the bishops at the council or just of Nicon, the Pamphylian representative at the synod.

42. CTh 16.5.65, 2 (issued at Constantinople, May 30, 428); ed. Mommsen-Meyer, p. 878: Messaliani, Euchitae sive Enthusiastae . . . et qui ad imam usque scelerum nequitiam perverunt Manichaei nusquam in Romano solo conveniendi orandique habeant facultatem. The law was issued when Nestorius was bishop: see below, ch. 6, p. 213.

ted for inspection both a copy of the synodal letter of 426 and a copy of "that noxious heresy's book, which they call *Asceticon*."[43] The council anathematized this book and any other "writings of their impiety that might be found among anyone."[44] It authorized that any cleric or layman "even suspected of such disease" be forced to anathematize his error,[45] and confirmed measures taken sometime earlier against Messalians at Alexandria.[46]

The Council of Ephesus thus marks the culmination of the effort to raise awareness about the Messalian heresy, now officially defined by the 426 synodal letter and the *Asceticon* brought to Ephesus. Authorities interested in pursuing the matter were advised to seek details from the Pamphylian bishops, who had become experts on Messalianism since the synod at Side in the 390s.[47] Fortunately, the Messalian characteristics condemned at both Constantinople and Ephesus are preserved by two later church writers, Timothy of Constantinople, in his early-seventh-century manual *On the Reception of Heretics,* and John of Damascus, in his eighth-century treatise *On Heresies.* Besides listing the doctrinal deviancies already noted,[48] Timothy's manual preserves the following items, taken from either the earlier synodal memoranda or from the synodal letter of 426:

> They say that after [attaining] what they call *apatheia,* then people are able to see the future and sensibly discern invisible powers. For this reason they suddenly jump up and imagine they are leaping over demons, and pretend to shoot them down with their fingers.[49]

43. *ACO* 1.1.7 [80]; ed. Schwartz, p. 118,4–7: τὸ βιβλίον τὸ προφερόμενον τῆς μιαρᾶς ἐκείνης αἱρέσεως τὸ λεγόμενον παρ' αὐτοῖς Ἀσκητικόν. For the council's anti-Messalian proceedings, see Fitschen (1998): 45–48.

44. *ACO* 1.1.7 [80], ed. Schwartz, p. 118,7–8: τι ἕτερον σύνταγμα τῆς ἐκείνων ἀνοσιότητος εὑρίσκοιτο παρά τισι.

45. *ACO* 1.1.7 [80]; ed. Schwartz, p. 117,15–16: ὥστε τοὺς ὄντας κατὰ πᾶσαν ἐπαρχίαν τῆς Μεσσαλιανιτῶν ἢ γοῦν Ἐνθουσιαστῶν αἱρέσεως ἢ καὶ ἐν ὑποψίαις τῆς τοιαύτης νόσου γεγενημένους, εἴτε κληρικοὶ εἶεν εἴτε λαικοί, μεθοδεύεσθαι.

46. *ACO* 1.1.7 [80]; ed. Schwartz, p. 117,13–14: βεβαίων ὄντων δηλαδὴ καὶ τῶν πεπραγμένων ἐν Ἀλεξανδρείᾳ. This probably refers to a synod held by Cyril of Alexandria in 430: see Fitschen (1998): 42–45. In his *Ep.* 82 to Amphilochius of Side (date unknown), Cyril recommends that Messalians be required only to anathematize their heresy since more technical inquiries on specific points would just "confuse those without much mental acumen, since most are simpletons": PG 77.376C: ἰδιῶται γάρ εἰσιν οἱ πολλοὶ καὶ οὐχ οὕτω νοεῖν δύνανται ὥστε πάντως τῶν καταγνωσέως ἀξίων. For Cyril's remarks, see Stewart (1991): 48–50 and Fitschen (1998): 43–45

47. Fitschen (1998): 41–47 believes that Atticus, Sisinnius, and Cyril sent letters to Pamphylia bishops because they suspected that clergy were lax or sympathetic toward Messalians.

48. For the relation of the lists in Timothy and John to proceedings at Antioch, Side, Constantinople, and Ephesus, see Fitschen (1998): 60–88 and Stewart (1991): 52–69.

49. Timothy of Constantinople, *De receptione haereticorum [DRH]* 10 (PG 86.49BC); cf. Theodoret, *HE* 4.11.1 and *HFC* 4.11 (PG 83.432B).

They say they know what state the souls of the dead have attained, and fancy themselves "knowers of the heart," so that they can tell exactly a person's disposition from their manners and habits.[50]

They say that manual labor must be avoided on the grounds that it is abominable. And for this reason they call themselves "spiritual ones," judging it neither possible nor righteous for such people to handle work in a literal sense. In this they violate the apostolic tradition.[51]

They say that alms must not be given to beggars or to widows or to orphans, or to those who have suffered disasters or are maimed in body, or to victims of brigandage or barbarian attacks or any such calamity, but rather all must be given to themselves, since they are "truly the poor in spirit."[52]

These points are reiterated by John of Damascus, who lists them after citing eighteen statements of Messalian doctrine. These statements, he says, he had "excerpted from their book," presumably the *Asceticon*. John also attributes to Messalians diverse activities that he borrowed from descriptions of other early heretics. All shared a similar trait, by his account, of scorning bishops while seeking to "exact a little power and authority for themselves."[53]

Such, then, were the practices by which early-fifth-century ascetics were identified and condemned as Messalian. They include a broad range of deviant behavior. To judge from Epiphanius' *Panarion* and other testimony of contemporary ascetic practices and exuberance, it is hardly surprising that Messalianism might be perceived to be such a widespread problem, especially when the Council of Ephesus included anyone "even suspected of the disease."[54] Nevertheless, two main traits are consistently repeated: refusal to practice manual labor for the sake of continuous prayer and a claim to material support from others. With the exception of the Eustathians and Manichaeans discussed below, these traits are not identified with

50. Timothy of Constantinople, *DRH* 17 (PG 86.52B).

51. Timothy of Constantinople, *DRH* 13 (PG 86.49D): Λέγουσιν τὴν τῶν χειρῶν ἐργασίαν ὡς βδελυρὰν ἀποστρέφεσθαι. Καὶ πνευματικοὺς ἐντεῦθεν ἑαυτοὺς ὀνομάζουσιν, οὐ κρίνοντες δυνατὸν οὐδὲ δίκαιον, ἔργον λοιπὸν αἰσθητοῦ τοὺς τοιούτους ἐφάπτεσθαι· ἀθετοῦντες καὶ ἐν τούτῳ τὴν τῶν ἀποστόλων παράδοσιν. Cf. Theodoret, *HFC* 4.11 (PG 83.429C). John of Damascus says Messalians considered manual labor "improper for Christians" generally: *De haeresibus* 80, ed. B. Kötter, p. 43: ὡς οὐ πρέπουσαν Χριστιανοῖς.

52. Timothy, *DRH* 15 (PG 86.52A): Λέγουσιν μὴ διδόναι ἐλεημοσύνην τοῖς προσαιτοῦσι μήτε μὴν χήραις ἢ ὀρφανοῖς, μήτε τοῖς ἐν διαφόροις περιστάσεσιν ἢ λώβῃ σωμάτων καθεστῶσιν, ἢ λῃστῶν ἢ βαρβάρων ἐπιδρομαῖς ἤ τισι τοιαύταις συμφοραῖς περιπεπτωκόσιν· ἀλλ' αὐτοῖς ἅπαντα μᾶλλον παρέχειν· διότι αὐτοί εἰσιν ὡς ἀληθῶς οἱ πτωχοὶ τῷ πνεύματι.

53. John of Damascus, *De haeresibus* 80; ed. Kötter, p. 45: δυναστείαν τινὰ καὶ αὐθεντίαν ἑαυτοῖς πραγματευόμενοι. For John's sources, see Fitschen (1998): 140–41.

54. For parallels, see esp. Elm (1994): 184–223 and Fitschen (1998): 97–104.

any other heretical group, and by the early fifth century they seem to have been considered definitively Messalian.[55] That such behavior became regarded as distinctly Messalian and cited to distinguish them from other ascetics is indicated by an apophthegm concerning Abba Lucius, a monastic leader outside Alexandria:

> Once some of the monks who are called 'Euchites' went to Enaton to see Abba Lucius. The old man asked them, "What kind of manual labor do you do?" They said, "We do not touch manual work but as the Apostle says we 'pray without ceasing.' "[56]

Should modern historians also regard these two traits to be specifically Messalian in origin and character? As we have seen, the monks labeled "Messalian" at Antioch and Side did not identify themselves as such. Should we nevertheless rely upon polemical characterizations for our understanding of such monks and ascetic phenomena? We shall see that the church authorities who produced the Messalian profile were confronted with ascetic assumptions that they considered new, but that actually had their origin in the way contemporary monks (like earlier ascetics) understood the paradigm for ascetic life presented by the Gospels. What then of the doctrinal deviancies that became associated with Messalians? Or of their relation to objectionable Messalian behavior? It will help to consider how modern research has illumined these questions.

TOWARD A BROADER DEFINITION OF THE MESSALIAN CONTROVERSY

Interest in the Messalian controversy revived in the twentieth century with the realization that John of Damascus' eighteen citations from the *Asceticon* were actually excerpted from spiritual homilies preserved under the name of Macarius, the founder of Scetis in Egypt.[57] This was an unsettling discovery, owing to the reverence this literature had attained over the centuries: "for indeed, if 'Macarius' is Messalian, [then] this entire tradition [of

---

55. Fitschen (1998): 60 maintains that the rejection of manual labor was not specifically Messalian, but his own methodology accepts anything Timothy introduces with the word Λέγουσι as definitively Messalian. Rejection of manual labor is introduced by these words in Timothy's list: see above, n. 51.

56. G Lucius 1 (PG 65.253BC): ἡμεῖς οὐ ψηλαφῶμεν ἐργόχειρον· ἀλλὰ, καθὼς λέγει ὁ Ἀπόστολος, ἀδιαλείπτως προσευχόμεθα. Trans. Ward, p. 120.

57. For correspondences between John of Damascus' citations and the Ps.-Macarian homilies, see Fitschen (1998): 145–60, 176–238 and Stewart (1991): 52–58. For their initial discovery, see Louis Villecourt, "La Date et l'origine des 'Homélies spirituelles' attribuées à Macaire," *Comptes Rendus des séances de l'Académie des Inscriptions et Belles-Lettres* (Paris 1920): 250–58 and Jean Darrouzès, "Notes sur les Homélies du Pseudo-Macaire," *Le Muséon* 67 (1954): 297–309.

Eastern Christian spirituality] is Messalian as well."[58] Despite initial reluctance to acknowledge the correspondences, further investigations have confirmed that John's citations did in fact derive from literature now commonly attributed to Pseudo-Macarius.[59]

The historical relationship between Messalian spirituality and fourth-century orthodox spirituality has gained further clarity from Reinhart Staats' demonstration that the Pseudo-Macarian *Great Letter,* an ascetic *protrepticus* (exhortation) and guidebook, provided the text that Gregory of Nyssa (ca. 330–394) followed when writing his own spiritual guidebook *On Christian Practice* (ca. 390).[60] It is now generally accepted that Gregory's work represents a modification of the *Great Letter* (ca. 381) and not the other way around, as was formerly believed.[61] In other words, not only are the Pseudo-Macarian homilies Messalian, but they also served as inspiration for at least one member of the Cappadocian orthodox triumvirate (Gregory of Nyssa, Basil of Caesarea, and Gregory of Nazianzus). Staats proposed that Gregory of Nyssa served as a cautious patron for the monks who had grouped around the author of the Pseudo-Macarian literature.[62] These Messalians Staats dissociates from the common or vulgar sort of Messalian that Epiphanius described in the *Panarion.*[63] He furthermore suggests that Gregory hoped to dissuade his own monastic circle from emulating such "vulgar Messalians" when he wrote his treatise *On Virginity* (ca. 375–378), a *protrepticus* toward ascetic moderation. Near the end of this work Gregory warns aspiring novices about misguided ascetic practice, noting that "certain peo-

58. John Meyendorff, "Messalianism or Anti-Messalianism? A Fresh Look at the 'Macarian' Problem," in *Kyriakon: Festschrift Johannes Quasten,* ed. P. Granfield and J. Jungmann, vol. 2 (Münster: Aschendorff, 1970), 586.

59. See Hermann Dörries, *Symeon von Mesopotamien. Die Überlieferung der messalianischen "Makarios"-Schriften* (Leipzig: J. C. Hinrichs'sche, 1941). Fitschen (1998): 218, 238 believes the extracts came from garbled paraphrases of Ps.-Macarian literature written by one of Adelphius' followers. He suggests that the name "Macarius" (Blessed One) became attached to its unknown author (as it did to the author of the *Liber Graduum*).

60. For the relation of Gregory's *De instituto christiano* to the *Epistula magna [EM],* see Reinhart Staats, *Gregor von Nyssa und die Messalianer* (Berlin: Walter de Gruyter, 1968), 1–15; id., *Makarios-Symeon: Epistola Magna. Eine messalianische Mönchsregel und ihre Umschrift in Gregors von Nyssa "De instituto christiano"* (Göttingen: Vandenhoeck und Ruprecht, 1984), 26–39; Fitschen (1998): 239–45. Staats (1984): 26–39 dates the *EM* ca. 381 and Gregory's work ca. 385–90: the trinitarian formula in *EM* 1.2 indicates a date after 381, and it must have been written before Gregory wrote his *De instituto christianorum.*.

61. Werner Jaeger, *Two Rediscovered Works of Ancient Christian Literature: Gregory of Nyssa and Macarius* (Leiden: Brill, 1954), first discovered the correspondences, but assumed that Ps.-Macarius was dependent on Gregory's work.

62. Reinhart Staats, "Die Asketen aus Mesopotamien in der Rede des Gregor von Nyssa *In suam ordinationem,*" *VC* 21 (1967): 173.

63. Staats (1967): 173 n.23, "jene 'Vulgärmessalianer' gehören doch schwerlich zu der von Symeon [i.e., Ps.-Macarius] geformten Gruppe." Cf. Fitschen (1998): 24.

ple in the past" had made a good start, but had become misled "because of blind conceit":

> Among them are those whom the Book of Wisdom calls "those who do not work, who let their ways get strewn with thorns" [Prov 15:19], who think devotion to labors ordained by God's commandments to be harmful to the soul, who take exception to apostolic instructions and do not eat their own bread "with propriety" [1 Thess 4:11–12] but gawk at what others have, making idleness *[argia]* their livelihood. Then there are dreamers who think the deceits of their dreams are more trustworthy than the Gospels' teachings, and call their fantasies "revelations." After these come those who insinuate themselves into houses, but there are others again who believe unsociability and savageness to be virtue. . . . We also know of those who starve themselves to death on the grounds that such a sacrifice is pleasing to God, and others again completely opposite to these, who practice not being married only in name, not only enjoying the pleasures of their stomach, but living openly with women, calling such cohabitation a "brotherhood."[64]

Noting that most of these characterizations—rejection of work, idleness, material dependency on others, identification of dreams with revelations, irregular fasting and cohabitation of sexes—correspond with those practices cited as Messalian in the *Panarion*, Staats concludes, "Gregory, like Epiphanius, is an early witness for the history of church opposition to Messalianism."[65]

Nowhere, however, does Gregory himself use the "Messalian" label to characterize those monks or any other. He simply presents them as poorly guided ascetic Christians. That raises a crucial problem of methodology. In his own reconstruction of the Messalian controversy, Columba Stewart deliberately restricts his evidence to those sources that refer to Messalians by name, arguing that "the alternative to such a cautious approach is to see Messalianism everywhere, using the term as a catch-all for every kind of charismatic religious phenomenon."[66] Such methodological caution would

---

64. Gregory of Nyssa, *De virginitate* 23.3; ed. Michael Aubineau, pp. 534–36: ἤδη γάρ τινες διὰ τοῦ τύφου ὑπεσκελίσθησαν . . . εἰ παραγραψάμενοι τὰς ἀποστολικὰς παραινέσεις καὶ μὴ τὸν ἴδιον ἄρτον "εὐσχημόνως" ἐσθίοντες, ἀλλὰ τῷ ἀλλοτρίῳ προσκεχηνότες τέχνην βίου τὴν ἀργίαν ποιούμενοι. ἐντεῦθεν οἱ ἐνυπνιασταὶ οἱ τὰς ἐκ τῶν ὀνείρων ἀπάτας πιστοτέρας τῶν εὐαγγελικῶν διδαγμάτων ποιούμενοι καὶ ἀποκαλύψεις τὰς φαντασίας προσαγορεύοντες· ἀπὸ τούτων εἰσὶν οἱ ἐνδύνοντες εἰς τὰς οἰκίας. . . .

65. Reinhart Staats, "Basilius als lebende Mönchsregel in Gregors von Nyssa *De virginitate*," *VC* 39 (1985): 250. Rita Lizzi, "'Monaci, Mendicanti e Donne' nella geografia monastica di alcune regioni orientali," *Atti dell' Istituto Veneto di Scienze, Lettere ed Arti* 140 (1981/1982): 350–52 had already argued that Gregory was referring to followers of Eustathius (discussed below).

66. Stewart (1991): 6 n. 4: "Staats recognizes the need to distinguish between narrow and broad uses of the term 'Messalianism' . . . and like many scholars, employs both." A similar methodology is defended by Fitschen (1998): 89–140, esp. 101–3 and 107.

reject Staats' identification of the monks described by Gregory of Nyssa as Messalians, and would exclude from consideration all testimony that seems to describe Messalian activities (as defined by Epiphanius and the councils), but does not label them as such.[67] Indeed, Staats has left his own conception of Messalianism rather open-ended: "Both Gregory and Epiphanius, as well as later documents, lead us to the conclusion that Messalianism in the fourth century was an ascetic movement which escapes definition, especially a dogmatic definition."[68] Thus, in Staats' final analysis, about the only thing distinct about Messalianism is its characterization as an "ascetic movement."

But was it even that?

No matter how loosely defined, the term "movement" requires explanation if it is to be a useful description of a historical phenomenon.[69] Its application to People Who Pray may be especially misleading. It has often been observed that Epiphanius' own Messalian profile responds to ascetic phenomena too diffuse to be considered features of any specific movement.[70] Earlier in his *Panarion*, Epiphanius describes a priest named Aerius and his followers who, circa 365–370, had broken with their mentor, Eustathius, upon his promotion as bishop of Sebaste (modern Sivas) in Armenia. They believed the promotion had corrupted Eustathius, who now seemed to be "inclined towards acquiring wealth and all sorts of property."[71] Rather than continue serving him in a Sebaste poorhouse, Aerius and his male and female recruits went back to nature, roaming along the fringe of the Anatolian plateau like the toughest of Armenian *boskoi*: "Driven from the churches, cultivated lands, and villages . . . he and his numerous band often lived under snow in the wild, making their home in the open air or under rocks, or taking shelter in the woods."[72] Under such circumstances

---

67. E.g., neither Stewart (1991): 50–52 nor Fitschen (1998): 138 accepts Cyril's *Ep.* 83 (cited above, ch. 1 n. 137) as evidence for Messalians in Egypt.

68. Staats (1985): 236: "eine Asketenbewegung gewesen ist, die sich einer Definition, gar einer theologisch-dogmatischen Festlegung entzieht."

69. Cf. Peter Brown's scepticism on the usefulness of the term "movement" in modern discussions of the North African circumcellions in Review of *Kirche und Staat im spätrömische Reich,* by H.-J. Diesner, *JThS* n.s. 15 (1964): 410.

70. See Jean Gribomont, "Le monachisme au IVe siècle en Asia Mineure: De Gangres au Messalianisme," *SP* 2.2 (1957): 414–15; Stewart (1991): 5; Fitschen (1998): 89–92.

71. Epiphanius, *Panarion* 75.2.3; ed. Holl-Dummer, p. 334: ἔκλινεν εἰς χρημάτων συναγωγὴν καὶ εἰς κτῆσιν παντοίαν. Epiphanius seems to draw on Aerius' own writings. For Aerius, see Elm (1994): 189–90 and Gribomont (1972): 614.

72. Epiphanius, *Panarion* 75.3.2; ed. Holl-Dummer, p. 334. The *boskoi* lifestyle in Armenia at this time is documented by Faustus of Byzantium, *Epic Histories* 5.128; 6.6, 16.

they pursued an ascetic existence marked by renunciation of property *(apotaxia)*, vagrancy, cohabitation of sexes, and, according to Epiphanius, irregular fasting.[73] Later Epiphanius attributes the same practices to Messalians as well. But clearly Aerius' lifestyle was not Messalian in origin. He and his followers had merely gone back to the uncompromising renunciations that had earlier been advocated and practiced by Eustathius (d. 377) himself. In the 340s or 350s a synod of bishops had gathered from several dioceses at Gangra (modern Tchankiri) in the Paphlagonian foothills of northern Asia Minor.[74] This synod condemned Eustathius and his male and female followers for various practices it considered deviant, including independent assembling and teaching, contempt for marriage, contempt for the church hierarchy, contempt for the rich who did not renounce all their wealth (whom Eustathius and his followers said "have no hope with God"), and claiming "for themselves and for those with them" the charitable offerings *(karpophoria)* given to the church, on the grounds that they were "holy ones."[75] The synod judged Eustathius and his followers to be "outside the church," and demanded that whoever displayed such behavior in the future be excommunicated as a heretic.[76]

Many such "Eustathian" practices became identified by Epiphanius with Messalians. As Jean Gribomont has observed, "the left wing of the movement started by Eustathius appears remarkably similar in its ascetic forms to the monasticism of neighboring provinces in northern Syria and Mesopotamia: admirable to our view, Messalian to Epiphanius."[77] In other words, the Messalianism that Epiphanius decried appears not to have been a specific movement, but rather a radicalism (defined in part by its emphasis on

73. Epiphanius, *Panarion* 75.2.3 (renunciation of possessions); 3.1 (cohabitation of sexes); 3.6–8 (rejection of rules on fasting, on the grounds that they were Judaic).

74. For Gangra and its canons, see Hefele and Leclerq (1973) 1:1029–45. Its date is disputed: Jean Gribomont, "Saint Basil et le monachisme enthousiaste," *Irénikon* 53 (1980): 126 argues ca. 340, while Timothy D. Barnes, "The Date of the Council of Gangra," *JThS* n.s. 40 (1980): 121–24 proposes ca. 355.

75. Gangra synod, *Epistula synodica;* ed. Périclès-Pierre Jaonnou: rejection of marriage, p. 86,9–12; irregular fasting, p. 87,17–23; contempt for wealth, p. 88,10–13: καταγνώσκοντες ... καὶ πλουσίων δὲ τῶν μὴ πάντων τῶν ὑπαρχόντων ἀναχωρούντων, ὡς ἐλπίδα παρὰ Θεῷ μὴ ἐχόντων; separation from church and independent teaching, p. 86,20–23; claim to church funds, p. 87,3–7: καρποφορίας τε τὰς ἐκκλησιαστικὰς τὰς ἀνέκαθεν διδομένας τῇ ἐκκλεσίᾳ ἑαυτοῖς καὶ τοῖς σὺν αὐτοῖς ὡς ἁγίοις τὰς διαδόσεις ποιούμενοι.

76. Gangra synod, *Epistula synodica;* ed. Joannou, p. 89,7–8: ὡς αἰρετικὸν αὐτόν. For Eustathius, see Gribomont (1957): 400–415 and *id.*, "Eustathe de Sébaste," *DGHE* 16 (1967): 26–33.

77. Gribomont (1972): 614. Later church manuals simply lump Eustathians and the charges against them under the Messalian rubric. Since Theodoret does not refer to any Eustathian charges when writing about Messalians, this assimilation probably did not occur until after the mid-fifth century: see Fitschen (1998): 141–42.

material renunciations and identification with the poor) found elsewhere in the fourth century, the most prominent exponent of which in Asia Minor was Eustathius of Sebaste. Gribomont suggests that Epiphanius, having heard of such People Who Pray, simply used the Messalian label to bring together all the practices of disparate ascetic groups that caused him distress, in order to fulfill his quota of "eighty concubines." Gribomont also suggests that Bishop Flavian, once alerted by reading the *Panarion* about Messalian heretics in his Mesopotamian diocese, took up pursuit of those who matched its descriptions and so discovered Adelphius and company. The doctrinal notions articulated by those few ascetics were then ascribed to whoever demonstrated behavior similar to what Epiphanius had described.[78]

In this way Gribomont challenged the specificity of Epiphanius' Messalian taxonomy, suggesting that what disturbed Epiphanius was a complex of ascetic practices that could be found diffused in varying shades throughout much of Asia Minor and the neighboring East.[79] Gribomont's discussion not only emphasizes that Messalianism must be understood as a polemical construction rather than a historical reality, but also brings ascetic practices to the forefront of the question of Messalian identity, reminding us that doctrinal issues arose secondarily. Indeed, Epiphanius, Ephrem, and the Gangra synod demonstrate that by the fourth century ascetic practices themselves could be deemed heretical without reference to specific doctrinal deviations.[80] Yet it may be objected that Gribomont, like Staats, has blurred important distinctions between Messalians and other fourth- and fifth-century ascetics. After all, no late antique author ascribes the Messalian notion of an "indwelling demon" or other such doctrinal tenets, together with continuous prayer and a rejection of manual labor, to Eustathians, Aerians, or any other known ascetic group.

Columba Stewart's study of the doctrinal aspects of the Messalian profile should resolve such objections and reorient historians toward a broader appreciation of what constituted Messalianism for contemporary church leaders. Stewart examines the remarkably graphic spiritual vocabulary and imagery of Messalian teachings as preserved in the anti-Messalian lists, noting how

> evil is depicted as adhering to human nature in ways characterized as indwelling, compounding or blending, coexisting, communing, being rooted so deeply that it must be cut out. One must pray for the coming of divine

78. Gribomont (1972): 616.

79. Fitschen (1998): 27–28 makes nearly the same point, but implies that doctrinal dimensions had the effect of narrowing rather than enhancing or expanding the Messalian profile.

80. Such practices were probably identified with *philonikia:* see below, ch. 4, p. 154.

help which is described as visitation, participation, communion, *parousia,* blending. The expulsion of evil and the coming of the divine are something to be *felt*. The result is ἀπάθεια, perfection, the experience of divine help in αἴσθησις, πληροφορία, ἐνέργεια, ὑπόστασις. Those who claim these experiences are dubbed "the spiritual ones," "the possessed ones," "the perfect ones."[81]

Stewart compares this terminology with its usage in Pseudo-Macarian literature.[82] He concludes that "Pseudo-Macarius has adopted, and then adapted . . . for his own purposes" such terminology in order to create his own spiritual "picture language," one rich in metaphor and experiential emphasis. Stewart observes that this unusual use of Greek technical terms would have seemed distinctly odd to Greek ears, as evinced by their citation in the anti-Messalian lists.[83] When set against orthodox literature of Syrian provenance, however, Stewart found that the idioms found in the Pseudo-Macarian texts (whose Eastern provenance had already been recognized) had equivalents in Syriac usage, and believes they would have passed for orthodox in the Syriac-speaking Christian milieu:

> The parallels with the *Liber Graduum* [*Book of Steps,* a Syriac text discussed below], especially noteworthy for the further evidence they provide of a Syriac background for Ps.-Macarian images, are not such as to demonstrate a direct dependence of one on the other. . . . Nevertheless both texts illustrate how elements of Syrian asceticism and Syriac idiom can be shaped according to an author's particular vision while remaining identifiable as parts of the larger tradition. This approach to the "Messalian" problem de-emphasizes doctrines and looks instead to the language in which doctrines are expressed . . . and points the modern student to the real significance of the controversy.[84]

This real significance, in Stewart's view, lies in Greco-Syrian cultural dissonance:

> Much of the language and many of the most striking descriptive images of the Ps.-Macarian writings are expressions in Greek of a spiritual argot characteristic of Syrian Christianity. This language sounded unusual, excessive, and even dangerous when translated for a Hellenistic audience. The graphic and sensual metaphors employed by Ps.-Macarius jarred theologically sensitive ears which normally heard such language used sparingly and cautiously. When used repeatedly and with great freedom, this language would captivate

81. Stewart (1991): 67–68.
82. The Greek terms in question are αἴσθησις, πεῖρα, and πληροφορία, either in combination with each other or with ἐνέργεια, δύναμις, ἀπάθεια, and ὑπόστασις.
83. Stewart (1991): 236.
84. Stewart (1991): 237.

readers by its beauty and vividness . . . or [could] challenge and threaten (as it did then, and later).[85]

Stewart thus confirms on linguistic grounds Staats' position that Pseudo-Macarius' spirituality (and so Messalianism) was "originally no more and no less than a dramatic manifestation of Syrian Christianity in Greek guise."[86] A half-century of doctrinal controversy, often turning on verbal distinctions of extreme subtlety, had hardened Greek ears to the florid tropes that Pseudo-Macarius, Adelphius, and others used to express their otherwise orthodox spirituality.[87]

Columba Stewart's assessment of the underlying causes of the Messalian controversy has important implications for understanding other Messalian matters, which he does not explore. If the Messalian idioms that raised doctrinal concern were simply acceptable Syriac usages misunderstood when transferred to a Greek-speaking, Mediterranean milieu, could not the same be said for Messalian ascetic practices? In other words, might not those ascetic practices that were routinely identified as Messalian—continuous prayer, rejection of manual labor, and a claim to material support from others—also be identified as idioms that were acceptable in traditional Syrian asceticism, but proved objectionable to Greco-Roman authorities who encountered them in their own milieu? To be sure, Stewart and others maintain that the rejection of manual labor, though repeatedly cited and decried in the ancient sources, is "difficult to relate to the Messalian controversy except in the most general terms."[88] Yet the documents from which Stewart draws his linguistic examples of traditional Syriac spirituality also reflect the same attitude toward manual labor, either explicitly or implicitly. This attitude should therefore be considered as equally Messalian as those "Messalian" linguistic idioms and metaphors that caused alarm—

85. Stewart (1991): 10; cf. 69: "Categorical denunciation of Messalian errors may be seen to rest largely on misunderstanding of unfamiliar terminology, and culture joins with (and perhaps supplants) doctrine as the basis of controversy." See also Lionel Wickham, "The 'Liber Graduum' Revisited," in *VI Symposium Syriacum 1992*, ed. R. Lavenant (Rome: Pontificio Istituto Orientale, 1994), 184.

86. Reinhart Staats, "Messalianforschung und Ostkirchenkunde," in *Makarios-Symposium über das Böse*, ed. W. Strothmann (Weisbaden: Harrassowitz, 1983), 53. Fitschen (1998): 13–14, 107 rejects Staats' and Stewart's thesis as an inadequate and historically implausible explanation for the Messalian controversy.

87. According to Stewart (1991): 239, Greek clergy "took the unfamiliar language to represent heretical doctrine; now it can be seen that the language in fact represents an unfamiliar culture. Unfamiliar to the Greek-speaking bishops; increasingly unfamiliar even to bilingual bishops like Flavian of Antioch: the controversy flared at precisely the time when Syriac Christianity was taking on more and more Hellenistic vocabulary and ways of thinking."

88. Stewart (1991): 51 and Fitschen (1998): 60.

or, rather, it should be considered as deeply rooted in traditional Syrian spirituality and ascetic practice as were those linguistic expressions that caused the Greek fathers concern. As we shall see, however, this Messalian attitude ultimately derived from interpretations of Scripture, and emerged wherever monks based their notions of ascetic propriety strictly upon the apostolic model that the Gospels present.

CONFLICTING ASSUMPTIONS OF ORTHODOX MONASTIC PRACTICE IN THE EAST

Gregory of Nyssa's talented brother Basil the Great (ca. 330–379) became bishop of Caesarea, Cappadocia (modern Kayseri) in 370. A former protégé of Eustathius of Sebaste, Basil had traveled in his youth to monasteries in Egypt, Palestine, Syria and Mesopotamia, and had been the "leader, guide, and guardian" to monastic communities he helped found at his family estate at Annesi, in rural Pontus, and around the city of Caesarea. He was already long familiar with monastic trends and ecclesiastical concerns of his time.[89] Before and during his nine-year tenure as bishop of Caesarea he wrote a series of recommendations for ascetic practice simply known as the "Shorter Rules" and "Longer Rules." Through Benedict of Nursia these rules would establish norms for Western monastic institutions, but they were first written to answer the needs of ascetic communities in Pontus and Cappadocia.[90] Among the questions posed to him was one that asked, "Whether we must neglect work for the sake of the prayers and singing psalms, what times are suitable for prayer, and first of all, whether we should work at all?"[91]

Basil's reply constitutes a diatribe against the same evil that Epiphanius associated with Messalians and Mesopotamian monks, namely *argia*. "We must not think the goal of piety as an excuse for *argia* or an escape from hardship," he says, but rather "as an opportunity for striving for more abundant toils, and for patience and tribulation."[92] Such a way of life is useful,

---

89. For Basil's ascetic background, see Jean Gribomont, "Eustathe le philosophe et les voyages du jeune Basile de Césaréa," *Revue d'histoire écclesiastique* 54 (1959): 115–24 and Philip Rousseau, *Basil of Caesarea* (Berkeley and Los Angeles: University of California Press, 1994), 61–92, 190–232 (quotation from 196). For Basil's ascetic household at Annesi (northwest of Armenian Sebaste) and his sister Macrina's influence, see Elm (1994): 60–105.

90. For the *Regulae brevius tractatae [RB]* and *Regulae fusius tractatae [RF]* and their MS tradition, see Jean Gribomont, *Histoire du texte des Ascétiques de S. Basile* (Louvain: Publications universitaires / Institut orientalique, 1953) with Rousseau (1994), 354–59. Benedict of Nursia cites Basil's rules as his model in *Regula Benedicti* 73.5–6.

91. Basil, *RF* 37 (PG 31.1009B). Gribomont (1953): 188, 262 believes this rule to have been Basil's own, and not a later addition to his corpus.

92. Basil, *RF* 37 (PG 31.1009C): Οὐ γὰρ πρόφασιν ἀργίας, οὐδὲ ἀποφυγὴν πόνου τὸν τῆς

he explains, both because it entails submission of the body and because it might provide resources for others who are sick and weak.[93] That a Christian should work diligently, Basil maintains, is "obvious," because the apostle Paul "has commanded us 'to toil and work with our hands that which is good, so that we may have something to share with the needy.' "[94] Citing a flurry of scriptural passages to illustrate how physical labor would enable Christians to provide food for themselves and others, Basil makes plain by contrast just "how great an evil is the evil of *argia*."[95]

Basil's confidence on this point came not only from his understanding of Paul and other scriptural passages, but from his commitment to the promotion of a new Christian economy and urban community. As bishop of a major metropolis and founder of his own "new city" for the poor, the *Basileiados*, outside it, Basil sought to harness ascetic energies in the service of his urban welfare projects. The result was a socially oriented vision of ascetic poverty in which manual labor was followed by divestment of its material yield, whereby the many little monastic brotherhoods of Cappadocia and Pontus might generate enough wealth to provide alms for the poor on a large scale in Caesarea.[96] This program required considerable time and industry. As Basil himself acknowledges, the practice of manual labor as an ascetic labor still needed justification, "since some people seek exemption from work on the pretext of prayers and psalm-singing."[97]

Citing Ecclesiastes 3:1, "For everything there is a season, and a time for every matter under heaven," Basil counters that there is an appropriate time for each different task, but then points out that prayers and psalms can be performed while working: if not with the voice, then "with the

---

εὐσεβείας σκοπὸν ἡγεῖσθαι χρὴ, ἀλλὰ ὑπόθεσιν ἀθλήσεως, καὶ πόνων περισσοτέρων, καὶ ὑπομονῆς τῆς ἐν θλίψεσιν. Trans. Clarke, 205.

93. Basil, *RF* 37 (PG 31.1009C).

94. Basil, *RF* 37 (PG 31.1009C), citing Eph 4:28: κοπιᾶν καὶ ἐργάζεσθαι ταῖς ἰδίαις χερσὶ τὸ ἀγαθὸν, ἵνα ἔχωμεν μεταδιδόναι τῷ χρείαν ἔχοντι, τὸ μὲν, ὅτι χρὴ ἐργαζέσθαι σπουδαίως, δῆλόν ἐστιν αὐτόθεν. Though Basil never uses the word "monk" or any synonym in his ascetic writings, I presume that *RF* 37 was intended primarily for monks under his care. Rousseau (1994): 357–59 includes it among those rules that reflect a "more institutional phase" in his monastic concerns at Caesarea.

95. Basil, *RF* 37 (PG 31.1011A) citing Mt 25:34–36; 2 Thess 3:8–10; Prov 6:6, 31.27; and Lk 12:48. Cf. *RB* 61 and 67.

96. Well described by Brown (1988): 289–91; see also Gregory of Nazianzus, *Or.* 43.35; Patlagean (1977): 21, 321–22; and Tomas Spidlík, "'Abbondare nell'opera di Dio' nel pensiero di S. Basilio," in *Spiritualità del lavoro nella catechesi dei Padri del III–VI secolo,* ed. S. Felici (Rome: Libreria Ateneo Salesiano, 1986), 95–104. For the *Basileiados,* see Basil, *Ep.* 94, 150, 176 and Gregory of Nazianzus, *Or.* 43.35 with Rousseau (1994): 139–43. It included a poorhouse with a house of prayer or memorial chapel attached, an episcopal residence, guesthouse, hospices for sick travelers, and workshops.

97. Basil, *RF* 37 (PG 31.1012B): Ἐπεὶ τινες προφάσει τῶν εὐχῶν καὶ τῆς ψαλμῳδίας παραιτοῦνται τὰ ἔργα, εἰδέναι δεῖ ὅτι ἐπὶ μὲν ἄλλων τινῶν ἑκάστου καιρός ἐστιν ἴδιος.

heart."[98] Only in this way, he says, is it possible to harmonize Paul's exhortations to constant prayer (1 Thess 5:17) and constant work (2 Thess 3:8), which might otherwise seem to conflict: "For unless these are our methods, how can we make what was said by the Apostle consistent: both his 'Pray without ceasing' and his 'working night and day'?"[99] Basil thus recognizes the problem of reconciling authoritative but apparently conflicting scriptural directives for ascetic practice. His discussion might not have been so defensive and extensive (it is one of the longest "Longer Rules") had he not been aware that certain ascetics considered prayer and psalm-singing a pretext for not performing manual labor. Cappadocian Caesarea was perched on the threshold of the Syrian East. Was Basil referring here to Messalians or just to lazy monks?

Like Gregory, Basil does not use the term "Messalian" here or anywhere else in his writings. Nevertheless, Basil's lengthy criticism of *argia* and special response to the justifications of certain ascetics who refrained from work for the sake of prayer is similar to Epiphanius' nearly contemporaneous response to Messalian and Mesopotamian *argia*. We must not simply presume that Basil, Epiphanius, and other authorities were merely annoyed with lazy monks or merely making a "commentary on, and condemnation of, a perennial monastic issue."[100] For in the late fourth and early fifth centuries such authorities were facing a Christian ascetic tradition that was already well entrenched and radically different from their own in its understanding of how Christian ideals and energies might best be put into practice. This was an apostolic ideology for monastic perfection that refrained from "worldly" labors in favor of purely spiritual pursuits in hope of emulating Jesus, his apostles, the angels, or Adam and his carefree existence before the Fall.

Both the Pseudo-Macarian *Great Letter* and the anonymous *Book of Steps* reflect such an alternative norm. Although neither can be dated with precision, both were probably written in northern Syria or Mesopotamia at more or less the same time that Basil and his brother Gregory were promoting their own monastic arrangements in central Asia Minor. Both works are notable for their expectation that Christian communities would be divided into two basic ranks, distinguished by degrees of worldly renunciations and spiritual dedication; and both works assume that the most spiri-

---

98. Basil, *RF* 37 (PG 31.1012C): εἰ δὲ μή γε, τῇ καρδίᾳ . . . καὶ τὴν προσευχὴν μεταξὺ τοῦ ἔργου πληροῦν.

99. Basil, *RF* 37 (PG 31.1013A): εἰ μὴ ταῦτα τοῦτον ἔχει τὸν τρόπον, πῶς δύναται συμβαίνειν ἀλλήλοις τὰ ὑπὸ τοῦ Ἀποστόλου εἰρημένα, τὸ τε "Ἀδιαλείπτως προσεύχεσθε," καὶ τὸ, "Νύκτα καὶ ἡμέραν ἐργαζόμεναι." Trans. Clarke, pp. 206–7.

100. Stewart (1991): 51. In my view Stewart does not take sufficient account of the historical context of this aspect of the Messalian controversy. Guillaumont (1979b): 125–26 also believes *RF* 37 and G Lucius 1 respond to fourth-century Messalian interpretations of Paul.

tually advanced in these communities would receive material support in return for the spiritual edification and services they provided.

Although written (probably) somewhere in northern Mesopotamia around the middle of the fourth century,[101] the *Book of Steps* returns us to the traditions of the *Acts of Thomas* and *Letters to Virgins*.[102] Its author expounds the Scriptures in order to harmonize relations and set expectations between various members of his community, ranging from ordinary householders to ordained clergy, from wealthy tradesmen to dedicated ascetics.[103] He believes that the New Testament contains different precepts enjoining greater or lesser demands upon Christians, corresponding to each person's degree of spiritual commitment.

Accordingly, the author distinguishes two levels or ranks of spiritual attainment, the "Upright" (or "Righteous," *kēnē*), and the "Perfect" (or "Fully Matured," *gmīrē*).[104] He explains the differences between these levels with the hope that "even simple people might attain insight, and everyone might

101. Fitschen (1998): 108–19 offers recent discussion of provenance and date for the Syriac *Ktābā d-massqātā* (*Book of Steps / Degrees / Ascents* or *Liber graduum [LG]*). He defends the conclusions of Michael Kmosko, the editor of the *LG* (PS 3.clxii–clxv), i.e., date ca. 358/59 (*LG* 8.4 alludes to Christian persecutions, possibly those of Shapur II) with origins in a mountainous region of Persia bordering the Roman Empire, perhaps in Adiabene near Nisibis (*LG* 30.14 refers to the lower Zab, a branch of the Tigris in northeastern Iraq). Irenée Hausherr, "Quanam aetate proderit 'Liber Graduum,'" *OCP* 1 (1935): 495–502 proposed on internal evidence (familiarity with Ephrem's writings and continued use of Tatian's *Diatessaron*) a date ca. 370–435. Most scholars assume a fourth-century date. Robert Kitchen has kindly advanced me a translation he is preparing for Cistercian Studies. I have used his translations throughout, but my citations refer to the columns of Kmosko's edition in *PS*.

102. Thus Vincent Desprez, "L'ascétisme mésopotamien au IVe siècle: III. Le 'Livre des degrés,'" *La Lettre de Ligugé* 262 (1992): 16. I have found the following most helpful for understanding the *LG*: Robert Kitchen, "Conflict on the Stairway to Heaven: The Anonymity of Perfection in the Syriac *Liber Graduum*," in *VII Symposium Syriacum 1996*, ed. R. Lavenant (Rome: Pontificio Istituto Orientale, 1998), 211–20; Juhl (1996): 99–128; Wickham (1994); Stewart (1991): 86–92; Robert Ratcliff, *Steps along the Way of Perfection: The Liber Graduum and Early Syrian Monasticism* (Ph.D. diss., Emory University, 1988); Antoine Guillaumont, "Situation et signification du Liber Graduum dans la spiritualité syriaque," in *Symposium Syriacum 1972* (Rome: Pontificio Istituto Orientale, 1974), 311–25.

103. For social ideals and tensions in the *LG*, see Kitchen (1998) and *id.*, "The Gattung of the Liber Graduum: Implications for a Sociology of Asceticism," in *IV Symposium Syriacum 1984*, ed. H. W. J. Drijvers (Rome: Pontificio Istituto Orientale, 1987), 173–82. Kitchen believes the *LG* was addressed to a specific community, but Wickham (1994): 185 thinks it was intended for a broad readership.

104. Wickham (1994): 179 prefers "Fully Matured" over "Perfect" for the term *gmīrē* (which can also mean "Fully Committed"), and suggests that the original title of the *LG* was "On the Mode of Life of Full Maturity and the Discrimination of Our Lord's Commandments" (*LG* was given to it later in the MS tradition). The two spiritual ranks / levels are defined broadly (e.g., in *mēmrē* 2, 4, and 5 the author discusses the "Sick" and the "Children," perhaps two intermediate ranks between the Upright and Perfect). The author hoped all Christians might aspire to higher spiritual levels.

struggle through the narrow gate of Perfection."[105] Christians content with mere righteousness could secure a place in heaven primarily by observing the Golden Rule. This especially meant being charitable to those in need— the author suggests they pool their resources in groups of five or ten if necessary.[106] The "lesser" scriptural precepts required them to abstain from vice, fast twice a week, and pray five times a day; otherwise, they were permitted to marry and engage in worldly commerce.[107] Those who wished to become Perfect, however, had to observe far more humbling precepts as taught and exemplified by Jesus himself. "Know this," insists the author in his characteristically strong voice, "If a person does not become poor and empty himself and sanctify [i.e., practice celibacy] and lower himself according to the example Jesus showed us . . . he will not be perfected and become great."[108]

The author's division of Christian society into two levels or ranks—and his assumption that ascetics would receive greater exposure to the Holy Spirit on earth, and therefore a higher station in the world to come—was not a radical proposition in the Syrian milieu. Indeed, the Pseudo-Clementine *Letters to Virgins* alludes to it.[109] Nor are the ascetic demands that the author places on his Perfect (poverty, celibacy, and, above all, lowliness or humility in imitation of Christ) any different from those demanded of Christians by Thomas in his *Acts*.[110] The *Book of Steps*, however, differs from anything we have seen so far (and in fact from all treatises written on voluntary poverty in this period) in its stark vision of ascetic poverty and frank discussion of what this meant in actual practice. Imitating Christ meant embracing poverty to the extreme. The author took literally Jesus' admonition in Matthew 19:21: "If you wish to be perfect, go, sell your possessions . . . and come follow me." Unlike the Upright, to whom Jesus' "lesser" precepts allowed property, those Christians who sought perfection had to give up everything:

> The Upright feed the hungry and clothe the naked and rescue the afflicted with their [own] possessions and riches; but the Perfect give away all of their possessions at once to the needy and afflicted, taking up their Cross and

105. *LG* 2.1 (PS 3.25).

106. *LG* 7.2 (PS 3.148). For communal demands on the Upright, see Deprez (1998): 17–23, Ratcliff (1988): 134–39; Guillaumont (1974): 312, 315.

107. *LG* 7 and 13.1–6 (PS 3.305–317).

108. *LG* 20.14 (PS 3.567).

109. *EV* I.4.2. On this aspect of the *LG* and Syrian Christian tradition, see Escolan (1999): 11–40; Persic (1986): 214–25; Arthur Vööbus, "Liber Graduum: Some Aspects of Its Significance for the History of Early Syrian Asceticism," *Charisteria Johanni Köpp* (Stockholm, 1954), 114–24. For the graded reception of the Holy Spirit in the *LG*, see *LG* 3.11 (PS 3.68–69) and Guillaumont (1974): 313–15.

110. As observed by Klijn (1962): 38.

following their Lord spiritually, and spiritually they serve him, loving all people and praying for them.[111]

The spiritual elite of the *Book of Steps* were apostolic vagrants. To recapture the divine "madness of the apostles," the author recommends imitating the deranged "fools of the world" who treat themselves "with contempt" by moving around in rags, without any home or possessions, eating whatever comes their way.[112] Transience itself was a goal, bringing liberty from all worldly attachments: "the Perfect do not take wives, nor do they work in the field, nor have a place to lay their heads on earth, like their teacher."[113] In the end, such voluntary hardship and self-abasement would render each aspirant nothing less than a "brother of our Lord," like the apostle Thomas.[114]

This went far beyond the ascetic poverty that Basil or his brother Gregory envisioned. The Perfect of the *Book of Steps* were forbidden to engage in any trade or manual labor. On this the author is quite emphatic: one seeking spiritual perfection "should not work, either for nourishment for oneself or for clothing for the body, in order to divest oneself from all one has."[115] Only in this way could they fulfill Jesus' great precept, to live free from care, and only this way could they recapture the angelic freedom that had characterized Adam before his Fall—before he had to work.[116] For, as the author explains, Adam had once "rejoiced with the heavenly angels without anxieties and pains, and was concerned about neither clothing nor food." He had eaten "heavenly bread."[117] Only after Adam's transgression did the need for physical labor arise, with its attendant economic anxieties.

The coming of Jesus, however, had made reconciliation with God possible. Whoever followed Jesus' precepts and examples to the fullest might become "like the angels" who "do not cultivate the earth," whose minds remain fixed not "on earth, but with the word of our Lord," and who are never "anxious for their food, because our Lord is concerned for them."[118] In fact God's concern for his Perfect would be made manifest on earth most concretely through the charity provided by the Upright. Thus the

111. *LG* 14.2 (PS 3.328); cf. 19.19 (481).

112. *LG* 16.7 (PS 3.401–402).

113. *LG* 15.13 (PS 3.367–368).

114. *LG* 7.20–21 (PS 3.185–188): such perfected Christians Jesus desired "more than thousands and ten thousands."

115. *LG* 20.1 (PS 3.528); equally explicit are 3.8 (61) and 14.1 (324).

116. *LG* 19.13 (PS 3.473). As with the *ATh*, emphasis on ἀμερίμνια is a major hallmark of the *LG*: see Guillaumont (1974): 313.

117. *LG* 21.7 (PS 3.600–601). For the *LG*'s emphasis on the Fall as the cause of human labor, see Aleksander Kowalski, *Perfezione e giustizia di Adamo nel Liber Graduum* (Rome: Pontificio Istituto Orientale, 1989b), 170–74 and Ratcliff (1988): 136–48.

118. *LG* 25.8 (PS 3.752).

author imagines Jesus had consoled his disciples and arranged for their support: "Do not be anxious, because I will tell the Upright who work the earth to nourish and clothe you."[119] The author assumes that the Perfect would likewise live free from care, depending on others for support, whether "begging food and clothing like a poor person,"[120] or subsisting "like a pauper in grace" off the alms supplied by the community.[121]

For their part, the Perfect had to devote themselves to intensive spiritual rigors by praising God "all their days" in a perpetual cycle of fasts, psalms, vigils, and prayers, performed in the manner that Jesus had shown his apostles, "with powerful groaning and tears, with great supplication and many prostrations."[122] Their physical exertions would generate a sweet odor, the author notes, and ultimately enable them to transcend all earthly "evil thoughts."[123] An ascetic who exerted himself with humility might even be visited by the Holy Spirit: "if he lowers himself more, the Lord will be revealed to him in this world." But only by fully emulating the apostles will he "receive the Paraclete and be perfected." Such an ascetic would ultimately become a master of discernment, able to discriminate between "the voice of God" and "the voice of Satan."[124]

The pursuits of this spiritual elite, it must be stressed, were not to be directed toward their own salvation alone. Their reception of the Paraclete and heightened powers of discrimination would qualify the Perfect to "preach the true Word and show all people how to be saved and how to grow."[125] The author's intention in all his ascetic prescriptions is to prepare them for an apostolic mission directed back towards the society they had forsaken:

> He who takes up the Cross . . . receives the burden of having to pray for all people, and humbly to give counsel and to teach them all. He does this by hoping they will listen to him, but whether they do listen to him or not, he is bound to continue humbly to teach all people, whether or not they are worthy, because our Lord wanted it this way.[126]

119. *LG* 25.3 (PS 3.737).

120. *LG* 20.2 (PS 3.529).

121. *LG* 14.1 (PS 3.324). *Mēmrā* 3.8 (61) qualifies, however, that "Whoever takes up the Cross and teaches the Word can neither . . . buy and sell, nor take care of himself, unless the matter is urgent."

122. *LG* 7.20 (PS 3.184–185) and 20.10 (552). *Mēmrā* 20 (esp. 8–10) offers a remarkable description of how Jesus taught his apostles genuflections. For the unusual prayers preserved in the *LG*, see Aleksander Kowalski, "Die Gebet im Liber Graduum," *OCP* 55 (1989a): 273–81.

123. *LG* 3.14 (PS 3.76); 7.20 (185); 15.6 (349); 20.10 (556).

124. *LG* 15.16 (PS 3.373); cf. 1.2 (12). Wickham (1994): 186 considers discernment the *LG*'s leitmotiv.

125. *LG* 3.14 (PS 3.77).

126. *LG* 3.8 (PS 3.61). For this emphasis of the *LG*, see Ratcliff (1988): 132–72, 195–219.

The Perfect's imitation of Christ's humility would give them an extraordinary capacity for empathy, which would enable them to teach without fear, even among murderers, since asceticism hardened them to fear and fortified them against temptations: "perfected in Christ, they will be able to be with any person and with whomever they wish to travel . . . for their intelligence . . . is complete in the knowledge of the Lord. Because of this they are all things with all people and know how to instruct every person as it is helpful for him."[127]

In the author's view, such expert ministrations entitled them to material support from the Upright.[128] For if, the author reasons, the Upright must refresh all passing strangers even if they be evil or have possessions of their own, then, a fortiori, they must also support "those who have no possessions or profession, who apply themselves wholly to the teaching of our Lord."[129] Such workmen, he argues, were spiritual "ministers of word and prayer," and so worthy of their pay.[130]

At the same time, the author did not consider the Upright qualified for spiritual ministries. Their charitable works required them either to possess property or to engage in commercial transactions, preventing them from devoting themselves to heavenly things and receiving the gifts of the Holy Spirit requisite for spiritual ministries. The author apparently includes church clergy among the Upright who were unable to perform the full range of spiritual ministries.[131] Indeed, such "corporeal" ministers ranked beside the Perfect as Martha ranked beside Mary (Lk 10:38–42), or as the stewards appointed to provide food and supplies (Acts 6:1–6) ranked beside the apostles "who occupied themselves with teaching the word of God." Of course, these corporeal ministers might also become spiritual ministers and "succor others with invisible things," as Stephen did, but in order to qualify, they first had to relinquish all possessions and thus fully "bear the Cross."[132]

The *Book of Steps* describes not so much a monastic community or even a single, unified ascetic elite as a reciprocal relationship that loosely binds spiritually advanced ascetics to other Christians. Like the wanderers of the *Letters to Virgins,* the ascetics of the *Book of Steps* were to provide charismatic

127. *LG* 19.31 (PS 3.504–5).
128. *LG* 3.10 (PS 3.65).
129. *LG* 3.1 (PS 3.48).
130. *LG* 3.15 (PS 3.77), referring to Lk 10:7 and the seventy apostles. Here the author defends his Perfect ("who do not possess anything") against blame for not giving alms: "this is not their ministry, nor does our Lord demand this of them."
131. See esp. *mēmrē* 3 and 19.31, where the author makes clear that worldly responsibilities rendered clergy unfit for perfection or spiritual ministries. This is not supposed to be a criticism either of the clergy or of their "visible" church, which the author lauds in *mēmrā* 12.
132. *LG* 3.13 (PS 3.71–72); 3.7 (57–60); 3.8 (61–62); 3.15 (77).

services and spiritual edification in exchange for material support. Pseudo-Macarius, on the other hand, describes something closer to the coenobitic communal life that would become predominant in the Mediterranean world. The community he addresses seems to have included some thirty members, living in or near some city on the northern Euphrates: perhaps Edessa, Melitene, or Amida (modern Diyarbakir).[133] Nevertheless, he similarly assumes the basic propriety of a two-tiered division in this monastery between, on the one hand, "overseers" and advanced ascetics, who pray, teach, or supervise the community, and, on the other, less advanced members, who provide for them.

Pseudo-Macarius encourages all members of the community to work harmoniously, like limbs of a body, moved by a single soul towards a common goal.[134] After discussing the basic requisites for all members (renunciation of property, separation from family and, above all, a shared sense of humility), he reminds readers that the "chief and highest" objective of their training was "perseverance in prayer." It was through such perseverance that all other virtues might be attained.[135] Those who dedicated themselves to this challenge merited special help and privileges:

> So if any of those brothers who contends with faith and prayer and repentance yearns to submit himself to the contest in his desire for heavenly goods, this one must be received and exceedingly praised by both God and mankind. For this reason let him be permitted and joyfully helped in his perseverance in prayer by the brotherhood as if by his own limbs . . . so that he who is praying might have . . . continuous solicitude and ceaseless contest . . . so that the fruits of his vigilance and perseverance might in this way become manifest day by day for the edification of all.[136]

One pictures an isolated monk supported day and night while at prayer in his cell. Pseudo-Macarius does not explicitly say that such people who pray must forego manual labor, but that is certainly implied. Indeed, he enjoins

133. See Fitschen (1998): 158–70 for the historical milieu gleaned from internal evidence of the corpus; Fitschen dates Ps.-Macarius' activities ca. 360–90. For "thirty [monks living] in unity," see Ps.-Macarius, *Hom.* 3.1 (Collection II); ed. Hermann Dörries, Erich Klostermann, and Matthias Kroeger, p. 20,13.

134. Ps.-Macarius, *EM* 11.3; ed. Reinhart Staats, p. 167.

135. Ps.-Macarius, *EM* 8.3; ed. Staats, p. 144: κορυφαῖον τῶν κατυρθωμάτων ἐστὶν ἡ τῆς προσευχῆς προκαρτέρησις, δι' ἧς καὶ τὰς λοιπὰς ἀρετὰς διὰ τῆς παρὰ θεοῦ αἰτήσεως.

136. Ps.-Macarius, *EM* 9.2–3; ed. Staats, p. 148: Εἴ τις τοίνυν τῶν ἀδελφῶν τῶν διὰ πίστεως καὶ προσευχῆς καὶ μετανοίας ἀγωνιζόντων ἀναδέξασθαι ἐπιποθεῖ τὸν ἀγῶνα ἔρωτι τῶν ἐπουρανίων ἀγαθῶν, ἀποδεκτέος καὶ πάνυ ἐπαινετὸς οὗτος καὶ ἀνθρώποις καὶ θεῷ. διὸ ἐάσθω καὶ βοηθείσθω ὑπὸ τῆς ἀδελφότητος τῶν συμμέλων ἀδελφῶν μετὰ χαρᾶς ὁ τοιοῦτος τῇ εὐχῇ προσκαρτερεῖν . . . ἵνα καὶ ἀδιάλεπτον μέριμναν καὶ ἄπαυστον ἀγῶνα ὁ εὐχόμενος ἔχῃ . . . ἵν' οὕτως οἱ καρποὶ τῆς παραμονῆς καὶ προσκαρτερήσεως εἰς οἰκοδομὴν ὁσημέραι πᾶσι φανεροὶ γίνωνται.

the overseers to ensure that no impediment might hinder those who take up the struggle of prayer.[137] They were to be supported by those not yet capable of such exertions, who also, adds Pseudo-Macarius, should not complain about their servitude:

> Those of you who on account of your inexperience are not yet sufficiently capable of dedicating yourselves to the work of prayer, prepare yourselves with faith and piety and fear of God in the ministration, service, work or relief of your brothers, trusting that you are fulfilling God's commandment and performing a spiritual task. Apply yourselves, not as if you might receive a reward from men or expect honor or thanks from them, but with alacrity, as if to God's work, ministering joyfully as slaves of Christ.[138]

Since "perseverance in prayer" is considered the most important and onerous activity, it is also the most privileged. Overseers were expected to encourage the more inexperienced in the community "to apply themselves keenly and seriously to this contest," but Pseudo-Macarius believed few would prove able to meet such a challenge, "according to the power of resolve given to him by the Lord."[139] Those who devoted themselves to supporting their brother in his regimen of prayer should consider his spiritual advancements "their own personal gain."[140]

Pseudo-Macarius devotes much of his letter to defending this two-tiered arrangement, which he considers "truly the angelic way of life on earth."[141] He justifies it (as does the author of the *Book of Steps*) by reference to Jesus' pronouncement of Mary's superiority over Martha and the example of the apostles, who appointed deacons to minister to their bodily needs so that they themselves could "persevere in the ministration of the word and prayer." In doing so they had "made the better choice," as had Mary.[142]

---

137. Ps.-Macarius, *EM* 9.5; ed. Staats, p. 150: μάλιστα οἱ προεστῶτες τῶν ἀδελφῶν ὀφείλετε . . . ἵνα μηδεὶς ἐγκοπὴν λαμβάνῃ εἰς ὃν προαιρεῖται ἀγωνίζεσθαι ἀγῶνα.

138. Ps.-Macarius, *EM* 10.1; ed. Staats, p. 162: οἱ δὲ μήπω δυνάμενοι ἄκρως ἐπὶ τὸ τῆς εὐχῆς ἔργον διὰ νηπιότητα ἑαυτοὺς ἀποδοῦναι τῇ διακονίᾳ ἢ ὑπηρεσίᾳ . . . τῶν ἀδελφῶν. . . . ἑαυτοὺς εὐτρεπίζετε . . . ὡς ἔργῳ θεοῦ νηφόντως προσέχετε καὶ ὡς δοῦλοι Χριστοῦ μετὰ χαρᾶς διακονεῖτε.

139. Ps.-Macarius, *EM* 9.9 and 10.2; ed. Staats, pp. 152, 162: ὁ κύριος . . . ἑκάστῳ ἔδωκεν ἐργασίαν κατὰ τὴν δύναμιν τῆς προαιρέσεως.

140. Ps.-Macarius, *EM* 9.4; ed. Staats, p. 148: ὡς βοηθοὶ αὐτῷ μᾶλλον συνεργείτωσαν . . . ἴδιον κέρδος ἡγούμενοι τὴν ἐπὶ τὰ κρείττονα τοῦ ἀδελφοῦ προκοπήν.

141. Ps.-Macarius, *EM* 11.5.

142. Ps.-Macarius on Mary and Martha, *EM* 11.9–10; on the apostles, *EM* 11.10–11; ed. Staats, p. 171: καὶ περὶ τὴν σωματικὴν διακονίαν τῶν τραπεζῶν ἀσχολούμενοι τὸ μεῖζον προέκριναν, τὸ τῆς εὐχῆς καὶ τοῦ λόγου μεταδιώκειν ἔργον . . . ἐκλεξάμενοι ἄνδρας πλήρεις. . . . ἡμεῖς δὲ τῇ διακονίᾳ τοῦ λόγου καὶ τῇ προσευχῇ προσκαρτερήσωμεν. In 1.2 (p. 88) he states that his monastic arrangement conformed to the apostolic paradigm (ἀποστολικὸν χαρακτῆρα) described in Acts.

Pseudo-Macarius stresses that both corporeal and spiritual ministrations should be viewed as "offshoots of the same, single root."[143] They were mutually beneficial, since those who persevered in prayer supplied the deficiencies of those who worked and served. In fact, Pseudo-Macarius considered this an "arrangement of simple unity," one that struck a balance and preserved "equality" between the two ranks.[144]

The *Book of Steps* is more explicit than Pseudo-Macarius in requiring its spiritual elite to go without property. It is also less defensive in asserting that others should provide their material support.[145] Nonetheless, both Pseudo-Macarius and the author of the *Book of Steps* reflect the same basic premise that ascetics who devoted themselves to the spiritual work of prayer and edification merited support from other members of the Christian community. This premise was closely bound to the Syro-Mesopotamian tradition of providing maintenance for the ascetic "Sons and Daughters of the Covenant," not to mention the tradition of the *Letters to Virgins* or first-century *Didache*.[146] Despite Basil's self-assurance that manual labor was an "obvious" necessity for all members of a monastic community, these treatises illustrate that this assumption was not at all obvious for many Christian ascetics in the late fourth century.

The concerns that lay behind Basil's pronouncement on manual labor will be explored in the next two chapters. Suffice to note here that Basil, whose monastic innovations tended to moderate ascetic practices that troubled church leaders, seems to have attempted reform in the area of material dependency too.[147] The same might be said for his brother Gregory. Significantly, the justifications elaborated by Pseudo-Macarius for the two-tiered arrangement of his communities fall mostly in that part of the *Great Letter* that Gregory declined to replicate in his own spiritual guidebook.[148]

---

143. Ps.-Macarius, *EM* 11.11; ed. Staats, p. 171.

144. Ps.-Macarius, *EM* 11.4; ed. Staats, p. 167: τὸ περίσσευμα τῶν ταῖς εὐχαῖς προσκαρτερούντων ἐπὶ τὸ ὑστέρημα τῶν διακονούντων καὶ ἐργαζομένων καὶ πάλιν τὸ περίσσευμα τῶν διακονούντων καὶ ἐργαζομένων ἐπὶ τὸ ὑστέρημα τῶν ταῖς εὐχαῖς σχολαζόντων.

145. Mees (1979): 62–63 and Fitschen (1998): 165 find references in the Ps.-Macarian homilies that suggest wandering in unknown villages and churches.

146. For this continuity see, in general, Escolan (1999) and Arthur Vööbus, *On the Historical Importance of the Legacy of Pseudo-Macarius* (Stockholm, 1972): 9–20. For the relation between the *LG* and the *Bnay* and *Bnāt Qyāmā* traditions, see Guillaumont (1974): 314 and Vööbus (1954): 114–20. The author of the *LG* was familiar with both the *Didache* and the *ATh*.

147. See Jean Gribomont, "Un aristocrate révolutionnaire, évêque et moine: s. Basile," *Augustinianum* 17 (1977b): 190–91; for the general reformist aspect of Basil's monastic rules, see Gribomont (1980); Rousseau (1994): 200–206; and Elm (1994): 60–77.

148. Fitschen (1998): 242–43 rejects any explanation for Gregory's omission of the last quarter of the *EM* (he stops at *EM* 10.4) other than lack of interest. As Staats (1984): 163 and Jaeger (1954): 206–7 observe, however, Gregory tends to obscure Ps.-Macarius' distinctions

Whatever Gregory's reasons were for passing over those features of Pseudo-Macarian spirituality, it should be clear that the ascetic practices identified by his Greek colleagues as "Messalian"—continuous prayer, refusal to work, claim to privileged support by others—were simply fourth-century manifestations of a very old Christian tradition of ascetic conduct, leadership, and support.[149] That, of course, does not mean that doctrinal issues were either irrelevant or mere side-issues to the Messalian controversy. Once Adelphius' views became known and Pseudo-Macarius' flamboyant expressions of spiritual experience caught the attention of Greek authorities, these, too, caused understandable alarm.

Ephrem, the earliest author to use the "Messalian" label, should instruct us. He lived in the milieu which produced the earliest known manifestations of these practices. He does not seem to identify Messalians with any specific group, movement, or doctrines, but seems to have used the label simply to deride people who were excessively flamboyant in their prayer.[150] Likewise, Pseudo-Macarius (probably writing probably somewhere in Ephrem's vicinity) regrets how some monks were performing their prayers with such a commotion that they scandalized others:

> They are really not laboring under any pain, nevertheless for the sake of ostentation or idiosyncrasy they pour forth disorderly cries, as if in this way they become pleasing to God. . . . This is the thinking of the simple-minded, for which reason they give scandal to some and are even a disturbance to themselves during prayer.[151]

We must remember that the *Weltanschauung* commonly held by Christians of this period was that the world was flourishing with demons. As soldiers of Christ, many ascetics considered it their job to combat these demons through self-mortification and prayers, hoping for God's favor in return.[152]

---

between Christians dedicated to prayer and those who supported them. Moreover, differences of scriptural interpretation seem to have been an issue. Whereas Gregory (and most other Greek fathers) interpreted the Gospel passage on Mary and Martha as a lesson on humility or the need not to forget spiritual goals while working, Ps.-Macarius (like the author of the *LG*) cite this passage to promote the priority of spiritual pursuits over earthly preoccupations: see Daniel Csányi, "Optima Pars: Die Auslegungsgeschichte von Lk 10,38–42 bei den Kirchenvätern der ersten vier Jahrhunderte," *SM* 2 (1960): 5–78.

149. So too concludes Desprez (1992): 16–29, focusing on the *LG*.

150. See above, n. 26.

151. Ps.-Macarius, *Hom.* 6.1,12–17 (Collection II); ed. Dörries, Klostermann, and Kroeger, p. 64–65: ἀλλ᾽ ὁρῶμεν ὅτι τὸ μέρος τοῦτο ἰδιωτῶν ἐστι, διὰ τὸ καὶ ἄλλους σκανδαλίζειν καὶ αὐτοὺς τεταραγμένους ποιεῖσθαι τὴν προσευχήν.

152. See Vööbus (1958b): 10–28. Heussi (1936): 53 neglected this dimension of ascetic enthusiasm when he restricted the term *Sonderwelt* to the spiritual world created by the monastic cloister, and used it to distinguish ascetic from monk. The alleged habit of Messalian monks to identify themselves with prophets, angels, etc. (Epiphanius, *Panarion* 80.3.5; cf.

Later in the fifth century, Isaac of Antioch (also a critic of the trend towards monks supporting themselves through manual labor) would describe monks graphically as spiritual warriors:

> Their prayers are arrows, which they aim at the target of mercy;
> their lips are bows, with which they fire to astounding heights.
> The words of the Holy Spirit are their armaments, since their
>   struggle is directed against a spiritual fortress.[153]

In light of such convictions it should be no surprise to find some monks giving dramatic expression to their spiritual combat, as did those criticized for imagining that "they are leaping over demons, and pretend to shoot them down with their fingers."

Moreover, the constant genuflections prescribed for ascetics in the *Book of Steps* reminds us that religious obeisance requiring the entire body was considered a necessary part of the devotional regimen ("in this way our Lord acted in front of his disciples . . . to give us an example to imitate") and was adopted by many notable ascetics of the period, though clearly not by Basil and other ascetic theorists.[154] Symeon Stylites' prayer regimen, for instance, reportedly included over 1,244 prostrations in a single day.[155] John "the Perfect Nazirite" bent down so many times he wore the hair off his head.[156] Hence we cannot presume that many of the Perfect would have recognized either Basil's recommendation that monks simply pray with the heart while they worked, or Abba Lucius' demonstration that they could say their prayers while sitting and weaving, as obvious solutions to Paul's apparently conflicting commands that they both pray without ceasing and work day and night. Pseudo-Macarius himself set aside a special time of prayer for novice brothers who were otherwise occupied with manual labor

---

Sulpicius Severus, *Vita Martini* 23.3–24.3) may be the result of immersion in their own spiritual *Sonderwelt* created through ecstatic prayer. See Stewart (1991): 74–233 and (1998): 114–22 for ecstatic prayer in this period.

153. Isaac of Antioch, "On the Perfection of Monks" (stanza 320), trans. Simon Landersdorfer, p. 94. For Isaac, see Vööbus (1960b): 146–50.

154. *LG* 20.10 (PS 3.552).

155. Theodoret, *HR* 26.22. Even if exaggerated, the report describes contemporary expectations: see *V.Alex.* 30, Evagrius Scholasticus, *HE* 1.21, and John of Ephesus, *Lives of the Eastern Saints* 13 (ed. Brooks, p. 204), counting 500 prostrations in a single night for Thomas in Amida.

156. John of Ephesus, *Lives of the Eastern Saints* 3 (ed. Brooks, pp. 40–41); cf. Palladius, *HL* 18.29. Adelphius was also believed to practice the severe asceticism of *nzirutā* (naziritehood): see Philoxenus, *Letter to Patricius* 108; ed. R. Lavenant, p. 850. On the credibility of the report, see Fitschen (1998): 94–95. On *nzirutâ* see Palmer (1990): 85–88.

to support the community—an indication that he, for one, did not consider prayer and manual labor to be simultaneously compatible occupations.[157]

But the monastic practices and problems that became defined as Messalian were not restricted to the East. They arose wherever monks took the Gospels and Jesus' precepts literally for guidance on proper ascetic conduct.

CONFLICTING ASSUMPTIONS OF ORTHODOX MONASTIC PRACTICE IN THE WEST

At the turn of the fifth century, while church leaders were rooting out Messalian heretics in the Eastern provinces, Bishop Aurelius in Carthage asked Augustine to address certain monastic problems that had arisen there and elsewhere in late fourth-century North Africa. Augustine explained the background of this episode in a later (ca. 427) retrospective:

> Necessity compelled me to write those things because when monasteries were beginning to exist at Carthage, some monks lived by supporting themselves through manual labor in obedience to the Apostle, but others wanted to live off the gratuitous offerings of pious people. Although they were not performing any work by which they might possess, or supply, their necessities, they assumed and even boasted they were better fulfilling the Gospel precept, where the Lord says, "Look at the birds of the sky and the lilies of the field." For this reason heated quarrels arose even among lay persons who were of lesser character but hot with zeal, who troubled the church, some defending one view and some another. Some of the ones saying work must not be done also had long hair.[158]

The attitudes of these long-haired monks toward manual labor, which Augustine addressed in his treatise *On the Work of Monks* in 401, bears remarkable similarity to the attitudes which Epiphanius had ascribed to Messalian heretics and long-haired Mesopotamian monks some twenty years earlier.

On the Work of Monks constitutes a lengthy rebuttal to the way certain monks, "gathered very idly together in some kind of holy society," were

157. For his divisions between work and prayer, see esp. Ps.-Macarius, *Hom.* 3.1–2 (Collection II); ed. Dörries-Klostermann-Kroeger, pp. 20–21, with commentary.

158. Augustine, *Retractationes* 2.21; ed. Almut Mutzenbecher, pp. 106–7: cum apud Carthaginem monasteria esse coepissent, alii se suis manibus transigebant obtemperantes apostolo, alii vero ita ex oblationibus religiosorum vivere volebant, ut nihil operantes, unde necessaria vel haberent vel supplerent, se potius implere praeceptum evangelicum existimarent atque iactarent, ubi dominus ait: Respicite volatia caeli et lilia agri. Unde etiam inter laicos inferioris propositi sed tamen studio ferventes existere coeperunt tumultuosa certamina, quibus ecclesia turbaretur, aliis hoc aliis aliud defendentibus.

using Gospel precepts "to justify not only laziness, but their arrogance as well."[159] According to Augustine, these monks defended their lifestyle by reference to Jesus' instruction that his followers not worry about providing for their food or clothing. They interpreted Jesus' words literally, but interpreted figuratively Paul's seemingly contradictory exhortation towards work, so as not to conflict with the Gospel ideal:

> They assert that when the Apostle says: "If any man will not work, neither let him eat" he does not refer to bodily labor at which farmers or artisans work. For, they maintain, St. Paul's attitude cannot be in contradiction to the Gospel, where the Lord Himself says: "Therefore I say to you, do not be anxious about your life, what you shall eat. . . ." They say: "Behold the passage where the Lord bids us to be free from care in regard to our food and clothing. How then can the Apostle, opposing the direction of the Lord, command us to be solicitous about what we are to eat and drink and how we are to be clothed and thus burden us with the arts, cares and labors of workmen?" They insist, therefore, that we ought to understand the passage: "If any man will not work, neither let him eat," as referring to spiritual works.[160]

These North African monks, like their Eastern counterparts, rejected manual labor on the grounds that they must "be free for prayers, for singing psalms, for readings, and for the word of God."[161] Moreover, they claimed for themselves the prerogative of living by the support of others that Jesus had granted to his apostles.[162] Augustine counters that it is Jesus' prescriptions that must be read figuratively, and Paul's literally. Although Augustine recognizes that Jesus had given his apostles the right to be supported by the faithful, he denies that the monks in question can claim this apostolic right for themselves: "Have they ever filled the lands from Jerusalem to Illyricum with the Gospel? Have they undertaken to approach and to fill with the peace of the Church whatever barbarian peoples remain?"[163] At the beginning of his treatise, however, Augustine indicates that there was more to their assertion of apostolic prerogatives than mere arrogance. In keeping with their belief that Paul must have meant spiritual rather than

---

159. Augustine, *De opere* 14.15 and 3.4; ed. Joseph Zycha, pp. 535–36: evangelica illa precepta, de quibus nonnulli non solum pigritiam, sed etiam adrogantiam suam fovent.

160. Augustine, *De opere* 1.2; ed. Zycha, pp. 532–33: neque enim evangelio posset esse contrarius, ubi ait ipse dominus [Mt 6:25–34]. . . . quomodo ergo apostolus sentire adversus dominum posset, ut nos praeciperet ita esse debere sollicitos quid manducemus et quid bibamus et unde cooperiamur, ut nos etiam opificum artibus, curis, laboribus oneraret? quapropter in eo [2 Thess 3:10] opera spiritalia, inquiunt, debemus accipere. See also 19.22 and 23.27. Trans. Mary Muldowney, pp. 331–32.

161. Augustine, *De opere* 17.20; ed. Zycha, p. 564: qui operari corporaliter nolunt, cui rei vacent scire desidero. orationibus, inquiunt, et psalmis et lectioni et verbo dei.

162. Augustine, *De opere* 20.23, 21.24, 24.31.

163. Augustine, *De opere* 14.15; trans. Muldowney, p. 355.

corporeal work, they were applying themselves, they affirmed, to spiritual works. As Augustine represents their defense,

> What profit is there [they say] in a spiritual repast, that is, in feasting on the word of God, if one does not then work for the edification of others? . . . We act in this fashion. We read with our brothers who come to us weary from the tumult of the world seeking in our company rest in the word of God, in prayers, psalms, hymns, and spiritual songs. We converse with them, comfort them, exhort and edify them in whatever we notice is needed for their progress. If we did not do such works, we would be taking the Lord's sustenance itself at our peril, for the Apostle has said, "If any man will not work, neither let him eat." In this way they imagine that they are obeying both the apostolic and the Gospel precept. . . . [164]

Although Augustine does not mention their pastoral activities or evangelic justifications again, these monks clearly viewed themselves as spiritual guides and instructors, and therefore as legitimate heirs to the Gospels' apostolic paradigm for monastic life.

Who were these North African monks? Where did they get such presumptions? Augustine's description of their refusal to work for the sake of prayer, of their claim to support from others, and of their long hair (Augustine claims they grew it long to remind people of Old Testament heroes) bear such remarkable resemblance to Epiphanius' Messalian profile that some historians have surmised that Augustine was unwittingly dealing with Messalian monks who had sought refuge in Carthage after their excommunication in Syria and Asia Minor.[165] By such reasoning, *On the Work of Monks* would represent testimony for the further westward progression of the Messalianism across the Roman Empire. Yet, Augustine never draws a connection between these monks and the Messalians or any other heretical group.[166] Nor does he suggest they came from the East; rather, he insinuates that they were North African peasants who had adopted monasticism solely in order to escape harder labors.[167] The modern supposition of a Messalian connection is unfounded and historically unwarranted.[168] Augustine's trea-

---

164. Augustine, *De opere* 1.2; ed. Zycha, pp. 533–34: alloquimur eos, consolamur, exhortamur, aedificantes in eis, si quid eorum vitae pro suo gradu esse perspicimus. . . . ita se isti arbitrantur apostolicae et evangelicae obtemperare sententiae.

165. Proposed by Georges Folliet, "Des moines euchites à Carthage en 400–401," *SP* 2 (1957): 386–99.

166. Folliet (1957): 390 demonstrates that Augustine did not have Epiphanius' *Panarion* when he wrote this treatise or when he included Messalians in his own *De haeresibus* in 426.

167. Augustine, *De opere* 22.25; ed. Zycha, pp. 570–71: vitam inopem et laborosam fugientes vacui pasci atque vestiri voluerint.

168. Stated most recently by Fitschen (1998): 57–60 and Biagio Amata, "S. Agostino: 'De Opere Monachorum.' Una concezione (antimanichea?) del lavoro," in *Spiritualità del lavoro nella catechesi dei Padri del III–VI secolo,* ed. S. Felici (Rome: Libreria Ateneo Salesiano, 1986),

tise simply attests the attitudes of early Christian ascetics in North Africa who, like the authors of the *Book of Steps* and the *Great Letter,* assumed the propriety of a monastic arrangement and vocation that was different from, and older than, the one that Augustine and Aurelius were trying to promote within their ecclesiastical domain.

What we know about early ascetic tradition at Carthage supports this hypothesis. As Augustine recalled in his retrospective, the problem with these monks arose just at the time when monasteries were being founded. By "monasteries" Augustine, of course, meant those that conformed to his own notions of proper communal practice, derived from what he had heard about Pachomian institutions, from his understanding of Paul, and from his reading of Acts: in other words, self-sufficient coenobitic monasteries based on manual labor and the sharing (as much as the renunciation) of property.[169] It has been estimated, however, that monasteries of this type had existed for only twelve years or so when Augustine wrote *On the Work of Monks,* and their existence was largely due to his own promotional efforts.[170] While in this treatise Augustine admits no alternative monastic model, he elsewhere informs us that there had already existed in Carthage (and other North African cities) another Christian ascetic group whose spiritual elite also claimed to "care nothing for tomorrow, unsolicitous as to how the stomach will be filled or the body will be clothed."[171]

These were Manichaean Christians, whom Augustine once refers to as *pseudo-Christiani* because they called members of Augustine's church *semi-Christiani.*[172] As discussed in the previous chapter, Mani and his followers took the Gospels as the blueprint for their ascetic arrangement and ideals.

59–77. The *De opere* has received little attention from social historians. Church historians, focusing on Augustine alone, have neglected both the arguments that Augustine ascribes to the monks he is refuting and their similarity to arguments made by other monks at the time.

169. Augustine first described his notion of ideal monastic arrangements in *De moribus ecclesiae catholicae et moribus manichaeorum* (written 388) 33.70; ed. John Coyle in *Augustine's "De Moribus Ecclesiae catholicae": A Study of the Work, Its Composition, and Its Sources* (Fribourg: University Press, 1978), 297: Romae etiam plura cognovi, in quibus. . . . ne ipsi quidem cuiquam onerosi sunt, sed Orientis more, et Pauli apostoli auctoritate manibus suis se transigunt. Coyle, pp. 214–15 and 230, thinks he knew of Pachomian rules through Latin translations. For Augustine's notion of monastic poverty, see Domingo Sanchis, "Pauvreté monastique et charité fraternelle chez Augustin: le commentaire augustinien des Actes 4, 32–35 entre 393 et 403" *SM* 4 (1962): 7–33 and Leyser (2000): 8–19, 45–46.

170. Folliet (1957): 399. Possidius, *Vita Augustini* 11 (PG 32.42) says Augustine was responsible for promoting monasteries that produced clergy for "Catholic" churches. For Augustine's views on monasticism, see George Lawless, *Augustine of Hippo and His Monastic Rule* (Oxford: Clarendon Press, 1987) and Coyle (1978).

171. Augustine, *Contra Faustum* 5.1 (written ca. 397–99), alluding to Faustus' defense of the evangelical basis of Manichaean asceticism. Augustine refers to Carthaginian Manichaeans in *De utilitate credendi* 14.32 (ca. 392); cf. Possidius, *V. Augustini* 6.

172. Augustine, *Contra Faustum* 1.3.

They divided their communities into two ranks, the ascetic "elect" and the "hearers." Like less advanced monks in the Pseudo-Macarian *Great Letter* or the Upright of the *Book of Steps*, Manichaean hearers were supposed to provide material support so that the elect could fulfill Jesus' evangelic ideal of living utterly free from material concerns. In return, the elect provided spiritual edification.[173] This arrangement was often targeted for ridicule in the polemics of orthodox or catholic authors. In 348 Cyril of Jerusalem had described the Manichaean elect as "children of *argia*, who do not work themselves, but devour the fruits of those who do; who welcome with smiling faces those who bring them their food, and give back curses instead of blessings."[174] Epiphanius had similarly scorned them in his *Panarion:* "Their so-called elect . . . are drones who sit around and 'do not work, but are busybodies' [2 Thess 3:11]. . . . Manichaeans bid their catechumens feed these people in abundance. They offer their elect everything, whatever they need, so that whoever nourishes the elected souls may look 'pious.' "[175]

As we have seen, such Manichaeans were simply practicing the arrangement for ascetic leadership and support that had long been used by their Syro-Mesopotamian contemporaries and predecessors. Moving westward with missionary intent, they had settled in North Africa by the early fourth century.[176] Thus the precedent they set for Christian leadership and monastic practice had nearly a century's head start on the arrangements espoused by Augustine and his colleagues in Carthage and neighboring cities. It would therefore be no surprise if other Christians embracing monasticism in fourth-century Carthage formed their notions of proper monastic practice from the example of Manichaean ascetics living in their vicinity.

Augustine's treatise does not provide evidence for the westward spread of specifically Messalian activities, but rather for the widespread fourth-century diffusion of the assumption that dedication to an ascetic life lived strictly according to Gospel precepts included a certain dependence upon, and entitlement to, material support from other Christians. That assumption may have ultimately derived from the East, but not necessarily.[177] By

173. For this aspect of Manichaean monasticism, see esp. François Decret, "Aspects de l'Église manichéenne: Remarques sur le Manuscript de Tébessa," in *id., Essais sur l'Église manichéenne en Afrique du nord et à Rome au temps de saint Augustin: recueil d'études* (Rome: Institutum Patristicum Augustinianum, 1995), 37–51; Persic (1986): 227–32; and Samuel N. C. Lieu, "Precept and Practice in Manichaean Monasticism," *JThS* n.s. 32 (1981): 153–73. Providing alms would assure a "hearer" rebirth as an "elect": see Coyle (1978): 201 n. 783.

174. Cyril of Jerusalem, *Catechesis* 6.32 (PG 33.596B).

175. Epiphanius, *Panarion* 66.53.1–4; ed. Holl-Dummer, p. 89: ἵνα δῆθεν εὐσεβὴς, ὀφθείη <ὁ> τρέφων τὰς ψυχὰς τὰς ἐκλελεγμένας.

176. See above, ch. 2 n. 139 and Lieu (1992): 121–24.

177. Tertullian, *De virginibus velandis* 14 may refer to a custom of providing material support for virgins in third-century Carthage: see Lane Fox (1987): 359.

their own explanation, the Carthaginian monks (like Pseudo-Clement, Manichaean Christians, Pseudo-Macarius, or the author of the *Book of Steps*) found the basis and justification for their practices in the apostolic models set forth in the Gospels. For this reason Manichaean practices should not be presumed to have inspired their monastic assumptions, any more than Messalian influences should. Rather, we must recognize that the precepts ascribed to Jesus in the Gospels (and regularly heard in church sermons) served as precepts for many Christians who sought prescriptions for proper monastic life in the late fourth and early fifth centuries. For them, strict imitation of Jesus' poverty and obedience to his command to live without worldly cares took obvious precedent over Paul's admonition to continue laboring with their own hands for their daily bread.

Indeed, the anonymous treatise *On Riches* (probably written in Sicily ca. 414) shows that literal interpretation of the Gospel was not restricted to ascetics of Syrian (or Carthaginian) origin in this period.[178] In its author's view, to give surplus wealth to the poor and to live content with just a little, as Basil wished his monks to do, was all right in itself—if you merely aspired to live by Old Testament standards.

> More praiseworthy is the man who wishes to fulfill the commandments not only of the Old Testament but also of the New, especially when our Lord and Savior has taught us by word as well as by example—by word, in that he said: No man who does not renounce all his possessions can be my disciple; by example, in that we read that after his assumption of the form of a man he was so poor that he did not possess even a place of his own where he might lay his head.[179]

This was polemical literature that decried the mounting wealth of the fifth-century clergymen. The worldliness of the bishops of Rome and other cities had already caught the eye of Ammianus Marcellinus in the late fourth century. Their freedom from care *(securi)*, he observed, was maintained through the offerings of rich matrons, who enabled them to ride in carriages and "serve banquets that outdo the tables of kings." Such urban churchmen would truly be blessed, he adds, if they would adopt the plain

178. For introduction, date, and provenance, see John Morris, "Pelagian Literature," *JThS* n.s. 16 (1965): 26–51 and Brinley Rees, *The Letters of Pelagius and His Followers* (Rochester, N.J.: Boydell Press, 1991), 12–25, 171–74.

179. Ps.-Pelagius, *De divitiis* 5.3 (PLS 1.1384), citing Lk 14:33, cf. Mt 19:21; and Mt 8:20 and Lk 9:29, cf. 2 Cor 8:9: *secundum adsumpti hominis formam tam pauperem fuisse legimus, ut nec, ubi caput declinaret, proprium possideret.* Trans. Rees, p. 178. For tensions between Old and New Testament precepts in this treatise, see Carlo Scaglioni, "'Guai a voi ricchi!' Pelagio e gli scritti pelagiani," in *Per foramen acus. Il cristianesimo antico di fronte alla pericope evangelica del "giovane ricco"* (Milan: Vita e Pensiero, 1986), 361–98.

clothes and meager diet of their provincial counterparts.[180] The author of *On Riches* was more demanding. Since priests and bishops claimed to be the heirs of the apostles, he reasons that they must also fully imitate the poverty Jesus imposed on his apostles. "Clearly we believe that our teachers, after Christ, are the apostles. Why then do we blush to live by the example of those whose disciples we profess to be?"[181]

Indeed, genuine dedication to the apostolic tradition must be demonstrated—the author is quite emphatic about this—by living like strangers, with as few possessions as travelers from far-off India, Arabia, or Upper Egypt.[182] He scorns the insincerity of those who defend their property through "that most notorious argument" that Christians stripped of wealth would be unable to give alms or do good works.[183] He likewise castigates the faithlessness of those who think material renunciations and poverty would leave them unable to feed themselves, since Jesus had promised God's care.[184] Against the assertion that it is better to support oneself with one's own wealth than to live off another's charity, the author replies that it is in fact better to live as the apostles did—supported by others—than to possess property at all.[185] Indeed, those placed in need through their voluntary adoption of poverty should feel no shame in receiving a layman's support, he contends, portraying this as a normal expectation between clergymen and those they instruct.[186] But in his view church leaders (*saeculi amatores,* he calls them) had twisted the clear meaning of the Gospels' "counsels of perfection" in order to preserve their material comforts "under the appearance of piety."[187]

Although this author is addressing ecclesiastical trends of his Western milieu, his sentiments match those of the author of the *Book of Steps.* Besides sharing a conviction that truly dedicated Christians could ascend *ad perfectionis gradum,*[188] these Eastern and Western authors both considered poverty

180. Ammianus Marcellinus, *Res gestae* 27.3.14; text and trans. John C. Rolfe, *Ammianus Marcellinus* 3 (LCL 331; Cambridge: Harvard University Press, 1986), 20–21: ita securi, ut ditentur oblationibus matronarum . . . beati re vera, si . . . ad imitationem antistitum quorundam provincialium viverent, quos tenuitas edendi potandique parcissime, vilitas etiam indumentorum . . . ut puros commendant.

181. Ps.-Pelagius, *De divitiis* 14.2 (PLS 1.1403): Quid ergo erubescimus eorum exemplo vivere, quorum nos discipulos confitemur? Trans. adapted from Rees, p. 197.

182. Ps.-Pelagius, *De divitiis* 19.4 (1.1415).

183. Ps.-Pelagius, *De divitiis* 12.1 (PLS 1.1400–01): illam famosissimam propositionem.

184. Ps.-Pelagius, *De divitiis* 13.1 (PLS 1.1402).

185. Ps.-Pelagius, *De divitiis* 15.1 (PLS 1.1403–4): meliores fuisse apostolos, qui de alieno sustentabantur, quam qui propria possidebant.

186. Ps.-Pelagius, *De divitiis* 15.3 (PLS 1.1405–6).

187. Ps.-Pelagius, *De divitiis* 12.1 (PLS 1.1401): sub specie pietatis perfectiora evangelica praecepta minime custodiri debere contendunt. Trans. Rees, p. 194.

188. Ps.-Pelagius, *De divitiis* 10.2 (PLS 1.1394); cf. Brown (1988): 414 and Leslie W. Bar-

to be the essential criterion for spiritual leadership, and both assumed such leaders should be supported by others, with no other care than contemplating and instructing other Christians about "the things of heaven." Paul's admonition that "If any man will not work, neither let him eat," was either not considered at all, or was interpreted figuratively to conform with Jesus' statements, or was otherwise regarded as a precept set down for Christians who aimed well below "perfection." As explained in the *Book of Steps,*

> The Perfect road is this: "Do not be anxious about what you shall eat and what you shall wear." But the path that leads you away from it is this: "Work and eat the bread [you have earned] and do not be a burden on anyone." This is said to whoever is dissolute because he does not work [for] heavenly things with fasting and prayer, with vigils and lowliness. He said to him "Work, even if in earthly matters, and give alms; do not cease completely from either one, [for] evil could triumph over you and you could contrive all sorts of evil."[189]

We should note that such a handling of Paul with respect to the Gospels would have seemed odd to most learned church authorities of the day. Their own notions of proper Christian conduct had, for the most part, been informed by the interpretive priority given to Paul in a flurry of commentaries on Paul's letters that began to appear in the middle of the fourth century. This Pauline approach to interpreting Jesus' utterances helped Christian leaders cope with increasingly complex institutional challenges, including competition with the Manichaean ascetic elect who lived in their cities.[190]

Nevertheless, despite the efforts of Augustine, Basil, and others to elevate Paul's authority on the matter, Jesus' apostolic command to live free from care continued to exert superior influence on Christian ascetics all around the empire. From Mesopotamia to North Africa, even to the interior of Gaul (where Martin of Tours founded a two-tiered community similar to Pseudo-Macarius', and reportedly told his fellow monks, "let the church both feed and clothe us, as long as we do not appear to have provided

---

nard, "Pelagius and Early Syriac Christianity," *Recherches de théologie ancienne et mediévale* 35 (1968): 193–96.

189. *LG* 19.13 (PS 3.473–476); cf. 19.19, quoting Mt 6:25 and 2 Thess 3:12.

190. See Maria Grazia Mara, "Il significato storico-esegetico dei commentari al corpus paolino dal IV al V secolo," *Annali di storia dell' esegesi* 1 (1984): 59–74 (the Manichaean challenge is at 66–67). Attestations of commentaries on Paul begin in the third century with Origen and rise sharply ca. 350–450, with 14 in Greek, 7 in Latin, and 1 in Syriac. For Augustine's own "turn to Paul," see now Thomas F. Martin, "*Vox Pauli:* Augustine and the Claims to Speak for Paul: An Exploration of Rhetoric at the Service of Exegesis," *JECS* 8 (2000): 237–72. More arguments defending Paul on manual labor in this period are Chrysostom, *In Johannem hom.* 44.1 and Cassian, *Inst.* 10.21, *Coll.* 24.10–13.

in any way for our own wants"),[191] the notion that an ascetic elite should be supported by others while devoting itself to prayer and spiritual services had become rooted in Christian monastic ideology before more orthodox authorities like Basil and Augustine initiated their reforms. Indeed, it is their promotion of a monastic arrangement based on manual labor and self-sufficiency for all members of an ascetic community that must be considered the truly novel movement of this period.

The reasons why church and monastic leaders sought to supplant the traditional apostolic way of ascetic life requires further exploration. There was more to the repudiation of People Who Pray than "indwelling demons" and other points of doctrine. The spiritual perfectionism pursued by such old-time ascetics provoked considerable social as well as a doctrinal misgivings, in no small part because the ascent that they advocated *ad perfectionis gradum* was grounded in the belief that Christian leaders must prove their worth by conforming to Gospel precepts. As the author of *On Riches* observed, the thought of actually living like the apostles caused many early-fifth-century church leaders to "blush," and nothing better illustrates the vexations and embarrassment such leaders might face when monks with apostolic pretensions came to town than the controversial career of Alexander the Sleepless.

191. Sulpicius Severus, *Dialogus* 3.14.6; ed. Karl Halm, p. 212: nos . . . ecclesia et pascat et vestiat, dum nihil nostris usibus quaesisse videamur. For Martin's community at Marmoutier, see *V. Martini* 10.5–6; ed. Jacques Fontaine, p. 274: Ars ibi, exceptis scriptoribus, nulla habebatur; cui tamen operi minor aetas deputabatur: maiores orationi vacabant; also 26.3–4 and Fontaine's commentary in *Sulpice Sévère: Vie de Saint Martin* vol. 2 (SC 134; Paris: Éditions du Cerf), 676. Some scholars have suggested Messalian influence, but more likely Martin found his precedents in the Gospels and Acts. See Claire Stancliffe, *St. Martin and His Hagiographer* (Oxford: Oxford University Press, 1983), 260–61 n. 51. Cassian's emphasis on manual labor in his *De institutis* and *Collationes* may have been intended to counter the influence of Martin's regimen in Gaul: see above, introduction, n. 37.

4

Apostle and Heretic

The Controversial Career of Alexander the Sleepless

Across the waters from Constantinople, in the oak-shaded suburbs of Chalcedon (modern Kadıköy) stood an impressive martyr's shrine dedicated to Peter and Paul, called "the Apostles." In 403 it saw the rancorous deposition of John Chrysostom, bishop of Constantinople; some twenty-five years later it became the scene of an armed confrontation with another persona non grata of the imperial city. This was Alexander, a Greek archimandrite (leader of a flock or fold) who had "come from the East" and settled in Constantinople with nearly a hundred followers:

> His way of life became known to all, for he was a zealot to the extreme. Carried by zeal he would denounce the magistrates, if he ever noticed them doing something reprehensible. These took common counsel and banished him so that he might go back to his own country. When he and his brothers left the city, they took refuge in the Apostles, close to the monastery of Hypatius.[1]

So writes Callinicus, a member of Hypatius' monastery since 426 and possibly an eyewitness to the violence that followed. "By order of the magistrates," he explains, the bishop of Constantinople sent a mob to evict Al-

---

1. Callinicus, *Vita Hypatii* 41.1–4; ed. G. J. M. Bartelink, p. 242: Ἀλέξανδρος ἐλθὼν ἐκ τῆς ἀνατολῆς. . . . ἡ πολιτεία αὐτοῦ ἐπίδοξος πᾶσιν ἐγένετο· ζηλωτὴς γὰρ ἦν εἰς ἄκρον, καὶ ζήλῳ φερόμενος ἤλεγχε τοὺς ἄρχοντας, εἴ τι ἂν συνέγνω ἄτοπον. Ἐκεῖνοι δὲ μίαν βουλὴν ποιήσαντες ἐξώρισαν αὐτόν, ἵνα ἀπέλθῃ εἰς τὴν ἰδίαν πατρίδα. The probable date of these events is discussed below. Callinicus entered Hypatius' monastery ca. 426, and wrote his *vita* ca. 447–451: see Bartelink's introduction, 9–12. For the history of this *martyrium* and monastery at the Rouphinianai (modern Caddebostan, four kilometers south of Chalcedon), see Jules Pargoire, "Rufinianes," *BZ* 8 (1899b): 429–77.

exander and company from the shrine.[2] These monks, some wounded, turned to Hypatius' monastery for help. The bishop of Chalcedon now dispatched a force of "officers of the martyr shrines, beggars, some factory workers, and clerics."[3] Surely more violence would have ensued—Hypatius was offered aid by peasants nearby—had not one of Hypatius' admiring patrons, the emperor's sister Pulcheria, sent soldiers from her retinue to intervene.[4] Under military protection Alexander lingered a few days longer, then set off with his monks to found a monastery at the mouth of the Bosphorus, near the Black Sea coast. It was here that Alexander the Sleepless (Akoimētos) finally found his rest.

If we had only this passage, Alexander, like so many other figures of this period, would remain little more than a name. But for Alexander we are remarkably well informed. Two other accounts indicate that his banishment from Constantinople occurred under more complex circumstances and in response to more complex issues than Callinicus suggests. Callinicus gives the impression that Alexander's troubles arose only because he spoke out against the city's civil officials; that these were the only authorities who took counsel against him and contrived his sentence; and finally, that church authorities became involved in the affair only insofar as they were pressured to make sure that Alexander's sentence and banishment were carried out. An anonymous biography of Alexander probably written in the late fifth or early sixth century tells us more. It reveals that the civil authorities involved had acted only after Alexander had already been identified as a heretic who aimed to "corrupt God's church."[5] It does not specify the exact nature of Alexander's heresy, but Nilus of Ancyra (ca. 390–430) provides the necessary clue. Writing his treatise *On Voluntary Poverty* soon

2. Callinicus, *V.Hypatii* 41.5; ed. Bartelink, p. 242: καὶ ἀποστέλλει ὁ ἐπίσκοπος ὄχλους διὰ τὸ κέλευσμα τῶν ἀρχόντων, ἵνα διώξωσιν αὐτοὺς ἐκεῖθεν. Presumably this was the bishop of Constantinople, since the bishop of Chalcedon is introduced at 41.8 as sending a new mob against the monks. The identity of the bishops involved depends on the date: see Pargoire (1899b): 446–47.

3. Callinicus, *V.Hypatii* 41.10; ed. Bartelink, p. 244: δεκανοὺς τῶν μαρτυρίων καὶ πτωχοὺς καὶ ἐκ τῶν ἐργαστρίων τινὰς καὶ κληρικούς.

4. Callinicus, *V.Hypatii* 41.11–15. For Pulcheria's involvement, see Kenneth Holum, *Theodosian Empresses: Women and Imperial Dominion in Late Antiquity* (Berkeley and Los Angeles: University of California Press, 1982), 132 n. 86, 134–36; and *V.Hypatii* 37.3–4.

5. *Vita Alexandri* [*V.Alex*] 48; ed. E. de Stroop, p. 697: ἀναφέρεται τοῖς ἐπάρχοις ὅτι ὁ μοναχὸς Ἀλέξανδρος αἱρετικός ἐστιν καὶ βούλεται λυμᾶναι τὴν ἐκκλησίαν τοῦ θεοῦ. For date of the *vita*, see below, appendix. Another description of Alexander's activities in Constantinople, too vague for use here, is the sixth-century *Vita Marcelli* 4–5; ed. Gilbert Dagron, "La *Vie* ancienne de saint Marcel l'Acémète," *AB* 86 (1968): 290–92. For a general history of Alexander and the Akoimētē monastery, see Venance Grumel, "Acémètes," *DSp* 1 (1937): 169–76; Jules Pargoire, "Acémètes," *DACL* 1 (1924): 307–21; and S. Vailhé, "Acémètes," *DHGE* 1 (1912): 274–81.

after the event, Nilus warns his readers not to succumb, "when emulating
the holy ones in their continuous occupation with things divine, to the
argia of Adelphius, the one from Mesopotamia, and of Alexander, who
recently churned up the imperial city of Constantinople."[6] This warning
comes in a section where Nilus has been describing the "possessionless ones
of the New Testament"—namely John the Baptist and the apostles. These
had demonstrated their trust in God through their utter lack of possessions
and provisions, refusing even to carry a traveler's staff or beggar's pouch,
"so as not to appear to take hope in these rather than in God." From these
exemplars, Nilus maintains, the monastic life originated.[7] Adelphius and
Alexander exemplified a perversion of that apostolic ideal.

This was the same Adelphius of Edessa whose statements at Antioch and
Side helped shape the official Messalian profile identifying those who rejected manual labor for the sake of continual prayer as heretics. Alexander's coupling with Adelphius indicates that he was banished from Constantinople as a Messalian himself.[8] The fact that Nilus presents him as an
example of *argia* in contrast to the apostles suggests why Alexander was
identified and banished as such.

There is no doubt that Alexander, who led over a hundred monks
around Syria and Asia Minor in absolute poverty and "sleepless" doxology,
was charged and banished from Constantinople as a Messalian heretic.
What remains in dispute is why and under what circumstances he was identified as a Messalian, and whether that identification has any significance
for our understanding of the Messalian controversy itself. The evidence
suggests that he was banished from Constantinople in the late 420s. This
raises the question whether he was the subject of synodal deliberations held
there against Messalians in 426, or else was later charged and banished

6. Nilus of Ancyra, *De voluntaria paupertate ad Magnam* [*De vol. paup.*] 21 (PG 79.997A):
ἀλλ᾽ ἄρα μὴ τῇ τῶν ἁγίων διηνεκεῖ περὶ τὸ θεῖον ἀσχολίᾳ τῆς ἀπὸ Ἀδελφίου τῆς Μέσης τῶν ποταμῶν
καὶ Ἀλεξάνδρου τοῦ πρὸς ὀλίγον τὴν βασιλευομένην Κωνσταντινούπολιν θολώσαντος ἀργίας
ἀνοίγωμεν θύραν. The usual date given to this work (ca. 426–430) rests mainly on the phrase
πρὸς ὀλίγον: see Karl Heussi, *Untersuchungen zu Nilus dem Asketen* (Leipzig: J. C. Hinrichs'sche,
1917), 51–52. Nilus will receive further attention below and in the next chapter.

7. Nilus, *De vol. paup.* 21 (PG 79.996CD): Ἴστε δὲ καὶ τοὺς νέας προθήκης ἀκτήμονας, Ἰωάννην
. . . καὶ τὸν χορὸν τῶν ἀποστόλων ὁμοῦ, ἐξ ὧν ὁ μοναδικὸς ἤρξατο βίος . . . οἱ δὲ Κυριακῇ παραινέσει
. . . οὐδὲν κτησάμενοι ὡς ἐδιδάχθησαν ὅλως ἕως ῥάβδου, καὶ πήρας τῶν μάλιστα διὰ πολλὰ τοῖς ὁδίταις
χρησίμων, ἵνα μὴ τούτοις τάχα δοκοῦντες θαρρεῖν τὴν ἐπὶ Θεὸν ἀμβλύνωσιν ἐλπίδα. . . .

8. Fitschen (1998): 142–43 dismisses Alexander's relevance to Messalianism on the
grounds that Nilus does not explicitly call him a Messalian, and that Nilus sees similarity
between Alexander and Adelphius on only one point (their attitude toward work). Fitschen
also says Nilus fails to call Adelphius a Messalian because Adelphius' name had become so
closely associated with that heresy; but the same could be argued for Alexander. Nilus is
discussing only ascetic work and prayer, and has no reason to discuss other aspects of the
Messalian profile.

under the 428 imperial law that banned all Messalians, Euchites, or Enthusiasts from assembling and praying on Roman soil.[9] More important is the question of historical significance. Because neither Nilus, nor Callinicus, nor Alexander's biographer attributes to him any specific Messalian doctrine, few historians have taken his example seriously for understanding the Messalian controversy. Instead, they have questioned whether the charge was accurately lodged against him, arguing that the authorities were either mistaken in assimilating Alexander with "real" Messalian heretics, or that they simply used the Messalian charge against him as matter of convenience, in order to rid themselves of a monk who was troubling for other reasons.[10]

These are important questions to resolve. At stake, however, is not whether late Roman authorities accurately applied the Messalian label to Alexander (for them, he definitely was a Messalian), but whether we ourselves fully understand the concerns that motivated authorities to lay charges of Messalianism in the first place. Although it is impossible to determine Alexander's own doctrinal beliefs (and, therefore, whether the charge was accurate on doctrinal grounds), our sources do indicate what other features of Alexander's profile prompted his condemnation. These included not only his ascetic regimen, which combined continual prayer with refusal to work (described as *argia* by his detractors) and an aggressive assertion of a right to support from others, but also his charismatic assertion of authority against church and civil leaders. Charges of doctrinal deviance were probably included, but as Nilus suggests, Alexander was identified, prosecuted, and banished as a Messalian as much because of the social issues he raised as because of any doctrinal deviancies.

Interesting in its own right, Alexander's case has broader significance for the Messalian controversy. If (as I will argue) the problems he raised at Constantinople and elsewhere prompted the Messalian deliberations at the synod of 426, and if these problems were of a social as much as a doctrinal nature, then we must reconsider modern assumptions of what prompted ecclesiastical authorities to raise Messalian charges. Though historians have focused almost solely on doctrinal aspects of the Messalian profile, the testimony shows that the social objections to Messalian monks were ever present, perhaps even fundamental. Despite the numbers of "sleepless" monks he led in perpetual prayer around the cities and steppes of the Roman Near East, Alexander's ascetic way of life was not too idiosyncratic. His controversial career simply casts in high relief the problems raised by

9. Arguments and chronology will be discussed below.

10. Thus Stewart (1991): 46 does not consider Alexander's case important for the Messalian controversy: "A taxonomy for heretics and misfits had developed, whatever basis it had in reality, and it was soon to be enforced by law."

other People Who Pray who likewise continued to pursue and advocate the apostolic paradigm for monastic life in the late fourth and early fifth centuries.

Apostle and heretic: the main question posed by Alexander the Sleepless is not which of these labels accurately described this monk, but how the same monk could be viewed by contemporaries as both.

ALEXANDER THE APOSTOLIC MAN

Sometime after Alexander's death a Syrian monk drew on his own or others' recollections to compose his *Life and Conduct of Our Sainted Father Alexander*. This biography, preserved in a single manuscript, provides our only account of any Messalian heretic written by an admirer rather than an opponent. Its author may have even known Alexander.[11] Because the biography is hagiographic, its representation of Alexander's life and motives cannot be assumed to be any more accurate than if it were heresiological literature.[12] Nonetheless, it offers a detailed account of Alexander's activities and movements together with an admirer's appreciation for the ideals that motivated them.

According to his biographer, Alexander came from a well-to-do family of the Greek Aegean islands. His parents sent him to Constantinople to complete his secondary education in grammatical studies, no doubt hoping this would be the first step in a rewarding career for their son. After he finished (he was then probably sixteen or seventeen) Alexander enrolled in the civil service as a clerk or a scribe.[13] Had he continued in that path he might have ended up a very rich technocrat in the imperial bureaucracy. But "in a short time," we are told, Alexander began to look for a more rewarding occupation and to study the Old and New Testaments. Like Antony, Alexander took fire when he read Mt 19:21, "If you wish to be perfect, sell what you have, give to the poor . . . and follow me." Accordingly he gave away all his possessions and embarked on a course of ascetic *xeniteia*, wishing "to estrange himself from his homeland, friends, and relations, and

---

11. Two authors and stages seem to have been originally involved in the composition of the text, and *V.Alex* 29 implies that one of these was a member of Alexander's original troupe: see below, appendix, p. 266. Scholars reckon Alexander's ascetic *floruit* ca. 380–430 based on chronological references and details in the text (*V.Alex* 4, 48 and 52 give fifty total years for his ascetic career). I discuss the chronological possibilities suggested by the text in appendix n. 25, proposing a birth ca. 355–360 with ascetic *floruit* ca. 375–427.

12. The biographer claims to make only a partial (or selective, ἐκ μέρους) account of Alexander's life (sect. 4). Clearly he has left out some controversial incidents (i.e., the troubles Alexander caused Bishop Porphyry in Antioch, mentioned only in sect. 40).

13. *V.Alex* 5.

to commune with his sole Master Christ."[14] He traveled to Syria and joined a coenobitic community governed by the archimandrite Elias.

Alexander's presence in Constantinople around 370 may well have exposed him to ascetic ideals inspired by Eustathius of Sebaste, whose uncompromising emphasis on material renunciations and solidarity with the poor we have already noted.[15] In any case, Alexander left Elias' monastery after only four years. His departure was precipitated, we are told, by his realization that the community did not fully live up to the standards of *aktēmosynē* (freedom from possessions, i.e., voluntary poverty) and *amerimnia* (freedom from care) espoused by the Gospels. Indeed, his biographer dramatizes the confrontation that followed as a turning point in Alexander's ascetic career. "Are the things in the holy Gospel really true?" Alexander demanded of Elias and the other monks.

> After hearing from all that they were true, because they were the utterances of God, he asked in response, "Then why do we not put them into practice?" They all said to him, "No one can possibly observe them." Then [Alexander] was seized by an irrepressible rage in the belief that he had lost all the preceding years and wasted them for nothing. Bidding the brothers all farewell, he struck out, holy Gospel in hand, to follow what is written and to imitate our holy fathers.

Alexander passed the next seven years on the fringe of the Syrian desert, "free of all earthly cares."[16]

Eventually Alexander settled down for twenty years to a regime of perpetual prayer on the eastern banks of the Euphrates, where other monks gathered around him, "four hundred . . . represent[ing] four languages in all: Romans, Greeks, Syrians, and Egyptians."[17] Alexander divided these disciples into fifty-man choirs and marshaled them according to a schedule of prayer that conformed to that of the apostles. Later, aware of Psalm 1:2 ("on the law of the Lord he will meditate day and night"), he scrupulously devised a more ambitious cycle of genuflection, hymn-singing, and doxology, performed in liturgical shifts that never ceased: hence their later epithet, *Akoimētoi*, the "Sleepless Ones."[18]

14. *V.Alex* 6.

15. For the influence of Eustathius at Constantinople in the fourth century, see Gilbert Dagron, "Les moines et la ville: Le monachisme à Constantinople jusqu'au concile de Chalcédoine (451)," *Travaux et Mémoires* 4 (1970): 238–39, 246–53. Pierre-Louis Gatier, "Un moine sur la frontière: Alexandre l'Acémète en Syrie," in *Frontières terrestres, frontières célestes dans l'antiquité,* ed. A. Rousselle (Paris: Presses Universitaires de Perignan, 1995), 441, suggests that Alexander received monastic training under Isaac (*fl.* ca. 370–415), on whom see ch. 5.

16. *V.Alex* 7–8.

17. *V.Alex* 26–27.

18. *V.Alex* 26–27. For Alexander's liturgical practices, see Iohannis Fountoules, *Hē Eikositetraōros Akoimētos Doxologia* (Athens: Papademetriou, 1963), 49–52.

Having perfected this regimen, Alexander selected seventy disciples ("zealots of the faith, capable of proclaiming God's word to the gentiles") to accompany him on an apostolic expedition down the Euphrates and back, continuously singing psalms as they traveled "through night and day."[19] After a period of faith-testing in the desert, Alexander turned to the fortress-settlements along the Roman-Persian border: "and as he passed along the entire stretch of frontier he strengthened all in their faith."[20] After being barred from the desert city of Palmyra, they turned north to Antioch.

Here they received a taste of the troubles they would experience at Constantinople. When Theodotus, bishop of Antioch (ca. 420/21–428/29),

> learned that the blessed Alexander had entered the city with a multitude of monks ceaselessly singing psalms, he cruelly ordered that they be driven out with blows and violent assaults. Those who took this as license abused the slaves of God without pity and chased them out.[21]

Alexander nonetheless managed to sneak back at night and settled his company down in an ancient bathhouse. He is said to have become a "tutor and teacher of all" through both his preaching and his care for the city's poor.[22] Eventually Theodotus and his clergy pressed the resident military commander (the highest imperial presence) to banish Alexander from the city permanently. This sent him eastward and confined him to the city of Chalcis; but here he eluded his guards and slipped back on the road again, stopping at the monasteries along the way to test their ascetic standards.

Finally Alexander arrived at Constantinople after nearly fifty years' absence. With twenty-four monks he settled on the old acropolis, near the church of St. Menas, a martyr shrine built in a former temple of Poseidon overlooking the city's imperial center and episcopal complex. Soon three hundred monks, Romans, Greeks, and Syrians, had abandoned their monasteries to join his ranks.[23] These Alexander marshaled into more sleepless

---

19. *V.Alex* 31.

20. *V.Alex* 33; ed. de Stroop, p. 684: διελθὼν διὰ παντὸς τοῦ λιμίτου πάντας ἐστήριξεν ἐν τῇ πίστει.

21. *V.Alex* 38. Theodotus held the see of Antioch ca. 420/421–428/429 (at least from 421–428): see Robert Devreesse, *Le patriarcat d'Antioche, depuis la paix de l'Église jusqu'à la conquête arabe* (Paris: Gabalda, 1945), 110 n. 4, 117.

22. *V.Alex* 38 and 39; ed. de Stroop, p. 689: παιδαγωγὸς πάντων καὶ διδάσκαλος.

23. *V.Alex* 43; ed. de Stroop, p. 692: παραμείναντος αὐτοῦ πλησίον τοῦ οἴκου τοῦ ἁγίου μάρτυρος Μηνᾶ. For the location of St. Menas, see Gilbert Dagron, *Naissance d'une capitale: Constantinople et ses institutions de 330 à 451* (Paris: Presses Universitaires de France, 1974), 376, 395 and Raymond Janin, *La géographie ecclésiastique de l'empire byzantin* 1.3: *Les églises et les monastères* (Paris: Institut Français d'Études Byzantines, 1953), 345–47.

choruses that carried on night and day as at Antioch, until authorities took action.

Besides offering this description of Alexander's career, the biographer emphasizes certain principles that he believed had guided him. Foremost was his concern for *akribeia* (strict, scrupulous ascetic discipline). The church historian Sozomen uses the same term to describe Antony's asceticism as well as the open-air "philosophy" he supposed the monk Aones had introduced to Syria. For Alexander, *akribeia* meant truly living by the letter of the Scriptures.[24] It was concern for *akribeia,* we are told, that made him question whether his "life was consonant with the Scriptures" while living in Elias' community. Later in the desert he observed "with *akribeia* the things written in the God-inspired Scriptures" and strove "that not a single line of God's commandments should escape him, so that he might become indeed an imitator of all the great men on record."[25]

The lines that apparently taxed him most in this regard were Mt 6:34 ("care not for tomorrow") and Mk 9:22 ("all things are possible for one who believes"). For Alexander, these meant living in absolute poverty. Thus his biographer repeatedly joins the ideal of freedom from care with that of freedom from possessions as the dominant leitmotivs of the hagiography.[26] Although Alexander could not bear to see "any" of God's commandments corrupted,[27] he chose to observe these particular ideals to the fullest. It was the failure of Elias and his monks to fulfill these ideals with *akribeia* that caused Alexander to storm off on his own.[28] He is said to have made sure that the monks who gathered round him maintained strict evangelic standards of poverty:

> Although he assumed oversight of so many brothers, he did not at all worry about any provisions for their needs. Rather, in accordance with the holy Gospel, they kept only what sufficed for the day, and all the rest he gave to the destitute poor. They wore only a single tunic and in all these things took cheer from the words of God and nourished themselves on their hope for things to come.[29]

24. Alexander's emphasis on "going by the book" is represented in the *V.Alex* by his traveling with only the Scriptures in hand (sect. 8, 32, 44). Callinicus, *V.Hypatii* 41.13 describes Alexander and his monks each taking with them a Bible from Hypatius' monastery as a εὐλογίαν εἰς τὴν ὁδόν.

25. *V.Alex* 28; ed. de Stroop, p. 678: προσεῖχεν ... Ἀλέξανδρος ἀκριβῶς τοῖς γεγραμμένοις ἐν ταῖς γραφαῖς ... ὅπως μὴ ἐκ τῶν ἐντολῶν τοῦ θεοῦ μία κεραία παρέλθῃ αὐτόν. See also *V.Alex* 4, 8, 44.

26. See sect. 7, 8, 27, 31, 35, 36, 44, 45, 52.

27. *V.Alex* 8.

28. *V.Alex* 7; ed. de Stroop, p. 662: προσεῖχε δὲ ἀκριβῶς εἰ συμ[π]νεῖ ὁ βίος ταῖς θείαις γραφαῖς· δὲ οὐχ εὕρισκε.... μὴ ἔχειν τὴν ἀκτημοσύνην καὶ ἀμεριμνίαν τοῦ ἁγίου εὐαγγελίου, ἐπειδὴ περὶ τοῦ προισταμένου ἐστὶν προβλέπειν καὶ σπουδάζειν περὶ ἑκάστης χρείας τῶν ἀδελφῶν.

29. *V.Alex* 27; ed. de Stroop, p. 678: τοσούτων ἀδελφῶν πρόνοιαν ποιούμενος, οὐδενὸς τῶν

Even when Alexander and his disciples entered the desert, they reportedly carried "nothing at all for provisions except the parchments on which they kept the holy Scriptures," and subsisted on nuts (causing some to rebel: "did you lead us out to this desert to kill us with hunger?").[30] Alexander viewed such hardship as a necessary trial of faith: "better to trust in God," he would say, "than to trust in men."[31] His refusal to compromise apostolic standards in regard to material renunciations is later illustrated by his inspection of a monastery he passed along the road. To his astonishment, it conformed to his own ascetic standards in all but one respect: it maintained a garden. This Alexander censured as a "distraction," on the grounds that it was "a possible impediment to perfect virtue." According to the biographer, Alexander's insistence on utter material renunciations caused the monks of this monastery to recognize him as "Alexander, the one who cast light in regions of the East." The biographer thus considered Alexander's most distinguishing feature to be not so much his sleepless regimen of prayer as his uncompromising standard of ascetic poverty.[32]

This emphasis on poverty and evangelic fervor renders Alexander a fifth-century avatar of the apostle Thomas. In fact, the biographer presents Alexander as nothing less than an "apostolic man" who "pursued a course unswerving like the sun in order to proclaim . . . the 'Sun of Righteousness.'"[33] We are told that his determination to fulfill the commandments was not directed merely towards his own salvation; he aimed to "deliver the whole world to his Master Christ as well."[34] This apostolic objective is said to have guided Alexander's selection and training of seventy disciples for the road, forming (as Jesus did in Lk 10) an elite ascetic corps that was "capable of edifying others."[35]

ἐπιτηδείων πρὸς τὰς χρείας ἐφρόντιζεν, ἀλλὰ κατὰ τὸ ἅγιον εὐαγγέλιον τὸ τῆς ἡμέρας μόνον καὶ πᾶν τὸ περισσεῦον τοῖς πτωχοῖς διεδίδοτο. ἦσαν δὲ καὶ μονοχίτωνες, καὶ ἐν τούτοις πᾶσιν, ηὐφραίνοντο ἐπὶ τοῖς λόγοις τοῦ θεοῦ, τρεφόμενοι τῇ τῶν μελλόντων ἐλπίδι.

30. *V.Alex* 32; cf. 44. In sect. 33 Roman soldiers provide relief; in sect. 35, camel-drivers.

31. *V.Alex* 32 and 35; ed. de Stroop, pp. 683, 686.

32. *V.Alex* 42; ed. de Stroop, p. 691: τὸν μακάριον θεασάμενοι, ἐμπόνως ἐπερωτῶντα ἕκαστα καὶ αἰτιασάμενον τοῦ κήπου τὸν περιπασμὸν ὡς δυνάμενον τῇ τελείᾳ ἀρετῇ ἐμπόδιον γενέσθαι . . . ἔγνωσαν ἀληθῶς ὅτι οὗτός ἐστιν . . . Ἀλέξανδρος ὁ ἐν τοῖς ἀνατολικοῖς μέρεσι διαλάμψας. Interestingly, the biographer never describes Alexander's appearance—only his uncompromising practices and attitude characterize him and his holiness. For Alexander's emphasis on poverty, see esp. *V.Alex* 18–19 and Vööbus (1960b): 151–53.

33. A characterization introduced in the opening sentence of *V.Alex* 1; ed. de Stroop, p. 658: Ἀλέξανδρος, ἀποστολικὸς ἀνὴρ γενόμενος. See also sect.2 and 9, with Vööbus (1960b): 193–95.

34. *V.Alex* 4; ed. de Stroop, p. 660: οὐ περὶ τῆς ἰδίας σωτηρίας ἐφρόντισε μόνον, ἀλλὰ καὶ τὴν οἰκουμένην ὅλην προσενέγκαι τῷ δεσπότῃ Χριστῷ ἔσπευδεν. The biographer explains Alexander's apostolic aspirations by reference to his determination to fulfill the "commandments."

35. *V.Alex* 25 and 31.

There is no reason to doubt that this was so. In the early fifth century much of the area in which Alexander moved—southeast of the highway between Antioch and Beroea (modern Aleppo)—was still unconverted. Its villages and hilltop temples offered many opportunities for apostolic zealots with time on their hands.[36] Alexander is said even to have considered leading his monks as far as Egypt "to instruct unbelievers there."[37] But his apostolic ambitions seem to have been mostly directed towards strengthening the faith of isolated Christian communities on the desert steppes of Syria, especially along the Mesopotamian frontier.

According to his biographer, Alexander's manifest poverty and *akribeia* served as credentials along the way, securing his reception as a legitimate Christian teacher and leader. At Constantinople, for example,

> When the urban masses observed . . . their perpetual hymn-singing, their absolute poverty, and the visible and quite wondrous performance of their prodigious mysteries, they came to Alexander with devotion as a true benefactor and teacher and were instructed by him about hope and the life to come. . . . When [the people] saw their voluntary poverty, how great it was, and their *akribeia*, and that they possessed nothing more than the parchments on which they kept the holy Scriptures . . . they were astounded, and glorified God for revealing His prodigious mysteries even in those regions.[38]

Similarly, when the people of Antioch "saw and heard his marvelous deeds," they identified Alexander as "one of the prophets." Like the apostle Thomas, Alexander is said to have been accused of sorcery, but in his case the accusation was made by abandoned clergy rather than abandoned husbands.[39]

Such, at any rate, is the biographer's account of Alexander's ideals and popularity. Alexander may well have formed his initial notions about what constituted proper ascetic conduct from early exposure to Eustathian monastic ideals.[40] He is best understood, however, within the Syro-

36. See Liebeschuetz (1979): 18; for a survey of apostolic activities by monks in this area, including Alexander, see Escolan (1999): 216–17, 228–65.

37. *V.Alex* 31.

38. *V.Alex* 44; ed. de Stroop, pp. 692–93: Θεωροῦντες δὲ οἱ ὄχλοι τῆς πόλεως . . . τὴν ἀκατάπαυστον ὑμνολογίαν, καὶ τὴν τελείαν ἀκτημοσύνην . . . ἀληθῶς ὡς πρὸς εὐεργέτην καὶ διδάσκολον οὕτως προθύμως ἤρχοντο καὶ ἐδιδάσκοντο παρ᾽ αὐτοῦ. . . . μάλιστα δὲ ὁρῶντες τὴν τηλικαύτην αὐτῶν ἀκτημοσύνην καὶ ἀκρίβεια . . . ἐκπληττόμενοι. . . .

39. *V.Alex* 38 and 40; ed. de Stroop, pp. 688–89. Chrysostom notes complaints that monks had "bewitched" young men with songs in fourth-century Antioch: *Adversus oppugnatores vitae monasticae* 2.2 (PG 47.334). For accusations of sorcery and tensions between institutional and charismatic authority, see Peter Brown, "Sorcery, Demons, and the Rise of Christianity: From Late Antiquity into the Middle Ages," in *Religion and Society in the Age of Saint Augustine* (London: Faber and Faber, 1972), 119–47.

40. See above, n. 15; but I do not wish to suggest strong distinctions between Eustathian ideals and those of Syro-Mesopotamian milieu represented by the *Book of Steps*.

Mesopotamian context in which he spent most of his career. After deliberately estranging himself from his Greek homeland, Alexander had gone native in the most rigorous ascetic traditions of that milieu. Similar regimens of perpetual prayer and psalm-singing were being devised in the same period in monasteries along the Euphrates and at the church of Seleucia-Ctesiphon in Persia. Such monks were called *Shāhrē* (Vigilant Ones) because they sang hymns and doxologies all night and day.[41] But the mid-fourth-century Syriac *Book of Steps* provides the most striking parallels for Alexander's way of life, in commanding that the ascetic Perfect bind themselves to God at all times, "whether you are standing or sitting . . . walking or singing in the Holy Spirit."[42] Alexander and the *Book of Steps* agreed that proper asceticism must literally conform to the apostolic precepts uttered by Jesus in the Gospels. Both were also concerned that monks of their day were being held back from perfection through specious justifications for "righteous labor," that is, for practicing the manual labors that properly occupied the Upright. According to the *Book of Steps,* such justifications came from "the Evil One," who sought to corrupt the Perfect by "promising under the guise of fine [actions] these things which our Lord had commanded only to the Upright ones."

> Deluding the Perfect one, [the Evil One] says the following: "It is virtuous that you should acquire a little [wealth] through Uprightness, sufficient for your own comfort and for whoever comes to you. Plant a little crop and make for yourself a vegetable garden that will be for the healthy and the sick." Under the pretext of the comfort of the afflicted [the Evil One] schemes to make [the Perfect one] fall from that major commandment which [Jesus] directs to the Perfect, "Do not be anxious even about yourself" [Mt 6:25], and by that [other] commandment, "Think about what is above and not of what is on the earth" [Col 3:2].[43]

This author would have thoroughly approved Alexander's censure of monastic garden work as an impediment to perfect virtue. Indeed, Alexander's commitment to absolute poverty, his ceaseless prayer and doxologies,[44] his apostolic preaching, and, as we shall soon discuss more fully, his dependence on others for support would have easily made him pass for one of the ascetic Perfect in the *Book of Steps.*

Thus, within the Syro-Mesopotamian milieu, Alexander's way of life

---

41. See Fountoules (1963): 47–48.

42. *LG* 27.5 (PS 3.777–80).

43. *LG* 25.5 (PS 3.741–44).

44. Alexander's habit of saying Lk 2:14 before hitting the road (e.g., *V.Alex* 36) recalls the brief *LG* doxologies discussed by Kowalski (1989a): 276–78.

would not have appeared too idiosyncratic. His troubles arose when he so forcefully brought back home what he had learned.

ALEXANDER THE HERETIC

The blessed one feared neither imperial power, nor the threats of magistrates, nor the accusations of the populace, nor the wicked recommendations of bishops. . . . Instead he reduced all his detractors to shame through his right way of life and perfect faith.[45]

Callinicus' testimony confirms this summation of Alexander's obstinacy. Here and elsewhere, Alexander's biographer is, in fact, remarkably candid about the hostility Alexander and his monks encountered during their wanderings and portrays it to their credit. His narrative becomes noticeably less candid, however, once it begins to describe Alexander's final troubles in Constantinople. While acknowledging that Alexander was persecuted and banished under a charge of heresy, the biographer cloaks events in an allegorical fog by presenting Satan as Alexander's main adversary, making it difficult to reconstruct what happened to him there.[46] However, Alexander's presence in (and expulsion from) Constantinople almost certainly fell in the late 420s, while Theodotus was still bishop of Antioch and before Nestorius had been appointed bishop of Constantinople (in 428).[47] It quite possibly coincided with the episcopal synod of 426, whose anti-Messalian proceedings were noted in the last chapter. Why this ceremonial gathering of bishops, assembled for the inauguration of Sisinnius as bishop of Constantinople, felt the (rather incongruous) need to address Messalian matters at all is a question that has never been addressed. Did Alexander give them the reason?

Alexander's biographer divides the events into two stages. First came Alexander's trial before a tribunal arranged by *eparchikoi*, deputy magistrates working for the city's urban prefect, "The appointed jurists, not mak-

45. *V.Alex* 3; ed. de Stroop, p. 659: Ὁ δὲ μακάριος οὐκ ἐξουσίαν βασιλικὴν ἐφοβήθη, οὐκ ἀπειλὴν ἀρχόντων, οὐ δήμου ψόγον, οὐκ ἐπισκόπων πονηρὰς παραινέσεις.

46. The biographer's reluctance to discuss events in Constantinople is underscored by his failure ever to mention that Alexander had entered the city. Whereas he names other cities where Alexander encountered trouble (Palmyra, Antioch, Chalcis), only his allusion to the St. Menas shrine in *V.Alex* 43 indicates that Alexander is in Constantinople.

47. Alexander's arrival in Constantinople followed (after an interlude of unknown length, but apparently brief) his presence at Antioch while Theodotus was bishop there ca. 420/21–29: see below, appendix n. 25. This allows the possibility that Alexander arrived and was tried in Constantinople ca. 428, but the lack of any reference to Nestorius in either the biography or Callinicus' *V.Hypatii*, or of any evidence that Alexander was banished from Roman soil, indicate that he was banished before 428, i.e., before Nestorius and *CTh* 16.5.65 first appeared.

ing a righteous decision, passed sentence against the great judge. This they did so that, once released, [Alexander] would be torn to shreds by the people and the champions of the devil." Nevertheless, Alexander held out, for "terror fell upon" his opponents and "their resolve broke down."[48] Then further actions were taken to banish and isolate him:

> Mindful how countries and cities were often betrayed by their own people, the enemy advanced against the blessed one in this way, enlisting as allies men of his own kind to help take him away. They seized the blessed Alexander together with his holy brothers, threw chains around them and inflicted on them a cruel beating. Then for a few days their incessant hymn-singing was interrupted, and sorrow truly rose among the brothers. . . . For those who had previously been these brothers' shepherds were each ordered to take back his own.[49]

These two successive actions are probably related to the two successive mobs of Callinicus' account, one sent (it seems) by the bishop of Constantinople, the other by the bishop of Chalcedon. According to Callinicus, the former bishop was acting by order of the magistrates who had condemned and banished Alexander.[50]

Some have thought that the involvement of a civil tribunal in Alexander's case is conclusive evidence that Alexander was exiled under the law of 428 that banned "Messalians, Euchites or Enthusiasts" from praying or assembling on Roman soil. From this it has also been reasoned that civil magistrates were mainly responsible for the legal proceedings and that Alexander was not "really" a Messalian, only a victim of the law applied through assimilation.[51] However, the fact that civilian proceedings were

---

48. *V.Alex* 49; ed. de Stroop, p. 698: οἱ οὖν καταστάντες δικασταί, τὴν δικαίαν κρίσιν μὴ καταλαβόντες, ἐπὶ τὸν μέγαν κριτὴν ἐδικαίωσαν. τοῦτο δὲ ἐποίησαν ὥστε ἀπολυθέντα σπαραχθῆναι αὐτὸν ὑπὸ τῶν δήμου. . . . θάμβος . . . κυρίου ἐπέπεσεν ἐπ' αὐτοὺς καὶ ἡ βουλὴ αὐτῶν διεσκεδάσθη.

49. *V.Alex* 50.

50. Callinicus, *V.Hypatii* 41.5; ed. Bartelink, p. 242: καὶ ἀποστέλλει ὁ ἐπίσκοπος ὄχλους διὰ τὸ κέλευσμα τῶν ἀρχόντων, ἵνα διώξωσιν αὐτοὺς ἐκεῖθεν. Presumably the two accounts describe the same incidents differently. Eugen Wölfe, "Der Abt Hypatios von Ruphinianai und der Akoimete Alexander," *BZ* 79 (1986): 304, notes that Callinicus compresses events in Alexander's life in Constantinople. The return of Alexander's followers to their monasteries (*V.Alex* 50) occurred before or after Alexander took refuge in Hypatius' monastery; if before, it might account for the discrepancy between the 300 monks attributed to Alexander in *V.Alex* 43 and the 100 Callinicus attributed to him in *V.Hypatii* 41.1.

51. So Jean-Marie Baguenard, *Les moines acémètes: Vies des saint Alexandre, Marcel, et Jean Calybite* (Bégrolles-en-Mauges: Abbaye de Bellefontaine, 1988), 45–46 and Dagron (1970): 235 n. 38, both apparently following Venance Grumel, *Les regestes des actes du Patriarcat de Constantinople* 1.1 (Constantinople: Socii Assumptionistae Chalcedonenses, 1932), 24: "It seems probable that [Alexander's condemnation and banishment as a "Messalian"] occurred after the Theodosian law [was issued, i.e., after 428] because Alexander was impeached before

brought against Alexander does not diminish the likelihood that he was tried and banished as a Messalian heretic in 426. First, it is unnecessary to assume that Alexander could only have been exiled as a Messalian heretic under the law of 428. Already by 425 the emperor had issued a law that "banished from the very sight of the cities" anyone determined to be outside the faith.[52] That law sufficiently accounts for Alexander's banishment from Constantinople (and Chalcedon) by a civil tribunal, and for his subsequent relocation to the wilds of Gomon, at the mouth of the Bosphorus. Second, the involvement of a civil tribunal in his punishment should be no surprise. Civil magistrates had to be involved in the sentencing of a Roman citizen to exile, whatever the charge. It was for this reason that Theodotus and his clergy had to petition the Roman military commander to banish Alexander from Antioch. This was the highest imperial authority at Antioch; he quickly passed the sentence on Alexander "as a favor" to Theodotus, and thereby gave the bishop legal sanction to drive Alexander out.[53]

A similar scenario played out at Constantinople. The biographer makes clear that the civilian magistrates at Constantinople took action only after they had received notice from elsewhere that Alexander was a heretic.[54] No doubt this identification came from church leaders, who, having already identified Alexander as a heretic, turned to civil officials for the legal action necessary to stop him from "corrupting God's church."

---

civil judges." Grumel also speculates that Alexander might have first been indicted by the synod of 426.

52. *CTh* 16.5.64; ed. Mommsen-Meyer, p. 878: Manichaeos haereticos sive schismaticos omnemque sectam catholicis inimicam ab ipso aspectu urbium diversarum exterminari praecipimus (issued at Aquileia, August 6, 425). This law makes the exile of heretics universally applicable, modifying *CTh* 16.5.62 issued for Rome alone. Had Alexander been sentenced under the 428 law, he should have been banished beyond imperial borders, certainly beyond Gomon (*CTh* 16.5.65, 2). Again, the best indication that Alexander was not tried ca. 428–430 under *CTh* 16.5.65 is the failure of either Callinicus or the *V.Alex* to mention the notorious Nestorius under whom that law was issued. Nestorius' involvement would have provided an easy opportunity to portray Alexander (or his defender Hypatius) as a defiant martyr; it would also have enabled the Akoimēte monks to defend themselves from later accusations of Nestorian sympathies. See appendix, n. 173.

53. *V.Alex* 43; cf. *CTh* 16.5.9 (issued in 382). Jill Harries, *Law and Empire in Late Antiquity* (Cambridge: Cambridge University Press, 1999), 210 n. 69, says that heresy could be handled as an internal disciplinary matter, citing Augustine's statement in *Ep.* 236 that he had a Manichaean expelled from the city. But his phrase, *eum cohercitum pellendum de civitate curavi*, does not rule out the involvement of imperial officials. Of course, a bishop might employ his own henchmen (e.g., *parabalani, lectarii, decani*) to deal with opponents without involving the civil machinery: this is how Theodotus first approached Alexander, and perhaps how Flavian dealt with Adelphius.

54. *V.Alex* 48 (PO 6.697): τότε ἀναφέρεται τοῖς ἐπάρχοις ὅτι ὁ μοναχὸς Ἀλέξανδρος αἱρετικός ἐστιν καὶ βούλεται λυμᾶναι τὴν ἐκκλησίαν τοῦ θεοῦ.

That neither Alexander's biographer nor Callinicus says anything about this ecclesiastical background to Alexander's civil trial is not surprising: neither would have wanted to suggest that either Alexander or Hypatius was truly involved either with heresy or heretics.[55] Indeed, the fact that Nilus received news in Ancyra of Alexander's activities and coupled him with the Messalian heresiarch Adelphius, indicates that Alexander's case was not just routine, but had quickly become something of a Messalian cause célèbre. The only known proceedings against Messalians in the 420s took place at Constantinople during the synod of 426. We actually know little about its circumstances.[56] Nothing directly links Alexander to it or otherwise explains why the synod took up Messalianism at this time. Nothing, that is, except for the presence and guiding role of Theodotus of Antioch, Alexander's main episcopal opponent before his move to Constantinople.

This connection has never been adequately stressed.[57] As one of Sisinnius' most senior colleagues, Theodotus would have attended his inaugural synod as a matter of course. But the evidence specifically indicates that he also assumed leadership of its Messalian deliberations. Besides coauthoring the letter that the synod sent afterwards to Pamphylia,[58] Theodotus is also said to have prepared certain *acta (prepragmata)* that could be used against later Messalian groups. In fact, Timothy of Constantinople names him as one of five major church authorities (beside Bishops Flavian of Antioch, Amphilochius of Iconium, Letoïus of Melitene, and Cyril of Alexandria) who combated Messalian heretics in the late fourth and early fifth centuries.[59] The other four are all known to have acted in response to activities

55. Baguenard (1988): 51 suggests Hypatius' involvement with Alexander guarantees the latter's orthodoxy, while Wölfe (1986): 306–7 argues Pulcheria would not have intervened for a heretic. Both scholars may be assuming too much sympathy between Hypatius, Pulcheria, and the civic or episcopal authorities in either Constantinople or Chalcedon. For Pulcheria's strained relations with the court at this time, see Holum (1982): 131–33.

56. As noted in ch. 3, p. 93, the only sure evidence we have from this synod is the short excerpt from a letter it sent to Pamphylian bishops (and perhaps to others). Its contents reveal only that one member of the synod, a Pamphylian bishop named Neon, was concerned that some clerics had been harboring Messalian heretics. See Stewart (1991): 44 n. 72.

57. Noted by Lenain de Tillemont, *Mémoires pour servir à l'histoire ecclésiastique des six premiers siècles*, vol. 12 (Venice, 1732), 497 and Jules Pargoire, "Les débuts du monachisme à Constantinople," *Revue des questions historiques* n.s. 21 (1899a): 134. Both believe Alexander was the cause and subject of the synod of 426.

58. Theodotus' name is coupled with Sisinnius' without mention of other senior colleagues in Photius, *Bibliotheca* 52; ed. Henry, p. 38: ἔγραψε δὲ καὶ Σισίννιος ὁ Κωνσταντινουπόλεως καὶ Θεόδοτος ὁ Ἀντιοχείας κοινὴν ἐπιστολὴν . . . ἧς ἡ ἐπιγραφή· "Τοῖς . . . ἐν Παμφυλίᾳ ἐπισκόποις. Σισίννιος καὶ Θεόδοτος καὶ πᾶσα ἡ ἁγία σύνοδος ἡ κατὰ θεοῦ χάριν συγκροτηθεῖσα ἐν τῇ μεγαλοπόλει Κωνσταντινουπόλει τῆς χειροτονίας ἕνεκα τοῦ θεοφιλεστάτου καὶ ἁγιωτάτου ἐπισκόπου Σισιν- νίου. . . ."

59. Timothy of Constantinople, *DRH* prol. (PG 86.48A): Ἠγωνήσαντο δὲ ἐγγράφως κατὰ τῆς πολυωνύμου ταύτης αἱρέσεως . . . οἵτινες καὶ πεπραγμένα συνεστήσαντο κατὰ τῆς τοιαύτης

either in or near their episcopal territories. As for Theodotus, the only record of his experience with anyone implicated in Messalianism at Antioch comes from Alexander's biography, which so vividly describes Theodotus' early confrontations with Alexander before he moved to Constantinople.

Even more intriguing for the connection between Theodotus, Alexander, and the synod of 426 is Timothy's notice that among the various groups identified as Messalian was one that was also known as the *Choreutai* (People of the Choir). This is the only Messalian group label mentioned by Timothy that historians have not yet identified with an otherwise known ascetic circle (e.g., the "Adelphians," the "Eustathians").[60] *Choreutai* is, however, a singularly apposite label for describing Alexander's highly organized company of psalm-singing monks (his *choroi*, as Alexander's biographer three times calls them).[61] Timothy probably found it in patriarchal records, which would have given more information about Theodotus and the synod of 426 than either he or Photius, the ninth-century epitomizer of those records, have preserved for us.

This confluence of evidence leads to the conclusion that Alexander and his choirs of psalm-singing monks were in fact subjects of the anti-Messalian deliberations at the synod of 426. Indeed, it was probably their activities that provoked those deliberations in the first place. Alexander had already settled in Constantinople and "churned it up" before Theodotus arrived for Sisinnius' ordination that year. Theodotus' prior experiences with Alexander at Antioch qualified him to direct (and perhaps inspired him to initiate) this peculiar part of the inaugural proceedings at Constantinople. While noting the name *Choreutai* in their records, Theodotus and his fellow bishops formally identified and condemned Alexander and his *choroi* as Messalians according to the established heretical taxonomy.[62] They then

---

πολυκεφάλου τε καὶ πολυωνύμου . . . αἱρέσεως. For Timothy's prologue, see Stewart (1991): 55 and Fitschen (1998): 69, 76. The activities of bishops Flavian, Amphilochius, Letoïus, and Cyril have already been noted: see ch. 3, pp. 90–91, 94n. 46. Sisinnius' name is absent from Timothy's list, which either attests Theodotus' greater prominence in the anti-Messalian proceedings in 426 or means that Theodotus drew up other (lost) *acta* at a different time.

60. Timothy of Constantinople, *DRH* prol. (PG 86.45D–48A): Μαρκιανισταὶ καὶ Μεσσαλιανοὶ καὶ Εὐχῖται καὶ Ἐνθουσιασταὶ καὶ Χορευταὶ καὶ Λαμπετιανοὶ καὶ Ἀδελφιανοὶ καὶ Εὐσταθιανοί· οὕτως προσαγορευόμενοι, διὰ τὸ πολυώνυμον εἶναι τὴν αἵρεσιν. Timothy does not list these groups chronologically; the others derive from fourth-century figures (Adelphius and Eustathius, discussed in ch. 3) or from figures later in the fifth (Lampetius) and sixth (Marcian). See Fitschen (1998): 273–83; at 282 he suggests that *Choreutai* was simply a generic label, like *Enthusiastai*.

61. The biographer uses χοροί with special reference to psalm-singing, *V.Alex* 26, 27, 43. This use of the plural to describe an ascetic group is not typical, though χορός (singular) was often used for a group of disciples in the fourth and fifth centuries (e.g., as Nilus describes Jesus' χορὸν τῶν ἀποστόλων in *De vol. paup.* 21 [PG 79.996C]; full text above, n. 7).

62. The same group could go by several titles in the records: Adelphius' "Spiritual Ones"

notified the city's civil authorities to set the state's legal machinery rolling.[63] Once the civil tribunal had passed sentence, Sisinnius was legally sanctioned to drive Alexander across the Bosphorus and break up his band. In the meantime, the synodal bishops notified their Pamphylian colleagues, involved in Messalian proceedings since the synod at Side in the late fourth century, of their recent findings and concerns.[64]

Why did this particular Messalian and his *Choreutai* cause such a stir? While we cannot assess the accuracy of the Messalian charge against Alexander on doctrinal grounds,[65] his biographer offers a glimpse of how Alexander had troubled Theodotus and his clergy before his arrival in Constantinople, and Callinicus and Nilus can guide us from there. All three emphasize the behavioral aspects of Alexander's Messalian profile: clearly he and his *Choreutai* raised as much alarm on their travels as they did psalms, doxologies, and prayers.

Alexander's troupe combined the charismatic dynamism of a mobile house of prayer with the potential menace of any well-organized, hundred-man gang. It would have been impossible to ignore their appearance on the urban scene as they rotated in choral shifts, swaying with their multiple prostrations and singing of psalms. Though punctuated with doxologies in praise of God and peace on earth, many of the psalms they sang would have rung out with imprecations against God's enemies, threatening violence.[66] Already in the 380s the approach of monks ominously chanting

---

are dubbed "Adelphians" as well as "Messalians." Fitschen (1998): 41, 52 thinks the label "Enthusiasts" gained currency before 428, but we do not know with what group it was first associated.

63. The biographer's vague reference to Alexander's defiance of ἐπισκόπων πονηρὰς παραινέσεις (*V.Alex* 3) may allude to this synod.

64. The synod's dispatch to the bishops of Pamphylia is best explained by the fact that bishops of that province had been dealing with Messalians under Sisinnius' predecessor, Bishop Atticus, and were the last to host a synod on that problem. Wölfe (1986): 308–9 and Gribomont (1972): 619, 625 hypothesize that Alexander arrived at Constantinople with a Messalian *Asceticon* (i.e., Ps.-Macarian writings). We are informed that Alexander was in the habit of carrying the Scriptures with him on his travels—perhaps he carried other writings as well. However, all we know for sure is that he arrived at Constantinople with monks he picked up at a monastery somewhere in western Asia Minor: see *V.Alex* 42–43 and below, appendix n. 153.

65. Some have sought to exonerate Alexander of Messalian charges by reference to the *V.Alex*, which does not ascribe to him any specific doctrines that fit the profile; but inclusion of controversial doctrinal points would have been unlikely in the *vita*. It is tempting to associate the allegations in Timothy of Constantinople's list (see ch. 3) with the synod of 426 and Alexander, but the source-criticism in Fitschen (1998): 60–88 reveals what was deemed Messalian in 426 and earlier synods, not what was deemed Messalian at the 426 synod alone.

66. Monks considered psalms special weapons against demons because of the heavy curses they directed against God's enemies: see below, appendix n. 41; in *V.Alex* 50 Satan realizes Alexander's psalms are directed against him. Michael Gaddis, *There Is No Crime for Those Who*

had set an imperial governor running from his judicial bench at Antioch.[67] Not surprisingly, when Bishop Theodotus first heard that Alexander had entered the city "with a multitude of monks ceaselessly singing psalms," he tried to secure his own position by dispatching pallbearers from his church's staff to greet them "with blows and violent assaults."[68]

As it turned out, the worst that he and other Antiochenes had to suffer from Alexander's presence was acute embarrassment. That, however, was enough. The biographer emphasizes how Alexander received "honor and glory" in the city at the expense of Theodotus and his clergy, as congregations "quit the church and devoted themselves" to Alexander, "listening to his wondrous teachings." Regarding him as "one of the prophets," they listened to him "gladly" and were "ready to do what he commanded."[69] The biographer attributes Alexander's popularity not only to his "marvelous deeds" and teachings but also to his unflagging *parrhēsia*. No wonder Theodotus and his colleagues were dismayed: Alexander evidently wielded this bold speech on behalf of the poor without restraint.[70] "Carried by zeal" he is said to have directed it against wealthy citizens, whom he admonished to finance a hospice.[71] But his tongue evidently fell most sharply on Theodotus and the resident military commander. Both he reproached "on many matters he felt they had neglected."[72] The antipathies Alexander raised at Antioch are most fully conveyed in a tirade ascribed to a subdeacon named Malchus:

> My authority in the courts was the one source of revenue I had, and the monk Alexander has deprived me of this. Not only that, but he has also stripped the Church of its glory: our sudden discovery of this "tutor" has made us a laughingstock to all. This is the conjurer who made the city rebel in our blessed father Porphyry's day and caused him countless evils. . . . This is the one who terrifies bishops and magistrates, perhaps even demons. Everywhere it is the same single-minded one. . . . Now he has come here, doing the same

---

Have Christ: Religious Violence in the Christian Roman Empire (Ph.D. diss., Princeton University, 1999), 249, notes that chanting monks "stood out in popular imagination as symbols of violence" associated with Christian zeal.

67. Libanius, *Or.* 45.26, describing Tisamenus' actions ca. 386; cf. *Or.* 30.11. Libanius says that monks usually came into Antioch in the summer (ed. Norman, p. 184: ὃ ποιεῖν τοῦ θέρους εἰώθασιν), when Epiphanius also found "Messalians" sleeping in city streets: see *Panarion* 80.3.4.

68. *V.Alex* 38.

69. *V.Alex* 38–39; ed. de Stroop, p. 688.

70. *V.Alex* 39; ed. de Stroop, p. 688: παρρησίαν πολλὴν δὲ κτημένος. The biographer uses the word παρρησία three times to explain Alexander's behavior in Antioch (*V.Alex* 38–39), and once in Constantinople (*V.Alex* 44).

71. *V.Alex* 39; sect. 34 describes how Alexander angered the rich in a fortress town by forcing them to burn debt records.

72. *V.Alex* 39; ed. de Stroop, pp. 688–89.

things. If he remains in this city, you can be sure that it will be uninhabitable for us, since we have already become a disgrace to all.[73]

The biographer tells us nothing more about Alexander's role in this earlier "rebellion" against Porphyry, bishop of Antioch circa 404–414. Evidently Alexander already had a record of stirring the city's populace against their church leaders.[74] The biographer claims that Theodotus and his clergy were prevented from driving Alexander out "because of the people's exertions on his behalf."[75] Only after they petitioned the military commander to banish him as a favor was order restored.

The biographer ultimately attributes Alexander's expulsion from Antioch to the envy of hypocritical men who chafed at his popular acclaim and usurpation of clerical prerogatives.[76] Whether or not he gives us the full story we cannot tell: Theodotus may have already identified him as a heretic and sought to evict him on that charge. But we must not underestimate the hostility Alexander would have provoked at Antioch simply through his bold speech. Contemporary writers celebrated *parrhēsia* as the distinctive mark of a holy man, partly because it took a holy man's nerve to talk back to a powerful member of late Roman society or his equally proud staff.[77] As John Chrysostom had observed some forty years earlier, "There are not many who can bear insult, insolence, impolite language, or taunts from inferiors, whether or not spoken justly."[78] But no one was more aware of the cautious etiquette needed to get by in this intensely hierarchical world than the author of the *Book of Steps*:

> You should call whoever is like you, "my brother," and "my sister," and whoever is younger than you, "my son," and "my daughter," and whoever is older than you, "my father," and "my mother;" and those who are clergy, "my Lords," and "my patrons." . . . and to whom honor [is due, give] honor, and to whom love [is due, give] love, and to whom fear [is due, give] fear.

73. *V.Alex* 40; ed. de Stroop, p. 689. Malchus refers to episcopal law courts.

74. For Porphyry at Antioch, see Devreesse (1945): 42, 117. Baguenard (1988): 109 n. 123 suggests this alludes to riots that broke out at Antioch when Porphyry backed opponents of Chrysostom after the latter's deposition at Constantinople, described by Palladius, *Dial.* 16 and Sozomen, *HE* 8.24. The reference to Porphyry shows how little we know about Alexander's career.

75. *V.Alex* 41.

76. *V.Alex* 38 and 40; ed. de Stroop, p. 689: τοιαῦτα καθ᾽ ἑκάστην ἡμέραν ὁρῶντες οἱ κληρικοί . . . ἔνδον τῷ φθόνῳ ἐτήκοντο.

77. See G. J. M. Bartelink, "Die *Parrhesia* des Menschen vor Gott bei Johannes Chrysostomos," *VC* 51 (1997): 263–64.

78. Chrysostom, *De sacerdotio* 3.10, 134–38; ed. Anne-Marie Malingrey, p. 174: τὰ παρὰ τῶν ἐλαττόνων σκώμματα . . . οὐ τῶν πολλῶν ἐνεγκεῖν.

To avoid difficulties, his Perfect had to be careful about what they said to whom: "If we owe honor [to someone] greater than us, let us not give him teaching so he might find fault and say, 'Are you teaching me?' "[79]

Alexander was not so deferential at Antioch, and evidently he carried on the same in Constantinople. Here, the biographer reports, he "continuously rebuked those who debased the commandments; and if these persisted unreformed, he used the bold speech *(parrhēsia)* he possessed to chasten them."[80] His outspokenness against urban magistrates is cited by Callinicus as the main reason for his later banishment from Constantinople. Both authors would have had reasons for stressing zeal as the cause of Alexander's troubles at Constantinople, rather than other things he might have done or said that would have implicated him in heresy. Nonetheless, both make clear that there was more to the Messalian charge against Alexander than doctrinal error. By raising his voice against church or civil authorities who "debased the commandments," Alexander challenged their social leadership. By luring away their congregations with spiritual instruction of his own, he displayed a measure of apostolic authority officially reserved for vested leaders of the church.

That may get to the heart of the reason Alexander and his *Choreutai* became the subject of anti-Messalian deliberations in 426. But Nilus, who was chronologically the closest of our three authors to these events, offers a different perspective in his treatise *On Voluntary Poverty*.[81] In his view, Alexander and Adelphius were culpable of the same fault that Epiphanius had found most reprehensible in other People Who Pray, namely their *argia*. In fact, Nilus reports that Alexander had even "made it a rule" in Constantinople "that young men and adults in vigorous health . . . must not work."[82] As an ascetic teacher, Nilus realized the problems that might arise from such a rule. His criticisms of Adelphius and Alexander were intended to dissuade readers from following their example:

> Those who excuse themselves from manual labor on the pretense that they must devote themselves to prayer do not really pray, since their thought cannot remain aloft without becoming lost in absent-mindedness. . . . They also render [their body] unsuitable for prayer by the very fact that they imagine

79. *LG* 16.2 (PS 3.389–92) and 27.6 (781). Cf. Antony's exemplary humility before bishops and clergy, *V.Ant* 67.

80. *V.Alex* 44; ed. de Stroop, pp. 692–93.

81. Nilus, *De vol. paup.* 21 (PG 79.997A); Nilus wrote earlier than Callinicus, who began his *V.Hypatii* after Hypatius' death in 447: see above, nn. 1 and 6.

82. Nilus, *De vol. paup.* 21 (PG 79.997A): καὶ νέοις παισὶ καὶ ἀνδράσι σφριγῶσιν ἔτι κατὰ τὴν ἰσχὺν τοῦ σώματος . . . νομοθετῆσαι τὸ μὴ ἐργάζεσθαι.

their *argia* gives their soul freedom from care. But really they are entangling it in a maze of cogitations from which there is no escape.[83]

"The innocent must not be deceived," he warns, "by men who exhort those who are inexperienced in both prayer and ascetic training to forgo what seems to be an inferior task [manual labor] for what they fancy to be greater [continuous prayer]."[84] Nilus criticizes their ascetic idleness mainly on theoretical grounds: to pray constantly without providing an anchor (manual labor) for the mind invites distracting daydreams or passions to well up and overwhelm a monk.[85] But Nilus betrays more concrete misgivings about monks like Adelphius and Alexander: "Rather than living in a way beneficial to the soul and body, it seems more their goal to eat food provided by others without sullying their own hands, speciously veiling their demands for bodily provisions under the respectable pretense of prayer."[86] Although their ostentatious genuflections might impress spectators with their devotion, Nilus suspected their minds were focused on other delights.[87] Paul, he adds, had warned about such people when he wrote, "He who does not work, let him not eat."[88]

Nilus draws attention to a feature of Alexander's ascetic profile—rejection of manual labor—that matched the Messalian profile circulating at the time, but has received little recognition from modern scholars as a serious factor in his condemnation as a Messalian.[89] Although Nilus does not mention the ecclesiastical proceedings directed against either Adelphius or Alexander, his specific contention that such ascetics made it their goal to eat food "provided by others without sullying their own hands" and justified it under "the respectable pretense of prayer" recalls the Messalian testimony from Timothy of Constantinople's list, which may go back

---

83. Nilus, *De vol. paup.* 26 (PG 79.1001CD): οἱ προφάσει τοῦ δεῖν προσκαρτερεῖν τῇ προσευχῇ παραιτούμενοι τὸ τῶν χειρῶν ἔργον, οὔτε προσεύχονται . . . ἀνεπιτήδειον ποιοῦσι πρὸς τὴν προσευχὴν αὐτῷ τούτῳ, ᾧ δοκοῦσι τῇ ἀργίᾳ παρέχειν τῇ ψυχῇ τὸ ἀμέριμνον.

84. Nilus, *De vol. paup.* 22 (PG 79.1000A). Nilus may be taking issue with ascetic teachers like the author of the *LG* who distinguish between "greater" and "lesser" precepts, in this case with regard to manual labor (e.g., *LG* 19.13).

85. Nilus, *De vol. paup.* 22 (PG 79.997BD); 24 (1000C); 25 (1001AB).

86. Nilus, *De vol. paup.* 23 (PG 79.1000AB): Σκοπὸς γὰρ αὐτοῖς μᾶλλον ὡς ἔοικε τὰ παρ' ἑτέρων ἐσθίειν, οὐ σκυλλομένοις ταῖς χερσί, σεμνῇ τῇ περὶ τὴν προσευχὴν προφάσει τὰ τοῦ σώματος εὐπροσώπως ἐρανιζομένοις ὀψώνια.

87. Nilus, *De vol. paup.* 22 (PG 79.997D): καὶ τὸ μὲν σχῆμα δείκνυσι προσευχῆς· κεκλικότες γὰρ ἐπὶ τὰ γόνατα, τοῦτο τοῖς ὁρῶσι φαινόμεθα, τῇ δὲ ἐννοίᾳ τὰ τέρποντα φανταζόμεθα. . . . On this point see Vincenzo Messana, "Πρᾶξις et Θεωρία chez Nil d'Ancyre," *SP* 18 (1989): 239.

88. Nilus, *De vol. paup.* 25 (PG 79.1001A).

89. For Alexander's material dependency as a factor in his identification as a Messalian, see Gribomont (1972): 617–18.

to the synod of 426: "They say that manual labor must be avoided on the grounds that it is abominable. And for this reason they call themselves 'spiritual ones,' judging it neither possible nor righteous for such people to handle work in a literal sense. In this they violate the apostolic tradition."[90] It should be recalled that Nilus had introduced Adelphius and Alexander in a discussion of the proper imitation of apostolic poverty.[91] It is possible that Nilus mentioned Alexander on this point because he had recently seen the Messalian charges drawn up against him.

In order to understand the implications of material dependency in Alexander's case, we must remember the size of his ascetic band and the sheer scale of their poverty. Alexander's biographer makes clear not only that Alexander "possessed nothing at all" but that manual labor had no place in his scrupulous regimen of poverty, prayer, and "freedom from care."[92] Although he assumed care of so many brothers, we are told that he never looked after their daily needs, worrying only lest they might compromise their "great freedom from care."[93] One episode shows how menacing such freedom from care might appear to urban residents. When citizens of the desert city of Palmyra saw Alexander's "multitude of brothers" drawing near, they immediately barred their city's gates: "Who can feed all these men? If they enter our city, we shall all starve."[94] In Constantinople his brotherhood encamped by the Menas shrine swelled to three hundred. Alexander taught all of them his brand of "voluntary poverty," and "arranged everything according to his original regimen."[95] According to Nilus, this included enforcing a rule that none of them should work.[96] With this rule, he adds, Alexander "churned up" the city. What Nilus really meant by this last remark is suggested by an invective preserved among his letters that is addressed to a certain "monk Alexander."

90. Timothy of Constantinople, *DRH* 13 (PG 86.49D): Λέγουσιν τὴν τῶν χειρῶν ἐργασίαν ὡς βδελυρὰν ἀποστρέφεσθαι. Καὶ πνευματικοὺς ἐντεῦθεν ἑαυτοὺς ὀνομάζουσιν, οὐ κρίνοντες δυνατὸν οὐδὲ δίκαιον, ἔργου λοιπὸν αἰσθητοῦ τοὺς τοιούτους ἐφάπτεσθαι· ἀθετοῦντες καὶ ἐν τούτῳ τὴν τῶν ἀποστόλων παράδοσιν. Cf. Theodoret, *HFC* 4.11 (PG 83.429C). For the relation of items in Timothy's list introduced by the phrase Λέγουσι and Messalian testimony in 426 or earlier, see Fitschen (1998): 70.

91. Nilus, *De vol. paup.* 21 (PG 79.996CD); text above, n. 7.

92. *V.Alex* 39 and 42.

93. *V.Alex* 27; ed. de Stroop, p. 678: τοσούτων ἀδελφῶν πρόνοιαν ποιούμενος, οὐδενὸς τῶν ἐπιτηδείων πρὸς τὰς χρείας ἐφρόντιζεν. *V.Alex* 31; p. 681: Μήποτε ἐν τῇ ἀμεριμνίᾳ ταύτῃ τῇ πολλῇ ἡ ῥαθυμία παρεισέλθῃ.

94. *V.Alex* 35; ed. de Stroop, pp. 685–86.

95. *V.Alex* 43; ed. de Stroop, p. 692: ἐδίδασκεν αὐτοὺς τὴν ἀκτημοσύνην, καὶ κατὰ τὸν ἀρχαῖον κανόνα πάντα διετυπώσατο. Three hundred is a figure commonly given for large monasteries: cf. Dalmatius' and Eutyches' monasteries at Constantinople discussed below, ch. 6.

96. Nilus, *De vol. paup.* 21 (PG 79.997A); text above, n. 82.

You seem to me to have an outlandish practice, using insults and rage to compel people to furnish you with "offerings" *[karpophoria]*. This is not what is meant by "offerings." Rather, it is a shameful act of force that is inappropriate to the extreme and harsher than the most oppressive public taxation and impositions. Please stop this improper behavior and devote yourself instead to prayers and spiritual tranquility. Then God will rouse people who are worthy and of good character to bring you everything sufficient for your needs.[97]

If, as seems likely, this invective was written with Alexander Akoimētos in mind, then it makes clear that Alexander and his monks achieved notoriety in Constantinople not merely for begging, but for aggressive begging.

We must beware, however, of regarding that as the "real" story. "Some faithless men," the biographer explains, wanted to "put God's grace to the test" to see "how the slaves of God were supplied with food" at Constantinople. They noticed that the brothers received food daily, but that after eating it "took no concern at all for the next day." The reason, they soon learned, was that Alexander's monks received bread daily through the care of an angel.[98] Clearly, the biographer was aware of controversy surrounding Alexander's material dependency. But we must not ignore his pious understanding of how Alexander obtained his support. The biographer offers a totally spiritualized vision of Alexander's economic existence. He sees beyond the human agencies involved, and views such transactions as giving and receiving solely in terms of God's providence and grace. Thus Alexander and his monks are said to have considered any offerings they received to be, in fact, a gift from God.[99]

Alexander seems to have benefited from unquestioning trust in a "miraculous economy" with very different laws and expectations from those that govern modern marketplaces. It was based partly in the Christological notion that God, whose majesty produced all human bounty, had made Himself poor (2 Cor 8:9), and so in His human aspect was pleased to

---

97. Nilus, *Ep.* 1.129 (PG 79.137C): Ἀλεξάνδρῳ μοναχῷ · Ἄτοπον δρᾶν πρᾶγμα δοκεῖς μοι, ἐν τῷ μεταξὶ ὕβρεων καὶ θυμοῦ καταναγκάζειν καρποφορεῖν σοί τινας. Τοῦτο δ' οὐκ ἂν λεχθείη καρποφορία . . . Ἀλλὰ παῦσαι, παρακαλῶ, τῆς ἀπρεπείας ταύτης . . . καὶ ὁ Θεὸς διεγείρει τοὺς ἀξίους ὄντας τῆς καλοκαγαθίας προσφέρειν σοι μεθ' ἱκεσίας πᾶσαν χρείαν. Gribomont (1972): 617–18 identifies the intended recipient as Alexander Akoimētos. Many letters in Nilus' corpus are either not genuine or misaddressed: see Alan Cameron, "The Authenticity of the Letters of St. Nilus of Ancyra," *Greek, Roman and Byzantine Studies* 17 (1976a): 181–96; reprinted in *id., Literature and Society in the Early Byzantine World* (London: Variorum, 1985), VI. I assume that those addressed to monks may be accepted as authentic. Writers often composed satirical letters not meant to pass outside their own circle: see Morton Smith, "The Manuscript Tradition of Isidore of Pelusium," *Harvard Theological Review* 47 (1954): 207.

98. *V.Alex* 45; ed. de Stroop, p. 69.

99. *V.Alex* 44; cf. 33.

receive offerings in alms given to the poor. Perhaps its most radical law was that the character of a beggar did not matter, since any alms given to him or her were actually being given to God. In turn, all spiritual labors, acts of charity, and faith were believed to merit blessings as recompense from God. Such blessings often came to monks in the form of alms *(eulogiae)*.[100] No doubt Alexander and his monks assumed their spiritual labors were worthy of the blessings they received. Already in the fourth century John Chrysostom had explained that singing psalms night and day in churches at Antioch constituted legitimate work for destitute widows and deserved alms, if performed with piety.[101] But Alexander earned his pay mainly by doing God's work on behalf of the poor. The author of the *Book of Steps* forbade his apostolic Perfect from physically working or performing charitable ministries that might distract them from prayer, but he believed they were otherwise obliged to teach Christians to "see" the afflicted and give to those in need.[102] Likewise, Alexander, when not at prayer, is said to have admonished the rich to relieve the poor, and to have given whatever surplus charity his monks received "to their brothers, the destitute poor."[103] It was largely because of Alexander's poverty and solidarity with the poor that his biographer considered him to be a man of apostolic stature, exemplifying the most scrupulous fulfillment of Jesus' precepts.

However, the values and expectations of this charitable new economy were only beginning to be established in Alexander's day. Nilus probably speaks for most people living in Constantinople at the time. Many could have simply avoided the streets around St. Menas' while Alexander and his *Choreutai* were in town, but the bishops gathered for Sisinnius' ordination could not so easily ignore his vocal presence. Alexander's combination of poverty, prayer, and refusal to work matched the known Messalian profile so closely that Theodotus would have had little trouble convincing his colleagues: to them, Alexander must have represented Messalianism writ large. In fact, Sisinnius' ordination provided a perfect symbolic and practical setting for asserting the authority of the church leadership against the apostolic challenge that Alexander represented.

100. See Vincent Déroche, *Études sur Léontios de Néapolis* (Uppsala: Uppsala Universitet, 1995), 238–49 ("L'économie miraculeuse"), 249–54 ("Une spiritualité proche du messalianisme"); also Escolan (1999): 193. Déroche deals primarily with sixth-and seventh-century sources but finds precedents in the *V.Alex* and *LG*. As he notes, those who gave alms were believed to be giving them to God; conversely, those who begged for alms were begging for God. Alexander's religious begging should be seen in that light. For parallels from other cultures, see above, ch. 2 n. 117. I thank Peter Brown for referring me to Déroche's study.

101. Chrysostom, *In Epistulam I ad Corinthios hom.* 30.4 (PG 61.254–55).

102. *LG* 3.7 (PS 3.59–60).

103. *V.Alex* 45; ed. de Stroop, p. 694: τὰ περισσὰ ἔδωκαν τοῖς ἀδελφοῖς τοῖς πτωχοῖς. Cf. sect. 35.

SPIRITUAL AUTHORITY AND THE MESSALIAN CONTROVERSY

Alexander may not have typified all ascetics accused of Messalianism in the late fourth and early fifth centuries, but his case forces us to consider again why church authorities viewed Messalians with such alarm. Though born in the Greek Aegean and educated at Constantinople, Alexander by the 420s could be regarded as one who had "come from the East."[104] After nearly fifty years' absence he had returned as an enthusiastic proponent of an ascetic lifestyle that had long been traditional in the Syro-Mesopotamian milieu, but had become increasingly outmoded even there. It is useful to remember Columba Stewart's thesis that doctrinal aspects of the Messalian controversy arose through the misapprehension of traditional Syrian devotional idioms when translated into the Greek milieu. The identification of Alexander as a Messalian heretic may also be explained, to some degree, as the reaction of Mediterranean bishops to the provocative devotional practices and ascetic assumptions he had brought back "from the East."

Yet, as discussed in the previous chapter, we should not view the Messalian controversy simply as a conflict between old "Eastern" and new "Western" cultures; and as Alexander's case demonstrates, we must not view it simply as a controversy over doctrinal issues. It was a conflict between church leaders and ascetic laymen that hinged in no small part on different interpretations of the Gospels, particularly on points where Jesus and Paul appeared to conflict. As portrayed by his biographer, Alexander, like the author of the *Book of Steps*, Pseudo-Macarius, and the long-haired monks of Carthage, believed that Jesus' apostolic command to live "free of care" for food and clothing took precedent over Paul's command to practice manual labor to provide for one's needs. All believed themselves heirs to Jesus' apostolic paradigm, providing spiritual edification to others in return for material support. Such apostolic presumptions, however, raised real concerns for bishops and clergy, which need to be spelled out.

First but not necessarily foremost, material dependency. Though considered the sine qua non for imitating Jesus' humility by the author of the *Book of Steps*, this ascetic practice was criticized by contemporary Greco-Roman authorities like Epiphanius as "baleful presumption" and *ametria* (lack of moderation).[105] Augustine helps explain why it provoked such a response. After refuting the claims of the Carthaginian monks to support from others on scriptural grounds, he warns readers that following such examples might identify them with the many "hypocrites in the garb of

---

104. Callinicus, *V.Hypatii* 41.1 and 3; ed. Bartelink, p. 242.

105. Epiphanius, *Panarion* 80.4.1; ed. Holl-Dummer, p. 488: ἔσχον δὲ τὸ βλαβερὸν τοῦτο φρόνημα ἀπὸ τῆς ἀμετρίας τῆς τινων ἀδελφῶν ἀφελείας. . . . μὴ γινώσκοντες τὸ μέτρον τῆς ἐν Χριστῷ πολιτείας.

monks" whom Satan had scattered everywhere: "they go around the provinces nowhere sent, nowhere still, nowhere stable, nowhere settled." Such
wandering monks turned monasticism into "base commercialization," and
confirmed public suspicions that monks were simply frauds looking for a
free meal.[106] Already in the fourth century Aphrahat had warned Mesopotamian covenanters not to make themselves despised by "begging for their
belly's sake." The active promotion of ascetic *argia* by Messalian monks like
Alexander impeded the efforts of Augustine and his peers to strike a balance between monastic ideals and the dominant social *mores* of the world
and thereby render monasticism socially acceptable. We must not dismiss
the impact of ascetic begging on contemporary attitudes towards the new
monastic profession. Nilus was particularly sensitive to public opinion on
this matter, for reasons we shall see.

Yet we must not reduce the concerns raised by Messalian claims to support to a mere problem of begging. By focusing on the alleged hypocrisies
of mendicant monks, Augustine deflects attention from the more sensitive
social and ecclesiastical issue of spiritual authority and privilege. This was
the main issue that both the long-haired monks of Carthage and their
Messalian counterparts in the East raised by their assumption of apostolic
prerogatives. Not only did the Carthaginians justify their support from others by reference to evangelic services they provided, but they evidently were
receiving considerable acclaim for these services. "Who can endure the
fact," Augustine asks, "that insolent men . . . are not only tolerated as weak
members, but are even extolled as if more holy, so that monasteries established on more wholesome principles are corrupted by a twofold evil, the
license of relaxed leisure and the false name of sanctity?"[107] In his later
retrospective on the work Augustine also indicates that these monks were
enjoying support from lay members of local church congregations.[108] Such
unbounded assumption of apostolic identity infringed on the authority and
prerogatives of local clergy, including their own right to material support
from their church communities. "In my estimation those brothers claim
for themselves privileged authority of this kind rashly. For if they are

106. Augustine, *De opere* 28.36; ed. Zycha, pp. 585–86: eis anputetis occasionem turpium
nundinarum, quibus existimatio vestra laeditur et infirmis offendiculum ponitur? Trans. Muldowney, p. 384. For the rest of the passage, see above, introduction, nn.1 and 2. Cf. Epiphanius, *Panarion* 80.3.3, and Augustine, *Ep.* 262.5–6.

107. Augustine, *De opere* 30.38; ed. Zycha, p. 589: quis ferat homines contumaces . . . non
sicut infirmiores tolerari, sed sicut sanctiores etiam praedicari, ut monasteria doctrina saniora
fundata gemina inlecebra corrumpantur, et dissoluta licentia vacationis et falso nomine sanctitatis. Trans. adapted from Muldowney, p. 388. On their "false" sanctity, see also 19.22 and
31.39.

108. Augustine, *Retractationes* 2.21; ed. Mutzenbecher, p. 107: etiam inter laicos inferioris
propositi, sed tamen studio ferventes existere coeperant tumultuosa certamina.

preachers, they have it, I admit; if they minister at the altars or confer the sacraments, they do not arrogate that privilege, but clearly substantiate their claim."[109] In Augustine's view, the privilege that Jesus granted to his apostles not to work and to rely upon others for their support extended only to official church leaders: "learn the labors of our occupations . . . and the established traditions of the church that we serve," Augustine tells monastic readers. "All these things prevent us from performing those manual labors to which we exhort you."[110] Though ostensibly written to promote proper monastic conduct, Augustine's *On the Work of Monks* is also a defense of his own ecclesiastical position. In fact, this seems to be the main reason the Carthaginian monks roused his indignation: they claimed for themselves the apostolic authority and privileges which Augustine as bishop reserved for vested ministers of the institutional church.

Ecclesiastical outrage had arisen in the East for similar reasons. Both Eustathius and Alexander were accused of claiming for themselves and their followers *karpophoria* (charitable offerings), a term used to designate church offerings made by congregations for clergy to take for themselves and share with the needy.[111] Most small churches depended on such offerings to support their clergy and welfare programs. It is important to note, however, that there was no established tithe in the late antique church.[112] While this meant that members of the laity were not obliged to make offerings, it also meant there were no set rules as to whom such offerings should go when they were made. The result was that the privilege of receiving them was open to dispute. Eustathian or Messalian claims to such offerings on the grounds that they were "holy ones" or "truly the poor in spirit" are presented in the conciliar records as a novel, outrageous pre-

109. Augustine, *De opere* 21.24; ed. Zycha, pp. 569–70: fratres nostri temere sibi adrogant, quantum existimo, quod eius modi habeant potestam. si enim evangelistae sunt, fateor, habent; si ministri altaris, dispensatores sacramentorum, bene sibi istam non adrogant, sed plane vindicant potestatem. Trans. Muldowney, p. 368.

110. Augustine, *De opere* 29.37; ed. Zycha, p. 586: quaerite et cognoscite labores occupationum nostrarum et in aliquibus nostrorum etiaam corporum infirmitates et ecclesiarum, quibus servimus, talem iam consuetudinem, ut nos ad illa opera, ad quae vos hortamur, vacare non sinant. Augustine defends the clergy's subsequent right to alms in numerous passages, e.g., *De opere* 3.14; p. 537: illi enim tamquam apostolo praedicatori evangelii . . . plantori vineae, pastori gregis constituerat dominus, ut de evangelio viveret. See also 5.6; 16.19; 20.23; 25.33; and 29.37; and the similar defensiveness prompted by Messalian *argia* in Epiphanius, *Panarion* 80.5.4–6.4.

111. For its contemporary ecclesiastical usage, see esp. *Constitutiones Apostolorum* 2.25,13–14; also Lampe, s.v. καρποφορέω 4–5, καρποφορία 4–5, and καρποφόρος. Under καρποφορέω 4, Lampe claims this term also referred to alms given to monks, but the only example he gives is Nilus' *Ep.* 1.129.

112. See A. H. M. Jones, "Church Finances in the Fifth and Sixth Centuries," *JThS* 11 (1960): 85

sumption.[113] Yet none other than Basil himself was ready to acknowledge the special sanctity of Christians who voluntarily adopted poverty. Drawing distinctions between the common poor and the ascetic poor, Basil maintained that

> poverty is not always praiseworthy, but only that which is practiced as a matter of choice, in conformity with the evangelic aim. For many are poor in their resources, but very grasping in their intention; poverty does not save these; on the contrary, their intention condemns them. Accordingly, it is not he who is in need who is blessed, but he who has considered the command of Christ better than the treasures of the world. These the Lord also pronounces blessed when he says, "Blessed are the poor in spirit" [Mt 5:3], not those poor in resources, but those who from their soul have chosen poverty.[114]

This line of Basil's thought perhaps shows the influence of his early ascetic mentor, Eustathius; at least it reveals that some orthodox authorities shared the view that ascetics who humbled themselves through voluntary poverty deserved special honor as the Gospels' "truly poor in spirit." But the self-identification attributed to Eustathians and Messalians, namely as "holy ones" who deserved material support, may well have derived not so much from Jesus' beatitudes as from Paul's repeated defense (Rom 15:25–27; cf. Gal 2:10, 1 Cor 1:2) of his collecting alms for the "holy ones" and "the poor among the holy ones" within the original apostolic community at Jerusalem. These, Paul argues, deserved *karpoi* (gifts) from other Christians because of "the spiritual things" they had shared with them.[115] Significantly, Augustine cites these same Pauline passages and arguments in his defense of the right of the church clergy to live off alms.[116]

113. See Timothy of Constantinople, *DRH* 15 and Gangra synod, *Epistola synodica* with texts above, ch. 3 nn. 52 and 75.

114. Basil of Caesarea, *Homilia in Psalmum XXXIII* 5 (PG 29.361A): οὐκ ἀεὶ ἐπαινετὴ ἡ πτωχεία.... οὐ τοίνυν ὁ ἐνδεὴς πάντως μακαριστός, ἀλλ᾽ ὁ κρείττονα ἡγησάμενος τῶν τοῦ κόσμου θησαυρῶν τὴν ἐντολὴν τοῦ Χριστοῦ. Trans. adapted from Agnes Clare Way, p. 256. Cf. Basil, *RB* 205. For Christian ascetics as "the truly poor," see e.g., Aphrahat, *Demonstratio* 20.17 and the Syriac *Life of Symeon* 42.

115. Rom 15:25–28; ed. Aland et al., p. 573: πορεύομαι εἰς Ἰερουσαλὴμ διακονῶν τοῖς ἁγίοις. εὐδόκησαν γὰρ Μακεδονία καὶ Ἀχαία κοινωνίαν τινὰ ποιήσασθαι εἰς τοὺς πτωχοὺς τῶν ἁγίων τῶν ἐν Ἰερουσαλήμ. εὐδόκησαν γὰρ καὶ ὀφειλέται εἰσὶν αὐτῶν · εἰ γὰρ τοῖς πνευματικοῖς αὐτῶν ἐκοινώνησαν τὰ ἔθνη, ὀφείλουσιν καὶ ἐν τοῖς σαρκικοῖς λειτουγῆσαι αὐτοῖς. This passage could be interpreted in literal conformity with Jesus' sayings. Those who did so may have also interpreted the Jerusalem "holy poor" as nazirs: see Num 6:1–21, Acts 21:23–26 and Hamel (1990): 190, 221. Epiphanius' and Augustine's discussions of long hair in *Panarion* 80.6.5–7.5 and *De opere* 31.39–32.40 suggest both were dealing with monks who viewed themselves as nazirs. Although this ascetic identity became common for elite monks in the East, it seems to have been viewed with suspicion by Greco-Roman churchmen: see below, n. 117.

116. Augustine, *De opere* 16.17; ed. Zycha, pp. 558–62.

Thus rival claims to apostolic identity, privilege, and authority were at stake in this contention over material support. From Eustathius to Alexander, all those who made such claims seem to have justified them not only by reference to evangelic precepts, but also by virtue of their material renunciations, their subsequent ministries to the poor (and other Christians), and their demonstrative asceticism, i.e., by their ascetic appearance or behavior that signaled their spiritual dedication as well as their renunciation of worldly norms. Such apostolic ascetics brought into the community the exotic spirituality Christians otherwise had to seek among recluses in the desert.[117] Augustine, Basil, and others complained that long-haired enthusiasts took on the appearance of biblical heroes solely to win alms.[118] If true, the fact that they did so is our best indication that at least some members of the Christian laity encouraged such behavior and were willing to support it with alms.

Although already attested in the *Didache* and third-century *Letter to Virgins,* this monastic profile first received ecclesiastical scrutiny at the synod of Gangra, which decreed that anyone who displayed the behavior or attitudes associated with Eustathius was a heretic and outside the church. The bishops at Gangra did not explain themselves, but it is likely that they condemned Eustathian practices for the same reason that Epiphanius criticized the Mesopotamian and Messalian practices of wearing sackcloth or growing hair long. Such practices signaled not only the *ametria* (lack of moderation) of the monks in question, but also their *philonikia* (spirit of rivalry), which Paul himself had pronounced alien to "the churches of God" (1 Cor 11: 16).[119]

It should be noted that this ascetic spirit of rivalry troubled some ordi-

117. See Frank (2000): 13–14, 29. The spiritual services offered by wandering enthusiasts included not only readings, exhortations, and prayer but also dramatic manifestations of faith in action: e.g., the Messalian display of archery against demons, or Alexander's prayer regimen, whose spectacular impact is noted in *V.Alex* 38,44 and suggested by Nilus, *De vol. paup.* 22 (PG 79.997D).

118. Epiphanius, *Panarion* 80.3.5; Augustine, *De opere* 31.34; ed. Zycha, pp. 590–91: illi . . . venalem circumferentes hypocrisin (Augustine insinuates that long-haired monks sought to impress and profit by emulating antiquos illos quos legimus . . . Samuelem et ceteros, qui non tondebant); Basil, *Ep.* 169; ed. and trans. Deferarri (LCL 215), pp. 438–39: on Glycerius, who "invested himself with the name and appearance of a patriarch" (πατριαρχίας ὄνομα ἑαυτῷ καὶ σχῆμα περιθείς), "adopting this course, not from any motive of obedience or of piety, but because he preferred this source of livelihood (ἀμφορμὴν βίου) just as another man would chose one or another occupation." Cf. Sulpicius Severus, *V. Martini* 23–24.

119. 1 Cor 11:16; ed. Aland, p. 603: εἰ δέ τις δοκεῖ φιλόνεικος εἶναι, ἡμεῖς τοιαύτην συνήθειαν οὐκ ἔχομεν οὐδὲ αἱ ἐκκλησίαι τοῦ θεοῦ. Epiphanius, *Panarion* 80.7.3–5; ed. Holl-Dummer, pp. 492–93: οὐ γὰρ διὰ θεὸν ἡ ἀρετή . . . ἀλλὰ διὰ φιλονεικίαν ὁ τρόπος. For the Gangra synod, see above, ch. 3, p. 100.

nary Christians as well as the clergy. Augustine reports that lay people took sides both for and against the long-haired monks of Carthage; both Eustathius and Alexander apparently divided communities with their fundamentalist demands; and both Pseudo-Macarius and the author of the *Book of Steps* seem to justify the apostolic privileges of their ascetic elites in defensive tones.[120] Yet the author of the *Book of Steps* would have agreed with Alexander's biographer that the problems facing his ascetics arose mainly from clerical envy.[121] The spiritual ministries he was advocating for his Perfect had come under attack from local church leaders, who in his view should welcome the Perfect precisely because their ministries transcended all geographical and institutional bounds:

> The leaders [of the church] have only such and such a region where, as is necessary, they may discipline with mercy, and wherever it is right they may [minister] justly what is better for the congregations in each place, and what is better for the infants and also for the sick, the corrupt and the rebels. [But] the Perfect, because they travel to many places, speak to each one the word which is helpful to him and leave for another place, say what is befitting to each, and then move on.[122]

Just at a time when the church was formalizing the prerogatives of its own ranks and restricting clergy to their appointed spheres of influence, the author of the *Book of Steps* sought to preserve an open range of preaching and spiritual services for ascetic members of the "church of the heart."[123] Unlike church leaders who exercised jurisdiction in fixed areas, such ascetics, he explains,

> since they are fulfilled in every respect with truth and are without fear, do not say because of this, "This is our place" and "this is not ours" or "this person is ours" or "this [person] is not one of us" . . . [the Perfect] invite

120. Augustine, *Retractationes* 2.21 (above, n. 108); *V.Alex* 34; for Ps.-Macarius, see Fitschen (1998): 241–45, for the *LG*, see Kitchen (1998). It might be supposed that opposition to such ascetics reflected socioeconomic perspective, but Eustathius' ascetic demands would have affected all members of the church, and Alexander's biographer notes how easily "the people" were swayed against Alexander at Constantinople, *V.Alex* 49.

121. See above, n. 76.

122. *LG* 19.31 (PS 3.505), trans. adapted.

123. For his distinction between the "visible church" and the "church of the heart," see *LG* sermon 12, esp. 12.2. For fourth-century efforts to define and organize ecclesiastical jurisdictions, see (for Syria) *Constitutiones Apostolorum* 8.28.1–8 and 47.14–15; and (more generally) Patricia Karlin-Hayter, "Activity of the Bishop of Constantinople outside His *Paroikia* between 381 and 451," in *Kathegetria: Essays Presented to Joan Hussey on Her Eightieth Birthday* (Camberley: Porphyrogenitus, 1988), 179–182 with Jones (1964): 874–83, 915–20. The author of the *LG* may have been responding to institutional developments in the Persian Empire, where church organization became even more centralized.

everyone by their word, since the truth of our Lord wins them over at all times. . . . [124]

He emphasizes that he is not advocating insubordination toward official church clergy or any separation from the "visible" church.[125] Yet the unbounded assumption of spiritual authority he was advocating for his Perfect had evidently brought some of them into dire conflict with local church leaders, to whom the author makes an urgent plea:

> Take notice of the ways of Perfection and do not complain about us, or accuse us in matters that concern us, or hate us at random and chase us away for nothing from the ministry in which it is right for us to walk—going to everyone, instructing and teaching everyone in love and lowliness—which is what our Lord Jesus taught and showed us in his person.[126]

Some of the Perfect, he reports, had actually been persecuted and killed by "members of the household of faith," apparently under suspicion of heresy.[127] Whether or not the author of the *Book of Steps* was referring here to ecclesiastical persecution of Messalian monks, as some historians believe, remains an open question.[128] What his writings do attest is the other side of the debate over apostolic ministries and prerogatives that pitched church leaders and ascetic enthusiasts against each other during the late fourth and early fifth centuries.

The author of the *Book of Steps* knew that his ideals were becoming outmoded through the growing reach of the institutional church and the alternative forms of monastic life it promoted in the post-Constantinian

---

124. *LG* 19.31 (PS 3.504–505).

125. E.g., *LG* 27.5 (PS 3.780): "No one should doubt the church or its priest, [for] from the Catholic church all truth shall be known." Escalon (1999): 5, 91–119 asserts that Messalian ascetics sought to separate themselves from the institutional church. But I have found no evidence for this in Ps.-Macarius, the *V.Alex*, or *LG*. It that seems to have been a polemical characterization. The willingness expressed by Adelphius to renounce his "beliefs" was rejected by bishops as insincere only because he did not cease communicating with other Messalians: see Photius, *Bibliotheca* 52.

126. *Ibid.* (PS 3.508).

127. *LG* 30.4 (PS 3.872–873): "The martyrs of love [i.e., the Perfect] are persecuted and killed by the members of the household of faith . . . since the members of the household of faith believe that they have understood the whole truth through faith. When a person of love speaks something which is hidden from them, they are stirred up against him, [saying] 'Why do you teach something that is not proclaimed in the whole church?' They do not understand that if a person does not love as our Lord and his apostles loved, he will not understand the whole truth."

128. For troubled relations between the wandering Perfect and church authorities in the *LG*, see Ratcliff (1988): 50–57 and Guillaumont (1974): 322. However, Kitchen (1998): 215–16 believes the author refers to troubles with "local church members, the laity in traditional terms of the church."

world.[129] The career of Alexander the Sleepless illustrates the troubles that arose when charismatic ascetics continued to pursue and advocate the apostolic model into the fifth century. As long as Alexander and his monks kept to the distant desert steppes like other Syrian anchorites, they seem to have had no problems. It was when they settled in cities like Antioch and Constantinople that they came under ecclesiastical notice and fire.[130] By the 420s even Constantinople had become a city on whose streets, according to most orthodox monastic thinkers, no decent monk should have appeared, and where respected archimandrites remained sequestered in monastic cells. That had not always been so. To see why that change occurred we must enter the late Roman urban environment in which wandering, begging monks could achieve notoriety no matter where their doctrinal sympathies actually lay.

129. For the increasing limitations placed by ecclesiastical power on ascetic options in the late fourth- and early fifth-century West, see Burrus (1995): 103–23.

130. See Vööbus (1960b): 188. Messalian monks first attracted Epiphanius' attention when they entered Antioch to sleep and beg on its streets.

5

Hypocrites and Pseudomonks

Beggars, Bishops, and Ascetic Teachers
in Cities of the Early Fifth Century

At the turn of the fifth century, about the same time Augustine was complaining that so many "hypocrites in the garb of monks" could be found everywhere seeking alms for their "pretended piety," Paulinus of Nola described how a young novice monk named Martinianus worried lest he might be thought "to be feigning destitution for love of gain" if, after his shipwreck near Marseilles, he were seen traveling "through army camps, hamlets, and towns" in tattered clothes, "just as greedy beggars habitually wander over land and sea, who solemnly swear they are monks or shipwrecked survivors, telling their story of misfortune for a price." Martinianus preferred to brave the sea again rather than risk being mistaken for such an impostor on the road.[1] Slightly later in the East we find similar concerns being expressed by Nilus of Ancyra:

> The monastic way of life, formerly much beloved and admired, has now, as you can see, become an abomination. This is because all the cities and villages are being weighed down by pseudomonks running around to no purpose, in much vulgarity and lack of distinction. Meanwhile all residents are being mobbed, and are truly offended at the sight of them planted at their gates, begging utterly without shame.

1. Paulinus of Nola, *Carmen* 24,325–38; ed. Wilhelm von Hartel, p. 217: ne nomen novum adquirat inposter sibi. Martinianus was enroute to Sulpicius Severus' monastery in Aquitania. The poem is dated ca. 400 by Pierre Fabre, *Essai sur la chronologie de l'oeuvre de saint Paulin de Nola* (Paris: Belles Lettres, 1948), 120. The association of fraudulent beggars with wandering monks and shipwreck survivors became a late antique topos, adapted in apophthegm G Bessarion 12 (PG 65.144BC).

For this reason, Nilus laments, even the conduct of monks who live "correctly and virtuously . . . is considered a deceit and a joke."[2]

In the last two chapters we have seen how ascetics in the late fourth and early fifth centuries raised ecclesiastical alarm by claiming for themselves the apostolic prerogatives set forth in the Gospels, including a right to material support from others. Now we must view such People Who Pray, as Augustine did the presumptuous monks of Carthage, as the crest of a more broadly vexing ascetic phenomenon. Augustine, Paulinus, and Nilus all bear witness that by the early fifth century, wandering, begging monks could be regarded not only as a problem in cities and towns across the Roman Empire, but as a threat to the reputation of monasticism itself. This chapter explores how ascetic begging troubled two particular authorities in this period: John Chrysostom, bishop of Constantinople (398–403/ 404), and Nilus, a monk himself (*fl.* 390–430).

It would be easy to accept these writers' characterizations and dismiss such monks simply as "hypocrites," "impostors" or "pseudomonks." No doubt many adopted the monastic *schēma* (garb or appearance) solely for gain, as these critics imply. But we must be wary of taking literary representation for a complete or accurate rendering of historical reality. Uncertainty surrounding wandering monks and the poor was easily exploited and helped shape polemical discourse. As already seen, both wandering and dependence on others for material support were still regarded by many in this period as the highest expressions of an ascetic life modeled on Jesus' humility and apostolic principles. Such practices could not be adopted, of course, without real social risk, as a fourth-century Syriac homily warns:

> *Xeniteia [aksnāyutā]* is a difficult and extremely harsh way of life. . . . [Whoever adopts it] trades honor for insult. . . . The ground will be his bed, a rock his pillow, and in winter he will knock on every door. . . . Although he may perish from hunger, he will still be mocked as a glutton and assailed everywhere. He will be called a thief and wicked slave, vagrant or vagabond, imposter or traitor, spy or housebreaker, a lunatic or fool. These insults and more await all who practice *xeniteia*.[3]

---

2. Nilus, *Ep.* 3.119 (PG 79.437C): τῶν μοναζόντων βίος, νῦν βδελυρὸς γέγονε . . . Διὸ βαροῦνται μὲν πᾶσαι πόλεις καὶ κῶμαι ὑπὸ τῶν ψευδομονάχων περιτρεχόντων μάτην καὶ ὡς ἔτυχεν, ἐν πολλῇ χυδαιότητι καὶ ἀδιαφορίᾳ· ἐνοχλοῦνται δὲ πάντες οἰκοδεσπόται, καὶ ἀηδῶς ἔχουσιν ἀληθῶς καὶ πρὸς αὐτὴν τὴν ὄψιν, βλέποντες αὐτοὺς τῶν προσαιτῶν ἀναιδέστερον ταῖς ἑαυτῶν παραμένοντας θύραις. Ὅθεν καὶ ἡ τῶν ὀρθῶς καὶ κατ᾽ ἀρετὴν βιοτευόντων κρίσις καὶ πολιτεία, διὰ τούτους ἀπάτη καὶ χλεύη ἀρτίως νομίζεται. This letter (to the archimandrite Nicon) constitutes either a précis or a reprise of Nilus' longer description in his *De monastica exercitatione* 9 discussed below.

3. Ps.-Ephrem, *Sermo* 16. Ed. with Latin trans. by Stefan Assemani, pp. 650–51. For date and discussion, see Arthur Vööbus, *Literary Critical and Historical Studies in Ephraem the Syrian* (Stockholm, 1958a), 91–93 and Guillaumont (1968): 47–48.

This homily anticipates the terms of abuse projected on wandering, begging monks by authors like Augustine, Paulinus, and Nilus, and alerts us that such terms were expressions of a more general suspicion that extended toward all homeless wanderers in the late Roman Empire, as in similarly stratified societies.[4]

It is therefore necessary to read such characterizations not so much as representations of fact as reflections of their authors' own social standing and outlook.[5] This is not to say that wandering, begging monks were a mere specter on the pages of polite ascetic discourse. But to understand the concerns they raised we must appreciate the position and social perspective of their critics. This becomes especially clear in Nilus' letters and treatises, our most detailed source for wandering, begging monks in urban settings of the early fifth century. His writings reveal the outlook of a monk who was steeped in aristocratic sensibilities and acutely embarrassed by the fact that his monastic colleagues had become either overly occupied by agricultural or commercial pursuits or too openly solicitous for material support from others. For him, the image of "pseudomonks" begging at rich men's gates provided the grossest illustration of how excessive concern for corporeal needs had mired too many of his day "in much vulgarity and lack of distinction" *(en pollē chydaiotēti kai adiaphoria)*.[6] Significantly, these were the same words the emperor Julian had used some fifty years earlier to ridicule the way Christians had lowered their *mores* in order to attract and accommodate "people of the baser sort: market hawkers and publicans, dancers and pimps."[7] In Nilus' view, his monastic vocation was in danger of being similarly identified with the urban rabble.

Against this trend Nilus urged his readers to return to the strict *akribeia* of their predecessors. He represents this as an ascetic life based on moderate poverty, manual labor, and seclusion from cities, with its main objective being philosophical contemplation and repose. This was a very different conception of monasticism from what we have studied in the past three

4. For similar characterizations (taken mostly from the early Muslim Near East), see Edwin Eames and Judith G. Goode, *Urban Poverty in a Cross-Cultural Context* (New York: Free Press, 1973), 36–38.

5. For the prevailing stereotypes and suspicions, see Ramsay MacMullen, *Enemies of the Roman Order: Treason, Unrest, and Alienation in the Empire* (Cambridge: Harvard University Press, 1966). For representations of "the poor" in literary sources of this period, see Patlagean (1977): 17–35.

6. Nilus, *Ep.* 3.119 (PG 79.437C). Nilus (like Julian, below) here seems to use the term ἀδιαφορία (usually translated "indifference") to refer to monks who mixed with the urban mob, a problem noted in *De monastica exercitatione* 7 (PG 79.728A).

7. Julian, *Contra Galileos*, frg. 238B. In Wilmer C. Wright (LCL 157), p. 388: τὴν ὑμετέραν ἀσέβειαν ἔκ... τῆς παρὰ τοῖς ἔθνεσιν ἀδιαφορίας καὶ χυδαιότητος συγκειμένην.... Frg. 238E (p. 390): ἐπιτεῖναι τὴν παρ' ἡμῖν ἐφιλοτιμήθητε χυδαιότητα.... βίοις ἀνθρώπων εὐτελῶν, καπήλων, τελωνῶν, ὀρχηστῶν, ἐταιροτρόφων καὶ ἁρμόττειν ᾠήθητε τὰ παρ' ὑμῖν.

chapters. It had more in common with Greco-Roman philosophical traditions emphasizing social withdrawal and tranquility than with apostolic traditions stressing social engagement. What makes Nilus' ascetic *akribeia* striking is the emphasis he places on its aristocratic aims: for him it meant, above all, a monastic lifestyle that would distinguish monks from the common herd. At the same time, it is plain from his writings that Nilus never sought to entirely extricate himself or his readers from the world they had renounced. In fact, his recommendations for manual labor were intended not so much to render his fellow monks respectably self-sufficient, as to inculcate appropriate ascetic manners that might rouse "pious souls to minister to us in all that pertains to our needs."[8] Like Alexander, Nilus believed in the charitable ideals of a "miraculous economy." Yet his prescriptions for monastic practice must be understood primarily within the normal framework of late Roman society, which "differed little except in scale from other pre-modern societies, [where] people resorted to the same mechanisms, chiefly patronage and dependence, in order to get around the sheer practical difficulties of living. This was recognized by all parties, but some practices upset the established pattern. . . ."[9] Upon closer examination we find that what Nilus calls "shameless begging" was not so much outright mendicancy as the pursuit of patronage by his urban monastic counterparts. His recommendations for proper monastic practices and his anxieties about wandering, begging monks tell us as much about his own sense of rivalry and concern for displaying proper decorum while competing for patronage, as it does about the extent to which such monks actually "weighed down" the cities, towns, and villages of the empire.

This chapter therefore explores monastic patronage in its urban social context and its consequences for both monastic and ecclesiastical developments in this period. Despite the complaints that Nilus and John Chrysostom report concerning monks roaming their cities, this problem arose in no small part because so many wealthy urban Christians were "contending to receive" such spiritual experts into their homes.[10] The apostolic model for monastic life easily melded with traditional Greco-Roman philosophical relationships, in which wealthy patrons maintained private ascetic teachers who provided spiritual edification. Such patrons could also

8. Nilus, *Ep.* 2.105 (PG 79.245D–248A): ψυχὰς εὐσεβεστάτας πρὸς τὸ πάντα τὰ πρὸς τὰς χρείας διακονῆσαι ἡμῖν.

9. Averil Cameron, *The Later Roman Empire* (Cambridge: Harvard University Press, 1993), 106–7. For a discussion of the importance of patronage in late Roman social structure, economy, and thought, see Patlagean (1977): 156–235 and Jens-Uwe Krause, *Spätantike Patronatsformen im Westen des Römischen Reiches* (Munich: Beck, 1987), 8–67. For an overview of monastic patronage in the East (mostly in the fifth and sixth centuries), see Escolan (1999): 182–225.

10. As Ps.-Ephrem also predicted would happen to those who persevered in *xeniteia* in *Sermo* 16; ed. Assemani, p. 651.

provide a monk with considerable power and influence beyond direct epis-copal control. So John Chrysostom learned during his troubled years in Constantinople. Like Nilus, Chrysostom considered wandering, begging monks to be an "insult to philosophy." Yet he discovered that the influence one such monk named Isaac achieved through his aristocratic patrons was sufficient to pose a serious challenge to Chrysostom's own spiritual authority as bishop of Constantinople.

BEGGARS AT THE GATES

Increasingly in the fourth century it became the task of church leaders to speak for the social conscience of their cities.[11] Bishops who censured monks for refusing to work and living off others were more often occupied with mustering charitable sentiments from wealthy congregations, slow to sympathize:

> I rise before you today on a righteous embassy for those who are living in your city destitute. . . . For as I was hastening to this congregation through the markets and alleyways, I saw many cast out in the middle of the street, some missing hands, some eyes, others covered with ulcers and incurable wounds. . . . People often subject those in need to intense scrutiny, examining where they come from, their life history, habits, and daily pursuits, making good physical condition grounds for accusation, demanding countless explanations about their health. For this reason many fake disabilities, to bend our hard-heartedness. . . . [12]

Through such rhetorical cadenzas Chrysostom and fellow preachers strained to make their audiences see the poor living in the porticoes, streets, and squares of their cities and hear the recriminations and abuse they habitually received from the rest of society.[13] Generally speaking, Greco-Roman society wasted little charity on those who could not in some way return a benefit, and this approach to almsgiving persisted among Christians in late antiquity.[14] Chrysostom and his colleagues were well aware

11. See Brown (1992): 89–117; Lizzi (1987): 34–84; and Blake Leyerle, "John Chrysostom on Almsgiving and the Use of Money," *Harvard Theological Review* 87 (1994): 29–47.

12. John Chrysostom, *De eleemosyna* 1 and 6 (PG 51.261, 269).

13. Examples are collected in Michael De Vinne, *The Advocacy of Empty Bellies* (Ph.D. diss., Stanford University, 1995). For the congregations addressed, see Ramsay MacMullen, "The Preacher's Audience (A.D. 350–400)," *JThS* 40 (1989): 503–11; with cautions from Wendy Mayer, "John Chrysostom: Extraordinary Preacher, Ordinary Audience," in *Preacher and Audience: Studies in Early Christian and Byzantine Homiletics,* ed. P. Allen and M. B. Cunningham (Leiden: Brill, 1998a), 123–29.

14. See Hands (1968): 30–31, 46–47 for earlier periods and 60–61 for the fourth century.

of the challenge they faced in trying to soften attitudes towards the homeless, especially toward any beggar who looked fit enough to work.

Fourth-and fifth-century sermons and patristic writings offer the first sustained and sympathetic view of the urban poor in the Greco-Roman world. The picture is deliberately grim. At Constantinople and Antioch, men and women competed with chained prisoners for alms by juggling, whistling, or banging on cups in marketplaces while crowds cheered them on to chase after coins. As Chrysostom reports, "some of them have surpassed even our wonderworkers in the perverse spectacles they put on: chewing on leather sandals, driving sharp nails into their heads, lying naked on frozen puddles in the icy cold, and worse" to attract alms.[15] Chrysostom estimated that ten percent of Antioch's quarter-million population was utterly destitute.[16] His fellow citizen Libanius (314–393) considered this no more than average for his times.[17] To appreciate what this meant, it must be remembered how densely the buildings, streets, and squares were concentrated within the walls of late Roman cities.[18] The "piteous and bitter spectacle" Chrysostom described would have been familiar to anyone living in them. "Our age has brought no shortage of people stripped and homeless," observed Gregory of Nyssa in Cappadocia in 382. "There's no lack of strangers and transients: you can see the begging hand stretched out everywhere."[19]

Under the influence of such rhetoric there is, perhaps, some danger of overstating the plight of the able-bodied poor in the eastern Mediterranean at this time. These were not yet cities in economic decline. Urban construction and expansion picked up in the fifth century and continued, in most places, late into the sixth.[20] Since no technological innovations had dimin-

15. Chrysostom, *In epistulam I ad Corinthios hom.* 21.5 (PG 61.177); *In epistulam I ad Thessalonicenses V hom.* 11.3 (PG 62.465); *In Johannem hom.* 60.4 (59.333); and *In Matthaeum hom.* 15.10 (57.236). For the conditions that Chrysostom's rhetoric addressed, see Brown (1988): 309–13.

16. Chrysostom, *In Matthaeum hom.* 66.3 (PG 58.630). For Antioch's population, the fourth largest in the empire at this time, see Liebeschuetz (1972): 92–98.

17. Libanius, *Ep.* 61; ed. Albert F. Norman, p. 36: οἵ γέ τοι παρ' ἡμῖν προσαιτοῦντες πόλεως μέτριον. See also Liebeschuetz (1972): 98.

18. See Glanville Downey, *A History of Antioch in Syria from Seleucus to the Arab Conquest* (Princeton: Princeton University Press, 1961), 404–10, 434–39 and Liebeschuetz (1972): 92.

19. Gregory of Nyssa, *De pauperibus amandis I;* ed. A. van Heck, p. 17.

20. For Antioch ca. 365–455, see Downey (1961): 404–10, 452; Liebeschuetz (1972): 97–98; and Alan Walmsey, "Byzantine Palestine and Arabia: Urban Prosperity in Late Antiquity," in *Towns in Transition: Urban Evolution in Late Antiquity and the Early Middle Ages,* ed. N. Christie and S. T. Loseby (Aldershot: Scholar Press, 1996), 126–58. Nonetheless, the urban socioeconomic structure had changed markedly from the earlier period: see Patlagean (1977): 181–88 and Jones (1964): 737–757.

ished the need for unskilled labor, the able-bodied poor might find day-to-day employment as grunt laborers in construction, in portage, in the fields outside the city, or on ships.[21] Though access to free or subsidized grain was largely restricted to propertied citizens,[22] by the mid-fourth century, churches began to use their wealth to make food, clothing, hostels, and hospitals available, on a large scale, to the destitute.[23] Nor were the poor necessarily neglected outside the church. In Antioch, for instance, contributions of some sort were made for them every month, apparently by shopkeepers.[24] Despite the impression left by church contemporaries, urban residents of this period were neither completely callous towards the poor nor, it seems, completely unjustified for associating able-bodied beggars with laziness.[25] Even Chrysostom, who usually urged his congregations not to examine beggars too closely ("for if we start scrutinizing people's lives, we'll never pity any human being"), acknowledged that alms-givers had justification for questioning why able-bodied men were begging in summertime.[26]

Yet there are indications that the level of urban homelessness was rising in the late fourth century, most noticeably in the East.[27] Already in the second and third centuries unemployment had run high for anyone not securely attached to some landowner's estate. Able-bodied men could be found milling about town squares at all hours of the day, even during harvest time.[28] This unemployment would have been exacerbated in the late fourth century by a rise in the rural population of northern Syria and a rapid conversion of regional estates for olive production. Although the new olive groves eventually brought prosperity to both landowners and peasants

21. Thus Chrysostom, *De eleemosyna* 1 (PG 51.261); see also P. A. Brunt, "Free Labor and Public Works at Rome," *JRS* 70 (1980): 92–93.

22. Robert J. Rowland, "The 'Very Poor' and the Grain Dole at Rome and Oxyrhynchus," *ZPE* 21 (1976): 69–72 and Jean Durliat, *De la ville antique à la ville byzantine: Le problème des subsistances* (Rome: École français de Rome, 1990).

23. See Brown (1992): 95–97; Judith Herrin, "Ideals of Charity, Realities of Welfare: The Philanthropic Activity of the Byzantine Church," in *Church and Peoples in Byzantium*, ed. R. Morris (Chester: Bemrose Press, 1990), 151–58; and Demetrios J. Constantelos, *Byzantine Philanthropy and Social Welfare*, 2d ed. (New Rochelle, N.J.: A. D. Caratzas, 1992), 45–71.

24. Libanius, *Or.* 46.21 (*Contra Florentium*, ca. 392); ed. Richard Foerster, p. 389. Noted by Liebeschuetz (1972): 128.

25. See Brown (1992): 92–93 and Hands (1968): 65–67.

26. Chrysostom, *De eleemosyna* 6 (PG 51.269–270).

27. Patlagean (1977): 132, 178–81, 301–40.

28. Hamel (1990): 93–98, 153 and Patlagean (1977): 170. The chronic nature of urban poverty in late antiquity is further illustrated by a name given to the poor in Alexandria: *anexodoi* (those with no exit or hope of escape from that condition). See Christopher Haas, *Alexandria in Late Antiquity: Topography and Social Conflict* (Baltimore and London: Johns Hopkins University Press, 1997), 61 and n. 39.

of the region, at first it may have displaced peasants and contributed to Antioch's influx.[29] But the main cause of this migration was no doubt the series of natural calamities and barbarian invasions that one church historian, Philostorgius, says his era (ca. 360–430) suffered on an unprecedented scale.[30] Thus we read of peasants driven into Antioch by successive bouts of drought, hail, locusts, and famine between the years 360 and 393 (especially from 383 to 385, when the effects of drought and famine were felt throughout the empire); similar circumstances drove peasants into Gaza in 396, into Constantinople circa 440–446, and into Jerusalem circa 431–451, when the drought was so severe that city wells dried up and the poor had to beg for water.

Peasants usually proved resilient to such natural calamities in the long term. Far more disruptive were the barbarian raids that followed the massive defeat of the East Roman army at Adrianople (modern Edirne) in 378.[31] After that, as Jerome lamented in 396, Roman blood had "gushed daily" between Constantinople and the Alps under invasions by Goths and other tribes. During the previous year the eastern provinces had been overrun by the "Caucasian wolves," the White Huns: "How many monasteries captured, how many rivers turned red with human gore!"[32] A more persistent menace in the East arose from the Isaurian natives of Pamphylia and Cilicia, "men who spared neither city nor village, but plundered and burned all they could seize."[33] In 405 their approach drove Jerome and his fellow monks from their Bethlehem monastery to the Mediterranean coast.

Dislocated by events like these, peasants migrated to large cities as ref-

29. Suggested by Hugh Kennedy and J. H. W. G. Liebeschuetz, "Antioch and the Villages of Northern Syria in the Fifth and Sixth Centuries A.D.: Trends and Problems," *Nottingham Medieval Studies* 32 (1988):70–71. For rural population growth in Syria, see George Tate, "La Syrie a l'époque byzantine: Essai de synthèse," in *Archeologie et histoire de la Syrie*, ed. J.-M. Dentzer and W. Orthmann, vol. 2 (Saarbrücken: Saarbrücker, 1989), 107–9, noting the fragility of the new economy at 104–5. See also Patlagean (1977): 231–35.

30. Philostorgius, *Historia ecclesiastica* 11.7; documented by Patlagean (1977): 75–84 and Liebeschuetz (1972): 128–32. See also Hamel (1990): 44–54, describing the effects of regular famines (one every twenty years) in earlier Palestine.

31. For the anxieties triggered by this event, see Noel Lenski, *"Initium mali Romano imperio:* Contemporary Reactions to the Battle of Adrianople," *Transactions of the American Philological Association* 127 (1997): 129–68.

32. Jerome, *Ep.* 60.16.2–4; ed. and trans. J. H. D. Scourfield, pp. 68–70. Jerome refers to invasions by the Goths, Alani, and Huns (ca. 377–82, 395–96), Quadi and Sarmatae (Pannonia in ca. 374), Marcommani and Vandals. Theodosius' army was probably still in Italy after fighting against Eugenius (ca. 394) when the "White Huns" invaded in eastern provinces. For the general context, John Matthews, *The Roman Empire of Ammianus* (Baltimore: Johns Hopkins University Press, 1989), 304–82.

33. Theodoret, *HR* 10.5; ed. Pierre Canivet and Alice Leroy-Molinghen, p. 444. Cf. also 12.6 and 21.27. For the effects of Isaurian brigandage, see Matthews (1989): 362–67 and Patlagean (1977): 297–98.

ugees, where they were often mistaken for career beggars or vagrants. Indeed, the disruptions and insecurities of the late fourth century made conditions ripe for the appearance of organized beggar bands like the roving Banū Sāsān of the ninth-century East, or the Coquillards of fifteenth-century France.[34] Gregory of Nyssa was not the only one alarmed in 382 at the rise in mendicant strangers "whose home is the open air and whose shelters are the porticoes, streets, and emptier spaces of the market."[35] In the same year—four years after Adrianople and the subsequent pillaging of Thrace—the emperors Gratian, Valentinian, and Theodosius issued the first law against vagrant beggars in Roman history. It authorized Roman officials to inspect thoroughly "any persons who adopt the profession of mendicancy and are induced to seek their livelihood at public expense."

> The soundness of body and vigor of years of each one of them shall be investigated. In the case of those who are lazy and not to be pitied on account of any physical disability . . . the zealous and diligent informer shall obtain the ownership of those beggars who are slaves; as for those beggars who are distinguished by free birth alone, let whoever demonstrates this sort of sloth be sustained by perpetual serfdom.[36]

A similar hardening against strangers and able-bodied beggars took place at more local levels. Soon after this law was issued, the prefect of Rome, faced with prolonged famine and idle mouths to feed, ordered all "strangers" to be expelled from the city.[37] Contemporaries considered this to be an extreme measure, but it was one which leaders of eastern cities, given similar circumstances, were ready to imitate.

Between 382 and 392 Antioch suffered repeatedly from food shortages.[38] At the same time, its citizens, like those of other eastern communities, had to shoulder the heavy tax imposed after 378 to rebuild the Roman

34. See Clifford Edmund Bosworth, *The Medieval Islamic Underworld: The Banū Sāsān in Arabic Society and Literature.* Part 1: *The Banū Sāsān in Arabic Life and Lore* (Leiden: Brill, 1976), 4–23. I thank Peter Brown for recommending this study. Cf. Chrysostom, *De eleemosyna* 6 (PG 51.270) with Patlagean (1977): 178–81 and Eames and Goode (1973): 25–29. Alexander's troupe and other Messalian bands would have seemed very similar to the Banū Sāsān—though we have no references to Messalians crippling themselves or others to attract alms.

35. Gregory of Nyssa, *De pauperibus amandis* 1; ed. van Heck, p. 18.

36. *CTh* 14.18.1: *De mendicantibus non invalidis* (issued June 20, 382 in Padua); ed. Mommsen-Meyer, p. 847; trans. adapted from Pharr, p. 420. Cf. *CTh* 14.14.1 (397). The rise of able-bodied beggars in Milan is noted by Ambrose, *De officiis ministrorum* 2.16.76.

37. In 383 or 384: see Matthews (1989): 13. Ambrose, *De officis* 3.7.46 (PL 16.168A) says it was common in time of famine for citizens to demand that strangers or foreigners (*peregrini*) be banned from the city.

38. Liebeschuetz (1972): 128–29 notes food crises in 375, 382–386, 388–389, and 392 (in 383–384 famine was reported throughout the empire).

army.[39] It was during this time that Libanius pressed home some basic civic distinctions in order to identify those whom the city might expel. Sometime between 382 and 387 he advised the imperial governor to disregard the protests being led by theater claques, since

> these are all outsiders who have come here up to no good . . . , driven out of their own hometowns, shirking the crafts that their parents taught them and that fed them while they were young, . . . wanting to live in idleness *[argia]*. Do you think our city consists of these people who have no cities or homes, are not married, and have not one good reason to live except to be evil and do wicked things?[40]

He recommended that the governor cultivate instead those citizens who represented the proper civic order: "council members and their children, teachers, legal advocates," followed by "those who till the earth, who make a living by the work of their hands, who keep the markets filled." Compared to these, the "idle" theater claques represented a "sickness" that Antioch would gain to lose.[41] Their continuing disturbances caused him to take a firmer stand around 387, this time urging fellow council members to distinguish the better-behaved resident aliens from "those who should have been rooted out long ago."

> What is the criterion? Those who have a house, a wife, and trade deserve a share of the city; for from these things of theirs comes good order *(eutaxia)*.[42]

Libanius had already expressed such views when clamors arose at Antioch during the food crisis of the early 360s.[43] In the 380s we find him repeating them more forcefully, urging stronger measures against agitators of the city's growing unemployed and hungry population.[44] Although Libanius

39. Entire villages were reportedly abandoned because of this taxation: Liebeschuetz (1972): 164. Cf. Chrysostom, *In Matthaeum hom.* 66.4 (PG 58.651).

40. Libanius, *Or.* 41.6 and 11 *(Ad Timocratum)*; ed. Richard Foerster, pp. 297–98: οὗτοι ξένοι πάντες εἰσὶ κακῶς δεῦρο ἥκοντες . . . ἐκπεσόντες τῶν ἑαυτῶν πατρίδων. . . . ζῆν μὲν ἐν ἀργίᾳ βουλόμενοι. . . . (p. 300): πόλιν γὰρ ἡγῇ τουτουσὶ τοὺς ἀπόλιδας πόλιν τοὺς ἀοίκους. For the date, see Liebeschuetz (1972): 214 n. 7.

41. Libanius, *Or.* 41.11; ed. Foerster, p. 300: οὐ κέρδος ἂν ἦν ἀπηλλάχθαι τὴν πόλιν.

42. Libanius, *Or.* 56.22–23 *(Contra Lucianum)*; ed. Richard Foerster, p. 143: ἐν τούτοις αὐτῶν τῆς εὐταξίας δηλουμένης. Trans. adapted from Liebeschuetz (1972): 215–16, dating it to 387. For Libanius' association of citizenship with self-support and property, see Paul Petit, *Libanius et la vie municipale à Antioche au IVe siècle après J.C.* (Paris: Geuthner, 1955), 221–22 and Patlagean (1977): 131, 179. His views reflect traditional views: see Hands (1968): 64–67.

43. *Or.* 11.151 (ca. 360) identifies the city's *demos* as those having wives, children, houses, and property. *Or.* 16.31–33 (ca. 362–363) identifies agitators during the food shortages as ἄποροι ξένοι.

44. See also *Or.* 26.8. For Libanius' contentions with theater claques, see Liebeschuetz (1972): 214–16.

was specifically targeting Antioch's theater claque for attack, his criteria for civic inclusion and exclusion made plain his distrust of all males who appeared to be homeless, single, and idle.

Libanius' hard posturing, though it failed to move fellow council members to act, worked on the common suspicions about able-bodied vagrants in the late fourth and early fifth centuries. As John Chrysostom attests, citizens of Antioch and Constantinople instinctively dismissed beggars as lazy idlers ("why is he not working? why feed a lazy person?"), and regularly accused even the sick of being impostors with no legitimate claim to charity.[45] Others they suspected more darkly, as Libanius did, of being "runaways, rogues, and strangers" who had "fled from their own homelands to stream into our city."[46]

These were the prevailing sentiments when Epiphanius first attacked Messalian vagrants for begging on the streets of Antioch in summertime. Suspicion towards able-bodied idlers was deeply ingrained in Greco-Roman urban society, but this suspicion was exacerbated by urban migration, food shortages, and heavy taxation during precisely the period that monasticism took root and apostolic zealots like Alexander achieved notoriety. Already in the third century one Christian author had imagined that apostolic bands had sent out scouts to secure lodgings in each town they approached "so as to appear less like vagabonds."[47] Around 370 or 373 the emperors Valentinian and Valens had made their own suspicions clear by ordering the seizure of those who had abandoned city council obligations for the Egyptian desert "under the pretense of religion," calling them "devotees of idleness."[48] In the early fifth century at least one itinerant monk, Peter the Iberian, was mistaken for an escaped slave while traveling through Asia Minor and pressed into service by the imperial assessor who captured him: an application, perhaps, of the law of 382.[49] Such incidents remind us that the suspicions of secular life had impact upon ascetic life as well. Nor did church leaders view able-bodied vagrants much differently. As Basil re-

45. Chrysostom, *In epistulam ad Hebraeos VI hom.* 11.3 (PG 63.94); cf. *In Matthaeum hom.* 35.3–5 (57.409–411).

46. Chrysostom, *De eleemosyna* 6 (PG 51.269–70); *In Matthaeum hom.* 35.3 (57.409).

47. Ps.-Clement, *Recognitiones* 7.2.6; ed. Bernard Rehm and revised Georg Strecker, p. 198: per singulas civitates parata invenientes hospitia minus vagari videantur.

48. *CTh* 12.1.63; ed. Mommsen-Meyer, p. 678: ignaviae sectatores desertis civitatum muneribus captant solitudines ac secreta et specie religionis cum coetibus monazonton congregantur. Trans. Pharr, p. 351. This law was reissued as *CJ* 10.32.26, extending the possible seizure of monks to all provinces.

49. See John Rufus, *Vita Petri Iberi,* trans. Richard Raabe, pp. 30–31. Peter was traveling to Jerusalem in 437 with a box of martyrs' bones. For the date, see Paul Devos, "Quand Pierre l'Ibère vint-il à Jérusalem?" *AB* 86 (1968): 337–50.

minded a colleague, "he who gives to every wanderer casts it to a dog that is troublesome because of his shamelessness, but not pitiable in his need."[50] We must therefore consider how such *mores* and suspicions impinged upon John Chrysostom, Nilus, and their notions about how one should properly live in voluntary poverty.

JOHN CHRYSOSTOM AND THE CHRISTMONGERS OF CONSTANTINOPLE

John Chrysostom devoted his youth to an ascetic study group in Antioch, spent two years in solitude among the monks of Mt. Silpius overlooking the city, and wrote a number of stylized essays in defense of this new Christian way of philosophy, but in later years he referred to monks only for the edification of his church audiences. Although he remained an ascetic in private life, Chrysostom became more of an apologist than a theorist for the monastic movement.[51] Whether preaching as a priest in Antioch (386–398) or as bishop of Constantinople (398–403/404), he considered the "brothers of the hills" his stock exemplars for illustrating how an angelic life could be attained by ordinary humans through hard work and a sufficient determination to abandon the "things of this life."

We learn from other sources, however, that Chrysostom proved so harsh toward many ascetics that they actively supported his deposition from episcopal office in 403. Soon after becoming bishop of Constantinople in 398 he came into conflict with Isaac, the leading monastic figure in the city at the time, whom Chrysostom's admirer Palladius describes as "the little Syrian street tramp and leader of pseudomonks, the one who spent all his time slandering bishops."[52] According to Sozomen,

> Discord arose between John and many of the monks, especially Isaac. For while [John] would praise and respect those who stayed quietly practicing philosophy in their monasteries, and while he took exceeding care that these might not be harassed and might have their daily necessities, he reproached

50. Basil, *Ep.* 150; ed. and trans. Roy J. Deferrari (LCL 215), p. 368. Cf. Basil, *RB* 100–101, and Bishop Atticus' letter describing the proper distribution of alms in Socrates, *HE* 7.25.

51. For Chrysostom's social background, see A. H. M. Jones, "St. John Chrysostom's Parentage and Education," *Harvard Theological Review* 46 (1953): 171–73; for his ascetic experiences and essays, see J. N. D. Kelly, *Golden Mouth: The Story of John Chrysostom: Ascetic, Preacher, Bishop* (London: Duckworth, 1995), 14–54, with important observations about his urban *askēterion* at 19–20. John became a reader ca. 371 and a deacon ca. 380/81. For his homiletic treatment of monks, see Jean-Marie Leroux, "Saint Jean Chrysostome et le monachisme," in *Jean Chrysostome et Augustin: Actes du colloque de Chantilly, 22–24 septembre 1974*, ed. C. Kannengiesser (Paris: Éditions Beauschesne, 1975), 125–27 and Dagron (1970): 258–59.

52. Palladius, *Dial.* 6; ed. Anne-Marie Malingrey and Phillipe Leclercq (SC 341) pp. 126–28: Ἰσαακίῳ Συρίσκῳ περιτρίμματι, ἀφηγητῇ ψευδομοναζόντων.

and rebuked those who went outdoors and appeared in the city, on the grounds that they were insulting philosophy.[53]

Here Sozomen reveals an episcopal policy towards monastic discipline at Constantinople that Chrysostom initiated but does not mention in his own writings. While Chrysostom liked to make his audience ponder "true and pure philosophy" by reference to Christian solitaries who had "fled cities and marketplaces" to go "where they have no communication with anyone, philosophizing unhindered in the tranquility of isolation,"[54] modern historians have found in his writings nothing "either in praise or blame that might be applicable to monks roaming the streets of the capital."[55] Yet in his sermons at both Constantinople and Antioch Chrysostom did allude to ascetic problems of his day. His remarks show not only that he was mindful of wandering, begging monks, but also that he was very concerned with their impact upon the reception of monasticism as a whole.

In Antioch Chrysostom had routinely addressed complaints about beggars who faked their wounds for alms; now, as bishop of Constantinople, he had to answer charges against impostors of a different sort.[56] "We have now come to such a pitch of unreasonableness," he one day told his listeners,

> that not only are we [suspicious] towards the poor who walk in the alleyways, but even towards men who lead a monastic life *[monazontes andres]*. "This guy is an impostor," you say. . . . What do you mean? Does seeking bread make him an imposter? If he asked for pounds of gold and silver, or for expensive clothing, servants, or some such thing, you might rightly call him a fraud. But

---

53. Sozomen, *HE* 8.9.4; ed. Bidez-Hansen, p. 362: ἠρεμοῦντας μὲν γὰρ ἐν τοῖς αὐτῶν φροντιστηρίοις τοὺς ὧδε φιλοσοφοῦντας εἰσάγαν ἐπήνει . . . ἐξιόντας δὲ θύραζε καὶ κατὰ τὴν πόλιν φαινομένους ὡς τὴν φιλοσοφίαν ἐνυβρίζοντας ἐλοιδόρει καὶ ἐπέστρεφεν.

54. E.g., John Chrysostom, *In epistulam ad Ephesios VI hom.* 21.3 (PG 62.153); *In Matthaeum hom.* 69.3 (58.643); *De Lazaro hom.* 3.1 (48.992).

55. See J. H. G. W. Liebeschuetz, "Friends and Enemies of John Chrysostom," in *Maistor: Classical, Byzantine, and Renaissance Studies for Robert Browning,* ed. A. Moffat (Canberra: Australian National University, 1984), 90–93 (quoted at 92) and Dagron (1970): 262–64. Neither treats the nexus of patronal support and spiritual authority explored in this chapter. I agree with Escolan (1999): 222 that Chrysostom considered Isaac's patronage a threat, but do not think *In I Corinthios hom.* 6.3 (PG 61.53–54) shows that he encouraged monks to act as spiritual teachers in people's houses, as Escolan implies.

56. Pauline Allen and Wendy Mayer have challenged the traditional criteria for assigning date and provenance to Chrysostom's sermons: see esp. Allen and Mayer, "The Thirty-Four Homilies on Hebrews: The Last Series Delivered by Chrysostom in Constantinople?," *Byzantion* 65 (1995): 309–48; "John Chrysostom's Homilies on I and II Thessalonians: The Preacher and his Audience," *SP* 31 (1997): 3–21; and Wendy Mayer, *The Provenance of the Homilies of St John Chrysostom: Towards a New Assessment of Where He Preached What* (Ph.D. diss., University of Queensland, 1996). I thank Wendy Mayer for her advice on those used here.

if he seeks none of these things but only food and shelter—things proper to philosophy—tell me, does this make him a fraud?[57]

This was a kindly defense of such *monazontes andres,* as monks of Constantinople were often called.[58] The homily reveals, however, not so much Chrysostom's concern for the welfare of these monks (whom he merely defended in the same charitable spirit he publicly extended towards all beggars accused of deceit), as his awareness that some had provoked ill will through their pursuit of alms. Chrysostom, in fact, took such monastic behavior quite seriously, to judge from other sermons. "If those among us are scandalized by such things," he observed on another occasion in Constantinople, "how much the more so are outsiders scandalized?" Chrysostom was referring to the non-Christians in the city: "These find grounds for countless jabs and accusations when they see a healthy man who is capable of supporting himself out begging, seeking his support from others." For this reason, he added, "they are even calling us 'Christmongers.' "[59]

No doubt Chrysostom was extemporizing against those same monks whom Sozomen says he considered an insult to philosophy, the ones Palladius would later call "pseudomonks." Although his concern for monasticism's reputation usually kept him from airing ascetic problems at church,[60] he let those remarks slip while expounding Paul's command to "work with your hands . . . so as to conduct yourselves decorously toward outsiders" (1 Thess 4:11–12). By work, he emphasized, the apostle had meant manual labor, not "receiving [alms] or living in *argia.*" Thus Chrysostom attacked ascetics who defined "work" as purely spiritual labors: "Where then are those who seek spiritual work? Do you see how he has removed from them every excuse by saying 'with your hands'? But does anyone work with his hands at fasting? or at all-night vigils? or at sleeping on the ground? No one would say so."[61] True, by manual labor Paul had meant spiritual labors, Chrysostom explains, but only in the sense that manual labor enabled a Christian to perform the spiritual work of giving alms. "See how he rebukes them?" he continues. Although Paul did not explicitly

57. John Chrysostom, *In Hebraeos VI hom.* 11.4 (PG 63.96). Allen and Mayer (1995): 343–45 express caution, but do not reject this sermon's attribution to Constantinople.

58. Dagron (1970): 251.

59. John Chrysostom, *In I Thess IV hom.* 6.1 (PG 62.430): Διὸ καὶ Χριστεμπόρους καλοῦσιν ἡμᾶς.

60. As suggested by Leroux (1975):127.

61. John Chrysostom, *In I Thess IV hom. 6.1* (PG 62.429–430): μὴ λαμβάνειν μηδὲ ἀργεῖν, ἀλλ' ἐργαζόμενον ἑτέρους παρέχειν. . . . Ποῦ τοίνυν εἰσὶν οἱ τὸ ἔργον ζητοῦντες τὸ πνευματικόν; ὁρᾷς πῶς αὐτοῖς πᾶσαν πρόφασιν ἀνεῖλεν εἰπὼν, "ταῖς χερσὶν ὑμῶν." Ἄρα νηστείαν ἐργάζεταί τις ταῖς χερσίν; ἀλλὰ παννυχίδας; ἀλλὰ χαμευνίας; Οὐδεὶς τοῦτο ἂν εἴποι. These were stereotypical monastic practices: see *V.Antonii* 5 and Chrysostom, *De sacerdotio* 3.16.

say that Christians must perform manual labor "in order to avoid the shamefulness of begging," he nonetheless had "insinuated the same."[62]

Clearly there was more at issue between the bishop and the *monazontes andres* of Constantinople than their mere appearance in the city. As Sozomen's account implies, their begging on the streets troubled Chrysostom enough that he made it a matter of policy to provide "daily necessities" to any who remained inside. Their leader, Isaac, was particularly active in soliciting alms from wealthy citizens, as we shall see, and such behavior had evidently caused complaints among both Christians and non-Christians in the city. But there was more to Chrysostom's animosity towards Isaac and his monks than the insult their begging was causing philosophy. He also sensed that it threatened the reputation of his own church office. Their "idleness" and pursuit of alms, he claims, had exposed him (and other Christians, probably clergy) to accusations of "selling Christ." This of course was the same accusation that had earlier troubled the author of the *Letters to Virgins*.[63] In another sermon we find Chrysostom speaking more defensively about the proper qualifications for charity. After noting Paul's remark, "I have heard that some of you are living in idleness, mere busybodies, not doing any work" (2 Thess 3:11), Chrysostom began to clarify exactly who had a legitimate claim to alms and who did not. Alms, he explained,

> are given only to those who do not have the strength to support themselves by the work of their hands, or to those who teach, and are wholly occupied in the business of teaching . . . for "the workman is worthy of his pay," so that [the teacher] is not idle, but receives his pay for work that is, in fact, a great work.

"But to pray and fast, being idle," he immediately adds, "is not manual labor."[64] Thus Chrysostom again made clear that the spiritual labors of the city's ascetic "idlers" did not constitute a fulfillment of Paul's command to work (or render them worthy of alms). But here he was also drawing a distinction between ascetics and church preachers like himself, who performed no manual labors but were not to be accused of idleness. Their dedication to the "great labor" of teaching justified their dependence on alms.[65] At the same time Chrysostom was also implying that monks who devoted themselves to prayer and fasting were not actively teaching. Deliv-

---

62. *Ibid.* (PG 62.430): Οὐκ εἶπεν, " Ἵνα μὴ ἀσχημονῆτε ἐπαιτοῦντες," ἀλλὰ τὸ αὐτὸ μὲν ᾐνίξατο.

63. Above ch. 2. In the fourth century the term Χριστεμπόρος was usually applied to heretics and schismatics: see Telfer (1939): 265–66.

64. Chrysostom, *In epistulam II ad Thessalonicenses III hom.* 5.2 (PG 62.494): οὐδὲ οὗτος ἀργός ἐστιν, ἀλλ᾽ . . . ἐργασίας μεγάλης λαμβάνει τὸν μισθόν. Τὸ δὲ εὔχεσθαι καὶ νηστεύειν ἀργοῦντα, οὐκ ἔστιν ἔργον χειρῶν.

65. Chrysostom defended provisioning church teachers "so that they may labor for spiritual things with no care for earthly things": *In epistulam I ad Timotheum V hom.* 15.2 (PG 62.581).

ered before a church audience and evidently mindful of the claims and presumptions of Constantinople's ascetics, these hasty, paratactic remarks represented a public defense of Chrysostom's own vocation and funding.

As a clergyman in Antioch during the 380s and early 390s he would have become highly sensitized to accusations of idleness. These were the same lean, troubled years in which Libanius repeatedly denounced the theater claques, contrasting them to workers who deserved to live in the city. Chrysostom's church had also adopted a hard stance against "idlers" within its own ranks. We learn much about the ecclesiastical culture in which Chrysostom rose from a church manual that was probably compiled at Antioch just before Chrysostom became a deacon there.[66] An entire section of these *Apostolic Constitutions* was devoted to work, self-sufficiency, and the evils of *argia:*

> You younger members of the church, . . . apply yourselves to your works with great dignity, in order to be sufficient at all times both for yourself and for those who are poor, so as not to burden God's church. . . . Work without ceasing, because idleness is an incurable vice. Among you, "If anyone does not work, let him not eat." For even the Lord our God hates idle people. None who serve God should be idle.[67]

Bishops were entitled to use church alms as "appropriate to their need and dignity" since they bore the weight of their office and "the laborer is worthy of his pay," but the manual requests that they show moderation.[68] Apart from widows and orphans, church funds were to be given only to those "*proven* in distress," or "*truly* in need."[69] Those who suffered as a consequence of their idleness were "not worthy of assistance, nor even of the Church of God." The manual recommends vigilance against anyone who might try to "take [alms] out of hypocrisy or idleness, instead of working to help others."[70]

Such frugal principles and concern for "idleness" Chrysostom brought with him and tried to impose on the Great Church of Constantinople. He

66. For provenance and date (Antioch, ca. 380) of the *Constitutiones Apostolorum* [*Const.App.*], see Marcel Metzger, *Les constitutiones apostoliques* (SC 320; Paris: Éditions du Cerf, 1985), 54–60.

67. *Const.App.* 2.63.1–6; ed. Metzger (SC 320), pp. 336–38: ἦτε ἐπαρκοῦντες καὶ ἑαυτοῖς καὶ τοῖς πενομένοις, πρὸς τὸ μὴ ἐπιβαρεῖν τὴν τοῦ Ἐκκλησίαν. . . . ἀργοὺς γὰρ μισεῖ καὶ ὁ Κύριος ὁ Θεὸς ἡμῶν· ἀργὸς γὰρ εἶναι οὐκ ὀφείλει οὐδεὶς τῶν Θεῷ προσανεχόντων.

68. *Const.App.* 2.25.1, 13; ed. Metzger (SC 320), pp. 226, 232.

69. *Const.App.* 3.3.2; ed. Metzger (SC 329) p. 124: τοῖς ἐν θλίψει ἐξεταζομένοις. 3.4.4; p. 126: τῷ χρήζοντι κατὰ ἀλήθειαν; see also 2.4.1, 2.25.2, 3.4.1–2, 3.3.1. This continues a trend toward limiting the range of people eligible for alms already noticeable in the third century and fully established as policy by the early fifth: see Hamel (1990):233 and Bishop Atticus' letter on use of alms in Socrates, *HE* 7.25.

70. *Const.App.* 2.4.4–7; ed. Metzger (SC 320), p. 150; 4.4.1 (SC 329), p. 174.

approached his new role there as chief "Steward of Christ" with great earnestness.[71] His predecessor, Nectarius (381–397), a mild-mannered senator who had been baptized on the same day he was ordained, had not kept a strict watch on the flow of money around the church during his sixteen years as bishop.[72] Apparently slander was being directed against the church for "selling Christ" at all levels. Chrysostom soon initiated reforms.[73] Besides cutting extravagances previously enjoyed in the episcopal palace (Palladius says that he wanted to set an example for other bishops by preaching like Paul "at his own expense"),[74] Chrysostom took over church accounts to prevent stewards from embezzling alms meant for the poor,[75] and kept vigilant against other abuses that jeopardized the church reputation: "He made trouble for that group that glued their eyes on others' purses. He took concern for their way of life, asking them to be satisfied with their own wages and not to seek fatty drippings from the wealthy, . . . pursuing the life of the parasite and flatterer."[76] Palladius reports that Chrysostom also mocked those who used ascetic poverty as a pretense to enrich themselves.[77] Judging from Palladius, when the new bishop arrived, there were few clerics or monks in Constantinople who did not assume that others would provide for their support. Chrysostom urged one of their major benefactors, the grand deaconess Olympias, to stop pouring her wealth out upon those who did not need it, "as if into the sea."[78]

Although Chrysostom did air concern for clergy seeking alms ("if he calls himself a priest, check his credentials"),[79] he was mostly concerned with the practices of the city's ascetic population. This may be partly explained by the fact that Chrysostom so keenly regarded monks as exemplars

71. Palladius, *Dial.* 12,35–38; ed. Malingrey-Leclercq (SC 341), p. 235. Cf. *De sacerdotio* 3.15–16 (written in Antioch ca. 390). For his reform of church finances at Constantinople, see Dagron (1974): 493–94.

72. Socrates, *HE* 5.8.12; Sozomen, *HE* 7.8.2 and Kelly (1995): 118.

73. For these reforms, see Kelly (1995): 120–23; Liebeschuetz (1984): 89–90; Dagron (1974): 493–94; and Chrysostomus Baur, *John Chrysostom and His Times*, trans. M. Gonzaga, vol. 2 (Westminster: Newman Press, 1960), 56–71.

74. Palladius, *Dial.* 5,127–32 and 17,205–209; ed. Malingrey-Leclercq (SC 341), pp. 348–50 (citing Acts 28:30).

75. Palladius, *Dial.* 12,33–35.

76. Palladius, *Dial.* 5,120–126; ed. Malingrey-Leclercq (SC 341), p. 120: ταράσσεται . . . τὸ μέρος τῶν βαλαντιοσκόπων . . . κολάκων καὶ παρασίτων μεταδιώξαντες βίον. Trans. adapted from Robert Meyer, p. 38. The context suggests Palladius means Chrysostom's reform of the clergy as Liebeschuetz (1984): 89 interprets it, but others in the church community may be meant as well.

77. Palladius, *Dial.* 19.

78. Sozomen, *HE* 8.9.2, to be read with Palladius, *Dial.* 17. For Olympias' support of church clergy at Constantinople, see Dagron (1974): 503–6.

79. Chrysostom, *In Hebraeos VI hom.* 11.4 (PG 63.96). See Leyerle (1994): 44–46.

for Christianity as a whole. Anyone attending his church at Antioch during the 380s or 390s would have grown accustomed to hearing how monks imitated the apostle's zeal and earned their bread through their "righteous toils."[80] As he explained one day to catechumens when some monk-priests had appeared, having come in from the Syrian hinterland, "the philosophy we try to teach with words they display through their deeds, fulfilling the apostolic precept on work, the one that commands each to obtain his daily sustenance through the work of his hands."[81] When associating such exemplars with philosophy, Chrysostom was also addressing audiences (both Christian and non-Christian) for whom Greco-Roman figures like the begging Cynic philosopher Diogenes still provided the most radical exemplars of philosophic renunciations. Chrysostom repeatedly cites monastic recluses as proof that Christian philosophers had achieved through apostolic humility what pagan philosophers had only appeared to achieve.[82] They were heirs to both the voluntary poverty and the "strict decorum" that Jesus had required of his representatives.[83] It is therefore not surprising that some of his remarks against begging monks were prompted by Paul's explanation (1 Thess 4:12) that Christians should work so as to conduct themselves with *euschēmosynē* (good form, or social decorum) with respect to "outsiders." As Chrysostom elsewhere notes, his contemporaries considered begging to be an extreme form of *aschēmosynē* (bad form, or lack of decorum). "Better to die," he quotes them as saying, "than to be caught begging."[84]

It is usually thought that Chrysostom encountered a type of monasticism at Constantinople that was different from what he had previously known.[85]

80. E.g., Chrysostom, *In Matthaeum hom.* 8.5 (PG 57.88); 69.3 (58.653); and 72.4. For Chrysostom's views on manual labor, see Ottorino Pasquato, "Vita Spirituale e Lavoro in Giovanni Crisostomo: 'Modelli' di un rapporto," in *Spiritualità del lavoro nella catechesi dei Padri del III–VI secolo,* ed. S. Felici (Rome: Libreria Ateneo Salesiano, 1986), 105–39.

81. Chrysostom, *Catechesis ad illuminandos hom.* 8.2; ed. Antoine Wenger, pp. 248–49. Frans van de Paverd, *St. John Chrysostom: The Homilies on the Statues: An Introduction* (Rome: Scuola Tipografica S. Pio X, 1991), 260–93 concludes that these monks had been ordained to serve as priests in the countryside and came into Antioch for monthly consultations.

82. See Chrysostom, *In Matthaeum hom.* 10.4; 22.4; *In Ephesios VI hom.* 21.3. For the popular image of the philosopher at this time, see Derek Krueger, *Symeon the Holy Fool* (Berkeley and Los Angeles: University of California Press, 1996), 82–86; Johannes Hahn, *Die Philosoph und die Gesellschaft: Selbstverständnis, öffentliches Auftreten und populäre Erwartungen in der hohen Kaiserzeit* (Stuttgart: Franz Steiner, 1989), 180–81; and MacMullen (1966): 59–61.

83. Chrysostom, *In Matthaeum hom.* 33.4 (PG 57.392): κοσμιότης ἠκριβωμένη. Jesus called his apostles "workmen" so they would not be "shamed" by begging: *In Matthaeum hom.* 32.5 (57.382D–383A).

84. Chrysostom, *In Hebraeos VI hom.* 11.4 (PG 63.95): τί δὲ ἀσχημονέστερον τοῦ ἐπαιτεῖν; κρεῖσσον ἀποθανεῖν ἢ ἐπαιτεῖν.

85. E.g., Kelly (1995): 123 and Dagron (1970): 253–54; but see Wendy Mayer, "Monasticism at Antioch and Constantinople in the Late Fourth Century: A Case of Exclusivity or

Although we have little evidence (besides Epiphanius) that monks roamed the streets of Antioch before Alexander's day, Chrysostom had in fact dealt with spiritual "idlers" there before moving to the imperial city. Once while expounding John 6:27 ("work not for the food that perishes, but for the food that endures for eternal life"), Chrysostom complained about certain Christians who had "abused this saying" by thinking that Jesus had meant to "put an end to the need to work."[86] In order to refute their justification for "living in idleness," Chrysostom proceeded to explain that Jesus' approval of Mary over Martha and his command to "have no care for tomorrow" must be understood in harmony with Paul's position on manual labor. He conceded, however, that Jesus' remarks might seriously conflict with Paul if taken literally.[87]

These were, of course, the same scriptural passages used by ascetics like Pseudo-Macarius, the author of the *Book of Steps*, and the monks of Carthage to justify their total poverty and dependence on others. In the late 370s Epiphanius had similarly criticized this literal interpretation of John 6:27 while discussing Messalian heretics, some of whom he located in Antioch. Indeed, Chrysostom may well have attended the synod that had investigated Adelphius and other Messalian monks at Antioch and had launched the church's anti-Messalian campaign. At any rate, he was here making his own contribution against presumptions that were becoming especially identified with Messalian heretics.[88] It is important to note, however, the specific reason he gives for criticizing such men. "They slander all Christianity, causing it to be ridiculed on the charge of *argia*."[89]

Chrysostom had to confront similar ascetic troubles in Constantinople. As Epiphanius had already observed in the 370s, one problem with Messalian *argia* was that it forced monks "to share the idle tables of the rich" out of need.[90] Chrysostom saw another problem: such ascetic "idlers" exposed other Christians, especially churchmen eligible to support by alms, to charges of "idleness" and "selling Christ." It is therefore not surprising that tensions arose between him and the city's "pseudomonks" or their

---

Diversity," in *Prayer and Spirituality in the Early Church*, ed. P. Allen et al. (Brisbane: Australia Catholic University, 1998b), 275–88. Most telling is Libanius, *Or.* 45.26: monks usually came into the city during summer.

86. Chrysostom, *In Johannem hom.* 44.1 (PG 59.248): τινες τῶν βουλομένων ἀργῶς τρέφεσθαι, ἀποκέχρηνται τούτῳ τῷ λόγῳ, ὡς τὴν ἐργασίαν ἐκκόπτοντος τοῦ Χριστοῦ.

87. *Ibid.* (PG 59.249): ἀλλὰ ταῦτα τὴν μάχην δείκνυσι σφοδροτέραν κατὰ τὸ ῥητόν.

88. Csányi (1960): 34–36 proposed that Chrysostom was addressing Messalians. Fitschen (1998): 134 challenges this view on the grounds that Chrysostom here only discusses the problem of *argia*.

89. Chrysostom, *In Johannem hom.* 44.1 (PG 59.248–249): εὔκαιρον καὶ πρὸς αὐτοὺς εἰπεῖν. Ὅλον γάρ, ὡς εἰπεῖν, διαβάλλουσι τὸν Χριστιανισμόν, καὶ ἐπὶ ἀργίᾳ κωμῳδεῖσθαι παρασκευάζουσι.

90. Epiphanius, *Panarion* 80.4.8; ed. Holl-Dummer, p. 490.

leader, Isaac. There was, however, another side to Chrysostom's troubles with the wandering monks of Constantinople, which neither he nor Palladius discloses. While criticizing other members of the church for skimming "fatty droppings" off tables of the rich and advising Olympias to refrain from lavishing wealth on these (including not only clergy but "innumerable ascetics" as well), Chrysostom himself continued to rely on the deaconesses' wealth and services to supply his own needs. Although Palladius defends this, saying Chrysostom "did not have to touch church funds and took his daily food as it came, ever eluding this sort of anxiety," it evidently raised talk of double standards.[91] Moreover, Chrysostom's justification for such support, based as it was on teaching, could only have sparked animosity among the city's ascetics, as it implied that they were not teachers themselves. Yet their leader, Isaac, who was probably the main target of Chrysostom's remarks,[92] had a better claim to support on this score than either Chrysostom or Palladius suggests. For one thing, Isaac was an ordained priest and therefore had rights to alms as a teacher according to Chrysostom's own criterion for eligibility.[93] But it was his reputation as a monk and spiritual teacher that most impressed his supporters. In fact, this particular monk, far from being a street tramp, had been revered and supported as the city's chief spiritual master by much of the nobility long before Chrysostom ever attempted to assert that role himself.

Such undercurrents of rivalry and reform only occasionally surfaced in Chrysostom's public discourse at Constantinople. The problems raised by monks there were found in other cities too. We will return to Chrysostom's troubles with Isaac and the city's monastic establishment after we have seen the light cast on its circumstances by Nilus of Ancyra.

NILUS AND THE ASCETIC PARASITES OF ANCYRA

Located at the juncture of major highways connecting Constantinople with Antioch, Jerusalem, Alexandria, and the eastern frontiers, Ancyra (modern Ankara) was no provincial backwater.[94] Although we know little about Nilus

91. Palladius, *Dial.* 17,185–221; ed. Malingrey-Leclercq (SC 341), pp. 348–50. Palladius' remarks are apologetic. Olympias' house was linked to the episcopal palace: for the support she gave Chrysostom, see Wendy Mayer, "Constantinopolitan Women in Chrysostom's Circle," *VC* 53 (1999): 286–87 and Brown (1988): 283–84.

92. Palladius calls Isaac ὁ ἡσυχαστής, referring sarcastically to his absorption in spiritual pursuits: *Dial.* 8; ed. Malingrey-Leclercq (SC 341), p. 176.

93. *Ibid.*, where Isaac is mentioned as one of two priests sent to summon Chrysostom to the Oak. See Baur 2 (1959): 64 n. 41.

94. For Ancyra, see Clive Foss, "Late Antique and Byzantine Ankara," *Dumbarton Oaks Papers* 31 (1977): 29–54. Its links to the cultural mainstream are illustrated by Libanius' correspondence.

apart from his own writings (ca. 390–430),[95] he evidently considered himself well informed about problems arising from ascetic begging in Constantinople and other cities. For Nilus these problems were by no means distant. As a monk himself, he was highly concerned with the impact of ascetic vagrancy on the reputation of his vocation. Indeed, the letter he wrote describing the pervasion of "pseudomonks" in cities and villages of his day merely epitomized a lengthier criticism of their activities in a treatise he wrote on proper monastic practice called the *Ascetic Discourse*. This treatise, which became quite popular in later orthodox circles,[96] also preserves our most detailed contemporary account of monastic life in early fifth-century urban society. Nilus' perspective, however, requires careful analysis. What Nilus found objectionable in these monks was not just their begging, but a pursuit of patronage and spiritual leadership that jeopardized his own.

By the early fifth century, Ancyra's Christian population included at least two thousand virgins and several aristocrats whom Palladius celebrates for their generosity. Prominent among both groups was Magna, a wealthy deaconess known for her support of hospitals, traveling bishops, and the poor.[97] It was to her that Nilus dedicated what was probably his last work, *On Voluntary Poverty*.[98] In it Nilus proposed a light regimen of manual labor, "following the footsteps of the apostles, working so as to not burden anybody."[99] Its intermittent practice, he said, would refresh the body for contemplative pursuits.[100] It would also supplement the moderate course of voluntary property that he recommended so as to liberate his readers from the empty concerns of worldly life and help them attain such spiritual ben-

95. Nilus is something of an enigma. He is not mentioned by name until the ninth century. His only secure dates begin with a letter written ca. 390 and end with his treatise *De voluntaria paupertate*, mentioning Alexander. On this and other questions, see Marie-Gabrielle Guérard, "Nil d'Ancyre," *DSp* 11 (Paris: Éditions Beauschesne, 1981), 345–56; Cameron 1976a; Harald Ringshausen, *Zur Verfasserschaft und Chronologie der dem Nilus Ancyranus zugeschriebenen Werke*. Inaugural Diss., Frankfurt am Main (1967); Heussi (1917). Guérard provides extended commentary on Nilus' style in *Nil d'Ancyre: Commentaire sur le Cantique des Cantiques* (SC 403; Paris: Éditions du Cerf, 1994).

96. Nilus' Λόγος ἀσκητικός *(De monastica exercitatione)* was included in the eighteenth-century *Philocalia*. Its importance is indicated by MS traditions and *florilegia* from the seventh century on; already in the sixth century Cyril of Skythopolis was quoting it in hagiography. See Binns (1994): 64 and Guérard (1981): 354.

97. Palladius, *HL* 66–67 with Foss (1977): 50–52. For earlier monasticism in Ancyra, see Elm (1994): 113–24.

98. The title *De voluntaria paupertate* (Περὶ Ἀκτημοσύνη) has the subscript πρὸς τὴν σεμνοπρεπεστάτην Μάγναν διάκονον Ἀγκύρας (PG 79.968). For her probable identification with the Magna of *HL* 67, see Foss (1977): 52.

99. Nilus, *De vol. paup.* 42 (PG 79.1020CD).

100. Nilus, *De vol. paup.* 29 (PG 79.1004D).

efits as freedom from care.[101] Although he nowhere describes what such poverty actually meant in practice, Nilus was probably advising his readers to adopt the same standard that he praised Magna for zealously preserving (despite her wealth) "uncorrupted, as it held from the beginning."[102]

As we have seen, Nilus was partly responding to extreme forms of ascetic poverty and idleness that had been made notorious by Adelphius and Alexander the Sleepless.[103] For Nilus, however, such Messalians merely provided outstanding examples of monasticism thrown off its proper balance of work and contemplation. His own ascetic prescriptions aimed to restore some measure of the strict apostolic discipline he considered lost on his monastic peers, whose pursuit of wealth and reputation for worldliness he had already surveyed in his *Ascetic Discourse*.[104] At stake was nothing less than rehabilitating true philosophy in the public eye, so that its image might "shine forth its own beauty" and no longer become grounds for mockery.[105] As Nilus saw it, ambition for material things had rendered most of his contemporaries unfit for the kingdom of heaven. Many were acquiring as much land and livestock as possible to supply the demands of the market, focusing more attention on field boundaries and water rights than on the divine.[106] For this reason,

> today most people think piety is procuring, and that we apply ourselves to the detached and blessed life of old for no other reason than that, through a feigned reverence for God, we might evade burdensome obligations of service [leitourgeias] and obtain license for relaxation.[107]

Consequently, he complains, "we are now regarded as a useless rabble even by those who should revere us, and are derided by the common throng for

101. Nilus, *De vol. paup.* 2 (PG 79.972A): μεσότητα τῆς ἀκτημοσύνης νῦν μετερχόμενοι. See also sect. 3 (972D). For *amerimnia:* sect. 36.

102. Nilus, *De vol. paup.* 1 (PG 79.968D): τὸν τῆς ἀκτημοσύνης κανόνα ὡς εἶχεν ἐξ ἀρχῆς ἀπαράτρωτον. Nilus defines moderate poverty only by explaining what it is not: i.e., that it is neither involuntary poverty that "grinds down the mind" (sect. 2) nor the completely possessionless and homeless state of the "saints of old" (sect. 3: i.e., prophets, John the Baptist, and the apostles, as explained in sect. 21) and certainly not the acquisitiveness displayed by contemporary monks (sect. 4–18).

103. Nilus introduces the subject in his discussion of Adelphius and Alexander, *De vol. paup.* 21.

104. Nilus refers to his *De monastica exercitatione* in *De vol. paup.* 1 (PG 79.968): Πρώην μὲν πρὸς τοὺς ἀμελέστερον μετιόντες τὸν μοναδικὸν βίον γράφοντες λόγον, ἱκανῶς κατηψάμεθα τούτων, ὅσον ὑπέβησαν τῆς ἀποστολικῆς ἀκριβείας....

105. Nilus, *De mon. ex.* 75 (PG 79.809B). Cf. sect. 3–4 (722BC).

106. Nilus, *De mon. ex.* 6–7, (PG 79.725A–D), 12 (732D); *De vol. paup.* 30 (1005BC).

107. Nilus, *De mon. ex.* 7 (PG 79.725D–728A): τοὺς πολλοὺς πορισμὸν ἡγεῖσθαι τὴν εὐσέβειαν ... διὰ τῆς ἐπιπλάστου θεοσεβίας, τὰς μὲν ἐπιπόνους λειτουργείας φύγωμεν, ἄδειαν δὲ ἀπολαύσεως πορισάμενοι.

having no special distinction from the rest of them, not least because of our involvement in the markets."[108]

As this passage indicates, Nilus considered monasticism a highly aristocratic enterprise, to be elevated above the "common throng." Not least responsible for its degradation were monks whose rumored evasion of onerous liturgies suggests that their social origins lay in the curial class and that they had abandoned traditional municipal obligations in order to retire to property in Ancyra's countryside.[109] But such country monks and their forays in the marketplace worried Nilus far less than those who permanently left for the cities to pursue their vocation "without scruple, among promiscuous mobs."[110] These were monks, he says, who had run away from their monasteries because they could not endure a life of strict discipline.

> They go reveling through the cities. Overpowered by the needs of their stomachs, they bear around a semblance of piety as bait for the deception of many, submitting to anything the needs of their bodies compel—for nothing is more compelling than physical necessity . . . and as their accustomed idleness increases to a greater degree, they advance their pleas in even more knavish fashion.[111]

Nilus regarded such ascetic idlers as woefully endemic in cities of his day:

> The cities are being overwhelmed by those who wander around them at random. People in their houses are being mobbed and look in disgust at the very sight of them planted at their gates, begging utterly without shame. Many even gain entry into houses where they feign piety for a while. Cloaking their mischief with the mask of hypocrisy, they later go away after defrauding their hosts.[112]

Nilus devotes far more space in his *Ascetic Discourse* to such urban wanderers than to monks involved with agricultural trade, clearly because he believed their activities posed the more serious threat to monasticism's reputation.

> They bring discredit upon the entire monastic way of life. For this reason those who once taught self-restraint are now driven out as corrupters of cities,

---

108. Nilus, *De mon. ex.* 7 (PG 79.728A): ὡς εἰκαῖος ὄχλος . . . καὶ . . . οὐχ ἥκιστα ταῖς ἀγοραῖς ἐμφερόμενοι γελώμεθα οὐδὲν παρὰ τοὺς λοιποὺς . . . ἐξαίρετον ἔχοντες.

109. These rumors echo the suspicions Valentinian and Valens aired in *CTh* 12.1.63.

110. Nilus, *De mon. ex.* 46 (PG 79.776C): ἀδεῶς τοὺς πεφυρμένους ὄχλους συνδιαιτᾶσθαι.

111. Nilus, *De mon. ex.* 8 (PG 79.728C): διὰ τὸ μὴ φέρειν τοῦ βίου τὴν ἀκρίβειαν, ἐπικωμάζωσι ταῖς πόλεσι . . . ἐπὶ ἀπάτῃ τῶν πολλῶν τὴν τῆς εὐσεβείας μόρφωσιν ὡς δέλεαρ περιφέρουσι . . . καὶ μάλιστα ὅταν καὶ ἀργία προσῇ μεμελετημένη, τότε καὶ πανουργότερον ἡ σκῆψις προχωρεῖ.

112. Nilus, *De mon. ex.* 9 (PG 79.729A): ἐνοχλοῦνται δὲ οἱ ἐν ταῖς οἰκίαις καὶ πρὸς αὐτὴν τὴν ὄψιν ἔχουσιν ἀηδῶς, προσαιτεῖν ὁρῶντες αὐτοὺς ἀναιδέστερον . . . πολλοὶ δὲ καὶ εἰσοικισθέντες, καὶ εὐλάβειαν ἐπ᾽ ὀλίγον ὑποκρινάμενοι . . . ὕστερον ἀποσυλήσαντες αὐτοὺς ἀπέρχονται.

as if they were cursed with leprosy. A person might put more trust in brigands or burglars than in those who adopt the monastic life, reckoning it easier to guard against open mischief than against credentials that have been contrived for ambush.

Such monks merely "use the monastic *schēma* as a cloak for importuning richer gains, wanting tribute for their bodies."[113] On their account, he bitterly concludes, "the much-beloved life has become an abomination."[114]

Here Nilus provides our most vivid and sordid depiction of wandering, begging monks in cities of the early fifth century. In fact, these passages of his *Ascetic Discourse* create such an unflattering impression of contemporary monasticism that some early scholars could accept them only as interpolations to his treatise, reflecting a later period of monastic decline.[115] What Nilus was describing, however, was the same "insult to philosophy" that Chrysostom had encountered already at Antioch and Constantinople, and Augustine at Carthage: monks whose "accustomed idleness" required their dependence on others for material support. Nilus represents them mainly as failed monks or opportunists who behaved like ordinary beggars. Yet another vignette indicates he was addressing a far more complex monastic and social phenomenon than his depiction of their begging might otherwise suggest. "For indeed," he says,

> they attend the gates of the rich no less than parasites. They run beside them through the marketplaces like slaves, scaring away those nearby, driving off anyone blocking the way, zealous to give them an easy passage. These things they do because of the neediness of their tables, having not learned to suppress their delight in delectable meals.[116]

Such characterizations of parasites hanging on rich men's gates and escorting them slavishly through marketplaces were, in fact, stock motifs satirists had used to parody the self-abasement that clients often showed wealthy patrons in Greco-Roman society in order to receive meals and support.[117]

In the second century Lucian had devoted an entire work to satirizing this "art of the parasite," which he described as the skill "concerned with

---

113. Ibid. (PG 79.729AB): παρασκευάζουσι τὴν δυσφημίαν.... ἁδροτέρων λημμάτων δυσώπησιν προβάλλοιντο τὸ σχῆμα καὶ βουλόμενοι δασμὸν τῷ σώματι. Here (as in 728A) Nilus puns σχῆμα, which means both "monastic garb" and "outward appearance."

114. Ibid. (PG 79.728D).

115. See Heussi (1917): 50–51.

116. Nilus, *De mon. ex.* 8 (PG 79.728CD): Θεραπεύουσι ... τὰς τῶν πλουσίων θύρας παρασίτων οὐκ ἔλαττον.

117. See Cynthia Damon, *The Mask of the Parasite: A Pathology of Roman Patronage* (Ann Arbor: University of Michigan Press, 1997).

food and drink and what must be said and done to procure them."[118] Their most famous representation is found in Juvenal's first *Satire:*

> Look now at the meager dole set down upon the outer threshold for the toga-clad mob to scramble for! . . . the day itself is marked out by a fine order of business: first come the doles, then the forum . . . wearied and hopeless, the old clients leave [their patron's] gates, though the last hope that a man relinquishes is that of dinner.[119]

Martial calls such clients *anteambulones,* or "those who walk in front" of their patron in public venues in order to receive their *sportula* (dole). Martial also considered such attendance in the great halls of the nobility one of the few ways a newcomer to Rome might avoid *casu vivere* (living hand-to-mouth).[120] Through such motifs these authors ridiculed the *avaritia* and self-interest that they believed characterized the typical patron-client relationship of their times.[121] However, these parasites could not exist without a willing host.[122] Though rarely described in anything other than satirical terms, it was commonly expected that the wealthier members of Greco-Roman society would be regularly visited by a large constituency *(clientela)* of dependent clients, whom they would support with food or money. This institution assumed both economic and social reciprocity. While clients sought protection or advancement by providing various services, patrons sought the prestige of having numerous clients at their gates during the morning greeting ceremony *(salutatio)* and a large entourage *(adsectatio)* in the marketplace and other public venues.

Late antiquity saw little change in such traditional features of patron-client relationships, or in the motifs used to criticize them.[123] Whether or not Nilus based his description of urban monks on earlier satire (we know he was remarkably well versed in Greco-Roman literature),[124] he clearly was

---

118. Lucian, *De parasito* 9 and 12.

119. Juvenal, *Satura* 1,95–134; ed. and trans. adapted from G. G. Ramsey, pp. 10–13.

120. Martial, *Epig.* 3.7 and 3.38; see R. P. Saller, "Martial on Patronage and Literature," *Classical Quarterly* n.s. 33 (1983): 246–57.

121. See Damon (1997): passim and Duncan Cloud, "The Client-Patron Relationship: Emblem and Reality in Juvenal's First Book," in *Patronage in Ancient Society,* ed. A. Wallace-Hadrill (London and New York: Routledge, 1989), 209–14.

122. The remarks of Damon (1997): 3–8 on the rhetorical significance of this figure pertain to Nilus as much as to Juvenal and Martial.

123. See Krause (1987): 6–67, esp. 20–31, and Patlagean (1977): 156–231. See esp. Ammianus Marcellinus, *Res gestae* 14.6.14, noting that the Roman rich often received a client who "pretended to know certain secret things" [secretiora quaedem se nosse confingit].

124. Guérard (1994): 46–47 detects his familiarity with a range of classical authors, including Vitruvius (!). But such imagery would have also been perpetuated through mime shows.

adapting well-known imagery (including begging at rich men's gates) in his *Ascetic Discourse* to ridicule the scramble for patronal support and the *obsequium* he saw among his urban monastic counterparts. Unlike their Old Testament forebears, who "did not flatter any of the well-to-do on account of corporeal need," monks of his day showed no reservations. Thus, Nilus observes, "Whenever we need something, then just as dogs leap for scraps or wag their tails to beg for bones, so too do we run to the rich, calling them 'benefactors' and 'providers of Christians,' declaring that they possess every virtue, even if they be bad to the extreme."[125] Yet such monks were offering their benefactors more than adulation: for "with his monastic appearance," Nilus says, each "professes skill and knowledge about things which he has not even had a taste."[126] It was this profession of ascetic skill and knowledge that most upset Nilus, yet gave many access to the rich. Indeed, despite his representation of their fraudulent intent, it is clear from his own account that numerous monks were being invited into Christian households, where as dependent clients—or rather, as Christian philosophers—they offered spiritual knowledge in return for patronal support.

We get a better understanding of the phenomenon Nilus was dealing with by turning to the satirist Lucian, who had caricatured the "many self-styled philosophers" of second-century Rome. These he portrayed as wandering around the streets of Rome, crowding the gates of the rich, searching for meals like common flatterers while "philosophizing for a wage and fixing a price on virtue as if it were something you could buy."[127] Indeed, Lucian devoted an entire essay entitled *Domestic Servants Hired for a Wage* to such house philosophers. While Lucian says that most of them were driven to their patron-client arrangements by poverty, he suggests that others simply believed it offered the easiest form of earning a wage without having to toil like other men.[128] He then details the real labors the occupation involved: much time on the road, continual attendance on doorsteps, and jockeying beside personal athletic trainers and other flatterers,

125. Nilus, *De mon. ex.* 19 (PG 79.744C): εὐεργέτας αὐτούς, καὶ τῶν Χριστιανῶν κηδεμόνας ἀποκαλοῦντες, καὶ πᾶσαν αὐτοῖς ἁπλῶς μαρτυροῦμεν ἀρετήν. John Climacus, *Scala Paradisi* 22 (PG 88.955C) criticizes monks who look to visitors for gifts and call them δεσπότας ... καὶ προστάτας.

126. Nilus, *De mon. ex.* 8 (PG 79.728BC).

127. Lucian, *Nigrinus* 22–25; ed. and trans. A. M. Harmon, pp. 120–24. Heinz-Gunther Nesselrath, *Lukians Parasitendialog: Untersuchungen und Kommentar* (Berlin: Walter de Gruyter, 1985), 75–80, considers Lucian's description of such philosophers as extension of the parasite stereotype.

128. Lucian, *De mercede conductis potentium familiaribus* 5–6; ed. A. M. Harmon, pp. 420–22: οἱ μὲν δὴ πολλοὶ τὴν πενίαν καὶ τὴν τῶν ἀναγκαίων χρείαν.... ἄλλοι δὲ πενίαν μὲν αὐτὴν οὐκ ἂν φοβηθῆναι ... ἐπὶ τήνδε ῥᾴστην οὖσαν τὴν μισθοφορὰν ἀπηντηκέναι.

while receiving daily abuse from ignorant patrons who merely wanted to appear learned by having a philosopher in their entourage.[129] Those who subjected themselves to such humiliation, he suggests, were driven by their desire to mingle with the rich and drink from golden cups.[130] Lucian also claims there were many who, "once given entry to houses, supply prophesies, potions, and love-charms because they know nothing else; yet they claim to be educated and wrap themselves in philosophic cloaks and beards that cannot be lightly scorned." Patrons deceived by such frauds, Lucian complains, thereafter held all philosophers equally suspect of slavishly seeking gain.[131]

Lucian's representation of the client philosophers of his day offers striking parallels for Nilus' representation of wandering, begging monks in cities of the early fifth century. Just as Lucian provides rare evidence for the phenomenon of house philosophers supported by wealthy aristocrats in second-century Rome,[132] so does Nilus in his *Ascetic Discourse* provide a glimpse of the christianized version of that arrangement in later Roman cities, where ascetic exemplars now taught virtue in the monastic *schēma* rather than the philosophic *tribōn,* providing in-house spiritual services to Christian aristocrats in return for material support.

"Let those who undertake leadership of others realize how much knowledge they need."[133] Nilus warns such monks not to assume spiritual leadership irresponsibly, that is, without proper training or experience. "How can those," he asks, "who do not yet know how to discern obvious sins, rush at the leadership and care of others, having not yet attended to care of their own passions?" While mundane skills like husbandry and medicine require much time and instruction for success, "only on the skill of skills, on reverence of God, do untrained people boldly lay their grasp, thinking it easier than anything else." Nilus complains that novice monks who knew only "how and when they should pray, and what their daily routine should be," were immediately passing themselves off as teachers, each "leading a chain of disciples while being in need of teaching himself." Moreover, what they taught was strictly limited to corporeal ascetic practice: "How can a person who conceives of nothing more than bodily asceticism be able to correct the habits of those placed under his care?" Such monks, Nilus concludes, "only look after their own fulfillment, imposing tasks on their broth-

---

129. Lucian, *De mercede conductis* 4, 10, 20–25.

130. Lucian, *De mercede conductis* 7–9.

131. Lucian, *De mercede conductis* 40; trans. adapted from Harmon, p. 476.

132. For second-century house philosophers, see Hahn (1989): 150–53; for Cicero's treatment of such figures see, Damon (1997): 235–51.

133. Nilus, *De mon. ex.* 41 (PG 79.769C).

ers as if they were slaves, staking their reputation *(doxa)* on this alone, namely how many they lead."¹³⁴

While dwelling mostly on the vanity and ineptitude of ascetic teachers who "think that glory lies in leading people,"¹³⁵ Nilus also displays indignation at the low social status he identifies with their "dire mania" for leadership and reputation. Such ambitions were more appropriate for market hawkers than for teachers and proved them unfit for the honor of that name:¹³⁶ "For who would not ridicule the man who just yesterday fetched water for the tavern, when today he is seen accompanied by disciples as a teacher of virtue? or having withdrawn from his morning's mischief in the city, in the evening struts through every marketplace with a multitude of disciples?"¹³⁷ To pursue such leadership rather than *hēsychia* in seclusion, Nilus remarks, "is clearly the way of petty, irresponsible men who have no source of support from home."¹³⁸ He casts similar doubts on those who importune at the gates of the rich. "These," he says,

> have no idea what profit comes from tranquility. They must have been recklessly driven to the solitary life by some necessity, perhaps thinking this business is an opportunity for trade and procuring their necessities.

"I think they might pursue it in more dignified fashion *(semnoteron)*," he adds, "if they did not press themselves upon everyone's gates."¹³⁹

"How shameful it is," he concludes, "to see those concerned with enjoying eternal goods to be seen groveling in the dust of earthly things, shaming their vocation with inappropriate pursuits."¹⁴⁰ Nilus' emphasis on social decorum was not just a reflection of snobbery. His description of urban monastic vulgarity serves chiefly as a foil for highlighting what he considered more appropriate monastic behavior: "As for ourselves, dear readers, who yearn for virtue by renouncing this worldly life and casting aside its desires, as we claim . . . why do we share in the folly of those who pursue

134. For these remarks, see Nilus, *De mon. ex.* 21–24 (PG 79.748C–752C); cf. sect. 74. For Cassian's similar concern for qualifications of ascetic leaders, see Leyser (2000): 54–55. The complaint that unqualified teachers focused on physical asceticism rather than contemplation was very old: see Lucian, *Nigrinus* 27–28 and Francis (1995): 75–76.

135. Nilus, *De mon. ex.* 22 (PG 79.749B).

136. Nilus, *De mon. ex.* 24 (PG 79.752C): καπήλων μᾶλλον ἢ διδασκάλων κατάστασιν ἐπιδεικνύμενοι. For their "dire mania," see sect. 33 (761B); also sect.5 (724C) and 7 (728A).

137. Nilus, *De mon. ex.* 22 (PG 79.749A).

138. Nilus, *De mon. ex.* 26 (PG 79.753C): Ὅτι δὲ εὐχερῶν ἀνθρώπων καὶ μηδεμίαν οἴκοθεν ἐχόντων ὠφέλειαν ἐστὶ δὲ τὴν ἑτέρων ἀναδέχθαι προστασίαν, δῆλον.

139. Nilus, *De mon. ex.* 9 (PG 79.729B): ἐξ ἀνάγκης ἴσως τινὸς συνωσθέντες ἀκρίτως ἐπὶ τὸν μονήρη βίον, καὶ ἐμπορίας ὑπόθεσιν εἰς πορισμὸν τῶν ἀναγκαίων ἡγούμενοι τὸ πρᾶγμα τοῦτο ἂν οἶμαι σεμνότερον μετέλθοιεν, εἰ μὴ ταῖς πάντων θύριας προσίενται.

140. Nilus, *De mon. ex.* 63 (PG 79.796D).

this activity *ou deontōs,* so indecently?"[141] Above all he urges his readers to flee the cities, in order to regain the "good old blessedness" that typified early saints. They should at least remain indoors and avoid the agitations of the world.[142] It was imperative to sequester oneself in solitude, "the mother of philosophy," in order to subdue passions and attain serenity.[143] This also required reducing bodily wants down to what was absolutely necessary—a single tunic, bread, and water—trusting in God for sustenance. This they could do with confidence, Nilus affirms, for "who would not provide enough daily necessities for one who lives according to virtue?"[144]

In fact, it was this assumption, that virtuous monks will be honored by others with material support, that underscored Nilus' emphasis on decorous ascetic conduct, and fueled his animosity towards his urban counterparts. Their behavior concerned him all the more because his own monastic circle was itself dependent upon good will for its support. As his *Ascetic Discourse* and correspondence make plain, Nilus considered such material dependence on patrons to be perfectly acceptable. What mattered was how it was solicited and whether it was deserved. As he wrote to a monk named Maurianus,

> If we seek tranquility and persist in prayers and singing psalms in our monasteries, and if we don't press upon people of the world, then God will take care and provide for us by rousing those very people, compelling them to furnish our bodily needs gladly. God cares for us, since we care for spiritual work.[145]

Nilus similarly advised another monk to "strive to live in tranquility as the monastic life requires, and God will rouse ministers for you from the trees, wind, and rocks themselves."[146] Indeed, Nilus' correspondence indicates that some of the anxious monks he comforted were already being well served by impressive social connections. As he reminded one named Hadrian,

141. Nilus, *De mon. ex.* 10 (PG 79.729CD): Ἡμεῖς δ᾽, ὦ ἀγαπητοί, οἱ πόθῳ τῆς ἀρετῆς, ὡς νομίζομεν, ἀποταξάμενοι τῷ βίῳ καὶ ἀρνησάμενοι τὰς κοσμικὰς ἐπιθυμίας . . . τί τῶν τῆς οὐ δεόντως μετερχομένων τὸ πρᾶγμα κακοβουλίας παραπολαύομεν.

142. Nilus, *De mon. ex.* 20 (PG 79.745CD) and 46 (776D).

143. Nilus, *De mon. ex.* 45 (PG 79.776B); *hēsychia* is discussed in sect. 46–54.

144. Nilus, *De mon. ex.* 16 (PG 79.741A): Τίς γὰρ οὐ μεθ᾽ ἱκεσίας παρέξει τὰ ἐπιτήδεια τῷ κατ᾽ ἀρετὴν βιοῦντι. See also sect. 6, 14, 67–68.

145. Nilus, *Ep.* 3.58 (PG 79.417C): Ἐὰν ἡσυχάζωμεν, καὶ τῇ εὐχῇ καὶ ψαλμῳδίᾳ ἐν τῷ μοναστηρίῳ προσκαρτερῶμεν, καὶ μὴ παρενοχλῶμεν τοῖς κοσμικοῖς, ὁ Θεὸς ἐκείνους αὐτοὺς φέρει πρὸς ἡμᾶς, προνοῶν καὶ φροντίζων ἡμῶν, καὶ ἀναγκάζει αὐτοὺς μετὰ προθυμίας ποιεῖν ἡμῶν τὰς σωματικὰς χρείας.

146. Nilus, *Ep.* 2.136 (PG 79.257A): Σὺ μόνον θέλησον ἡσυχάσαι . . . καὶ ὁ Θεὸς ἐκ τῶν δένδρων, καὶ τῶν ἀνέμων, καὶ ἐκ τῶν λίθων τούτων ἐξεγερεῖ τοὺς διακονοῦντάς σοι.

Why . . . do you risk falling into disbelief, expecting that God will abandon you, and that you'll become bereft of your daily necessities? Hitherto you have had people attending you . . . including his eminence the Illustrious Heron, who reveres monks very much in his heart, and the most holy bishop's nephew Theodoulus, both a lover of monks and a most dignified deacon of God. Even if these were to die before you, then God who ever looks upon the tranquil gentleness of your soul . . . will send ministers for your needs from out of the blue. . . . For who wouldn't provide the necessities and even more for those who live in pious, dignified, and virtuous fashion?[147]

Nilus did, of course, consider manual labor to be a spiritual activity incumbent on a monk,[148] but not once in his correspondence does he recommend it for self-support. Nor does he mention it explicitly in his *Ascetic Discourse*.[149] In fact, when he discusses manual labor in his treatise *On Voluntary Poverty*, he treats it primarily as a contemplative aid. Like his elder and equally well-educated contemporaries Evagrius and Jerome, Nilus probably considered his own obligation to practice manual labor fulfilled by writing treatises like the *Ascetic Discourse*.[150]

What emerges from Nilus' writings is a monastic world that was highly conditioned by concerns for material support and patronage.[151] They also show that monks of his day were truly divided over the proper setting for monastic life: in cities among other people or in seclusion. Nilus publicized his own preference in another treatise, entitled *On the Superiority of Solitaries*. "It is no wonder," he says,

that those who have not learned by experience how virtue is achieved scorn monks who live in tranquility in caves or mountains, and reckon monks who live in cities and go among men to be far worthier of esteem than those who are fully withdrawn. So much the more do they think them worthier of praise, as much as athletes who grapple with opponents in the ring are more genuine than those who merely shadow-box.[152]

In this treatise Nilus acknowledges that some monks considered the urban environment to be an ascetic challenge itself. He nevertheless maintains

147. Nilus, *Ep.* 2.60 (PG 79.226C–228A): Ἔχεις γὰρ δὴ τέως τινὰς ἐπικουροῦντας . . . παντῶς βλέπων ὁ Θεὸς τὸ πρᾶον, καὶ ἡσύχιον τῆς ψυχῆς σου . . . ἐξ ἀμηχάνου πέμψει σοι τοὺς διακονῆσαι πρὸς τὴν χρείαν ὀφείλοντες. . . . Τίς γὰρ δὴ οὐ μετ᾽ ἱκεσίας πολλῆς χορηγήσει, οὐ μόνον τὰ τῆς χρείας, ἀλλὰ καὶ τὰ ὑπὲρ χρείαν, τοῖς εὐσεβῶς καὶ σεμνῶς καὶ ἐναρέτως βιοῦσιν;

148. Nilus, *Ep.* 1.310 (PG 79.196AB); 2.135 (256D–257A); 3.101 (432D).

149. His only allusions to it are in *De mon. ex.* 14–15 (PG 79.736C, 740D).

150. For Jerome and Evagrius, see J. N. D. Kelly, *Jerome: His Life, Writings, and Controversies* (New York: Harper and Row, 1975), 134, 226 and Palladius, *HL* 38.10. N 375 notes that scribal writing was also considered manual labor.

151. Similar anxieties and ambitions are revealed by Jerome's correspondence: see Rebenich (1992): 159–80.

152. Nilus, *De monachorum praestantia* 1 (PG 79.1061A); cf. 27 (1093B).

that those who conquered their passions in seclusion must be more honorable than those who adopt a "promiscuous life among the common herd [agelaion kai migada bion], even if they distinguish themselves with dignity [semnotēti]."[153] In the end it came down to vainglory: for while monks who live in cities may claim to profit those who see them, what they really cared about (even if they were unaware of it) was winning glory by virtue of "pleasing mankind" (anthropareskia). Such urban monks he calls "pigeon-doves," an inferior species to the ascetic "turtle-doves" of the wild who answered only to God.[154]

Both the *Ascetic Discourse* and *On the Superiority of Solitaries* show two forms of monastic life competing in the early fifth century, one urban-oriented, the other country-based. Nilus is presenting just one side of a debate between two fundamentally different conceptions of monasticism and its purpose: one apostolic, emphasizing engagement with society and spiritual guidance; the other philosophic, emphasizing withdrawal from society and spiritual contemplation.[155] Nilus leaves his reader no doubt about which he considered more virtuous and why. Yet, while he probably wrote these treatises primarily to persuade and instruct monks (at least those able to navigate his looping syntax) to share in his choice, there should be no doubt that he intended them to be read by interested patrons as well.[156] Throughout his *Ascetic Discourse* Nilus presents himself as the consummate arbiter of ascetic manners. Knowing what behavior was attractive to sympathetic patrons, he implores his readers to avoid actively pursuing them in the streets: "Let us flee living in cities and villages, in order that those in cities and villages might run to us. Let us seek out solitary places, that we might draw to us those who now flee from us—if it please any of them to do so."[157] And while expounding his notions of proper conduct and scriptural exe-

153. Nilus, *De monachorum praestantia* 12 (PG 79.1076A).

154. Nilus, *De monachorum praestantia* 26 (PG 79.1092B): περιστερὰς μὲν τοὺς ἐν πόλισιν ἀσκοῦντας ὠνόμασαν, τρυγόνας δὲ τοὺς ἐν ἐρημίας καὶ ἀβάτοις ἐμβιωτεύοντας, ὅτι οἱ μὲν ὑπὸ θεαταῖς τὴν ἀρετὴν μετέρχονται, καὶ μολύνουσι ταύτην ἑκόντες, ἢ ἄκοντες ἀνθρωπαρεσκείᾳ ... καὶ γνώμῃ τὸ δοξασθῆναι πολλάκις προτιθέμενοι πρὸς τὸ δῆθεν ὠφελῆσαι τοὺς θεωμένους.

155. For the early monastic debate between proponents of the *migas bios* ("promiscuous," "useful," "lived in the world") and *erêmikos bios* (characterized by philosophic withdrawal and *hêsychia*), see Elm (1994): 207–10. It can be detected in letters of Antony and Ammonas: see McNary-Zak (2000): 37.

156. Guérard (1994): 380 observes that Nilus' elaborate style would have put his work beyond most readers.

157. Nilus, *De mon. ex.* 20 (PG 79.745D). Jerome, *Vita Hilarionis* 1 (PL 23.29B) observes that a monk "who has been seen by many people" will likely "be deemed vile and cheap" [qui a multis visus est, vilis existimetur]. I discuss the similarities between Nilus' and Jerome's situation and outlook in "Nilus of Ancyra and the Promotion of a Monastic Elite," *Arethusa* 33 (2000): 401–10.

gesis, his *Ascetic Discourse* also made clear that competent teachers were rare.[158] It effectively advertised to potential patrons that Nilus and his circle were superior to the usual throng of ascetic philosophers who came knocking on their doors. To that end we know it proved successful. Not only did Nilus dedicate the *Ascetic Discourse*'s companion volume, *On Voluntary Poverty,* to Ancyra's "most dignified" deaconess, Magna, but his introduction assures her that those who showed "compassion to kin" would receive as much honor from God as those who dedicated themselves to philosophy.[159] Nilus had evidently secured the best patron in town.

As for the wandering monks he describes, Nilus surely had good reason to complain that many were abusing their vocation. His treatise responds to the annoyance some were evidently causing his fellow Ancyrans. Yet his numerous remarks suggest not only that such monks came from a socioeconomic background different from his own, but also that his perspective was colored by his notions of social rank and decorum. His supposition that they lacked any "support from home" indicates at least that Nilus was writing from a relatively secure economic position. Indeed, the sophisticated style and broad education exhibited in his writings leave no doubt that Nilus came from an elevated, if not aristocratic, rank.[160] We may, therefore, suspect that his sensitivity to the behavior and low social status of his urban counterparts derived partly from his discomfort at having to compete for patronage with such vulgar *parvenus.*

It is, in any case, clear from Nilus' own testimony that such monks were being sought out by wealthy urban Christians themselves to minister to their spiritual needs. In one letter he even had to admonish monks of his own circle not to comply when "men of the world" summoned them to

158. Nilus, *De mon. ex.* 10–11, 28 (PG 79.756C–757A): σπάνιος δὲ ὁ τοιοῦτος καὶ οὐ ῥᾳδίως εὑρισκόμενος.

159. Nilus, *De vol. paup.* 1 (PG 79.969BC): Κακεῖνοι γὰρ τῆς πρὸς τὸ συγγενὲς εὐσπλαγχνίας ...ὁμοίως εἰσὶ...ἄξιοι. Here τὸ συγγενὲς presumably refers to kindred interest; otherwise, Magna may have been Nilus' own "source of support from home." His allusion at the beginning of the treatise (968C) to the *De mon. ex.* assumes her familiarity with it.

Nilus' correspondence includes letters thanking other patrons: *Epp.* 2.84, 105, and 157. Also preserved among his works is a treatise called the *Peristeria* after a woman extolled in its preamble for providing monks with freedom from care by ministering to their daily needs: PG 79.813CD. It ends with a section praising those who give alms. If, indeed, Nilus did write it, his credentials may have first been established by his *Commentary on the Song of Songs,* to which the *Peristeria* shows close affinity. See Guérard (1981): 348 and Ringshausen (1967): 20–24. If not by Nilus, then the *Peristeria* provides another example of a literate monk concerned to secure or maintain patronal connections.

160. See Guérard (1994): 373–80 for these points of style and education, as reflected in Nilus' *Commentary on the Song of Songs.* In the ninth century, George the Monk believed Nilus to have been a student of Chrysostom: see Heussi (1917): 11–16.

their houses "in order to make prayers on their behalf."[161] Although Nilus characterizes this patron-client arrangement as a recent corruption of his profession,[162] it was, in fact, both a practical and traditional arrangement for supporting ascetic teachers in both Greco-Roman society and Christian communities, especially in the East. Gregory of Nyssa seems to have alluded to it in his treatise *On Virginity,* in noting how some ascetics "insinuated themselves into houses."[163] We may suspect that Nilus was using his Greco-Roman satirical motifs to marginalize an apostolic ascetic lifestyle that had been known in northern Asia Minor since at least the days of Eustathius and Aerius.

At any rate, the trend toward urban monasticism that Nilus laments had probably always been the norm, and it only accelerated in Asia Minor during the fifth century. Writing in the middle of the fifth century, Sozomen observed that most monks in Galatia (where Ancyra was located), Cappadocia, and neighboring northern provinces were living in cities and villages. Although he suggests (as does Nilus) that these monks had fallen away from the "traditions of their predecessors," he also offers a practical explanation for the phenomenon: desert asceticism was impossible in those regions because the winters were so severe.[164] In Ancyra at least one group took shelter in the old imperial temple of *Roma et Augustus* in the center of the city, which may have been converted into a monastery as early as the mid-fifth century. Perhaps its inhabitants were the "pigeon-doves" Nilus criticizes.[165]

Yet the city where the earliest traces of urban monasticism are most clearly visible is Constantinople. There we must now return to investigate how patronal support was a factor in the discord that arose between John Chrysostom and the city's wandering monks, especially their leader, Isaac.

JOHN CHRYSOSTOM AND THE MONKS OF CONSTANTINOPLE

Monasticism at Constantinople did not begin with Isaac. Sozomen informs us that monasteries had already been founded there during the reign of

---

161. Nilus, *Ep.* 2.46 (PG 79.217): εἰς τοὺς ἑαυτῶν οἴκους βιωτικοῖς ἀνδράσιν, ὥστε ὑπὲρ αὐτῶν ποιήσασθαι προσευχάς.

162. Nilus, *De mon. ex.* 4–6.

163. Gregory of Nyssa, *De virg.* 23.3; ed. Aubineau, p. 536: ἀπὸ τούτων εἰσὶν οἱ ἐνδύνανοτές εἰς τὰς οἰκίας. Basil, *Ep.* 42, discourages its recipient, a monk, from going from village to village and house to house ostentatiously.

164. Sozomen, *HE* 6.34.7–8; ed. Bidez-Hansen, p. 291. Epiphanius notes the snows which Aerius' *boskoi* had to endure in this region: *Panarion* 75.3.2.

165. See Foss (1977): 65–66. The temple still stands with its inscription of Augustus' *Res gestae.*

the emperor Constantius II (324–361) by the Arian Bishop Macedonius and his deacons Eleusius and Marathonius. Significantly, the controversial Eustathius of Sebaste is said to have encouraged the deacon Marathonius, who was also a man of considerable wealth, to found not only urban monasteries, but also hospitals and poorhouses served by the city's monks.[166] These monks served Bishop Macedonius in another way: during his contentions with the previous bishop's supporters, Macedonius is said to have "fortified himself with the many monasteries he had founded at Constantinople," whose forces he allegedly used to harass his opponents into exile, even to death.[167]

Such were the Eustathian origins and politicized background of the monastic establishment that John Chrysostom encountered when he became bishop of Constantinople in 398. In its earliest history we see the first of many instances when monastic patrons called upon their client monks to support their bid for ecclesiastical power. Since both Macedonius and Marathonius were later implicated in heresy and exiled, we know little about the subsequent fate of the monks they had patronized.[168] No doubt some took refuge with "Macedonian" monks already dwelling outside the city walls in the house and garden where Eusebia (a deaconess from Macedonius' church) kept the bones of the Forty Martyrs of Sebaste.[169] This group itself apparently dwindled after Eusebia's death—an example of how monastic circles at Constantinople depended on sympathetic patrons for their survival. Most of them probably turned to the new star rising on the city's monastic scene, the Syrian monk Isaac.[170]

Isaac owed his rise to prominence to the new religious sympathies that came with a sudden change in government.[171] According to his sixth- or

166. For Eustathius of Sebaste's influence on Marathonius and thus on early monastic developments in Constantinople, see Sozomen, *HE* 4.27.4; Dagron (1970): 239, 246–53; and Elm (1994): 111–12. For Eleusius, see Sozomen, *HE* 4.20.2 and Dagron (1970): 239.

167. Sozomen, *HE* 4.2.3; ed. Bidez-Hansen, p. 141: μοναστηρίοις πολλοῖς ἃ συνεστήσατο . . . περιφράξαι ἑαυτὸν, λέγεται διαφόρως κακῶσαι τοὺς τὰ Παύλου φρονοῦντας.

168. Because of their Arian, or *homooiousian*, affiliations, such Eustathian institutions were eventually suppressed or outlawed: see *CTh* 16.5.11–13 (issued 383–384) and Elm (1994): 217–23. Sozomen, *HE* 4.2.3, notes that some persisted into his day.

169. Sozomen, *HE* 9.2.1–8; ed. Bidez-Hansen, p. 393: rumors about Eusebia's relics later prompted efforts to find "the monks who once lived in the place."

170. As suggested by Dagron (1970): 248.

171. See Dagron (1970): 231–38 on the hagiographic tradition, which ignored all Arian forerunners, to make Isaac the "first" monk at Constantinople, and Neil McLynn, "A Self-Made Holy Man: The Case of Gregory Nazianzen," *JECS* 6 (1998): 480–82, who believes Isaac benefited from the "reorientation of competitive lay piety" towards holy men and "heightened responsiveness among the elite at Constantinople to ascetic ideals," which attended the Theodosian regime and its suppression of doctrinal disputation ca. 378–381.

seventh-century *vita*,[172] Isaac had first come to Constantinople "from the desert of the East" in the 370s to combat the Arian creed, then dominant. He is said to have established his spiritual credentials by confronting the emperor Valens (364–378) and cursing his Arianism at the city gates just before the battle of Adrianople. Valens vanished in that battle, probably incinerated in a farm house.[173] The new emperor, Theodosius I (378–395), coming from the Nicene West, reversed his predecessor's doctrinal policies. Now Isaac's Nicene creed received imperial favor and, in fact, became law in the land. Members of the new Theodosian court rushed to show their piety by embracing Nicene ascetics.[174] Two trusted officers of the former emperor, Saturninus and Victor, seeing the change, were first to claim Isaac for themselves. Although Isaac is said to have wanted to return to the desert (after helping, we are told, make the transition to orthodoxy at the Council of Constantinople in 381), his two admirers competed to keep his company, each building hermitages for him on their suburban estates.[175] Isaac finally chose the residence Saturninus built just outside Constantine's walls, near the Psamathian district, some three miles from the city center.[176] Eventually Saturninus gave Isaac full legal rights to the property, having seen "how many monks were increasing his fold."[177]

Operating from this base, Isaac planted other monasteries around the city and "incited them to zeal."[178] As Callinicus recalled later in the fifth century,

> The blessed Isaac spent his time watching over [the city's monks] as if they were his children. . . . Wherever he knew there were any who lacked things to live, if he did not have something himself, he informed well-heeled Chris-

172. *Vita Isaacii* 2.4–7 (*AASS Maii* VII.246B). The MS identifies the author as a member of the monastery of Dalmatius (as Isaac's monastery later was known), and therefore may be based on that monastery's records: see Dagron (1970): 231–33. It cannot be credited in all details (e.g., that Isaac was the city's first monk, that he died in 383 and therefore never met Chrysostom), but its testimony for Isaac's relationship with the city's aristocracy is corroborated by Callinicus, writing a generation after Isaac died.

173. *V.Isaacii* 2.8. The confrontation between Isaac and the Arian emperor became a culminating episode in Nicene triumph narratives: see Sozomen *HE* 6.40.1 and Theodoret, *HE* 4.31. For Valens' death at Andrianople, see Matthews (1989): 379.

174. See John Matthews, *Western Aristocracies and Imperial Court, A.D. 364–425* (Oxford: Clarendon Press, 1975), 109–45.

175. *V.Isaacii* 4.15 (*AASS Maii* VII.251F). For Saturninus, see *PLRE* 1 (Flavius Saturninus 10); for Victor, *PLRE* 1 (Victor 4). Matthews (1975): 120–21 and 130–31 describes their competition to become Isaac's patrons.

176. For the location, see Janin (1953): 86–89. Victor's property was in the Psamathian district itself.

177. *V.Isaacii* 4.16.

178. Callinicus, *V.Hypatii* 11.1; ed. Bartelink, p. 110: τότε συνεκροτοῦντο ... μοναστήρια ζῶντος τοῦ μακαρίου Ἰσαακίου καὶ εἰς ζῆλον αὐτοὺς ἄγοντος.

tians, and they would send [it]: for he was esteemed by all and listened to as a father.[179]

It is notable that this description of Isaac's role focuses on the economic aspects of his paternity. That raises important questions about the source and scale of his provisions. Where did Isaac get such resources? Who were those well-heeled urban Christians who esteemed him as a father?

Isaac's *vita* is particularly illuminating in the emphasis it gives to his aristocratic connections. Indeed, it represents Isaac as spending as much time strengthening the faith of the city's aristocracy as inciting its monks to zeal. Foremost in his care were his earliest champions, Victor and Saturninus, who "would not go up to the palace, unless they had come to the holy one's side before dawn. Once he had blessed them, they would go away, rejoicing."[180] As an expert on the new emperor's creed, Isaac would have been particularly helpful in preparing these generals for their imperial encounters. What the *vita* itself emphasizes, however, is the joy these men derived from intimacy with their own Syrian *hēsychast* (tranquility seeker), as Palladius refers to him.[181] Word of Isaac's powers spread and soon demand for his services rose, as Victor and Saturninus "roused many others to spiritual zeal by describing the saint's ways. These, too, began to come to him each day from every quarter, in order to be edified and strengthened in the Lord's faith through his saintly words. Most of them also thought it proper for the saint to come to their houses for the sake of prayer. When he saw their faith, he would go." Sometimes Isaac stayed so late in their houses, we are told, that after nightfall he had to make the sign of the Cross upon the city gates to open them so he could return to his cell.[182] Besides Victor (honored as consul in 369) and Saturninus (consul in 383), his impressive admirers included Aurelian (praetorian prefect in 399, consul in 400, and then praetorian prefect again from 414 to 416), as well as a member of the imperial guard named Dalmatius, who eventually joined Isaac's monastery and became abbot upon Isaac's death.[183]

Insofar as Isaac offered in-house spiritual edification to wealthy urban patrons, his activities appear rather similar to those associated with the

179. Callinicus, *V.Hypatii* 11.2–4; ed. Bartelink, p. 110: ὅπου ἂν ἔγνω λειπομένους τὰ πρὸς ζωήν, εἰ μὴ εἶχεν αὐτός, τοῖς ἁδροῖς καὶ Χριστιανοῖς ἔλεγεν καὶ ἀπέστελλον.

180. *V.Isaacii* 4.15 (*AASS Maii* VII.252A).

181. Palladius, *Dial.* 8; ed. Malingrey-Leclercq (SC 341), p. 176. Palladius may be mocking the way admirers referred to Isaac in Chrysostom's day.

182. *V.Isaacii* 4.15 (*AASS Maii* VII.252B): ἤρχοντο πάντοθεν πρὸς αὐτὸν ἐφ' ἑκάστης ἡμέρας, οἰκοδομούμενοι καὶ στηριζόμενοι ἐν τῇ πίστει τοῦ κυρίου τοῖς ὁσίοις λόγοις αὐτοῦ. Οἱ δὲ πλεῖστοι αὐτῶν ἠξίουν παραγενέσθαι εὐχῆς χάριν εἰς τοὺς οἴκους αὐτῶν τὸν Ὅσιον.

183. See *V.Isaacii* 4.16–17 with Matthews (1975): 131 and *PLRE* 1:128–29 (Aurelianus 3) and 2:341 (Dalmatius 1). Even the emperor sometimes visited him: *V. Isaacii* 4.14.

frauds in Nilus' *Ascetic Discourse.* (Significantly, Isaac's *vita* maintains that when he left his benefactors' houses, he always displayed a lack of vainglory, this being a trait that Nilus especially identified with urban monastic "pigeon-doves.")[184] What needs emphasis is that Isaac's patrons pursued him as much for their own edification as he pursued them for material donations, and that when he solicited their support for the monks under his care, they willingly gave. Isaac is also said to have sought relief for destitute beggars whom he passed en route to their houses.[185] Indeed, he probably took on responsibility of running the urban hospices and hospitals formerly run by Arian monks under Marathonius' and Macedonius' patronage. Thus Isaac's aristocratic connections served him well. They enabled him to become an important benefactor himself and to carry out pastoral activities on the street without any need for episcopal funding.

Such was the person Palladius describes as the "little Syrian street tramp and leader of pseudomonks." Callinicus sufficiently corroborates the hagiographic biography for us to trust its representation of Isaac as the preeminent spiritual leader of Constantinople's monks and aristocrats alike. This position Isaac had enjoyed since at least 381.[186] Seventeen years later John Chrysostom arrived in the city and initiated his reforms.

As we have seen, the new bishop soon repudiated Isaac and his monks and called those who adopted ascetic poverty in Constantinople "give-me guys."[187] Not surprisingly, many of the monks came to hate their bishop, we are told, calling him an "irascible, gloomy, and overbearing man."[188] Within two years Chrysostom had also helped arrange the exile of two of Isaac's patrons, Saturninus and Aurelian (these men returned, no doubt resentful, in 401).[189] Such actions did not bode well for Chrysostom's tenure as bishop of the city. At the same time, he incurred the enmity of numerous clergy and resident bishops (many of whom were friends of Isaac) and became increasingly embroiled with Theophilus, bishop of Alexandria (385–412). Ultimately Isaac joined forces with the numerous other disgruntled clerics and bishops. He aligned himself and his monks, as they did, with the Alexandrian bishop's efforts to remove Chrysostom

---

184. *V.Isaacii* 4.15 (*AASS Maii* VII.252B): τὸ ἀκενόδοξον ἐπιδεικνύμενος. For Nilus' view, see above, p. 188.

185. *V.Isaacii* 4.16 (*AASS Maii* VII.252B).

186. Dagron (1970): 232 dates Saturninus' construction of Isaac's cell ca. 381.

187. Palladius, *Dial.* 19,99–100; ed. Malingrey-Leclercq (SC 341), p. 384: ἀπεκάλει... τὸν ἀκτήμονα "πλεονέκτην." Trans. Meyer, p. 128.

188. Sozomen, *HE* 8.8.5; ed. Bidez-Hansen, p. 362.

189. For Chrysostom's role in their exile and date, see Alan Cameron and Jacqueline Long, *Barbarians and Politics at the Court of Arcadius* (Berkeley and Los Angeles: University of California Press 1993), 164–66, 234–36 and Liebeschuetz (1984): 93, 97–98.

from office. In fact, Isaac became one of Chrysostom's most vocal denouncers at the Synod of the Oak that Theophilus orchestrated for Chrysostom's deposition in 403.[190]

Isaac's prominence during these proceedings needs further explanation. Although Saturninus and Aurelian must have encouraged him, scholars have rightly emphasized that Isaac's alliance with Theophilus was mainly provoked by the insulting and possibly threatening treatment Isaac had received under the new bishop's direction.[191] During the Synod of the Oak, Isaac claimed to have personally suffered many abuses under Chrysostom's new episcopal appointees.[192] We must ask why Chrysostom applied such pressure on him. Obviously he disapproved of Isaac's monastic style, as Sozomen attests. Yet Chrysostom's sermons indicate that the real problem lay in rival claims for the city's spiritual leadership: who had a legitimate claim to the laity's support through alms, and for what reason?

The fact is that Chrysostom took a monarchical view of his new position as head of the church.[193] Later, the church historian Socrates, describing the bishop's haughty manner towards his clergy, referred to them as Chrysostom's *hypēkooi* (subjects). The disciplinary actions Chrysostom took against them were probably intended to subordinate them to his control.[194] This included Isaac and his monks. Before his move to Constantinople, Chrysostom had described the difference between a priest (or bishop; he makes no distinction) and a monk as being tantamount to that between "a king and a commoner," since a monk's corporeal rigors, like vigils, fasts, and sleeping on the ground, "do not contribute towards our not being self-willed, irascible, and headstrong, or to being prudent, orderly, and astute and having all the other virtues with which the blessed Paul filled out for us the image of the best priest."[195] Therefore, a monk could not possibly

190. For the Synod of the Oak and its political background, see Susanna Elm, "The Dog That Did Not Bark: Doctrine and Patriarchal Authority in the Conflict between Theophilus of Alexandria and John Chrysostom of Constantinople," in *Christian Origins: Theology, Rhetoric, and Community*, ed. L. Ayers and G. Jones (London and New York: Routledge, 1998), 68–93; Kelly (1995): 211–27; and Timothy Gregory, *Vox Populi: Popular Opinion and Violence in the Religious Controversies of the Fifth Century* A.D. (Columbus: Ohio State University Press, 1979), 50–58.

191. Thus Dagron (1970): 263–64, followed by Liebeschutz (1984): 93.

192. Isaac, Synod of the Oak grievances #16–17, in Photius, *Bibliotheca* 59; ed. Henry, p. 56: ἐχειροτόνησεν ἐπισκόπους . . . αὐτὸν Ἰσαάκιον πολλὰ παρ᾽ αὐτῶν συνέβη κακωθῆναι.

193. Liebeschuetz (1984): 92; also Istrán Baán, "L'évêque Chrysostome: exigences et réalisations," in *Vescovi e pastori in epoca teodosiana*, vol. 2 (Rome: Institutum Patristicum Augustinianum, 1997), 426; Kelly (1995): 120–21, 126–27; and Lizzi (1987): 52–55.

194. Socrates, *Historia ecclesiastica* 6.4.1; ed. Günther Christian Hansen and Manja Sirinian, p. 315: τῇ ὀφρύι κατὰ τῶν ὑπηκόων ἐκέχρητο. Noted by Kelly (1995): 120.

195. Chrysostom, *De sacerdotio* 6.5–6; ed. Malingrey, pp. 320–22: μέγας ὁ τῶν μοναχῶν ἀγὼν

qualify as a spiritual leader. In Constantinople Chrysostom referred to these ascetic practices again in his sermons, this time indicating that they neither counted as work, nor qualified the monks who performed them to receive alms like church teachers. We should interpret this not merely as an asser-tion of his own monastic principles but as a clarification of a bishop's qual-ifications over a monk, and as one of a number of maneuvers in a political rivalry for influence and control—with Isaac's alliance to Theophilus being a maneuver of defense.

To repeat, in his sermons Chrysostom publicly challenged the city's monks in two respects: the way they sought material support by demanding alms from others and the way they justified this support through their as-cetic practices. In doing so, he was effectively telling his congregations not to patronize Isaac's monks or support their activities. As both Callinicus and Isaac's biography attest, Isaac's influence and prestige was founded on his long-established reputation as both a spiritual master and a solicitor of alms for the city's ascetic and ordinary poor. He was the central link in a chain of patron-client relationships that ran from the city's palaces down to its streets. Indeed, the material patronage that he received from aristo-crats allowed him to furnish the needs, and thus become patron himself, of his own *clientela* among the monks and poor. It was this chain of patron-age and largely independent influence that Chrysostom had to strike if he wished to assume Isaac's position as the city's preeminent spiritual leader.

There was not much that Chrysostom could officially do to break the influence of Isaac and his monks besides denouncing their activities in church. Until the Council of Chalcedon in 451, there were no specific church canons that could be used to discipline monks directly; in Chrysos-tom's day, monks, like other laypeople, were outside the official ecclesias-tical hierarchy and therefore outside a bishop's formal jurisdiction.[196] Nor could Isaac be charged with heresy, because of his early role in defending and establishing its Nicene orthodoxy. Isaac was, however, a priest as well as a monk, and for this reason ultimately had to seek help from Theophilus, a bishop whose power was equal to Chrysostom's. Until then, Isaac still had powerful patronal connections in the city, and their protection hampered Chrysostom's ability to act against him directly.[197] Therefore the bishop had

---

... ἀλλ᾽ εἴ τις τῇ καλῶς ἱερωσύνῃ διοικουμένῃ τοὺς ἐκεῖθεν ἱδρῶτας παραβάλοι, τοσοῦτον εὑρήσει τὸ διάφορον ὅσον ἰδιώτου καὶ βασιλέως τὸ μέσον. For context, method, and aims of Chrysostom's self-representation, see Kelly (1995): 25–28, 83–85.

196. See Liebeschuetz (1984): 92.

197. The importance of such secular patronal connections for protection against episcopal adversaries is especially apparent in the case of Eutyches: see below ch. 6. Cf. also Alexander Akoimētos, who lacked patronal connections in Constantinople and was banished through episcopal and governmental collaboration.

to find alternative ways to subvert the monk-priest's influence and assert his own.

It has been suggested that Chrysostom did so mainly by assuming supervision of the city's charitable institutions. Since Marathonius' day the hospitals and poorhouses had been supervised and operated by monks. By placing them under his own supervision and funding, Chrysostom could claim to be the main patron of the city's poor.[198] Certainly by 403 his preaching on behalf of the poor, and management of the city's charitable institutions had won him the allegiance of many. In Chrysostom, Isaac faced a rival who was not only an eloquent ambassador to the rich for the poor, but was also determined to back up his words with the considerable wealth of his church.[199]

With church wealth at his disposal, a bishop could also establish himself as the material benefactor of monks in a city. Sozomen indicates that this is precisely what Chrysostom did in Constantinople. In fact, John Chrysostom is the first bishop known to have provided protection and daily necessities for monks as a general matter of policy.[200] This policy, according to Sozomen, was especially meant to reward those monks who "stayed quietly practicing philosophy in their monasteries"—those who conformed to his notions of proper monastic practice. Of course, by defining monasticism primarily as a philosophic activity rather than as an apostolic vocation, Chrysostom was not only imposing a Greco-Roman paradigm of philosophic contemplation and withdrawal, but he was also, in effect, reserving the apostolic identity and authority for vested teachers like himself.[201] We know that his policy benefited fifty retiring intellectual (Origenist) monks from Egypt, whom he sheltered for two years in a hospice. These monks, we are told, dutifully "worked with their hands" while Olympias supplied them with daily meals.[202] This policy established him as a competitor for

198. Thus Dagron (1970): 264 and Rita Lizzi, "Ascetismo e predicazione urbana nell'Egitto del V secolo," *Atti dell'Istituto Veneto di Scienze, Lettere ed Arti* 141 (1982/1983): 137–38. Liebeschuetz (1984): 92 is skeptical. For Chrysostom's reorganization of the charitable institutions, see Palladius, *Dial.* 5; for the wealth of the church in the early fifth century and the institutions it supported, see Dagron (1974): 496–98, 509–13.

199. The influence Chrysostom gained through preaching and charitable organizations is discussed by Gregory (1979): 47–50 and 67–68. For the importance of the poor for episcopal power in general, see Brown (1992): 97–98.

200. Sozomen *HE* 8.9.4; ed. Bidez-Hansen, p. 362: ὅπως μὴ ἀδικοῖντο καὶ τὰ ἐπιτήδεια ἔχοιεν, σφόδρα ἐπεμελεῖτο. Sozomen's phrase implies both legal protection and material support, the two main benefits traditionally conferred by patronage. Callinicus, *V.Hypatii* 11.5 also notes that Chrysostom took great care for monks.

201. For Chysostom's definition of monasticism as a philosophic pursuit incompatible with church leadership, see *De sacerdotio* 6.6 and Lizzi (1987): 22–32.

202. Palladius, *Dial.* 7; ed. Malingrey-Leclercq (SC 341), p. 150: γυναῖκες δὲ φιλόθεοι

the wandering monks in Isaac's *clientela*. Nilus knew that maintaining monastic leadership could depend on providing daily necessities. To win new recruits, he warns, abbots had to be ready to offer "every aid and service as if they were drawing up contracts about food and clothing."[203] Those who could not live up to their promises risked abandonment. Although Isaac could count on his aristocratic patrons to provide him with resources to provide for most of his ascetic "children," some evidently went begging. Callinicus says Isaac often reminded Hypatius to help feed those who came by his monastery in Chalcedon.[204] Such monks may have been easy recruits for Chrysostom's institutions, especially if they believed their new bishop (who had been elected to office for life, and was only in his fifties) was there to stay.[205]

Such maneuvers may have outflanked Isaac and his monks, but did not neutralize them. Needing to defend his beleaguered standing in the church and city, Isaac found ready support from Alexandria's Theophilus. Chrysostom later alleged that his adversary had used money to turn the city's monasteries against him.[206] This was partly true: Theophilus had presented himself as an alternative episcopal patron and found in Isaac's company his own ascetic *clientela* in the heart of Constantinople. This was a method that later bishops of Alexandria would also use to influence events in the distant capital, as we shall see in the next chapter. But Isaac and his monks had already been provoked by Chrysostom's policies against them. The result was a patron-client collaboration in the old Roman political mold. Isaac rallied his monks to defend Theophilus' cause to the end. When they heard that Chrysostom had been recalled from exile following the Synod of the Oak, they provoked a riot inside the city's Great Church that killed several Chrysostom supporters and left as many of their own numbers dead.[207]

Thus the discord between Chrysostom, Isaac, and the wandering monks of Constantinople came to an end. Isaac apparently did not join the riot

---

ἐπήρκουν αὐτοῖς τὴν δίαιταν, καὶ συνεισφερόντων ἐκ μέρους τῇ τῶν χειρῶν ἐργασίᾳ. See also Kelly (1995): 196–97.

203. Nilus, *De mon. ex.* 33 (PG 79.761B): πᾶσαν ἐπαγγελλόμενοι θεραπείαν, καθάπερ οἱ πρὸς μισθωτοὺς συνθήκας περὶ τροφῆς καὶ ἐνδυμάτων τιθέμενοι. See also sect. 34 and *V.Alex* 7.

204. Callinicus, *V.Hypatii* 11.2–3. The context indicates that Isaac was here referring to monks.

205. Kelly (1995): 106.

206. John Chrysostom, *Sermo post reditum ab exilio* 1 (PG 52.443) and 3 (444), remarks that Theophilus corrupted the monasteries and used money to influence events in 403, whereas his own supporters relied on prayers. See Timothy Gregory "Zosimus 5, 23 and the People of Constantinople," *Byzantion* 43 (1973): 79.

207. It is not clear who made the protest turn violent: see Gregory (1973): 61–83 and F. van Ommeslaeghe, "Jean Chrysostome et le peuple de Constantinople," *AB* 99 (1981): 333–39.

himself, but prudently sailed with Theophilus to Alexandria soon afterwards.[208] Chrysostom lasted just a few months longer, only to be banished again in 404, this time for good. Now his own supporters (the Johnites) responded with violence, burning the Great Church and part of the senate house to the ground.[209] Chrysostom died while being driven in exile to the eastern Black Sea coast in 407. Isaac returned to the city. Secure at last, he probably resumed his former spiritual services until his death, perhaps as late as 416. His patron Aurelian laid him to rest in a shrine he had dedicated to Stephen, the Protomartyr, across from Isaac's monastery. Chrysostom's memory would not be so honored for many years to come.[210]

MONASTIC PATRONAGE AND SOCIAL MOBILITY

In September of 390 Emperor Theodosius I issued a law that ordered all who adopted the monastic profession to live in "deserted places and empty solitudes," effectively prohibiting them from living in cities. Two years later he retracted it.[211] Theodosius' reason for issuing the law remains unclear. He is said to have remarked, following the burning of a synagogue in Mesopotamia in 388, that "monks commit many crimes." His law is usually assumed to have been intended to prevent such urban violence, but we do not know of any disturbance monks caused in 390.[212] A different explanation is suggested by legislation that he issued (and similarly retracted) slightly earlier in the summer of that year, which prohibited wealthy widows and deaconesses from expending any superfluous wealth in support of religion or designating as heirs any "church, cleric, or pauper." It was intended to prevent any cleric from "plundering" such women "even in the name of the Church" and from "conducting himself as an heir of the living

208. Sozomen, *HE* 8.19.3.

209. For this incident, see Gregory (1979): 62–68. Gregory (1973): 70 excludes monks from the ranks of the Johnites, but their participation is likely.

210. Chrysostom was rehabilitated ca. 428–438: see Kelly (1995): 289–90. For Isaac's internment, see *V.Isaacii* 4.18 (*AASS Maii* VII.253E). Dagron (1970): 233 dates his death ca. 405, but Cameron and Long (1993): 72–75 argue ca. 416, which better fits with evidence for the passing of his monastery's leadership to Dalmatius: see below, ch. 6.

211. *CTh* 16.3.1 (issued at Verona, September 2, 390); ed. Mommsen-Meyer, p. 853: quicumque sub professione monachi repperiuntur, deserta loca et vastas solitudines sequi adque habitare iubeantur. Trans. Pharr, p. 449. Cf. *CTh* 16.3.2. This law (like *CTh* 16.2.27, below) was issued while the pagan Tatian was praetor, and therefore may be the product of pagan antipathies: see *PLRE* 1: 878 (Tatianus 5). Its retraction in 392 coincided with the praetorship of Rufinus, who in 394 imported monks from Egypt to perform liturgies in his shrine at the Rouphinianai: see Matthews (1975): 134–36.

212. For Theodosius' remark, see Ambrose, *Ep.* 41.27, dated 388. Another well-known act of monastic violence, the destruction of the Serapeion in Alexandria, did not occur until 391 or 392.

under the cover of catholic discipline."[213] Twenty years earlier a law had already threatened both churchmen and "those who wish to be called Continents [monks]" with banishment, in order to prevent them from doing the same.[214]

Theodosius' law sending monks to the desert may indicate how many rushed to Constantinople and other cities after 379, once the Theodosian court had demonstrated its interest in Nicene holy men. Dependence on wealthier members of society was simply the way most of the late Roman secular world worked, but the closer a cleric or monk came to eating from tables of the rich, the more suspicions he raised of flattery, fraud, or "Christmongering." This was perhaps even more true for men like John Chrysostom or Nilus of Ancyra, both of whom came from relatively affluent backgrounds, yet continued to depend on wealthy deaconesses. The concern both expressed for the behavior of wandering, begging monks stemmed partly from the fact that they felt the reproaches being directed against such monks could also be extended against themselves. Their sensitivity to charges of Christmongering indicates how social pressures impinged on the formulation and promotion of orthodox Christian practices, especially with regard to acceptable forms of ascetic poverty.

"The whole human race," wrote John Cassian at the end of his *Conferences*, "relies on the charitable compassion of others, with the sole exception of the race of monks which, in accordance with the Apostle's precept, lives by the daily toil of its own hands."[215] Even when put in the mouth of an Egyptian hermit, these words expressed more of an ideal than a reality. Nevertheless, Cassian's statement alerts us that self-sufficiency through manual labor would have been radical in the late fourth and early fifth century. In fact, it was this proposition—and not the apostolic dependency of monks like Isaac or Alexander—that would have radically differentiated Christian monasticism from other ancient forms of philosophy, had it become the norm.

The reasons for promoting and embracing this "orthodox" ascetic work ethic must be understood in its contemporary social context. It was not

213. *CTh* 16.2.27 (issued June 21, 390 at Constantinople); ed. Mommsen-Meyer, p. 843: nullam ecclesiam, nullum clericum, nullam pauperem scribat heredes, and *CTh* 16.2.28 (issued August 23, 390 at Constantinople). Trans. Pharr, p. 445. On deaconesses' wealth and laws against clerical legacy-hunting, see Dagron (1974): 500–506.

214. *CTh* 16.2.20 (issued July 30, 370 at Rome); ed. Mommsen-Meyer, pp. 841–42: ecclesiastici aut ex ecclesiasticis vel qui continentium se volunt nomine nuncupari, viduarum ac pupillarum domos non adeant.

215. Cassian, *Collatio* 24.12; ed. Pichery (SC 64), p. 183: nam utique omne hominum genus absque illo tantum genere monachorum, quod secundum praeceptum apostoli cotidianis manuum suarum laboribus vivit, agapem alienae miserationis expectat. Trans. Ramsey, p. 834.

simply a matter of fulfilling Paul's precepts, or of being able to provide alms, or of avoiding being a burden on others, although these aims were important and often expressed. Achieving self-sufficiency meant, above all, that a monk could keep honest. "Desire not the meats of the rich," warns Proverbs 23:3, "for these are near to a life of falsehood." As Epiphanius explained, monks who worked "will not become needy and fall into human hypocrisies, no longer able to speak the truth to impious people."[216] That was especially important for monks who were supposed to wield *parrhēsia* in order to improve people's souls. Epiphanius made the same claim for priests and bishops, who "enjoyed a clear conscience in teaching and preaching" because they supported themselves in imitation of Paul, despite their right to be supported by their congregations. Most, he says, performed some kind of labor, if not for support, then "for the sake of righteousness," having found trades that "befit their rank."[217]

Given this correlation between manual labor and honesty, it is not surprising that self-sufficiency was touted by many monastic authorities as the most virtuous way to live in voluntary poverty.[218] For them, orthodox ascetic poverty came closer to resembling the ordinary penury *(penia)* of the working poor than the destitute poverty *(ptōcheia)* of idle beggars grasping for coins on the street.[219] Equally important for understanding this promotion of manual labor is the Greco-Roman civic notion of *eutaxia* that the orator Libanius repeatedly expressed in these years at Antioch. While attacking itinerant outsiders who led demonstrations in the theaters, Libanius claimed that citizens who worked "with their hands," living in their own houses under the guidance of an educated elite, represented *eutaxia:* "good, stable order." As the ecclesiastical community began to replace the classical *polis* as the basis for social cohesion, *eutaxia* remained a civic ideal that church and monastic authorities valued no less than Libanius. This

216. Epiphanius, *Panarion* 80.4.7; ed. Holl-Dummer, p. 489. The connection between self-sufficiency and *parrhēsia* is illustrated by Mare the Solitary's independence and reputation as a critic under Justinian: see John of Ephesus, *Lives of the Eastern Saints* 36 (PO 18.638–39).

217. Epiphanius, *Panarion* 80.6.1–4; ed. Holl-Dummer, p. 491: οἵαν ... συμπρέπουσαν τῷ ἀξιώματι ... εὕροιεν <ἐργάζονται> τέχνην, ὅπως μετὰ τοῦ λόγου καὶ τοῦ κηρύγματος ἡ συνείδησις χαίρῃ. Epiphanius' identification of manual labor with righteousness is underscored by his praise for the schismatic Audian clergy, which denounced clerical wealth and practiced manual labor: see *Panarion* 70.2.1. On appropriate labor for clergy, see Emilio Herman, "Le professioni vietate al clero bizantino," *OCP* 10 (1944): 23–44.

218. E.g., Palladius, *HL* 38.10; 45.3–4; 47.2; 58.1; 71.4: such *exempla* lived by the work of their hands and did not take charity from others.

219. This holds true despite the survey in Patlagean (1977): 32–33, which shows that hagiography uses the term πτωχός more frequently to describe monks than πένης. This preference may derive from references to Christ's πτωχεία in 2 Cor 8:9. Patlagean, 33, observes that πένης, when used, "désigne ... une condition sociale à travers une condition économique."

concern may be seen not only in episcopal opposition to the *philonikia* associated with radical Eustathian and Messalian ascetics, but also in the episcopal promotion of work-based monastic arrangements like the one Basil promoted to support his city of the poor at Caesarea, the *Basileiados*.[220]

At the same time, however, philosophic ascetic theorists like Nilus and Evagrius were careful not to identify their voluntary poverty with the mundane, involuntary *penia* that "grinds down the mind."[221] Since their monasticism was aimed at philosophic contemplation through physical and social detachment, they conceived ascetic poverty as a moderate "freedom from possessions" *(aktēmosynē)* rather than a complete divestment of property. In this way Nilus promoted a more aristocratic form of ascetic poverty, one that would distinguish its practitioners from banausic country monks who spent too little time in contemplation and from avaricious urban monks who spent too much time mobbing potential benefactors on the street.

One suspects, however, that Nilus' recommendations for decorous dependency would not have been so practicable for monks who were not so well connected with affluent society as he was, or who "had no source of support from home." The notions one held of voluntary poverty and its proper circumstances depended greatly on social rank and perspective. Chrysostom reports how aristocrats in Antioch complained that the agriculture being performed by monks in the hinterland constituted the lowest form of penury and was too demeaning to be performed by their sons.[222] That attitude, not very different from what we find in Nilus' writings, reminds us that for ascetics of high social birth in this period to practice any form of manual labor was to adopt a more humble status. Indeed, hagiography of the period regularly highlights the *downward* social mobility of men and women whose voluntary embrace of poverty, despite family wealth and status, made them outstanding exemplars of Christ's voluntary condescension.[223] In the most well-known examples, such aristocratic *ptōcheia* meant austerity, manual labor, mixing with social inferiors, and carefully

---

220. Libanius, *Or.* 56.23; text above, n. 42. Basil uses the term εὐταξία to describe ideal church conditions in *Ep.* 161; ed. Deferrari (LCL 215), p. 412; cf. *Const. App.* 8.31.3; ed. Metzger (SC 336), p. 234: ἡ γὰρ Ἐκκλησία οὐκ ἀταξίας, ἀλλ᾽ εὐταξίας ἐστὶ διδασκαλεῖον. Such ecclesiastical order (and the place of monks in it) is graphically presented in Pseudo-Dionysius, *Ep.* 8.1 (PG 3.1088D–1089A). For agreement between orthodox monasticism and structural ideals of late Roman society, see Philip Rousseau, "Orthodoxy and the Coenobite," *SP* 30 (1997): 246–51. For Basil, see Gribomont (1977b): 179–91.

221. Nilus, *De vol. paup.* 2 (PG 79.969D): οὐ ... τὴν ἀκούσιον πενίαν ... ἥτις ἐξ ἀνάγκης συμβαίνουσα θλίβει τὴν γνώμην.

222. Chrysostom, *Adversus oppugnatores* 2.2 (PG 47.333–334): πενίας τῆς ἐσχάτης.

223. E.g., *V.Antonii* 1–3; Jerome, *Vita Pauli* 17; Greek *vita* of Pachomius 29, 33; Theodoret, *HR* 3, 5, 8, 10, 12; Syriac *vita* of Symeon Stylites 11; John of Ephesus, *Lives of the Eastern Saints* 57. For Basil, Gregory of Nyssa, and Gregory of Nazianzus, see Angstenberger (1997): 105–30 and Hamel (1990): 195–96.

distributing or sharing one's resources as alms rather than divesting oneself of possessions. The object was to become "poor in spirit" if not poor in fact. Thus Basil's affluent sister Macrina humbled herself by wearing a single garment and preparing food with the slaves in her community, while Basil emphasized his own *penia* (his "mother of philosophy") but still had the means to construct his *Basileiados* outside Caesarea.[224] When Melania the Younger and her husband arrived in Jerusalem in the early fifth century, they are said to have reached such a state of deprivation that they considered putting themselves on a church register to be fed with other beggars, yet they were soon building monasteries and dispersing gold in Egypt.[225] These, of course, were exceptional figures, but it was to such ascetics that authors like Nilus wrote and dedicated their orthodox treatises on voluntary poverty.

By contrast, the wandering urban monks Nilus assumed had "no source of support from home" provide fascinating examples of how monasticism and monastic patronage opened new opportunities for upward mobility in the late Roman period. Nilus repeatedly expresses concern that his apostolic vocation was being overrun by "the mania of those who are contending for greater renown."[226] These were the same ascetic *humiliores* who Augustine believed should keep on performing the manual labor that had characterized their previous existence. Like Nilus, Augustine suspected some of having adopted monasticism merely to escape toil and "above all, to be honored by those who would otherwise despise them."[227] Augustine notes the possibility of questioning whether it would really profit a person who had adopted a religious life to continue performing the labors that had characterized his secular existence. His response, that the nature and goals of work itself had changed upon entry to a monastery, was certainly novel, and perhaps not obvious to the monks in question.[228]

224. See Gregory of Nyssa, *Vita Macrinae* 5, 7, 11, 29 with Elm (1994): 98–102; Basil, *Ep.* 4 and *Homilia in Psalmum XIV* 2.2–4 (PG 29.273A–276B). In his poem *In monachorum obtrectatores* (PG 37.1349) Gregory of Nazianzus responds to criticism he received for his wealth from certain monks ("false" ones, of course).

225. Gerontius, *Vita Melaniae Junioriae* 35; ed. Denys Gorce, p. 194: εἰς τοσαύτην δὲ ἤλασαν ἀκτημοσύνην. For their dispersal of gold, see sect. 37–38, 41. See also Elizabeth Clark, *The Life of Melania the Younger: Introduction, Translation, and Commentary* (New York: Edwin Mellen Press, 1984), 92–119.

226. Nilus, *De mon. ex.* 5 (PG 79.724): ἡ τῶν πλέον δοξάζεσθαι φιλονεικούντων μανία, cf. 7 (728A) and 33 (761B). See also Jerome *Ep.* 125.16.

227. Augustine, *De opere* 22.25; ed. Zycha, p. 571: insuper honorari ab eis, a quibus contemni conteri convenuerant. Described as *ex paupertate* in 25.32 (578) and *ex vita humiliore* in 25.33 (580).

228. Augustine, *De opere* 25.32; ed. Zycha, p. 577: Dicet aliquis: quid ergo prodest servo dei . . . si adhuc eum oportet tamquam opifices exercere negotia. For Augustine's response, see Robert Marcus, "Vie monastique et ascétisme chez saint Augustin," in *Atti, Congresso in-*

In any case, rural monasteries could not long hold such monks on the move. Both Nilus and his Egyptian contemporary Isidore of Pelusium (modern Tell al-Farama) indicate that, by the early fifth century, many monks were heading back to the cities to secure their livelihood.[229] Once there, poverty put them on level with the promiscuous throng.[230] Some subsisted on the charity of "lovers of Christ and holy men" like Moses of Oxyrhynchus, who gave half his annual income to beggars and needy monks alike.[231] Others seem to have supported themselves as day laborers or by hanging around law courts, where they may have served as advocates (a law of 398 gave monks the right to make appeals for condemned criminals before imperial tribunals; Nilus says those who did so provoked contempt).[232] From such urban monks must have come the dark-cloaked *dēmodidaskaloi* (popular teachers) whose appearance on fifth-century streets was criticized by Synesius, bishop of Ptolemais (modern Tulmaytha) in Africa.[233] But Nilus indicates that even more sought positions in wealthy households. Although Nilus alleges that these offered benefactors more corporeal asceticism than spiritual knowledge, and although Chrysostom claims they spent more time in vigils and sleeping on the ground than in teaching, many evidently found interested patrons. It was through such patronage that some, like Isaac, were able to recruit and maintain their own urban monastic followings, and conduct their ministries beyond direct episcopal control.[234] Isaac's ordination as a priest (common for abbots of large monasteries, so they could perform liturgies and preach within monastery walls) made his status at Constantinople all the more ambiguous.[235]

---

ternazionale su S. Agostino nel XVI centenario della conversione, Roma, 15–20 settembre 1986 (Rome: Institutum Patristicum Augustinianum, 1987), 120–22.

229. Nilus: *Ep.* 1.292 (PG 79.189B: to Linnius, who was "determined to wander around like an utter fool"); 1.295 (189D–191A); 2.56 (224CD); 2.62 (228D); 2.71 (232D); 2.77 (234D–235A); 2.117 (252A); 2.136 (257A): to Eusebius, who "wanders around every region and land, city or village." Isidore of Pelusium (*fl.*390–435): *Ep.* 1.41 (PG 78.208C); 1.173 (296BC); 1.314 (364CD): all driven back to the cities "to fill their bellies."

230. Escolan (1999): 194.

231. John Rufus, *V. Petri Iberi;* trans. Raabe, p. 61. See also Palladius, *HL* 52, *Dial.* 7 and Theodore of Petra, *Vita Theodosii* 27.

232. Nilus, *Ep.* 2.78 (PG 79.234D–235A); see *CTh* 9.40.16 (398).

233. Synesius considered them "barbarians." See *Ep.* 154 with *Dion* 5. For discussion, see Lizzi (1987): 17–22.

234. Harry Maier, "Religious Dissent, Heresy, and Households in Late Antiquity," *VC* 49 (1995): 49–63, notes the importance of private houses in this period for those who wished to establish influence outside the dominant bishop's control. In Isaac's case, however, this should be viewed as a continuation of old philosophic / apostolic arrangements rather than a strategy of dissent.

235. For the origin of the monk-priest status and the problems caused by its ambiguity, see Escolan (1999): 267–311, mostly addressing developments from the late fifth century onward. Ambiguities surrounding monk-priests in the fourth century are illustrated by Chry-

While it made him formally subject to his bishop, it also meant he combined both ascetic and priestly credentials and, therefore, bridged the gap which Chrysostom had compared to that between a king and a commoner. As a monk-priest, Isaac blurred such distinctions, making him an especially potent rival.

Of course, not many monks were likely to attain such prestige as Isaac. The future of respectable urban monasticism lay with the philosophic withdrawal that articulate spokesmen like Nilus and Chrysostom taught aristocratic patrons to appreciate. Yet the legacy that Isaac left in Constantinople as chief spiritual guide to its nobility, as patron to its needy monks, and as rival to its bishop, would be inherited by his successors, Dalmatius and Eutyches. These monk-priests and the wandering, begging monks under their care would not only "throw" church politics "into confusion" for the next two generations, but would also give rise to new laws aimed at defining proper monastic behavior, and at settling church and monastic relations once and for all.

---

sostom's *Catechesis ad illuminandos hom.* 8.2 and the attempt to clarify their status by Paverd (1991): 260–93.

6

Monastic Patronage and the Two Churches of Constantinople

The council held at Chalcedon in 451 marked a watershed in official church policy toward monks. It issued the first disciplinary canons specifically aimed at bringing them under episcopal control. As stated in its fourth canon,

> Let those who truly and sincerely adopt the solitary life be considered worthy of the appropriate honor. But since some have used the monastic cover to throw church and civil affairs into confusion, moving indiscriminately around the cities, even making it their business to establish monasteries for themselves, let no one construct or establish anywhere a monastery or house of prayer against the will of the city's bishop; but let those who pursue a monastic life in each city and village be subordinate [hypotetachthai] to their bishop, and let them embrace tranquility and attend to fasting and prayer alone, persevering in those places to which they have withdrawn. Let them neither aggravate nor participate in ecclesiastical or temporal affairs by leaving their monasteries, unless they be permitted at some time by the bishops of the city through pressing need. . . . Whoever should transgress this our decision we decree to be excommunicated, lest he blaspheme the name of God. But the bishop of the city must make the necessary provision [tēn deousan pronoian poieisthai] for the monasteries.[1]

1. Council of Chalcedon, canon 4; ed. Périclès-Pierre Joannou, pp. 72–74: Οἱ ἀληθινῶς καὶ εἰλικρινῶς τὸν μονήρη μετιόντες βίον τῆς προσηκούσης ἀξιούσθωσαν τιμῆς. Ἐπειδὴ δέ τινες τῷ μοναχικῷ κεχρημένοι προσχήματι, τάς τε ἐκκλησίας καὶ τὰ πολιτικὰ ταράσσουσι πράγματα, περιιόντες ἀδιαφόρως ἐν ταῖς πόλεσιν, οὐ μὴν ἀλλὰ καὶ μοναστήρια ἑαυτοῖς συνιστᾶν ἐπιτηδεύοντες, ἔδοξε μηδένα μηδαμοῦ οἰκοδομεῖν μηδὲ συνιστᾶν μοναστήριον ἢ εὐκτήριον οἶκον παρὰ γνώμην τοῦ τῆς πόλεως ἐπισκόπου. Τοὺς δὲ καθ᾽ ἑκάστην πόλιν καὶ χώραν μονάζοντας ὑποτετάχθαι τῷ ἐπισκόπῳ, καὶ τὴν ἡσυχίαν ἀσπάζεσθαι, καὶ προσέχειν μόνῃ τῇ νηστείᾳ καὶ τῇ προσευχῇ, ἐν τοῖς τόποις ἀπετάξαντο προσκαρτεροῦντες, μήτε δὲ ἐκκλησιαστικοῖς μήτε βιωτικοῖς παρενοχλεῖν πράγμασιν ἢ

The immediate provocation for this and other canons arose during the council's fourth session.[2] Certain supporters of Eutyches (the leading monastic figure in Constantinople at the time, whose christological views were under attack) had petitioned to be heard. All claimed to be archimandrites. When their names were read out, seven were not known at all, and seven more were identified as *memoritai* or *memorophylakes*—monks who lived by or tended the martyr shrines scattered around Constantinople.[3] Several archimandrites present at the council (themselves residents of Constantinople, who were allied as Eutyches' opponents) immediately requested that these petitioners' "monasteries" be investigated, so that any whose martyr-shrine dwellings did not support their claim to be either legitimate monks or monastic leaders might be expelled from the city as imposters.[4] The emperor heard their request. The pronouncements he gave in response served as the basis for canons that granted bishops unprecedented legal authority and jurisdiction over monks and their habitats.

The fourth canon of the Council of Chalcedon imposed official distinctions on monastic legitimacy that would influence secular and canonical law on monks for centuries to come.[5] By its provisions, those who remained tranquilly in monasteries approved by a local bishop were recognized as legitimate and worthy of honor, while those who wandered in cities and established themselves wherever they pleased became liable for excommunication. Eutyches had kept what his peers considered bad company. Besides such dubious archimandrites as "Leontius, the former bearkeeper," "Hypses, who has two or three names at the shrine near the Wooden Circus," and "Gaudentius, the *memoritês* who has five names in the shrines of

---

ἐπικοινωνεῖν, καταλιμπάνοντες τὰ ἴδια μοναστήρια, εἰ μή ποτε ἄρα ἐπιτραποῖαν διὰ χρείαν ἀναγκαίαν ὑπὸ τοῦ τῆς πόλεως ἐπισκόπου.... Τὸν δὲ παραβαίνοντα τοῦτον ἡμῶν τὸν ὅρον ὡρίσαμεν ἀκοινώνητον εἶναι, ἵνα μὴ τὸ ὄνομα τοῦ θεοῦ βλασφημῆται. Τὸν μέντοι ἐπίσκοπον τῆς πόλεως χρὴ τὴν δέουσαν πρόνοιαν ποιεῖσθαι τῶν μοναστηρίων. Cf. canon 23.

2. See Hefele-Leclerq 2.767–828 and Leo Ueding, "Die Kanones von Chalkedon in ihrer Bedeutung für Mönchtum und Klerus," in *Das Konzil von Chalkedon,* ed. A. Grillmeier and H. Bacht, vol. 2 (Würzburg: Echter, 1953), 600–612.

3. *ACO* 2.1.2 [64]; ed. Schwartz, pp. 114,27–115,5. For the text, see below, n. 86.

4. *ACO* 2.1.2 [64]; ed. Schwartz, p. 115,12: ἐξελθεῖν ἀπὸ τῆς πόλεως ὡς ἐπιθέτας.

5. Its influence on secular law is evident in *CJ* 1.31.29 (issued by Emperor Leo in 471, prohibiting monks from wandering in cities) and Justinian's *Novella* 123.41–42 (issued 542): see Ueding (1953): 632–35 and Charles Frazee, "Late Roman and Byzantine Legislation on the Monastic Life from the Fourth to the Eighth Centuries," *Church History* 51 (1982): 272–74. For its reception in the West, see Jenal (1995): 709–14, 783–812 and later references in Lawrence Mayali, "Du vagabondage à l'apostasie: le moine fugitif dans la société medievale," in D. Simon, ed. *Religiöse Devianz: Untersuchungen zu sozialen, rechtlichen, und theologischen Reaktionen auf religiöse Abweichungen im westlichen und östlichen Mittelalter* (Frankfurt am Main: Klostermann, 1990), 121–42. Its actual application and effectiveness are another matter.

Philip," there stood the more notorious presence of the Syrian archimandrite Barṣawma. This grim "Son of Fasting" (ca. 403–457) had spent his youth as a *boskos* in the foothills of northern Syria near Samosata (modern Samsat). He was the dangerous monk writ large. In the 430s he led a hundred iron-clad monks on a rampage against pagans, Samaritans, and Jews in the Holy Land: "Frequently his appearance alone convinced his victims to embrace Christianity."[6] Having deployed his monks against the bishop of Constantinople during the second Council of Ephesus just two years before (449), he was vigorously denounced ("Barṣawma has destroyed all Syria! He sent a thousand monks against us!") and nearly lynched ("The murderer to the lions!") when he appeared uninvited at the fourth council session.[7] The canons issued at Chalcedon were meant to ensure that such rogue monks would never exert their pressure upon ecclesiastical or civil affairs again.

That monks were largely responsible for "elevating urban violence into one of the major problems of the late Roman world" has long been observed.[8] Their role in the christological controversies that led up to the Council of Chalcedon is particularly notorious.[9] More must be said, however, about the economic and social circumstances through which monks became agents of ecclesiastical and civil confusion, and how those circumstances were addressed by the fourth Chalcedonian canon in particular. The conciliar *acta* offer a fascinating glimpse of what might be called inner-city monastic life, lived in or around the martyr shrines of Constantinople. Though regarded as imposters by their opponents, such martyr-shrine monks may be regarded as so many little Alexanders, whose activities around the shrine of St. Menas had caused such a stir in the mid-420s. Equally illuminating parallels for understanding their circumstances (as

6. Holum (1982): 187. Little is known for sure about the historical Barṣawma (whose name means "Son of Fasting"), but his Syriac *vita* is a hagiographical masterpiece. In Palestine he is said to have razed temples, torched synagogues, and terrorized Samaritans, apparently to redefine the Holy Land once and for all. His monastery corresponds to Borsun-Kaleshi on Nemrud Dag (southeastern Turkey). See the summary of the *Vita Barsaumae* by François Nau, "Résumés de monographies syriaques," *ROC* 18 (1913): 272–76, 379–89; *ROC* 19 (1914): 113–34, 278–79. Also *id.*, "Deux épisodes de l'histoire juive sous Théodose II (423 et 438) d'après la vie de Barsauma le Syrien," *Revue des études juives* 83 (1927): 184–206; Ernest Honigmann, *Le couvent de Barsauma et le patriarcat jacobite d'Antioche et de Syrie* (Louvain: Durbecq, 1954), 6–29; Vööbus (1960b): 196–208; and Gaddis (1999): 184–86, 244–45.

7. *ACO* 2.1.2 [78–81]; ed. Schwartz, p. 116,29–39.

8. Alan Cameron, *Circus Factions: Blues and Greens at Rome and Byzantium* (Oxford: Clarendon Press, 1976b), 291.

9. For the role of monks in these controversies and councils, see Heinrich Bacht, "Die Rolle des orientalischen Mönchtums in den kirchenpolitischen Auseinandersetzungen um Chalkedon (431–519)," in *Das Konzil von Chalkedon*, ed. A. Grillmeier and H. Bacht, vol. 2 (Würzburg: Echter, 1953), 193–245 and Dagron (1970): 353–76.

well as their potential threat) may be found in the so-called circumcellions of fourth- and early fifth-century North Africa, whom contemporaries describe as wandering ascetics (false ones, to be sure) who had gravitated to martyr shines to receive both religious inspiration and material support.

Such North African examples need occupy us insofar as they help us tap into a monastic world outside hagiography. Circumcellions exemplify how ascetic zealots impoverished by ideology or circumstance might not only use violence to assert their ideals but also provide a constituency ready to support a patron's cause. We have seen how such a monastic *clientela* contributed to the authority and influence of Isaac at Constantinople. After Isaac's death, his clientela had been led by Dalmatius, and then by Eutyches. All three were known for using (or threatening to use) monks under their care to agitate against bishops of Constantinople. Besides having influence over the city's less reputable monastic population, all three had strong links to influential patrons both at the imperial court and in the Alexandrian church. It was through such patronal connections, extending from the imperial court to the city streets, that these three monk-priests were able to wield *parrhēsia* and oppose their bishops nearly to the point of establishing a rival church in the imperial capital.[10] As one of Constantinople's deposed bishops, Nestorius, bitterly described Eutyches' position before the Council of Chalcedon:

> Although he was not a bishop, he granted himself another role, thanks to imperial power: that of bishop of bishops. It was he who directed all the affairs of the church. . . . [On the inside] he was driving out of the church as heretics all those who were not holding his views; but those who were aiding him he raised up and gave support. On the outside he used imperial power, firm power. . . . [11]

Nestorius reminds us that institutional definitions were as much at stake at Chalcedon as doctrinal definitions.[12] The council had to make clear ex-

---

10. Dagron (1970): 274, "Le concile pense . . . à l'indépendance d'un ordre monastique qui, dans la capitale, avait provoqué la rivalité de deux hiérarchies et presque l'affrontement de deux Églises."

11. Nestorius, *Liber Heraclidis* [*LH*] 2.2 [460]; trans. Godfrey R. Driver and Leonard Hodgson, p. 336 (cf. François Nau's trans. with more extensive notes, pp. 294–95). Nestorius wrote this apology while exiled at Egypt's Great Oasis. It received interpolations (mostly of a theological nature) ca. 451–470, and is preserved only in a sixth-century Syriac translation. See Luise Abramowski, *Untersuchungen zum Liber Heraclidis des Nestorius* (Louvain: Secrétariat du CorpusSCO, 1962). Bracketted numbers in citations refer to pages in Paul Bedjan's critical edition of Nestorius' text.

12. Several narratives describe the complex issues and events between the first Council of Ephesus (431) and the Council of Chalcedon (451) in greater detail than I do here. For doctrinal issues and ecclesiastical maneuvers, see esp. Aloys Grillmeier, *Christ in Christian Tradition*, vol. 1, *From the Apostolic Age to Chalcedon (451)* (New York: Sheed and Ward, 1965), 363–

actly who would control the affairs of the church, and how. Controlling monastic patronage was crucial, as Nestorius indicates. Yet, despite the emphasis Nestorius places on patronage as the basis of Eutyches' quasi-episcopal power, the role of monastic patronage in events leading up to the council has received little scholarly attention. Nor has the relevance of such patronage to the fourth Chalcedonian canon been observed. Of course, it has long been recognized that the canon addressed fluid monastic circumstances at Constantinople that had enabled monastic leaders to exert their influence since at least the days of Isaac.[13] What has not been observed is how the bishops at Chalcedon attempted to wrest control over the monastic forces such leaders had under their care. The fourth canon did not simply forbid monks from wandering or planting monasteries in cities at will. It also included the brief but crucial stipulation that "the bishop of the city must make the necessary provision [deousan pronoian poieisthai] for the monasteries."

This phrase, *deousan pronoian poieisthai,* has usually been interpreted as a mere summation that bishops should keep close watch on the monks and monasteries now officially under their supervision.[14] It certainly can and does mean that here. The word *pronoia,* however, was often used in this period with the additional connotation of supplying material provisions.[15] For example, Nilus uses it (in verb form) to describe how God provides (*pronoōn*) for monks who remained tranquilly praying in their monasteries by compelling outsiders to furnish their bodily needs.[16]

In fact, Sozomen attributes a similar monastic policy to John Chrysostom, who "took greatest care" that those who stayed quietly in urban monasteries would "have their daily necessities." Such was also the policy of

---

495 and Robert Sellers, *The Council of Chalcedon: A Historical and Doctrinal Survey* (London: S.P.C.K., 1953). For the rhetorical positions and discourse adopted by different parties, see Gaddis (1999): 296–349. For their political circumstances, see Holum (1982): 147–216 and Gregory (1979): 81–201.

13. Dagron (1970): 270–74; Ueding (1953): 610.

14. E.g., Hefele-Leclerq 2.780: "L'évêque de la ville doit surveiller d'une manière très exacte les couvents;" Dagron (1970): 273: "L'évêque de la ville doit exercer la surveillance nécessaire sur les monastères." Dionysius Exiguus' Latin translation is ambiguous: ed. Joannou, pp. 73–74: Verumtamen episcopum convenit civitatis competentem monasteriorum providentiam gerere.

15. E.g., *Didache* 12.4; *HM* 2.3 (Abba Or providing for his monks) ed. Festugière, p. 36: πᾶσαν πρόνοιαν αὐτῶν ἐποιεῖτο ... ἵνα ἐν μηδενὶ λείπωνται τῶν ἀναγκαίων. ... *V.Alex* 47 (PO 6.695,18–696,1): πρόνοιαν ἐποιεῖτο ὁ μακάριος τοῦ εὐκρατίου διὰ τοὺς ἀρρωστοῦντας ἀδελφούς. Also used for a bishop's distribution of alms: Socrates, *HE* 7.25.3; ed. Hansen-Sirinian, p. 373: ἦν μεταδοτικός, ὡς ... τῶν ἐν ταῖς αὐτοῦ παροικίαις πτωχῶν προνοεῖν. For other examples, see Lampe, s.v. πρόνοια A.2.

16. Nilus, *Ep.* 3.58 (PG 79.417C): ὁ Θεὸς ἐκείνους αὐτοὺς φέρει πρὸς ἡμᾶς, προνοῶν καὶ φροντίζων ἡμῶν, καὶ ἀναγκάζει αὐτοὺς ... ποιεῖν ἡμῶν τὰς σωματικὰς χρείας.

Nestorius, bishop of Constantinople (428–431), and that most monarchical Syrian bishop, Rabbula of Edessa (411/12–435/36). Rabbula's legacy includes monastic rules that not only restricted the movement of monks outside their monasteries, but also limited their ability to become economically independant, placing them under the financial care and control of his clergy instead. In this way Rabbula imposed episcopal hegemony and ecclesiastical order upon monastic populations deep in the Syrian heartland decades before Chalcedon.[17]

In 451 at Chalcedon the bishops enacted a similar policy, only now at an ecumenical level. The *deousan pronoian poieisthai* clause effectively established them as the official (if not exclusive) monastic patrons in their cities. Given the role of patronage and material support in helping Isaac, Dalmatius, and Eutyches rise to power, this policy (which they added to emperor's original pronouncements) was more political than philanthropic. Providing material support may have rewarded monks who lived a quiet, orthodox monastic life. But more importantly, it kept them within the episcopal fold, so that they would not need outside patrons who might encourage them to throw church affairs "into confusion."

With Eutyches, the bishops at Chalcedon faced problems that were in many respects similar to those Chrysostom had faced with Isaac nearly fifty years before. But time had brought important changes to Constantinople's monastic scene. No longer did respectable archimandrites let themselves be seen in the streets as Isaac had. Indeed, the sequestered style of Dalmatius and Eutyches more closely resembled the aristocratic ideal propounded by Nilus, than the wandering ways of many of the monks in their *clientelae*. In other words, the fourth canon of Chalcedon rewarded—and institutionalized—a monastic lifestyle that was already being practiced by the city's monastic elite.

This elite, however, was no longer a united elite. The policies adapted

---

17. Rabbula, *Rules for Monks* 2–3, 13–15 (monks shall not leave their monasteries or roam in villages or towns), 9 (monasteries shall possess only a single donkey), 11 (monasteries shall not conduct business beyond what suffices for their needs), 12 (no private possessions), 25 (no selling of crops for profit); *Rules for the Clergy and the Bnay Qyāmā* 15 (priests and deacons must take charge of monks in their territories and take care of them; cf. 12 and 19), ed. and trans. Arthur Vööbus, pp. 27–32, 39–41. Their attribution to Rabbula is strengthened by allusions to them in the *Life of Rabbula*, written soon after his death, probably by a member of the Edessan clergy. In her unpublished paper, "Bishop Rabbula: Ascetic Tradition and Change in Fifth-Century Edessa," Susan Ashbrook Harvey discusses Rabbula's policy of controlling monks around Edessa by making these economically depended on his church and clergy. See also Harvey, "The Holy and the Poor: Models from Early Syriac Christianity," in *Through the Eye of a Needle: Judeo-Christian Roots of Social Welfare*, ed. E. A. Hanawalt and C. Lindberg (Kirksville: Thomas Jefferson University Press, 1994), 52–53; Escolan (1999): 187–88; and Georg Günther Blum, *Rabbula von Edessa: Der Christ, der Bischof, der Theologe* (Louvain: Secrétariat du CorpusSCO, 1969), 56–60.

at Chalcedon were supported by archimandrites who were opposed to Eutyches and had everything to gain from aligning themselves with his episcopal adversaries. The fourth Chalcedonian canon itself must be viewed as a collaborative effort between these "orthodox" monks and their episcopal patrons. For this and other canons issued by the council did not merely represent an attempt to subject monks to episcopal control, but also an attempt to establish a distinct, stable, and unified spiritual hierarchy for the Roman world once and for all.

DALMATIUS AND ASCETIC ENTHUSIASTS IN THE DOWNFALL OF NESTORIUS

The quarter-century between the deposition of John Chrysostom and the ordination of Nestorius as bishop of Constantinople was a quiet period in relations between the monks and bishops of the city. Except for the appearance of Alexander and the proceedings against him in 426, there is no record of monastic disturbances. That may be attributed to the forbearance of Atticus, bishop of Constantinople for nineteen years from 406 to 425. Himself an ascetic from an early age and a native of Eustathius' Sebaste, Atticus may have felt at home with the urban monastic lifestyles exemplified by Isaac and others.[18] Indeed, while still a priest at Constantinople Atticus had aligned himself with those who opposed Chrysostom at the Synod of the Oak,[19] and as their bishop he proved more tolerant and open to compromise. As the church historian Socrates fondly recalls, "he became all things to all people."[20]

This climate of peaceful coexistence changed with the ordination of Nestorius in 428. Formerly a monk and deacon at Antioch, Nestorius was, like Chrysostom, appointed bishop of Constantinople because of his reputation for eloquence. And like Chrysostom, he quickly became known for his assertive and irascible disposition, particularly exhibited in his dealings with heretics. For his ardent campaigns against them he was soon branded an incendiary by friends and foes alike.[21] Speaking in church on the day of

---

18. Socrates, *HE* 6.20.3. Dagron (1970): 265 assumes that Atticus had been raised on Eustathian asceticism. As bishop, Atticus took action against Messalians, writing a letter urging the Pamphylian bishops to drive them out as an abomination. However, the letter fragment that Photius preserves does not otherwise indicate what Atticus considered Messalianism to be: see Fitschen (1998): 40–41. Between Chrysostom and Atticus, the bishop of Constantinople was Arsacius (404–406).

19. Photius, *Bibliotheca* 59.

20. Socrates, *HE* 7.2.2–4; Gregory (1979): 83 notes that Atticus was criticized for laxity.

21. Socrates, *HE* 7.29.10; ed. Hansen-Sirinian, p. 378. Socrates describes Nestorius' temper at 7.29.6–8. For his imperial appointment, see Holum (1982): 145–46.

his ordination, Nestorius offered the emperor Theodosius II (408–450) an unprecedented bargain:

> Emperor, give me the earth cleared of heretics, and I will give you heaven in return. Help me wipe out the heretics, and I will help you wipe out the Persians.

Under the influence of this new bishop (whom he backed with great loyalty until 431), Theodosius reversed the tolerant stance he had previously taken toward heretics in his empire.[22] Within days of his ordination Nestorius was permitted to demolish a house of prayer where some of the city's Arians met; thus commenced his purge of old sects whose congregations had continued to gather in the city or neighboring suburbs. Six weeks later the emperor himself contributed his own sweeping law against heretics, which denied such old and formerly tolerated groups their churches, and prohibited all others (including "the Messalians, the Euchites or Enthusiasts") from assembling or praying on Roman soil.[23]

Towards monks in the city Nestorius' actions were just slightly less severe. As he himself noted later, the monastic front that agitated for his deposition in 431 included "those who had been separated and removed from the monasteries by reason of their lives and strange manners, and had for this reason been expelled."[24] Unfortunately, none of Nestorius' extant sermons shed light on his attitude towards monks the way Chrysostom's do. According to a later apologist, Nestorius took such disciplinary actions against those who wandered through public places, drank in taverns, or spoke with women. Such monks he considered not only "a cause for scandal in the city," but also "a cause for blasphemy against true monks." Nestorius reportedly forbade all monks except their leaders from going out "so that this might no longer happen," while at the same time "he also made sure to give them food and whatever was necessary for their maintenance."[25]

22. As noted by Gregory (1979): 118 n. 20, correcting Colm Luibhéid, "Theodosius II and Heresy," *JEH* 16 (1965): 13–38. For Nestorius' ordination speech, see Socrates, *HE* 7.29.5; ed. Hansen-Sirinian, p. 377. Seven years earlier (420–421) the emperor's Persian war had ended in stalement.

23. Socrates, *HE* 7.29 (persecution of Arians, Novatians, and Quartodecimans) and 7.31 (persecution of Macedonians); *CTh* 16.5.65 (May 30, 428).

24. Nestorius, *LH* 2.1 [373]; trans. Driver-Hodgson, p. 271.

25. Barḥadbeshabba 'Arbaya, *Historia ecclesiastica* [*HE*] 21; ed. with French translation François Nau (PO 9.528–29). Barḥadbeshabba was a sixth-century dyophysite (Nestorian) bishop of Halwan (in Persian Mesopotamia). His account may be based on Nestorius' lost apology, the *Tragoedia,* and on lost episcopal *acta:* see Abramowski (1963): 38–43. His description of wayward monks uses standard polemical tropes of the period, on which see Gaddis (1999): 220–26.

By this account Nestorius' monastic policy resembled that which Chrysostom had adopted thirty years earlier: both bishops considered monks who wandered outside their monasteries as an insult to their profession and both provided material support to encourage them to stay inside. Yet by his own account, Nestorius went further: he even had expelled some from their monasteries because of their "strange manners." A later source explains that "he excommunicated monks who were accustomed to insinuating themselves into houses and appearing in the public thoroughfares."[26] Nestorius evidently encountered the same behavior at Constantinople that had provoked Chrysostom, but Nestorius responded more directly and aggressively. That was not all. Nestorius also criticized the city's abbots for not looking after their monks' deportment. One in particular he is said to have reprimanded numerous times, namely Dalmatius, the city's chief archimandrite in these years. As in the case of Chrysostom and Isaac, that did not bode well for Nestorius' tenure. Not only did the wandering monks he disenfranchised prove especially zealous agitators for his deposition, but Dalmatius, we are told, soon also "conceived a hatred" for him.[27]

Nestorius is said to have suspected the monks in Dalmatius' monastery of plotting "seditious activities" long in advance.[28] It was through his doctrinal pronouncements, however, that the bishop exposed himself to attack. Early in 428 he was asked to settle a dispute over the proper title for Mary. Should she be called the *Theotokos,* the "God-bearing" mother (emphasizing her role in the mystical generation of the God Jesus) or as *anthrōpotokos,* the "human-bearing" mother (restricting her role to the generation of the human part of Jesus)? Choosing between these designations involved making profound decisions on the matter of God's incarnation. Had divinity come down, as it were, to settle in Jesus' human body while remaining distinct from its corporeal being and carnal sufferings, or had divinity become wholly fused with Jesus' humanity at birth, to remain thereafter inseparable from Jesus' flesh as soul to body?

Two schools of thought developed regarding this christological question of how divine and human natures were unified in Jesus.[29] The Antiochene

26. See Emil Goeller, "Ein nestorianisches Bruchstück zur Kirchengeschichte des 4 und 5 Jahrhunderts," *Oriens Christianus* 1 (1901): 95. Goeller defends the credibility of this ninth-century (?), pro-Nestorian document at pp. 82–83. Its reference to excommunication may be anachronistic, reflecting post-Chalcedonian policies; nonetheless, it more closely resembles the monastic policy Nestorius himself describes than do the policies which Barḥadbeshabba ascribes to him.

27. On Nestorius' relations with Dalmatius, see Barḥadbeshabba, *HE* 21 (PO 9.529) and 27 (566); also Nestorius, *Letter to Cosmus* 3 (PO 13.277).

28. Barḥadbeshabba, *HE* 27 (PO 9.566); cf. Nestorius, *LH* 1.2 [153].

29. For a technical introduction to these points, see Grillmeier (1965): 369–412. The

school (with which Nestorius was most familiar) tended to keep the divinity and humanity of Jesus separate (without denying that at some level the two had been united). It viewed any identification of his divine nature with his historical humanity as implying that divinity itself might be subject to historical change through biological generation and suffering at birth and at death. For similar reasons it refrained from conceding that Mary was involved in giving birth to the divine in Jesus along with his human nature. The Alexandrian school, on the other hand, affirmed that his divinity and humanity had become inseparably conjoined at birth (as soul to flesh), while maintaining that differences between these two natures had not become lost in the incarnation. By this Alexandrian Christology, God could be said not only to have suffered and died on the cross, but also to have been born at Bethlehem through Mary (hence the appropriateness of *Theotokos*).

Designating Mary as either *Theotokos* or *anthrōpotokos* also had implications for the view one took of humanity's relation to Jesus Christ as one's savior. The preference of most late Roman congregations for the Alexandrian Christology has been explained in the following way:

> The one-nature christology [of the Alexandrian school] implied confession in unequivocal terms that "Christ is God" and associated the suffering and redemption of mankind with divine suffering and glorification, whereas "two natures inseparably united" [of the Antiochene school] either seemed nonsense or implied the existence of "two Christs" (pre-and post-Incarnation), one of which could not be God.[30]

If oversimplified or misconstrued, the Antiochene approach could either suggest a God who ultimately remained aloof from human needs and suffering, or else that Jesus was "a mere man." This helps explain why monks (whose ascetic endurance depended in part on their assurance that God had voluntarily suffered too) numbered so high among those who took to the streets at Constantinople when Nestorius began preaching against use of the *Theotokos*.[31]

Antiochene school (including Theodoret of Cyrrhus and Nestorius) developed primarily out of the teachings of Theodore of Mopsuestia (350–428) against the views of Apollonarius of Laodicea (ca. 310–390). The latter stressed (among other tenets) the use of the *Theotokos* to combat the Arian subordination of the Son (Jesus) to the Father (God).

30. W. H. C. Frend, "Popular Religion and Christological Controversy in the Fifth Century," in *Popular Belief and Practice,* ed. G. J. Cumming and D. Baker (Cambridge: Cambridge University Press, 1972a), 26.

31. At first Nestorius tried to avoid controversy by proposing the term *Christotokos* [Mother of Christ]: *LH* 1.2 [152]. His own preaching against the *Theotokos* began in defense of a cleric who had criticized its use. Socrates, *HE* 7.32.6 reports most people believed Nestorius himself preached that Jesus was a "mere man." Nestorius complained that his own partisans

A petition directed to the emperor from an archimandrite named Basil and "the rest of the Christian monks" recounts what followed. Some of the city's clergy who began to preach against Nestorius' views were beaten and dragged off (together with their congregations, crying "we have an emperor; a bishop we have not") to an ecclesiastical prison. A monk among them who dared to call Nestorius a heretic was handed over to the civil magistrates for a public flogging. Basil then describes what he himself suffered when he led a group to confront the bishop in his episcopal palace:

> He immediately ordered us to be seized by his throng of *decani*. After we were beaten there we were led away to the church prison where, naked and chained, we were beaten on the feet, drawn on benches, and flogged.

Basil petitioned the emperor to prevent Nestorius ("who does these things emboldened by wealth, by the force of corrupt men, and, to speak without fear, by your power") from terrorizing them any further. As Nestorius had done, he also offered the emperor a bargain: if he would summon an ecumenical council to settle the *Theotokos* dispute, the monks would "send up our prayers to God in harmony for our common salvation and for your empire."[32]

Basil's petition gives some idea of what monks were ready to risk at Constantinople in order to oppose their bishop before 431. Later tradition remembered Basil as a heroic outsider whom Providence had roused from his distant Cilician cell to expose Nestorius and arrange his deposition at Ephesus in 431.[33] As in 403, however, the monks at Constantinople needed the help of an episcopal outsider who could exert decisive ecclesiastical pressure. Enter Cyril, who was bishop of Alexandria from 412 to 444. Cyril was Theophilus' nephew and the leading exponent of Alexandrian Christology at the time. The "Nestorian" problem mounting in the capital gave him the perfect opportunity to champion his christological views and assert the preeminence of Alexandria over Constantinople in episcopal (and, thus, political) power.[34] Like his uncle Theophilus, Cyril realized the stra-

---

misrepresented him. For the outbreak of the controversy at Constantinople, see Gregory (1979): 88–100 and Hefele-Leclerq, 2.219–47.

32. Basil's petition is preserved in *ACO* 1.1.5 [143]; ed. Schwartz, pp. 8,8–10,11. It was used at the Council of Ephesus in 431 in order to portray Nestorius as a tyrant acting above the law: see Gaddis (1999): 297.

33. John Rufus, *Plerophoriae* 35 (PO 8.78–81). Basil evidently was influential in the early fifth century. He is said to have been responsible for Peter the Iberian's conversion to asceticism in the early 420s at Constantinople, where he served as a deacon. His own ascetic career began in Egypt; later he trained under the *boskos* Heliodorus in Cilicia and planted monasteries in Lycia. Rufus says he was exiled for his confrontation with Nestorius at Constantinople, whither a divine voice had called him.

34. When Cyril became involved in the controversy is unknown: see Gregory (1979): 89

tegic need for collaboration with the monks in the capital. In 430 he sent a letter to the "Fathers of the Monasteries" at Constantinople, urging them to take courage as God's slaves and to "do everything on behalf of Christ's glory."[35] What he meant became clear the following year.

On the first day of the Council of Ephesus in 431, Cyril and his clerical allies deposed Nestorius without even giving him a hearing. So began a long summer of maneuvering among partisans on both sides of the christological debate.[36] Faced with the emperor's staunch support of Nestorius (whose peremptory deposition Theodosius considered illegal), Alexandrian agents at Constantinople set to work rallying popular demonstrations on behalf of Cyril and the *Theotokos*. As Nestorius later explained, "They took with them those who had been separated and removed from their monasteries by reason of their lives and strange manners" and "for this reason had been expelled."

> There is indeed much to say on the subject of the dreams they recounted, which they say that they saw concerning me. . . . They amazed their hearers by the saints (to be sure!) and by the revelations that were recounted by them and by a prophesy that was fabricated. . . . For they were persuading all men of all the things that they were seeing, likening themselves to angels of light.

Nestorius alludes here to Paul's warning about false apostles and Satan's appearance as "an angel of light" (2 Cor 11:12–15), but the contribution of these monks with "strange manners" to his downfall is nonetheless clear: "With all these things," Nestorius concludes, "they disturbed the emperor's mind."[37] Their demonstrations culminated when Cyril, now in house arrest at Ephesus, had a letter smuggled into Constantinople describing his need to be heard by Theodosius himself. Among those it addressed was "the archimandrite Dalmatius, Lord of the Monasteries."[38] With the stirrings of this sequestered ascetic, the emperor began to abandon his bishop.

Dalmatius had been the leading monastic figure in Constantinople since the death of Isaac. What we know of him before 431 comes mostly from a

and Sellers (1953): 3–4. Nestorius *LH* 1.2 [153–57] explains that Cyril held a grudge against him going back to his failure to send Cyril *eulogiae* [gifts] after his ordination and to support Cyril's envoys at Constantinople.

35. *ACO* 1.1.5 [144]; ed. Schwartz, p. 13,15–19. Socrates, *HE* 7.7.4 notes that Cyril's political reach extended even farther than his uncle Theophilus' had.

36. For disturbances created by both sides at Ephesus, see Gregory (1979): 102–8.

37. Nestorius, *LH* 2.1 [373–74]; trans. Driver-Hodgson, pp. 271–72. Callinicus, *V.Hypatii* 32.3–3 records that Hypatius foretold Nestorius' demise in a prophesy that circulated among the city's monks.

38. *ACO* 1.1.2 [67]; ed. Schwartz, p. 66,10–11: τῷ ἀρχιμανδρίτῃ τῶν μοναστηρίων κυρίῳ Δαλματίῳ. For the title, see Dagron (1970): 269. Nestorius still had on his side clerical supporters and imperial forces who blocked communications between Ephesus and the capital. Still, letters got by: see Gregory (1979): 108.

biography of unknown date.[39] Having come from the East he had served Emperor Theodosius I as a *scholaris* in the palace guard and had visited Isaac for daily blessings. Eventually with the holy man's encouragement he left his wife and moved into the monastery on Saturninus' property (ca. 384), together with his son, Faustus. He became known for his assiduous prayer, fasting, and visions. When Isaac died, Dalmatius was made head of the monastery because, we are told, "he had emulated his teacher in asceticism and every way of life . . . especially in giving alms." His election was confirmed by Bishop Atticus, who was probably responsible for ordaining him a priest.[40]

Dalmatius distinguished himself from Isaac in one respect, however. By 431 he had not left his monastery once in forty-eight years. "Despite frequent earthquakes," he had refused to come out, even to perform special liturgies (probably rogations) at the emperor's bidding.[41] Such long-term enclosure was considered a singular feat, noted by all as Dalmatius' special source of prestige. He therefore did not visit monks or go to the homes of aristocrats to provide spiritual services, as Isaac had done; instead, aristocrats came to him. These admirers included none other than Theodosius himself, who used to cross town just to see him.[42] When they visited they also brought gifts: "All who came to show reverence would place contributions in Dalmatius' hand." These proceeds he shared, we are told, "with prisoners and with those who came to the holy monastery."[43] The abbot became no less a provider to the city's indigent monks. In fact, to judge from his biography, monastic tradition associated his reputation as the city's chief archimandrite not so much with his feat of enclosure as with his capacity and his readiness to provide material "blessings" (alms) to all, especially to monks. As his biographer remarks,

39. See *PLRE* 2, "Dalmatius 1." There are two Greek versions of the *Vita Dalmatii;* neither is comparable to the *V.Isaacii:* see Dagron (1970): 231 n. 11. The first (ed. Anselmo Banduri), however, includes letters to Dalmatius that match those in conciliar records, so the other information it gives may also have been drawn from accurate records. It is preferable to the second version (ed. Manouel Gedeon), which errs chronologically by placing Dalmatius' assumption of leadership of the city's monasteries under Bishop Nectarius (i.e., before Chrysostom), and claims that Dalmatius' son Faustus took over this leadership after his death (which we know was not so: see below).

40. Dalmatius' origin and entry into Isaac's monastery, *V.Dalmatii* 1.1; ascetic training, 1.3–5; election as Isaac's successor because of emulation, 1.6; ed. Banduri 699A: ἐξαιρέτως δὲ καὶ ἐν τῇ ἐλεημοσύνῃ. Atticus is said to have confirmed his election and was probably the one responsible for ordaining him priest, as Dalmatius is titled in *ACO* 1.1.3 [86].

41. *ACO* 1.1.2 [66]; ed. Schwartz, p. 65,25–29. Cf. Barḥadbeshabba, *HE* 27.

42. *ACO* 1.1.2 [66]; ed. Schwartz, p. 65,27.

43. *V.Dalmatii* 1.2; ed. Banduri, p. 697DE: πάντες οἱ ἐρχόμενοι εἰς προσκύνησιν αὐτῶν φέροντες προσφορὰς εἰς τὰς χεῖρας τοῦ ἁγίου Δαλματίου ἐδίδουν . . . μετεδίδουν αὐτὰ εἰς αἰχμαλώτους καὶ εἰς τοὺς ἐρχομένους εἰς τὸν ἅγιον μοναστήριον.

The name "Lord Dalmatius" remains attached to the monastery to this day, because whenever the brothers would go to its gates in order to ask to receive a blessing *(eulogia)*, they also would use his name and say to each other, "Let's go to Lord Dalmatius, for he has resources from God to nourish us with."[44]

In this way Dalmatius became their patron and "Lord."

To appreciate Dalmatius' position and the responsibilities that went with it we must note his monastery's size: with three hundred monks inside, it operated in the midst of the city on a village scale.[45] His ability to provide both for its residents and for those who came begging must have mainly derived from a steady flow of gifts from those who came for spiritual blessings.[46] Dalmatius, like Isaac, forged his reputation as leading monk in Constantinople not only through ascetic prowess, but through the patron-client relationships he extended from wealthy admirers in the imperial court on down to the monks on the street.

It was a memorable event in 431 when the abbot emerged from his cell. This time the demonstrations included Dalmatius himself, who was carried by "troops of monks" all the way to the palace in order to "overwhelm the emperor with amazement." Their procession was a spectacular success. As Nestorius reports,

> A multitude of monks surrounded [Dalmatius] in the middle of the city, chanting the offices, in order that all the city might be assembled with them and proceed before the emperor in order to hinder his purpose. . . . When the emperor saw Dalmatius, he shook his head and put up his hands as if astonished at the sight.[47]

Inside the palace Theodosius received the holy man, read his letter, and finally agreed to hear Cyril's case. Cyril's supporters rightly took this development as victory assured.[48] Carried back to the Psamathian district amid

---

44. *V.Dalmatii* 1.2; ed. Banduri, p. 697EF: ἐν τῷ ἔρχεσθαι τοὺς ἀδελφοὺς ἐν τῷ πυλεῶνι, καὶ αἰτοῦντας λαμβάνειν παρ' αὐτοῖς εὐλογίαν, αὐτοὶ καὶ τὸ ὄνομα ἐπέθηκαν λέγοντες πρὸς ἀλλήλους· ἀγώμεθα εἰς τὸν κύριον Δαλματίον· αὐτὸς ἔχει τῶν παροχῶν τοῦ θεοῦ θρέψαι ἡμᾶς. The title Κύριος (Lord) is not attested for any other monk at Constantinople, but it may be Greek for the Syriac title *Mār*, often used to honor archimandrites and holy men (Dalmatius, like Isaac, came from somewhere in the Roman East).

45. Barḥadbeshabba, *HE* 27. Three hundred is given frequently for monastery size (e.g., *V.Alex* 43 and Eutyches' monastery) and may just mean "big."

46. As a former imperial *scholaris*, Dalmatius probably brought with him considerable wealth: see Jones (1964): 647.

47. Nestorius, *LH* 2.1 [375]; trans. adapted from Driver-Hodgson pp. 272–73 with Nau, p. 241.

48. The immediate results of Dalmatius' audience with Theodosius were simply Cyril's release and the reopening of communications with his party in Ephesus, but both sides considered it crucial in turning the emperor and his courtiers against Nestorius: see *ACO* 1.1.2 [67]; Holum (1982): 168–71; and Gregory (1979): 111–12.

acclamations and chants ("reclining on a couch spread with coverlets," imagines Nestorius), Dalmatius read Cyril's letter and described his encounter with the emperor to supporters waiting at the shrine of St. Mocius by his monastery. "Thus it was made known that a victory had been gained over the purpose of the emperor, amid great assemblies of people and monks, who were dancing and clapping their hands and crying out all that can be said against one who has been deposed for iniquity."[49]

By all accounts Dalmatius' sudden emergence made an impression on the emperor—as Nestorius laments, "the *schēma* of the monks was very dear" to him. It is also clear that the archimandrite had been working in close concert with the Alexandrian bishop. The two had corresponded during the summer of 431,[50] during which Dalmatius communicated that he was ready to fulfill any command that Cyril might make.[51] Indeed, Cyril and Dalmatius probably orchestrated his dramatic appearance long in advance: Cyril had been in contact with the emperor's ministers, and the holy man's embassy would have helped the emperor save face if he decided to abandon the bishop he had appointed and, until then, so adamantly supported.[52]

But their collaboration was sustained on the street by the zeal of the city's monks. As Nestorius complains, "those who were furnishing [them] with money and supplies . . . were both preparing them and demanding them to be ceaselessly engaged" in agitations against him at Constantinople.[53] Indeed, their job was not over yet. By the end of the summer the emperor had summoned representatives from both sides to Chalcedon for a final settlement. When Nestorius and his allies arrived, they were met by "an assemblage of men practiced in sedition." According to Nestorius this mob included

> those who were renegade from monasticism, together with all those who for whatever reason had been driven out and were zealous for the work of agitators. With their monastic robes they were receiving food and provisions from the monasteries, given to them as wages of fervor and charity. . . . From the

49. Nestorius, *LH* 2.1 [382]; trans. adapted from Driver-Hodgson, p. 277, with Nau, p. 246. For other descriptions, see *ACO* 1.1.2 [66]; *V.Dalmatii* 1.14; and W. Kraatz, ed., *Koptische Akten zum ephesinischen Konzil vom Jahre 431. Übersetzung und Untersuchungen* TU 26.2 (Leipzig: J. C. Hinrichs'sche, 1904), pp. 47–50. For the location of St. Mocius' *martyrium*, see Dagron, (1974): 395 and Janin (1953): 371.

50. See *ACO* 1.1.2 [67] and Bacht (1953): 197–98.

51. *ACO* 1.1.7 [*Fragmentum Garnerianum*]; ed. Schwartz, p. x,16–20.; cf. 1.1.3 [86].

52. Nestorius suspected the complicity of Theodosius' ministers: see *LH* 2.1 [375]. Until then, Theodosius had been on closest terms with him: see Barḥadbeshabba, *HE* 20 (PO 9: 523) and Holum (1982): 172.

53. Nestorius, *LH* 2.1 [384]; trans. Driver-Hodgson, pp. 278–79.

things which you [Cyril] were sending and bringing from your granaries and deposits of wine. . . . You filled the monasteries that had been chosen for this and [you filled] other places, so that even the holy houses of prayer were being encumbered. . . . You were paying them with the things that are called "blessings," giving these instead of wages.

"And so you were acting," Nestorius maintains, "that you might not be thought to be sending these to cause sedition but, since they were coming into the monasteries and were being received by the monasteries," people would simply credit the violence at Chalcedon to zealous monks, rather than to Cyril's connivance.[54]

It was partly through such zealous intimidation that Cyril was able to obstruct Nestorius' appeal and confirm his deposition for good.[55] Nestorius indicates that his opposition at Chalcedon largely consisted of monks he had earlier "separated," "removed" or "expelled" from their monasteries across the Bosphorus in Constantinople. Who were those monks? To Nestorius they were obviously false ones, who wandered in the streets and frequented taverns, and had "strange manners": they had visions of saints and amazed their hearers with descriptions of revelations, fuelling the demonstrations. The enthusiastic behavior Nestorius attributes to them recalls the behavior being identified with Messalian heretics in these same years: perhaps Nestorius had expelled some through application of the law banning Messalians and Enthusiasts, issued six months into his tenure. Cyril, in fact, was accused by Nestorius' party of having recruited at Ephesus "those who are Euchites or Enthusiasts and so were excommunicated by their diocesan and metropolitan bishops."

> In contempt of ecclesiastical order [eutaxia] they have received these into communion, mustering for themselves a multitude from all sides . . . thinking a flow of money can prevail against the faith of the Fathers.[56]

Whatever Cyril's opponents meant by "Enthusiasts" in their letter,[57] his agents found similarly disenfranchised and enthusiastic supporters ready

54. Nestorius, *LH* 2.1 [397–98]; trans. adapted from Driver-Hodgson, pp. 288–89 with Nau, p. 255.

55. See Theodoret of Cyrrhus, *Ep.* 169 (*ACO* 1.5.2 [22]) for his stoning by "false" monks and daily fear of ambush. For the effect of the Chalcedon demonstrations on the emperor, see Holum (1982): 171–72.

56. John of Antioch *et al.*, *Ep.* to Rufus of Thessalonica, *ACO* 1.1.3 [97]; ed. Schwartz, p. 42,4–11: Εὐχῖται γάρ εἰσιν εἴτ' οὖν Ἐνθουσιασταί, δι' ὃ καὶ ἀκοινώνητοι ἦσαν... τῆς ἐκκλησιαστικῆς εὐταξίας καταφρονήσαντες εἰς κοινωνίαν αὐτοὺς ... χρημάτων ῥεύμασιν οἰόμενοι τὴν τῶν πατέρων καταγωνίζεσθαι πίστιν.

57. Stewart (1991): 48–50 and Fitschen (1998): 48–49 think the Antiochene reference to Messalians was simply meant to tar the supporters of Cyril at Ephesus. John of Antioch also

at Constantinople and Chalcedon as well. Nestorius' repudiation of such monks of "strange manners," combined with their opposition to his teachings, explains their zeal against him. Once expelled from their monastic homes, however, such monks were especially in need of patrons. Those who furnished them with material necessities could expect their allegiance in return. Thus material circumstances combined with other grievances made those monks enthusiastic recruits against Nestorius, "zealous for the work of agitators."

More will be said later about Cyril's use of "houses of prayer" in supplying such monks. Writing many years afterward in his Egyptian exile, Nestorius emphasized the role Cyril had played in orchestrating his downfall, saying that Cyril had directed a flow of wealth and false holy men against him.[58] His claims were well founded. A letter preserved from these years documents that Cyril's clergy at Constantinople distributed 1,080 pounds of gold "blessings" as well as other precious items (ivory stools, embroidered drapes, ostrich-eggs, and peacocks) to members of the imperial court in order to maintain their allegiance.[59] The monks Nestorius had driven out of their monasteries were useful recipients of such Alexandrian "blessings," and more in need of them, too. It was Dalmatius' participation, however, that made Cyril's "gilded arrows" particularly effective, both at Constantinople and Chalcedon. The same letter that lists Cyril's handouts to the court advises that Dalmatius should be asked to bind the emperor and his advisors "with a terrible oath not to mention that man [Nestorius] ever again."[60] As the city's leading monk and spiritual exemplar (perhaps Theodosius' first choice for bishop in 428),[61] Dalmatius alone could provide the moral weight needed to counter Bishop Nestorius' influence with the emperor.

That was not all. It was Dalmatius who controlled the city's monks and monasteries. Those whom Nestorius had expelled because of their "strange

---

sent a letter to the emperor referring to Cyril's communion with "twelve Messalians from Pamphylia," which Fitschen interprets as a reference to Cyril's clerical allies from that region: see *ACO* 1.1.3 [154]; ed. Schwartz, p. 26,28–34 and Fitschen (1998): 49–50.

58. See Gaddis (1999): 300–302 on Nestorius' characterizations of these events.

59. *ACO* 1.4.2 [293]; ed. Schwartz, p. 223,5–21, written ca. 432 to the new bishop of Constantinople, Maximianus, by Cyril's archdeacon Epiphanius. For different discussions of the context of this letter, see Holum (1982): 179–81 and Brown (1992): 15–17.

60. ACO 1.4.2 [293]; ed. Schwartz, p. 223,21–25: et dominum meum sanctissimum Dalmatium abbam roga ut et imperatorem emendet, terribili cum coniuratione eum constringens, et ut cubicularios omnes ita constringat. For Cyril's "gilded arrows," see Barḥadbeshabba, HE 27 (PO 9.566).

61. Nestorius, *LH* 2.1 [377]. Dagron (1970): 268 n. 184 is skeptical, but Dalmatius was clearly thought worthy of the honor: see Liberatus, *Brevarium causae nestorianorum et eutychianorum* 7; *ACO* 2.5. Liberatus wrote ca. 555–556 from good sources (e.g., Cassiodorus): see Schwartz, *ACO* 2.5, pp. xvi–xviii and Hefele-Leclerq, 2.767.

manners" naturally turned to their Lord Dalmatius, not only for handouts, but for recognition of their legitimacy. Although he did not share their lifestyle, he was still their patron; as Nestorius remarked, he remained their organizer and chief.[62] If Cyril needed them, he especially needed Dalmatius: ultimately, the wandering enthusiasts of Constantinople were his *clientela*.

To city residents, the events of 431 must have seemed much like what they had seen some thirty years earlier. Once again a bishop of Constantinople had been deposed through the collaboration of the city's leading monk and a powerful Alexandrian bishop. In both conflicts Isaac and Dalmatius ultimately depended on outside bishops to depose their adversaries through formal ecclesiastical proceedings. Yet, at the same time, both were able to establish considerable spiritual authority within the imperial city by virtue of their ascetic practices, and could effectively raise sedition against their bishop through the wealth of aristocratic admirers and the enthusiasm of the needy, disenfranchised monks at their command. Similar patron-client relationships would also enable Dalmatius' successor, the archimandrite Eutyches, to assert himself as "bishop of bishops," until imperial and Alexandrian support finally collapsed for him and his *clientela*.

EUTYCHES AND THE CIRCUMCELLIONS OF CONSTANTINOPLE

Religious affairs at Constantinople calmed after Nestorius' dismissal in 431, but partisan fervor still simmered outside the city over doctrinal issues that the Council of Ephesus had left unresolved. The formal reconciliation struck between Cyril and his Antiochene colleagues in 435 was unstable at best: bishops of the Antiochene school continued to defend Christ's distinct humanity, while wandering monks pressed allegiance to the Alexandrian Christology in cities and monasteries throughout the East.[63] When Cyril died in 444, his successor, Dioscorus, proved even more ambitious for the Alexandrian cause. Though Bishop Proclus of Constantinople (434–447) managed to maintain peace within the imperial capital for seventeen years by steering between the two parties, his successor, Flavian, was forced to take sides in 448, when the city's leading archimandrite and monk-priest Eutyches (Dalmatius having died ca. 440) was accused of heresy.

Like other opponents of Nestorianism in these years, Eutyches is said to have preached an extreme version of Alexandrian Christology, one that

---

62. Nestorius, *LH* 2.1 [375]; trans. adapted from Driver-Hodgson, p. 272.

63. Liberatus, *Brevarium* 8. *ACO* 2.5; ed. Schwartz, p. 112,9–15; John Rufus, *Plerophoriae*, appendix 97.3. For developments between the years 431–448, see Gregory (1979): 129–31; Bacht (1953): 198–206; and Sellers (1953): 15–29.

blurred all distinction between the human and divine natures of Christ. He reportedly taught that these natures had solidified in Jesus "just as the atmosphere becomes rain or snow under the influence of wind." To some it seemed that his teachings vaporized Christ's humanity entirely. Proclus had avoided the issue when complaints first arose in 447, but the new bishop, Flavian, was reluctantly forced to make Eutyches respond at a synod *endēmousa,* that is, a local synod, of bishops at Constantinople in 448.[64]

Flavian knew he was getting into trouble. For many days the archimandrite refused to answer the synod's summons, claiming he had sworn an oath not to leave his monastery unless by "fatal compulsion." Monks stood guard at the gate.[65] When he finally presented himself at the synod, he arrived with soldiers, monks, and imperial officers at his side.[66] Nonetheless, his opponents were not deterred: when Eutyches refused to concede that two distinct natures persisted in Christ after their union, he was stripped of his priestly rank and excommunicated. And something else happened that portended change: twenty-three archimandrites of the city signed the decree that condemned him.[67]

We will turn to the possible causes of this schism among the city's monastic leaders below. The accusation of heresy and subsequent conviction made this confrontation between Flavian and Eutyches different from those between previous bishops and monastic leaders of Constantinople. Condemnation as a heretic rendered the archimandrite a virtual outlaw, exposing him to public abuse, as Alexander had been after his conviction as a Messalian heretic in 426. Indeed, as Eutyches later complained, after the synod *endēmousa,* Bishop Flavian "delivered me to a multitude, which had been prepared for this, both at the episcopal palace and in the marketplace, to be killed as a heretic, a blasphemer, and a Manichaean. Only God's

64. Eutyches managed to prevaricate to such a degree that it is impossible to know exactly what he believed. For the quotation, Ps.-Zachariah, *Chronicle* 2.2; trans. F. J. Hamilton and E. W. Brooks, p. 21. For interpretation, see Thomas Camelot, "De Nestorius à Eutychès: L'opposition de deux christologies," in *Das Konzil von Chalkedon,* ed. A. Grillmeier and H. Bacht, vol. 1 (Würzburg: Echter, 1951), 213–42. The archimandrite Maximus identified as his teacher at the Council of Chalcedon may be the same Maximus who agitated against Nestorianism in the East and reported to Cyril: see *ACO* 1.4.2 [285, 297] and 2.1.2 [64]; Liberatus, *Brevarium* 8; and Bacht (1953): 209 and 237. For the synod *endēmousa,* see Hefele-Leclerq 2.518–38; Gaddis (1999): 308–9; Gregory (1979): 131–43; and Bacht (1953): 210–17.

65. *ACO* 2.1.1 [397]; ed. Schwartz, pp. 128,36–129,20.

66. *ACO* 2.1.1 [464]; ed. Schwartz, p. 138,5–6.

67. See *ACO* 2.1.1 [552]; ed. Schwartz, pp. 145–47; for prosopography, see Bacht (1953): 217–20 and Dagron (1970): 240–42. Eutyches later claimed Flavian had compelled them to sign. Though this was perhaps true for some (two of those who signed named Carosus and Dorotheus appeared among Eutyches' loyal supporters at Chalcedon), it was clearly not true for all: see Bacht (1953): 216 n. 107 and Gregory (1979): 134–35.

Providence saved me."[68] Officially, no sanctuary was open to a heretic. Eutyches was not only prohibited from entering any church or receiving its sacraments (as were all who accepted his teachings), but he was also banned by Flavian's order from all of the city's monasteries.[69]

The heresy charge thus isolated Eutyches and put him in need of patronal support to an extent that neither Isaac nor Dalmatius had experienced. It had one immediate and predictable result: Eutyches turned to the bishop of Alexandria, Dioscorus, who was ready to help. Indeed, Eutyches' condemnation in 448 galvanized forces that were already at work elsewhere against representatives of the Antiochene Christology. Once again events moved towards Ephesus, where a second ecumenical council was scheduled for August 449.[70]

Meanwhile, Eutyches had to rely on local patrons. The task before them was prodigious: for Eutyches to function normally in Constantinople after being charged with heresy, the whole church community had to be reconstituted around him and his teachings. His supporters, therefore, had to wield influence at the highest level. In Nestorius' view, this is precisely what happened: Five months after the synod *endēmousa,* the emperor was persuaded to use his authority to cause church leaders to secede from Bishop Flavian and to recognize Eutyches' orthodoxy. In this way, according to Nestorius, the emperor helped the abbot become the "bishop of bishops." Even Eutyches' partisans agreed that ecclesiastical affairs at Constantinople verged on major schism.[71]

That Eutyches was able to challenge Flavian and circumvent his heresy conviction is testimony to his patronal leverage. Indeed, the fluster surrounding his presence at the synod in 448 attests the stature he had attained by that time in monastic and imperial circles around Constantinople. He was one of the last of Isaac's generation. In a letter he sent Pope Leo of Rome in 448, Eutyches claimed to have been living "in complete chastity" for seventy years, which indicates that he had become a monk around 378, even before Dalmatius.[72] Eutyches had collaborated with Dalmatius against Bishop Nestorius in 431, and by 448 had assumed Dalma-

68. *Ibid.* Cf. *V.Alex* 49. For events at Constantinople after the synod *endēmousa,* see Gregory (1979): 135–37.

69. *ACO* 2.1.1 [185]; ed. Schwartz, p. 95,33–34.

70. For the background to Ephesus II and its proceedings, see Hefele-Leclerq 2.545–66, 585–621 and Gregory (1979): 129–61. For the role of monks, see Bacht (1953): 221–31.

71. Eutyches' monks petitioned Emperor Marcian to prevent an impending schism: *ACO* 2.1.2 [76]; ed. Schwartz, p. 116,9. Cf. Nestorius, *LH* 2.2 [465–468]; trans. Driver-Hodgson, p. 340.

72. Leo, *Ep.* 23. *ACO* 2.4 [108]; ed. Schwartz, p. 144,37. Some mss give him 66 years: see Bacht (1953): 207 n. 203 (206–9 for Eutyches in general).

tius' title as "Archimandrite of the Monasteries."[73] He did not, however, belong to Dalmatius' monastery. His was in the city's Hebdomon suburb (modern Bakirköy), about five miles southwest of the city center. Called the Monastery of Job, it rivaled Dalmatius' in size, and by the late 440s had become "the most celebrated in Constantinople."[74]

The reason was clear even to hostile observers. Eutyches' life of ascetic enclosure did not prevent him from having important admirers any more than it had Dalmatius. As one writer attests, "This man was visited by many who happened to be in the city, who resorted to him ostensibly on account of his chastity and piety, and especially soldiers of the palace, who were lovers of doctrine."[75] Despite Pope Leo's description of Eutyches as "an ignorant old man," Eutyches had, in fact, become spiritual mentor to an unusually prestigious set of admirers. Besides the members of the palace guard who accompanied him to the synod *endēmousa* in 448, they included the eunuch chamberlain Chrysaphius (the emperor's closest advisor) and Nomus, a wealthy patrician, former consul, and master of offices whose dependent clients were themselves said to be "ardently devoted to Eutyches."[76] No doubt they all had adopted Eutyches' christological teachings. Chrysaphius, however, had special reason to defend his cause. As Eutyches' godson, he would have prepared for his baptism with instruction in the same faith now being declared heretical. After Eutyches' condemnation, the emperor's most trusted advisor might be considered a heretic himself.[77]

With such patrons it is no wonder that Eutyches caused such a stir or enjoyed such a reversal of fortune at Ephesus in 449.[78] The emperor had

73. For the title, see Dagron (1970): 270 n. 203. His partisanship against Nestorius in 431 is attested by *ACO* 1.4.2 [293] and *ACO* 2.1.1 [147]; also Barḥadbeshabba, *HE* 21 (PO 9.534).

74. Liberatus, *Brevarium* 11. *ACO* 2.5; ed. Schwartz, p. 113,61–62. For the monastery, see Janin (1953): 281–82 and *id., Constantinople byzantine, developpement urbain et répertoire topographique* 2d ed. (Paris: Institut Français d'Études Byzantines, 1964), 446–49.

75. Ps.-Zachariah, *Chronicle* 2.2; trans. F. J. Hamilton and E. W. Brooks, *The Syriac Chronicle Known as That of Zachariah of Mitylene*, p. 19. Leo, *Ep.* 47; *ACO* 2.4; ed. Schwartz, p. 22,23 describes Eutyches' teachings as haeresim unius imperitissimi senis.

76. For Chrysaphius, see *PLRE* 2 (Chrysaphius *qui et* Ztummas) and Holum (1982): 191–92. He first appears in the early 440s as Theodosius' *spatharius*. For Nomus and his circle see *PLRE* 2 (Nomus 1), with Theodore Lector, *Historia ecclesiastica [HE]* frg.346; ed. Günther Christian Hansen, p. 98: οἱ περὶ Νόμον τὸν ὕπατον ἐκθύμως τῷ Εὐτυχεῖ προσκείμοι. As *magister officiorum* Nomus was in charge of the palace guard; perhaps this constituted "Nomus' circle" and the "soldiers of the palace" noted among Eutyches' followers. Eutyches also seems to have been on close terms with the tribune and *notarius* Aristolaus, whom Theodosius had sent around the East to secure reconciliations after Ephesus: see *PLRE* 2 (Aristolaus).

77. Cf. Evagrius Scholasticus, *HE* 2.2. For Chrysaphius' role in defending Eutyches, see Gregory (1979): 137–41 and Paul Goubert, "Le rôle de Sainte Puchérie et de l'eunuque Chrysaphios," in *Das Konzil von Chalkedon*, ed. A. Grillmeier and H. Bacht, vol. 1 (Würzburg: Echter, 1951), 303–21. His baptism by Eutyches is mentioned by Liberatus, *Brevarium* 11.

78. Theodore Lector, *HE* frg. 346 says Chrysaphius and Nomus persuaded the emperor

sent his representatives ahead with clear instructions that those who had condemned "the most devout archimandrite" Eutyches in 448 were now to be put on trial themselves.[79] Such imperial pressure did not reflect mere favoritism. Faced with the growing menace of Attila's pagan Huns on the Balkan frontier, Theodosius wanted his empire to be firmly unified in the Christian faith already declared orthodox in 325 at Nicaea and 431 at Ephesus. The second Council of Ephesus was therefore not to wrangle over Christ's different natures. Its purpose was to reassert previously established Alexandrian tenets and to silence opposition by any means necessary.[80]

The result was the notorious *Latrocinium* (Robber Council). At the council's first session Eutyches was reinstated; by its last session, Bishop Flavian had been deposed and beaten, to die afterwards under mysterious circumstances. Other bishops with Antiochene sympathies were deposed *in absentia*. The emperor had guaranteed unanimity at the council not only by placing Alexandria's Bishop Dioscorus fully in charge, but by inviting the formidable Syrian archimandrite Barṣawma to represent the empire's monks at its sessions. Barṣawma was later said to have "slain" Bishop Flavian.[81] Yet Barṣawma was not the only archimandrite who brought his monastic forces to bear at the council. Eutyches brought some three hundred who proved equally intimidating: "All those with Eutyches—they were monks—enjoyed great liberty and authority . . . so that they delivered unto their leaders and unto the inhabitants of the city all those who were indicated to them. For every man was made subject to them and served them whether willing or not."[82] The bishop of Ephesus later claimed that Eutyches' monks had arrived at his palace with soldiers "about to kill me, saying I had received the enemies of the emperor. . . . so all came to pass through violent compulsion."[83]

Who were these monks whom Eutyches had brought to Ephesus? Nestorius distinguishes them from "those enclosed in their monasteries," that is, the archimandrites who had signed Eutyches' condemnation in 448 and had come down from Constantinople to support Flavian at Ephesus.[84] No

to convene the second Council of Ephesus to judge Flavian; Liberatus, *Brevarium* 12 says Dioscorus persuaded him, after receiving Eutyches' letter.

79. Theodosius, *Mandate on Conciliar Discipline*, trans. P. R. Coleman-Norton, *Roman State and Christian Church*, pp. 752–57.

80. My understanding of this council owes much to Gaddis (1999): 317–31.

81. For Barṣawma's imperial invitation and role at the council, see *ACO* 2.1.1 [48]; Gaddis (1999): 317; Gregory (1979): 143; and Bacht (1953): 225–26. For Flavian's fate, see Henry Chadwick, "The Exile and Death of Flavian of Constantinople," *JThS* n.s. 6 (1955): 17–34.

82. Nestorius, *LH* 2.2 [482]; trans. adapted from Driver-Hodgson, pp. 351–52 with Nau, p. 308.

83. *ACO* 2.1.1 [58]; ed. Schwartz, p. 75,33: οἱ μονάζοντες Εὐτυχέος, ὀνόμαντα ὡς τριακόσια.

84. Nestorius, *LH* 2.2 [482]; trans. Driver-Hodgson, p. 351.

doubt most of Eutyches' forces came from his Hebdomon monastery.[85] He had other monastic supporters in the capital, however. These included the archimandrites who would later be challenged as imposters at the Council of Chalcedon in 451, about half of whom were identified as *memorophylakes* (martyr-shrine guardians) or *memoritai* (martyr-shrine attendants). As their opponents identified them at that time,

> Elpidius is the *memorophylax* of the shrines of Procopius. Photinus, we don't know who he is. Eutychius is in the *martyrium* of Celerina, since he doesn't have a monastery. Theodore is a *memoritēs*. Moses we don't know. Maximus is an archimandrite, Eutyches' teacher. Pherontius we don't know. Nemesinus we don't know, and his name is strange to us. Theophilus' name we don't recognize. Thomas likewise we don't know.[86] Leontius is a former bearkeeper. Hypses is a *memoritēs* with two or three names at the Wooden Circus. Callinicus has ten names at the shrine *[memorin]* at the Wooden Circus. Paul the Bithynian lives by himself at a shrine. Gaudentius is a *memoritēs*, with five names in the shrine of Philip. Eugnomonius we don't know.[87]

The location of these martyr shrines in Constantinople is unknown, but the Wooden Circus *(Xylokerkos)* was probably near the gate of that name southwest towards the Hebdomon suburb.[88] Significantly, it was a priest from a shrine in this district that had been sent down to investigate rumors that Eutyches was plotting sedition before his hearing at the synod *endēmousa* in 448.[89] At that time such fears proved unfounded, but not in 449

85. Thus Bacht (1953): 209 n. 63 and 228 n. 43. Monks from Eutyches' monastery complained at Ephesus II about the abuse they had received from Flavian since 448.

86. *ACO* 2.1.2 [64]; ed. Schwartz, pp. 114,27–115,5: Ἐλπίδιος μεμοροφύλαξ τῶν Προκοπίου ἐστί. Φωτεινὸν οὔτε οἴδαμεν τίς ἐστιν. Εὐτύχιος ἐν μαρτυρίῳ Κελερίνης ἐστίν · μοναστήριον γὰρ οὐκ ἔχει. Θεόδωρος μεμορίτης ἐστί. Μωσῆν οὐκ οἴδαμεν. Μάξιμος ἀρχιμανδρίτης ἐστί, διδάσκαλος Εὐτυχοῦς. Φερόντιον οὐκ οἴδαμεν. Νεμεσῖνον οὐκ οἴδαμεν καὶ τὸ ὄνομα αὐτοῦ ξενίζει ἡμᾶς. Θεοφίλου τὸ ὄνομα ξενιζόμεθα. Θωμᾶν ὁμοίως οὐκ οἴδαμεν. Λεόντιος ἀπὸ ἀρκοτρόφων ἐστίν. Ὕψης μεμορίτης ἐστὶν ἔχων δύο ἢ τρία ὀνόματα εἰς τὸ ξυλόκιρκον. Καλλίνικος ἔχει δέκα ὀνόματα εἰς μεμόριν εἰς τὸ ξυλόκιρκον. Παῦλος ὁ Βιθυνὸς κατὰ μόνας ἐστὶν εἰς μεμόριν. Φαυδέντιος <μεμορίτης> ἐστίν, ἔχει πέντε ὀνόματα εἰς τὰ Φιλίππου. Εὐγνωμόνιον οὐκ οἴδαμεν.

87. For the terms μεμόρις and μεμορίτης (attested only here) as "martyr shrine" and "dweller of a martyr shrine," see Dagron (1970): 243 n. 80 and Gregory (1979): 167–69. Dionysius Exiguus translates μεμόρις, μεμορίτης and μεμοροφύλαξ as *monumentum* and *in monumentis habitat*, and *custos monumentorum*, respectively: *ACO* 2.3.2; ed. Schwartz, p. 119,26–29. I follow Hefele-Leclerq 2.707 in interpreting ὀνόματα as a reference to monks under their care (e.g., "Callinicus has ten monks under his care at the shrine at the Wooden Circus"). For previous discussions of them, see Gregory (1979): 169–70; Dagron (1970): 243–244; and Bacht (1953): 237–38.

88. For the location, see Janin (1964): 440–441, correcting earlier scholarship that located the gate at the northwestern end of the Anthemian wall.

89. *ACO* 2.1.2 [381]; ed. Schwartz, p. 126,34–36: ὄντα τὸν πρεσβύτερον τὸν ἐν μαρτυρίῳ τοῦ Ἑβδόμου.

when Eutyches' martyr-shrine supporters proved as dangerous as they were disreputable. Martyr-shrine monks were not unique to Constantinople in this period, however. We get a better understanding of Eutyches' supporters, their circumstances, and the menace contemporaries saw in them by turning to reports of other monks who lived "around the shrines" in the late fourth and fifth centuries.

In late antiquity an ascetic subculture arose around martyr shrines that was as varied as the shrines themselves, but only half-seen and half-acknowledged. When the Spanish pilgrim Egeria visited Edessa in 384, she records that she saw "many martyr shrines as well as holy monks, some living among the shrines." These she distinguished from others who had monasteries in secluded regions outside of the cities.[90] In fact, monks had been using shrines as temporary shelters or as residences in the cities and countryside of Syria and Mesopotamia since at least the mid-fourth century.[91] Temple precincts and empty tombs had long provided shelter for religious devotees and other homeless misfits in the Roman Empire.[92] The chapels and shrines that Christians built in commemoration of martyrs exerted a particularly strong attraction upon monks, who often identified with the martyrs' voluntary sufferings and religious ardor. The Christian conviction in the continuing presence of the martyr's spirit with his buried physical remains gave these shrines a numinous power.[93] Known for miracles, they became places where a monk might perform special penance surrounded by images of a suffering saint[94] or incubate in close contact with the divine, to emerge hyped-up and supercharged for faith-healings and other charismatic exploits.[95]

90. Egeria, *Itinerarium* 19.4; ed. Maraval, p. 204: in eadem civitate martyria plurima nec non et sanctos monachos, commanentes alios per martyria, alios longius de civitate in secretioribus locis habentes monasteria.

91. E.g., Theodoret, *HR* 2.21 (outside Cyrrhus); *Vita Danielis Stylitae* 10 and 13 (Constantinople); John of Ephesus, *Lives of the Eastern Saints* 7 (outside Amida); *Life of Theodore of Sykeon* 12 (outside Sykeon). Fiey (1970): 111 dates this development in Mesopotamia ca. 360–390; for the attraction of martyr shrines for monks, see Vööbus (1958b): 208–302 and (1960b): 160. For examples of shrines themselves, see Lassus (1947): 158–61.

92. The most vivid example in the Roman East is Philostratus, *Vita Apollinii* 1.8–16; cf. Lucian, *De dea Syria* 43. *LG* 7.15 (PS 3.173) indicates that tombs were places where the insane might live.

93. See Peter Brown, *The Cult of the Saints: Its Rise and Function in Latin Christianity* (Chicago: University of Chicago Press, 1981) and Raymond Van Dam, *Saints and Their Miracles in Late Antique Gaul* (Princeton: Princeton University Press, 1993). Eastern martyr shrines have not received comparable attention.

94. See John of Ephesus, *Lives of the Eastern Saints* 12 and 13 for penance in monastery martyr shrines.

95. For incubation and dreams in *martyria*, see Peter Brown, "Eastern and Western Christendom in Late Antiquity," in *Society and the Holy in Late Antiquity* (Berkeley and Los Angeles:

In North Africa such zealots were called "circumcellions." We know of them primarily through the writings of critics who coined this label and disapproved of their behavior. The most temperate portrayal of their activities comes from the North African grammarian and theologian Tyconius. He considered their religious practices to be "over and beyond established devotional observance."

> These men do not live in the same manner as other brothers do but kill themselves as if in love of martyrdom, so that when they depart from this life they might also be called martyrs. In Greek they are called "Cotopices," but in Latin we call them "Circumcellions," since they live in the country. They roam around the provinces because they do not allow themselves to be in one place with the brothers in single-mindedness or partake in communal life, so that they might live with a single heart and soul according to the apostolic custom. Instead, as I remarked, they go around different places and visit the tombs of the saints as if for the salvation of their own souls.[96]

These circumcellions were said to receive revelations and did not, in fact, call themselves "monks." That was a label they associated with the monasteries promoted by Augustine and other leaders of the imperial church. Instead, they preferred to call themselves *agonistici* (contenders) or *milites Christi* (soldiers of Christ).[97] Some sacrificed themselves in suicidal raids on

---

University of California Press, 1982), 188. John of Ephesus, *Lives of the Eastern Saints* 15, indicates that such practices were suspect: monks incubating in Amida received visions from Satan and needed to submit themselves to their bishop for penance.

96. Tyconius (writing ca. 380) *apud* Beatus of Libana, *In Apocalypsim* 5.53; in Traugott Hahn, *Tyconius Studien. Ein Beitrag zur Kirchen-und Dogmengeschichte des 4. Jahrhunderts* (Leipzig: Dietrich, 1900), 68 n. 1: pseudoprophetae quattuor membra sunt . . . alius est superstitiosus. Superstitio dicta est, eo quod superflua aut super instituta religionis observatio. Et isti non vivunt aequaliter ut ceteri fratres, sed quasi amore martyrum semetipsos perimunt, ut violenter de hac vita discedentes et martyres nominentur. Hi graeco vocabulo Cotopices dicuntur, quos nos latine Circumcelliones dicimus, eo quod agrestes sint. Circumeunt provincias, quia non sinunt se uno in loco cum fratribus uno esse consilio et unam vitam habere communem, ut anima una et corde uno vivant apostolico more, sed ut diximus diversas terras circuire et sanctorum sepulcra pervidere, quasi pro salute animae suae; sed nihil proderit, quia hoc sine consilio communi fratrum faciunt.

Tyconius was a Donatist who was excommunicated by Donatist bishops because he opposed rebaptism. W. H. C. Frend, "Circumcellions and Monks," *JThS* n.s. 20 (1969): 544 n. 4, suggests Beatus may have conflated Tyconius' original description with accounts of circumcellions from Augustine and Isidore, but his reference to circumcellion use of martyr shrines is independent of those accounts, and so likely reflects Tyconius' own observations.

97. Augustine, *Enarratio in Psalmum CXXXII* 6 (PL 37.1732): Agonisticos eos vocant . . . sic eos, inquiunt, appellamus propter agonem. In this passage Augustine notes their rejection of the label *circumcelliones;* for their alleged repudiation of *monachi,* see Augustine, *Enarratio in Psalmum CXXXII* 3 and *Contra Litteras Petiliani* 3.40.48. The name *agonistici* reflects the common ascetic conception of life as an *agon.* For *milites Christi,* see Frend (1985): 174. Contemporary opponents knew circumcellions defined themselves as ascetics: e.g., Possidius, *V.Augustini* 10

pagan festivals. Others in the 340s set out to right social wrongs by freeing slaves, destroying records of debt, and terrorizing rich creditors.[98] They sang the Psalms as they wandered the Numidian countryside with their "Captains of the Saints" and shouted "Praise to God" as they fell upon their targets. Such holy men proved particularly zealous recruits for the Church of the Martyrs during the brutal Donatist schism which rent North African congregations in the fourth and fifth centuries. Their violence and willingness to die for the Donatist cause brought them lasting discredit in the writings of Catholic opponents, especially Augustine.

Only recently have historians seen beyond the polemical uses of the "circumcellion" label.[99] These ascetics were the North African counterparts of equally controversial Messalian monks. The most striking parallels are found in the career of Alexander the Sleepless, who similarly led bands of psalm-singing monks against church and secular authorities, forced the rich to burn records of debt, and shouted "Glory to God" as he took to the road, before settling at St. Menas' shrine in Constantinople.[100] What makes

---

(PL 31.41): sub professione continentium ambulantes. For emphasis on their wandering, Augustine, *Enarratio in Psalmum CXXXII* 3 (37.1730): circumcelliones dicti sunt, qui circum cellas vagantur: solent ire hac, illac, nusquam habentes sedes.

98. Optatus of Milevi, *De schismate Donatistarum* 3.4.3 (written ca. 364–367); ed. J. Labrousse (SC 413), pp. 38–40: per loca singula vagarentur, cum Axido et Fasir ab ipsos insanientibus duces sanctorum appellarentur.... terrabantur omnes. Augustine, *Contra epistulam Parmeniani* 1.10.16; *Enarratio in Psalmum* CXXXII 3, 6; and *Ep.* 108.3.12 and 5.14; ed. Al. Goldbacher, p. 628: in hac patria cum suis cuneis deduxerunt, deo laudes inter cantica conclamantes quas vocas velut tubas praeliorum in suis omnibus latrociniis habuerunt. For other details of the circumcellion profile, see Frend (1985): 171–77, culled from various sources.

99. I am sidestepping nearly a century's debate over "circumcellion" identity: see Gaddis (1999): 88–98. The theory that circumcellions represented a distinct peasant order in revolt against landlords was based on a misreading of *CTh* 16.5.52: see Alfred Schindler, "Kritische Bemerkungen zur Quellenbewertung in der Circumcellionforschung," *SP* 14 (1984): 238–41 and J. E. Atkinson, "Out of Order: The Circumcellions and Codex Theodosianus 16.5.52," *Historia* 41 (1992): 488–99. As with polemical representations of "Messalian" heretics, we must not assume that representations of circumcellions as a single, organized group under specific leaders reflects historical reality. That they should be viewed primarily as wandering monks was first suggested by Reizenstein (1916): 50–52 and strongly affirmed by Salvatore Calderone, "Circumcelliones," *La parola del passato* 113 (1967): 99–101. Though religious explanations for their activities have gained wide acceptance, scholars continue to mince over the terminology applied by their critics: e.g., Rudolf Lorenz, "Circumcelliones-Cotopitae-Cutzupitani," *ZKG* 82 (1971): 54–57.

100. See *V.Alex.* 33, 36, 43. For circumcellion assaults on the rich in the 340s, see Optatus of Milevi, *De schismate Donatistarum* 3.4.4–5. They were also accused of revelations, cohabitation with women, and liberation of slaves, as were Eustathian and Messalian monks. The parallels with Alexander are noted by W. H. C. Frend, *The Rise of the Monophysite Movement: Chapters in the History of the Church in the Fifth and Sixth Centuries* (Cambridge: Cambridge University Press, 1972b), 90, but dismissed on the assumption that circumcellions were more organized. I find no evidence for that. What makes circumcellions different is their emphasis on martyrdom,

these North African monks important for our purposes is the information provided about their connection to martyr shrines, or *cellae*.[101]

Tyconius' religious explanation of the circumcellion phenomenon may be adequate, but salvation was not the only reason such monks hung around the shrines. Augustine observes that they got their name by "wandering around country shrines *(cellas circumiens rusticanas)* for the sake of food," and claims they were otherwise "idle, shirking work."[102] Evidence of such *cellae* has been unearthed in central Algeria, the Numidian hotbed of circumcellion activities. Excavations here of early churches and chapels (from two to seven per village) have yielded not only commemorative inscriptions[103] but also distinctive structural features: storage bins planted in chapel floors and separate, single-room structures built within church compounds. These seem to have been used for receiving offerings of firstfruits, for holding grain to be distributed to the poor, or both.[104] Country martyr shrines were thus equipped to provide material as well as spiritual salvation for circumcellions who either lived in them permanently or wandered by in need of food. Presumably this was how many Numidian holy men subsisted when not foraging or peddling martyr bones, as Augustine elsewhere indicates they did.[105]

---

which can be understood only within the historical context and the ideology of their fourth- and fifth-century "Church of the Martyrs." This point is emphasized by Gaddis (1999): 80–142, with brilliant discussion of the polemical representation of circumcellion *furor* for suicide. Inscriptions commemorating their martyrdoms (which may have been executions) are still visible on Algerian cliff surfaces: see Frend (1985): 175–76.

101. Other scholars have interpreted *cellae* as either "country farm houses" or "monasteries": see Ch. Saumagne, "Ouvriers agricoles ou rôdeurs de celliers: Les circoncellions d'Afrique," *Annales d'histoire économique et sociale* 6 (1934): 363 and Calderone (1967). I consider the evidence for the "martyr shrine" interpretation to be conclusive: see W. H. C. Frend, "The *Cellae* of the African Circumcellions," *JThS* n.s. 3 (1952): 87–89 and (1969). Frend presents epigraphical data that demonstrate that the word *cella* was used to denote "martyr shrine" in Numidian Africa by 361, and therefore before the label *circumcelliones* first appeared in the writings of Optatus of Milevi. Strangely, Tyconius' phrase "diversas terras circuire et sanctorum sepulcra pervidere quasi pro salute animae suae" has generally been ignored as a explanatory gloss for "superstitious circumcellion" *(sepulcra* is used in conjunction with *cellam* in *C.I.L.* 8.9585). Augustine notes that circumcellions gathered around *martyria* to honor the martyrs: *Contra Epistulam Parmeniani* 3.6.29 (PL 43.105–106).

102. Augustine, *Contra Gaudentium* 1.27.32 (written ca. 418); ed. Michael Petschenig, p. 231: ab utilibus operibus otiosum . . . ab agris vacans et victus sui causa cellas circumiens rusticanas.

103. CIL 8.9585 lists an "aream et sepulchra. . . . et cellam"; *cellam* has been interpreted as a reference to a martyr chapel built beside a church and tomb by Henri Leclerq, "Area," *DACL* 1.2.2796 and Frend (1952): 89. An inscription from Mauretania Sitifensis dated 361 refers specifically to a *cella martyrum:* see Frend (1969): 546.

104. This interpretation is especially championed by Frend (1952): 89 and (1969): 547–48; for the structures, see André Berthier et al., *Les vestiges du Christianisme antique dans la Numidie centrale* (Algiers: Maison Carrée, 1942), 167–213.

105. Augustine, *De opere* 23.28 (foraging on estate fields) and 28.36; ed. Zycha, p. 585: alii

There are reports, however, that some Donatist church leaders provided such support for specific purposes. When imperial forces advanced on southern Numidia in 347, Bishop Donatus of Bagai was said to have turned his basilica into a silo so as to furnish sufficient grain for the *circumcelliones agonistici* he had invited for combat and a siege.[106] Similar recruitment and provisioning by clergy must have occurred at many martyr shrines in North Africa during its religious civil war.[107] Church patronage and a shared sense of identity in the Church of the Martyrs combined with ascetic poverty to make circumcellion monks ready recruits, and helped channel their zeal for the Donatist cause.

Analogous circumstances could be found in Constantinople. The Spanish pilgrim Egeria remarks how many martyr shrines (as distinct from other church structures) the city had.[108] These shrines, sometimes called "houses of prayer," became especially known as outlets for charity. John Chrysostom told congregations in Constantinople that they would see "true kingdoms" if they visited the "prayer-houses of the martyrs;" here they would see "the poor and possessed and the destitute, the elderly, blind, and crippled" huddled on the thresholds of the shrines.[109] As another homilist explains, Christians might do God's bidding not just by giving alms at existing shrines but by funding new ones themselves.[110] As conduits for alms, they became places where the poor and destitute tended to cluster. No doubt that is why Alexander settled with his monks near a shrine in the city, and why one of Eutyches' supporters, Eutychius, was said to be in one "since he doesn't have a monastery." Beggars of any kind might turn to an urban martyr shrine for shelter and support: indeed, monks probably moved along a network of such shrines. Under

---

membra martyrum si tamen martyrum venditant. Basil *RF* 40 prohibits monks from plying trades at martyr shrines.

106. Optatus of Milevi, *De schismate Donatistarum* 3.4.2 and 10; ed. Labrousse (SC 413), pp. 38 and 42: circumcelliones agonisticos nuncupans, ad praedictum locum ut concurrerent invitavit . . . annonam competentem constat fuisse praeparatam. De basilica quasi publica fecerant horrea. For the incident, see Gaddis (1999): 104–7 and Frend (1985): 178–79. Donatus and his recruits were massacred.

107. Augustine, *Ep.* 108.5.14 notes circumcellion collaboration with clerics in their acts of brigandage.

108. Egeria, *Itinerarium* 23.9. For shrines attested at Constantinople before 451, see Dagron (1974): 388–401. Eusebius, *Vita Constantini* 3.25–48 says Constantine dedicated several himself.

109. John Chrysostom, *In I Thess XI hom.* 4 (PG 62.446): ἐν τοῖς μαρτυρίοις προκάθηνται τῶν προπυλαίων οἱ πένητες, ὥστε ἡμᾶς ἐκ τῆς τούτων θέας πολλὴν δέχεσθαι τὴν ὠφέλειαν. . . . εἰς δὲ τὰ ὄντως βασίλεια, τὴν ἐκκλησίαν λέγω καὶ τοὺς εὐκτηρίους οἴκους τῶν μαρτύρων, διαμονῶντες ἀνάπηροι πένητες γέροντες τυφλοὶ διεστραμμένοι τὰ μέλη. Cf. *De statuis hom.* 1.9 (PG 49.29). The charitable function of *martyria* in the late Roman West is discussed by Brown (1981): 33–47.

110. Ps.-John Chrysostom, *De eleemosyna* 3 (PG 64.433D–436A).

their porticoes or by their gates, the ordinary poor and the voluntary poor might meld into one.[111]

Moreover, just as martyr shrines were built through private initiative and funding, so too did they remain in private hands until 451, when they officially came under episcopal control.[112] In 386 Emperor Theodosius I had tried to regulate their proliferation by requiring that they be built only where martyrs' bodies were found, but otherwise he allowed his citizens to construct "whatever building they wished . . . in any place whatever." Such *martyria* were concentrated on the outskirts of the city; some were hidden, subterranean structures.[113] Logically their owners would install monks to serve as custodians or perform liturgies, as the Macedonian deaconess Eusebia did in her shrine of the Forty Martyrs outside the walls, and as the prefect Rufinus did in his outside Chalcedon. These, we may assume, went by the titles *memorophylakes* and *memoritēs* used in the Chalcedonian *acta*. Their duties would have included receiving alms and distributing them to the poor.[114] Whether living with the poor or simply controlling access to charity, such custodians were in an opportune position both to establish themselves as archimandrites over needy monks who hung around the shrines (e.g., the five "names" associated with a *memoritēs* in the shrine of Philip), and exert influence on other members of the city's volatile fringe population.

Not surprisingly, church leaders viewed martyr shrines with ambivalence and suspicion. A kind of transient Christian *demi-monde* took root around them: a shrine by the racetracks (e.g., at the Wooden Circus where some of Eutyches' supporters lived) was just the right place to find an archimandrite who was formerly a bearkeeper.[115] And because they were usually lo-

111. As Barṣawma and his monks mixed with beggars under a temple portico by the Dead Sea: *Vita Barsaumae*, Nau (1913): 385. Cf. *Life of Theodore of Sykeon* 9–15, 36.

112. For the proliferation and private operation of such shrines in Constantinople, see John Philip Thomas, *Private Religious Foundations in the Byzantine Empire* (Washington, D.C.: Dumbarton Oaks, 1987), 14–37. As Brown (1981): 9–10 observes, in the Roman East the typical martyr shrine "tended to go its own way."

113. *CTh* 9.17.7 (issued at Constantinople, February 386); trans. Pharr, p. 240. Although the law seems to have been widely ignored, an example of compliance may be Eusebia's shrine (*euktērion*) for the Forty Martyrs of Sebaste, built in the 380s outside the Constantinian walls. It was so hidden that, when the property was sold, its new owner, Caesarius (consul 397), built a new shrine over it (for the martyr Thyrsus) without knowing: Sozomen, *HE* 9.2.1–10. Shrines built outside the Constantinian walls in Theodosius' time would have been inside the city once the Anthemian wall was finished in 413.

114. Escolan (1999): 196 cites legislation by John of Tella addressing the problem of martyr-shrine attendants who pocket offerings rather than using them for the upkeep of the shrine and the sick.

115. See Gregory of Nazianzus, *Anthologia Palatina* 8.166–74 with Gregory (1979): 169. Ps.-Athanasian canon 92 prohibits monks and virgins from going to *martyria* at festival times;

cated some distance from the episcopal headquarters at the center of town, they provided meeting places for groups who were excluded from the dominant church community.[116] It was to a shrine in the outlying Psamathian district that Dalmatius was carried to proclaim the imminent demise of Nestorius (whose clergy still held the churches at the center of town), and Nestorius noted how "holy houses of prayer" were stocked with grain to supply seditious enthusiasts—just as Donatist shrines were stocked during the North African schism. No doubt some of those monks with "strange manners" whom Nestorius expelled had already ended up at those shrines, fomenting sedition with visions of saints.

By 448, Constantinople had plenty of martyr shrines, plenty of needy monks, and a church and monastic schism on the rise. The circumcellion examples from North Africa bring us back to Eutyches' martyr-shrine monks with a greater appreciation of why Bishop Flavian sent a martyr-shrine priest down to the Hebdomon suburb to see if a monastic "sedition" was stirring in that year. As chief "Archimandrite of the Monasteries of Constantinople," Eutyches would have ultimately been responsible for provisioning the monks in shrines on the outskirts of town, where his own monastery was located. Indeed, Eutyches' influence at the outlying martyr shrines may explain why Flavian had notices read out "in different prayer-houses and at the tombs of holy ones" proclaiming Eutyches' excommunication,[117] and later tried to interfere with the way Eutyches' monastery disposed of its property "in the name of the destitute."[118] Despite such efforts, Eutyches' martyr-shrine monks remained zealous supporters to the end. As Nestorius attests, Eutyches was able to become "bishop of bishops" not only through imperial forces he received but through the patronage he provided: "Those who were aiding him he raised up and gave support."

TOWARD A NEW ERA IN CHURCH AND MONASTIC RELATIONS

Fully rehabilitated at the Robber Council in 449, Eutyches returned to Constantinople in triumph, but his fortune did not last for long. The next

---

Evagrius Scholasticus, *HE* 1.14, offers a lively vignette of celebrations at the shrine of Symeon Stylites.

116. Chrysostom's Johnites met at the Xylokerkos after their expulsion from the city: Sozomen *HE* 8.21. During the sixth-century persecution at Amida, a martyr shrine built in a rented room sheltered as many as 15 to 20 people (probably monks) at night: John of Ephesus, *Lives of the Eastern Saints* 12 (PS 17.177). For other examples, see Harry O. Maier, "The Topography of Heresy and Dissent in Late-Fourth-Century Rome," *Historia* 44 (1995): 245–49.

117. *ACO* 2.1.1 [185]; ed. Schwartz, p. 95,35–37: ἐν διαφόροις εὐκτηρίοις οἴκοις ἔν <τε> ταῖς τῶν ἁγίων μνήμαις.

118. *ACO* 2.1.1 [887]; ed. Schwartz, p. 187,1: τὰ τοῦ μοναστηρίου φυλάττειν αὐτῷ τῷ τῶν πτωχῶν ὀνόματι (τοῦτο γὰρ ἐπραγματεύετο). On Eutyches' influence with the poor, see Gregory (1979): 142.

year his godson and most influential patron at the imperial court, Chrysaphius, was driven into exile, and Emperor Theodosius died after falling off a horse. Out of this sudden collapse of leadership the deceased emperor's sister Pulcheria emerged to take control, together with Marcian, an officer and senator she made her husband and emperor. These changes created opportunities for Eutyches' opponents. Pope Leo (whose envoys had been silenced in 449) was intensively courting Pulcheria to arrange another ecumenical council to reverse the decisions made at Ephesus.[119] By the summer of 451 Flavian's bones had been brought back to Constantinople and Eutyches was banished, at Leo's request, "so that he might not enjoy or make use of the support repeatedly being offered by those whom he has drawn into his impiety."[120] In the fall of 451, 520 bishops met under close imperial guard at Chalcedon. Their overriding concern was to overturn Ephesus II and restore order by establishing a clearly defined ecclesiastical hierarchy and faith.[121]

No repudiation of Constantinople's monastic past could have been better orchestrated than the one that transpired at the Council of Chalcedon's fourth session.[122] Seated in honor among episcopal ranks were the monks who had sided with Flavian against Eutyches in 448 and 449. Their leader, Faustus, was given the privilege of reading the petition of Eutyches' monastic supporters. After reading off the names of the martyr-shrine archimandrites, Faustus addressed the council with a petition of his own:

> We request that some men be sent . . . to go out and see their monasteries to learn if they have monasteries, or if they are mocking and abusing the prerogatives of archimandrites and should therefore be punished, so that those who dwell in martyr shrines might not claim to be archimandrites. We also request that those who call themselves monks but are neither recognized by your clemency nor by the most holy archbishop nor by ourselves might be expelled from the city as impostors, because of the scandal they have tried to make.[123]

119. For a general narration of events of 449–451, see Gregory (1979): 163–67; Sellers (1953): 88–103; and Hefele-Leclerq 2.630–67. For Pulcheria's role and connections to Leo, see Holum (1982): 203–5 and Goubert (1951): 315–21; also Leo, *Ep.* 30 and 45. It was Leo (*Ep.* 95) who coined the name *Latrocinium* for Ephesus II.

120. Leo, *Ep.* 84; *ACO* 2.4; ed. Schwartz, p. 44,11–14: ne frequentioribus solatiis eorum, quos ad impietatem suam traxit, utatur. Theodore Lector, *HE* frg. 356 says Eutyches was exiled to Doliche (modern Dülük) in northwestern Syria. This put him dead center in the Antiochene sphere of influence and supervision.

121. See Gaddis (1999): 331–33 for this portrayal of the council.

122. For the fourth session, see esp. Bacht (1953): 236–40.

123. *ACO* 2.1.2 [64]; ed. Schwartz, p. 115,5–12: πεισθῆναι εἰ ἔχουσιν μοναστήρια ἢ χλευάζουσι καὶ βλάπτουσι τὰς ὑπολήψεις τῶν ἀρχιμανδριτῶν καὶ ἀπὸ τούτων ὀφείλουσιν ἐπιτιμασθῆναι, ὥστε μὴ ἑαυτοὺς ἀρχιμανδρίτας λέγειν τοὺς ἐν μεμορίοις οἰκοῦντας. παρακαλοῦμεν δὲ τοὺς λέγοντας

Only the intervention of imperial mediators at the council enabled Eutyches' supporters to speak. Their request that they not be forced to declare doctrinal allegiances in the absence of Dioscorus (who had been deposed in the previous session) was met with episcopal indignation: "Throw them out! Remove the insult from the council!"—to which Faustus and his monks added their chant, "Remove insult from the monasteries!" Constantinople's archdeacon then read out a canon from an earlier council that excommunicated any member of the clergy who defied his bishop. This canon, they were informed, now applied to monks as well.[124] Then they heard the petition Faustus had sent Emperor Marcian sometime before the council had begun:

> Your Christ-loving power has exiled Eutyches . . . but his disciples . . . have kept fighting in stiff-necked opposition against the correct confession of the fathers, despite the frequent exhortations being offered to them by their God-loving archbishop Anatolius. . . . For this reason we think it right that your power . . . allow us to subject to the spiritual orders of monks those who disgracefully rebel against our correct faith. . . . As for the cave where they dwell like savage beasts and blaspheme Christ daily . . . may your Christ-loving majesty entrust us to give it a rule.[125]

As a threat, the reading of this petition had little effect: Eutyches' monks remained defiant. It effectively signaled, however, that a new monastic leadership had emerged in Constantinople and was already collaborating with the new bishop, Anatolius, and new emperor, Marcian, to discipline the city's monastic population.

At its forefront were the monks whom Nestorius had characterized as "those enclosed in their monasteries," and who had been driven into hiding at Ephesus in 449. Now it was their turn. Their ascendancy in 451 was confirmed at Chalcedon's sixth session when the emperor himself presented several recommendations for restoring monastic order. The first made clear which monks the new emperor had listened to and favored:

> Those who truly and sincerely adopt the solitary life we deem worthy of the honor they deserve. But since some have used the monastic cover to throw church and public affairs into confusion, let no one construct a monastery against the will of the city's bishop or dwell on property against the will of

---

ἑαυτοὺς μονάζοντας καὶ μὴ γνωριζομένους. . . . ἐξελθεῖν ἀπὸ τῆς πόλεως ὡς ἐπιθέτας διὰ τὸ σκάνδαλον ὃ ἐπεχείρησαν ποιῆσαι.

124. *ACO* 2.1.2 [83–90]; ed. Schwartz, pp. 117–18. The fifth canon of the Council of Antioch (344) was now being applied to "monks and all who live as Christians." At this time the assembled bishops also decried Barṣawma.

125. *ACO* 2.1.2 [105]; ed. Schwartz, pp. 119,32–120,7: ἀξιοῦμεν. . . . ἐπιτραπῆναι δὲ ἡμῖν τοῖς πνευματικοῖς τῶν μοναχῶν ὅροις ὑποβαλεῖν τοὺς οὕτως ἀναισχύντως τῆς ὀρθῆς ἡμῶν ἀποστατήσαντας πίστεως. . . . περὶ τοῦ σπηλαίου. . . . τύπον δοθῆναι παρ' ἡμῶν.

that property's owner. Let those who pursue a monastic life in each city and village be subordinate to their bishop, embrace tranquility, and attend to fasting and prayer alone, and not trouble church and civic affairs, unless they be permitted at some time by the bishops of the city through pressing need.[126]

Thus Marcian sided with Faustus and his fellows over martyr-shrine monks and effectively gave the bishops his imperial sanction to subject all monks to church canons and episcopal control. His recommendations, in fact, served as the basis for the council's fourth canon.[127] Those whom the emperor described as having "used the monastic cover" to cause disturbances were now more specifically identified as "those who move indiscriminately around the cities." Prohibitions were also added against constructing any "house of prayer" (euktērion) or leaving monasteries without episcopal consent. Marcian's point that monks should be occupied only in prayer and fasting was underscored by the notice that monks must "persevere in those places to which they have withdrawn." Those who violated the canon were subject to excommunication. The revisions, however, concluded with a stipulation addressed to bishops themselves: "But [mentoi] the bishop of the city must make the necessary provision [deousan pronoian] for the monasteries."

Commentators have observed that this canon made stabilitas loci the official touchstone of orthodox monastic practice.[128] What was particularly novel, however, was its final clause. It asserted that the material welfare of urban monasteries would now be an episcopal responsibility, not that of an archimandrite or outside patrons. Thus the ideal of economic self-sufficiency, promoted to prevent monks from becoming subservient to patrons, was eclipsed at Chalcedon by the more pressing need to keep monks in their place. Indeed, the bishops at Chalcedon seemed to have approved such dependency as long as monks were dependent on episcopal providers: another canon prohibited monks (and members of the clergy) from man-

126. *ACO* 2.1.2 [17]; ed. Schwartz, p. 157,1–10: τοὺς ἀληθινῶς καὶ εἰλικρινῶς τὸν μονήρη μετιόντες βίον τῆς ὀφειλομένης ἀξιοῦμεν τιμῆς. Ἐπειδὴ δέ τινες τῷ μοναχικῷ κεχρημένοι προσχήματι, καὶ τάς τε ἐκκλησίας καὶ τὰ κοινὰ διαταράττουσι πράγματα, ἔδοξε μηδένα οἰκοδομεῖν μοναστήριον παρὰ γνώμην τοῦ τῆς πόλεως ἐπισκόπου μήτε δὲ ἐν κτήματι παρὰ γνώμην τοῦ δεσπότου τοῦ κτήματος. Τοὺς δὲ καθ' ἑκάστην πόλιν καὶ χώραν μονάζοντας ὑποτετάχθαι τῷ ἐπισκόπῳ, καὶ τὴν ἡσυχίαν ἀσπάζεσθαι, καὶ προσέχειν μόνῃ τῇ νηστείᾳ καὶ τῇ προσευχῇ, εἰ μή ποτε ἄρα ἐπιτραπεῖεν διὰ χρείαν ἀναγκαίαν ὑπὸ τοῦ τῆς πόλεως ἐπισκόπου.

127. For the fourth canon text, see above, n. 1. For the relation between it and Marcian's recommendations, see Ueding (1953): 604–16 and Hefele-Leclerq 2.767–828. Marcian had told the council that he preferred his recommendations to be issued as church canons rather than imperial law.

128. Dagron (1970): 272–74; Emilio Herman, "La 'stabilitas loci' nel monachismo bizantino," *OCP* 21 (1955): 125–42; and Ueding (1953): 607.

aging secular property or "occupying themselves with worldly finances."[129] From now on their job would be "fasting and prayer alone, persevering in those places to which they have withdrawn."[130]

The council took other measures to prevent archimandrites like Isaac, Dalmatius, or Eutyches from throwing church and secular affairs back into confusion. Of course, subversive gatherings of monks or clerics were expressly forbidden,[131] but the council also required beggars to register with their city's bishop,[132] and warned officials in poorhouses, monasteries, and martyr shrines not to "arrogantly rebel" against him.[133] In this way the bishops at Chalcedon rounded off their urban domain. By placing the various charitable institutions of the cities under their control, they made them satellites of their own authority and influence.

What makes the efforts of the council particularly interesting is the role that Eutyches' monastic opponents played along the way. Already in 449 Pope Leo had made contact with Faustus, Martinus, and other archimandrites at Constantinople who had signed Eutyches' condemnation in 448. These monks had received special treatment from Flavian (only bishops were supposed to sign such documents, as Eutyches noted), and had proven their loyalty to him during the Robber Council.[134] Afterwards, Leo courted them as trustworthy agents in the imperial capital. Early in 450 he requested their active support so that Eutyches "might no longer have power to deceive the simple-minded." He desired that they cure Eutyches' followers "with a higher medicine, by the remedy of correction."[135] Once Eutyches

129. Council of Chalcedon, canon 3 with commentary, Hefele-Leclerq, 2.775–776. Canon 24 prevents monasteries and monastery property from ever reverting to secular use, which may also have been intended to bolster monastic security.

130. In 539 Justinian's *Novella* 133.6; ed. Rudolf Schoell and Wilhelm Kroll, p. 675, considers ἐργόχερια along with scriptural study to be the "twofold work" appropriate to a monk, but, as in Nilus' writings, it considers manual labor a contemplative exercise (that keeps monks out of trouble) rather than an economic activity: διάνοια γὰρ μάτην σχολάζουσα οὐδὲν ἂν τῶν ἀγαθῶν ἀποτέκοι.

131. Council of Chalcedon, canon 18.

132. Council of Chalcedon, canon 11; cf. Dagron (1974): 516 and Brown (1992): 98. The canon says nothing about monks, but by its provisions ascetic vagrants would have also become subject to episcopal certification and control.

133. Council of Chalcedon, canon 8; cf. canons 6 and 10.

134. Leo probably first learned their names from the synod *endēmousa* transcript he had received from Flavian: *Ep.* 72 addresses them in the same order in which they had signed their names in 448. For their early contact with Leo and Pulcheria, see Bacht (1953): 226–27 and Holum (1982): 203. For the irregularity of their signing of Eutyches' condemnation, see Eutyches' letter to Leo (Leo, *Ep.* 21) with Gaddis (1999): 305–6.

135. Leo, *Ep.* 71 in ACO 2.4; ed. Schwartz, p. 31,14–16. On the letter, see Bacht (1953): 234.

had been removed, Leo's archimandrites could act with impunity, and they apparently did.[136]

We may presume that the archimandrites Leo courted shared his doctrinal objections to Eutyches' radical Alexandrian teachings. Nonetheless, they had other reasons for opposing Eutyches and his monks. During the fourth Chalcedonian session these archimandrites, represented by Faustus, not only accused those among Eutyches' supporters who lived at martyr shrines of "abusing the prerogatives [hypolēpseis] of archimandrites," but also denounced them as imposters, proposing their exile so that they could not claim to be archimandrites. Their indignation in this respect is reminiscent of Nilus' scornful attitude towards former tavern boys who presented themselves as monastic leaders and ascetic teachers. Indeed, it has been suggested that their opposition to Eutyches' monks reflects social divisions in Constantinople's monastic community that had been developing for decades, pitting monks whose origins aligned them with the city's bishop against "a kind of monastic proletariat" drawn from less privileged ranks.[137]

The rivalry in the monastic community, however, was about more than social backgrounds. The fact that Faustus led the opposition to Eutyches suggests that it was driven by political rivalry, for this was none other than Dalmatius' son Faustus, who had entered Isaac's Psamathian monastery with his father around 384.[138] Although entrusted with leadership of that prestigious monastery when Dalmatius died in the early 440s, Faustus did not inherit his father's title, "Archimandrite of the Monasteries." That honor seems to have passed first to the old archimandrite Hypatius—Alexander's defender—who held it until his death in 446.[139] It then passed to Eutyches only two years before Flavian sought monastic allies to oppose Eutyches at the synod of 448. Why Eutyches was recognized as the city's leading archimandrite over Faustus is not known. Both had spent nearly equal time in the monastic profession, with Eutyches having some two or three years' more experience. Perhaps the decisive factor was Eutyches'

136. Eutyches' monks appealed to the emperor that "no one be cast from a monastery, church, or martyr shrine" before the council had come to a decision: ACO 2.1.2 [76]; ed. Schwartz, p. 116,12–18. This was one of two petitions they sent to Marcian to have read at Chalcedon: see Gregory (1979): 167–68.

137. Thus Bacht (1953): 240, based on his prosopographical study at 217–20.

138. Thus Gregory (1979): 134–35; Dagron (1970): 240; and Janin (1953): 86. Bacht (1953): 218 is too skeptical.

139. Callinicus, V.Hypatii 23.3; ed. Bartelink, p. 146: μετὰ γὰρ τὴν κοίμησιν τοῦ ἁγίου Δαλματίου αὐτὸν [i.e., Hypatius] λοιπὸν εἶχον πάντες ὡς πατέρα. Bacht and Dagron both assume the leadership passed directly to Eutyches, but there is no reason to doubt what Callinicus implies here. Dalmatius died while Proclus was bishop (434–446) and a few years before Hypatius' death in 446: see Callinicus, V.Hypatii 23.3 and Dagron (1970): 233.

special connection to Chrysaphius, whose influence as a patron could not be matched in the late 440s. Faustus' readiness to support Bishop Flavian against Eutyches from 448 onward may have stemmed, therefore, from his sense that he had not received appropriate honors. Certainly he vented resentment during the Council of Chalcedon: his reference to "that cave" where Eutyches' followers dwelt "like savages, blaspheming Christ daily" undoubtedly meant Eutyches' grand monastery in the Hebdomon.

The ecumenical policy towards supporting monks initiated at the Council of Chalcedon did not burden the Roman Empire with so many "idle mouths" to feed as to push it into economic decline.[140] Chalcedon did, however, initiate further doctrinal schism, pitching partisans against each other to such a degree that novice monks were sometimes recruited according to physical strength and furnished with clubs.[141] Nevertheless, the measures taken at Chalcedon seem to have inaugurated a new era of unity in church and monastic relations in the imperial city itself. Never again did an Isaac, Dalmatius, or Eutyches lead his monks against a bishop of Constantinople.[142] This, we may conclude, stemmed partly from the fact that the monks' economic interests were now intertwined with those of their new episcopal patrons. This common concern provided no small basis for common cause. Some twenty-five years after the Council of Chalcedon, when the imperial usurper Basiliscus tried to lay hands on the wealth of the Constantinopolitan church, its bishop, Acacius, threatened with exile, had only to call on his monks to protect their common welfare. As a contemporary reports, Basiliscus was immediately "beaten back by a multitude of the so-called monks."[143]

140. We do not know what percentage of the Roman Empire's population was monastic, but it must have been small overall. On these questions, see Jones (1964): 930–31, 1046–47, and 1063.

141. See Arthur Vööbus, *History of Asceticism in the Syrian Orient* 3 (1988), 203–6 and Escolan (1999): 347–99.

142. After 451 the title Archimandrite of the Monasteries of Constantinople disappears from record and is replaced by *eparchos*, which denotes the monastic representative of the bishop responsible for enforcing canonical rules in the monasteries: see Dagron (1970): 269 and Escolan (1999): 340.

143. Malchus, *Byzantine History* frg. 9; ed. Blockley, p. 416: Βασιλίσκος . . . τῶν ἐκκλησιῶν τοὺς ἐπισκόπους εἰσέπραττε χρήματα καὶ Ἀκάκιον τὸν Κωνσταντινουπόλεως ἐπίσκοπον μικροῦ δεῖν ἀπώσατο, εἰ μὴ τῷ πλήθει τῶν λεγομένων μοναχῶν ἀπεκρούσθη. For this incident, see *Vita Danielis Stylitae* 70–85 and Dagron (1974): 508. Acacius was remembered for indebting members of the church to him through patronage: see *Suda* A783, s.v. Ἀκάκιος. Cf. Cyril of Scythopolis, *Vita Sabae* 31, for the funding of an urban monastery by the new bishop, Elias, to collect, house, and feed the monks scattered around Jerusalem in 494.

Epilogue

As Muslim armies bore down upon Roman Syria and Egypt in the early seventh century, a monk named John (ca. 580–649) was living in the Theotokos monastery (now St. Catherine's) below Mount Sinai. Safe within its walls, John culled the sayings and writings attributed to the desert fathers, Evagrius Ponticus, Nilus of Ancyra, and other luminaries of the philosophic monastic tradition to compose his famous *Ladder of Divine Ascent*. This spiritual guidebook would soon gain the same normative stature as a repository of ascetic wisdom among monks of the East as Benedict's *Rule* did among monks of the West.[1]

Comparison of the two books yields a notable difference. John, unlike Benedict, places little emphasis on manual labor: in his pages there is definitely more on *ora* than on *labora*.[2] Both, however, took a dim view of ascetic wandering. In keeping with the philosophic monastic tradition, John treats the impulse to wander as a failure to resist temptation. In his view, the "pleasure-loving demon of wandering" was the first that awaited novice monks. It perverted their *xeniteia* by making them maintain bonds with the world and wander back and forth "on account of their passions" rather than "alienating themselves for the sake of the Lord."[3] Another temptation awaited those who resisted the first. Having acquired a certain

---

1. See Chitty (1966): 168–71 and John Chryssavgis, "The Sources of St. John Climacus, ca. 580–649," *Ostkirchliche Studien* 37 (1988): 3–13.

2. The contrast diminishes when it is recognized that Benedict promoted manual labor as a contemplative aid rather than as a means of economic production. See Rotraut Wisskirchen, "Das monastische Verbot der Feldarbeit und ihre rechtliche Gestaltung bei Benedikt von Nursia," *JbAC* 38 (1995): 91–96.

3. John Climacus, *Scala paradisi* 3 (PG 88.664D): ὁ ξενιτεύσας διὰ τὸν Κύριον, οὐκ ἔτι σχέσεις ἔσχησεν, ἵνα μὴ φανῇ διὰ πάθη πλαζόμενος.

degree of ascetic mastery and self-control, "then vain thoughts come over us," John explains, "telling us to travel back to our homelands for the edification of many, as an example and benefit for those who know the former lawlessness of our deeds. Moreover, if we possess the gift of eloquence and a little knowledge, these thoughts suggest to us that we might also become saviors of souls and teachers in this world."[4]

As John observes, the impulse of monks to return to the world they had abandoned with the intention of "saving others, having been saved themselves," remained constant.[5] Alexander the Sleepless and his kind are merely outstanding examples of an apostolic form of Christian monasticism that would later become identified with Patrick of Ireland, Francis of Assisi, or, more often, monks and priests identified as heretics in the Middle Ages.[6] Often accompanied by a fundamentalist emphasis on apostolic poverty, this impulse to teach proved a perennial challenge for the definition of orthodox monasticism and its relation to the Gospels, the world, and the church.

What makes Alexander and the other wandering monks so historically important is their appearance when orthodox monasticism and church institutions were still evolving and only beginning to take root. This evolutionary process was not confined to the Roman Empire. The fourth Chalcedonian canon found its complement in legislation passed by bishops at the Persian capital of Seleucia-Ctesiphon in 486:

> Concerning these impostors who put on black cloaks to give themselves a false, seductive appearance and to deceive the simple-minded with a guise of holiness, asceticism *[nzirutā]*, abstinence, and voluntary poverty *[msam'lutā]*—which the ancient ones practiced in deserted and uncultivated regions, who served God and pleased God by fixing their dwellings far from human society and cities and villages—we decree: If they truly be sons and disciples of those Blessed Ones and conform to their way of life, let them also live in places appropriate to that way of life; but it is not permitted to them to enter and inhabit cities and villages where bishops, priests, and deacons are found, lest they become an occasion for strife, rousing dispute between the clergy and their flock, between teachers and their disciples.

This legislation recalls the Council at Chalcedon's distinction between legitimate and illegitimate monks, as well as Augustine's account of the dis-

---

4. John Climacus, *Scala paradisi* 3 (PG 88.665AB): οἱ λογισμοὶ τῆς ματαιότητος ἐπιστάντες πορεύεσθαι ἡμῖν πάλιν ἐπὶ τὴν οἰκείαν πατρίδα ἐπιτρέπουσιν εἰς οἰκοδομὴν πολλῶν. . . . Εἰ δὲ καὶ λόγου καὶ φίλης γνώσεως εὐποροῦντες τυγχάνομεν, ὡς σωτῆρας ψυχῶν, καὶ διδασκάλους ἡμᾶς ἐν αὐτῷ κόσμῳ ὑποβάλλουσιν.

5. *Ibid.*: σκοπῷ τοῦ μετὰ σωθῆναι σῶσαι τινας.

6. See Phyllis Jestice, *Wayward Monks and the Religious Revolution of the Eleventh Century* (Leiden: Brill, 1997); Malcolm Lambert, *Medieval Heresy: Popular Movements from the Gregorian Reform to the Reformation*, 2d ed. (Oxford: Basil Blackwell, 1992), 9–87; and Giles Constable, "Monachisme et pèlerinage au Moyen Âge," *Revue historique* 258 (1977): 3–27.

turbances that arose in Carthaginian communities when apostolic "long-hairs" appeared in town. With this legislation, monks in the Persian Empire, as in the Roman, were ordered to remain "obedient to the bishops, priests, and *periodeutae* who control the places and monasteries where they dwell." Any caught entering cities to erect monasteries were liable to excommunication.[7]

The apostolic impulse we have been studying could not be legislated out of existence, however. Monks determined to "make a show of sanctity with their long hair and staffs" or carry sacks of martyrs' bones continued to attract attention around the Byzantine East, despite attempts to confine them to monasteries.[8] It has often been recognized that wandering in emulation of Christ and his apostles remained fairly common in the Byzantine world and later in Russia.[9] We must note, however, that such wanderers were accommodated in orthodox tradition primarily by being relegated to the ranks of the *saloi* (Fools for Christ). These figures began to appear in hagiographic literature in the early fifth century.[10] With their sanctity concealed either by self-effacing humility or vulgar behavior, such ascetics could either be praised or ignored; they posed no serious challenge to episcopal authority or institutional stability. An early example is found in the Syriac *Legend of the Man of God*. Probably written in the late fifth or early sixth century, it tells how a Roman aristocrat abandoned all his family's wealth and prestige to become, like Christ, a beggar living among the destitute in a martyr's shrine at Edessa.[11] This was a fitting hero for a city that, two centuries earlier, had produced the legend of Christ's apostolic dop-

7. Synod of Mâr Acacius in Bet Armāyē, canon 2; ed. with Latin trans. Michael Kmosko (PS 3.cclxxiv–cclxxix). For the canon and context, see Arthur Vööbus, "Les messaliens et les réformes de Barsauma de Nisibe dans l'Église perse," *Contributions of the Baltic University* 34 (1947): 1–27 and Escolan (1999): 298–300.

8. See Rabbula, *Rules for Monks* 5–6, ed. and trans. Vööbus, p. 28. Quotation from Isaac of Antioch, describing monks in Bet Hur ca. 457–466, in Segal (1970): 169. Andrew Palmer, "*Semper Vagus:* The Anatomy of a Mobile Monk," *SP* 18 (1989): 255–60, describes a late-seventh-century monk who carried martyrs' bones around Syria and Egypt; Leslie S. B. MacCoull, "A Coptic Marriage-Contract," in *Actes du XVe congrès international de papyrologie*, ed. J. Bingen and G. Nachtergael, vol. 2 (Brussells: Fondation égyptologique Reine Élizabeth, 1979), 116–23, presents a document requiring an Egyptian cleric to swear he would neither consort with wandering monks nor offer them use of his church.

9. See Elisabeth Malamut, *Sur la route des saints byzantines* (Paris: CNRS, 1993); Donald Nicol, "*Instabilitas Loci:* The Wanderlust of Late Byzantine Monks," in *Monks, Hermits, and the Ascetic Tradition*, ed. W. J. Sheils (London: Basil Blackwell, 1985), 193–202.

10. For the evolution of this figure, see Krueger (1996): 57–71. Early examples occur in Palladius, *HL* 34 and 37 (the Egyptian monk Sarapion Sindonites) and Nilus, *Ep* 1.292. The *boskoi* were also identified as *saloi:* see Evagrius Scholasticus, *HE* 1.21 and apophthegm N 62. Living like a deranged vagrant was advised for the Perfect in *LG* 16.7.

11. *Legend of the Man of God of Edessa;* ed. and trans. Arthur Amiaud, *La légende syriaque de Saint Alexis, l'homme de Dieu* (Paris: Vieweg, 1889).

pelgänger, Thomas. This new Man of God, however, neither preaches, nor exercises *parrhēsia*, nor even has a name: his *imitatio Christi* achieves sublimity by remaining utterly anonymous.[12]

Through Greek and Latin translations the Man of God passed into popular medieval legend.[13] By contrast, we would know almost nothing about Alexander the Sleepless if not for the survival of a single manuscript preserving his biography. That does not mean, however, that the enthusiasm of monks like Alexander left no mark in either Christian hagiography or ascetic tradition. In the early 440s Bishop Theodoret of Cyrrhus (modern Nebi Ouri) wrote his *Religious History,* a work famous for its gallery of ascetic life found east of Antioch: monks who hid in cramped enclosures, roamed the hills under a mass of hair and chains, or stood on columns of increasing height, as in the case of Symeon Stylites (387–459), whom Theodoret recognized as the first "pillar saint."

Most remarkable is that Theodoret recognized such flamboyant practices as commendable at all. Few authorities before him would have.[14] His validation of such behavior must be understood as an accommodation, perhaps possible only in a Christian milieu where demonstrative asceticism had been considered a "beautiful pattern for believers" since the third century at least. Of course, his *Religious History* is selective. It makes no reference to urban wanderers, and does not mention either Alexander or Barṣawma, although Theodoret was writing in the area and period in which they made themselves known.[15] Against their example it makes sense that Theodoret preferred to promote Symeon Stylites as his consummate holy man. Perched high in Antioch's hinterland, Symeon on his column combined spectacular ascetic display with utter dependence on the goodwill of admirers below. In contrast to enthusiasts like Alexander who agitated in the streets, Symeon must have seemed a perfect symbol of Christian stabil-

12. See Harvey (1994): 59–66; *id.* (1990): 18–21; H. J. W. Drijvers, "Die Legende des Heiligen Alexius und der Typus des Gottesmannes im syrischen Christentum," in *Typus, Symbol, Allegorie bei den östlichen Vätern und ihren Parallelen im Mittelalter,* ed. M. Schmidt and C. F. Geyer (Regensburg: Pustet, 1982b), 87–217; and *id.,* "Hellenistic and Oriental Origins," in *The Byzantine Saint,* ed. S. Hackel (London: Fellowship of St. Alban, 1981a), 26–28.

13. Over time he received the name Alexius. For Greek and Latin versions of the text, see Amiaud (1889): xxviii–lxxix.

14. E.g., Nilus, *Ep.* 2.114–15 (PG 79.249) berates an unknown stylite for κενοδοξία and demands that he come back down to earth; *Historia Monachorum in Aegypto* 8.59; ed. Festugière, p. 70, where the Egyptian monk Apollo finds fault with "those who wear irons and grow hair long" so as to win "approval from men" (ἀνθρωπαρέσκεια, the word Nilus uses to describe ambitious urban monks, *De monachorum praestantia* 26 [PG 79.1092B]); also Jerome, *Ep.* 22.28; Augustine, *De opere* 31.39; Epiphanius, *Panarion* 80.7; and Basil, *Ep.* 169.

15. Theodoret's selectivity is discussed by Escolan (1999): 342; Pierre Canivet, *Le monachisme syrien selon Théodoret de Cyr* (1977), 75–76, 225; and *id.,* "Théodoret et le messalianisme," *Revue Mabillon* 54 (1961): 26–34.

ity, towering above Theodoret's other "living images and statues" of divine philosophy.[16]

By the late sixth century, Eastern bishops could entertain guests with tales of *boskoi* seeking solace at the base of a rural stylite's pillar.[17] Theodoret's *Religious History* had brought a more harmonious generation of heroic enthusiasts to the fore. Although their way had been cleared by wandering ascetics of the third to the early fifth centuries, their future was fixed on pillars of monks like Symeon, who, while still alive, became recognized throughout the empire as an icon of human sanctity on earth.[18]

16. Theodoret of Cyrrhus, *Historia religiosa* prol. 2; ed. Pierre Canivet and Alice Leroy-Molinghen, p. 128: οἷον τινας εἰκόνας αὐτῶν ἐμψύχους καὶ στήλας σφᾶς αὐτοὺς πεποιήκασι. For stylitism as a solution to tensions between ascetic enthusiasm and episcopal power, see Susan Ashbrook Harvey, "The Stylite's Liturgy: Ritual and Religious Identity in Late Antiquity," *JECS* 6 (1998): 523–39 and Robin Lane Fox, "The *Life of Daniel*," in *Portraits: Biographical Representation in the Greek and Latin Literature of the Roman Empire*, ed. M. J. Edwards and S. Swain (Oxford: Clarendon Press, 1997), 208–10 and 223.

17. John Moschos, *Pratum spirituale* 129.

18. For icons of him hung in Rome, see Theodoret of Cyrrhus, *HR* 26.11; cf. *V.Danielis* 59, 99.

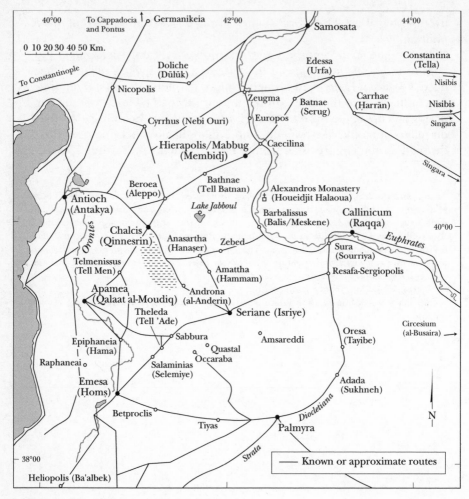

Roman Syria in the Early Fifth Century

The *Life* of Alexander Akoimētos

INTRODUCTION TO THE TEXT

The *vita* of Alexander Akoimētos (Sleepless) is preserved in a single tenth- or eleventh-century manuscript (*Parisinus* 1452, fols. 159v–174v) of a Greek menologion that commemorates Alexander on February 2.[1] My translation is based on E. de Stroop's critical edition of the text, *La Vie d'Alexandre l'Acémète*. It was made in consultation with translations by de Stroop, Jean-Marie Baguenard, and Elizabeth Theokritoff.[2] The section divisions and bracketed numbers represent the numbered section divisions and pagination of de Stroop's edition. In those places where the biographer's scriptural allusions seem to inform the meaning of the text, I have either paraphrased or quoted the relevant scriptural passage in the footnotes.

The date of this *vita* is not certain. De Stroop proposed a date around 460, noting that the biographer claims to describe what he himself had seen (section 54; see also 29), and that the style of his Greek and certain other details suggests a fifth-century witness (e.g., the description of fortifications on the Persian frontier, section 33).[3]

---

1. Two Slavic menologia also commemorate Alexander, one on February 23, the other on July 3: see Joanne Martinov, *Annus ecclesiasticus Graeco-Slavicus* (reprint Brussels: Société des Bollandistes, 1963), 78–79. In *AASS* he is commemorated on January 15, apparently by association with John Calybites, a saint of Akoimēte origin whose cult was brought to Italy and already celebrated on that day. See Baguenard (1988): 201–3.

2. See bibliography. De Stroop's Latin translation revises the earlier Bollandist Latin translation, *De S. Alexandro, Fundatore Acoemetorum Constantinopoli*, in *AASS Januarii* I.1020–1029 (based on the unedited MS).

3. See de Stroop's introduction, PO 6.652–54. In further support of an early-sixth-century *terminus ante quem*, the description of Roman-Persian negotiations in 539 in Procopius, *De bello Persico* 2.1–15 suggests that fortifications along the frontier were no longer held and patrolled by Roman *limitanei*, as described in *V.Alex* 33–35: see J. H. W. G. Liebeschuetz, "The Defences

Some scholars have suggested a much later date.[4] Yet it is evident that the *vita* was written while the Akoimēte monastery outside Constantinople was flourishing (see sections 51–53). Such prosperity arose under the monastery's third leader, Marcellus (ca. 430/448–484), but began to suffer under the emperor Justinian in the 530s, when the monastery's hard-line Chalcedonian stance against monophysite doctrines exposed it to charges of Nestorian sympathies.[5] A late fifth- or early sixth-century date is therefore probable.

Our text, however, seems to be the work of more than one hand. Linguistic peculiarities (e.g., frequent use of sentence-initial καί, redundant adverbial use of the participle λέγων) in certain sections suggest that a lost Syriac text lay behind our Greek version. Arthur Vööbus therefore posits two early authors: the first, a member of Alexander's original band, wrote down details of his itinerary and experiences in Syriac; the second, a later member of the Akoimēte monastery, not only translated the Syriac material into Greek, but also interpolated those sections (9–23) describing Alexander's conversion of Rabbula, the anti-Nestorian bishop of Edessa.[6] Vööbus' thesis is defended by Pierre-Louis Gatier,[7] who believes that the Greek translation and Rabbula interpolations were made in the early sixth century to counter allegations that the Akoimēte monks harbored Nestorian sympathies. Finally, some minor additions to the text seem to have been made later, perhaps by the tenth- or eleventh-century redactor who transcribed the *vita* into the Greek menologion.

For further discussion and scholarship on Alexander, see chapter four.

TRANSLATION AND COMMENTARY

[658]

THE LIFE AND CONDUCT OF OUR SAINTED FATHER ALEXANDER

1. The most holy and blessed Alexander, who was an apostolic man, furnishes the occasion for my discourse with you, who are lovers of Christ.[8] For my part I think the same power is needed both for achieving virtue in deeds and for describing good deeds as they deserve in words.[9] Yet with the assistance of God, who loves

---

of Syria in the Sixth Century," in *Studien zu den Militärgrenzen Roms,* vol. 2 (Cologne: Rheinland, 1977), 489.

4. E.g., Carolus van den Vorst, Review of *Vie d'Alexandre l'Acémète,* by E. de Stroop, *AB* 31 (1912): 107–8 cautions against interpreting the author's remarks as evidence for an early date.

5. See below, n. 173.

6. Arthur Vööbus, "La Vie d'Alexandre en grec: un témoin d'une biographie inconnue de Rabbula écrite en syriaque," *Contributions of the Baltic University* 61 (1948): 2–3.

7. Gatier (1995): 440–41.

8. The title is Βίος καὶ πολιτεία τοῦ ὁσίου πατρὸς ἡμῶν Ἀλεξάνδρου. The usual designation of Alexander as Alexander Akoimētos is modern, deriving from the name of the monastery he founded at Constantinople (below, sect. 53) and its liturgical regimen (sect. 29–30). For discussion of this regimen (and its reformation after his death), see Fountoulis (1963).

9. Cf. Gregory of Nyssa's preamble to *De vita Gregorii Thaumaturgi,* ed. G. Heil (Leiden: Brill, 1990) p. 2,2–4.

mankind, I will describe where this holy man came from and the origin of his mode of athletic training. For all who receive benefits from God who loves mankind must acknowledge His mercy, rejoice in His works, and glorify Him with the Apostle, saying, "O the depth of the riches and wisdom and knowledge of God! How unsearchable His judgments, and how inscrutable His ways!"[10]

2. So let us consider the outcome[11] of the victorious athlete who passed among us **[659]** and pursued a course unswerving like the sun to proclaim the Master of the Contest[12] and Sun of Righteousness.[13] Let us take up the full armor by which he entirely cast down the enemy's full armor.[14] With this armory he not only repulsed the magistrates, authorities, and cosmic rulers of this age's darkness and spiritual forces of wickedness,[15] but did not even yield when the whole world turned against him. For after the enemy had tried everything, and since he was always repelled by the power of God and had no success, he [the enemy] summoned the entire human populace to his alliance, and they set upon our noble athlete in manifold, crafty ways.[16]

3. But the blessed one feared neither imperial authority, nor the threats of magistrates, nor the accusations of the populace, nor the wicked recommendations of bishops;[17] nor could any other pretext turn him away from truth. Instead, he reduced all his detractors to shame through his right way of life[18] and perfect faith, for he ever heard the Apostle saying, "Who will separate us from the love of Christ? Will tribulation, or worry, or persecution, or hunger, or nakedness, or peril, or a sword?"[19] And [by these words] he was guided in his deeds.

4. And he alone shone forth in our wicked generation, which our Master attests is wicked,[20] and obtained for himself a double crown. Therefore since all who write histories[21] have kept silent on account of the sheer feebleness of words for narrating

---

10. Rom 11:13.

11. Cf. Heb 13:7, "Remember your leaders who spoke to you the word of God, and as you consider the outcome of their way of life, imitate their faith."

12. ἀγωνοθέτης, a common designation for Jesus in early ascetic literature.

13. Cf. Mal 4:2, "But for you who revere my name the sun of righteousness shall rise with healing on its wings."

14. Cf. Eph 6:11, "Put on the full armory of God so that you can withstand the machinations of the devil." This armor *(panoply)* is the Psalter: see below, sect. 7 and n. 41.

15. Cf. Eph 6:12, "Our struggle is not against enemies of blood and flesh, but against the magistrates, the authorities, the cosmic rulers of this present darkness, and the spiritual forces of wickedness in the heavens."

16. ποικίλως. For probable context, see below, sect. 48–50.

17. οὐκ ἐξουσίαν βασιλικὴν ἐφοβήθη, οὐκ ἀπειλὴν ἀρχόντων, οὐ δήμου ψόγον, οὐκ ἐπισκόπων πονηρὰς παραινέσεις. Perhaps "exhortations" for παραινέσεις, but the biographer seems to be alluding to the actions taken against Alexander in sect. 38–42, 48–50.

18. ὀρθὸς βίος. Considering Alexander's association with heresy (sect. 48), ὀρθός may be used here and in sect. 52 to stress his orthodoxy.

19. Rom 8:35.

20. Cf. Mt 12:39, 45; 16:4.

21. πάντες οἱ ἱστορήσαντες, referring either to hagiographers who wrote *vitae*, or to church historians like Socrates, Sozomen, and Theodoret, who included excursus on monks in their

[his life], and **[660]** since this silence has borne no fruit for those who want to emulate [it], for their sake do I, like worldly merchants who risk near death for temporary gain, readily bear the charge of recklessness for the profit of those who want to emulate [it], and take this opportunity to make a partial[22] description [of his life]. For it is impossible for a man to describe this noble athlete's virtues as thoroughly as they deserve.

Come, then, let us make a start of our contest and show how the noble athlete equipped himself in faith. Alexander, whose memorial is in [his] blessings,[23] proved by his very deeds that he loved his Master with his whole heart and with all his strength. That he did not neglect any of the commandments, his fruits bear witness: for the Lord says, "You will know them by their fruits."[24] Nor did he take thought only for his own salvation, but he eagerly strove to deliver the whole world to his Master Christ as well. Even in this he had partial success. For just as if he held in his hands the requital of those he was saving, so he strove with a resolute soul and undivided heart for fifty years[25] on behalf of those who wished to be saved, but all the more for his own salvation.

---

narratives. In fact, Alexander's alleged Messalianism may have caused his exclusion from Theodoret's *HE* and *HR:* see Canivet (1977): 75–76.

22. ἐκ μέρους, perhaps "selective." The biographer evidently left out controversial episodes in Alexander's career: e.g., the troubles he caused Bishop Porphyry of Antioch (sect. 40).

23. τὸ μνημόσυνον ἐν εὐλογίαις. Perhaps a literal reference to "blessings" (*eulogiae,* usually oil) taken as souvenirs from a saint's tomb. See Cynthia Hahn, "Loca Sancta Souvenirs: Sealing the Pilgrim's Experience" in *The Blessings of Pilgrimage,* ed. Robert Ousterhout (Urbana and Chicago: University of Illinois Press, 1990), 85–96, and below, sect. 53.

24. Mt 7:16.

25. The *V.Alex* gives this figure repeatedly (sect. 4, 48, 52) for the length of Alexander's ascetic career, and provides several other figures for different episodes within his career: at a coenobitic community 4 years (sect. 8); in the desert west of the Euphrates 7 years (sect. 8); in the desert east of the Euphrates 20 years (sect. 26, 27), with 7 years devising a prayer regimen (sect. 26, 29), and 3 years devising a sleepless doxology (sect. 29); visit to Peter for first time in 30 years (sect. 37); visit to "children" outside Syria for first time in 20 years (sect. 41). Such chronological figures in hagiography are often undependable, and Gatier (1995): 438–39 considers these incoherent. But the biographer seems to have been concerned to keep track of such details in Alexander's life, and the figures given do, in fact, reasonably cohere if the 20 years mentioned in sect. 26 and 27 for Alexander's time east of the Euphrates be understood to include the 10 (7 plus 3) years also noted for his activities there in sect. 26 and 29. (The 20 years given for this period is probably a rounded figure). The *V.Alex* thus reckons that Alexander's ascetic training lasted (from his entry to Elias' coenobitic community to the end of his withdrawal east of the Euphrates) ca. 30 years; his wanderings in Syria another 20 years; this 50-year career ended with his trip to Constantinople, and his death evidently soon after (sect. 51–52). This chronology would also allow for Alexander's visit to his "children" 20 years after he left them outside Syria (sect. 41). The 3 years mentioned in sect. 34 are clearly based on scriptural allusion and probably should not be factored into this chronology (*pace* Gatier, 453), nor should the 30 years given for the time since Alexander last saw Peter (sect. 37), because the *V.Alex* does not mention when they last saw each other (perhaps before Alexander first left Syria).

In ch. 4 I argue that Alexander was charged with Messalianism in 426. The chronology established above permits this date and, moreover, coheres with the only other chronological

5. This blessed one was an Asian by birth, of distinguished parents, and an inhabitant of the Islands.[26] At Constantinople he received a full education in grammatical studies,[27] and when he had reached [661] an age mature in dignity and honesty he entered the civil service as a member of the prefect's staff *[praefectianus]*.[28] But in a short time he perceived that the things of this life are infirm and insecure, and that "its glory withers like a flower of grass."[29] And he became scornful of the passing nature of the things of this life, and decided upon a better way of life. And by making a taxing study of the words in the Old and New Testaments,[30] he found in the holy Gospels a treasure safe from theft and inexhaustible[31] for those who come in faith to Him who says "If you wish to be perfect, sell what you have and give to the poor and you will have a treasure in heaven: and come, follow me."[32]

6. Upon hearing this and sincerely believing it, he immediately distributed to the needy and destitute the portion allotted to him from his father's estate and the proceeds that came from his civil service (and these were many, since he had been a noble and honest *praefectianus*).[33] It was his wish, in view of the hope set before

---

indicators mentioned in the text (sect. 38–41): his troubles at Antioch with bishops Porphyry (ca. 404–414) and Theodotus (ca. 420–429). I therefore propose that Alexander began his ascetic training ca. 375 and traveled around Syria (visiting Antioch at least twice) ca. 405–425. In ca. 425–426 he visited his "children" outside Syria, went to Constantinople, was charged with Messalianism and banished, dying shortly afterwards at Gomon. Since Alexander probably would have been between 16 and 20 years old when he began his ascetic training (sect. 5), by my reckoning he was born ca. 355–360.

26. The account follows late Roman administrative distinctions between dioceses and their provincial subdivisions: Alexander was born in the diocese of *Asiana* (western Turkey) within its province of *Insulae* (Aegean islands). See Jones (1964): 1456–57. Alexander's family was evidently wealthy (sect. 6) and Christian; we learn nothing more about them except that his brother Peter also became an archimandrite in Syria (sect. 37).

27. πᾶσαν τὴν γραμματικὴν ἐπιστήμην. This refers to the secondary course of ancient education, emphasizing classical poetry and prose: see Robert Kaster, *Guardians of Language: The Grammarian and Society in Late Antiquity,* Transformation of the Classical Heritage 11 (Berkeley and Los Angeles: University of California Press, 1988), 12–40. Alexander would have been about sixteen when he finished.

28. στρατεύεται ἐπαρχικός. Alexander joined the staff *(militia)* of either the praetorian prefect or the urban prefect at Constantinople, probably as an entry-level clerk. This post was attractive to young men from wealthy provincial families because it relieved them from serving their municipal councils: see Jones (1964): 592.

29. Cf. Jas 1:10; 1 Pet 1:24; Isa 40:6–7.

30. ἐπιπόνως φιλολογῶν τὴν παλαιὰν καὶ τὴν καινὴν διαθήκην. His exacting approach to reading Scripture (cf. sect. 7–8, 12, 28–31) is exactly how grammatical studies approached classical texts: see Kaster (1988): 11–31.

31. Cf. Mt 6:19–20, "Do not store up treasures on earth where moths and rust consume and where thieves break in and rob, but store up treasures in heaven."

32. Mt 19:21. An interesting parallel to Alexander's ascetic conversion is that of Marathonius: see Sozomen, *HE* 4.27.4.

33. John Lydus in the sixth century says he accumulated one thousand *solidi* in his first year as a praetorian *praefectianus* by serving σωφρόνως [honestly], the word used here to describe Alexander. Such wealth came mostly from extra fees *(sportulae)* a clerk charged for his services (perhaps those who charged modest fees became regarded as σώφρων and attracted

him,[34] to estrange himself from his homeland, friends, and relations, and to commune with his sole Master Christ. And he heard that in Syria there were coenobitic communities that in those regions pursued such conduct in a venerable way. And after nobly completing the journey he came to them, made his request, and entered the monastery of the most God-beloved archimandrite Elias, who was renowned in those regions for the brotherhood, liturgical order, and standards of his community.[35] **[662]**

7. During the four years he spent there he made progress in the Lord, fighting the good fight[36] and obedient in every respect. But he was scrupulously attentive[37] whether this way of life was consonant with the divine Scriptures, and discovered that this was not the case. For, as those who are dedicated well know, coenobitic communities do not keep the holy Gospel's freedom from possessions and freedom from care,[38] since it is incumbent on the one placed in charge to anticipate and attend to his brothers' every need. But since God's slave Alexander burned with the Spirit[39] and continuously heard his Master's [words] "care not for tomorrow" and "you are worth more than many sparrows,"[40] he was deeply disturbed and could no longer bear to restrain himself. Yet he was not able to express his thoughts from the start, for the time was not right. First he waited to receive his full spiritual armor, which was the Psalter.[41]

---

more clients): see A. H. M. Jones, "Roman Civil Service (Clerical and Sub-Clerical Grades)," *JRS* 39 (1949): 51–53.

34. Cf. Heb 6:18–19, "We have this . . . sure and steadfast anchor of the soul, a hope that enters the inner shrine behind the curtain where Jesus, a forerunner on our behalf, has entered."

35. συστήματος ἕνεκεν ἀδελφότητος καὶ ἀκολουθίας καὶ τύπων. Elias and his monastery are otherwise unknown. Gatier (1995): 441 locates it in the Syrian agricultural plateau east of Antioch and north of Emesa (Homs, northeastern Syria).

36. Cf. 2 Tim 4:7.

37. προσεῖχε δὲ ἀκριβῶς. The *V.Alex* stresses Alexander's concern for ἀκρίβεια, his concern that his faith and lifestyle conform as literally as possible to scriptural precepts and models. I translate this word as "strict discipline" in sect. 44, where it refers to his ascetic regimen; I variously translate its adverbial form as "scrupulously" (sect. 7, 28), "precisely" (8, 14) and "literally" (17).

38. τὴν ἀκτημοσύνην καὶ τὴν ἀμεριμνίαν τοῦ ἁγίου εὐαγγελίου. The ideals prescribed by Mt 6: 25–34 are central themes in Alexander's *V.Alex.* ἀκτημοσύνη is usually translated "voluntary poverty," as I have below, sect. 37 and 43–44. For the problem addressed here cf. the Syriac *Canons of Marūtā* 48.3; trans. Vööbus, p. 129: "[The abbot] shall with his entire soul take that nothing be in want in the monastery, in order that, through want, the community of brothers may not be scattered and the monks perish immediately when they find no rest."

39. Rom 12:11.

40. Cf. Mt 10:29–31 (Jesus to his disciples), "Are not two sparrows sold for a penny? Yet not one of them will fall to the ground apart from your Father. Even the hairs of your head are counted. So be not afraid: You are worth more than many sparrows."

41. The Psalms were memorized by novice monks, not only for recitation during liturgical services, but also because their imprecations against God's enemies were considered a monk's most effective scriptural weapon for fighting demons: see John Moschos, *Pratum Spirituale* 152 (specifying Ps 7, 36, 61, and 67); Athanasius, *Epistula ad Marcellinum* 18, 33; many examples

8. This desire he fulfilled in the fourth year; and it was not because he had trouble learning that he spent years in the exercise of learning, but rather because he wanted to know precisely what each verse meant. Then, once he had become worthy of knowledge through his prayers and petitions, he could no longer bear to see any corruption of the commandment.[42] All of a sudden he picked up the holy Gospel, approached the abbot and said, "Father, are the things written in the Gospel really true?" When Elias, who was truly a father and shepherd of flocks endowed with reason, heard this outburst of questioning, he thought his brother had been deceived by the wicked one and had fallen into disbelief. For the moment **[663]** he said nothing to the brother, but fell on his face and summoned his brothers so they might pray for [Alexander] who, he said, had been ensnared by the devil. For two hours all cried and petitioned God on his behalf. After this he stood up and said to him, "Brother, what has happened to you that you have these thoughts?" But [Alexander] stood firm saying, "Are the things in the holy Gospel really true?" After hearing from all that they were true, because they were the utterances of God, he asked in response, "Then why do we not put them into practice?" They all said to him, "No one can possibly observe them."

Then [Alexander] was seized by an irrepressible rage in the belief that he had lost all the preceding years and wasted them for nothing. Bidding the brothers all farewell, he struck out, holy Gospel in hand, to follow what is written and to imitate our holy fathers. And in that time he imitated the prophet Elijah by going down to the desert.[43] There he passed seven years free of all earthly cares, since he was truly governed by the Holy Spirit.

[Sections 9–23: Rabbula's Conversion and Discipleship][44]

9. And when he thought his faith had reached full strength he also endeavored to proclaim the Gospel, so as **[664]** not to be condemned with the idle and lazy slave.[45]

---

in Evagrius, *Antirrheticus*. The biographer calls the Psalms Alexander's armor (sect. 2) and suggests that his monks' psalm-singing was specifically directed against Satan (50).

42. παρὰ τὴν ἐντολήν, probably referring to Jesus' command to "care not for tomorrow" (see sect. 7).

43. Cf. 1 Kings 17:2–6 (God sends Elijah to hide in the Wadi Cherith, east of the Jordan river, where ravens bring him meat and bread each morning and night). Elijah was the scriptural exemplar for anchoretic monasticism par excellence: see *Vita Antonii* 7 and the *Canons of Marūtā* 53. Gatier (1995): 442–44 identifies this desert with the steppe southeast of Chalcis.

44. Sections 9–23 are considered an interpolation; see Vööbus (1948) and Blum (1969): 36–39. Its description of the conversion of Rabbula, bishop of Edessa ca. 411/12–435/36, conflicts with that given by the Syriac *Life of Rabbula* (written ca. 440), which does not mention Alexander. But Gatier's discussion of the topographical allusions in these sections of the *V.Alex* assumes some basis in fact, and I note parallels between *V.Alex* and the *Life of Rabbula*, referring to the relevant pages of J. J. Overbeck's edition in *S. Ephraemi Syri, Rabulae Episcopi Edesseni, Balai aliorumque opera selecta* (Oxford: Clarendon Press, 1865), 159–209.

45. Cf. Mt 25:26 (Parable of the Talents): the slave who failed to invest talents he received

Then he heard of a city[46] where the energies of the wicked one reigned supreme; for [its people] were constantly holding festivals for their idols and rejoicing in their lawless deeds.[47] Having girded his loins with the preparation of the Gospel[48] he entered their renowned temple,[49] and with divine power he set it on fire and overthrew it. Although he had taken this prize he did not withdraw from the place, but sat down in the temple itself.

10. The people went up in a great frenzy to drive him out, but were quelled by the man's bold speech and backed down. Yet he was protected even more by the grace of God as he raised the apostolic cry, "I too am human and like you in nature, and I too have wasted time in these vanities. Flee eternal judgment. I commend to you the Kingdom of Heaven."[50]

11. They continued in their activities for a long time but were utterly incapable of causing the noble athlete any harm. Then a certain member of the city council named Rabbula—[then] a collaborator with the devil and a Father of the City[51] (for he was distinguished in both eloquence and wealth), but later a denouncer of idols and a herald of the truth—in his madness for idol-worship addressed the people with a loud voice, "Brothers and fathers, let us not abandon our ancestral gods, [665] but let us perform our sacrifices in our usual fashion. The gods take no account of this Galilean despite the outrages he has done them. They are not defending themselves against him either because they are kindly disposed towards humans, or [because] the god of the Christians is great." Confident in his civic authority and blinded by all the devil's meddlings, he told the gathered throng, "I will go up to him alone, and after I have cast down his sorcery and deceit, I will avenge the gods and all of us who have been wronged by him."

---

from his master is called a "wicked and lazy slave." This passage was allegedly used by monks at Carthage to justify their own pastoral activities: see Augustine, *De opere* 1.2; ed. Zycha, p. 533.

46. Identified by Gatier (1995): 445 with Chalcis.

47. Here (as below, sect. 24) ἀθεμίτα probably means both sacrilegious and illegal. Gatier (1995): 444 suggests that Alexander was encouraged by edicts against pagan temples issued from 392 to 408 (*Codex Theodosianus* 16.10.12, 14, 16, 19). For the influence of these laws on monks, see Vööbus (1960b): 342–46 and Trombley (1994): 246–312.

48. Cf. Eph 6:14–15, "Stand and gird your loins in truth, put on the breastplate of righteousness, and wrap your feet with the preparation of the Gospel of peace."

49. Identified by Gatier (1995): 445–46 with an ancient sanctuary of Ba'al above Chalcis.

50. Cf. Acts 14:15 (addressed to the citizens of Lystra who thought Paul and Barnabas were Zeus and Hermes and tried to sacrifice to them), "Friends, why are you doing these things? We are human and like you in nature, and are preaching the Gospel that you might turn from these vanities to the living God. . . ." Here and elsewhere in sect. 9–23, Vööbus (1948) detects use of a different version of Scriptures from that used in the rest of the *V.Alex.* Vööbus suggests that this different version was Tatian's *Diatessaron.*

51. A title given to a prominent city councilor in charge of civic revenues. Common in the sixth century, it is not securely attested before the middle of the fifth. This is the only attestation for its use in Syria. See Denis Feissel, "Nouvelles données sur l'institution du πατὴρ τῆς πόλεως," in *Inscriptions de Cilicie*, ed. G. Dagron and D. Feissel (Paris: De Bocard, 1987), 215–20. The *Life of Rabbula*, ed. Overbeck, p. 161,4–5 says that a Roman emperor (probably Julian) had made Rabbula a distinguished honorary governor.

So he went up to [Alexander] in a great frenzy and began to dispute with him. At first he was brash in his words, saying "What demon sent you to this city to overthrow the temple of the gods our masters? It is not just our temple you want to destroy through your sorcery, but all of us, whom you want to make like yourself, impious towards all the gods! Tell the truth. What sort of hope do you Christians have, that you despise your life so much as to dare such things?" But the blessed Alexander laughed and said, "We do not despise our life, as you put it, but rather, since we desire life eternal, we scorn this one, which is temporal. For we have it written that 'He who loses his life in this world will find it in everlasting life.'"[52] Then Rabbula said to him, "What hope can you expect when you depart from this life?" The blessed one replied, "For those who want to learn the truth, and to move from darkness into the light of truth, we prove this saying's truth [666] through our deeds. We have no need for wordy, fabricated myths like those you Hellenes believe in."

12. Then [Rabbula] said, "I too am ready to learn about all this madness of yours by which you have not only astounded us, but have even dishonored our gods without respite." When he heard this the blessed one replied, "Hear the power of our God and the mysteries of our faith." So he began to tell him of God's compassion for mankind and the power of the holy Scriptures from the world's creation to the dispensation of the Cross, and they argued back and forth with each other the whole day and night. And they kept at it without taking any food, nor did they allow themselves any sleep, as [Alexander] pointed out the virtues of the holy men recorded in Scripture and the freedom of speech they had with their Master.

And as he went through the God-inspired Scriptures he came to the prophet Elijah, the one who three times brought fire down from heaven.[53] At this point, after hearing many chapters, Rabbula began to object contentiously, "All these stories of yours are lies and fabricated myths! Let me advise you to your advantage: join us in our festivals and sacrifice to the gods. As for your offenses against them, they will forgive you because you were ignorant and because they love mankind." But the blessed one said, "If those were gods, why did they not reply with fire to those who petitioned them [667] from dawn till dusk?[54] God's slave Elijah was just one man but he slew all the false prophets with divine power. When he prayed that it not rain on account of human madness for idols, no rain fell on earth for three years and six months, till the Master Himself assuaged His slave's severity out of compassion for the widow,[55] persuading him to renounce his oath and to petition Him on the world's behalf. For [Elijah] had said, 'As the Lord lives, let it not rain

---

52. Cf. Mt 10:39, "He who finds his life will lose it and he who loses his life for my sake will find it."

53. Cf. 1 Kings 18:38 (answering Elijah's call), "the fire of the Lord fell and consumed the burnt offering" of the 450 priests of Ba'al. The use of this scriptural episode for justifying violence by fifth-century Christian zealots is discussed by Gaddis (1999): 180–93.

54. Cf. 1 Kings 18:26, Ba'al's priests "called on Ba'al's name from morn till noon crying, 'Ba'al, answer us!' But there was no voice, and no answer."

55. Referring to the widow of Zarephath sent to feed Elijah in 1 Kings 17:8–16.

on earth unless by my word.'[56] And God the Master did not ignore His slave's oath, but it happened just as the prophet said it would."

13. But [Rabbula] laughed in scorn and said to the blessed Alexander, "If these stories are really true and your god is such as to hearken so readily to his slaves, then go pray yourself for fire to come down before us. If it does, I will say there is no god but the god of the Christians. Otherwise the things in your writings are false, for as you say, you are a slave of that god." But the blessed Alexander believed without question that God the Master would consent to his request. And because it is written that "to one who believes, all things are possible,"[57] he said to [Rabbula], "Go call on your own gods, many as they are, for fire to come down before us. Then I will call on my God, and fire will come down and consume the rush-mats **[668]** lying before us."[58] But Rabbula said, "I have no such authority. You pray instead."

Hearing this the holy man burned with the Spirit. And he rose and said, "Let us pray." Facing the east he stood, stretched out his hands, and so prayed as to move creation itself. And fire came down and consumed the mats spread round the building just as the noble athlete said it would. Although it did them no harm, when Rabbula saw the miracle's sudden rush he thought the fire would consume him too and he fell on his face, clinging to the blessed one's feet until the fire subsided. Then he exclaimed, "Great is the God of the Christians!"[59] And though he wanted to proclaim the miracle to everyone, the holy man made him swear that he would not confess the mystery to anyone while he was still alive, and so he did. But thirty years after the miracle had happened and the holy man had died, Rabbula made his confession before bishops and monks, and the testimony of the new disciple is true.[60]

And by this portent the faithful should also be fully assured that [Alexander] overthrew the temple in a similar way.

14. After seeing this miracle Rabbula remained with the blessed Alexander a week to learn the word of truth more precisely. Then, persuaded by the preceding events, he requested to receive enlightenment.[61]

As Easter drew near and he was ready to be honored with the holy baptism, the

---

56. 1 Kings 17:1, "As the Lord God of Israel whom I stand before lives, there will be no dew or rain these years lest by my word."

57. Mk 9:23.

58. Cf. 1 Kings 18:24 (Elijah to the priests of Ba'al), "You call the name of your god and I will call the name of the Lord's name; the god who answers with fire is God indeed."

59. Cf. 1 Kings 18:39, "When all the people saw [fire fall and consume their offerings], they fell on their faces and said, 'The Lord indeed is God.'"

60. Cf. Jn 19:35: "He who saw this [blood and water pouring from Jesus' wound on the cross] has testified, and his testimony is true; and he knows he tells the truth so that you may believe."

61. φωτισθῆναι, i.e., receive baptism. Escolan (1999): 40–44 adduces this passage to show that baptism could still have strong ascetic consequences in the fifth century. Zealous Christians often chose to be baptized on Easter following an intensive catechumenate during Lent (as here in Rabbula's case). The *Life of Rabbula*, ed. Overbeck, p. 165,4–6 has Rabbula baptized in the Jordan during a pilgrimage to Jerusalem.

enemy of the truth saw his power being broken on all fronts and made haste to deprive the new disciple Rabbula of **[669]** eternal life. He suggested to [Rabbula] that he not be baptized in the city, but that he go to a certain martyr's shrine and receive his enlightenment there, three staging-posts from the city.[62] Then he arranged for a consecrated virgin to be possessed by a demon in this shrine.[63] When they entered the shrine they found her convulsing and foaming at the mouth. At this sight Rabbula immediately recoiled, saying "I will not become a Christian. For surely the gods are teaching her a lesson for becoming a Christian. If I too become one, I will have to suffer the same."

15. When the blessed one saw him deterred, he urgently petitioned God to confound the wicked one's scheme and take pity on the new disciple. When three hours had passed he managed with difficulty to persuade [Rabbula] by telling him, "This is the enemy's scheme. This woman is being chastised because of her evil deeds, since she disgraced the [religious] garb that she wears. If we enter and the demon does not confess through her own mouth that this is so, do not listen to me." After hearing this Rabbula was persuaded to return (for he had withdrawn from the shrine) expecting to hear if the things the blessed one said were true. When they entered, they found her being chastised and confessing aloud the reason she had been possessed by the demon. And when Rabbula heard her shameful deeds and was persuaded thereby that it had come about just as the blessed one had told him, he said, "Truly this woman is being punished on account of her evil deeds." And so then with sincere faith he was honored with the holy baptism. **[670]**

16. And God in turn performed many wonders through him. For when he had received his enlightenment and had risen from the baptismal font, his cloak was found entirely covered with crosses from top to bottom.[64] By this sign Rabbula was all the more strengthened in faith. Then, when the citizens saw the wonder and the thoroughness of his conversion, they believed in our Lord Jesus Christ together with their wives and children. And so fervently did they come to the faith that they hastened to receive the seal of holy baptism before they had even heard the word of God.

17. But since the blessed Alexander wanted to learn if they literally believed, he said to them all, "First prove your faith through your deeds and then you can receive the seal. If anyone has idols in his house, let him bring them out in public and

62. Three days' distance.

63. "Consecrated virgin" renders κανονικήν τινα, perhaps referring to a member of a *Bnāt Qyāmā*. The shrine mentioned here is identified by Gatier (1995): 446–47 n. 62 with the sanctuary of Cosmas and Damian at Cyrrhus (Nebi Ouri, northern Syria), which became especially known for curing women under demonic possession. The *Life of Rabbula*, ed. Overbeck, pp. 163,27–164,1 says that Rabbula while praying here saw a healing miracle that confirmed his faith. At Cyrrhus there remains an ancient Christian *martyrium* now dedicated to a Muslim saint, known for its cures.

64. For this motif as a sign of God's power to convert, see John Chrysostom, *Expositio in psalmum* 110.4–5; Socrates, *HE* 3.20; Sozomen, *HE* 5.22; and Theodoret, *HE* 3.15 (all referring to the same event). The *Life of Rabbula*, ed. Overbeck, p. 165,6–11 describes Rabbula's garment after baptism as shining on all sides with a sign of the cross in the color of Christ's blood.

smash them with his own hands." On hearing this each one hastened to be the first to display his zeal and smash his own idols.[65] And on that day it was possible to see God's mysteries, because if anyone was merely pretending to believe and wanted to hide his idols, he could not. For each of them hastened to bring out his own idols before he was accused by someone else, since they knew each other's secrets. And so they were purified together with their houses. And in a short time they were confirmed in the faith and all were honored with the holy baptism's grace. And thus in a short time they and their wives and children became such zealots of the faith that they petitioned the authorities to exile whoever spoke against the truth of the faith. **[671]**

18. When the blessed one saw them all exulting in the faith and giving thanks to God, he said to them, "Till now you have partaken of milk. If anyone wishes to partake of solid food and wants to become a perfect Christian,[66] let him sell what he has, give to the poor, take no care for tomorrow, and he will have a treasure in heaven. Let him strive as it is written for the Kingdom of Heaven and God's righteousness, and all these things will be given to him as well, in abundance."[67] These words weighed heavily on some of those who heard them and possessed much property. The disciple Rabbula said, "Am I not yet a perfect Christian? How can I do this? For if I do this, who will feed my multitude of domestic slaves?[68] This alone is false. But if you want, persuade me through deeds. Sustain me and my servants for just one day, and then I will believe you and what you say. But if you cannot do this within the city, what if we go out to the desert?" The blessed Alexander replied, "Take your servants and as many others more as you wish and lead them out to the desert wherever you want. And if our Lord does not care for us, do not listen to me." And Rabbula said, "If you do this I will follow everything that is written."

19. Then, since he wanted to test the blessed Alexander, he took his own servants and very many others that he chose and led them to a place in the desert where no human was ever **[672]** seen. After traveling all day they settled down around the eleventh hour[69] between two mountains.[70] Rabbula surveyed the roads and laughed. But the blessed Alexander hastened to prayers in his habitual way, and as soon as they had completed their evening hymn the Lord acted in accordance with the faith of the noble athlete of Christ. For his Master Christ dispatched His angel in the

---

65. Cf. Acts 19:18–19, When Paul's exorcisms proved Jesus' powers, the Ephesians "confessed and disclosed their practices. A number of those who practiced magic collected their books and publicly burned them."

66. Cf. Heb 5:13, "Everyone who lives on milk is inexperienced in the word of righteousness and still an infant. Solid food is for the perfect, who have been trained in their faculties so they can discern between good and evil."

67. Mt. 6:33, "But strive first for the kingdom of God and his righteousness, and all these things [i.e., food and clothing] will be given to you as well."

68. τὸ πλῆθος τῶν οἰκετῶν, perhaps "household dependents" including wife and daughters as well as slaves. The *Life of Rabbula*, ed. Overbeck, p. 166,22–23, 26 records that Rabbula also had sons.

69. One hour before sunset, or about five o'clock.

70. Gatier (1995): 447–48 identifies these mountains with Jebel Hass and Jebel Shbeyt near Anasartha (modern Hanaser), some 35 miles southeast of Chalcis.

guise of a peasant with an ass laden with fresh,[71] warm bread and straddled by two cooking pots containing vegetables and lentils. Then the blessed Alexander said to Rabbula, "Rise, receive, and become a believer, not a doubter."[72]

But Rabbula remained for a long time wondering to himself, and saying, "How has this come to appear in a deserted place, and how can a peasant have so much bread of such quality? We barely made it to this place after traveling the whole day. Likewise this man too must have set out during the night to arrive here at this hour. But the bread could not also have been made today. So why is it still warm?" As he pondered all these things he marveled at the power of Christ. He said to the one who had come, "Where do you come from and who sent you here?" The angel of God replied, "My Master sent me." And after receiving the food they sent the supposed peasant back. And when he had gone a short distance away from them, he suddenly disappeared. But they thankfully enjoyed what their Master Jesus had sent and stayed in that place through the night. After passing the night they returned to the city. [**673**]

20. So Rabbula was strengthened in the faith by this portent too.[73] And since he wished to be undisturbed in his contemplation of God, he gave the city council its property[74] and gave his wife's property to his wife, daughters, and their handmaids. His wife agreed to her husband's plan and organized an ascetic community where she remained with her daughters and maids, serving the Lord with her whole heart. Rabbula himself set his own servants free after giving them sufficient means for a degree of comfort. Then after selling off all his clothing and possessions he gave to the destitute poor and went out to the desert. He applied himself to asceticism so severely that one could not reckon him clad in a human body as he persevered in fasts, vigils, and prayers, ceaselessly trying to make amends to the Lord with lamentations for his former error.[75]

21. But our merciful God who loves mankind, who alone does not remember wrongs, and who has said, "I will glorify those who glorify me,"[76] fulfilled His promise

---

71. Literally "clean" (as below, sect. 45). Wheat bread was so described to distinguish it from the more common bread of coarsely milled barley. Wheat bread was usually eaten only by the rich, or used for ritual purposes: see Hamel (1990): 32. For a close parallel, see Cyril of Scythopolis, *Vita Iohannis Hesychastae* 12; ed. Schwartz, p. 211,1–5, answering Ps 78:19: "Can God spread a table in the wilderness?"

72. Jn 20:27 (Jesus to Thomas after the resurrection), "put your hand in my side, and do not be a doubter but a believer.'"

73. A letter from Rabbula to Gemellinus, bishop of Perrhe (Pirun, north of Samosata) expresses worry over "certain brothers whose cloisters are unknown and others of distinguished archimandrites" in the vicinity who boasted they did not need to drink or eat on their travels, because they received food from God instead: meaning bread and wine from the eucharist they would celebrate "two or three times in one day." See Ps.-Zachariah, *Chronicle* 10.4; trans. E. W. Brooks and F. J. Hamilton, pp. 301–2.

74. Presumably this refers to Rabbula's renunciation of his former financial responsibilities as πατὴρ τῆς πόλεως: see above, sect. 11 and n. 51.

75. The *Life of Rabbula*, ed. Overbeck, pp. 166,23–167,1 similarly describes Rabbula's dispersal of property, slaves, and family before setting out to practice desert asceticism, but emphasizes that Rabbula did so in imitation of Antony the Great.

76. 1 Sam 2:30.

to him and did not keep His good slave hidden for long, but displayed him as a beacon of light to the world. For when the bishop of Edessa was laid to rest,[77] the whole city and surrounding territory sought [Rabbula] as their shepherd, and he was elected leader of the people by many votes. Edessa is the metropolis of Mesopotamia.[78]

22. Once ordained bishop he became a haven of knowledge of God not only for Syria, Armenia, **[674]** and Persia,[79] but for the whole world as well. For in this city the Lord long ago established schools for the Syriac language,[80] and governors and wealthy men of influence (leaders of nearby cities)[81] send their children to be educated here. So when he came into office Bishop Rabbula hastened with the help of the Holy Spirit to unify all in true and firm belief, ever striving to act according to his teacher's example. And in this case one must truly say, "It is enough for the disciple to be like his teacher."[82]

I will also describe the following good thing this blessed one accomplished, since it will profit those who take heed. To widows and orphans he became nothing less than a father. As for the foreign children of the Hellenes,[83] twice a month he would

77. Named Diogenes by the *Life of Rabbula*, ed. Overbeck, p. 170,23, which notes that Rabbula was elevated as his successor by bishops gathered at Antioch. This happened ca. 412: see Blum (1969): 7.

78. This is an error. Although Edessa lay within the area generally considered Mesopotamia in antiquity, it was officially the metropolis of the province of Osrhoene. Amida (modern Diyarbakir) was the metropolis of Mesopotamia. Such distinctions were blurred by the Muslim conquests: in the eighth century, Edessans claimed their city had been metropolis (i.e., center for church and imperial administration) of Mesopotamia "from the time of Addai" (i.e., the first century): see Segal (1970): 209. The error suggests a late date for the remark, though not necessarily for the whole section. The sentence seems tacked on as a gloss (as found in the next section and sect. 38), probably added by the tenth-or eleventh-century redactor at Constantinople. De Stroop notes here that the MS spelling, Αἴδεσσα, is attested for the European Edessa, in Macedonia.

79. A reference to Edessa's three theological schools. The "Schools of the Armenians, and of the Persians, and of the Syrians" are listed in the second Council of Ephesus *acta* as being among those who were opposed to Ibas, Rabbula's successor at Edessa. The Persian school later became viewed as Nestorian and was forced out of Edessa in 489. Relocated at Nisibis in the Persian Empire, it became a major center for the Dyophysite Persian church. See Arthur Vööbus, *History of the School of Nisibis* (Louvain: Secrétariat du CorpusSCO, 1965), 24–32.

80. Edessa became famous as a center of Syriac literature, but this is the only evidence of elementary schools (παιδευτήρια, perhaps schools for grammatical studies) that taught the Syriac language there: see Segal (1970): 149–50.

81. De Stroop considers the words placed here in parentheses to be a later gloss, and considers the whole section to be corrupt.

82. Mt 10:25. See the *Life of Rabbula*, ed. Overbeck, pp. 117,16–178,18 and 179,19–181,26 for a general description of Rabbula's pastoral efforts.

83. I.e., children from pagan families outside Edessa. The closest major city to Edessa was Carrhae (modern Ḥarrān, southeastern Turkey). Close to the Persian border, it remained staunchly polytheist throughout late antiquity; the Council of Chalcedon referred to it as ἡ Ἑλλήνων πόλις [the City of the Hellenes]: *ACO* 2.1.3 [73]; ed. Schwartz, p. 25,3–4; *ACO* 2.3.3; p. 30,16–17.

summon them from the schools, gather them round, and teach them the word of truth. When they had received the seal of the Holy Spirit (and thus the greatest profit of all) they would return to their own homelands; and having come into good habits, over the years they pass these on to their own children, to the present day.[84] And so God's grace shone forth in those regions too. And [Rabbula] did not just do this for two or three years, but for thirty.

But let us show the achievements and virtues of this one through the struggles of his teacher.[85] For [Alexander] struggled no less than this one. I can truly say his deeds were such as to rank him beside the prophet Elisha[86]—and among these was the new disciple. [**675**]

23. When Alexander, the father of reasoning flocks, saw how nobly he [Rabbula] had renounced the world and knew he was capable of guiding others toward God and that all in due time would follow in the faith, he rejoiced in his heart, fully assured by these deeds that all things are possible for one who believes, and that God the Master is ready to give to those who ask things that please Him.[87] So he thought again what next he might ask from the merciful Christ. But the people were employing every device to keep him among them,[88] because their excessive love for him made them demand him for their shepherd. Knowing this, he planned to leave the city in secret, but when the people of the city became aware of his plans they posted guards at the city gate and watched over him night and day, so as not to lose their true father. Since he was unable to exit freely, the blessed one was lowered over the walls at night in a basket by his disciples. In this way he left the city just like the blessed Paul.[89]

24. Making a two-day journey into the desert he found a place inhabited by brigands.[90] Here was a brigand chief with thirty pestilent men under him whom no city had escaped, nor was there a countryside [**676**] that had not been polluted by the lawless deeds of their hands. Having heard this from many people, the blessed Alexander called on God and asked that he might deliver the wicked men's souls to Him; and God, knowing Alexander's intention was good, granted his request. When he met with the brigand chief and made the word of faith known to him, the chief was stung to contrition by the blessed one's words, and he received the holy baptism's grace with sincere faith. After he had been honored with the grace of

84. This passage seems to describe the creation of a *Bnay* or *Bnāt Qyāmā*. See *Canons of Marūtā* 25.7 and 26.2–4, ed. Vööbus, pp. 120–22.

85. The Greek is corrupt; Theokritoff translates "Let us point out that this man's achievements and his virtues came about through the efforts of his teacher." The awkward phrasing may reflect that this is the point of transition from the interpolated sections to the original *V.Alex* narrative. The next section mentions disciples who have otherwise not yet appeared, and may have originally described Alexander's encounter with someone other than Rabbula.

86. Cf. 2 Kings 1–9, describing the numerous miracles of Elisha's early career.

87. Cf. Mt. 7:11.

88. This section apparently returns to Rabbula's home city, i.e. Chalcis.

89. Cf. 2 Cor. 11:33 (Paul's escape from Damascus).

90. Located by Gatier (1995): 448–49 on the southern slopes of Jebel Shbeyt, 50 miles southeast of Chalcis.

holy baptism and had risen from the holy font, the blessed Alexander said to him, "Did you ask for anything when you approached the holy font?" "Yes," he replied. Then Alexander said, "What did you ask?" "I asked," he said, "that the Lord might soon take my soul." He lived a week more, repenting for the things he had done, and on the eighth day the Lord took him away.

25. When the thirty men who had been with him saw this prodigious wonder, they also approached and petitioned the blessed Alexander that they too might be honored with the gift of Christ. And since they sincerely believed in our Lord Jesus Christ, they too received the holy baptism. So fervently did they embrace the faith that they made that brigands' camp into a monastery where they stayed and served the Lord with their whole heart, so that in a short time they were found precious in God's sight.[91] When the blessed Alexander observed that they were powerful in faith so as to be capable of edifying others as well, **[677]** he appointed for them an abbot. Then having strengthened their faith more fully he bade them farewell, said a prayer, and set out on his way rejoicing.

26. After traveling two days he reached the Euphrates river and crossed it like a spiritual Jacob. And having found a storage jar set in the ground, he filled out his prayers on the mountains by day but spent the nights in this jar.[92] That man [Jacob] crossed [the Jordan] with [only] a staff,[93] and spent twenty years there praying for bread to eat and clothing to wear.[94] With him in mind the blessed Alexander petitioned God to grant him to be revealed a second Jacob, and God, who loves mankind, granted what was asked of Him.

Comparing Jacob's life to his own, Alexander said to himself, "Jacob became a shepherd of flocks devoid of reason; I am striving to become a shepherd of flocks endowed with reason. He after seven years demanded to receive his rightful pay from [Laban];[95] but I after seven years will coax from my Master His grace. He after serving a man for twenty years took four wives and became a father of assemblies;[96]

---

91. Cf. 1 Pet 2:4, "Come to him like a living stone rejected by humans but chosen and precious in God's sight, and like living stones let yourselves also be built into a spiritual house, becoming a holy priesthood offering spiritual sacrifices acceptable to God through Jesus Christ."

92. Gatier (1995): 449 locates Alexander's crossing of the Euphrates at Barbalissus (near Meskene/Balis, 44 miles east of Jebel Shbeyt) and identifies his mountain with Jebel Sheikh Sinn al-Aabed that rises steeply along the Euphrates' eastern bank (see below, n. 98). Its valley was fertile agricultural land in antiquity but is now under Assad dam waters. *Pithoi* [storage jars] like Alexander's were often planted in the ground as cisterns.

93. Cf. Gen 32:10, "I am not worthy of . . . the steadfast love and all the faithfulness you have shown your servant, for with only my staff I have crossed this Jordan."

94. Cf. Gen 28:20–21, "Jacob made a vow, saying 'If God be with me and keep me in the way I am going and give me bread to eat and clothing to wear . . . then the Lord will be my God.' "

95. Cf. Gen 29:18–21, "Jacob loved Rachel; so he said, 'I will serve you seven years for your younger daughter Rachel.' . . . So Jacob served seven years for Rachel. . . . Then Jacob said to Laban, 'Give me my wife . . . for my time is complete.' "

96. Cf. Gen 35:11, "God said to him, be fruitful and multiply. A nation and an assembly of nations shall come of you, and kings shall come out of your loins."

but I after serving my Master for twenty years will furnish Him with four choruses in different languages. He in fear of his brother ransomed his life with eight flocks of animals;[97] but I will secure my salvation with eight **[678]** choruses of men singing hymns to God. He had twelve sons from the flesh; but I have twelve recitations from the divine Scriptures."

27. These things he pondered while living partly in his jar for twenty years. Meanwhile there gathered round him four hundred men who were eager to be brought into Christ's family through his admirable and irreproachable conduct, convinced that through him they would be deemed worthy of the Kingdom of Heaven. They represented four languages in all: Romans, Greeks, Syrians, and Egyptians. These he separated into eight choruses that sang and chanted psalms to God with zeal and understanding. And so he established his monastery.[98] As for its liturgical observance and sequence, he arranged this into twelve parts in accordance with the prayers he recited in his jar. And in this too one must admire the faith of our noble athlete. For although he assumed oversight of so many brothers, he did not worry about any provisions for their needs.[99] Rather, in accordance with the holy Gospel, they kept only what sufficed for a day, and all the rest he gave to the destitute poor. They wore only a single tunic[100] and in all these things took cheer from the words of God and nourished themselves on their hope for things to come.

28. God's slave Alexander was scrupulously attentive to the things written in the God-inspired Scriptures and was adamant that not a single line of God's commandments should escape him so that he might become indeed an imitator of all the great men on record. First he took the apostles' example for his own regimen[101] of spiritual activity, **[679]** performing his prayers at the third hour,[102] the sixth

---

97. Cf. Gen 32:11–20 (Jacob's gift to appease Esau, who was coming to kill him).

98. Excavations of a monastery church at Houeidjit Halaoua on Sheikh Sinn al-Aabed (8 miles northeast of ancient Barbalissus) have recovered Greek and Syriac mosaic inscriptions dated January 471 with the words μον[ή] τοῦ ἁγόυ Ἀλεξάνδρου / *Dayrā d-ṭubānā Mār Aleksandros*, [Monastery of the blessed Lord Alexander]: see Pauline Donceel-Voûte, *Les pavements des églises byzantines de Syrie et du Liban*, vol. 1 (Louvain-La-Neuve: Collége Érasme, 1988), 148–50. Gatier (1995): 450 believes that this refers to Alexander Akoimētos. If so, it probably marks the site which Alexander left to his disciple Trophimus (sect. 31), perhaps also the one he visits outside Syria in sect. 41. The inscriptions commemorate work completed through alms or "blessings" (ἐλεημοσύναι / *burkātā*) given to the monastery.

99. τοσούτων ἀδελφῶν πρόνοιαν ποιούμενος, οὐδενὸς τῶν ἐπιτηδείων πρὸς τὰς χρείας ἐφρόντιζεν. Alexander did not ensure his monks had a dependable food supply as did, e.g., the Egyptian Abba Or for his monks: see *HM* 2.3. Gatier (1995): 451 notes that Alexander's monks could have scavanged off the rich agricultural fields along the Euphrates.

100. Mt 10:10 (Jesus' instructions to his apostles), "Take no gold, silver, or copper in your belts, nor bag for your journey, nor two tunics, sandals, nor a staff; for workers are deserving of their food."

101. ἐν τῷ κανόνι τῆς πνευματικῆς διαγωγῆς τὸν τύπον τῶν ἀποστόλων λαμβάνει. I translate κανών "regimen" throughout because it suggests a broader program of monastic discipline than the usual translation, "rule," does.

102. Mid-morning, or about nine o'clock. Cf. Acts 2:14–15 (Peter addressing the Jews at

hour,[103] the ninth hour,[104] and once during the night.[105] Then he considered what next he might ask from God. He saw that God his Master everywhere proclaims the number seven, as when He says, "Seven times a day I praise you."[106] So he endeavored to carry out this too, and did so by performing his prayers seven times a day and seven times a night.

29. After passing seven years this way he made another search to see what else to ask. And he found the prophet saying, "On the law of the Lord he will meditate day and night."[107] And pondering this he said to himself, "How is this possible?" And again he reasoned and said, "Of course, were it not possible, the Holy Spirit would not have commanded it to us through His prophet." And though he wanted to ask for this, he did not dare, realizing that the request was beyond human capacity. But again he realized that Christ encourages us every day by saying, "Ask and it will be given to you, knock and it will be opened for you"[108] and again, "Each who asks, receives, and to him who knocks, it will be opened"[109] and again, "All things are possible to one who believes." Reflecting on this he said to himself, "If our Master in His love of mankind encourages us to ask of Him all good things, why then in our idleness do we neglect to ask?" And so he spent three years devoting himself to fasting and prayers while petitioning God both night and day that this too could be performed by him on earth, although it was the work of heavenly powers. Our merciful God, who loves mankind, seeing His good slave's love, devotion, and burning [680] zeal, granted him this too, revealing Himself to [Alexander] visibly and saying, "Make your request, and it will endure on earth until the end of eternity according to your word."

And this he confessed to us himself as if it had happened to another person. Just as the blessed Apostle Paul described his own vision as if it had belonged to someone else,[110] so too did Alexander, the Apostle's disciple.

30. After this mystery was revealed to him he sought a regimen by which this work could be accomplished. But seeing the feebleness of [human] nature he was utterly at a loss. For though he scoured through all the writing of the Old and New Testaments and closely observed all the great men who had arisen in their times, he could not find anyone who had accomplished this marvel on earth, that by imitation

---

Jerusalem at Pentecost before reciting the Psalms), "Let this be known to you . . . these people are not drunk, as you suppose, for it is only nine in the morning."

103. Noon. Cf. Acts 10:9, "About noon the next day as they were on their journey and approaching the city, Peter went up on the roof to pray."

104. Mid-afternoon, or about three o'clock. Cf. Acts 3:1, "One day Peter and John went up to the temple at the hour of prayer at the ninth hour."

105. Cf. Acts 16:25, "Around midnight Paul and Silas prayed and sang hymns to God."

106. Ps 119:164, "Seven times a day I praise you for your righteous ordinances."

107. Ps 1:2, "Their delight is the law of the Lord, and on his law they meditate day and night."

108. Mt 7:7.

109. Mt 7:8.

110. Cf. 2 Cor 12:1–5, "I know a man in Christ who fourteen years ago was taken up to the third heaven. . . . On behalf of such a man I will boast, but on my own behalf I will not boast."

he might fulfill his good yearning for the salvation of many souls. Therefore he took as a teacher the Creator of the universe, and just as He imposed limits on His creation,[111] so too did Alexander arrange his way of life, saying, "My Christ in His creation allotted twenty-four hours for day and night; so let us also pass the course of the day and night with twenty-four services singing hymns to God. Our Savior bids us forgive our fellow slaves their sins against us seventy times seven;[112] so let us also raise our petitions to our good God on their behalf by making seventy-seven genuflections. My Master has [681] made the days and nights increase in orderly fashion; so let us also ceaselessly offer hymns to Him in such an orderly arrangement. The angels glorified my Savior even on earth;[113] so let us also glorify Him along with the angels." So when the full liturgical sequence had been performed and the recitations kept and the services finished, then in addition he sang the hymn of the holy angels seventy-seven times both night and day, the one that goes "Glory to God in the highest, and on earth peace, goodwill toward men."[114]

31. When he had accomplished these things in the name of the Father, Son, and Holy Spirit, he searched again for what to ask from God. He found in the Gospel that the number of disciples appointed to proclaim the Kingdom of our Lord Jesus Christ was seventy.[115] So he petitioned God that the same number from his own disciples might be appointed zealots of the faith, capable of proclaiming God's word to the gentiles. And God granted him this too, and in accordance with the saint's petition appointed seventy of his disciples who were powerful in the faith.

I will truthfully describe how this happened. For when his eight companies had equipped themselves in perfect faith and had long been raising their prayers and hymns to God with joy and with cheerful hearts, he reflected to himself, saying, "Relaxation must never be allowed into this great freedom from care." So once more he imposed on himself bodily afflictions, as was his habit. He summoned by name one hundred and fifty noble soldiers of Christ [682] who were truly armed with the breastplate of faith and helmet of salvation and sword of the Holy Spirit,[116] and he said to them, "Brothers, let us test ourselves to see if we are perfect in our faith. Let us pass through that fearsome desert of unbelievers and show through our deeds that we believe in God with our whole heart and not in word alone." At first he wanted to go to Egypt and instruct the unbelievers there who trust in the works of their own hands, but he was prevented by the Holy Spirit.[117] When his true disciples

---

111. Cf. Acts 17:26–27 (Paul to the Athenians), "From one man [God, the Creator of the Universe] made all nations inhabit the whole earth and allotted the times of their existence and limited the places where they would live so that they would search for God, and that by groping for him they might find him."

112. Cf. Mt 18:21–22 (Peter to Jesus), "'Lord, if my brother sins against me, how often should I forgive? seven times?' Jesus said to him, 'I say to you not just seven times but as many as seventy times seven.'"

113. Lk 2:13.

114. Lk 2:14.

115. Lk 10:1.

116. Cf. Eph 6:16–17.

117. Cf. Acts 16:6–7, "[Paul and Timothy] went through the region of Phrygia and Galatia, having been prevented by the Holy Spirit from speaking the word in Asia."

heard this plan they agreed to follow him without hesitation. But the blessed Alexander wanted to withdraw from the place for good. He did not let anyone know this but remarked instead, "I am going away to visit our brothers in the desert." He appointed as abbot for the brotherhood a gentle, tranquil, and holy man of God whose name was Trophimus. After exhorting them all in his usual way, he bade them farewell, made a prayer, and set out.

32. After crossing the Euphrates river once more,[118] the blessed Alexander went out to the Persian desert with the disciples he had chosen, carrying with them nothing at all for supplies except the parchments on which they had the holy Scriptures.[119] They lived in the desert with just a single cloak and observed their regimen of hymn-singing unbroken through day and night. In that time it happened that they were tested by the needs of the flesh in order that they might prove their virtue.[120] For many days they had nothing but nuts to eat and satisfy themselves. Thirty of their number **[683]** began to rail against the blessed one and spoke to him as if to Moses, "Did you lead us out to this desert to kill us with hunger?"[121] They secretly wanted to return to the monastery and discussed this plan among themselves. But the blessed one knew about their plan through the Spirit, for there was nothing which escaped him, since he was truly a second Moses, faithful in all his house.[122] Calling them together, he reproached them and censured their lack of faith, then released them to return to the monastery he too had left, and told them in a loud voice, "Believe me, brothers, today the Lord will visit us and shame your lack of faith."

33. And when they had gone off a short distance God sent, as the holy man predicted, Roman tribunes and soldiers carrying goods for them from God. And these

118. Gatier (1995): 451 believes that Alexander recrossed the Euphrates, moving south, probably at Sura (modern Sourriya), and suggests that the "Persian desert" means the steppe zone south of the Euphrates between Circesium (al-Busaira, southeastern Syria) and Palmyra. In Alexander's day it was largely controlled by Bedouins allied to Persia. By the sixth century the area between Sura and Resafa was known as *Barbarikon:* see Elizabeth Key Fowden, *The Barbarian Plain: Saint Sergius Between Rome and Iran.* The Transformation of the Classical Heritage 28 (Berkeley and Los Angeles: University of California Press, 1999), 1.

119. Callinicus, *Vita Hypatii* 41.13; ed. Bartelink, p. 244 perhaps corroborates this description by reporting that when Alexander and his monks were later preparing to leave their shelter in Hypatius' monastery at Chalcedon, each took with him a "Bible as a blessing (εὐλογία) for the road." Callinicus does not describe them taking other provisions. Bartelink, 245 n. 5 suggests each carried a Bible (or a fragment of one) as a phylactery.

120. Cf. Deut 8:2–3 [Moses to the Israelites]: "Remember the long way that the Lord your God led you for forty years in the desert so as to humble you, to test you, and to know your inmost heart, whether you would keep His commandments or not. He humbled you, He made you feel hunger, He fed you with manna . . . to make you understand that human beings do not live on bread alone but on every word that comes from the Mouth of the Lord."

121. Cf. Ex 16:2–3, "The whole congregation of Israelites railed against Moses and Aaron in the desert [saying], 'If only we had died by the hand of the Lord in the land of Egypt, where we sat by the pots and ate our fill of bread; for you have led us out into this desert to kill our whole assembly with hunger.'"

122. Cf. Heb 3:5, "Moses was faithful like a slave in all [God's] house, to bear witness to things that would be spoken of in the future."

asked them to go to their fortresses and give them a blessing, for between the Roman and Persian territories there are fortresses built every ten to twenty milestones from each other for defense against the barbarians.[123] When the brothers who had deserted them observed the soldiers coming from afar, they realized it was happening just as their sainted father said it would and were strengthened in their faith. Some of them cast themselves on the ground and rejoined the brotherhood with contrition. The others who were with him returned to the inner desert[124] and dwelled there [684] to their death. But the blessed Alexander, just as happened in the holy Apostle Peter's case,[125] was commanded by the Holy Spirit to go with [the soldiers], and he followed them without question. As he passed along the entire stretch of frontier[126] he strengthened all in their faith. And he nourished the poor like a father and taught the rich to do good deeds. So stung were they by his words that they brought before him the records they had kept against their debtors and burned them up.

34. But certain pestilent men who were conceited in their wealth and darkened in their minds[127] rose up against him saying, "Did you come to us to make us poor?" Because they were ungrateful for the gifts of God the blessed one cursed them, and on their account it did not rain at that fortress camp for three years.[128] Then when all learned the cause of his wrath, they joined together in one accord to drive those

123. κάστελλοι γὰρ εἰσιν μεταξὺ τῶν Ῥωμαίων καὶ τῶν Περσῶν τὰ ἀντέχοντα τοὺς βαρβάρους, ἀπὸ δέκα καὶ εἴκοσι σημείων ὄντα ἀπ᾽ ἀλλήλων. For the fortress camps and frontier troops along the *Strata Diocletiana*, see Fowden (1999): 20–21, 65–77; Thilo Ulbert, "Villes et fortifications de l'Euphrate à l'époque paléo-chrétienne (IVe–VIIe siècle)" in *Archeologie et Histoire de la Syrie*, ed. Jean-Marie Dentzer and W. Othman (Saarbrücken: Druckerlei und Verlag, 1989), 283–96; and August Brinkmann, "Der römische Limes im Orient," *Bonner Jahrbücher* 99 (1896): 252–57. Brinkmann notes that the Peutinger map gives 19 to 20 Roman miles between the fortresses. Sura to Resafa were 20 miles apart, with Tetrapyrgium halfway between. The *Strata* was a major caravan route to Emesa and Damascus. Its fortresses were built to monitor Bedouin movements and protect caravans from raids as well as for defense against Persia. The region may have seen fighting about the time that Alexander passed through: see O. J. Schrier, "Syriac Evidence for the Roman-Persian War of 421–422," *Greek, Roman, and Byzantine Studies* 33 (1992): 75–86, and below, sect. 34.

124. εἰς τὴν ἐσωτέραν ἔρημον, referring again to the "Persian desert" between the fortresses and the Euphrates: see Liebeschutz (1977).

125. Cf. Acts 10:20 (when soldiers were looking for Peter), "The Spirit said to him, 'Behold the three men who seek you. Now get up, go down and travel with them without hesitation, for I have sent them.'"

126. διὰ παντὸς τοῦ λιμίτου, i.e., along the *Strata Diocletiana*. Army camps and fortress towns were frequently noted as magnets for wandering holy men: e.g., Origen, *Contra Celsum* 7.9; Julian, *Or.* 7.224C; Paulinus of Nola, *Carmen* 24,328; Jerome also places his *remnuoth* in both cities *et castellis: Ep.* 22.34.

127. Cf. Eph 4:18, "[The Gentiles] are darkened in their minds, estranged from the life of God because of their ignorance and hardness of heart."

128. Identified by Gatier (1995): 452–54 with the fortress camp at Oresa (modern Tayibe) 62 miles northeast of Palmyra. The *Notitia Dignitatum* assigns it to the *Legio IIII Scythica*. The three-year drought brought by Alexander's curse is no doubt meant to recall the one brought by Elijah's curse (see above, sect. 12).

responsible out of the camp; and these in fright took refuge in the church, tearfully apologizing for their sinful act.

Seeing this and fearing lest they suffer the same, the rest of the throng approached the Roman bishops in order that they might supplicate the blessed Alexander on their behalf through letters, since they heard he had appeared in Antioch.[129] They were greatly alarmed at this, believing he had gone to Antioch to plead with the military commander[130] against them. When the bishops heard this they hastily wrote the blessed one, asking that he might petition God on the camp's behalf [685] and pity those who lived in it. When he received the letters and learned of the people's distress, the holy man cried out bitterly before the Lord, saying, "Who am I, my Lord, that You have so listened to me and caused evils for this innocent people? I will ever thank You, Master, for taking heed of me, a sinner. But now I beseech Your Mercy that You pity the poor and give them back the crops lost to three years of dearth, and let me know that I am Your servant."[131] Thus he prayed and dismissed the messengers with unstinting belief that God would act on his request, saying, "Brothers, go in the name of our Lord Jesus Christ."

And in accordance with his word, in the fourth year there arose at that camp a harvest such as had never been before. But afterwards God's wrath fell upon those pestilent ones responsible. For within a few days their children suddenly died, their livestock was seized by barbarians, and their houses were plundered by brigands, so that all were fully convinced that these calamities had befallen them because of the vexations they had caused the holy man.

35. The blessed one traversed the entire desert with his brothers ceaselessly singing their psalms. They came to the city of Solomon named in the Book of Kings, a city he built in the desert called Palmyra.[132] When its citizens observed from afar the multitude of brothers drawing near (and since they were, in fact, Jews, although they called themselves Christians), [686] they shut tight the city gates and said to one another, "Who can feed all these men? If they enter our city, we will all starve!" When the holy man observed this he glorified God by saying, "It is better to trust in God than to trust in men.[133] Take heart, brothers, that the Lord will visit us when we least expect it."

Then the barbarians who lived in those parts showed them unusual compassion. They had spent three days in the desert when, as the holy man had said, God sent them camel drivers who lived four staging posts' distance from the city,[134] all bearing

129. This probably refers to Alexander's sojourn in Antioch, described below (sect. 38–41). But sect. 40 also alludes to his presence there earlier under Bishop Porphyry (ca. 404–414): perhaps the trip mentioned here is related to that earlier visit.

130. στρατηλάτης, the *magister militum per Orientem* [supreme military commander for the eastern Roman provinces] whose headquarters were in Antioch.

131. Cf. Jas 5:17–18, "Elijah was human like us, and he prayed fervently that it not rain, and for three years and six months it did not rain on earth. Then he prayed again, and the heaven gave rain and the earth yielded its harvest."

132. Cf. 1 Kings 9:18.

133. Ps 118:8.

134. Escolan (1999): 216 suggests these camel drivers were Bedouins attached to caravanserais on the city outskirts, and that Alexander may have temporarily served as their preacher.

supplies. These they received and shared after giving thanks to God. There was so much in abundance that even after receiving their own portions they found themselves providing the city's poor with the things sent to them.

36. Certain earnest brothers wanted to make refreshments for their multitude of brothers in consolation for their recent affliction. So against his will they prepared various foods which they knew would be agreeable to the brothers. But Alexander wanted to teach them to transcend their sufferings; so when all the food had been carefully prepared, he suddenly took up the parchments of the holy Gospel and set off down the road in his habitual way, saying "Glory to God in the highest, and on earth peace, goodwill toward men" (for such was his habit whenever he wanted to move on). **[687]** He commanded them to touch none of the things prepared for them, so they left it all and went back on the road.

37. And after four days of travel they reached the place where his own brother by birth was archimandrite of a large brotherhood.[135] Alexander wanted to learn if he conducted himself according to the Gospel of the Lord. So taking just one brother he knocked on the door. The doorkeeper in the usual way said to him, "Be patient. First I will tell the abbot, then you can enter." But he did not wait. Instead he followed, wanting to see if the abbot would become angry with the brother. But his holy brother Peter (for that was his name), although it was the first time he had seen his true brother in thirty years, recognized him immediately—for it is natural to recognize one's own even when appearances are unclear. [Peter] fell down and embraced his feet, begging forgiveness for what had happened. But the blessed one reproached him harshly, saying, "Our father Abraham welcomed strangers and ministered to them himself,[136] and our Lord Jesus Christ laid down these same laws."[137] After shaking his cloak[138] he went on his way. The most holy Peter and all his brothers begged him in sorrow to stay just one day with them, but he did not consent. Instead, after teaching them this lesson about voluntary poverty and divine love,[139] he went off to Antioch.

38. The bishop of this city, Theodotus,[140] had come under the influence of some wicked and **[688]** hypocritical people (meaning *periodeutae*).[141] When he learned

---

135. Gatier (1995): 455 suggests this monastery was near Emesa.

136. Cf. Gen 18:1–2, "The Lord appeared to Abraham by the oaks of Mamre as he sat at the entrance of his tent in the heat of the day. He looked up and saw three men standing near. When he saw them, he ran from the tent entrance to meet them and bowed down to the ground."

137. Cf. Mt 25:35, "I was hungry and you let me eat, I was thirsty and you let me drink, I was a stranger and you welcomed me."

138. Cf. Lk 9:5, "Wherever they do not welcome you, as you are leaving shake the dust off your feet as a testimony against them."

139. By making Alexander wait at the monastery entrance Peter had failed to show proper hospitality or concern for a poor stranger. This section implies criticism of the careful screening that monastic leaders authorized for those who came to the door seeking alms: see *Regula magistri* 95 and Dietz (1997): 129–32.

140. Bishop of Antioch ca. 420–429.

141. The parenthese enclose a later gloss. *Periodeutae* were itinerant priests who performed liturgies and represented bishops in the countryside. They often would have been the only church officials to appear in villages outside Antioch at this time. For inscriptions reflect-

that the blessed Alexander had entered the city with a multitude of monks cease-lessly singing psalms, he cruelly ordered that they be driven out with blows and violent assaults. Those who took this as license abused the slaves of God without pity and chased them out. But the holy man perceived the devil's craft and secretly entered the city with his brothers around midnight. He found an ancient bathhouse and made their perpetual hymn-singing rise up in the usual way. When the bishop learned of their boldness[142] he was extremely vexed, but did not dare lay hands on them again. For he feared the people of the city, since they regarded the blessed man as one of the prophets, having seen and heard his marvelous deeds. For this reason they quit the church and devoted themselves to him instead, listening to his wondrous teachings.[143]

39. When Alexander saw he had liberty to speak with them all and that everyone listened to him gladly, and that they were ready to do the things he commanded, and that he had much honor and glory, he found the time opportune to take earnest care of the city's destitute poor. In this too the holy man's magnanimity must be admired. For though he was being chased from one place to another and possessed nothing at all, he was carried by zeal even to attend to the construction of a hospice. Assembling the city's wealthy citizens before him, he admonished them according to the divine wisdom he possessed and caused them to provide the things the hos-pice needed. With the great boldness of speech he possessed he also reproached both the military commander and the bishop **[689]** for many matters he felt they had neglected. Simply put, he became the teacher and tutor of all.

40. When the clergy saw these and similar things every day, they showed admiration to his face but were inwardly consumed with envy. A certain subdeacon and arrogant man named Malchus approached the bishop and said, "My authority in the courts was the one source of revenue I had,[144] and the monk Alexander has deprived me of this. Not only that, but he has also stripped the Church of its glory: our sudden discovery of this 'tutor' has made us a laughingstock to all. This is the conjurer who made the city rebel in our blessed father Porphyry's day and caused him countless evils.[145] This is the one who cast soot in the eyes of heretics.[146] This is the one who

---

ing their prominence in northwest Syria in the fourth and early fifth centuries, see Trombley (1994): 250, 254, 257–63.

142. παρρησία.

143. Cf. Acts 2:42 (at Pentecost), "They devoted themselves to the apostles' teaching and to their fellowship, in their breaking of bread and prayers."

144. μίαν ἐξουσίαν εἶχον τῶν δικῶν τὴν παραμυθίαν. For παραμυθία as "allowances drawn from church revenues," see Lampe, s.v. παραμυθία. The subdeacon Malchus is refering to his role in the episcopal lawcourts. By the early fifth century the clergy were being accused of using them for profit: Socrates, *HE* 7.37. This passage indicates that fees were collected from dis-putants in these courts just as in secular courts, *pace* John C. Lamoreaux, "Episcopal Courts in Late Antiquity," *JECS* 3 (1995): 152.

145. Bishop of Antioch ca. 404–414. These troubles may refer to the controversy over Porphyry's erasure of John Chrysostom's name from the diptychs at Antioch after the latter's exile from Constantinople in 404: see Palladius, *Dial.* 16; Sozomen, *HE* 8.24.

146. A method of publicly shaming someone. Ps.-Zachariah, *Chronicle* 3.8 describes how a zealous monk dumped dust and ash on the head of Juvenal, bishop of Jerusalem, after he sided with the Council of Chalcedon.

terrifies bishops and magistrates, perhaps even demons. Everywhere it is the same single-minded one.[147] This is the one who scorns death and makes troubles for everyone. Now he has come here, doing the same things. If he remains in this city, you can be sure that it will be uninhabitable for us, since we have already become a disgrace to all. I entreat your Angel that I be given license to drive him out of the city."

41. Once Malchus had received this license against him he set upon the blessed one with a multitude of pallbearers.[148] Seized by irrepressible rage he immediately gave Alexander a beating and said, "Get out of this city, law-breaker."[149] Like an innocent little lamb the blessed one meekly endured his audacity with no response **[690]** but this: "And the slave's name was Malchus."[150] Those present admired the man's wit when they heard this quick and ready remark. And though many had been sent against him, they could not harm the blessed one because of the people's exertions on his behalf. They reported this to the bishop, and after deliberating together they approached and petitioned the military commander, asking just one favor: that he exile the holy man to the city of Chalcis in Syria and expel from the city the brothers who were with him. But God, who loves mankind, turned their wickedness to his advantage, because by leaving Syria through divine dispensation the blessed one was destined to visit his spiritual children for the first time in twenty years.[151] After this came to pass he entered the city and strengthened everyone in the faith. He spent some time there guarded by the city's municipal slaves, since the magistrates feared him, and by the citizens, since they yearned to keep him. Aware of the wicked people's contrivance, he marveled at God's forbearance, and at the thwarting of their intention.

42. After some time he wished to go off again to a foreign land and renounce the world as he had done six times before.[152] But since the orders of the military commander prevented him from making an open exit, he changed his garb and went out by night dressed as one of the beggars. After many days on the road he came to a certain place where he found a monastery of men renowned for their piety. This was called the Barley Corn.[153] He went in, and after greeting them all **[691]**

147. μονότροπος, often used synonymously for "monk": see Guillaumont (1972b): 51–52.

148. μετὰ πλήθους λεκτικαρίων. These *lecticarii* were the Antiochene equivalent to the 600 *parabalani* [hospital attendants] and 950 *decani* [gravediggers or orderlies] used as muscle by the bishops of Alexandria and Constantinople at this time: see Jones (1964): 911.

149. παράνομε.

150. Cf. Jn 18:10 (Jesus' arrest at Gethsemane), "then Simon Peter drew the sword he had, struck the high priest's slave and cut off his right ear. And the slave's name was Malchus."

151. Alexander's departure from Syria suggests that he was visiting the monastery he left to Trophimus across the Euphrates in Osrhoene (sect. 31).

152. ἐβουλήθη πάλιν εἰς ξένον τόπον ἀπελθεῖν καὶ ἀποτάξασθαι ὁ ἕκτον ἀποταξάμενος. The biographer may be referring to the following six renunciations: Alexander's initial withdrawal to Elias' monastery (sect. 6), then to the Syrian desert (8); back again to the same desert (24–25); over to the desert east of the Euphrates (26); then to the "Persian desert" (31–32); then to the desert outside Palmyra (35–36).

153. τὸ Κριθήνιον. This monastery is otherwise unknown. It may have been named "Barley Corn" because barley was a main staple for slaves and the poor: see Hamel (1990): 34–35. Its probable location in western Asia Minor (perhaps near Constantinople) is indicated by two

he was amazed to see the condition and order of their way of life, and the great love the holy brothers displayed. Upon reflection he said, "I recognize this condition of living and their observances as my own in origin. But I wonder how they were spread into these parts. On all my travels I have seen nothing like it. Even the faces of their superiors are unknown to me." As he reflected on these things, he learned who had first organized the monastery in those regions and realized that it was one from his own flock. He praised God, who had displayed the fruits of his labors in those regions too. While approving their love and devotion, he set out again to hunt out those ensnared by the devil. When the most holy brothers saw the blessed man carefully questioning each one and saw him censuring the distraction of their garden as a possible impediment to perfect virtue,[154] they were stung to contrition by the Holy Spirit and knew that this truly was Alexander, the great shepherd of flocks endowed with reason, the one who cast light in regions of the East.

43. When he left, twenty-four of the brothers followed him as soldiers of Christ bearing the breastplate of righteousness, the helmet of salvation, and the sword of the Spirit,[155] asking that through him they too might be rendered blameless to Christ. When the blessed one saw the brothers' great devotion, **[692]** zeal, and faith, he pondered what this might mean, and he learned through the Holy Spirit that he was being summoned to a contest in those regions too. Roused by this thought he began to prepare himself by asking Christ that His will for him might soon be accomplished. God, who loves mankind, promptly answered his petitions. Having settled near the shrine of the holy martyr Menas,[156] within a few days there gathered round him noble athletes of Christ who were sound in their judgment from all the monasteries of those parts. Romans, Greeks, and Syrians: there were three races, and three hundred in number.[157] He divided these into six choruses to perform their ceaseless hymn-singing; he taught them voluntary poverty, and he arranged everything according to his original regimen; and within a short time he showed

---

phrases. First, Alexander is here for the first time identified as having been in the East (ὁ ἐν τοῖς ἀνατολικοῖς μέρεσι διαλάμψας; similarly Callinicus *V.Hypatii* 41.1 describes him at Constantinople as ἐλθὼν ἐκ τῆς ἀνατολῆς). Second, the biographer refers to the monastery's location as ἐν τοῖς μέρεσι ἐκείνοις (which Alexander reaches only many days after leaving Chalcis). In the next section that phrase clearly refers to Constantinople itself.

154. For similar criticism of a vegetable garden in the *Vita Barsaumae*, see Nau, "Résumé de monographies syriaques," *ROC* 8 (1913): 386.

155. Eph 6:14–17.

156. This is the only precise indication that Alexander is now in Constantinople. The shrine of St. Menas at this time was inside a former temple of Poseidon on the old Byzantine acropolis, in the Mangana district: see Dagron (1974): 376, 395. By living near it Alexander resorted to a practice that was common among the city's vagrant monks at least until 451: see Dagron (1970): 253–61 and above, ch. 6. Menas was an Egyptian martyr whose cult quickly spread around the Mediterranean East.

157. *Vita Marcelli* 4–5 (perhaps written in the mid-sixth century) states that Alexander came to the city in response to God's call when "the city was in need of such a teacher": see Dagron (1968): 290. The only details it provides are the names of three of his disciples there (Jacob, John, and Marcellus: John became the second Akoimēte leader, Marcellus the third). It also says he was visited by "many people from Bithynia" (i.e., across the Bosphorus) as well as imperial officials (*eparchikoi*), but it makes no reference to the troubles described here.

his followers to be equipped in every virtue. He introduced them to the foundation of their struggle,[158] for he appointed marshals to supervise them in their regimen in companies of ten and of fifty. And so at all hours they persevered in singing the glories of God.

44. When the urban masses observed their organized struggle, their perpetual hymn-singing, their absolute poverty, and the visible and quite wondrous performance of their prodigious mysteries, they came to Alexander with devotion as a true benefactor and teacher and were instructed by him about hope and the life to come. In a short time he had become a haven of salvation and a tutor of righteousness to all.[159] And if he himself kept silent, his way of life cried aloud and continuously rebuked those who [693] debased the commandments; and if these persisted unreformed, he used the bold speech he possessed to chasten them. But especially when [the people] saw their voluntary poverty, how great it was, and their strict discipline,[160] and that they possessed nothing more than the parchments on which they kept the holy Scriptures, and that they performed their hymn-singing without a pause, and that they lived in their bodies as if they had none, they were astounded, and glorified God for revealing His prodigious mysteries even in those regions. For as I said before, they held earthly things in contempt and took no concern for things of the present.

45. Certain faithless men tried to put [God's] grace to the test. They stayed with the brothers day and night, wanting to see how the slaves of God were supplied with food. For they saw that their daily food was always found ready without fail and that, after taking what sufficed for themselves, they would distribute the leftovers to the destitute poor, with no concern at all being taken for the next day. But since the blessed one knew through the Spirit what they were thinking he said to the brother who attended him, "Go out and receive the things sent by our Master," though no one was knocking at their door. But before he reached the door there came a man dressed in white vestment, knocking hard. When the brother opened the door he found a basket filled with fresh, warm loaves of bread, but did not see the one who had knocked—for an angel of God had produced the man with the bread and had gone away. Therefore, the brother said to the man who had come, "Who sent you here?" and he replied, "As I was taking the loaves out of my oven [694] a very tall man dressed in white appeared beside me and urgently pressed me, saying, 'Take all that bread to the slaves of the Most High.' Since I did not know where to go, he made me follow him here. It was he who knocked on your door, but now he has disappeared."

After hearing these things the brother reported them to his blessed abbot. The brothers were already sitting at their tables. The saintly Alexander took the warm bread and served it up; when they had enjoyed it with thanks, they gave the leftovers to their brothers, the destitute poor. And they were astounded by the great liberality

158. τὸν θεμέλιον τοῦ ἀγῶνος.

159. Θεωροῦντες δὲ οἱ ὄχλοι τῆς πόλεως τὸν ἀγῶνα συσταθέντα, καὶ τὴν ἀκατάπαυστον ὑμνολογίαν, καὶ τὴν τελείαν ἀκτημοσύνην, καὶ τὰ παράδοξα μυστήρια . . . ἐπιτελούμενα, καὶ ἀληθῶς ὡς πρὸς εὐεργέτην καὶ διδάσκαλον οὕτως προθύμως ἤρχοντο . . . γέγονε . . . παιδαγωγὸς δικαιοσύνης.

160. τὴν τηλικαύτην αὐτῶν ἀκτημοσύνην καὶ ἀκρίβειαν.

of the man, seeing that in accordance with the Scripture he showed no care for tomorrow. In order to make the brothers believers, he summoned the man who had come among them and made them hear everything from his own mouth. In this way the brothers' souls were bound to him with love and awe. And he did these things not because he wished to glorify himself, but because they were about to enter a contest. He was training them and strengthening the faith in their souls first, so they would not expire through lack of faith when they entered the central arena.

46. I will describe a few of his many miracles that were made visible even to the multitude; for in this way I want to prove how this noble athlete became a second Moses, faithful to God in all his house. The blessed one was in the habit of using new disciples to represent him on monastery business,[161] but it happened that one of these was living promiscuously in the city off the resources [695] that God the Master had dispensed to the brothers. Knowing this through the Spirit, the blessed one confronted and reproached him in cryptic fashion, for he said to him in local language[162] just this: "Thief." Then he kept silent, wanting to see if this remark would make him turn to repentance and confess his sin. Nor did he make a fuss about the matter, lest the enemy of truth destroy [the brother] through shame. But the brother did not fully realize his father knew about his sin; instead he took the remark as a joke and persisted in the same activities.

The holy shepherd lamented for him and petitioned God on his behalf. Wanting to show he had known all about the previous sin, he found a suitable occasion to punish [the brother] and drive him from his sight. But Satan hardened his heart once again, and he refused to make amends. After three days he grew contrite and ashamed of himself and wanted to atone for his punishment. The blessed one instantly recognized through the Spirit that the brother was having these thoughts. He said to the [monk] attending him, "Go tell the brother, 'Since your heart has softened and you have repented, you are released from your punishment.'" When he heard this the brother truly understood from the portent of this second notice that [Alexander] had known about his previous sin as well, and with tears he apologized for that sin too. Thus saved, the brother thereafter followed in the footsteps of his teacher.

47. I want to describe another portent that surpassed human nature. The blessed one had foresight [696] to make a potion[163] for brothers who were sick. They had clay pots that he had set in the ground to keep hot. He assigned four brothers to take turns in attending them each day. But one day there occurred a lapse, or rather, the Lord allowed a lapse to happen in order to make His slave manifest to all. On

---

161. τὰς ἀποκρίσεις διὰ τῶν νέων μαθητῶν ποεῖσθαι. Here ἀποκρίσεις must refer to the duties of an *apocrisiarius*, a deputy used to deal with outside monastery business.

162. ἐπιχωρίῳ λόγῳ. Gatier (1995): 440 and others consider this evidence that the *V.Alex* was originally written in Syriac, with its author here seeking to clarify that Alexander used the language of Constantinople, i.e., Greek.

163. εὐκρατίον. Theodore the Studite, the late-eighth-century abbot of the Studite monastery in Constantinople (which received rules from the Akoimēte monastery in the fifth century) uses this word for a Lenten beverage made from pepper, cumin, and anise (specifically *not* taken by the sick or old): see PG 99.1716B.

that day no one tended the pots, but after washing and filling them with cold water in the morning, they left them. But now when the hour of need arrived and compelled them to remember, they were ashamed even to look at their brothers and did not dare approach and tell their abbot. But one of them took courage and approached him, saying, "We have no wood and did not make the hot water." When he heard this the blessed one said, "Why did you not remember in the morning? But I see—you want to test me. Go back and you will have hot water." Though dubious, they went and found the pots boiling, though it was evident that nothing at all had been put underneath [to heat] them that day. This again made the brothers marvel at the man's faith.

These select miracles I have set forth so that from a few we might believe the many others, and so that we might believe all things were possible for him because he was perfect in faith.

48. The enemy could not bear to see Alexander's service so well performed with God's aid, or his disciples advancing in the faith, exulting in their psalms, hymns, and spiritual songs and living in peace. So he advanced against the noble athlete as if in a pitched battle between enemies. [697] For enemies while at first still distant attack each other with arrows; then with one accord they rush upon each other with swords, and victory falls to the stronger side. So, too, did the enemy of truth proceed. For although he had made war against the valiant man for fifty years, he had not been able to break him down, but the war had always turned back upon his own head.[164] Now at last he came at him with his whole demonic army. Having summoned the human populace to his alliance, he flung his shaft against the slave of God once more.

At that time it was reported to the prefects that "the monk Alexander is a heretic and wants to corrupt God's church."[165] But while the blessed one nobly held out through his prayers, they could not withstand even his shadow, as the saying goes. For it is the nature of falsehood to be overcome by truth; and, to tell the truth in figurative terms, righteousness weathered the storm.[166] The blessed Alexander stood by naked in appearance but fully equipped in determination. And though the human populace had been moved against him by the devil, the slave of God kept saying to himself the words of the divine Scriptures: "Rulers sat and railed against me, but your slave kept meditating upon your decrees. For your testimonies are my study, your decrees my counsels. I have stuck by your testimonies, Lord. Do not put me to shame."[167] [698]

49. Then the enemy of truth stood before him and shouted, "Slave of God, why are you punishing me before my time? I have my own Master and Judge." Then the appointed jurists, not making a righteous decision, passed sentence against the great judge.[168] This they did so that, once released, he would be torn to shreds by the

164. Cf. Ps 7:16: "His mischief shall return upon his own head, and his violence shall come down on his own pate."

165. αἱρετικός ἐστιν καὶ βούλεται λυμᾶναι τὴν ἐκκλησίαν τοῦ θεοῦ. For this charge, see ch. 4.

166. εἰπεῖν ἐν τοῖς ἀδήλοις, ἡ δικαιοσύνη χειμάζεται. I have followed Baguenard's translation, "dire la vérité de manière figurée."

167. Ps. 119:23–25.

168. οἱ οὖν καταστάντες δικασταί, τὴν δικαίαν κρίσιν μὴ καταλαβόντες, ἐπὶ τὸν μέγαν κριτὴν

people and the champions of the devil. Yet he passed through their midst[169] encouraged by God's protection. For the Lord's terror fell upon them, and their resolve broke down. Petitions had risen from the holy brothers to God on his behalf, and what happened in the holy apostles' time happened this time too. For in both cases God Himself was acting with them.[170]

50. Although this battle had been brought to an end through the power of Christ, the enemy of truth did not stay quiet, but made every effort to stop their incessant hymn-singing since it had been raised against him. He devised a means by which he thought he might finally be able to end it. Mindful how countries and cities are often betrayed by their own people, the enemy advanced against the blessed one in this way, enlisting as allies men of his own kind to help take him away.[171] They seized the blessed Alexander and his holy brothers, threw chains around them, and inflicted on them a cruel beating. Then for a few days their incessant hymn-singing was interrupted, [699] and sorrow truly rose among the brothers and the holy powers. For those who had previously been these brothers' shepherds were each ordered to take back his own.

51. God's slave Alexander alone was released, or so they thought—but he was not alone, since he had Christ with him. And after his release all the brothers gathered together with one accord as if summoned by a trumpet.[172] They resumed their service to God and the same regimen that very day, as though nothing had happened at all; in fact, they exulted all the more, as if they had discovered a spiritual treasure. And as they advanced in the Lord many other brothers joined their ranks. Should anyone wish to traverse the whole earth under heaven—not just the land of the Romans but that of the barbarians too—you will find this blessed one's disciples flourishing. For at that time they established the famous monastery of the

---

ἐδικαίωσαν. Theokritoff follows the common biblical usage of δικαιόω by translating "failing to reach a just verdict, justified him before the great Judge [i.e., God]." But μέγαν κριτὴν probably refers to Alexander, not God: John Climacus, *Scala paradisi* 5 (PG 88.772B) specifically uses the title τὸν κριτὴν τὸν μέγαν to designate a venerable abbot in charge of his monks' souls.

169. Cf. Lk 4:29–30 (Jesus' rejection at Nazareth), "They cast him out of the city and led him to . . . the hill on which their city was built in order to throw him down. But passing through their midst he went on his way."

170. Cf. *Acts* 12:5–18 (when Peter is imprisoned by Herod, the apostles pray for him; God sends an angel to break his chains and lead him out in disguise; having escaped from prison, Peter returns to the apostles while Herod searches for him in vain).

171. ὁμόφυλοι: "men of the same race, tribe, stock" corresponding to the aforementioned συμφυλέτοί who betray their own communities. Since the people (δῆμος) of Constantinople have already turned against Alexander (sect. 48, 49) the kinship here seems to be one of vocation, i.e., other abbots or monks in the city. But it could also be those who gave orders to the abbots to "take back their own," i.e., church officials. These events must somehow relate to those described by Callinicus, *V.Hypatii* 41.4–10 (see ch. 4), though Callinicus does not mention abbots or monks, but credits the assaults on Alexander first to a mob (who drove them out of Constantinople), then to a group of martyr-shrine attendants, beggars, factory workers, and clerics sent by the bishop of Chalcedon against them.

172. Cf. Callinicus, *V.Hypatii* 41.18.

Sleepless Ones *[Akoimētōn]* and many other very large ones. These are visible to all like the sun in the sky.[173]

52. If we were to recount the virtues of this noble athlete one by one, then as the blessed Apostle Paul has said, "Time would fail me to tell."[174] For who might be so great or honored by such inspiration as to be able to describe his fifty-year struggle in detail? Perhaps those who lack faith and hate goodness will think I have said some things that are impossible, **[700]** exaggerated, and beyond human nature. That is because they are utterly bound to the flesh. But those who have faith, who think like us and regard their neighbors' goods as their own, will accept that we are telling the truth. For they trust what the Lord promised when his disciples marveled at the withering of the fig-tree: "Not only will you do the things I do, but you will do things even greater than these,"[175] and again, "All things are possible to one who believes."

But we ourselves know that the highest portent of all is the right way of living this perfect teacher attained. Therefore let us end our account here, where he, too, finished his life. In his fifty years of ascetic practice this blessed one never took pause from affliction, persecution, nakedness, hunger, or thirst. Even in these he rejoiced and boldly taught the word of truth, gathering many people together and delivering them to Christ, just as his disciples do to this day. Through these deeds he shone forth and came to a blessed and carefree end that relieved him of his toils. He fell asleep in saintly fashion and is buried in the regions of Bithynia, at a place called Gomon.[176]

53. After his departure from life, his disciples multiplied through his intercessions and gained prominence, as I have said, not only in those regions but everywhere in creation. For after the leaders of their brotherhood had established the monastery we mentioned before—a monastery worthy of his conduct called "of the Sleepless Ones" on account **[701]** of their ceaseless doxology that never sleeps—they translated his holy and blessed relics there.[177] And his saintly relics have worked miracles

---

173. This describes an expansion and prominence that did not arise until Marcellus became abbot (ca. 430/448–484). According to *V. Marcelli* 12–14, the brotherhood was joined by a senator's son named Pharetrius, whose wealth Marcellus used first to build up Akoimēte facilities at Eirenaion (see below, n. 177), then to propagate its rules and liturgical style εἰς πᾶσαν τὴν οἰκουμένην. By the late fifth century the Eirenaion monastery reportedly housed a thousand monks. After the Council of Chalcedon (451) the monastery's vigorous opposition to monophysitism exposed it to charges of Nestorianism, especially in the sixth century, when it opposed Emperor Justinian's compromise "theopascite" doctrine. In 534 Justinian pressed for its condemnation by John II (Bishop of Rome, 533–535), but it provided a patriarch for Jerusalem in 583. Its existence is still attested in the thirteenth century. See Ps.-Zachariah, *Chronicle* 7.7; also Baguenard (1988): 219–40 and Dagron (1968): 270–76.

174. Cf. Heb 11:32–33.

175. Cf. Jn 14:12.

176. *V. Marcelli* 4 describes Gomon as being toward the mouth of the Black Sea. Janin (1964): 485 suggests its identification with modern Anadoloufeneri, about 18 miles north of Istanbul.

177. *V. Marcelli* 7 describes how the Akoimēte monastery's second leader (John) moved

every day, so that God, who loves mankind, might show even there that "He will honor those who honor Him"[178] and that all the blessed one's acts were performed according to God's will. Impure spirits cannot bear to hear his name, but are scorched by its sound as if by fire.

54. With brotherly love and affection we have [recorded] in our unskilled way what we observed, concerned only for truth. We hope by the Lord that others who are moved by the Holy Spirit and are more learned in these matters than we are will tell them more clearly, for the edification and profit of those who wish to pursue this way of life. May we all become disciples worthy of him [Alexander], and may we attain through his intercessions those things which he now enjoys by the grace and goodwill of our Lord Jesus Christ, for whom is the glory to the ages of ages, Amen.

---

the brotherhood soon after Alexander's death to Eirenaion (modern Tchubuklu) about 8 miles north of Constantinople on the eastern (Bithynian) shore of the Bosphorus.

178. Cf. 1 Sam 2:30.

SELECT BIBLIOGRAPHY

PRIMARY SOURCES

Acts of Thomas [ATh]. Coptic version. Ed. with French trans. Paul-Hubert Poirier, *La version copte de la Prédication et du Martyre de Thomas*. SH 67. Brussels: Société des Bollandistes, 1984.

———. Greek version. Ed. Maximilian Bonnet and R. A. Lipsius, *Acta Apostolorum Apocrypha* 2.2. Leipzig: Mendelsson, 1903; repr. Hildesheim: Georg Olms, 1959. Trans. H. J. W. Drijvers in *New Testament Apocrypha*. 2d. ed. Vol. 2, 339–411. Ed. Edgar Hennecke, Wilhelm Schneemelcher, and Robert McL. Wilson. Westminster: John Knox Press, 1992.

———. Syriac version. Ed. and trans. A. F. J. Klijn, *The Acts of Thomas. Introduction, Text, Commentary*. Supplements to Novum Testamentum 5. Leiden: Brill, 1962.

Ambrose. *De officiis ministrorum*. PL 16:23A–184B.

Antony. *Epistulae*. Ed. and trans. Samuel Rubenson, *The Letters of St. Antony: Monasticism and the Making of a Saint*. Studies in Antiquity and Christianity. Minneapolis: Fortress Press, 1995.

Aphrahat. *Demonstratio* 6. PS 1:239–312. Ed. with French trans. Jean Parisot. Paris: Firmin-Didot (1894). Trans. John Gwynn, *Aphrahat: Select Demonstrations*. NPNF 13.2 2d series. Grand Rapids: Eerdmans, 1956.

Apophthegmata Patrum. Ethiopic Collection [Eth.Coll.]. Ed. with Latin trans. Victor Arras, *Collectio Monastica*. CSCO 238–39. Scriptores Aethiopici 45–46. Louvain: Secrétariat du CorpusSCO, 1963.

———. Greek Alphabetical Collection [G]. PG 65:72A–440D. Supplementary material [S] ed. Jean-Claude Guy, *Recherches sur la tradition grecque des Apophthegmata Patrum*. SH 36. Brussels: Société des Bollandistes, 1984. Trans. Benedicta Ward, *The Sayings of the Desert Fathers*. CS 59. Kalamazoo: Cistercian Publications, 1984.

———. Greek Anonymous Collection [N]. Ed. François Nau, "Histoires des solitaires égyptiens (MS Coislin 126, fol.158f.)." *ROC* 12 (1907): 43–68, 171–81, 393–404. *ROC* 13 (1908): 47–57, 266–83. *ROC* 14 (1909): 357–79. *ROC* 17

(1912): 204–11, 294–301. *ROC* 18 (1913): 137–46. Trans. Columba Stewart, *The World of the Desert Fathers*. Kalamazoo: Cistercian Publications, 1986.

———. Latin Systematic Collection [PJ]. PL 73:855A–1022B.

———. Syriac Collection. *Paradisus patrum*. Ed. Paul Bedjan, *Acta martyrum et sanctorum*, vol. 7. Paris: Harassowitz, 1897; repr. Hildesheim: Georg Olms, 1968. Trans. Ernest A. Wallis-Budge, *The Wit and Wisdom of the Christian Fathers of Egypt: The Syrian Version of the Apophthegmata Patrum by 'Ānān Īshō' of Bēth 'Ābhe*. London: Oxford University Press, 1934.

Athanasius. *Vita Antonii*. Ed. with French trans. G. J. M. Bartelink, *Athanase d'Alexandrie: Vie d'Antoine*. SC 400. Paris: Éditions du Cerf, 1994.

Athanasius, Pseudo. Ed. and trans. Wilhelm Reidel and W. E. Crum, *The Canons of Athanasius, Patriarch of Alexandria*. Text and Translation Society 9. London: William and Norgate 1904; repr. Amsterdam: Philo Press, 1973.

Augustine. *Contra Faustum*. Ed. Joseph Zycha, *S. Aureli Augustini scripta contra Manichaeos*. CSEL 25.1. Vienna: F. Tempsky; Leipzig: G. Freytag, 1891.

———. *Contra Gaudentium*. Ed. Michael Petschenig, *S. Aureli Augustini scripta contra Donatistas*. CSEL 53.3. Vienna: F. Tempsky, 1908.

———. *De moribus ecclesiae catholicae et moribus manichaeorum*. Ed. John K. Coyle, *Augustine's "De moribus ecclesiae catholicae": A Study of the Work, Its Composition, and Its Sources*. Paradosis 25. Fribourg: University Press, 1978.

———. *De opere monachorum*. Ed. Joseph Zycha, *S. Aureli Augustini De fide et symbolo*, etc. CSEL 41. Vienna: F. Tempsky, 1900. Trans. Mary Muldowney in *St. Augustine: Treatises on Various Subjects*, ed. Roy J. Deferrari. Fathers of the Church 16. New York: Fathers of the Church, 1952.

———. *Enarratio in Psalmum CXXXII*. PL 37:1729–1736.

———. *Retractationes*. Ed. Almut Mutzenbecher. CCSL 57. Turnhout: Brepols, 1984.

Babylonian Talmud. See *Pe'ah*, below.

Barḥadbeshabba 'Arbaya. *Historia ecclesiastica [HE]* (part 2). Ed. with French trans. François Nau, *La seconde partie de l'Histoire de Barhadbesabba 'Arbaïa*. PO 9:501–667. Paris: Firmin Didot, 1913.

Basil of Caesarea. *Epistulae*. Ed. and trans. Roy J. Deferrari and Martin R. P. McGuire, *St. Basil: Letters*. LCL 190, 215, 243, 270. Cambridge: Harvard University Press, 1970–1987.

———. *Homilia in Psalmum XXXIII*. PG 29.349B–385C. Trans. Agnes Clare Way in *Saint Basil: Exegetic Homilies*. Fathers of the Church 46. Washington, D.C.: Catholic University Press, 1963.

———. *Regulae brevius tractatae [RB]*. PG 31:1080A–1305B. Trans. W. K. Lowthar Clarke, *The Ascetic Works of Saint Basil*. London: S.P.C.K., 1925.

———. *Regulae fusius tractatae [RF]*. PG 31:889A–1052C. Trans. W. K. Lowthar Clarke, *The Ascetic Works of Saint Basil*. London: S.P.C.K., 1925.

Benedict of Nursia. *Regula Santi Benedicti*. Ed. and trans. Timothy Fry et al., *RB 1980: The Rule of St. Benedict in Latin and English with Notes*. Collegeville, Minn.: Liturgical Press, 1981.

Callinicus. *Vita Hypatii*. Ed. with French trans. G. J. M. Bartelink, *Callinicus: Vie d'Hypatios*. SC 177. Paris: Éditions du Cerf, 1971.

Chalcedon, Council. *Acta*. Ed. Eduard Schwartz in *Acta Conciliorum Oecumenicorum [ACO]*. Vol.2: *Concilium universale Chalcedonense*. Berlin and Leipzig: Walter de

Gruyter, 1924–1935. French trans. André-Jean Festugière, *Actes du Concile de Chalcédoine: Sessions III–VI (La Définition de la Foi)*. Cahiers d'Orientalisme 4. Geneva, 1983. *Canons*. Ed. Périclès-Pierre Joannou, *Fonti. Fascicolo IX: Discipline générale antique (IVᵉ–IXᵉ s.)*. Vol.1.1: *Les canons des conciles oecuméniques*. Rome: Tipografia Italo-Orientale "S. Nilo," 1962.

Clement, Pseudo. *Epistolae ad virgines/de virginitate [EV]*. PG 1:379A–452B. Latin trans. T. Beelen, *Patres Apostolici*. 2.2, ed. F. X. Funk. Tübingen, 1901. Trans. B. P. Pratten, *Two Epistles Concerning Virginity*. ANF 8. Grand Rapids: Eerdmans, 1978.

———. *Recognitiones*. Ed. Bernard Rehm; revised Georg Strecker, *Die Pseudoklementinen II: Recognitionen in Rufins Übersetzung*. GCS. Berlin: Akademie Verlag, 1994.

Codex Theodosianus [CTh]. Ed. Theodor Mommsen and P. M. Meyer, *Theodosiani Libri XVI cum Constitutionibus Sirmondianis et Leges novellae ad Theodosianum pertinentes*. Berlin: Weidmann, 1954. Trans. Clyde Pharr, *The Theodosian Code and Novels and the Sirmondian Constitutions*. Princeton: Princeton University Press, 1952.

Constitutiones Apostolorum [Const.App.]. Ed. with French trans. Marcel Metzger, *Les constitutiones apostoliques*. SC 320, 329, 336. Paris: Éditions du Cerf, 1985–1987.

Consultationes Zacchaei et Apollonii. Ed. with French trans. Jean Louis Feiertag and Werner Steinmann, *Questions d'un païen à un chrétien (Consultationes Zacchaei christiani et Apollonii philosophi)*. SC 401, 402. Paris: Éditions du Cerf, 1994.

Corpus iuris civilis. Vol. 2: *Codex Iustinianus [CJ]*, ed. Paul Krüger. Vol. 3: *Novellae*, Ed. Rudolf Schoell and Wilhelm Kroll. Berlin: Weidmann, 1963.

Cyril of Alexandria. *Epistolae I–LVIII*. PG 77:9A–321D.

———. *Epistula LXXXII*. PG 77:376A.

———. *Letter to Calosirius [Ep 83]*. Ed. and trans. Lionel Wickham, *Cyril of Alexandria. Select Letters*. Oxford: Clarendon Press, 1983.

Cyril of Jerusalem. *Catechesis* 6. PG 33:538A–604A.

Didache. Ed. with French trans. Willy Rordorf and André Tuilier, *La Doctrine des Douze Apôtres (Didachè)*. SC 248. Paris: Éditions du Cerf, 1978.

Egeria. *Itinerarium*. Ed. with French trans. Pierre Maraval, *Égérie: Journal de voyage (Itinére)*. SC 296. 2d ed. Paris: Éditions du Cerf, 1997.

Ephesus, First Council of. *Acta*. Ed. Eduard Schwartz, *Acta Conciliorum Oecumenicorum [ACO]*. Vol.1: *Concilium universale Ephesenum*. Berlin and Leipzig: Walter de Gruyter, 1924–1935.

Ephrem. *Homily on Admonition and Repentence*. Trans. A. Edward Johnston, *Three Homilies of Ephraem*. NPNF 13.2. 2d series. Grand Rapids: Eerdmans, 1956.

Ephrem, Pseudo. *On Hermits and Desert Dwellers*. Trans. Joseph P. Amar in *Ascetic Behavior in Greco-Roman Antiquity: A Sourcebook*, ed. Vincent L. Wimbush. Minneapolis: Fortress Press, 1990.

———. *Sermo* 16. *De peregrinatione*. Ed. with Latin trans. Stefan Assemani, *Sancti Ephraem Syri Opera Omnia*. Vol. 3, 650E–651F. Rome: Typographia Pontificia Vaticana, 1743.

Epiphanius of Salamis. *Ancoratus*. Ed. Karl Holl, *Epiphanius Werke*. Vol. 1. GCS 25. Leipzig: J. C. Hinrichs'sche, 1910.

———. *Panarion*. Ed. Karl Holl, revised Jürgen Dummer, *Epiphanius Werke*. 2 vols. GCS. Berlin: Akademie Verlag, 1980, 1985.

Eugippius. *Regula.* Ed. Fernand Villegas and Adalbert de Vogüé, *Eugippii Regula.* CSEL 87. Vienna: F. Tempsky, 1976.

Eusebius of Caesarea. *Historia ecclesiastica [HE].* Ed. with French trans. Gustave Bardy, *Histoire ecclésiastique et les martyrs en Palestine.* SC 31, 41, 55, 73. Paris: Cerf, 1952–1960.

Evagrius of Pontus. *Ad monachos.* Ed. Hugo Gressmann with trans. Jeremy Driscoll in *The "Ad monachos" of Evagrius Ponticus: Its Structure and a Select Commentary.* Studia Anselmiana 104. Rome: Abbazia S. Paolo, 1991.

———. *Antirrheticus.* Ed. with Greek retroversion Wilhelm Frankenberg, *Euagrius Ponticus.* Abhandlungen der königlichen Gesellschaft der Wissenschaften zu Göttingen, Philologisch-historische Klasse, n.F. 13.2. Berlin: Weidmann, 1912.

———. *De malignis cogitationibus.* PG 79:1199D–1233A.

———. *De octo spiritibus malitiae.* PG 79:1145A–1164D.

———. *Epistulae.* Ed. with Greek retroversion Wilhelm Frankenberg, *Euagrius Ponticus.* Abhandlungen der königlichen Gesellschaft der Wissenschaften zu Göttingen, Philologisch-historische Klasse, n.F. 13.2. Berlin: Weidmann, 1912.

———. *Practicus.* Ed. with French trans. Antoine and Claire Guillaumont, *Évagre le Pontique: Traité pratique ou le moine.* SC 170, 171. Paris: Éditions du Cerf, 1971. Trans. John E. Bamberger, *Evagrius Ponticus: The Praktikos and Chapters on Prayer.* CS 4. Kalamazoo: Cistercian Publications, 1978.

———. *Tractatus ad Eulogium.* PG 79:1093C–1140A.

Evagrius Scholasticus. *Historia ecclesiastica [HE].* Ed. Joseph Bidez and Léon Parmentier, *The Ecclesiastical History of Evagrius with the Scholia.* London, 1898; repr. Amsterdam: A. M. Hakkert, 1964.

Gangra, Synod. *Epistula synodica.* Ed. Périclès-Pierre Joannou, *Fonti. Fascicolo IX: Discipline générale antique (IVᵉ–IXᵉ s.).* Vol.1.2: *Les canons des synodes particuliers.* Rome: Tipografia Italo-Orientale "S. Nilo," 1962.

Gerontius. *Vita Melaniae Junioris.* Ed. with French trans. Denys Gorce, *Vie de Sainte Mélanie.* SC 90. Paris: Éditions du Cerf, 1962. Trans. Elizabeth A. Clark, *The Life of Melania the Younger: Introduction, Translation, and Commentary.* Studies in Women and Religion 14. New York: Edwin Mellen Press, 1984.

Gospel of Thomas. Trans. Thomas O. Lambdin in *The Nag Hammadi Library in English,* ed. James M. Robinson and Richard Smith. 3d ed. San Francisco: Harper and Row, 1988.

Greek New Testament. Ed. Kurt Aland, Matthew Black, Carlo Martini, Bruce Metzger, and Allen Wikgren. 3d ed. Stuttgart: Biblia-Druck, 1983.

Gregory of Nazianzus. *In monachorum obstrectatores et ad falsi nominis monachos.* PG 37: 1349A–1353A.

———. *Oratio 21. In laudem Athanasii.* PG 35:1081A–1128C.

Gregory of Nyssa. *De instituto christiano.* Ed. Reinhart Staats, *Makarios-Symeon: Epistola Magna. Eine messalianische Mönchsregel und ihre Umschrift in Gregors von Nyssa "De instituto christiano."* Abhandlungen der Akademie der Wissenschaften in Göttingen, Philologische-historische Klasse, F. 3.134. Göttingen: Vandenhoeck und Ruprecht, 1984.

———. *De pauperibus amandis.* Ed. A. van Heck, *Gregorii Nysseni De pauperibus amandis orationes II.* Leiden: Brill, 1964.

————. *De virginitate*. Ed. with French trans. Michel Aubineau, *Grégoire de Nysse: Traité de la Virginité*. SC 119. Paris: Éditions du Cerf, 1966.

Historia monachorum in Aegypto [HM]. Greek version. Ed. André-Jean Festugière, *Historia monachorum in Aegypto*. SH 34. Brussels: Société des Bollandistes, 1961. Trans. Norman Russell, *The Lives of the Desert Fathers*. CS 34. Kalamazoo: Cistercian Publications, 1981.

————. Latin version. Ed. Eva Schulz-Flügel, *Tyrannius Rufinus. Historia monachorum sive De vita sanctorum patrum*. PTS 34. Berlin: Walter de Gruyter, 1990. Trans. Norman Russell, *The Lives of the Desert Fathers*. CS 34. Kalamazoo: Cistercian Publications, 1981.

Isaac of Antioch. *On the Perfection of Monks*. German trans. Simon K. Landersdorfer, *Ausgewählte Schriften der Syrischen Dichter: Cyrillonas, Baläus, Isaak von Antiochien und Jacob von Sarug*. Munich: Kösel, 1913.

Isaiah of Scetis. *Asceticon*. Ed. with French trans. René Draguet, *Les cinq recensions de l'Ascéticon syriaque d'Abba Isaïe*. Vol.1: *Les témoins et leurs parallèles non-syriaques. Édition des logoi I–XIII*. Vol.2: *Édition des logoi XIV–XXVI*. CSCO 289–90. Scriptores Syri 120–21. Louvain: Secrétariat du CorpusCSO, 1968.

Isidore of Pelusium. *Epistulae*. PG 78:177A–1646D.

Jerome. *Dialogus adversus Pelagianos*. Ed. C. Moreschini. CCSL 80. Turnhout: Brepols, 1990.

————. *Epistula 22*. Text and trans. by F. A. Wright, *Select Letters of St. Jerome*. LCL 262. Cambridge: Harvard University Press, 1933.

————. *Epistula 60*. Ed. and trans. J. H. D. Scourfield, *Consoling Heliodorus: A Commentary on Jerome, Letter 60*. Oxford: Clarendon Press, 1993.

————. *Vita Hilarionis*. PL 23:29–54.

John Cassian. *Collationes patrum xxvi*. Ed. with French trans. E. Pichery, *Jean Cassien: Conférences*. SC 42, 54, 64. Paris: Éditions du Cerf, 1955–1959. Trans. Boniface Ramsey, *John Cassian: The Conferences*. ACW 57. New York: Paulist Press, 1997.

————. *De institutis coenobiorum et de octo principalium vitiorum remediis libri xii*. Ed. with French trans. Jean-Claude Guy, *Jean Cassien: Institutions cénobitiques*. SC 109. Paris: Éditions du Cerf, 1965.

John Chrysostom. *Adversus oppugnatores vitae monasticae*. PG 47:319–386.

————. *Catecheses ad illuminandos*. Ed. with French trans. Antoine Wenger, *Huit catéchèses baptismales inédites*. SC 50. Paris: Éditions du Cerf, 1957.

————. *De eleemosyna homilia*. PG 51:261–272.

————. *De Lazaro homiliae*. PG 48:963–1054.

————. *De sacerdotio*. Ed. with French trans. Anne-Marie Malingrey, *Jean Chrysostome: Sur le sacerdoce*. SC 272. Paris: Éditions du Cerf, 1980.

————. *De statuis homiliae*. PG 49:15–222.

————. *De suo reditu post reditum a priore exilio*. PG 52:439–442.

————. *In Acta Apostolorum homiliae*. PG 60:13–384.

————. *In epistulas ad Corinthios homiliae*. PG 61:299–392.

————. *In epistulam ad Ephesios homiliae*. PG 62:11–176.

————. *In epistulam ad Hebraeos homiliae*. PG 63:9–236.

————. *In epistulas ad Thessalonicenses homiliae*. PG 62:392–500.

————. *In epistulam I ad Timotheum homiliae*. PG 62:501–600.

————. *In Johannem homiliae.* PG 59:23–482.

————. *In Matthaeum homiliae.* PG 57:21–472; 58:473–794.

John Chrysostom, Pseudo. *De eleemosyna homilia.* PG 64:433C–444B.

John Climacus. *Scala paradisi.* PG 88:632A–1164D.

John of Damascus. *Liber de haeresibus.* Ed. Boniface Kötter, *Die Schiften des Johannes von Damaskos.* Vol. 4: *Liber de haeresibus.* PTS 22. Berlin: Walter De Gruyter, 1981.

John of Ephesus. *Lives of the Eastern Saints.* Ed. and trans. E. W. Brooks, PO 17:1–304; 18:513–697; 19:153–227. Paris: Firmin-Didot, 1923–1924, 1926.

John Moschus. *Pratum spirituale.* PG 87.3:2852A–3112B.

John Rufus. *Plerophoriae.* Ed. with French trans. François Nau, *Plérophories: Témoignages et révélations contre le Concile de Chalcédon.* PO 8:1–208. Paris: Firmin-Didot, 1912.

————. *Vita Petri Iberi.* Ed. with German trans. Richard Raabe, *Petrus der Iberer. Ein Charakterbild zur Kirchen- und Sittengeschichte des fünften Jahrhunderts.* Leipzig: J. C. Hinrichs'sche, 1895.

Julian. *Contra Galileos.* Ed. and trans. Wilmer C. Wright, *The Works of the Emperor Julian.* Vol. 3. LCL 157. Cambridge: Harvard University Press, 1959.

————. *Oratio 7.* Ed. and trans. Wilmer C. Wright, *The Works of the Emperor Julian.* Vol 2. LCL 29. Cambridge: Harvard University Press, 1990.

Juvenal. *Saturae.* Ed. and trans. G. G. Ramsay, *Juvenal and Persius.* LCL 91. Cambridge: Harvard University Press, 1979.

Legend of the Man of God of Edessa. Ed. with French trans. Arthur Amiaud, *La légende syriaque de Saint Alexis l'homme de Dieu.* Bibliothèque de l'École des Hautes Études, Sciences Philologiques et Historiques 79. Paris: F. Viewig, 1889.

Libanius. *Epistulae.* Ed. and trans. Albert F. Norman, *Libanius: Autobiography and Selected Letters.* LCL 478, 479. Cambridge: Harvard University Press, 1992.

————. *Oratio 11.* Ed. Richard Foerster, *Libanii opera.* Vol. 1. Leipzig: Teubner, 1903; repr. Hildesheim: Georg Olms, 1998.

————. *Oratio 16.* Ed. Richard Foerster, *Libanii opera.* Vol. 2. Leipzig: Teubner, 1904; repr. Hildesheim: Georg Olms, 1998.

————. *Oratio 26.* Ed. Richard Foerster, *Libanii opera.* Vol. 3. Leipzig: Teubner, 1906; repr. Hildesheim: Georg Olms, 1998.

————. *Oratio 41.* Ed. Richard Foerster, *Libanii opera.* Vol. 3. Leipzig: Teubner, 1906; repr. Hildesheim: Georg Olms, 1998.

————. *Oratio 45.* Ed. and trans. Albert F. Norman, *Libanius: Selected Works.* Vol. 2. LCL 452. Cambridge: Harvard University Press, 1977.

————. *Oratio 46.* Ed. Richard Foerster, *Libanii opera,* Vol. 3. Leipzig: Teubner, 1906; repr. Hildesheim: Georg Olms, 1998.

————. *Oratio 56.* Ed. Richard Foerster, *Libanii opera.* Vol. 4. Leipzig: Teubner, 1908; repr. Hildesheim: Georg Olms, 1998.

Liber graduum [LG]. Ed. with Latin trans. Michael Kmosko in PS 3:1–932. Paris: Firmin Didot, 1926. Trans. Robert A. Kitchen and Martien F. G. Parmentier, *The Syriac Liber Graduum, Ktaba dmasquata, "The Book of Steps": Translation, Introduction, and Notes.* (Kalamazoo: Cistercian Publications, forthcoming).

Liberatus. *Brevarium causae Nestorianorum et Eutychianorum.* Ed. Eduard Schwartz in *ACO* 2.2.5. Berlin and Leipzig: Walter de Gruyter, 1936.

Life of Saint Pachomius. Bohairic version. Ed. and trans. Armand Veilleux, *Pachomian Koinonia: The Lives, Rules, and Other Writings of Saint Pachomius and His Disciples.* Vol 1. *The Life of Saint Pachomius and his Disciples.* CS 45. Kalamazoo: Cistercian Publications, 1980.

Lucian. *De dea Syria.* Ed. and trans. Harold W. Attridge and Robert A. Oden, *The Syrian Goddess (De Dea Syria) Attributed to Lucian.* Missoula: Scholars Press, 1976.

———. *De mercede conductis potentium familiaribus.* Ed. and trans. A. M. Harmon, *The Works of Lucian.* Vol. 3. LCL 130. Cambridge: Harvard University Press, 1947.

———. *De morte Peregrini.* Ed. and trans. A. M. Harmon, *The Works of Lucian.* Vol. 5. LCL 302. Cambridge: Harvard University Press, 1936.

———. *De parasito.* Ed. and trans. A. M. Harmon, *The Works of Lucian.* Vol. 3. LCL 130. Cambridge: Harvard University Press, 1947.

———. *Nigrinus.* Ed. and trans. A. M. Harmon, *The Works of Lucian.* Vol. 1. LCL 14. Cambridge: Harvard University Press, 1934.

Lucian, Pseudo. *Asinus.* Ed. and trans. Matthew D. MacLeod, *The Works of Lucian.* Vol. 8. LCL 432. Cambridge: Harvard University Press, 1967.

Macarius, Pseudo. *Epistula magna [EM].* Ed. Reinhart Staats, *Makarios Symeon: Epistola Magna. Eine messalianische Mönchsregel und ihre Umschrift in Gregors von Nyssa "De instituto christiano."* Abhandlungen der Akademie der Wissenschaften in Göttingen, Philologische-historische Klasse, F. 3.134. Göttingen: Vandenhoeck und Ruprecht, 1984.

———. *Homiliae.* Collection 2. Ed. Hermann Dörries, Erich Klostermann, and Matthias Kroeger, *Die 50 geistlichen Homilien des Makarios.* PTS 4. Berlin: Walter de Gruyter, 1964.

Malchus. *Byzantine History.* Ed. and trans. R. C. Blockley, *The Fragmentary Classicising Historians of the Roman Empire.* Vol. 2. ARCA Classical and Medieval Texts, Papers, and Monographs 10. Liverpool: Francis Cairns, 1983.

Martial. *Epigrammata.* Ed. and trans. D. R. Shackleton Bailey in *Martial: Epigrams.* LCL 94, 95, 480. Cambridge: Harvard University Press, 1993.

Marūtā of Mayperqaṭ. *The So-called Canons of Marūtā.* Ed. and trans. Arthur Vööbus, *Syriac and Arabic Documents Regarding Legislation Relative to Syrian Asceticism.* PapETSE 11. Stockholm, 1960.

Nestorius. *Liber Heraclidis [LH].* Ed. Paul Bedjan, *Nestorius, Le livre de Héraclide de Damas.* Paris-Leipzig, 1910. Trans. Godfrey R. Driver and Leonard Hodgson, *The Bazaar of Heracleides, Newly Translated from the Syriac and Edited with an Introduction, Notes, and Appendices.* Oxford: Clarendon Press, 1925. French trans. François Nau, *Le livre d' Héraclide de Damas.* Paris: Letouzey et Ané, 1910.

Nilus of Ancyra. *De monastica exercitatione.* PG 79:719A–810D.

———. *De monastica praestantia.* PG 79:1061A–1093C.

———. *De voluntaria paupertate ad Magnam.* PG 79:968C–1060D.

———. *Epistulae.* PG 79:81A–581B.

———. *Peristeria seu Tractatus de virtutibus excolendis et vitiis fugiendis.* PG 79:812A–968B.

Optatus of Milevis. *De schismate Donatistarum.* Ed. with French trans. J. Labrousse, *Optat de Milève: Traité contre les Donatistes.* SC 412, 413. Paris: Éditions du Cerf, 1995–1996.

Origen. *Contra Celsum*. Ed. with French trans. Marcel Borret, *Origène: Contre Celse*. SC 132, 136, 147, 150, 227. Paris: Éditions du Cerf, 1967–1976. Trans. Henry Chadwick, *Origen: Contra Celsum*. Cambridge: Cambridge University Press, 1965.

Palladius. *Dialogus de vita Iohannis Chrysostomi [Dial]*. Ed. with French trans. Anne-Marie Malingrey and Philippe Leclercq, *Palladios: Dialoque sur la vie de Jean Chrysostome*. SC 341, 342. Paris: Éditions du Cerf, 1988. Trans. Robert T. Meyer, *Palladius: Dialogue on the Life of St. John Chrysostom*. ACW 45. New York: Newman Press, 1985.

———. *Historia Lausiaca [HL]*. Ed. G. J. M. Bartelink, *Palladio: La Storia Lausiaca*. Milan: Fondazione Lorenzo Valla, 1974. Trans. Robert T. Meyer, *Palladius: The Lausiac History*. ACW 34. Westminster: Newman Press, 1965.

Papohe. *Life of Phif*. Ed. Tito Orlandi with Italian trans. Antonella Campagnano, *Vite dei monachi Phif e Longino*. Testi e documenti per lo studio dell' antichita. Milan: Cisalpino-Goliardica, 1975.

Paulinus of Nola. *Carmen* 24. Ed. Wilhelm von Hartel, *S. Ponti Meropii Paulini Nolani carmina*. CSEL 30.2. Vienna: F. Tempsky, 1894.

Pe'ah. Ed. I. Epstein and trans. S. M. Lehrman, *The Babylonian Talmud: Seder Zera'im*. Vol. 2. London: Soncino Press, 1948.

Pelagius, Pseudo. *De divitiis*. PLS 1:1380–1418. Trans. Brinley R. Rees, *The Letters of Pelagius and His Followers*. Rochester, N.J.: Boydell Press, 1992.

Philoxenus. *Letter to Patricius*. Ed. with French trans. René Lavenant, *La lettre à Patricius de Philoxène de Mabboug*. PO 30.5. Paris: Firmin-Didot, 1963.

Photius. *Bibliotheca*. Ed. with French trans. René Henry, *La Bibliothèque de Photius*. Paris: Société d'édition "Les Belles-Lettres," 1959–1974.

Possidius. *Vita Augustini*. PL 32:33–66.

Priscus. *Byzantine History*. Ed. and trans. R. C. Blockley, *The Fragmentary Classicising Historians of the Later Roman Empire*. Vol. 2. ARCA Classical and Medieval Texts, Papers, and Monographs 10. Liverpool: Francis Cairns, 1983.

Psalmoi Sarakoton [Psalms of the Wanderers]. Ed. and trans. Charles Robert Cecil Allberry in *A Manichaean Psalmbook. Part 2: Manichaean Manuscripts in the Chester Beatty Collection*. Stuttgart: Kolhammer, 1938.

Psalms of Heracleides. Ed. and trans. Charles Robert Cecil Allberry, *A Manichaean Psalmbook. Part 2: Manichaean Manuscripts in the Chester Beatty Collection*. Stuttgart: Kolhammer, 1938.

Rabbula of Edessa. *Rules for Monks. Rules for the Clergy and the Bnay Qyāmā*. Ed. and trans. Arthur Vööbus, *Syriac and Arabic Documents Regarding Legislation Relative to Syrian Asceticism*. PapETSE 11. Stockholm, 1960.

Regula magistri [RM]. Ed. with French trans. Adalbert de Vogüé, *Le Règle du Maître*. SC 105, 106, 107. Paris: Éditions du Cerf, 1964–1965. Trans. Luke Eberle, *The Rule of the Master*. CS 6. Kalamazoo: Cistercian Publications, 1977.

Roman State and Christian Church: A Collection of Legal Documents to A.D. 535. Trans. P. R. Coleman-Norton. London: S.P.C.K., 1966.

Rufinus. *Historia ecclesiastica [HE]*. PL 21.467–540.

———. *Historia monachorum in Aegypto [HM]*. See above, *Historia monachorum*. Latin version.

Siricius. *Epistulae et decreta*. PL 13:1131B–1196A.

Socrates. *Historia ecclesiastica [HE]*. Ed. Günther Christian Hansen and Manja Sirinian, *Sokrates Kirchengeschichte*. GCS n.F.1. Berlin: Akademie Verlag, 1995.

Sozomen. *Historia ecclesiastica [HE]*. Ed. Joseph Bidez, revised Günther Christian Hansen, *Sozomenus Kirchengeschichte*. GCS n.F.4. Berlin: Akademie Verlag, 1995. Trans. Chester D. Hartnaft, *The Ecclesiastical History of Sozomen*. NPNF 2. 2d series. Grand Rapids: Eerdmans, 1989.

Sulpicius Severus. *Dialogus* 3. Ed. Karl Halm, *Sulpicii Severi libri qui supersunt*. CSEL 1. Vienna: C. Geroldi, 1866.

————. *Vita Martini*. Ed. with French trans. Jacques Fontaine, *Sulpice Sévère: Vie de Saint Martin*. SC 133, 134, 135. Paris: Éditions du Cerf, 1967–1969.

Synesius of Cyrene. *Opera*. Ed. Antonio Garzya, *Opere di Sinesio di Cirene*. Torino: Unione Tipografico-Editrice Torinese, 1989.

Theodore Lector. *Historia ecclesiastica [HE]*. Ed. Günther Christian Hansen, *Theodoros Anagnostes Kirchengeschichte*. GCS n.F.3. Berlin: Akademie Verlag, 1995.

Theodoret of Cyrrhus. *Haereticarum fabularum compendium [HFC]*. PG 83:336C–556A.

————. *Historia ecclesiastica [HE]*. Ed. Léon Parmentier, revised Günther Christian Hansen, *Theodoret Kirchengeschichte*. GCS n.F.5. Berlin: Akademie Verlag, 1998. Trans. Blomfield Jackson, *The Ecclesiastical History of Theodoret*. NPNF 3. 2d series. Grand Rapids: Eerdmans, 1979.

————. *Historia religiosa [HR]*. Ed. with French trans. Pierre Canivet and Alice Leroy-Molinghen, *Théodoret de Cyr: Histoire des moines de Syrie*. SC 234, 257. Paris: Éditions du Cerf, 1977, 1979. Trans. R. M. Price, *Theodoret of Cyrrhus: A History of the Monks of Syria*. CS 88. Kalamazoo: Cistercian Publications, 1985.

Timothy of Constantinople. *De receptione haereticorum [DRH]*. PG 86:12A–68B.

Tyconius. See Hahn, T., in secondary sources.

Vita Alexandri [V.Alex]. Ed. with Latin trans. E. de Stroop, *La Vie d'Alexandre l'Acémète*. PO 6:645–704. Paris: Firmin-Didot, 1911. Trans. Elizabeth Theokritoff, "The Life of Our Holy Father Alexander." *Aram* 3 (1991): 293–318. French trans. Jean-Marie Baguenard, *Les Moines Acémètes: Vies des saints Alexandre, Marcel et Jean Calybite*. Spiritualité orientale 47. Bégroles-en-Mauges: Abbaye de Bellefontaine, 1988.

Vita Antonii. See Athanasius, above.

Vita Augustini. See Possidius, above.

Vita Barsaumae (Summary). French trans. François Nau, "Résumés de monographies syriaques." *ROC* 18 (1913): 272–76, 379–89; *ROC* 19 (1914): 113–34, 278–79.

Vita Dalmatii. Version 1. Ed. Anselmo Banduri, *Imperium orientale; sive Antiquitates Constantinopolitanae in quatuor partes distributae*. Vol. 2: 697–710. Paris: J. B. Coignard, 1730.

————. Version 2. Ed. Manouel Io. Gedeon, *Vyzantinon heortologion*. Constantinople, 1899.

Vita Danielis Stylitae. Ed. Hippolyte Delehaye, *Les saints stylites*. SH 14. Brussels: Société des Bollandistes, 1923.

Vita Hypatii. See Callinicus, above.

Vita Isaacii. AASS Maii VII.243–253.

Vita Marcelli. Ed. Gilbert Dagron, "La *Vie* ancienne de saint Marcel l'Acémète." *AB* 86 (1968): 271–321.

Vita Pachomii. See *Life of Saint Pachomius,* above.

Vita Rabbulae. Ed. J. J. Overbeck in *S. Ephraemi Syri, Rabulae episcopi Edesseni, Balaei aliorumque Opera selecta.* Oxford: Clarendon Press, 1865.

Zachariah of Mitylene, Pseudo. *Chronicle.* Trans. E. W. Brooks and F. J. Hamilton, *The Syriac Chronicle Known as That of Zachariah of Mitylene.* London: Methuen, 1899.

SECONDARY SOURCES

Abramowski, Luise. 1962. *Untersuchungen zum Liber Heraclidis des Nestorius.* CSCO 242. Subsidia 22. Louvain: Secrétariat du CorpusSCO.

Adam, Alfred. 1953–1954. "Grundbegriffe des Mönchtums in sprachlicher Sicht." *ZKG* 65:209–39.

———. 1957. "Erwägungen zur Herkunft der Didache." *ZKG* 68:1–47.

Allen, Pauline, and Wendy Mayer. 1995. "The Thirty-Four Homilies on Hebrews: The Last Series Delivered by Chrysostom in Constantinople?" *Byzantion* 65:309–48.

———. 1997. "John Chrysostom's Homilies on I and II Thessalonians: The Preacher and His Audience." *SP* 31:3–21.

Amata, Biagio. 1986. "S. Agostino: 'De Opere Monachorum.' Una concezione (antimanichea?) del lavoro." In *Spiritualità del lavoro nella catechesi dei Padri del III–VI secolo,* ed. Sergio Felici, 59–77. Biblioteca di scienze religiose 75. Rome: Libreria Ateneo Salesiano.

Angstenberger, Pius. 1997. *Die reiche und der arme Christus. Die Rezeptionsgeschichte von 2 Kor 8,9 zwischen dem zweiten und dem sechsten Jahrhundert.* Studien zur Alten Kirchengeschichte 12. Bonn: Borengässer.

Arbesmann, Rudolf. 1973. "The Attitude of Saint Augustine toward Labor." In *The Heritage of the Early Church: Essays in Honor of Georges Vasilievich Florovosky,* ed. David Neiman and Margaret Schatkin, 245–59. OCA 195. Rome: Pontificio Istituto Orientale.

Atkinson, J. E. 1992. "Out of Order: The Circumcellions and Codex Theodosianus 16.5.52." *Historia* 41:488–99.

Baán, Istrán. 1997. "L'évêque Chrysostome: exigences et réalisations." In *Vescovi e pastori in epoca teodosiana.* Vol. 2, 423–28. Studia Ephemeridis Augustinianum 58. Rome: Institutum Patristicum Augustinianum.

Bacht, Heinrich. 1953. "Die Rolle des orientalischen Mönchtums in den kirchenpolitischen Auseinandersetzungen um Chalkedon." In *Das Konzil von Chalkedon,* ed. Aloys Grillmeier and Heinrich Bacht. Vol. 2, 193–314. Würzburg: Echter.

Bagnall, Roger. 1993. *Egypt in Late Antiquity.* Princeton: Princeton University Press.

Baguenard, Jean-Marie. 1988. *Les moines acémètes: Vies des saint Alexandre, Marcel, et Jean Calybite.* Spiritualité orientale 47. Bégrolles-en-Mauges: Abbaye de Bellefontaine.

Baker, Aelred. 1968. "Syriac and the Origins of Monasticism." *Downside Review* 86: 342–53.

Bammel, Caroline P. 1996. "Problems of the *Historia Monachorum.*" *JThS* n.s. 47:92–104.

Bardy, G. 1949. "Philosophie et philosophe dans le vocabulaire chrétien des premiers siècles." *Revue d'ascetique et de mystique* 25:97–108.

Barnard, Leslie W. 1968. "Pelagius and Early Syriac Christianity." *Recherches de théologie ancienne et mediévale* 35:193–96.

Barnes, Timothy D. 1980. "The Date of the Council of Gangra." *JThS* n.s. 40:121–24.

Bartelink, G. J. M. 1997. "Die *Parrhesia* des Menschen vor Gott bei Johannes Chrysostomos." *VC* 51:261–72.

Bäss, Peter. 1969. "Der Liber Graduum—ein messalianisches Buch?" In *XVII Deutscher Orientalistentag 1968,* ed. Wolfgang Voigt. Vol. 2, 368–74. Wiesbaden: Franz Steiner.

Bauer, Walter. 1971. *Orthodoxy and Heresy in Earliest Christianity.* 2d ed. Ed. and trans. Robert A. Kraft and Gerhard Krodel. Philadelphia: Fortress Press.

Baur, P. Chrysostomus. 1959–1960. *John Chrysostom and His Time.* 2 vols. Trans. M. Gonzaga. Westminster: Newman Press.

Bazell, Dianne M. 1995. "The Politics of Piety." In *Asceticism,* ed. Vincent L. Wimbush and Richard Valantasis, 493–50. Oxford: Oxford University Press.

Berthier, André, M. Martin, and F. Logeart. 1942. *Les vestiges du Christianisme antique dans la Numidie centrale.* Algiers: Maison Carrée.

Binns, John. 1994. *Ascetics and Ambassadors of Christ: The Monasteries of Palestine, 314–631.* Oxford: Clarendon Press.

Blum, Georg G. 1969. *Rabbula von Edessa. Der Christ, der Bischof, der Theologe.* CSCO 300. Subsidia 34. Louvain: Secrétariat du CorpusSCO.

Bosworth, Clifford Edmund. 1976. *The Mediaeval Islamic Underworld: The Banū Sāsān in Arabic Society and Literature.* Part 1: *The Banū Sāsān in Arabic Life and Lore.* Leiden: Brill.

Boulluec, Alain Le. 1985. *La notion d'hérésie dans la littérature grecque IIe–IIIe siècles.* Paris: Études Augustiniennes.

Bousset, Wilhelm. 1923a. *Apophthegmata: Studien zur Geschichte des ältesten Mönchtums.* Tübingen: Mohr.

———. 1923b. "Das Mönchtum der sketischen Wüste." *ZKG* 42:1–41.

Brock, Sebastian P. 1973. "Early Syrian Asceticism." *Numen* 20:1–19.

Brown, Peter Robert Lamont. 1964. Review of *Kirche und Staat im spätrömische Reich,* by H.-J. Diesner. *JThS* n.s. 15:409–11.

———. 1969. "The Diffusion of Manichaeism in the Roman Empire." *JRS* 59:92–103. Repr. in Brown (1977):94–118. References in text to this edition.

———. 1971. "The Rise and Function of the Holy Man in Late Antiquity." *JRS* 61:80–101. Revised in Brown (1982):103–52. References in text to this edition.

———. 1972. *Religion and Society in the Age of St. Augustine.* London: Faber and Faber.

———. 1976. "Eastern and Western Christendom in Late Antiquity: A Parting of the Ways." In *The Orthodox Churches and the West,* edited by Derek Baker, 1–24. Studies in Church History 13. Oxford: Basil Blackwell. Revised in Brown (1982): 166–95. References in text to this edition.

———. 1978. *The Making of Late Antiquity.* Cambridge: Harvard University Press.

———. 1981. *The Cult of the Saints: Its Rise and Function in Latin Christianity.* Haskell Lectures on History of Religions n.s. 2. Chicago: University of Chicago Press.

————. 1982. *Society and the Holy in Late Antiquity.* Berkeley and Los Angeles: University of California Press.

————. 1983. "The Saint as Exemplar in Late Antiquity." *Representations* 1:1–25.

————. 1988. *The Body and Society: Men, Women, and Sexual Renunciation in Early Christianity.* Lectures on the History of Religions, n.s. 13. New York: Columbia University Press.

————. 1992. *Power and Persuasion in Late Antiquity: Towards a Christian Empire.* Madison: University of Wisconsin Press.

————. 1995. *Authority and the Sacred: Aspects of the Christianisation of the Roman World.* Cambridge: Cambridge University Press.

————. 1998. "The Rise and Function of the Holy Man in Late Antiquity, 1971–1997." *JECS* 6:353–76.

Brunt, P. A. 1980. "Free Labor and Public Works at Rome." *JRS* 70:81–100.

Büchler, Bernward. 1980. *Die Armut der Armen. Über den ursprünglichen Sinn der mönchischen Armut.* Munich: Kösel.

Burrus, Virginia. 1995. *The Making of a Heretic: Gender, Authority, and the Priscillianist Controversy.* The Transformation of the Classical Heritage 24. Berkeley and Los Angeles: University of California Press.

Butler, Cuthbert. 1898. *The Lausiac History of Palladius.* Part 1: *A Critical Discussion together with Notes on Early Egyptian Monasticism.* TS 6. Cambridge: Cambridge University Press.

Calderone, Salvatore. 1967. "Circumcelliones." *La parola del passato* 113:94–105.

Camelot, Thomas. 1951. "De Nestorius à Eutychès: L'opposition de deux christologies." In *Das Konzil von Chalkedon,* ed. Aloys Grillmeier and Heinrich Bacht. Vol. 1:213–42. Würzburg: Echter.

Cameron, Alan. 1965. "Wandering Poets: A Literary Movement in Byzantine Egypt." *Historia* 14:470–509. Repr. in Cameron (1985): I. References in text to this edition.

————. 1976a. "The Authenticity of the Letters of St. Nilus of Ancyra." *Greek, Roman, and Byzantine Studies* 17:181–96. Repr. in Cameron (1985): VI. References in text to this edition.

————. 1976b. *Circus Factions: Blues and Greens at Rome and Byzantium.* Oxford: Clarendon Press.

————. 1985. *Literature and Society in the Early Byzantine World.* Collected Studies 109. London: Variorum.

Cameron, Alan, and Jacqueline Long 1993. *Barbarians and Politics at the Court of Arcadius.* The Transformation of the Classical Heritage 19. Berkeley and Los Angeles: University of California Press.

Cameron, Averil. 1991. *Christianity and the Rhetoric of Empire: The Development of Christian Discourse.* Sather Classical Lectures 55. Berkeley and Los Angeles: University of California Press.

————. 1993. *The Later Roman Empire.* Cambridge: Harvard University Press.

Campenhausen, Hans F. von. 1968. "The Ascetic Ideal of Exile in Ancient and Early Medieval Monasticism." In *Tradition and Life in the Church,* trans. A. V. Littledale, 231–51. Philadelphia: Fortress Press.

Canévet, Mariette. 1969. "Le 'De instituto christiano' est-il de Grégoire de Nysse?" *Revue des études grecques* 82:404–23.

Canivet, Pierre. 1961. "Théodoret et le messalianisme." *Revue Mabillon* 51:26–34.

———. 1977. *Le monachisme syrien selon Théodoret de Cyr.* Théologie historique 42. Paris: Beauchesne.

———. 1989. "Le Christianisme en Syrie des origines à l'avènement de l'Islam." In *Archeologie et histoire de la Syrie,* ed. Jean-Marie Dentzer and Winfried Orthmann. Vol. 2:117–48. Saarbrücken: Saarbrücker.

Ceran, W. 1970. "Stagnation or Fluctuation in Early Byzantine Society." *Byzantinoslavica* 31:192–203.

Chadwick, Henry. 1955. "The Exile and Death of Flavian of Constantinople." *JThS* n.s. 6:17–34.

———. 1993. "Bishops and Monks." *SP* 24:45–61.

Chitty, Derwas J. 1966. *The Desert a City: An Introduction to the Study of Egyptian and Palestinian Monasticism under the Christian Empire.* Oxford: Basil Blackwell.

———. 1971. "Abba Isaiah." *JThS* n.s. 22:47–72.

Chryssavgis, John. 1988. "The Sources of St. John Climacus, c. 580–649." *Ostkirchliche Studien* 37:3–13.

Clark, Elizabeth A. 1984. *The Life of Melania the Younger: Introduction, Translation, and Commentary.* Studies in Women and Religion 14. New York: Edwin Mellen Press.

———. 1992. *The Origenist Controversy: The Cultural Construction of an Early Christian Debate.* Princeton: Princeton University Press.

Cloud, Duncan. 1989. "The Client-Patron Relationship: Emblem and Reality in Juvenal's First Book." In *Patronage in Ancient Society,* ed. Andrew Wallace-Hadrill, 205–17. Leicester-Nottingham Studies in Ancient Society 1. London and New York: Routledge.

Constable, Giles. 1977. "Monachisme et pèlerinage au Moyen Âge." *Revue historique* 258:3–27.

Constantelos, Demetrios J. 1992. *Byzantine Philanthropy and Social Welfare.* 2d ed. New Rochelle, N.J.: A. D. Caratzas.

Coyle, John K. 1978. *Augustine's "De moribus ecclesiae catholicae": A Study of the Work, Its Composition, and Its Sources.* Paradosis 25. Fribourg: University Press.

Csányi, Daniel A. 1960. "Optima Pars: Die Auslegungsgeschichte von Lk 10,38–42 bei den Kirchenvätern der ersten vier Jahrhunderte." *SM* 2:5–78.

Curran, John. 1997. "Jerome and the Sham Christians of Rome." *JEH* 48:213–29.

Dagron, Gilbert. 1968. "La *Vie* ancienne de saint Marcel l'Acémète." *AB* 86:271–321.

———. 1970. "Les moines et la ville: Le monachisme à Constantinople jusqu'au concile de Chalcédoine (451)." *Travaux et Mémoires* 4:229–76.

———. 1974. *Naissance d'une capitale: Constantinople et ses institutions de 330 à 451.* Bibliothèque byzantine, Études 7. Paris: Presses Universitaires de France.

Damon, Cynthia. 1997. *The Mask of the Parasite: A Pathology of Roman Patronage.* Ann Arbor: University of Michigan Press.

Darrouzès, Jean. 1954. "Notes sur les Homélies du Pseudo-Macaire." *Le Muséon* 67: 297–309.

Dattrino, Lorenzo. 1986. "Lavoro e Ascei nelle 'Institutiones' di Giovanni Cassiano." In *Spiritualità del lavoro nella catechesi dei Padri del III–VI secolo,* ed. Sergio Felici, 165–84. Biblioteca di scienze religiose 75. Rome: Libreria Ateneo Salesiano.

Daumas, François. 1968. "Les travaux de l'institut français d'archéologie orientale pendent l'année 1966–67." *Comptes rendus de l'Académie des inscriptions et belles-lettres 1967*, 438–51. Paris.

Dechow, Jon F. 1988. *Dogma and Mysticism in Early Christianity: Epiphanius of Cyprus and the Legacy of Origen.* Patristic Monograph Series 13. Macon, Ga.: Mercer University Press.

Decret, François. 1995. "Aspects de l'Église manichéenne: Remarques sur le Manuscrit de Tébessa." In *Essais sur l'Église manichéenne en Afrique du nord et à Rome au temps de saint Augustin: recueil d'études*, 37–51. Studia Ephemeridis Augustinianum 47. Rome: Institutum Patristicum Augustinianum.

Degórski, Bazyli. 1997. "L''abate' come pastore in epoca teodosiana." In *Vescovi e pastori in epoca teodosiana.* Vol. 1:91–120. Studia Ephemeridis Augustinianum 58. Rome: Institutum Patristicum Augustinianum.

Déroche, Vincent. 1995. *Études sur Léontios de Néapolis.* Studia Byzantina Upsaliensia 3. Uppsala: Uppsala Universitet.

Desprez, Vincent. 1992. "L'ascétisme mésopotamien au IVe siècle: III. Le 'Livre des degrés.'" *La Lettre de Ligugé* 262:16–31.

Devreesse, Robert. 1945. *Le patriarcat d'Antioche, depuis la paix de l'Église jusqu'à la conquête arabe.* Paris: Gabalda.

Dietz, Maribel. 1997. *Travel, Wandering, and Pilgrimage in Late Antiquity and the Early Middle Ages.* Ph.D. diss., Princeton University.

Disdier, M. Th. 1931. "Nil l'Ascète." *DTC* 11:661–74. Paris: Letouzey et Ané.

Dörries, Hermann. 1941. *Symeon von Mesopotamien. Die Überlieferung der messalianischen "Makarios"-Schriften.* TU 55. Leipzig: J. C. Hinrichs'sche.

———. 1966a. "Die Vita Antonii als Geschichtsquelle." In *id., Worte und Stunde.* Vol. 1:145–224. Göttingen: Vandenhoeck und Ruprecht.

———. 1966b. "Mönchtum und Arbeit." In *id., Worte und Stunde.* Vol. 1:277–301. Göttingen: Vandenhoeck und Ruprecht.

———. 1966c. "Urteil und Verturteilung. Kirche und Messalianer: Zum Umgang der alten Kirche mit Häretikern." In *id., Worte und Stunde.* Vol. 1:334–51. Göttingen: Vandenhoeck und Ruprecht.

———. 1970. "Die Messalianer im Zeugnis ihrer Bestreiter: Zum Problem des Enthusiasmus in der spätantiken Reichskirche." *Saeculum* 21:213–27.

Downey, Glanville. 1961. *A History of Antioch in Syria from Seleucus to the Arab Conquest.* Princeton: Princeton University Press.

Drijvers, Han J. W. 1966. *Bardaisan of Edessa.* Assen: Gorcum.

———. 1981a. "Hellenistic and Oriental Origins." In *The Byzantine Saint*, ed. S. Hackel, 25–33. Studies Supplementary to Sobornost 5. London: Fellowship of St. Alban. Repr. in Drijvers (1984b): IV.

———. 1981b. "Odes of Solomon and Psalms of Mani: Christians and Manichaeans in Third-Century Syria." In *Studies in Gnosticism and Hellenic Religions Presented to Gilles Quispel*, ed. R. van den Broek and M. J. Vermaseren, 117–30. Leiden: Brill. Repr. in Drijvers (1984b): X.

———. 1982a. "Facts and Problems in Early Syriac-Speaking Christianity." *The Second Century* 2:157–75. Repr. in Drijvers (1984b): VI.

———. 1982b. "Die Legende des heiligen Alexius und der Typus des Gottesmannes im syrischen Christentum." In *Typus, Symbol, Allegorie bei den östlichen Vätern und ihren Parallelen im Mittelalter,* ed. Margot Schmidt and Carl Friedrich Geyer, 187–217. Eichstätter Beiträge 4. Regensburg: Friedrich Pustet. Repr. in Drijvers (1984b): V.

———. 1984a. "East of Antioch: Forces and Structures in the Development of Early Syriac Theology." In Drijvers (1984b), 1–27.

———. 1984b. *East of Antioch: Studies in Early Syriac Christianity.* Collected Studies 198. London: Variorum.

———. 1985. "Jews and Christians at Edessa." *Journal of Jewish Studies* 36:88–102.

———. 1992. "The Acts of Thomas." In *New Testament Apocrypha.* 2d ed. Ed. Edgar Hennecke, Wilhelm Schneemelcher, and Robert McL. Wilson. Vol. 2:324–37. Westminster: John Knox Press.

Duensing, Hugo. 1950. "Die dem Klemens von Rom zugeschriebenen Briefe über die Jungfräulichkeit." *ZKG* 63:166–88.

Eames, Edwin, and Judith G. Goode. 1973. *Urban Poverty in a Cross-Cultural Context.* New York: Free Press.

Edwards, M. J. 1989. "Satire and Verisimilitude: Christianity in Lucian's *Peregrinus.*" *Historia* 38:89–98.

Elm, Susanna. 1994. *"Virgins of God": The Making of Asceticism in Late Antiquity.* Oxford: Clarendon Press.

———. 1997. "The Polemical Use of Genealogies: Jerome's Classification of Pelagius and Evagrius Ponticus." *SP* 33:311–18.

———. 1998. "The Dog That Did Not Bark: Doctrine and Patriarchal Authority in the Conflict between Theophilus of Alexandria and John Chrysostom of Constantinople." In *Christian Origins: Theology, Rhetoric, and Community,* ed. Lewis Ayers and Gareth Jones, 68–93. London and New York: Routledge.

Escolan, Philippe. 1999. *Monachisme et Église. Le monachisme syrien du IVᵉ au VIIᵉ siècle: un ministère charismatique.* Théologie historique 109. Paris: Beauchesne.

Estal, Juan Manuel del. 1959. "Descertada opinión moderna sobre los monjes de Cartago." *La Ciudad de Dios* 172:596–616.

Evelyn-White, Hugh G. 1932. *The Monasteries of the Wadî'n Natrûn.* Part 2: *The History of the Monasteries of Nitria and Scetis.* Metropolitan Museum of Art Egyptian Expedition Publications 7. New York: Metropolitan Museum of Art.

Feiertag, Jean Louis. 1990. *Les Consultationes Zacchaei et Apollonii. Étude d'histoire et de sotériologie.* Paradosis 30. Fribourg: University Press.

Fiey, Jean-Maurice. 1962. "Aonès, Awun, et Awgin (Eugène) aux origenes du monachisme mésopotamien." *AB* 80:52–81.

———. 1970. *Jalons pour une histoire de l'Église en Iraq.* CSCO 310. Subsidia 36. Louvain: Secrétariat du CorpusCSO.

Fitschen, Klaus. 1998. *Messalianismus und Antimessalianismus: Ein Beispiel ostkirchlicher Ketzergeschichte.* Forschungen zur Kirchen- und Dogmengeschichte 71. Göttingen: Vandenhoeck und Ruprecht.

Folliet, Georges. 1957. "Des moines euchites à Carthage en 400–401." *SP* 2:386–99. TU 64. Berlin.

Foss, Clive. 1977. "Late Antique and Byzantine Ankara." *Dumbarton Oaks Papers* 31:29–87.

Fountoules, Iohannis M. 1963. *Hē Eikositetraōros Akoimētos Doxologia.* Athens: Papademetriou.

Francis, James A. 1995. *Subversive Virtue: Asceticism and Authority in the Second-Century Pagan World.* University Park, Penn.: Pennsylvania State University Press.

Frank, Georgia. 2000. *The Memory of the Eyes: Pilgrims to Living Saints in Christian Late Antiquity.* Transformation of the Classical Heritage 30. Berkeley and Los Angeles: University of California Press.

Frankfurter, David. 1990. "Stylites as *Phallobates:* Pillar Religions in Late Antique Syria." *VC* 44:168–98.

———. 1998. *Religion in Roman Egypt: Assimilation and Resistance.* Princeton: Princeton University Press.

Frazee, Charles A. 1982. "Late Roman and Byzantine Legislation on the Monastic Life from the Fourth to the Eighth Centuries." *Church History* 51:263–79.

Frend, William H. C. 1952. "The *Cellae* of the African Circumcellions." *JThS* n.s. 3: 87–89.

———. 1969. "Circumcellions and Monks." *JThS* n.s. 20:542–49.

———. 1972a. "Popular Religion and Christological Controversy in the Fifth Century." In *Popular Belief and Practice,* ed. G. J. Cumming and Derek Baker, 19–29. Studies in Church History 8. Cambridge: Cambridge University Press.

———. 1972b. *The Rise of the Monophysite Movement: Chapters in the History of the Church in the Fifth and Sixth Centuries.* Cambridge: Cambridge University Press.

———. 1985. *The Donatist Church: A Movement of Protest in Roman North Africa.* 3d ed. Oxford: Clarendon Press.

Fry, Timothy. 1981. *RB 1980: The Rule of St. Benedict in Latin and English with Notes.* Collegeville, Minn.: Liturgical Press.

Gaddis, John Michael. 1999. *There Is No Crime for Those Who Have Christ: Religious Violence in the Christian Roman Empire.* Ph.D. diss., Princeton University.

Gardner, I. M. F., and Samuel N. C. Lieu. 1996. "From Narmouthis (Medinet Madi) to Kellis (Ismant El-Kharab): Manichaean Documents from Roman Egypt." *JRS* 86:146–69.

Gatier, Pierre-Louis. 1994. "Villages du Proche-Orient protobyzantin (4ème–7ème siècles). Étude régionale." In *The Byzantine and Early Near East II: Land Use and Settlement Patterns,* ed. Averil Cameron and Geoffrey R. D. King, 17–48. Studies in Late Antiquity and Early Islam 1. Princeton: Darwin Press.

———. 1995. "Un moine sur la frontière: Alexandre l'Acémète en Syrie." In *Frontières terrestres, frontières célestes dans l'antiquité,* ed. Aline Rousselle, 435–57. Paris: Presses Universitaires de Perpignan.

Geoghegan, Arthur Turbitt. 1945. *The Attitude towards Labor in Early Christianity and Ancient Culture.* Studies in Christian Antiquity 6. Washington, D.C.: Catholic University Press.

Gilliard, Frank D. 1966. *The Social Origins of Bishops in the Fourth Century.* Ph.D. diss., University of California at Berkeley.

———. 1984. "Senatorial Bishops in the Fourth Century." *Harvard Theological Review* 77:153–75.

Goehring, James E. 1990. "The World Engaged: The Social and Economic World of Early Egyptian Monasticism." In *Gnosticism and the Early Christian World. In Honor of James M. Robinson,* ed. James E. Goehring and J. M. Robinson. Vol. 2: 134–44. Sonoma, Calif.: Polebridge Press.

———. 1992. "The Origins of Monasticism." In *Eusebius, Christianity, and Judaism,* ed. Harold W. Attridge and Gohei Hata, 235–55. Studia Post-Biblica 42. Leiden: Brill.

———. 1993. "The Encroaching Desert: Literary Production and Ascetic Space in Early Christian Egypt." *JECS* 1:281–96.

———. 1997. "Monastic Diversity and Ideological Boundaries in Fourth-Century Egypt." *JECS* 5:61–83.

Goeller, Emil. 1901. "Ein nestorianisches Bruchstück zur Kirchengeschichte des 4 und 5 Jahrhunderts." *Oriens Christianus* 1:80–97.

Gotoh, Atsuko. 1988. "*Circumcelliones:* The Ideology behind Their Activities." In *Forms of Control and Subordination in Antiquity,* ed. Toru Yuge and Masaoki Doi, 303–11. Leiden: Brill.

Goubert, Paul. 1951. "Le rôle de sainte Pulchérie et de l'eunuque Chrysaphios." In *Das Konzil von Chalkedon,* ed. Aloys Grillmeier and Heinricht Bacht. Vol. 1:303–21. Würzburg: Echter.

Gould, Graham. 1989. "Moving on and Staying Put in the *Apophthegmata Patrum.*" *SP* 20:231–37.

———. 1991. "The *Life of Antony* and the Origins of Christian Monasticism in Fourth-Century Egypt." *Medieval History* 1:3–11.

———. 1993. *The Desert Fathers on Monastic Community.* Oxford: Clarendon Press.

Green, W. S. 1979. "Palestinian Holy Men: Charismatic Leadership and Rabbinic Tradition." *Aufstieg und Niedergang der römischen Welt* II/19.2:619–647. Berlin: Walter de Gruyter.

Gregory, Timothy E. 1973. "Zosimus 5,23 and the People of Constantinople." *Byzantion* 43:63–83.

———. 1979. *Vox Populi: Popular Opinion and Violence in the Religious Controversies of the Fifth Century A.D.* Columbus: Ohio State University Press.

Gribomont, Jean. 1953. *Histoire du texte des Ascétiques de S. Basile.* Bibliothèque du Muséon 32. Louvain: Publications universitaires/Institut orientalique.

———. 1957. "Le Monachisme au IVe siècle en Asia Mineure: De Gangres au Messalianisme." *SP* 2.2:400–15. TU 64. Berlin.

———. 1959. "Eustathe le philosophe et les voyages du jeune Basile de Césaréa." *RHE* 54:115–24.

———. 1965. "Le monachisme au sein de l'Église en Syrie et en Cappadoce." *SM* 7:7–24.

———. 1967. "Eustathe de Sébaste." *DGHE* 16:26–33. Paris: Letouzey et Ané.

———. 1972. "Le dossier des origines du Messalianisme." In *Epektasis: mélanges patristiques offerts au Cardinal Jean Daniélou,* ed. Jacques Fontaine and Charles Kannengiesser, 611–25. Paris: Beauchesne.

———. 1977a. "Les apophthègmes du désert." *Rivista di storia e letteratura religiosa* 13:534–41.

———. 1977b. "Un aristocrate révolutionnaire, évêque et moine: s. Basile." *Augustinianum* 17:179–91.

———. 1980. "Saint Basil et le monachisme enthousiaste." *Irénikon* 53:123–44.

Griffith, Sidney H. 1993. "Monks, 'Singles,' and the 'Sons of the Covenant.' Reflections on Syriac Ascetic Terminology." In *Eulogema: Studies in Honor of Robert Taft, S.J.,* ed. E. Carr, 141–60. Studia Anselmiana 110. Rome: Pontificio Ateneo S. Anselmo.

———. 1995. "Asceticism in the Church of Syria: The Hermeneutics of Early Syrian Monasticism." In *Asceticism,* ed. Vincent L. Wimbush and Richard Valantasis, 220–45. Oxford: Oxford University Press.

Grillmeier, Aloys. 1965. *Christ in Christian Tradition.* Part 1: *From the Apostolic Age to Chalcedon (451),* trans. J. S. Bowden. New York: Sheed and Ward.

Grumel, Venance. 1932. *Les regestes des actes du Patriarcat de Constantinople* 1.1. Constantinople: Socii Assumptionistae Chalcedonenses; repr. Paris: Institut Français de Études Byzantines, 1972.

———. 1937. "Acémètes." *DSp* 1:169–76. Paris: Beauchesne.

Gryson, Roger. 1982. "The Authority of the Teacher in the Ancient and Medieval Church." *Journal of Ecumenical Studies* 19:176–87.

Guérard, Marie-Gabrielle. 1982. "Nil d'Ancyre." *DSp* 11:345–56. Paris: Éditions Beauschesne.

———. 1994. *Nil d'Ancyre: Commentaire sur le Cantique des Cantiques.* SC 403. Paris: Éditions du Cerf.

Guillaumont, Antoine. 1968. "Le dépaysement comme forme d'ascèse dans le monachisme ancien." *École Pratique des Hautes Études V section: Sciences Religieuses, Annuaire 1968–1969* 76:31–58.

———. 1972a "Monachisme et éthique judéo-chrétienne." *RevSR* 60:199–218. Repr. Guillaumont (1979d):47–66. References in text to this edition.

———. 1972b. "Un philosoph au désert: Evagre le Pontique." *RHR* 181:29–56.

———. 1974. "Situation et signification du Liber Graduum dans la spiritualité syriaque." In *Symposium Syriacum 1972,* 311–25. OCA 107. Rome: Pontificio Istituto Orientale.

———. 1975. "La conception du désert chez les moines d'Egypte." *RHR* 188:3–21.

———. 1978. "Les fouilles françaises des Kellia, 1964–1969." In *The Future of Coptic Studies,* ed. Robert McL. Wilson, 202–8. Leiden: Brill.

———. 1979a. *Aux origines du monachisme chrétien. Pour une phénoménologie du monachisme.* Spiritualité orientale 30. Bégrolles-en-Mauges: Abbaye de Bellefontaine.

———. 1979b. "Le travail manuel dans la monachisme ancien: contestation et valorisation." In Guillaumont 1979a:117–26.

———. 1979c. "Liber Graduum." *DSp* 9:749–54. Paris: Beauchesne.

———. 1979d. "Messalianisme." *DSp* 9:1074–83. Paris: Beauchesne.

———. 1982. "Christianisme et gnoses dans l'orient préislamique." *Annuaire du Collège de France 1981–1982,* 425–33. Paris.

Guy, Jean-Claude. 1984. *Recherches sur la tradition grecque des Apophthegmata Patrum.* SH 36. Brussels: Société des Bollandistes.

Hahn, Johannes. 1989. *Der Philosoph und die Gesellschaft: Selbstverständnis, öffentliches Auftreten und populäre Erwartungen in der hohen Kaiserzeit.* Heidelberger althistorische Beitrage und epigraphische Studien 7. Stuttgart: Franz Steiner.

Hahn, Traugott. 1900. *Tyconius-Studien. Ein Beitrag zur Kirchen- und Dogmengeschichte des 4. Jahrhunderts.* Studien zur Geschichte der Theologie und der Kirche 6.2. Leipzig: Dietrich; repr. Aalen: Scientia, 1971.

Hamel, Gildas. 1990. *Poverty and Charity in Roman Palestine, First Three Centuries C.E.* Near Eastern Studies 23. Berkeley and Los Angeles: University of California Press.

Hamman, A. 1964. "Le *Sitz im Leben* des Actes de Thomas." *Studia Evangelica* 3:383–89.

———. 1966. "*Sitz im Leben* des actes apocryphes du Noveau Testament." *SP* 8:62–69. TU 93. Berlin.

Hands, Arthur R. 1968. *Charities and Social Aid in Greece and Rome.* Ithaca: Cornell University Press.

Harnack, Adolf von. 1891. "Die pseudoclementinischen Briefe De virginitate und die Entstehung des Mönchthums." *Sitzungsberichte der königlich-preussischen Akademie der Wissenschaften zu Berlin* 21:361–85.

Harpham, Geoffrey G. 1987. *The Ascetic Imperative in Culture and Criticism.* Chicago: University of Chicago Press.

Harvey, Susan Ashbrook. 1990. *Asceticism and Society in Crisis: John of Ephesus and the Lives of the Eastern Saints.* The Transformation of the Classical Heritage 18. Berkeley and Los Angeles: University of California Press.

———. 1994. "The Holy and the Poor: Models from Early Syriac Christianity." In *Through the Eye of a Needle: Judeo-Christian Roots of Social Welfare,* ed. Emily Albu Hanawalt and Carter Lindberg, 43–66. Kirksville, Mo.: Thomas Jefferson University Press.

———. 1998. "The Stylite's Liturgy: Ritual and Religious Identity in Late Antiquity." *JECS* 6:523–39.

Hausherr, Irenée. 1935. "Quanam aetate proderit 'Liber graduum.'" *OCP* 1:495–502.

Hefele, Carl Joseph, and Henri Leclerq. 1973. *Histoire des conciles d'après les documents originaux* 1.1–2.2. Paris, 1907. Repr. Hildesheim: Georg Olms.

Hendriks, O. 1958. "L'activité apostolique des premiers moines syriens." *Proche-Orient Chrétien* 8:3–25.

Herman, Emilio. 1944. "Le professioni vietate al clero bizantino." *OCP* 10:23–44.

———. 1955. "La 'stabilitas loci' nel monachismo bizantino." *OCP* 21:125–42.

Herrin, Judith. 1990. "Ideals of Charity, Realities of Welfare: The Philanthropic Activity of the Byzantine Church." In *Church and Peoples in Byzantium,* ed. Rosemary Morris, 151–64. Chester: Bemrose Press.

Heuser, Manfred. 1998. "The Manichaean Myth according to the Coptic Sources." In Manfred Heuser and Hans-Joachim Klimkeit, *Studies in Manichaean Literature and Art,* trans. Majella Franzmann, 3–108. Nag Hammadi and Manichaean Studies 46. Leiden: Brill.

Heussi, Karl. 1917. *Untersuchungen zu Nilus dem Asketen.* TU 42.2. Leipzig: J. C. Hinrichs'sche.

———. 1936. *Der Ursprung des Mönchtums.* Tübingen: Mohr.

Hirschfeld, Yizhar. 1990. "Edible Wild Plants: The Secret Diet of Monks in the Judean Desert." *Israel Land and Nature* 16:25–28.

Holum, Kenneth G. 1982. *Theodosian Empresses: Women and Imperial Dominion in Late Antiquity.* The Transformation of the Classical Heritage 3. Berkeley and Los Angeles: University of California Press.

Holze, Heinrich. 1992. *Erfahrung und Theologie im frühen Mönchtum. Untersuchungen zur einer Theologie des monastichen Lebens bei den ägyptischen Mönchsvätern, Johannes Cassian, und Benedikt von Nursia.* Forschungen zur Kirchen- und Dogmengeschichte 48. Göttingen: Vandenhoeck und Ruprecht.

Honigmann, Ernest. 1954. *Le couvent de Barsauma et le patriarcat Jacobite d'Antioche et de Syrie*. CSCO 146. Subsidia 7. Louvain: Durbecq.

Hoven, Birgit van den. 1996. *Work in Ancient and Medieval Thought: Ancient Philosophers, Medieval Monks, and Theologians and the Concept of Work, Occupations, and Technology*. Dutch Monographs on Ancient History and Archaeology 14. Amsterdam: J. C. Gieben.

Jaeger, Werner. 1954. *Two Rediscovered Works of Ancient Christian Literature: Gregory of Nyssa and Macarius*. Leiden: Brill.

Janin, Raymond. 1953. *La géographie ecclésiastique de l'empire byzantin* 1:3: *Les églises et les monastères*. Paris: Institut Français d'Études Byzantines.

———. 1964. *Constantinople byzantine, developpement urbain et répertoire topographique*. 2d ed. Paris: Institut Français d'Études Byzantines.

Jargy, Simon. 1951. "Les 'fils et filles du pacte' dans la littérature monastique syriaque." *OCP* 17:304–20.

Jenal, Georg. 1995. *Italia Ascetica atque Monastica. Das Asketen- und Mönchtum in Italien von den Anfängen bis zur Zeit der Langobarden, ca. 150/250–604*. Monographien zur Geschichte des Mittelalters 39. Stuttgart: Hiersemann.

Jestice, Phyllis G. 1997. *Wayward Monks and the Religious Revolution of the Eleventh Century*. Studies in Intellectual History 76. Leiden: Brill.

Jones, Arnold Hugh Martin. 1953. "St. John Chrysostom's Parentage and Education." *Harvard Theological Review* 46:171–73.

———. 1964. *The Later Roman Empire, 284–602: A Social, Economic, and Administrative Survey*. Oxford: Basil Blackwell.

———. 1970. "The Caste System in the Later Roman Empire." *Eirene* 7:79–96.

Jones, Arnold Hugh Martin, J. R. Martindale, and J. Morris. 1971. *The Prosopography of the Later Roman Empire*. Vol. 1 (A.D. 260–395). Cambridge: Cambridge University Press.

Jones, C. P. 1978. "A Syrian in Lyon." *American Journal of Philology* 99:336–53.

Judge, Edwin Arthur. 1977. "The Earliest Use of Monachos for 'Monk' (P. Coll. Youtie 77) and the Origins of Monasticism." *JbAC* 20:72–89.

Juhl, Diana. 1996. *Die Askese im Liber Graduum und bei Afrahat. Eine vergleichende Studie zur frühsyrischen Frömmigkeit*. Orientalia Biblica et Christiana 9. Wiesbaden: Harrassowitz.

Karlin-Hayter, Patricia. 1988. "Activity of the Bishop of Constantinople outside His *Paroikia* between 381 and 451." In *Kathegetria: Essays Presented to Joan Hussey on Her Eightieth Birthday*, 179–210. Camberley: Porphyrogenitus.

Kasser, Rodolphe. 1976. "Sortir du monde: réflexions sur la situation et le développement des établissements monastiques aux Kellia." *Revue de théologie et de philosophie* 26:111–24.

———. 1978. "Fouilles suisses aux Kellia: passé, présent, et futur." In *The Future of Coptic Studies*, ed. Robert McL. Wilson, 209–19. Coptic Studies 1. Louvain: Brill.

Kelly, John Norman Davidson. 1975. *Jerome: His Life, Writings, and Controversies*. New York: Harper and Row.

———. 1995. *Golden Mouth: The Story of John Chrysostom: Ascetic, Preacher, Bishop*. London: Duckworth.

Kennedy, Hugh, and J. H. W. G. Liebeschuetz. 1988. "Antioch and the Villages of Northern Syria in the Fifth and Sixth Centuries A.D.: Trends and Problems." *Nottingham Medieval Studies* 32:65–90.

Kern-Ulmer, Brigitte. 1991. "The Power of the Evil Eye and the Good Eye in Midrashic Literature." *Judaism* 40:344–53.

Kirschner, Robert. 1984. "The Vocation of Holiness in Late Antiquity." *VC* 38:105–24.

Kitchen, Robert A. 1987. "The Gattung of the Liber Graduum: Implications for a Sociology of Asceticism." In *IV Symposium Syriacum 1984,* ed. Han J. W. Drijvers, 173–82. OCA 229. Rome: Pontificio Istituto Orientale.

———. 1998. "Conflict on the Stairway to Heaven: The Anonymity of Perfection in the Syriac *Liber Graduum.*" In *VII Symposium Syriacum 1996,* ed. René Lavenant, 211–20. OCA 256. Rome: Pontificio Istituto Orientale.

Klijn, A. F. J., see under *Acts of Thomas,* Syriac version, in primary sources.

Kraeling, Carl Herman. 1967. *Excavations at Dura-Europos Final Report 8.* Part 2: *The Christian Building.* New Haven: Yale University Press.

———. 1979. *Excavations at Dura-Europos Final Report 8.* Part 1: *The Synagogue.* 2d ed. New York: KTAV Publishing House.

Krause, Jens-Uwe. 1987. *Spätantike Patronatsformen im Westen des Römischen Reiches.* Vestigia 38. Munich: Beck.

Kretschmar, Georg. 1964. "Ein Beitrag zur Frage nach dem Ursprung frühchristlicher Askese." *Zeitschrift für Theologie und Kirche* 61:27–67.

Krueger, Derek. 1996. *Symeon the Holy Fool: Leontius' Life and the Late Antique City.* The Transformation of the Classical Heritage 25. Berkeley and Los Angeles: University of California Press.

Kowalski, Aleksander. 1989a. "Die Gebet im Liber Graduum." *OCP* 55:273–81.

———. 1989b. *Perfezione e giustizia di Adamo nel Liber Graduum.* OCA 232. Rome: Pontificio Istituto Orientale.

Lambert, Malcolm. 1992. *Medieval Heresy: Popular Movements from the Gregorian Reform to the Reformation.* 2d ed. Oxford: Basil Blackwell.

Lampe, G. W. H. 1961–1968. *A Patristic Greek Lexicon.* Oxford: Oxford University Press.

Lane Fox, Robin. 1987. *Pagans and Christians.* New York: Knopf.

———. 1997. "The *Life of Daniel.*" In *Portraits: Biographical Representation in the Greek and Latin Literature of the Roman Empire,* ed. M. J. Edwards and Simon Swain, 175–225. Oxford: Clarendon Press.

Lassus, Jean. 1947. *Sanctuaires chrétiennes de Syrie.* Bibliothèque archéologique et historique 42. Paris: Geuthner.

Lawless, George. 1987. *Augustine of Hippo and His Monastic Rule.* Oxford: Clarendon Press.

Lefort, Louis-Théophile. 1927. "Le 'de virginitate' de S. Clément ou de S. Athanase?" *Le Muséon* 40:260–64.

———. 1929. "S. Athanase, Sur la virginité." *Le Muséon* 42:265–69.

Leroux, Jean-Marie. 1975. "Saint Jean Chrysostome et le monachisme." In *Jean Chrysostome et Augustin: Actes du colloque de Chantilly, 22–24 septembre 1974,* ed. Charles Kannengiesser, 125–46. Théologie historique 35. Paris: Éditions Beauchesne.

Leyerle, Blake. 1994. "John Chrysostom on Almsgiving and the Use of Money." *Harvard Theological Review* 87: 29–47.

Leyser, Conrad. 2000. *Authority and Asceticism from Augustine to Gregory the Great.* Oxford: Clarendon Press.

Liebeschuetz, J. H. W. G. 1972. *Antioch: City and Imperial Administration in the Later Roman Empire.* Oxford: Clarendon Press.

———. 1977. "The Defences of Syria in the Sixth Century." In *Studien zu den Militärgrenzen Roms.* Vol. 2.: 487–99. Cologne: Rheinland.

———. 1979. "Problems Arising from the Conversion of Syria." In *The Church in Town and Countryside,* ed. Derek Baker, 17–24. Studies in Church History 16. Oxford: Basil Blackwell.

———. 1984. "Friends and Enemies of John Chrysostom." In *Maistor: Classical, Byzantine, and Renaissance Studies for Robert Browning,* ed. Ann Moffat, 85–111. Byzantina Australiensia 5. Canberra: Australian National University.

Liefeld, W. L. 1967. *The Wandering Preacher as a Social Figure in the Roman Empire.* Ph.D. diss., Columbia University.

Lieu, Samuel N. C. 1981. "Precept and Practice in Manichaean Monasticism." *JThS* n.s. 32:153–73.

———. 1992. *Manichaeism in the Later Roman Empire and Medieval China.* 2d ed. Wissenschaftliche Untersuchungen zum Neuen Testament 63. Tübingen: Mohr.

———. 1994. "From Mesopotamia to the Roman East: The Diffusion of Manichaeism in the Eastern Roman Empire." In *id., Manichaeism in Mesopotamia and the Roman East,* 23–53. Leiden: Brill.

Lizzi, Rita. 1981/1982. "'Monaci, Mendicanti e Donne' nella geografia monastica di alcune regioni orientali." *Atti dell' Istituto Veneto di Scienze, Lettere ed Arti* 140: 341–55.

———. 1982/1983. "Ascetismo e predicazione urbana nell' Egitto del V secolo." *Atti dell'Istituto Veneto di Scienze, Lettere ed Arti* 141:127–45.

———. 1987. *Il potere episcopale nell' Oriente romano: Rappresentazione ideologica e realtà politica (IV–V sec. d.C.).* Filologia e critica 53. Rome: Edizioni dell' Ateneo.

Lof, L. J. van der. 1974. "Mani as the Danger from Persia in the Roman Empire." *Augustiniana* 24:75–84.

Lorenz, Rudolf. 1966. "Die Anfänge des abendländischen Mönchtums im 4. Jahrhundert." *ZKG* 77:1–61.

———. 1971. "Circumcelliones—Cotopitae—Cutzupitani." *ZKG* 82:54–59.

Lucchesi, Enzo. 1981. "Compléments aux pères apostoliques en Copte." *AB* 99:405–8.

Luibhéid, Colm. 1965. "Theodosius II and Heresy." *JEH* 16:13–38.

MacCoull, Leslie S. B. 1979. "A Coptic Marriage-Contract." In *Actes du XVe congrès international de papyrologie,* ed. Jean Bingen and Georges Nachtergael. Vol 2:116–23. Papyrologia Bruxellensia 17. Brussells: Fondation égyptologique Reine Élisabeth.

MacMullen, Ramsey. 1964. "Social Mobility and the Theodosian Code." *JRS* 54:49–53.

———. 1966. *Enemies of the Roman Order: Treason, Unrest, and Alienation in the Empire.* Cambridge: Harvard University Press.

———. 1984. *Christianizing the Roman Empire,* A.D. *100–400.* New Haven: Yale University Press.

———. 1989. "The Preacher's Audience, A.D. 350–400." *JThS* 40:503–11.

Maier, Harry O. 1995a. "Religious Dissent, Heresy, and Households in Late Antiquity." *VC* 49:49–63.

———. 1995b. "The Topography of Heresy and Dissent in Late-Fourth-Century Rome." *Historia* 44:232–49.

Malamut, Elisabeth. 1993. *Sur la route des saints byzantines.* Paris: CNRS.

Mara, Maria Grazia. 1984. "Il significato storico-esegetico dei commentari al corpus paolino dal IV al V secolo." *Annali di storia dell' esegesi* 1:59–74.

Markus, Robert A. 1987. "Vie monastique et ascétisme chez saint Augustine." *Atti, Congresso internazionale su S. Agostino nel XVI centenario della conversione, Roma, 15– 20 settembre 1986,* 119–225. Rome: Institutum Patristicum Augustinianum.

———. 1990. *The End of Ancient Christianity.* Cambridge: Cambridge University Press.

Martin, Thomas F. 2000. "*Vox Pauli:* Augustine and the Claims to Speak for Paul: An Exploration of Rhetoric in the Service of Exegesis." *JECS* 8:237–72.

Martindale, J. R. 1980. *The Prosopography of the Later Roman Empire.* Vol. 2 (A.D. 395– 527). Cambridge: Cambridge University Press.

Matthews, Edward G. 1990. "'On Solitaries': Ephrem or Isaac?" *Le Muséon* 103:91– 110.

Matthews, John F. 1975. *Western Aristocracies and Imperial Court, A.D. 364–425.* Oxford: Clarendon Press.

———. 1989. *The Roman Empire of Ammianus.* Baltimore: Johns Hopkins University Press.

Mayali, Lawrence. 1990. "Du vagabondage à l'apostasie: le moine fugitif dans la société medievale." In *Religiose Devianz: Untersuchungen zu sozialen, rechtlichen, und theologischen Reaktionen auf religiöse Abweichungen im westlichen und östlichen Mittelalter,* ed. Dieter Simon, 121–42. Studien zur europaischen Rechtsgeschichte 48. Frankfurt am Main: Klostermann.

Mayer, Wendy. 1996. *The Provenance of the Homilies of St. John Chrysostom. Towards a New Assessment of Where He Preached What.* Ph.D. diss., University of Queensland.

———. 1998a. "John Chrysostom: Extraordinary Preacher, Ordinary Audience." In *Preacher and Audience: Studies in Early Christian and Byzantine Homiletics,* ed. Pauline Allen and Mary B. Cunningham, 105–137. Leiden: Brill.

———. 1998b. "Monasticism at Antioch and Constantinople in the Late Fourth Century: A Case of Exclusivity or Diversity." In *Prayer and Spirituality in the Early Church,* ed. Pauline Allen, Raymond Canning, and Lawrence Cross. Vol. 1:275– 88. Brisbane: Australia Catholic University.

———. 1999. "Constantinopolitan Women in Chrysostom's Circle." *VC* 53:265–88.

McDonnell, Ernest W. 1980. "Monastic Stability: Some Socioeconomic Considerations." In *Charanis Studies: Essays in Honor of Peter Charanis,* ed. Angeliki E. Laiou-Thomadakis, 115–50. New Brunswick: Rutgers University Press.

McLynn, Neil. 1998. "A Self-Made Holy Man: The Case of Gregory Nazianzen." *JECS* 6:463–83.

McNary-Zak, Bernadette. 2000. *Letters and Asceticism in Fourth-Century Egypt.* Lanham, Md.: University Press of America.

Mees, Michael. 1979. "Pilgerschaft und Heimatlosigkeit. Das frühe Christentum Ostsyriens." *Augustinianum* 19:53–73.

Messana, Vincenzo. 1989. "Πρᾶξις et Θεωρία chez Nil d'Ancyre." *SP* 18:235–39.

Meyendorff, John. 1970. "Messalianism or Anti-Messalianism? A Fresh Look at the 'Macarian' Problem." In *Kyriakon: Festschrift Johannes Quasten,* ed. Patrick Granfield and Josef Jungmann. Vol. 2:585–90. Münster: Aschendorff.

Milavec, Aaron. 1994. "Distinguishing True and False Prophets: The Protective Wisdom of the *Didache.*" *JECS* 2:117–36.

Millar, Fergus. 1993. *The Roman Near East, 31 B.C.–A.D. 337.* Cambridge: Harvard University Press.

Morard, Françoise. 1980. "Encore quelques réflexions sur Monachos." *VC* 34:395–401.

Morgenstern, Frank. 1991. "Kirchenspaltung in Nordafrika: Donatisten und Circumcellionen." *Alterum* 37:211–21.

Morris, John. 1965. "Pelagian Literature." *JThS* n.s. 16:26–60.

Murray, Robert. 1974/1975. "The Exhortation to Candidates for Ascetical Vows at Baptism in the Ancient Syriac Church." *New Testament Studies* 21:59–80.

———. 1975a. "The Features of the Earliest Christian Asceticism." In *Christian Spirituality: Essays in Honor of Gordon Rupp,* ed. Peter Brooks, 65–77. London: S. C. M.

———. 1975b. *Symbols of Church and Kingdom: A Study in Early Syriac Tradition.* Cambridge: Cambridge University Press.

———. 1982. "The Characteristics of the Earliest Syriac Christianity." In *East of Byzantium: Syria and Armenia in the Formative Period,* ed. Nina G. Garsoïan, Thomas F. Matthews, and Robert W. Thomson, 3–16. Washington, D.C.: Dumbarton Oaks.

Nagel, Peter. 1966. *Die Motivierung der Askese in der alten Kirche und der Ursprung des Mönchtums.* TU 95. Berlin: Akademie.

———. 1967. "Die Psalmoi Sarakoton des manichäischen Psalmbuches." *Orientalistische Literaturzeitung* 62:123–30.

———. 1973. "Die apokryphen Apostelakten des 2. und 3. Jahrhunderts in der manichäischen Literatur: Ein Beitrag zur Frage nach den christlichen Elementen im Manichäismus." In *Gnosis und Neues Testament,* ed. Karl-Wolfgang Trögen, 149–82. Berlin: Gutenslohor.

———. 1977/1978. "Action-Parables in Earliest Monasticism. An Examination of the Apophthegmata Patrum." *Hallel* 5:251–61.

Nau, François. 1927. "Deux épisodes de l'histoire juive sous Théodose II (423 et 438) d'après la vie de Barsauma le Syrien." *Revue des études juives* 83:184–206.

Nedungatt, George. 1973. "The Covenanters of the Early Syriac-Speaking Church." *OCP* 39:191–215, 419–44.

Nesselrath, Heinz-Gunther. 1985. *Lukians Parasitendialog: Untersuchungen und Kommentar.* Untersuchungen zur antiken Literatur und Geschichte 22. Berlin: Walter de Gruyter.

Nicol, Donald M. 1985. "*Instabilitas Loci:* The Wanderlust of Late Byzantine Monks." In *Monks, Hermits, and the Ascetic Tradition,* ed. W. J. Sheils, 193–202. Studies in Church History 22. London: Basil Blackwell.

O'Laughlin, Michael. 1992. "The Bible, the Demons, and the Desert: Evaluating the *Antirrheticus* of Evagrius Ponticus." *SM* 34:201–15.

Ommeslaeghe, F. van. 1981. "Jean Chrysostome et le peuple de Constantinople." *AB* 99:329–49.

O'Neill, J. C. 1989. "The Origins of Monasticism." In *The Making of Orthodoxy: Essays in Honor of Henry Chadwick,* ed. Rowan Williams, 270–87. Cambridge: Cambridge University Press.

Palmer, Andrew N. 1989. *"Semper Vagus:* The Anatomy of a Mobile Monk." *SP* 18: 255–60.

———. 1990. *Monk and Mason on the Tigris Frontier: The Early History of Tur Abdin.* University of Cambridge Oriental Publications 39. Cambridge: Cambridge University Press.

Pargoire, Jules. 1898/1899. "Un mot sur les Acémètes." *Échoes d'Orient* 2:304–8; 3:365–72.

———. 1899a. "Les débuts du monachisme à Constantinople." *Revue des questions historiques* n.s. 21:67–143.

———. 1899b. "Rufinianes." *BZ* 8:429–77.

———. 1924. "Acémètes." *DACL* 1:307–21. Paris: Letouzey et Ané.

Pasquato, Ottorino. 1986. "Vita Spirituale e Lavoro in Giovanni Cristomo: 'Modelli' di un rapporto." In *Spiritualità del lavoro nella catechesi dei Padri del III–VI secolo,* ed. Sergio Felici, 105–39. Biblioteca di scienze religiose 75. Rome: Libreria Ateneo Salesiano.

Patlagean, Evelyne. 1977. *Pauvreté économique et pauvreté sociale à Byzance, 4–7ème siècles.* Civilisations et sociétés 48. Paris: Mouton.

Paverd, Frans van de. 1991. *St. John Chrysostom: The Homilies on the Statues: An Introduction.* OCA 239. Rome: Scuola Tipografica S. Pio X.

Peel, J. D. Y. 1990. "Poverty and Sacrifice in Nineteenth-Century Yorubaland: A Critique of Iliffe's Thesis." *Journal of African History* 31:465–84.

Persic, Alessio. 1986. "La Chiesa di Siria e i 'gradi' della vita cristiana." In *Per foramen acus. Il cristianesimo antico di fronte alla pericope evangelica del "giovane ricco,"* 208–63. Studia Patristica Mediolanensia 14. Milan: Vita e Pensiero.

Peterson, Erik. 1929. "Zur Bedeutungsgeschichte von Παρρησία." In *Festschrift Reinhold Seeberg,* ed. Wilhem Koepp. Vol. 1:283–97. Leipzig: Werner Scholl.

Petit, Paul. 1955. *Libanius et la vie municipale à Antioche au IVe siècle après J.C.* Institut Français d'Archaeologie de Beyrouth, Bibliothèque archéologique et historique 62. Paris: Geuthner.

Poupon, P. 1981. "L'accusation de magie dans Les Actes apocryphes." In *Les Actes apocryphes des apôtres,* ed. François Bovon, 71–93. Geneva: Labor et Fides.

Pourkier, Aline. 1992. *L'hérésiologie chez Épiphane de Salamine.* Christianisme antique 4. Paris: Beauchesne.

Quacquarelli, A. 1982. *Lavoro e ascesi nel monachesimo prebenedettino del IV e V secolo.* Quaderni di "Vetera Christianorum" 18. Bari: Istituto di letteratura cristiana antica, Università degli studi.

Quispel, Gilles. 1964. "The Syrian Thomas and the Syrian Macarius." *VC* 18:226–35.

Ratcliff, Robert A. 1988. *Steps along the Way of Perfection: The Liber Graduum and Early Syrian Monasticism.* Ph.D. diss., Emory University.

Raynor, D. H. 1989. "Non-Christian Attitudes to Monasticism." *SP* 18.2:267–73.

Rebenich, Stefan. 1992. *Hieronymus und sein Kreis. Prosopographische und sozialgeschichtliche Untersuchungen.* Historia: Einzelschriften 72. Stuttgart: Franz Steiner.

Rees, Brinley R. 1992. *The Letters of Pelagius and His Followers.* Rochester, N.J.: Boydell Press.

Reitzenstein, Richard. 1916. *Historia Monachorum und Historia Lausiaca. Eine Studie zur Geschichte des Mönchtums und der frühchristlichen Begriffe Gnostiker und Pneumatiker.* Forschungen zur Religion und Literatur des Alten und Neuen Testaments 7. Göttingen: Vandenhoeck und Ruprecht.

Ringshausen, Harald. 1967. *Zur Verfasserschaft und Chronologie der dem Nilus Ancyranus zugeschrieben Werke.* Inaugural Diss., Frankfurt am Main.

Rousseau, Philip. 1978. *Ascetics, Authority, and the Church in the Age of Jerome and Cassian.* Oxford: Oxford University Press.

———. 1985. *Pachomius: The Making of a Community in Fourth-Century Egypt.* The Transformation of the Classical Heritage 6. Berkeley and Los Angeles: University of California Press.

———. 1994. *Basil of Caesarea.* The Transformation of the Classical Heritage 20. Berkeley and Los Angeles: University of California Press.

———. 1997. "Orthodoxy and the Coenobite." *SP* 30:241–58.

Rousselle, Aline. 1988. *Porneia: On Desire and the Body in Antiquity,* trans. Felicia Pheasant. Oxford: Basil Blackwell.

Rowland, Robert J. 1976. "The 'Very Poor' and the Grain Dole at Rome and Oxyrhynchus." *ZPE* 21:69–72.

Rubenson, Samuel. 1995. *The Letters of St. Antony: Monasticism and the Making of a Saint.* Minneapolis: Fortress Press.

Saller, R. P. 1983. "Martial on Patronage and Literature." *Classical Quarterly* n.s. 33: 246–57.

Sanchis, Domingo. 1962. "Pauvreté monastique et charité fraternelle chez Augustin: le commentaire augustinien de Actes 4,32–35 entre 393 et 403." *SM* 4:7–33.

Saumagne, Ch. 1934. "Ouvriers agricoles ou rôdeurs de celliers? Les circoncellions d'Afrique." *Annales d'histoire économique et sociale* 6:351–64.

Scagliono, Carlo. 1986. "'Guai a voi ricchi.' Pelagio e gli scritti pelagiani." In *Per foramen acus. Il cristianesimo antico di fronte alla pericope evangelica del "giovane ricco,"* 361–98. Studia Patristica Mediolanensia 14. Milan: Vita e Pensiero.

Schindler, Alfred. 1984. "Kritische Bermerkungen zur Quellenbewertung in der Circumcellionenforschung." *SP* 15:238–41.

Segal, Judah B. 1970. *Edessa "The Blessed City."* Oxford: Clarendon Press.

Sellers, Robert. 1953. *The Council of Chalcedon: A Historical and Doctrinal Survey.* London: S.P.C.K.

Spidlík, Tomas. 1986. "'Abbondare nell' opera di Dio' nel pensiero di S. Basilio." In *Spiritualità del lavoro nella catechesi dei Padri del III–VI secolo,* ed. Sergio Felici, 95–104. Biblioteca di scienze religiose 75. Rome: Libreria Ateneo Salesiano.

Staats, Reinhart. 1967. "Die Asketen aus Mesopotamien in der Rede des Gregor von Nyssa *In suam ordinatonem.*" *VC* 21:165–79.

———. 1968. *Gregor von Nyssa und die Messalianer.* PTS 8. Berlin: Walter de Gruyter.

———. 1982. "Beobachtungen zur Definition und zur Chronologie des Messalianismus." *Jahrbuch österreichische Byzantinistik* 32.4:235–44.

———. 1983. "Messalianforschung und Ostkirchenkunde." In *Makarios-Symposium über das Böse,* ed. W. Strothmann, 47–71. Göttinger Orientforschungen 1.24. Weisbaden: Harrassowitz.

———. 1984. *Makarios-Symeon: Epistola Magna. Eine messalianische Mönchsregel und ihre Umschrift in Gregors von Nyssa 'De instituto christiano.'* Abhandlungen der Akademie der Wissenschaften in Göttingen, Philologische-historische Klasse, F. 3.134. Göttingen: Vandenhoeck und Ruprecht.

————. 1985. "Basilius als lebende Mönchsregel in Gregors von Nyssa *De virginitate.*" *VC* 39:228–55.

Stancliffe, Claire. 1983. *St. Martin and His Hagiographer: History and Miracle in Sulpicius Severus.* Oxford: Oxford University Press.

Steinhauser, Kenneth B. 1993. "The Cynic Monks of Carthage: Some Observations on *De opere monachorum.*" In *Augustine: Presbyter Factus Sum,* ed. Joseph T. Lienhard, Earl C. Muller, and Roland J. Teske, 455–62. New York: P. Lang.

Stewart, Columba. 1989. "New Perspectives on the Messalian Controversy." *SP* 19: 243–49.

————. 1991. *"Working the Earth of the Heart": The Messalian Controversy in History, Texts, and Language to A.D. 431.* Oxford: Clarendon Press.

————. 1998. *Cassian the Monk.* Oxford: Oxford University Press.

————. 1999. Review of *Messalianismus und Anti-Messalianismus,* by Klaus Fitschen. *JEH* 50:552–53.

Tate, George. 1989. "Le Syrie à l'époque byzantine: Essai de synthèse." In *Archeologie et histoire de la Syrie,* ed. Jean-Marie Dentzer and Winfried Orthmann. Vol. 2:97–116. Saarbrücken: Saarbrücker.

Telfer, William. 1939. "The Didache and the Apostolic Synod of Antioch." *JThS* 40: 258–71.

Theissen, Gerd. 1992. "The Wandering Radicals." In *Social Reality and the Early Christians,* trans. Margaret Kohl, 33–60. Minneapolis: Fortress Press.

Thomas, John Philip. 1987. *Private Religious Foundations in the Byzantine Empire.* Dumbarton Oaks Studies 24. Washington, D.C.: Dumbarton Oaks.

Tillemont, Louis-Sébastien Lenain de. 1732. *Mémoires pour servir à l'histoire ecclésiastique des six premiers siècles.* 16 vols. Paris, 1701–1712. Repr. Venice.

Traina, G. 1987. "L'espace des moines sauvages." *Quaderni Catonesi di studi classici e medievali* 9:353–62.

Trombley, Frank R. 1993–1994. *Hellenic Religion and Christianization, c. 370–529.* 2 vols. Religions in the Graeco-Roman World 115.1–2. Leiden: Brill.

Ueding, Leo. 1953. "Die Kanones von Chalkedon in ihrer Bedeutung für Mönchtum und Klerus." In *Das Konzil von Chalkedon,* ed. Aloys Grillmeier and Heinrich Bacht. Vol. 2:596–676. Würzburg: Echter.

Vailhé, S. 1912. "Acémètes." *DHGE* 1:274–81. Paris: Letouzey et Ané.

Veyne, Paul. 1990. *Bread and Circuses: Historical Sociology and Political Pluralism,* trans. Brian Pearce. London: A. Lane.

Villecourt, Louis. 1920. "La Date et l'origine des 'Homélies spirituelles' attribuées à Macaire." *Comptes Rendus des séances de l'Académie des Inscriptions et Belles-Lettres,* 250–58. Paris.

Villey, Audré. 1994. *Psaumes des errants: Écrits manichéens du Fayyûm.* Sources gnostiques et manichéennes 4. Paris: Cerf.

Vinne, Michael J. de. 1995. *The Advocacy of Empty Bellies: Episcopal Representation of the Poor in the Late Roman Empire.* Ph.D. diss., Stanford University.

Visonà, Giuseppe. 1986. "Povertà, sequela, carità. Orientamenti nel cristianesimo dei primi secoli." In *Per foramen acus. Il cristianesimo antico di fronte alla pericope evangelica del "giovane ricco,"* 3–78. Studia Patristica Mediolanensia 14; Milan. Vita e Pensiero.

Vogüé, Adalbert de. 1984. "Le pauvreté dans le monachisme occidental du IVe au VIIIe siècle." *Collectanea Cisterciensia* 46:177–85.

Vööbus, Arthur. 1947. "Les messaliens et les réformes de Barsauma de Nisibe dans l'Église perse." *Contributions of the Baltic University* 34:1–27. Pinneberg.

———. 1948. "La Vie d'Alexandre en grec: un témoin d'une biographie inconnue de Rabbula écrite en syriaque." *Contributions of the Baltic University* 62:1–16. Pinneberg.

———. 1954. "Liber Graduum: Some Aspects of Its Significance for the History of Early Syrian Asceticism." In *Charisteria Johanni Kôpp*, 108–28. PapETSE 7. Stockholm.

———. 1958a. *Literary Critical and Historical Studies in Ephraem the Syrian.* PapETSE 10. Stockholm.

———. 1958b. *History of Asceticism in the Syrian Orient.* Vol. 1. CSCO 184. Subsidia 14. Louvain: Secrétariat du CorpusSCO.

———. 1960a. "Ein merkwürdiger Pentateuchtext in der pseudo-klementinischen Schrift De virginitate." *Oriens Christianus* 44:54–58.

———. 1960b. *History of Asceticism in the Syrian Orient.* Vol. 2. CSCO 197. Subsidia 17. Louvain: Secrétariat du CorpusSCO.

———. 1961. "The Institution of the *Benai Qeiama* and *Benat Qeiama* in the Ancient Syrian Church." *Church History* 30:19–27.

———. 1972. *On the Historical Importance of the Legacy of Pseudo-Macarius.* PapETSE 23. Stockholm.

———. 1988. *History of Asceticism in the Syrian Orient.* Vol. 3. CSCO 500. Subsidia 81. Louvain: Secrétariat du CorpusSCO.

Vorst, Carolus van de. 1912. Review of *Vie d'Alexandre l'Acémète,* by E. de Stroop. *AB* 31:107–108.

Walmsey, Alan. 1996. "Byzantine Palestine and Arabia: Urban Prosperity in Late Antiquity." In *Towns in Transition: Urban Evolution in Late Antiquity and the Early Middle Ages,* ed. N. Christie and S. T. Loseby, 126–58. Aldershot: Scholar Press.

Walters, C. C. 1974. *Monastic Archaeology in Egypt.* Warminster: Aris and Phillips.

Weidmann, Denis. 1991. "Kellia: Swiss Archaeological Activities." In *The Coptic Encyclopedia,* ed. Aziz S. Atiya, vol. 5, 1400–1406. New York: Macmillan.

Wenzel, Siegfried. 1963. "Ἀκηδία. Additions to Lampe's Patristic Greek Lexicon." *VC* 17:173–76.

Wickham, Lionel. 1994. "The 'Liber Graduum' Revisited." In *VI Symposium Syriacum 1992,* ed. René Lavenant, 177–87. OCA 247. Rome: Pontificio Istituto Orientale.

Williams, Michael A. 1982. "The *Life of Antony* and the Domestication of Charismatic Wisdom." In *Charisma and Sacred Biography,* 23–45. Journal of the American Academy of Religious Studies, Thematic Studies 48. Chico, Calif.: Scholars Press.

Winkler, G. 1983. "Ein bedeutsamer Zusammenhang zwischen der Erkenntnis und Ruhe in Mt 11, 27–29 und dem Ruhen des Geistes auf Jesus am Jordan. Eine Analyse zur Geist-Christologie in syrischen und armenischen Quellen." *Le Muséon* 96:267–326.

Wipszycka, Ewa. 1986. "Les aspects économiques de la vie de la communauté des

Kellia." In *Le site monastique des Kellia: Sources historiques et explorations archéologiques,* 117–44. Geneva. Repr. Wipszycka 1996:337–62. References in text to this edition.

———. 1994. "La monachisme égyptien et les villes." *Travaux et mémoires* 12:1–44. Repr. Wipszycka (1996):282–336. References in text to this edition.

———. 1996. *Études sur le christianisme dans l'Égypte de l'antiquité tardive.* Studia Ephemeridis Augustinianum 52. Rome: Institutum Patristicum Augustinianum.

Wisskirchen, Rotraut. 1995. "Das monastiche Verbot der Feldarbeit und ihre rechtliche Gestaltung bei Benedikt von Nursia." *JbAC* 38:91–96.

Wölfe, Eugen. 1986. "Der Abt Hypatios von Ruphinianai und der Akoimete Alexander." *BZ* 79:302–9.

INDEX

Compositor: Binghamton Valley Composition, LLC
Text: 10/12 Baskerville
Display: Baskerville
Printer and Binder: Edwards Brothers, Inc.